The Long Shadow

The Long Shadow

NUCLEAR WEAPONS AND SECURITY IN 21ST CENTURY ASIA

Edited by
Muthiah Alagappa

STANFORD UNIVERSITY PRESS
Stanford, California 2008

Stanford University Press
Stanford, California

Printed in the United States of America on acid-free, archival-quality paper

Library of Congress Cataloging-in-Publication Data

The long shadow : nuclear weapons and security in 21st century Asia / edited by Muthiah Alagappa.
p. cm.
Includes bibliographical references and index.
ISBN 978-0-8047-6086-7 (cloth : alk. paper)—
ISBN 978-0-8047-6087-4 (pbk. : alk. paper)
1. Nuclear weapons—Government policy—Asia. 2. National security—Asia. 3. Security, International—Asia. 4. Asia—Military policy—21st century. I. Alagappa, Muthiah.
UA830.L66 2008
355.02'17095—dc22

2008005320

Typeset by Thompson Type in 10/13 Bembo

Contents

Tables and Figures

Tables

Figures

Preface and Acknowledgments

Nuclear weapons played a central role in the strategic interaction of the two superpowers and their allies during the Cold War. Termination of the Cold War and the collapse of the Soviet Union quickly ended that centrality and raised doubts about the relevance and role of nuclear weapons in the new era. With their heyday deemed over, nuclear weapons were expected to play only a minimal security role in a dramatically altered strategic environment. Nuclear proliferation was seen as the gravest security threat; nonproliferation became the primary concern of nuclear policy in Western countries. A concerted effort was made to freeze the Cold War nuclear order and move toward a comprehensive ban on testing. Some hoped that this would lead to ridding the earth of nuclear weapons.

Within a decade, however, nuclear weapons started to command increasing attention. The United States unveiled a sweeping reappraisal of its nuclear policy; Russia began to emphasize nuclear deterrence as the major element to guarantee its sovereignty; and Britain and France reviewed and reiterated their commitment to retain their nuclear forces. In Asia, interest in nuclear weapons was undiminished. A fast ascending China is modernizing its nuclear arsenal; a rising India and a rather unstable Pakistan are now overt nuclear weapon states; Israel is upgrading its substantial nuclear force; North Korea has tested short- and medium-range missiles and carried out a partially successful nuclear test; and Iran is believed to be seeking a nuclear weapon capability. By the turn of the twenty-first century, old and new nuclear weapon states started to explore "new" roles and strategies for their nuclear forces (or those of their allies) to cope with their contemporary security challenges, including the threat of international terrorism posed by transnational nonstate actors. Uncertainty and debate still characterize discussion about the security significance, roles, and implications of nuclear weapons.

This study investigates the roles and strategies for the employment of nuclear weapons and their implications for security and stability in a dramatically altered strategic landscape and a substantially different nuclear environment. Its focus is Asia, which has emerged as a distinct and core world region. With a region dominant security system, fast-growing Asia has the potential to become the central world region in the twenty-first century. The broadly defined Asian security region has six nuclear weapon states (United States, Russia, China, India, Pakistan, and Israel), several nuclear weapon-capable states (Japan, South Korea, and Taiwan), and at least two aspirants (North Korea and Iran). There is also growing interest in Asia in developing nuclear energy to meet the demands of large and rapidly growing economies.

A chief conclusion of the study is that although they are not in the forefront, nuclear weapons continue to be important. They cast a long shadow that informs in fundamental ways the strategic policies of the major powers and their allies with far-reaching consequences for security and stability in the Asian security region. Although strategic defense and the counterforce role may increase in significance, deterrence will continue to be the dominant role and strategy for the employment of nuclear weapons. Deterrence, however, operates largely in a condition of asymmetry and with small nuclear forces. Some view this condition and the increase in the number of non-Western nuclear weapon states as destabilizing. The study argues that although it is possible to envisage destabilizing situations and consequences, thus far nuclear weapons have had a stabilizing effect in the Asian security region. They have contributed to regional stability by assuaging the national security concerns of vulnerable states, strengthening deterrence and the status quo, inducing caution, preventing the outbreak and escalation of major hostilities, and reinforcing the trend in the region that deemphasizes the offensive role of force and increases the salience of defense, deterrence, and assurance. Extended deterrence and assurance continue to be crucial in preventing the spread of nuclear weapons to additional states. The study posits that the Cold War nuclear order is not in sync with present realities and must be substantially adapted or constructed anew with a focus on Asia to address five key issues: sustaining deterrence in a condition of asymmetry and discouraging destabilizing capabilities and strategies; accommodating new nuclear weapon states; preventing the spread of nuclear weapons to additional states; preventing proliferation to nonstate actors; and supporting the peaceful use of nuclear energy with adequate safeguards. These and other findings of the study may be controversial and contested by those who see nuclear weapons as the primary drivers of insecurity and perceive the world through the dangers of nuclear weapons and other weapons of mass destruction.

It is important to subject the different perspectives and findings to rigorous analyses to develop a better understanding of the roles and implications of nuclear weapons. This is crucial as we enter a new strategic environment that is dramatically different from that of the Cold War, and which is likely to further evolve with the rise of Asian powers. In some ways the present period parallels the early phase of the Cold War when strategic analysts were grappling with the new bipolar situation and the advent of nuclear weapons. It is now opportune to undertake work on nuclear weapons as all relevant countries are modernizing and building their strategic arsenals, albeit at a relatively moderate pace, and developing strategies for their employment. Such an exercise is also difficult because of the tendency in the region to secrecy and ambiguity and to downplay the role of nuclear weapons in the interest of other national priorities and political correctness. The difficulty is compounded by the lack of a common discourse across Asian countries and the small number of analysts who can undertake rigorous work on nuclear strategy-related issues. Both situations need to be rectified, although care should be taken not to swing to the other extreme situation in which discussion of nuclear weapons and strategies becomes highly technical, jargon ridden, and the preserve of a group of analysts who live in an isolated strategic and technological world.

Covering fourteen relevant countries and actors in a broadly defined Asian security region that includes the Middle East; involving twenty authors and over forty senior scholars, readers, and reviewers; and spanning three years, the study was a major undertaking. The contributors, senior scholars, and discussants met in two stimulating and productive workshops: first in May 2006 in Washington, D.C. and then in Singapore in November 2006. I also discussed the preliminary findings of the study in seminars at the East-West Center Washington, the Fletcher School of Law and Diplomacy in Tufts University, the Weatherhead Center for International Affairs at Harvard University, the Shorenstein Asia-Pacific Research Center at Stanford University, and the East Asian Institute at the University of California, Berkeley. The project was intellectually challenging. And the experience, at least for me, has been humbling and rewarding. I learned a great deal from the project. The contributors and I hope that readers will find the book as useful and stimulating as it has been for us in writing it.

Many people have helped in this endeavor. I would like to express my deep appreciation to the contributors, senior scholars, readers, and reviewers of the manuscript in its various stages. Special thanks are due to the contributors. Their deep knowledge of the nuclear policies and strategies of the respective countries, their willingness to ground inquiry in a common framework, and their willingness to revise their chapters several times have been admirable and important in bringing this project to a successful conclusion. It was a great honor and privilege to have Noble Laureate Thomas Schelling participate fully in all sessions of the first workshop in Washington, D.C. Shlomo Brom, Devin Hagerty, Patrick Morgan, and Yoshihide Soeya participated in both workshops. Victor Cha, Charles Glaser, Avery Goldstein, Admiral Karat Rajagopalan Menon, Andrew Oros, Trita Parsi, Major General Guang Qian Peng, Joseph F. Pilat, Yuan-Kang Wang, and Major

General Noboru Yamaguchi participated in the first workshop. Farideh Farhi, Bharat Karnad, K. S. Nathan, Shinichi Ogawa, Brad Roberts, Tang Shipping, Richard Tanter, and William Tow participated in the second workshop. All these scholars read, reread, and commented on one or more chapters.

Avery Goldstein and Charles Glaser offered highly detailed and constructive reviews of the entire book manuscript. Their suggestions were helpful in the final revision of the manuscript. Patrick Morgan and T. V. Paul read the penultimate versions of Chapters 17 and 18, and Kenneth Waltz read the early chapters and offered helpful comments. Rajesh Basrur, Richard Bush, Stephen Cohen, Ralph Cossa, Farideh Farhi, David Kang, David Leheny, Mike Mochizuki, C. Raja Mohan, Chung-in Moon, Jonathan Pollack, Daryl Press, Richard Samuels, Phillip Saunders, Sheldon Simon, Scott Snyder, Nikolai Sokov, Gerald Steinberg, Ashley Tellis, and Hugh White read the penultimate versions of the country chapters and offered helpful comments and suggestions. Robert Pfaltzgraff, Alastair Iain Johnston, Daniel C. Sneider, and T. J. Pempel organized and chaired the seminars at the Fletcher School, Harvard University, Stanford University, and the University of California, Berkeley, respectively. To all these scholars I would like to express my sincere appreciation and gratitude for taking the time amid their busy schedules. The authors and I benefited greatly from their reviews and comments. However, because we did not fully embrace all suggestions we take responsibility for our views.

Thanks are due to the Center for Global Partnership, the Japan Foundation for providing funding support; Junichi Chano of the Japan Foundation for his support; the Institute of Southeast Asian Studies for cosponsoring the second workshop in Singapore; the Japan Institute of International Affairs for cosponsoring the dissemination meeting in Tokyo; Charles Morrison (presently President of the East-West Center) for his support of this and other projects that I have led over the past two decades; Janet Mowery for her copyediting of the prepeer review manuscript; In-Seung Kay and Farzin Farzad for their research assistance; June Kuramoto for so ably handling the logistics for the two workshops and the dissemination meeting in Tokyo; Megan Hayes for her assistance with the first workshop; and Jeremy Sutherland for his assistance in compiling the final version of the manuscript, managing the response to copyediting, and in proofreading the entire manuscript. Geoffrey Burn, John Feneron, Jessica Walsh, and Margaret Pinette assisted greatly in shepherding the manuscript through the review and production stages at Stanford University Press.

At a personal level, the East-West Center has been an invaluable home over the last two decades. A research scholar could not ask for a better home and environment. After several management positions (including first director of the integrated research program at the East-West Center in Honolulu and founding director of the East-West Center Washington, D.C.), I reverted to a full-time research position in early 2007 when the East-West Center appointed me as the first Distinguished Senior Fellow. I have also been fortunate over the years to work with a large number of senior and younger scholars, theorists, and regional and country specialists in the United States, Asia, Australia, Canada, and Europe. These interactions and networks have been enormously beneficial in my intellectual journey.

Finally, my deepest appreciation goes to my family. I have been blessed with a loving wife, three wonderful daughters, understanding and supportive sons-in-law, and three affectionate grandchildren. It has been a great pleasure to see Radha, Shanthi, and Padma blossom in their professional and personal lives with the love and support of Adotei and Stuart. And it is a great joy to be close to Vikram, Arjun, and Rohini and see them grow. I would like to dedicate this work to my wife Kalyani, without whose love, forbearance, and support this and other books would not have been possible.

Washington, D.C. Muthiah Alagappa

Contributors

MUTHIAH ALAGAPPA is Distinguished Senior Fellow at the East-West Center. He can be contacted at alagappm@eastwestcenter.org.

KANG CHOI is Director-General and Professor of the Department for American Studies at the Institute of Foreign Affairs and National Security (IFANS), Seoul. He can be contacted at kchoi05@mofat.go.kr.

CHU SHULONG is Professor at Tsinghua University, Beijing. He can be contacted at shulongc@yahoo.com.

AVNER COHEN is Senior Fellow, Jennings Randolph Fellowship Program, at the United States Institute of Peace (2007–08) and an affiliate of the University of Maryland. He can be contacted at cohenavner@msn.com.

YURY FEDOROV is Associate Fellow of the Royal Institute of International Affairs (Chatham House), London. He can be contacted at fedorovyury@googlemail.com

KATSUHISA FURUKAWA is a Fellow at the Research Institute of Science and Technology for Society, Tokyo. He can be contacted at katsu_furukawa@yahoo.com.

MICHAEL J. GREEN is Associate Professor at the Edmund A. Walsh School of Foreign Service at Georgetown University and Senior Advisor and Japan Chair at the Center for Strategic and International Studies, Washington, D.C. He can be contacted at mgreen@csis.org.

DEVIN T. HAGERTY is Associate Professor of Political Science at the University of Maryland, Baltimore County. He can be contacted at devinhagerty@gmail.com.

S. PAUL KAPUR is Associate Professor in the Department of Strategic Research at the United States Naval War College. He can be contacted at pkapur@stanford.edu.

FEROZ HASSAN KHAN is Senior Lecturer and Senior Research Fellow at the Center for Contemporary Conflict, Department of National Security Affairs at the Naval Postgraduate School, Monterey. He can be contacted at fhkhan@nps.edu.

PETER R. LAVOY is National Intelligence Officer for South Asia at the National Intelligence Council. At the time of this writing, he was director of the Center for Contemporary Conflict, Department of National Security Affairs at the Naval Postgraduate School, Monterey.

DONG SUN LEE is Assistant Professor of International Relations at Korea University. He can be contacted at ds0306@korea.ac.kr.

ROD LYON is Program Director (Strategy and International) at the Australian Strategic Policy Institute, Canberra. He can be contacted at rodlyon@aspi.org.au.

JOHN S. PARK is Director of the Korea Working Group at the U.S. Institute of Peace, Washington, D.C. He can be contacted at jpark@usip.org.

JOON-SUNG PARK is Distinguished Researcher in the Department for National Security and Unification Studies at the Institute of Foreign Affairs and National Security (IFANS), Seoul. He can be contacted at jspark01@mofat.go.kr.

RAJESH RAJAGOPALAN is Professor at the School of International Studies, Jawaharlal Nehru University, New Delhi. He can be contacted at r_rajesh@mail.jnu.ac.in.

RONG YU is a Ph.D. candidate at the School of Public Policy and Management, Tsinghua University, Beijing. She can be contacted at rongy03@mails.thu.edu.cn.

TAN SEE SENG is Associate Professor at the S. Rajaratnam School of International Studies, Nanyang Technological University, Singapore. He can be contacted at issstan@ntu.edu.sg.

VINCENT WEI-CHENG WANG is Chair and Associate Professor of Political Science at the University of Richmond. He can be contacted at vwang@richmond.edu.

JAMES J. WIRTZ is Professor of National Security Affairs at the Naval Postgraduate School, Monterey. He can be contacted at jwirtz@nps.edu.

The Long Shadow

Introduction
Investigating Nuclear Weapons in a New Era

MUTHIAH ALAGAPPA

Nuclear forces continue to play a critical role in the defense of the United States, its allies, and friends. They provide a credible deterrent [against] a wide range of threats . . . [and] give the United States options . . . to achieve strategic and political objectives.

U.S. Nuclear Posture Review, 2002

Russia [considers] nuclear deterrence as the main element guaranteeing its security. Maintaining a minimally sufficient number of nuclear weapons to ensure nuclear deterrence remains one of the most important policy priorities.

Vladimir Putin, 2006

China maintains a small but effective counterattacking nuclear force in order to deter possible attacks by other countries. Any such attack will inevitably result in a retaliatory nuclear counterstrike.

PRC Defense White Paper, 2000

India seeks to develop a "credible minimum deterrent" nuclear capability and adheres to a no first use policy . . . Nuclear retaliation to a first strike will be massive and designed to inflict unacceptable damage.

Indian Cabinet Committee on Security, 2003

We were compelled to show then, in May 1998, that we were not bluffing, and in May 2002 we were compelled to show that we do not bluff.

Pervez Musharraf, 2002

Israel won't say . . . whether we have nuclear weapons. It suffices that one fears that we have them and that fear in itself constitutes an element of dissuasion.

Shimon Peres, 2006

North Korea has built nuclear weapons to cope with the U.S. nuclear threat and is prepared to counter any U.S. pre-emptive strike.

Minju Joson, March 2006

To cope with the threat of nuclear weapons, Japan continues to rely on the nuclear deterrent provided by the United States . . . [It] will . . . introduce ballistic missile defense systems to cope effectively with ballistic missile attacks.

National Defense Program Guidelines, 2005

Leaders and governments in nuclear weapon states, their allies, and aspirants to the nuclear club believe that their nuclear forces or those of their allies can advance national security by providing a capability to counter specific threats; to achieve certain policy priorities; to demonstrate national power; to preserve freedom of action; or as insurance against uncertainty and risks in a changing international environment. Nuclear weapons, ballistic missiles, and strategic defense have entered or reentered the security thinking of the old, new, and prospective nuclear weapon states and their allies in a fundamentally different strategic environment and in a nuclear era that is substantially different from that of the Cold War. This study investigates the purposes and roles of nuclear weapons in the new security environment, the nature and content of the national nuclear strategies of relevant states, and their implications for international security and stability in the new era with the focus on the Asian security region. The latter is now a core world region and could become the geopolitical center of the world in the twenty-first century.

Persistence of Nuclear Weapons

Nuclear weapons played a central role in defining the strategic relations between the two superpowers—the United States and the former Soviet Union—and their key allies during the Cold War. At times, considerations relating to the strategic balance even eclipsed the underlying political struggle. Nuclear weapons and ballistic missiles dramatically elevated the importance of the strategy of deterrence (dissuasion by threat of enormous destruction known in the nuclear jargon as deterrence by threat of punishment) and downgraded strategies of defense (known as deterrence by denial) and offense.[1] From an "occasional stratagem" deterrence became an elaborate and comprehensive strategy that shaped all aspects of the national security policies of the two superpowers and a cornerstone of international politics (Morgan 2003: 3–4). After the 1962 Cuban missile crisis, avoiding war between the United States and the former Soviet Union became a central strategic goal of the two adversaries. Most political, strategic, and technological developments were evaluated in terms of their consequence for the stability of deterrence between the two superpowers, often associated with a set of strategic circumstances referred to as "mutual assured destruction" (MAD). Beginning in the 1970s, arms control agreements were designed to preserve strategic stability through mutual deterrence, and to prevent war. Nuclear weapons were credited for the "long peace" among the major powers during the Cold War (Gaddis 1987; Jervis 1989: 23–24; Morgan 2003: 27–28).[2]

Termination of the Cold War, which coincided with the dawn of the information age, raised doubts about the relevance and role of nuclear weapons in the new era. For reasons discussed below, initially there was a marked lack of interest in nuclear weapons in the so-called first and second worlds. The heyday of nuclear weapons was deemed over; nuclear weapons were expected to play only a limited security role in the new era. This was reflected in the U.S. Department of Defense 1994 Nuclear Posture Review (NPR), which stated "nuclear weapons are playing a smaller role in U.S. security than at any other time in the nuclear age." A concerted effort was made in the 1990s to freeze the nuclear order and move toward a comprehensive ban on testing in the hope of ridding the earth of nuclear weapons. In Asia, however, interest in nuclear weapons was undiminished by the termination of the Cold War. In fact the U.S.-dominated new international order combined with developments in the Asian security region and the international attempt to freeze the nuclear order, increased the incentives for certain countries to openly declare their nuclear weapon status and for others to accelerate acquisition and modernization of their nuclear arsenals. These developments, together with concerns over new security challenges and strategic uncertainty, contributed to renewed interest in nuclear weapons in the West as well. The net result has been increased attention to nuclear and missile forces in national security strategies.

Initial Disinterest in the West

Termination of the Cold War and the collapse of the Soviet Union quickly ended the centrality of nuclear weapons in national and international security in the first and second worlds. For about a decade there was a marked lack of interest in the security role of nuclear weapons. The lack of interest may be traced most fundamentally to the disappearance of the security rationale brought about by two interrelated transformations: change in the structure of the international system from bipolarity to unipolarity and the development of cordial relations between the Western powers and Russia. Demonstrating that arms, including nuclear weapons, are in large measure symptomatic and a consequence of political conflict, the two transformations quickly eliminated the centrality of nuclear weapons in relations among these countries. This, however, did not lead to the abandonment of nuclear weapons. Both inertia and concern over uncertainty caused the United States, Russia, France, and Britain to retain sizable nuclear arsenals.

A second reason for neglect of the security role of nuclear weapons was the changed international security situation and the focus on "new" threats like terrorism, rogue states, ethnic and religious conflicts, and pandemics (avian flu, HIV/AIDS, etc.). Such concerns redirected scholarly and policy community attention to "nontraditional" security threats arising from intrastate conflicts, "failed states," transnational terrorist networks and organizations, and rogue states. In this context, work on nuclear weapons and traditional interstate security seemed irrelevant and unfashionable. Concern with nuclear proliferation and nuclear terrorism, however, was an exception. Although proliferation was always a concern, the difference was that during the Cold War it ranked below the nuclear threat the two superpowers posed to each other. In the post-Cold War era, nuclear proliferation moved up the security agenda to become the primary concern for the United States and the Western international community. Nuclear proliferation became an even more acute concern in the post-9/11 era. President George W. Bush identified "the gravest danger" confronting the United States as lying "at the crossroads of radicalism and technology."[3] The states of concern for him were Iraq, North Korea, and Iran, which he collectively termed the "axis of evil."[4] Religious terrorist groups also became a concern. Though the probability is low that religious terrorist groups will be able to acquire nuclear weapon capabilities, their interest in doing so and the belief that traditional deterrence will not work against those groups underscore the concern with nuclear terrorism.

A third reason for the disinterest in the security roles of nuclear weapons was rooted in a reading of the Cold War as a highly dangerous era in which peace rested on a "delicate balance of terror" and threat of mutual annihilation that should never be repeated. In this view, nuclear weapons were dangerous and immoral and should be delegitimized and denaturalized. The proper focus should be on "cooperative nuclear threat reduction" that includes securing weapons and fissile material, especially in Russia and the former Soviet republics, preventing nuclear proliferation, and moving toward comprehensive disarmament. The world would be safer without nuclear weapons. Nonproliferation became the dominant lens for viewing nuclear weapons and security. It came to be seen as an end in itself rather than one of several approaches to a safer world. Downplaying or disregarding the changing strategic environment and national security imperatives, all proliferation was condemned.[5] A strong effort was made to indefinitely extend the Non-Proliferation Treaty (NPT).

Fourth, the antinuclear vision was reinforced by uncertainty over the role of nuclear weapons in the information age. Warfare was believed to be on the cusp of a new revolution in which the acquisition or denial of information was the key to victory (Gray 2001). The anticipation was that emphasis on surveillance and information (a presumed consequence of the revolution in military affairs [RMA]) combined with new, more accurate, long-range, and lethal conventional weapons would bring about a revolution in the conduct of warfare that would reduce the significance of nuclear weapons. This belief was due in part to the uncertainty over the role of nuclear weapons in a profoundly altered world. Conventional military capability was seen as the more relevant and useable instrument of policy in the new security environment.

A final reason for the lack of interest in the security role of nuclear weapons after the Cold War ended was the unwillingness to recognize the security rationales of the new and aspiring entrants to the club and the consequent labeling of these countries as "illegitimate" nuclear weapon states or "rogue" states with irrational leaders who cannot be deterred.[6] Contesting, downplaying, or disregarding the security imperatives of the new entrants and aspirants, Western scholarship in the "proliferation pessimism" mode emphasized the prestige that poor countries were apparently seeking through the acquisition of nuclear capability and the negative security, safety, and proliferation consequences that would flow from the spread of nuclear weapons to these states. Nonproliferation advocates, for example, argued the incompatibility of the third world states' logic and behavior patterns with Western rational deterrence concepts and stressed the possible negative safety consequences arising from the technological and organizational deficiencies of new nuclear forces (Sagan 1994). Though not unimportant, undue focus on the spread of nuclear material and weapons to "rogue" states and nonstate actors has hindered serious investigation of larger geopolitical issues; it has reduced attention to the salience and role of nuclear weapons in national security policies and strategies and their implications for regional and global interstate security and stability.

Continued Interest in Asia

Instead of diminishing interest in nuclear weapons, termination of the Cold War and regional developments stimulated interest in the acquisition of nuclear weapons and modernization of existing nuclear arsenals in Asia. The emergence of the United States as the sole superpower and its unilateral effort to construct a world order based on its unmatched military capability created apprehensions in several Asian countries, including China and especially in those countries that Washington labeled as "rogue" states. These concerns became a key driver of nuclear modernization in China and the quest for nuclear weapons by North Korea and Iran. Developments in Asia, such as the rise of China and India, intensified the security apprehensions of India and Pakistan, respectively, strengthening the case for nuclear weapons.

India's interest in nuclear weapons was grounded in security considerations relating to China and Pakistan and its vision of itself as a major power. These considerations were unaltered by the termination of the Cold War. In fact a rising China increased anxieties in India. Further, the proposed indefinite extension of the NPT and movement toward concluding a Comprehensive Test Ban Treaty (CTBT) increased the incentive for India to overtly declare its status as a nuclear weapon state. Likewise, Pakistan's perception of an existential threat from India remained unaltered. A rising India and improvement in U.S.-India relations were seen as further tilting the balance of power against Pakistan. Consequently Pakistan followed India in testing and declaring itself a nuclear weapon state. Similarly the termination of the Cold War did not affect Israel's rationale for its nuclear force, which is grounded in its view of history and the existential threat it perceives in the Middle East. The belief that Iran is seeking a nuclear weapon capability provides a new and in some ways regionally more palatable rationale for Israel's nuclear force.

Unilateralism on the part of the United States; demonstration of its might in the First Gulf War, Kosovo, Afghanistan, and the invasion of Iraq; and its emphasis on developing strategic defense (ballistic missile defense [BMD] and counterforce capabilities) to make the use of force a more effective instrument of U.S. foreign policy created apprehensions even in major powers like China and Russia, contributing to modernization of their nuclear arsenals. U.S. military action in Afghanistan and Iraq to oust hostile and "despicable" regimes created fear and concern in North Korea and Iran that were identified by President Bush as possible military targets for regime change and destruction of their nuclear facilities. Along with other considerations, fear of the United States has been a key factor accelerating the nuclear weapon programs of North Korea and Iran. North Korea views its missile and nuclear weapon programs as key elements in developing a self-reliant capability to deter the United States.

The rise of China, its nuclear modernization program, and the North Korean missile and nuclear programs also raised security concerns in Japan, contributing to further strengthening of the U.S.-Japan security alliance and reiteration of the U.S. extended deterrence commitment to Japan. A rising China reinforced Indian apprehensions and raised concerns in Washington as well about Chinese military power, including nuclear modernization. Concern with China is an important factor in the budding strategic relations among the United States, India, and Japan. The North Korean nuclear and missile programs raised security concerns in Northeast Asia, particularly in Japan and to a lesser degree in South Korea. In addition to seeking a more substantive demonstration of U.S. extended deterrence commitment, Tokyo became more committed to the development of BMD to protect Japan from North Korean missile threats. Likewise, Iran's nuclear weapon quest created apprehensions in Israel and certain Arab states. The basic point is that the interest in nuclear weapons in Asia and the Middle East was not diminished by the termination of the Cold War. The new strategic environment, with a dominating United States and a rapidly rising China, provided additional or new impetus for the acquisition and development of nuclear weapon capability.

Renewed Interest in Recognized Nuclear Weapon States

Beginning sometime around the turn of the twenty-first century, the five recognized nuclear weapon states began to rethink the purpose, roles, and strategies for the employment of nuclear weapons in a new strategic era. That rethinking was linked to several developments but three were particularly important. First, after a decade of post-Cold War experiences the outlines of the new strategic environment were becoming more visible. Countries were in a better position to assess "new" security challenges and their strengths and weaknesses in coping with them. It was evident that despite and, in some ways, because of the fundamental change in the security environment, nuclear weapons continued to be relevant although there was still uncertainty about specific roles and suitable nuclear postures. The United States, Russia, Britain, and France began to review and redesign their national nuclear postures for the new era. The second development was the perceived unraveling of the Cold War nuclear order with the Indian and Pakistani nuclear tests in 1998, the nonratification of the CTBT by the Bush administration, Iraq's expulsion of the United Nations Special Commission (UNSCOM) inspectors in 1999, the gradual erosion of the 1994 Agreed Framework with North Korea, and revelations of the A. Q. Khan proliferation network. The de facto expansion of the nuclear club, prospect of further increase in the number of nuclear weapon states, and the heightened prospect that nonstate actors may acquire weapons of mass destruction (WMD) capability stimulated interest in how to cope with the new nuclear situation and threats. The third development was the Bush administration's geopolitics-oriented worldview, its attempt to unilaterally construct a world order based on U.S. predominance and values, and its heavy handed prosecution of the global war on tyrants and terrorists in the wake of 9/11. Set out boldly in several reports and speeches, these policies and especially their manifestation in the various military actions became a key driving force in the review of the U.S. nuclear posture as well as that of other countries.

Of particular relevance to this study is the 2002 NPR, which is the first sweeping reappraisal of U.S. nuclear posture since the termination of the Cold War. Mandated by Congress, the 2002 NPR maintains that nuclear weapons play an important role in the defense of the United States and that they provide credible military options to deter a wide range of threats, including WMD and large-scale conventional military attacks. The new capability-based posture, it posits, should be capable of dealing with immediate contingencies (e.g., an Iraqi attack on Israel or its neighbors, a North Korean attack on South Korea, or a military confrontation over the status of Taiwan) as well as potential and unexpected contingencies. It identifies North Korea, Iraq, Syria, and Libya as countries that could be involved in all three types of contingencies. North Korea and Iraq are identified as chronic military concerns. China is identified as a country that could be involved in an immediate or potential contingency. Although the United States seeks a cooperative relationship with Russia, the NPR states that that country maintains the most formidable nuclear forces aside from the United States, and because it confronts many instabilities Russia remains a country of concern. The NPR downgrades deterrence by punishment and high profiles strategies of offense (preemption and prevention) and strategic defense (preemption, ballistic missile defense, counterforce, and passive defense). It seeks to build a new strategic triad with a mix of nuclear and nonnuclear capabilities to make military force a more useable instrument of policy. The goal is to develop a credible multipurpose force with a broad array of capabilities, including a significant nuclear component, to provide a spectrum of options in the pursuit of deterrence, assurance, offense, and defense. Although the programs envisioned in the NPR have not mustered the necessary political and funding support in the United States, and its future in the post-George W. Bush presidency remains uncertain, it remains official policy. The contents of the NPR combined with the statements and actions of the Bush administration, including the military action in Iraq, created apprehensions in several countries, forcing them to rethink their own policies and postures.

Russia's reappraisal of its nuclear policy is a function of several developments: the dramatic decline in its conventional military capability and more generally its descent from the position of great power; its perception that the unipolar structure, the growing power and influence of the United States, its unilateral approach to international governance, and the eastward expansion of the North Atlantic Treaty Organization (NATO) are marginalizing Russia and threatening its interests in Europe, the Middle East, Central Asia, and the Pacific region; and the belief that America's development of counterforce capability and BMD will negatively affect its strategic deterrent (Fedorov 2006; Sokov 2004). The reappraisal is also linked to the rise of China. Although Russia cooperates with China on several international issues and supplies advanced military technology to that country, a rapidly rising China is viewed in certain quarters as a long-term security concern. After much debate in the 1990s, Russia articulated a military doctrine in 2000 that emphasized nuclear deterrence as the major element that will guarantee its international security and underscore its status as a powerful nation. Russia's strategic posture appears to be shifting from its Cold War orientation to national defense, although the specific threats that Russian nuclear forces are supposed to deter remain unclear.

Though they are not in the Asian security region, it is pertinent to observe that Britain and France also reviewed and reiterated their commitment to retain their nuclear forces in the first decade of the twenty-first century. The British government tabled a white paper in Parliament in December 2006 arguing that it sees "an enduring role for the UK's nuclear forces as an essential part of our capability for deterring blackmail and acts of aggression against our vital interests by nuclear-armed opponents" (Secretary of State for Defense and the Secretary of State for Foreign and Commonwealth Affairs 2006). It proposes building a new class of submarines, participating in the U.S. life extension program for the Trident D5 missile, and developing a replacement warhead, all with a view to maintaining an effective submarine and ballistic missile-based deterrent system. In March 2007 the British House of Commons supported the plan to renew Britain's nuclear submarine system. French nuclear doctrine and capability have also evolved substantially. President Jacques Chirac indicated the changes in January 2006 when he announced a "new" nuclear deterrence doctrine (Chirac 2006). In addition to deterring threats from major powers, the doctrine posits that state sponsors of terrorism risk nuclear retaliation, that regional powers armed with WMD and threatening European territory would face "absolutely unacceptable damage," and that France has the right to "employ final warning to signify our determination to protect our vital interest" (Yost 2006). France has acquired or is seeking to acquire new air and sea capabilities for more discriminatory and controllable options in employing its nuclear weapons.

Although less explicit and less transparent, China has emphasized modernization and further development of a survivable nuclear deterrent capability as an integral part of its defense modernization program (State Council Information Office 2000). A primary purpose of nuclear modernization is to make China's deterrent capability more effective in the context of "new" security challenges, including a shift in U.S. nuclear posture, U.S. development of a BMD system, and the entry of new nuclear powers in Asia. Deterring possible U.S. military intervention in the event of a conflict across the Taiwan Strait is a major purpose of Chinese military modernization; the role of nuclear weapons in this conflict, however, seems more implied than explicit. Chinese scholars and officials are beginning to engage in more explicit discussion of nuclear doctrine, force posture, and operational planning. Arguing the case for using nuclear weapons in limited conflicts for escalation control and damage limitation, some Chinese officials and scholars advocate abandoning the policy of no first use (NFU) or at least making it conditional.[7] The *2006 China Military Power* report published by the U.S. Department of Defense suggests that the pace and scope of the modernization of China's strategic nuclear forces has exceeded expectations and has the potential to alter the regional military balance. China's success in destroying a defunct weather satellite in space with an antisatellite missile has raised concerns in the United States about the security of its space-based surveillance systems, with certain analysts arguing that it could stimulate military competition in space (e.g., Johnson-Freese 2007). Ashley Tellis (2007) asserts that China has surpassed the Soviet Union in its heyday by demonstrating a "unitary hit-to-kill payload" capability and that the Chinese purpose is not to compete in space-based weapons or compel the United States to negotiate space arms limitation agreements but to blunt the massive U.S. conventional superiority by threatening its "eyes and ears" in space. In his view Beijing's investment in space denial technologies is driven by strategic concerns, with China preparing for a prospective geopolitical rivalry with the United States.

"New" Nuclear Weapon States

Concurrent with the reorientation of national postures and the modernization of the arsenals of the five recognized nuclear weapon states, two (India and Pakistan) of the three undeclared nuclear weapon states that had remained outside the NPT became declared nuclear weapon states after May 1998. International efforts to freeze and roll back their nuclear weapon programs have not been successful. The international community appears to have accepted them as nuclear weapon states. Both countries view nuclear weapons as essential for national security and strategic autonomy, and they are in the process of developing doctrines and capabilities for an operational deterrent force. A series of crises between 1999 and 2002 compelled the two countries to recognize the possible roles and limitations of nuclear weapons in their security interaction. New Delhi also seeks to develop a deterrent capability against China. Israel is now the only undeclared nuclear weapon state, but it is believed to possess a substantial nuclear force that is comparable in numbers (though not in delivery vehicles or range) to China, Britain, or France. The Israeli government continues to be committed to an opaque status and existential deterrence, but a nuclear Iran may compel a reappraisal of the opaque nature of its nuclear arsenal and the nature of its deterrence strategy. Despite the assertion that it only seeks nuclear energy, the Iranian government's ultimate goal is widely believed to be the acquisition of nuclear weapons, or at least the development of the necessary infrastructure to realize such a capability on short notice (Chubin 2006).

North Korea is possibly the latest entrant to the nuclear club. The government in Pyongyang declared North Korea a nuclear weapon state after a partially successful low-yield atomic test on October 9, 2006. Producing widespread international condemnation, the test has been depicted as a threat to the national security of the United States and Japan, as increasing the prospects for the spread of nuclear weapons and material to additional states and nonstate actors, and generally as a threat to international peace and security with far-reaching strategic consequences for Northeast Asia. Pyongyang, however, sees the test, and more broadly its nuclear and missile programs, as a vital element in developing a self-reliant deterrent capability focused in the short to medium term against a perceived U.S. threat, including preemptive action.[8] In the long term, the capability may be seen as insurance to reduce North Korea's vulnerability and increase its options toward China, Japan, and Russia.

North Korea's nuclear test has reinforced apprehensions among U.S. allies in Northeast Asia, particularly in Japan. Although Japan has since reaffirmed its nonnuclear stance, certain political leaders and influential opinion makers have called for an open debate on Japan's nuclear future. Tokyo also sought reaffirmation of Washington's extended nuclear deterrence commitment. And support for Japanese participation in the American BMD effort has solidified. Though less concerned about North Korea's nuclear program, South Korea too sought reaffirmation of Washington's extended nuclear deterrence commitment in the wake of the test.

Nuclear Energy Renaissance

A final reason for increased international concern with nuclear weapons is linked to the worldwide renewed interest in nuclear energy and the potential for diversion of weapon-grade plutonium to undesirable state and nonstate actors. Rising fossil fuel cost, energy security concerns, favorable changes in nuclear technology and nuclear energy economics, and concern over the environment have all contributed to a nuclear energy renaissance (Holton 2005). The United States, Britain, France, Japan, Australia, China, and India along with many other countries envision nuclear energy as a central component of their energy policy. The International Atomic Energy Agency estimates that sixty new nuclear power plants will be built in the next fifteen years. Meeting the growing global demand for energy requires investment, trade, and nuclear energy-related technology transfer to ensure reliable supplies of reactor fuel to bona fide users. At the same time the international community is concerned about nuclear proliferation and seeks to put in place adequate international safeguards to lower the risk of diversion of proliferation-sensitive parts for noneconomic purposes (ElBaradei 2006).

Continued Security Relevance

The preceding overview and the epigraphs to this introduction suggest that nuclear weapons will persist and influence national security policies and strategies of major powers, certain second-tier powers, as well as isolated states in the foreseeable future, with consequences for national and international security. Initial anticipation in the West especially in the arms control and nonproliferation community of the decreasing security relevance of nuclear weapons was ill-founded. The effort in the last decade and a half to arrest and reverse the spread of nuclear weapons has not been any more successful than earlier ones. The United States and Russia have each undertaken to drastically cut back their nuclear arsenals, but at the end of the day they still would have large nuclear forces. And each is trying to develop new capabilities that would increase the effectiveness of their respective arsenals in new missions and blunt those of others. Other nuclear weapon states are building and modernizing their nuclear arsenals to retain or increase their robustness with a view to increasing their military options. The number of declared nuclear weapon states has increased and may further increase although only gradually. Nuclear weapons will continue to be relevant in the foreseeable future. It is imperative to investigate their security roles and implications. This is especially important in light of the dramatically altered security environment and a new nuclear age.

Unipolar System with Multiple Security Dynamics

Termination of the Cold War, collapse of the Soviet Union, and its succession by a weak Russia fundamentally altered the structure and dynamics of the international political system. Unipolarity replaced bipolarity. Early hopes and predictions that unipolarity would be short lived and the system would soon become multipolar have not been realized.[9] It is now commonly accepted that unipolarity will continue for another decade or two, possibly longer. At the same time it is widely anticipated that rising Asian powers, especially a fast rising China, and a united and expanding Europe will increasingly constrain U.S. dominance not only in Asia and Europe but also globally. In a few decades from now the international system could become multipolar, with the United States still remaining first among equals. The anticipated transition is contingent on the continued growth and modernization of Asian powers and the unity and ability of the European Union to act in a concerted manner in the political and security arenas.

Unlike the Soviet-American ideological and military confrontation that undergirded and shaped international politics and security in almost every region of the world during the Cold War, the post-1990 unipolar system does not have a single integrating security dynamic. Instead it is characterized by multiple dynamics flowing from the attempt of the United States to unilaterally construct a new world order based on its dominance and values (democracy, human rights, market economy); the interaction of the predominant United States with rising powers (principally in Asia with a focus on China); the U.S.-led global war on terrorism (GWT) that is enmeshed in local and domestic conflicts over political system, legitimacy, and national identity; unresolved regional conflicts in Asia (Taiwan, Korea, and Kashmir); concern over the spread of nuclear weapons, especially to so-called rogue states and terrorist groups; increasing economic interdependence and integration at the regional level; and economic globalization. Although there are some unresolved regional disputes and long-range apprehensions, there is no deep cleavage or confrontation among the major powers that overrides other considerations. The contemporary political, security, and economic dynamics are not necessarily congruent. Competing political, traditional security, and economic priorities and dynamics imply that states have to continuously balance short- and long-term interests within and across sectors.

The United States, Russia, and the Asian powers are all subject to multiple and competing dynamics, including interdependence, cooperation, conflict, and confrontation. Threat perceptions vary widely, with certain countries being viewed simultaneously as friend, partner, and potential security threat. Several states confront multiple threats of unequal urgency; threats are often long range and seldom articulated explicitly; only in a few cases is the threat perception clear and urgent (between North Korea and the United States, Taiwan and China, and Pakistan and India). The numerous explicit and "quiet" rivalries (China-United States, China-Russia, Russia-United States, India-China, Pakistan-India, North Korea-United States, Japan-North Korea, Japan-China, Taiwan-China, and South Korea-North Korea) make for a complex security environment with crosscutting lines of amity and enmity. This is compounded by widespread regional anticipation of change in the distribution of power and uncertainty over the "ultimate" configuration of power in the Asian security system. The numerous rivalries, anticipation of strategic change, and uncertainty contribute to the perception of a region in strategic flux and provides stimulus for military modernization to deal with unexpected developments.

Security during the Cold War was global. Regional security then was entwined with and subsumed by the global Soviet-American confrontation. Today security is largely regional. Although the United States is the sole global power, it has not been able to define the international security environment in terms of threats or architecture for managing security. Despite its efforts, the GWT and democratic development have not become primary drivers of international politics and security. Further, there is no political and security counterpart to economic globalization. Political and security dynamics have become largely regional. The United States is a key player in many regions but all other significant actors are largely regional players. The European Union is significant in adjacent areas but its security role in Asia or Latin America, for example, is limited. Likewise although the reach of Asian countries is expanding, their security role is effectively limited to Asia and adjoining regions. In geography as well as in substance, the contemporary international security environment is dramatically different from that of the Cold War.

A New Nuclear Age

Likewise, the contemporary nuclear environment, which has been referred to as the second or new nuclear age, is substantively different from that during the Cold War. At first glance the nuclear situation in contemporary Asia might appear rudimentary. A closer look, however, suggests a more complex nuclear environment that differs from that of the Cold War era in significant ways. Six major differences are discernible: asymmetry as the dominant condition, increasing salience of defense against nuclear weapons, blurring of the nuclear-conventional distinction, spread of nuclear weapons to more states, concern that nonstate actors will acquire nuclear weapons, and renewed interest in nuclear energy.

Asymmetry

A key difference is the condition of asymmetry created by the huge disparity in military capabilities, including those in the nuclear arena. Asymmetry did characterize the context for nuclear thinking in the early period of the Cold War when the United States enjoyed a nuclear monopoly into the mid-1950s and nuclear superiority well into the 1960s. Asymmetry also characterized nuclear thinking in Britain, France, and China (Goldstein 2000). It informed the U.S. effort to cope with Soviet conventional superiority in Europe, and it is possible (though not clear) that the Soviet Union was also seized with asymmetry in the early phase of the Cold War. Nevertheless, parity and mutual vulnerability between the two superpowers were the defining parameters in thinking about nuclear strategy from the mid-1960s onward.

In contrast, asymmetry is now the defining condition and the basis for strategic thinking and planning in nearly all nuclear weapon states. Asymmetry is manifest in the wide spectrum and many gradations in nuclear and missile capabilities that range from covert programs to develop nuclear weapons (North Korea and Iran), substantial but opaque nuclear capability (Israel), through minimum deterrence postures (India and Pakistan), a limited strategic triad (China), a shrinking conventional capability but still extensive range of nuclear capabilities (Russia), to a wide array of conventional and nuclear weapon capabilities possessed by the United States which it is trying to further expand. (For details about the nuclear weapon capabilities of states in the Asian security region, see Table I-1.)

Because of the overall power and technological differentials, nuclear and conventional asymmetry appears unlikely to be bridged in the foreseeable future. Asian nuclear forces would be much smaller than Russian and American forces. China is likely to make important advancements in its nuclear and missile arsenals but is unlikely to catch up with Russia or the United States, and Russian forces will continue to be more limited than those of the United States. Despite a substantial reduction in the number of warheads and the budgetary constraints on the development of new systems, the United States is likely to enjoy nuclear superiority for at least a few more decades. Asymmetry has important implications for the basis for deterrence, the construction of survivable nuclear forces, incentives for development of first strike capabilities, and crisis stability and instability.

Ballistic Missile Defense

The development and deployment of BMD constitutes the second and possibly the fundamental technological difference between today and the Cold War. Bernard Brodie (1946, 1959) emphasized that the significance of nuclear weapons "depends above all on the possibilities of defense against them in strategic attack." He stressed that all "conclusions about strategies and national policies must be largely governed by our estimate of probabilities for the future of defense" (1959: 173). Although there was always interest, effective defense against nuclear weapons was deemed not possible. Even if it had been possible, strategic defense was considered undesirable because it would threaten the strategic stability embodied in MAD. Mutual vulnerability and deterrence based on assured retaliation dominated security thinking during the Cold War, especially in the United States. The 1972 Anti-Ballistic Missile (ABM) Treaty that brought the first debate on ballistic missile defense (1965–72) to a conclusion embodied this understanding and was

TABLE I–1

Nuclear Forces of Countries in the Asian Security Region

		United States	Russia	China	Israel	India	Pakistan	North Korea	Britain	France
Weapons	Stockpile	5,400	14,000	~240	~100	~60-70	~60	<10	~185	348+
	Deliverable	4,075	5,569	~193	~80	~60	~60	?	<160	348
ICBM	Number	488	453	26						
	Warheads	764	1,743	26				?		
	Type	MMII: 0 MMIII: 488 MX PK: 0	SS-18: 75 SS-19: 123 SS-24: 0 SS-25: 201 SS-27: 48 SS-27M: 6	DF-5A: 20 DF-31A: 6[c]				TD-2: 0		
SRBM, IRBM, MRBM	Number			~100	50	<58	<150			
	Warheads			~100	~50	~20	~35	?		
	Type			DF-3A: 17 DF-4: 17 DF-21: 60 DF-31: 6[c]	Jericho 1: 0 Jericho 2: ~50 Jericho 3: 0	Prithvi I: <50 Agni I: ~8 Agni II: 0 Agni III: 0 Agni IV: 0 Danush: 0	Hatf-3: <50 Hatf-4: <50 Hatf-5: <50 Hatf-6: 0	TD-1: 0		
SLBM	Number	288	176	(12)					50	48
	Warheads	1,728	624	(12)					<144	288
	Type	Trident-I: 0 Trident-II: 1,728	SS-N-8: 0 SS-N-18: 80 SS-N-20: 0 SS-N-23: 80 SS-N-23M1: 16 Bulava: 0	JL-1: (12)[d] JL-2: (24)[d]		K-15: 0			Trident-II: 50	M-4: 0 M-45: 48 M-51: 0
	SSBN	Ohio: 14	Delta I: 0 Delta III: 5[b] Delta IV: 6 Typhoon: (2)[b] Borey: 0[b]	Xia (Type 092): (1)[d] Jin (Type 094): (2)[d]		(ATV: 0)			Vanguard: 4	Redoutable: 1 Triomphant: 3

(continues)

TABLE I-1 (continued)

Nuclear Forces of Countries in the Asian Security Region

		United States	Russia	China	Israel	India	Pakistan	North Korea	Britain	France
Strategic Bombers	Number	114	78	~100						
	Warheads	1,083	872	Bombs ~20 DH-10 LACM ~15[e]						
	Type	B-2: 20/16 B-1B: (65)[a] B-52: 94/56	Tu-95H6: 32 Tu-95H16: 32 Tu-160: 14	H-6: ~100/30[e]						
Theater Weapons	Number	—	—	?	—	—	—	—		—
	Warheads	500	2,330	Bombs ~20	~30	Bombs ~40	~25	?		ASMP 60
	Type	B61-3/4 bombs: 400 Tomahawk SLCM: 100	ABM: 100 SA-10 SAM: 600 Aircraft: ~974 Naval: ~656	H-5: 0 Q-5 / others? ?[e]	F-15I ? F-16	Jaguar M 2000H	Babur LACM: 0 F-16	Fighter-bombers?		M 2000N: 60 S Etendard: 10

SOURCE: Federation of American Scientists/Natural Resources Defense Council, www.fas.org/nuke/guide/summary.htm. Maintained by Hans M. Kristensen. Data current as of March 2008.

NOTES:

ABM: Anti-Ballistic Missile; DF: Dong Feng; ICBM: Intercontinental Ballistic Missile; IRBM: Intermediate-Range Ballistic Missile; JL: Julang; LACM: Land-Attack Cruise Missile; MRBM: Medium-Range Ballistic Missile; SLBM: Sea-Launched Ballistic Missile; SLCM: Sea-Launched Cruise Missile; SRBM: Short-Range Ballistic Missile; SSBN: Nuclear-Powered Ballistic Missile Submarine; TD: Taepo Dong.

[a]The B-1B bomber was officially removed from the SIOP in 1997, but retained in a Nuclear Rerole Plan until March 2003, when the Office of the Secretary of Defense directed the Air Force to discontinue the plan. The B-1B is no longer nuclear capable.

[b]The first Borey-class SSBN was launched in 2006 and might be entering operation in 2008 with the Bulava SLBM. A total of six Borey SSBNs are planned. Delta IVs are being upgraded to the modified SS-N-23 (Sineva). All but three of the original six Typhoon-class SSBNs have been retired. One has been converted to a test launch platform for the SS-N-30 (Bulava) SLCM. The Borey will probably replace Delta IIIs on a one-for-one basis.

[c]The Pentagon declared in May 2007 that the DF-31 had achieved "initial threat capability" in 2006.

[d]The first Jin-class (Type 094) was launched in 2004 and first spotted with commercial satellite images in July 2007. A second Jin-class SSBN has been launched, and a third appears to be under construction. U.S. naval intelligence has projected that China might build five SSBNs if it wants to have a more permanent sea-based deterrent, and the Department of Defense (DOD) report in March 2008 projected that Chinese forces by 2010 might include "up to five" Jin-class SSBNs.

[e]The DOD reported in 2008 that 50–250 DH-10 have been deployed in air- and ground-based versions. Only a portion of the H-6 force, perhaps 30 aircraft, are estimated to have secondary nuclear mission. The H-6 is being modified to carry the DH-10. The Q-5 may no longer be nuclear capable. There is no reliable information that newer tactical aircraft have been assigned a nuclear role.

justified primarily in terms of strengthening deterrence by protecting second-strike capability (Freedman 2004: 19).

A radical departure in thinking came in 1983. Seeking to escape from deterrence based on the threat of nuclear retaliation and mutual annihilation, President Ronald Reagan tasked the scientific community to explore the feasibility of strategic defense against nuclear ballistic missiles (Payne 1985). The idea elicited deep skepticism and was even ridiculed, and it failed to achieve much progress owing to technological limitations and the waning of the Cold War, but the Strategic Defense Initiative (SDI) did establish a national research program. Strategic defense gained new prominence during the George W. Bush administration, which scrapped the distinction between strategic and theater missile defense and made the development of missile defense a high priority. The U.S. commitment to develop and deploy a layered system to defend itself, its allies, and its friends against ballistic missile threats from "rogue" states, and the attraction of such systems to America's allies, such as Japan and Taiwan, complicate the strategic picture and calculations of Russia and China, which for the moment oppose such systems (Berry 2005; Ferguson 2000; Glaser and Fetter 2001; International Institute for Strategic Studies [IISS] 2004).

Thus far, missile defense development has been limited in scope, and the small number of tests under favorable conditions has had only partial success. According to Philip Coyle, the U.S. missile defense program is still struggling to deal with threats from decoys and countermeasures (Coyle 2002, 2006). Even if U.S. interceptors become more effective against threats posed by states like North Korea and Iran in the next several years (it should be noted here that for the present both these countries do not have long-range missiles that can reach the United States), the United States is still quite far from the development of effective defense against more substantial nuclear threats from countries such as Russia and China that do have nuclear-tipped missiles that can reach the United States and which can deploy decoys and countermeasures. Despite the substantial research and development investments by the United States, Japan, Taiwan, and Europe on tactical missile defense, the technology for such a system is also not proven. Further, such systems can be relatively easily countered by the development of more missiles (Coyle 2006).

However, if strategic defense against substantial threats becomes more effective, it could alter the balance between deterrence and offense, with far-reaching strategic consequences for the relationship between force and statecraft, for stability, and for the salience of small nuclear forces. With effective strategic defense, the assumption of mutual vulnerability that was at the heart of strategic thinking during the Cold War would become suspect. States with effective shields will have the option to exit from the MAD situation. The sword may become more potent and usable. The counterforce role may gain new prominence. For those without a missile defense system, force protection and effectiveness in penetrating the adversary's BMD system would assume high priority. Striking first could become attractive. Much more effort would be required to establish mutual vulnerability and stability. Credible minimum deterrence might require larger and more accurate forces. Development of effective missile defense would fundamentally alter the significance of nuclear forces, especially small ones. The implications of missile defense have not commanded much attention because of the continuing belief that effective defense against nuclear threats is technologically still not feasible. Only a few scholars have attempted systematic exploration of related questions (Glaser 1990; Glaser and Fetter 2001; Kartchner 2005; Powell 2003).

Blurring of the Nuclear-Conventional Distinction

The third difference lies in the development of long-range, highly lethal conventional weapons that can be deployed in roles previously assigned to nuclear weapons, and the development of small and more precise nuclear warheads that can be employed in bunker busting and targeting conventional military assets. These developments muddy the hitherto relatively clear distinction between conventional and nuclear war and could have implications for the integrity of the nuclear threshold and for stability. The so-called RMA also threatens to outmode existing conventional military forces. It provides the United States a level of conventional military power—demonstrated in operations in the First Gulf War, Afghanistan, and Iraq—that creates apprehension in other states.[10] The RMA advantages the strong; nuclear weapons might become an even more important means to cope with superior conventional military force (see, e.g., Metz and Kievit 1994). Although the RMA may revolutionize conventional military engagements, it does not undo the nuclear revolution (Gray 2001).

Increase in the Number of Nuclear Weapon States

A fourth difference between the contemporary and the Cold War nuclear environment is in the increase in the number of nuclear weapon states. The number of overt nuclear weapon states has increased from five to seven, with Israel still maintaining its opaque status. Although India and Pakistan had already developed nuclear weapon capabilities during the Cold War, their move to overt status necessitates further development of their nuclear postures, capabilities, command and control arrangements, doctrines, and strategies. North Korea is a new entrant, and Iran is widely believed to be seeking nuclear weapons. In reality, the spread of nuclear weapons has been more gradual than the alarmist readings of nonproliferation advocates.

However, even a small increase in the number of nuclear weapon states poses challenges for the existing nuclear order (ElBaradei 2006). First there is the question of how to deal with nuclear weapon states that are outside the NPT system.

The U.S.-India nuclear deal grounded in U.S. long-term strategic thinking is an attempt to deal with this issue on a country-specific basis. How to deal with Pakistan, Israel, and North Korea (if the effort to dismantle its nuclear program is only partially successful) remains a vexing issue. Second is the issue of additional proliferation. There is international concern that successful nuclear quests by North Korea and Iran would set off a new wave of proliferation in Northeast Asia and the Middle East. Nonproliferation experts see the spread of nuclear weapons and ballistic missiles primarily as a threat to the existing regimes. An equally if not more important challenge is how to adapt these institutions to changing conditions. Failure to adapt will undermine them.

Finally, an increase in the number of nuclear weapon states raises the issue of stability. Some argue that the spread of nuclear weapons is destabilizing, while others argue that it can have stabilizing effects (Knopf 2002; Sagan and Waltz 1995). Based largely on deductive reasoning and extrapolating behavior from the Cold War or discarding that experience altogether, the stability-instability debate is unlikely to be resolved. Nevertheless, it draws attention to the possible implications of the spread of nuclear weapons to more states. Although proliferation and stability were also concerns during the Cold War, the present situation is deemed to be different because of the close proximity of the new nuclear weapon states and the intractable conflicts between them (India-Pakistan and Israel-Iran), the totalitarian or theocratic nature and/or fragility of regimes (North Korea, Iran, and Pakistan), their irrational and "roguish" behavior (North Korea, Iran, and Pakistan), and because of safety concerns (Buchan et al. 2003: 22–23). The United States and the Soviet Union did not share a politically significant boundary, and their heartlands were separated by thousands of miles, allowing space and time for response in crisis situations. Although China and Russia, and China and India, border each other, their heartlands are also relatively far apart. In other dyads (India-Pakistan, Israel-Iran, North Korea-Japan, and North Korea-China), however, Asian nuclear powers are neighbors or very close to each other with very short missile flight times between major cities. In nearly every case, political boundaries are sensitive and disputed, or there is a high degree of mistrust and conflict. Some of these states are also fragile, with the potential for regime collapse and change. All these considerations have implications for force posture, force security, and crisis stability. The spread of nuclear weapons to more states, along with the multiplicity of threats, also necessitate thinking about nuclear strategy, and especially deterrence, as a complex multisided enterprise rather than in the more familiar bilateral mode.

Nuclear Terrorism

The concern that nuclear weapons may be acquired and used by terrorist organizations is peculiar to the contemporary era. The belief is that if terrorist organizations like Al-Qaeda were able to obtain such weapons, including dirty bombs, they would not hesitate to use them to attack populated areas in order to cause widespread death and fear. Proliferation to nonstate actors and nuclear terrorism have become major security concerns. Concerns under the heading of nuclear terrorism include theft of nuclear weapons or material, assistance to terrorist organizations by rogue states and black market networks like that of A. Q. Khan, attacks on nuclear facilities, and takeover of a collapsing nuclear weapon state by radical Islamic groups (Braun and Chyba 2004; Frost 2005; Sokolski 2006). Some have argued that the threat is exaggerated (Frost 2005); even if they acquire such weapons, terrorists are likely to use them strategically rather than in a punitive manner (Schelling 2006); and that deterrence can work against such threats.

Most analysts agree that the probability of terrorist organizations acquiring or producing nuclear weapons is rather low. However, given the enormity of destruction that can be caused, even a minuscule risk is considered too high. How to prevent the spread of nuclear material and weapons to nonstate actors is a key question that has to be addressed by the contemporary international community. This becomes more challenging when certain states are believed to be aiding and abetting terrorist groups or are in danger of failing. Another key question is how to deal with a nonstate actor that somehow comes into possession of nuclear weapons. How can deterrence be made to work against such groups? Deterrence against nonstate actors is commanding increasing policy and scholarly attention (Allison 2006; Galluci 2006). Transnational actors with nuclear weapons pose novel challenges to the construction and management of security order in a system of states. It compels us to think the unthinkable—about nuclear weapon roles, strategies, and implications outside the interstate system.

From the preceding overview it is clear that the contemporary nuclear context is significantly different from that of the post-1960s Cold War era. However, it is similar to the early period of the Cold War in two respects. One, both periods are formative. In the 1950s and 1960s, the United States and the Soviet Union were engaged in developing nuclear capabilities and strategies to deal with a new situation brought about by the nuclear revolution and the bipolar ideological and military confrontation. There was no established body of knowledge to draw on. The new civilian strategy analysts (Bernard Brodie, Thomas Schelling, and Herman Kahn, among others) considered earlier work by military strategists to be irrelevant to the new situation. The contemporary period is formative not so much from a technological perspective, but in the political-strategic context.[11] All states are rethinking their security policies, including nuclear policy and strategy, in the context of a radically altered strategic environment. Such rethinking, and this is the second similarity, is informed by the condition of asymmetry that was also a key parameter in the 1950s and early 1960s. The difference, however, is that nuclear weapons were central to the security thinking in the early

Cold War era. Today they appear less central and their role more indirect, but salient nevertheless.

Necessity, Opportunity, and Difficulty

In light of the dramatically altered strategic and nuclear environments and the persistence and in certain cases expansion of nuclear arsenals, it is imperative to investigate the "new" roles and strategies for the employment of nuclear weapons. The ideas and lessons from the Cold War experience with nuclear weapons may or may not be relevant. We need a firm empirically grounded understanding of the role of nuclear weapons in the contemporary era and to develop "new" ideas and concepts. Such a study is opportune because we can now draw on almost two decades of post-Cold War experience. The contours of the transformed Asian security landscape and the new driving forces of change like the rise of Asian powers are becoming clearer (see Chapter 1). The ongoing reappraisal, modernization, and development of national nuclear doctrines and capabilities also provide a good vantage point to comparatively investigate the role of nuclear weapons in Asian security. Some may consider two decades of experience insufficient evidentiary basis. Others have justified theoretical inquiry on the ground that the five decades of Cold War experience are insufficient because of their ambiguous nature (Harknett, Wirtz, and Paul 2001: 4). We have to go with what we have. History is always subject to different interpretation across actors and over time. There is no definitive history. By design this study is empirically grounded. Though informed by relevant concepts and theories, it is not theory driven.

A few studies have investigated certain concepts and strategies (for example the history and relevance of nuclear deterrence in the post-Cold War era), nuclear policies and strategies of specific countries (the United States, Russia, India, China, Pakistan, North Korea, and Iran), the role of nuclear weapons in specific conflicts or dyads (India-Pakistan and United States-China), or specific problems (nuclear proliferation, for example). However, there have been very few or no systematic comparative inquiries of national roles and strategies of all relevant states or explorations of their implications for security, stability, and conflict resolution in the Asian security region as a whole. This study seeks to make a modest contribution in this direction. It includes a reconsideration of conceptual and policy issues and illuminates their significance through the study of the nuclear policies and strategies of most of the countries that are likely to play a major role not only in Asian international relations but also in the twenty-first-century world.

Such an investigation is also difficult. Information on nuclear forces and strategies is relatively thin and often highly classified. There is also a tendency to secrecy and ambiguity in the belief that hiding limitations enhances the security value of the relatively small nuclear forces of Asian states. Difficulty also arises from the fact that nuclear strategies are in an early stage or at turning points with limited consensus on policy, posture, and strategy. In the case of Asian states, capabilities are often limited and do not match the requirements of professed strategies. Doctrines tend to be vague and in outline form. It is necessary to distinguish between declaratory policy, operational strategies, and actual behavior in crisis situations. These considerations will make analysis more difficult.

Purpose of Study

The central purpose of the study is to develop an intellectual framework and a strong empirical base for understanding and theorizing about nuclear weapons in the context of a dramatically altered international security environment. To enable this, a crucial first step is to develop a deep understanding in comparative perspective of the purposes and roles assigned to nuclear weapons in the security thinking and practice of relevant states and to explore their implications for regional security, stability, and conflict resolution. With this in mind, this bottom-up study investigates three sets of issues:

1. The purposes, roles, strategies, and significance of national nuclear forces. The study explores the security problems, threats, and contingencies for which nuclear weapons are deemed relevant (or irrelevant), the specific roles assigned to nuclear weapons in dealing with them, the basic nuclear strategies of states, how these have been framed and operationalized, and if they are likely to alter. It also investigates the relationship of nuclear weapons to conventional military capability and to other instruments of policy to ascertain their overall salience in national security policy.
2. Commonalities and differences. The study explores similarities and differences across countries in the relevance and roles assigned to nuclear weapons and in nuclear strategies to ascertain if there is anything distinctive about nuclear security in Asia, and if a common vocabulary and discourse is evolving.
3. Regional implications. Here the study explores the implications of national nuclear capabilities and strategies for regional security structure and dynamics, if they have hindered or fostered conflict resolution, and their impact on stability in the Asian security region.

Findings of the Study

The study advances five propositions on the significance and role of nuclear weapons in national security strategies and three propositions on the implications of nuclear weapons for security and stability in the Asian security region. Before outlining them, I would like to stress that these propositions must be considered a first cut, a basis for further research, debate, and refinement.

Significance of Nuclear Weapons in National Security Strategies

On the significance of nuclear weapons, the study first posits that they play an indirect but important role with far-reaching implications. On the surface, nuclear weapons appear less central, often an adjunct to conventional military force that seems more significant in dealing with the many security challenges confronting Asian states. Even in the situations in which nuclear weapons are relevant, they appear to be in the background augmenting conventional forces and deterrence. The emphasis on modernizing conventional military capabilities would appear to support such a line of thinking. However, a closer look suggests that the influence of nuclear weapons runs deeper.

Nuclear weapons cast a long shadow that informs in fundamental ways the national security strategies of major powers and their strategic interactions. Nuclear weapons induce caution, set limits to military options in conflict management, require careful management of crisis situations, shape the way conventional force is used, and provide foundational insurance in situations of conventional military imbalance and against unanticipated developments. Under certain conditions nuclear weapons can also enhance bargaining leverage. Likewise, the nuclear umbrella is a key defining parameter in the national security strategies of allied states, including their decision not to acquire nuclear weapons. For states with existential security concerns, nuclear weapons are bedrock "weapons of the weak." They are the ultimate security insurance to guarantee survival. By setting limits and shaping the way force and the threat of force may be used, nuclear weapons provide the all-important context for the management of key regional conflicts. In the absence of deep ideological conflict and strategic military confrontation like that during the Cold War, nuclear weapons are likely to continue to remain in the background but deeply influence the national security strategies of relevant states and international politics in the Asian security region. The concern that certain nonstate actors may acquire nuclear weapons also exerts a deep influence on national and international security threat perceptions, security policies, and strategies, including the prosecution of the global war on terrorism. The possible acquisition of the "ultimate" weapon by nonstate actors poses novel challenges to an international system constructed on the basis that states are the only legitimate containers and users of violence.

Second, the primary role of nuclear weapons in interstate relations in the foreseeable future is basic or central deterrence (deterring nuclear and large-scale conventional aggression against the homeland) in a condition of asymmetric power relationships. In addition, nuclear deterrence serves as a backstop or insurance to avoid blackmail, preserve strategic autonomy (freedom to act), and cope with unanticipated security developments in a changing strategic environment. The offensive (compellence, coercive diplomacy, war fighting) and defensive (counterforce damage limitation) roles of nuclear weapons as well as strategic defense against nuclear weapons are likely to remain relatively marginal in utility and unlikely to surpass the deterrence role of nuclear weapons in the foreseeable future. Only the United States is developing significant offensive and defensive capabilities and strategies. Technological limitations, funding constraints, the preferences and capabilities (conventional and nuclear) of other states, and the generally stable political and strategic environment in the Asian security region are likely to limit the employment of nuclear weapons in these roles.

Although deterrence continues to be the dominant strategy for the employment of nuclear weapons, the conception and practice of deterrence differ substantially across states and from that during the Cold War. This leads to the third and fourth propositions. The third finding is that widely differing goals and a broad spectrum of capabilities have resulted in an array of deterrence strategies ranging from existential deterrence through minimum deterrence to assured retaliation. All these strategies rely on the threat of punishment, but they differ on the force level and structure required to deter and on the scope of threats to be deterred. Because of their limited capabilities and small nuclear forces, weaker powers opt for deterrence strategies (existential and minimum deterrence) that emphasize uncertainty, risk of escalation to nuclear war, and absolute destruction rather than a secure second-strike capability that will result in certain retaliation and "unacceptable" damage as in an assured retaliation strategy. Weaker powers opt for existential and minimum deterrence strategies out of necessity; their preferred end point is assured retaliation. Countries with relatively large nuclear arsenals have retained assured retaliation capabilities against substantial nuclear weapon states. Although a range of deterrence strategies also existed during the Cold War, assured retaliation between the two superpowers provided the dominant frame for thinking about nuclear deterrence. All contemporary national deterrence strategies are still in a formative stage, and the new nuclear weapon states often do not have the requisite capability to effectively implement professed strategies. It is thus important to distinguish between declaratory and operational doctrines and actual behavior in particular crisis situations. These can vary substantially.

Fourth, the study argues that the absence of severe confrontations and the limited capabilities of the relatively small Asian nuclear forces have resulted in general deterrence postures. Although the United States has the largest and most sophisticated nuclear arsenal and seeks additional capabilities to deal with new threats, it has not issued actor-specific threats that would result in nuclear retaliation or developed actor threat-specific capabilities. Its threats to rogue states and terrorist groups, for example, tend to be general, and those in relation to contingencies involving China are vague and implied. Other countries have chosen to focus on their relatively more urgent concerns, deferring response to lesser ones or attempting to defuse them. Even on primary concerns, states rely on general and implied threats without specifying red lines or specific response. There are very few instances where hostilities are intense and immediate and have resulted in the issuance of specific nuclear threats and development of capabilities to carry out such threats. In all other cases, nuclear deterrence in Asia is implied and indirect. States maintain a broad range of capabilities, including nuclear weapons, and issue general threats to dissuade other states from seriously contemplating aggression.

The final proposition on the significance and role of nuclear weapons is that the strategy of extended nuclear deterrence continues to be relevant for the security of certain U.S. allies. In addition to deterring attacks on allies and preserving their strategic autonomy, extended nuclear deterrence reassures allies and prevents them from pursuing independent nuclear options. National sensitivities and competing threat perceptions and demands of allies make crafting and implementing an effective and credible strategy of extended deterrence more difficult.

Uniqueness and Common Discourse

The role and significance of nuclear weapons in Asian national security strategies do not appear unique. They appear to be a function of specific histories, strategic circumstances, security challenges, and national nuclear capabilities. The tendency toward ambiguity and secrecy, for example, is not a peculiar Asian cultural trait but a function of the belief that such ambiguity and secrecy enhance the deterrence value of small nuclear forces. During the Cold War, Henry Kissinger (1957) posited that a strategy of ambiguity was employed by the Soviet Union and China in their revolutionary struggle against the West. Asian nuclear weapon states are not immune to the logic of nuclear weapons and their consequences.

On common discourse, although certain states use similar terms such as *minimum deterrence* and *no first use,* their interpretations vary across countries. There is no common vocabulary, and a common discourse is noticeable by its absence. A U.S.-China nuclear dialogue appears to have started, but there is no such dialogue between the United States and other countries or among Asian countries. A common discourse has been hindered by the tendency toward secrecy and ambiguity, by the reluctance of the recognized nuclear weapon states to accept new entrants, and the tendency rooted in political correctness to downplay the security role of nuclear weapons. However, as nuclear weapons will continue to exist and nuclear arsenals will expand in size and capability, it is imperative to begin bilateral and multilateral dialogues to foster a common understanding of the roles and implications of nuclear weapons. Thomas Schelling even advocates educating terrorist groups on the catastrophic consequences of using nuclear weapons.[12]

Implications for National and Regional Security

In exploring the implications of national nuclear strategies and more broadly nuclear weapons for national and regional security, this study advances three propositions. First it posits that nuclear weapons strengthen weaker powers and have a modifying effect on structure and its consequences. However, they do not fundamentally alter the distribution of power to make a difference in system structure or the pattern of security interaction. Nuclear weapons have not substantially altered the security dynamics in Asia. Certain nuclear strategies such as compellence, counterforce, and limited war could and have intensified existing threat perceptions and lines of enmity. However, they have not created new ones. Other strategies such as existential, minimum, and extended deterrence, and a posture of general deterrence have not exacerbated security situations. In fact, they have had an ameliorating effect.

By contributing to greater self-reliance in deterrence, nuclear weapons reduce the salience of external balancing as a rationale for alliance among nuclear weapon states. However, alliances and alignments among them still make sense for other reasons. For nonnuclear weapon states that perceive a nuclear threat, alliance with a nuclear weapon state that can extend the deterrence function of its nuclear arsenal provides an incentive for alliance formation and sustenance. On conflict resolution, nuclear weapons do not advance or obstruct settlement of disputes. When they are relevant, nuclear weapons contribute to a situation of no war and no peace. The logic of the enormous destruction power of nuclear weapons argues against conflict resolution through the physical use of violence. However, nuclear weapons are not a barrier to peaceful conflict resolution. The grave risks associated with escalation to nuclear war in certain cases have induced parties to explore a diplomatic settlement. Dispute settlement, however, hinges on the willingness or unwillingness of conflicting parties to negotiate and compromise on political differences that underlie the dispute.

Second, the study posits that nuclear weapons have contributed to the security of states and reinforced stability in the Asian security region that is underpinned by several pillars. Although there could be some destabilizing consequences, thus far nuclear weapons have not undermined stability in Asia. In fact, they have contributed to stability by assuaging national security concerns, preventing the outbreak of major wars, strengthening the status quo, increasing deterrence dominance, and reinforcing the trend in the region toward a reduction in the salience of force in international politics. For a number of reasons (acceptance of the political and territorial status quo; increase in the political, diplomatic, and economic cost of using force in a situation of complex interdependence; and the impracticability of resolving conflicts through the use of force) the offensive roles of force have been on the decline in Asia. Nuclear weapons reinforce this trend by enhancing deterrence dominance and making the cost of war among nuclear weapon states catastrophic and prohibitive, especially in a situation of complex interdependence.

Finally, the study posits that if it is to continue to be relevant, the nuclear order that was forged during the Cold War era must adjust to accommodate contemporary strategic realities, including a focus on Asia that has already become a core world region and may become the geopolitical center of the world in the twenty-first century. The new nuclear order must sustain deterrence in a situation of asymmetry; accommodate change by bringing in nuclear weapon states outside the NPT system; deal with the further spread of nuclear weapons by addressing security concerns of relevant states as well as through denial strategies; prevent the spread of nuclear material, technology, and weapons to nonstate actors; and facilitate trade, investment, and technology transfer to promote the development of nuclear energy, with adequate safeguards in place to prevent leakage of proliferation-sensitive parts.

The above reading of the roles of nuclear weapons in national security strategies and their regional security implications is a consequence of a "politics in command" approach that sees nuclear weapons as an instrument of state policy and understands their roles and implications in the context of the overall national priorities of states in a complex Asian political, strategic, and economic landscape. Such a "benign" reading may be controversial and unacceptable to those who view nuclear weapons as the drivers of insecurity or for arms control, especially nonproliferation advocates who tend to see the world through the dangers of nuclear weapons.

Premises and Definition

Two premises inform this study. First, as will be evident by now, a security perspective that attaches importance to nuclear weapons but does not prejudge their salience girds this study. It takes seriously the security rationales advanced by states for the development of nuclear capabilities or reliance on those of an ally. In the aftermath of the Cold War, nonproliferation has been the dominant lens for the study of nuclear weapons. I argue that, while the spread of nuclear weapons remains a key international security concern, an exclusive or near exclusive reliance on the nonproliferation lens, by rejecting or according insufficient attention to the security value attached to nuclear weapons, obscures and limits our understanding of the broader salience and role of nuclear weapons in national security strategies and the international implications that flow from them.

Nuclear arsenals will continue to exist and inform the security policies of most major countries in the Asian security region for the foreseeable future. A perspective like that adopted in this study can provide valuable insights on a range of issues that cannot and would not be addressed by a nonproliferation approach. The insights would include a comprehensive understanding of the security policies and strategies of states and nonstate actors possessing or seeking to acquire nuclear weapons; the security challenges for which nuclear capabilities are considered relevant; the nature and content of national nuclear strategies; their impact on subregional and regional security dynamics; and consequences for security interdependence, stability, and security management. Investigation of these and related issues is crucial to understanding security in Asia and to the effort to build regional and global institutions to manage security, as well as to limit, control, and manage nuclear weapons and their consequences. An exclusive focus on preventing or countering proliferation would obscure these issues or deal with them only indirectly, leading to unnecessarily benign or alarmist readings of nuclear-related developments. The ethics of responsibility require us to address the nuclear situation in all its dimensions.

Second, this study proceeds on the basis that Asia has become a core region of the world with its own distinct dynamics and that it is likely to become more consequential in international affairs. The study also treats Asia defined broadly as a single security region. The distinctiveness and increasing significance of Asia are addressed in Chapter 1. Here I limit myself to the definition of Asia as a single security region and the broadening of that definition, if only tentatively, in this study to include the Middle East. This premise informs the delimitation of the study to states that are part of the Asian security region and the exclusion of Britain and France from it.

In line with my earlier work, Asia is conceptualized in this study as a single security region comprising several interconnected subregional clusters in Northeast, Southeast, South, and Central Asia, with Northeast Asia as its core (Alagappa 1998, 2003). This conceptualization is based on both security interdependence and growing internal and external recognition. The lines of amity and enmity that are regionally significant in Asia center largely on China but also on India and Japan. Beijing's security concerns span all four subregions, and China is a primary driver of international security for many countries in these subregions. India's security concerns span South, Southeast, Southwest, and Central Asia, and China in Northeast Asia. New Delhi's security relations with Tokyo appear to be on the uptick. Japan's security concerns span Northeast and Southeast Asia; South and Central Asia are also of increasing interest to the government in Tokyo. Conceptualizing Asia as a security region does not exclude countries from outside the region. Asia is the security footprint, but certain aspects of conflict formation and security governance in Asia, especially among the major powers, cannot be explained without reference to key outside powers, particularly the United States. As Chapter 1 will show, the United States plays a crucial security role in the region. Its policies influence major power relations in significant ways, and Sino-American relations are emerging as the central security dynamic affecting Asia. Thus, although not physically in the region, the United States is conceptualized in this study as part of the Asian security region. Although its impact does not compare with that of the former Soviet Union, Russia is part of the Asian security region by dint of its physical geography, its relevance to security in Northeast Asia, and its increasing interaction with China and India.

The delimitation of Asia as a single security region was received with skepticism in the 1990s, but developments since then have reinforced security interdependence among the various subregions in Asia and my case for such delimitation. All of the following are testimony to the increasing interconnectedness among the major powers in the Asian security region: the growing power and influence of China; rising concerns about international terrorism; Japan's developing strategic relations with Australia and India; India's sustained economic growth and its growing relations with all major powers, especially the growing economic, strategic, and defense relationship with the United States; the growing salience of the Sino-Indian relationship; the increasing Chinese, Russian, and Indian interest in Central Asia, and the newfound American interest and role in that region; the demonstrated interest of Japan and Southeast Asian countries to draw all relevant major powers into Asian regional institutions; the footprint and expanding membership of the Association of Southeast Asian Nations (ASEAN) Regional Forum and the East Asian Summit; the growing salience of the Shanghai Cooperation Organization; and trilateral dialogues such as those among China-India-Russia, the United States-Japan-India, and the United States-China-Japan. The deepening security connections among the subregions further contribute to the development of an Asia-wide security region. It should be noted that a region is used here to denote a group of countries whose in-group intensity of interaction is significant for their well-being or exceeds that with external actors (or both); it does not necessarily imply greater cohesion, identity, or ability to be a coherent actor in internal and international matters.

This study tentatively broadens the definition of Asia to include the adjoining Middle East region. Interactions based on religion, terrorist networks, energy supply, labor migration, and trade and investment, among others, have raised the importance of the Middle East for Asian countries. The strategic concerns of the major Asian countries increasingly include the Middle East. Islam and trade were historically important links connecting the Arab world, Persia, South Asia, Southeast Asia, and Central Asia. The oil supplies of the Arab world on which several major Asian countries are heavily dependent, the resurgence of Islam, the emergence and radicalization of some transnational Islamic groups, the Israeli-Palestinian conflict, the wars in Iraq and Afghanistan, and the regional aspirations of Iran are some of the modern-day issues that link the Middle East to Asia. This study investigates whether nuclear weapons deepen security interconnectedness between these regions or subregions. Nuclear weapons inform the security thinking of several states in the adjoining Middle East, which has one undeclared nuclear weapon state (Israel), and at least one other state (Iran) that is believed to have a covert nuclear weapon program. Recent developments appear to have rekindled interest in a nuclear option in Egypt. Concerned about the Iranian nuclear program, the Gulf Cooperation Council decided in December 2006 to establish a nuclear research program for the first time. A nuclear Israel has not directly affected security in Asia. Would a nuclear Iran, a state with regional ambitions, deepen connections among South Asia, Southwest Asia, and the Middle East? What would be the security implication of this, and would it justify broadening the definition of the Asian security region to include the Middle East?

About the Book

This study is organized in three parts. The Introduction and Part I set out the rationale, purpose, and propositions advanced in the study; they explore the contemporary security environment in and affecting Asia, as well as likely changes, with particular reference to drivers of insecurity and change; and they develop a historical and conceptual perspective to guide investigations in the ensuing chapters. Part II investigates the nuclear policies and strategies of six nuclear weapon states (the United States, Russia, China, India, Pakistan, and Israel) in the broadly defined Asian security region, four states that rely on the U.S. nuclear umbrella (Japan, South Korea, Taiwan, and Australia), two aspirant states (North Korea and Iran), nonstate organizations in Asia that may seek nuclear weapon capability, and the ASEAN states as a group that seek to make Southeast Asia a nuclear weapon-free zone. Drawing on the case studies in Part II, the two chapters in Part III explore the significance and roles of nuclear weapons in national security strategies and their implications for international security interdependence, conflict management, and regional stability.

Notes

1. Glenn Snyder (1961) first articulated the distinction between deterrence through punishment and deterrence through denial in 1959.

2. Other factors that have been advanced as contributing to the "long peace" include structural bipolarity (Waltz 1979), obsolescence of war among major powers (Mueller 1989), and reduction in the salience and spoils of war in the context of growing economic interdependence (Rosecrance 1986). It is important not to overstate the Euro-centric idea of a long peace. The first two to three decades of the Cold War era were in fact marked by several crises between the superpowers, and there were several "hot" wars involving them, especially in Asia (Korea, Vietnam, Afghanistan). The "long peace" in Asia only began in 1979.

3. George W. Bush, Graduation speech at West Point. June 1, 2002. Available at http://www.whitehouse.gov/news/releases/2002/06/20020601-3.html.

4. George W. Bush, State of the Union Address, 2002. Available at http://www.whitehouse.gov/news/releases/2002/01/20020129-11.html.

5. The George W. Bush administration did, however, seek to differentiate between responsible democratic states like India and "rogue" states like Iraq, North Korea, and Iran.

6. Mohamed ElBaradei (2006) states that "under the NPT there is no such thing as a 'legitimate' or 'illegitimate' nuclear weapon state." The recognition of five states as hold-

ers of nuclear weapons was regarded as a matter of transition. The NPT does not confer permanent status on the five countries.

7. In 1964 China adopted an NFU policy. In 1995 Beijing expanded this commitment when it issued an unconditional negative security assurance. See China's National Statement on Security Assurance of April 5, 1995 available at http://www.nti.org/db/china/engdocs/npt0495a.htm. Western analysts have tended to view the NFU commitment as symbolic and a reflection of operational constraints, rather than as a commitment to an altruistic principle. See, for example, Gill, Mulvenon, and Stokes (2001). Iain Johnston (1995/6) notes that many military strategists do not support the NFU policy. Major General (ret.) Pan Zhenqiang (2002) has presented certain scenarios (Washington's tactical use of nuclear weapons in the Taiwan Strait conflict, U.S. conventional attacks on China's nuclear weapons and facilities, and limited nuclear attack on China) that might force China to reconsider its NFU policy. See also Dingli Shen (2005).

8. See "DPRK Foreign Ministry Clarifies Stand on New Measure to Bolster War Deterrent." Korean Central News Agency of the DPRK, October 3, 2006.

9. Layne (1993) and Waltz (1993), for example, argued that unipolarity would be short lived.

10. Biddle (2000) disputes the claim that there has been an RMA and argues that the ability to manage complexity underpins the widening gap in military power.

11. It is possible to argue that missile defense, when it becomes effective against substantial nuclear threats and the RMA together, may mark a fundamental technological change with strategic consequences.

12. Thomas Schelling made this point in the discussion of the paper "Prospects for Nuclear Terrorism in Asia" at the first workshop of the East-West Center Washington project on "Nuclear Weapons and Security in 21st Century Asia" in Washington, D.C., May 1–3, 2006.

References

Alagappa, Muthiah. 1998. "Introduction." In *Asian Security Practice: Material and Ideational Influences,* ed. Muthiah Alagappa. Stanford, Calif.: Stanford University Press.

———. 2003. "Introduction: Predictability and Stability Despite Challenges." In *Asian Security Order: Instrumental and Normative Features,* ed. Muthiah Alagappa. Stanford, Calif.: Stanford University Press.

Allison, Graham. 2006. "Preface." In Graham Allison, guest editor, "Confronting the Specter of Nuclear Terrorism." American Academy of Political Science (AAPSS), *Annals* 607 (1): 6–9.

Berry, William E. 2005. "The Nuclear Posture Review and Northeast Asia: Theoretical and Policy Implications." In *Nuclear Transformation: The New U.S. Nuclear Doctrine,* ed. James J. Wirtz and Jeffrey A. Larsen. Basingstoke, U.K.: Palgrave Macmillan.

Biddle, Stephen. 2000. "Assessing Theories of Future Warfare." In *The Use of Force after the Cold War,* ed. H. W. Brands. College Station: Texas A&M University Press.

Braun, Chaim, and Christopher F. Chyba. 2004. "Proliferation Rings: New Challenges to the Nuclear Non Proliferation Regime." *International Security* 29, 2: 5–49.

Brodie, Bernard. 1946. "War in the Atomic Age'" and "Implications for Military Policy." In *The Absolute Weapon: Atomic Power and World Order,* Frederick S. Dunn, Bernard

Brodie, Arnold Wolfers, Percy E. Corbett, and William T. R. Fox. New York: Harcourt, Brace.

———. 1959. *Strategy in the Missile Age.* Princeton, N.J.: Princeton University Press.

Buchan, Glenn C., David Matonick, Calvin Shipbaugh, and Richard Mesic. 2003. *Future Roles of U.S. Nuclear Forces.* Santa Monica, Calif.: RAND.

Chirac, Jacques. 2006. Speech by President of the French Republic during his visit to the Strategic Air and Maritime Forces at Zlandivisiau/L'lle Longue. Available at www.elysee.fr.

Chubin, Shahram. 2006. *Iran's Nuclear Ambitions.* Washington, D.C.: Carnegie Endowment for International Peace.

Coyle, Philip. 2002. "Rhetoric or Reality? Missile Defense Under Bush." *Arms Control Today* 32 (4): 3–9.

———. 2006. *The Limits and Liabilities of Missile Defense.* Washington, D.C.: Center for Defense Information. Available at www. Ciaonet.org.proxyau.wrlc.org/wps/cdi022.html.

ElBaradei, Mohamed. 2006. "Rethinking Nuclear Safeguards." *The Washington Post,* June 14, page A23.

Fedorov, Yury E. 2006. "Old Wine in New Bottles: Russia's Nuclear Thinking and Policy in the 21st Century." Paper prepared for the East-West Center Washington first project meeting on Nuclear Weapons and Security in 21st Century Asia in Washington, D.C.

Ferguson, Charles. 2000. "Sparking a Buildup: U.S. Missile Defense and China's Nuclear Arsenal." *Arms Control Today* 30 (2): 113–18.

Freedman, Lawrence. 2004. *Deterrence.* Malden, Mass.: Polity.

Frost, Robin M. 2005. "Nuclear Terrorism after 9/11." Adelphi Paper no. 378. London: IISS.

Gaddis, John Lewis. 1987. *The Long Peace: Inquiries into the History of the Cold War.* Oxford: Oxford University Press.

Gallucci, Robert L. 2006. "Averting Nuclear Catastrophe: Contemplating Extreme Responses to U.S. Vulnerability. AAPSS, *Annals* 607 (1): 51–58.

Gill, Bates, James Mulvenon, and Mark Stokes. 2001. "The Chinese Second Artillery Corps: Transition to Credible Deterrence." In *The People's Liberation Army as an Organization,* ed. James C. Mulvenon and Andrew Yang. Santa Monica, Calif.: RAND (2002), pp. 510–86.

Glaser, Charles L. 1990. *Analyzing Strategic Nuclear Policy.* Princeton, N.J.: Princeton University Press.

Glaser, Charles L., and Steve Fetter. 2001. "National Missile Defense and the Future of U.S. Nuclear Weapons Policy." *International Security* 26 (1): 40–92.

Goldstein, Avery. 2000. *Deterrence and Security in the 21st Century.* Stanford, Calif.: Stanford University Press.

Gray, Colin S. 2001. "Nuclear Weapons and the Revolution in Military Affairs." In *The Absolute Weapon Revisited: Nuclear Weapons and the Emerging International Order,* ed. T. V. Paul, Richard J. Harknett, and James J. Wirtz. Ann Arbor: The University of Michigan Press.

Harknett, Richard J., James J. Wirtz, and T. V. Paul. 2001. "Introduction: Understanding Nuclear Weapons in a Transformed Role." In *The Absolute Weapon Revisited: Nuclear*

Arms and the Emerging International Order, ed. T. V Paul, Richard J. Harknett, and James J. Wirtz. Ann Arbor: The University of Michigan Press.

Holton, W. Conrad. 2005. "Power Surge: Renewed Interest in Nuclear Energy." In *Environmental Health Perspectives,* 113, 11: A742–A749.

International Institute for Strategic Studies (IISS). 2004. "The Impact of Missile Defence in Asia." *IISS Strategic Comments* 10 (6): 40–45.

Jervis, Robert. 1989. *The Meaning of the Nuclear Revolution: Statecraft and the Prospect of Armageddon.* Ithaca, N.Y.: Cornell University Press.

Johnson-Freese, Joan. 2007. "The Chinese Anti-Satellite Weapons Is a Challenge but the U.S. Would Be Better Off Not Overreacting." *YaleGlobal,* February 6. Available at http://yaleglobal.yale.edu/display.article?id=8714.

Johnston, Alastair Iain. 1995/6. "China's New 'Old Thinking': The Concept of Limited Deterrence." *International Security* 20 (3): 21–23.

Kartchner, Kerry M. 2005. "Implementing Missile Defense." In *Nuclear Transformation: The New U.S. Nuclear Doctrine,* ed. James J. Wirtz and Jeffrey A. Larsen. London: Palgrave Macmillan.

Kissinger, Henry A. 1957. *Nuclear Weapons and Foreign Policy.* New York: Council on Foreign Relations.

Knopf, Jeffrey W. 2002. "Recasting the Proliferation Optimism-Pessimism Debate." *Security Studies* 12, 1: 41–96.

Layne, Christopher. 1993. "The Unipolar Illusion: Why New Great Powers Will Rise." *International Security* 17 (4): 5–51.

Metz, Steven, and James Kievit. 1994. *The Revolution in Military Affairs and Conflict Short of War.* Carlisle, Penn.: Strategic Studies Institute, U.S. Army War College.

Morgan, Patrick M. 2003. *Deterrence Now.* Cambridge: Cambridge University Press.

Mueller, John. 1988. "The Essential Irrelevance of Nuclear Weapons." *International Security* 13 (2): 55–79.

———.1989. *Retreat from Doomsday: The Obsolescence of Major War.* New York: Basic Books.

Pan Zhenqiang. 2002. "On China's No First Use of Nuclear Weapons." *Pugwash Online.* November 26. Available at www.pugwash.org/reports/nw/zhenqiang.htm.

Payne, Keith. 1985. *Why SDI?* Fairfax, Va.: National Institute for Public Policy.

Powell, Robert. 2003. "Nuclear Deterrence Theory, Nuclear Proliferation, and National Missile Defense." *International Security* 27 (4): 86–118.

Rosecrance, Richard. 1986. *The Rise of the Trading State: Commerce and Conquest in the Modern World.* Ithaca, N.Y.: Cornell University Press.

Sagan, Scott D. 1994. "The Perils of Proliferation: Organization Theory, Deterrence Theory, and the Spread of Nuclear Weapons." *International Security* 18 (4): 66–107.

Sagan, Scott D., and Kenneth N. Waltz. *The Spread of Nuclear Weapons: A Debate.* New York: W. W. Norton and Company.

Schelling, Thomas C. 2006. "Nuclear Deterrence for the Future." *Issues in Science and Technology* 23 (1): 50–52.

Secretary of State for Defense and the Secretary of State for Foreign and Commonwealth Affairs. 2006. *The Future of the United Kingdom's Nuclear Deterrent.* London: Crown Copyright.

Shen, Dingli. 2005. "Nuclear Deterrence in the 21st Century." In *China Security* (World Security Institute China Program) (Autumn 2005): 10–14. Also available at http://wsichina.org/www/Focus.cfm?Focusid=20&charid=1.

Snyder, Glenn H. 1961. *Deterrence and Defense: Toward a Theory of National Security.* Westport, Conn.: Greenwood Press.

Sokolski, Henry. 2006. "Rethinking Nuclear Terrorism." Paper presented at the conference "Islamistic Terrorism and Means of Mass Destruction" at the Round Table of the Hanns-Seidel Stiftung in Wilbad/Kreuth, Germany.

Sokov, Nikolai. 2004. *Russia's Nuclear Doctrine.* Available at www.nti.org/e_research/e3_55a.html.

State Council Information Office. 2000. *PRC White Paper on China's National Defense 2000.* Beijing: State Council Information Office.

Tellis, Ashley J. 2007. *Punching the U.S. Military's "Soft Ribs": China's Antisatellite Weapon Test in Strategic Perspective.* Washington, D.C.: Carnegie Endowment for International Peace, Policy Brief 51.

U.S. Department of Defense. 1994. *Nuclear Posture Review.* Available at http://www.fas.org/nuke/guide/usa/doctrine/dod/95-npr.htm.

———. 2002. *Nuclear Posture Review in the DoD Annual Report to the President and the Congress.* Available at www.defenselink.mil/execsec/adr2002/toc2002.htm.

———. 2006. *Annual Report to the Congress: Military Power of the People's Republic of China 2006.* Available at http://www.defenselink.mil/pubs/pdfs/China%20Report%202006.pdf.

Waltz, Kenneth N. 1993. "The Emerging Structure of International Politics." *International Security* 18 (2): 45–73.

Yost, David. S. 2006. "France's New Nuclear Doctrine." *International Affairs* 82 (4): 701–21.

PART I

Historical, Strategic, and Conceptual Perspectives

1

Asia's Security Environment
From Subordinate to Region Dominant System

MUTHIAH ALAGAPPA

To provide the context for investigating the roles of nuclear weapons and their implications for regional security and stability, this chapter maps Asia's present security environment and likely changes in that environment. It advances four propositions. First, contemporary Asia's security environment is fundamentally different from that of the Cold War period when Asia was a subordinate security region penetrated and dominated by the ideological and strategic confrontation between the United States and the Soviet Union. Today, Asia has become a core world region with distinctive economic, normative, and institutional features. The dynamics of security in Asia are increasingly shaped by the interaction of interests and priorities of states in the Asian security region. Conflict formation, management, and resolution are grounded largely in regional and local dynamics. Extraregional actors are involved but their salience derives from their interaction with Asian state and nonstate actors on issues of mutual concern.

Second, Asia's security environment is likely to substantially alter over the next two to three decades. Escalation or resolution of regional conflicts (Taiwan, Korea, and Kashmir) and regime change in countries like China, Indonesia, and Pakistan could bring about interaction change at a subregional level. They may also trigger broader changes. More fundamental system-level consequences, however, are likely to result from two ongoing trends. One is the rise of Asian powers, their quests for power, status, and wealth, and differing visions of regional order set in a context of the continuing desire of the United States to remain the preeminent power in Asia. The sustained rise of Asian powers is likely to result in gradual structure change and make relative gain considerations and strategic competition more significant. China's rise would pose the most significant challenge to the U.S.-dominated security order in Asia making Sino-American relations the primary security dynamic with regionwide security implications. Sino-Japanese and Sino-Indian relationships would also become consequential. How these relationships evolve and interact with each other, and the "eventual" configuration of relations among major powers, however, remain uncertain. Although several outcomes are possible, I argue that a gradual transition from a U.S.-centered system to a loose informal balance-of-power system with the de facto purpose of preventing domination of Asia by a single power is likely. Although the U.S. power and influence in Asia will decline, it will remain the lead power over the next two decades.

The continuing dynamism of Asian economies and their increasing integration into regional and global economies is another important driver of change. It creates a dynamic that reinforces as well as counteracts strategic competition. As their economic power increases, Asian countries would be able to devote greater resources to build military capabilities and other capacities to pursue competing foreign policy objectives. This could intensify strategic competition. Growing economic integration and interdependence could, on the other hand, temper competition and modify adversarial relationships by creating alternative lines of interaction and vested interest in peace and stability. Regional cooperation and rule-governed interaction for mutual economic benefit could have spillover effects and reinforce peace and security. Interaction of the two drivers of change makes for a complicated strategic picture that defies single theory explanation and prediction. The Asian strategic situation is more akin to that of complex interdependence characterized by cooperation, competition, and conflict.

Third, the chapter posits that although it will not be free of tension and will be characterized by a significant degree of uncertainty and hedging, the gradual transition from a U.S.-centered system to an informal balance-of-power system is likely to be relatively peaceful. The primary attention of Asian states in the next decade or more would be internally directed toward economic growth, modernization, state and nation building, and addressing domestic challenges. Maintaining a stable international environment that is conducive to the pursuit of these national goals and preventing international interference in their domestic affairs will be a primary foreign policy objective and determinant of security order. This does not imply that states will not seek to build national power and influence, alter the status quo, or engage in strategic competition. These pursuits will be moderated by other concerns, priorities, and deep interest in stability. Finally, the chapter argues that military force will remain an important instrument of policy in the interaction of major powers, but largely in defense, deterrence, and assurance roles, not in aggression. States will seek to avoid strategic confrontation and full-scale war but at the same time hedge against uncertainty and unanticipated developments. In strategic matters, the behavior of major powers will approximate more closely to defensive realism than offensive realism.

From a Subordinate to a Region Dominant Security System

Over the past century, Asia has traveled from a position of imperial subordination and fragmentation to a position of substantial strength, with several Asian states having the power to influence regional and global affairs. From the sixteenth century to the mid-twentieth century, international politics in Asia was dominated by the intrusion of Western powers (much earlier in South and Southeast Asia than in Northeast Asia) and later by imperial Japan (from the late nineteenth century).[1] The colonial and semicolonial era ended the indigenous interstate systems that had operated in Asia and transformed the nature and boundaries of Asian political units and their economies. Upon independence, these countries (though some had long histories, almost all were new as modern nation-states) were integrated into the global international system still dominated by the West. For much of the Cold War, Asia was a subordinate security region penetrated and dominated by the ideological and strategic confrontation between the two superpowers.

Cold War Asia: A Subordinate Security Region

A loose Asia-wide regional security system emerged for the first time in history upon decolonization, which coincided with the onset of the Cold War. The intense zero-sum ideological and military confrontation between the United States (leader of the so-called free world) and the Soviet Union (leader of the socialist world), with Europe as the focal point, infused and shaped the Asian security environment. The intrusion of superpower confrontation created connections among Asian powers and subregions that otherwise would have been relatively isolated. At the same time, the Soviet-American struggle polarized Asia into two rival blocs, with China initially allying with the Soviet Union, and Japan deeply bound to the United States. In this context, some Asian countries, with India as a leader, opted for nonalignment. With the onset of the Sino-Soviet conflict, and Washington's adoption of the Guam doctrine, China aligned with the United States (and Japan) against the Soviet Union. After the 1962 Sino-Indian war, New Delhi gradually leaned toward Moscow while Washington, Tokyo, and Beijing drew closer. Local conflicts such as the many communist insurgencies in Southeast Asia, the Taiwan Strait conflict, the Vietnam wars, the Cambodian conflict, and to a lesser degree the India-Pakistan conflict were all penetrated, overlaid, or transformed by the conflicts and rivalries between the superpowers.

No Asian power could stand alone. India's initial attempt to develop a position independent of the bipolar confrontation was not successful. All three Asian powers (China, Japan, and India) chose alliance or alignment with one of the two superpowers. In the 1950s and early 1960s, China allied with the Soviet Union to deal with the threat posed by the United States. The latter perceived China as presenting the foremost security threat to the free world in Asia and had threatened a nuclear attack against it during the Korean War. However, Moscow's reluctant support of China during the Korean War and the 1958 Taiwan crisis, China's growing concern that an alliance with the Soviet Union might compromise its national interests and complicate military planning, fear of abandonment in the event of a crisis, and emerging tensions with Moscow argued the case for self-reliance, impelling Beijing to accelerate its nuclear program, leading to the 1964 atomic and 1967 hydrogen bomb tests (Goldstein 2000: 62–90). However, despite the tests, as a second-rank power still lacking an effective deterrence capability, and now perceiving its primary security threat as emanating from Moscow, Beijing entered into a strategic alignment with Washington. It stressed the common Soviet threat to free ride on the U.S. strategic deterrent. Only in the 1980s did China begin to assume a more independent security posture, mediating the impact of the bipolar confrontation on the strategic situation in Asia.

Under American tutelage and subsequent concern with the Soviet threat, Japan relied on its security alliance with the United States, including the nuclear umbrella of that country. However, unlike Washington, Tokyo did not perceive a security threat from Beijing and worried about becoming entrapped in the U.S. policy of containing China. Tokyo's concern eased with the development of the U.S.-China rapprochement and strategic alignment in the 1970s against the Soviet Union, which Japan perceived as the primary threat. As observed earlier, India's effort to position itself apart from the bipolar confrontation was not successful. New Delhi leaned toward Moscow because of its concern with China that became heightened after India's defeat in 1962, the U.S. pro-Pakistan position in the India-Pakistan conflict, and Sino-American rapprochement. India and the Soviet Union entered into a de facto alliance in 1971. Although like China, but much later, India took sides in the Cold War in pursuit of its own national interests, it was less deeply involved in the bipolar confrontation. India's nuclear weapon program had its roots in the confrontations with China and Pakistan. The drivers of the Indian nuclear program have been the subject of much debate, with some analysts arguing the primacy of domestic variables, and others positing greater salience of the international security rationale (Jones and Ganguly 2000; Tellis 2001: 20–115). Rajesh Rajagopalan notes in this volume that a strong case can be made that the need for and direction of the Indian nuclear weapon program was driven in large part by the security rationale, while its pace may have been influenced by limited technological capabilities in the 1960s and by domestic political and bureaucratic factors.

Pakistan more explicitly engaged in the Cold War through its alliance with the United States and later alignment with China, but its principal focus was India, not China or the Soviet Union. Pakistan's nuclear weapon program was initiated in the aftermath of its crushing defeat by India in the 1971 war, the ensuing dismemberment of Pakistan, and the peaceful Indian nuclear test in 1974. Subsequent development of the program had to do with military domination of politics in Pakistan and Islamabad's desire to counter and compete with India. The development of Pakistan's program, however, benefited from Chinese assistance in the context of the Sino-Indian conflict and U.S. diplomatic and military support during the Cold War. Perceiving Pakistan as a close ally, U.S. support included turning a blind eye to Pakistan's nuclear weapon program.

Unlike the India-Pakistan conflict, which was only marginally connected to the Cold War confrontation, the conflicts across the Taiwan Strait and on the Korean peninsula were produced by or became deeply enmeshed in the Cold War. In the conflict between the Chinese Communist Party (CCP) and the Guomindang or Nationalist Party (KMT) over which was the rightful government of China, the United States backed the KMT and became committed to defending Taiwan, while the People's Republic of China (PRC) relied on the Soviet Union. On the Korean peninsula, the Cold War divided the peninsula. The United States backed the Republic of Korea (ROK, or South Korea), and China and the Soviet Union backed the Democratic People's Republic of Korea (DPRK, or North Korea). Taiwan and South Korea became pawns in the game of great power competition. Their survival was contingent on the commitment of Washington. Both countries feared abandonment by the United States.

The Chinese nuclear test in 1964, U.S. refusal to bomb China's nuclear facilities, and virtual "abandonment" of Taiwan by Washington in its rapprochement with Beijing in the 1970s motivated Taipei to embark on an indigenous nuclear weapon program (Mitchell 2004). Under intense U.S. pressure, in 1976 Taipei committed itself not to acquire or engage in reprocessing. Despite this, Washington discovered in 1988 that Taiwan was within a year or two of building a nuclear bomb. Again under intense U.S. pressure, Taiwan agreed to conclusively and verifiably end the program. Similarly, the 1969 Guam doctrine (which sought to shift the burden of defense responsibility to Asian states) and the Sino-American rapprochement in 1971–72 (which marginalized Taiwan) created much insecurity in Seoul and led to the institution of a covert nuclear weapon program (Pollack and Reiss 2004). This program was ended under U.S. pressure, which included the threat of abrogation of the bilateral security treaty. In both cases, erosion of the credibility of the U.S. security commitment was the key variable in the decisions to embark on indigenous nuclear weapon programs.

From the preceding brief discussion, it is evident that the loose Cold War Asian security system was subordinate to and deeply penetrated by global bipolarity and the dynamics of superpower competition. Conflict formation and management, the responses of regional states and relations among them, and the security policies of Asian states (including nuclear policies) were heavily influenced by a global structure over which they had little control and by a set of largely external dynamics. Except in maritime Southeast Asia, which was the only Asian subregion until the 1980s to witness the development of indigenous multilateral subregional cooperation, all other regional efforts were led by one of the two superpowers and took the form of alliances or strategic alignments. During much of the Cold War era Asia was a subordinate region and a theater of several hot wars that had their primary drivers elsewhere.

Asia Becomes a Core World Region

Beginning in the mid- to late-1980s Asia emerged as a distinct core world region. Economic dynamism of Asian countries, growing interdependence among them and with other power centers, forging of a shared regional normative structure among Asian states, and development of regionwide institutions have been crucial drivers and indicators of regional distinctiveness and the emergence of Asia as a core world region.

Dramatic economic growth of East Asian countries (Japan, South Korea, Taiwan, and Hong Kong) and certain Association of Southeast Asian Nations (ASEAN) countries (Singapore, Thailand, Malaysia, and Indonesia) in the 1970s and 1980s combined with growing intraregional economic interaction (trade, investment, and manufacturing) centered on Japan provided the initial impetus for regionalization and recognition of East Asia as a significant economic region (Katzenstein and Shiraishi 1996). By 1990, East and Southeast Asian countries minus China had become major trading partners of the United States and the European Union. In the late 1980s, it was conventional wisdom to assert that with the meteoric rise of Japan and the newly industrializing countries (NICs), the center of the word economy was shifting to the Pacific Basin (Gilpin 1987). The opening up of the Chinese economy in 1979 and its sustained rapid growth since then has further increased the economic weight of Asia. Along with and rivaling Japan, China has become a key engine of growth in the world.

Economic stagnation in Japan for over a decade and the 1997–98 Asian financial crisis tarred the miracle economy image, but Asia has since recovered. The pace of growth of many Asian economies has slowed but is still advancing at a respectable rate. China continues to grow rapidly, and Japan appears to be recovering from its long stagnation. The gradual liberalization of the Indian economy beginning in 1991 and sustained high growth rates since 2003–04 adds to the economic weight of Asia. In current prices (using U.S. dollars), East Asian countries and India accounted for about 22 percent of the world's gross domestic product (GDP) in 2005. In purchasing power parity (PPP) terms the share was about 35 percent. Asia accounted for about 50 percent of world growth that year. The Economist Intelligence Unit's "Foresight 2020" estimates that Asia's share of the global economy will increase to 43 percent by 2020. Collectively, Asia accounted for more than 30 percent of total world trade in 2001. It is also an important destination for private capital flows, including foreign direct investment, a major consumer of energy, and is fast becoming the manufacturing and offshore base for the world. In 2005, East Asian countries and India collectively held over US$1.6 trillion in foreign exchange reserves. Several Asian countries (Japan, China, South Korea, and India) have or are becoming significant economic actors regionally as well as globally, with implications for trade, investment, energy sourcing and consumption, and the environment. The participation of Asian countries in addressing regional and global problems has become crucial, as for example in negotiating world trade arrangements and addressing the problem of global imbalances.

Concurrently, Asian economic interdependence has increased intraregional merchandise trade from 42 percent in 1990 to 50 percent in 2004. Intraregional production networks and investment have contributed to the increase in regional interdependence. And there is a desire in the Asian policy community for greater regional economic interdependence (Petri 2006). Numerous bilateral and multilateral trade agreements focused on the region are being negotiated or planned; new regional dialogues involving ASEAN, China, Japan, South Korea, and other countries are being explored; and there is growing interest in regional financial arrangements, including a common currency after the 1997–98 financial crisis. Asia's economic interaction with the rest of the world, especially the United States and Europe, has deepened. Through investments, energy exploration and pipeline contracts, trade and trade-related loans, aid, and political support for certain regimes, Asian countries (Japan and increasingly China) are also making significant inroads in the Middle East, Russia, Latin America, and Africa. It is possible to argue that growing economic significance in the aggregate does not matter since Asian countries, unlike their European counterparts, do not act collectively. This is partially valid. My point, however, is that Asian countries, individually and collectively, have moved or are moving to the core of the international economic system with power to shape the patterns of trade, investment, production, and the structure and governance of regional and global economies.

Along with economic growth and increasing economic interdependence, the development of indigenous subregional and regional institutions has contributed to the emergence of Asia as a distinct region. Initially limited to Southeast Asia, regional organizations have become more widespread and numerous. Asia is now home to several inclusive subregional organizations including ASEAN (formed in 1967), the South Asian Association for Regional Cooperation (SAARC, 1985), and the Shanghai Cooperation Organization (SCO, 2001), which has its origins in the Shanghai Five that was formed in 1996. Certain countries desire to convert the ongoing Six-Party Talks on North Korea into a security forum for Northeast Asia. Beginning with the formation of the Asia-Pacific Economic Cooperation (APEC) forum in 1989, Asia has also witnessed the development of several regionwide organizations including the ASEAN Regional Forum (ARF, 1994), the ASEAN Plus Three (APT, 1999), and the East Asia Summit (EAS, 2005). The region is also home to several significant U.S.-led military alliances (U.S.-Japan, U.S.-South Korea, and U.S.-Australia).

Not only is Asia home to several regional organizations, but over the years it has also developed a shared normative framework. The core norms of this framework can be traced to the Five Principles of Peaceful Coexistence articulated by India and China in 1955 and which were incorporated into the final Bandung communiqué of the twenty-nine nation Asia-Africa Conference held that year. The 1976 Treaty of Amity and Cooperation in Southeast Asia, which has since been signed and ratified by all ten Southeast Asian countries, reaffirms those principles. Interaction among signatories, according to the Treaty, is to be guided by the following values: mutual respect for the independence, sovereignty, equality, territorial integrity, and national identity of all nations; the right of every nation to lead its national existence free from external interference, subversion, or coercion; noninterference in the internal affairs of one another; settlement of differences or disputes by peaceful means; renunciation of the threat and use of force; and effective cooperation. The principles of the 1976 Treaty have been endorsed by the ARF, and the Treaty has been acceded to by several key non-Southeast Asian states including China, India, Japan, Russia, and Australia. Accession to the Treaty has been made a precondition for membership in the EAS. The principles have also been incorporated into the ASEAN Charter adopted in 2007. Similar principles inform the charters of SAARC and the SCO.

Certain observers, especially from the West, tend to disparage Asian regional organizations as mere talk shops with little substantive content and the normative framework as pro forma echoes of the United Nations (U.N.) Charter with little meaning, as the Asian states have failed to translate these norms into binding rules of behavior and, in fact, have frequently violated them (Jones and Smith 2007). The cynical view of a shared normative framework was indeed justified in the early postindependence period that coincided with the Cold War when Asian countries did frequently violate the norms they publicly articulated. However, in time the norms have become deeply imprinted in the mind-set of the Asian political elite across Asia—contributing to a shared set of norms that increasingly influences the behavior of states. Although Asian regional organizations suffer several shortcomings, especially in comparison with European ones, and their contribution may appear limited on the basis of rationalist and community-building criteria, they perform several invaluable functions. These include creating a sense of regional awareness and a sense of common good; providing a forum for discussion of regional disputes, common concerns, and issues; ameliorating bilateral and regional tensions; constraining the use of force; providing opportunities for cooperation and exercising a collective voice in international forums; and most significantly in socializing elites and in constructing a regional normative framework (Acharya 2003; Alagappa 2003b).

Asian regional institutions, however, have not played a transforming role except perhaps in Southeast Asia. And even in this subregion the much-touted transforming role of ASEAN is questionable. As Jones and Smith (2007) argue, ASEAN and related organizations have been long on community-building visions but very short in realizing them. A long-range vision of an East Asian community has been under discussion for some time now but there is little agreement on substantive content, footprint, membership, and the suitable institutional vehicle for pursuing such an objective. Competing national interests appear likely to hamper such efforts. Nevertheless, Asian regional institutions have become a visible sign of internal and international recognition of Asia as a distinct region. External actors like the United States and Europe now engage in regular dialogue with Asian regional institutions.

Post-Cold War Asia: A Distinct Regional Security System

Concurrent with the emergence of Asia as a core economic region and the development of regional norms and organizations, the security system in Asia has become more distinct and autonomous. Some see regional distinctiveness in the structure of the Asian system and its organizing principle. David Kang (2003), for example, posits that Asia is becoming China-centric and that hierarchy rather than anarchy is the organizing principle of the China-centered Asian system. Robert Ross (1999, 2003) posits that East Asia is already a bipolar system, with China dominant in the East Asian land mass and the United States dominant in maritime East Asia or the rimland. I disagree with these positions. The system in Asia is not Sino-centric, and sovereignty-conscious East and Southeast Asian states do not accept hierarchy or Chinese dominance. They seek good relations with China but several also seek to hedge, balance, and constrain China. There is no return to history. The view that a hierarchic Sino-centric order existed in historical times or that it was always hierarchic is also contested (Ledyard 1983; Rossabi 1983; Yang 1968). The present system in Asia is also not bipolar. China has become an economic powerhouse, and its diplomatic influence is increasing, but it is not a comprehensive power. It is still far behind the United States, especially in military power but also in several other dimensions of power. Though enjoying economic and diplomatic success, Beijing has limited positive ideational capital for regional political leadership. With erosion in the ideological underpinning of its Marxist-Leninist political system, Beijing itself is in search of a viable political model. Those who see East Asia as Sino-centric or bipolar often ignore Japan, which still has the second largest economy in the world, a strong conventional military capability, and is closely allied with the United States. My view is that global unipolarity also pervades Asia. Although Asia is home to several large powers, some of which may in due course substantially dilute the power and influence of the United States and challenge its primacy, for now none is able to compete with the United States.

The Asian regional system is distinctive not because of its structure or organizing principle but because of the centrality of regional and local dynamics in conflict formation, management, and resolution. Unlike during the Cold War, when internal and international conflicts in the region were overlaid by the Soviet-American ideological and strategic confrontation, regional actors and their interests now drive conflict formation and resolution in Asia. Extraregional actors are involved in certain conflicts, but their salience derives from their interaction with Asian state and nonstate actors on issues of mutual concern. They do not override indigenous actors and dynamics. Settlement or resolution of security problems in Asia now hinges on addressing indigenous roots rather than merely external ones. At the same time, there is no overarching regional security dynamic that permeates all or even most security challenges in Asia. Even when Asian states confront common security challenges, each internal and international conflict has its own dynamics that are only marginally linked to others. The ensuing discussion of the contemporary security challenges in Asia demonstrates the regional and local basis of conflict formation and resolution.

Internal Security Challenges. Internal conflicts over political identity and legitimacy have been a prominent feature of the Asian political-security landscape since 1945. Asia has witnessed numerous civil wars, armed insurgencies, coups d'etat, revolutions, and regional rebellions. Many have been protracted; several have had far-reaching implications. The civil war in Pakistan, for example, led to the breakup of the country in 1971. During the Cold War, many internal conflicts were penetrated and in some cases transformed by the overarching global security dynamic, with the two superpowers supporting rival groups and at times engaging directly in war as for example in Vietnam and over Cambodia. With the termination of the Cold War, the global strategic overlay has disappeared. There is no new global or regional equivalent.

Asian countries continue to witness numerous internal conflicts over political identity and legitimacy, many of which are rooted in contestations over center-elite-led nation- and state-building projects. Although there are common features across countries, each internal conflict has its own dynamic that has to be addressed on its own merit. For example, there are interconnections among the conflicts in Nepal, Northeast India, Bangladesh, and Burma, or in the Pakistan-Afghanistan border area. These interconnections are rooted in ethnic and religious ties, common ideology, or simply in pragmatism, and facilitated by porous borders and weak states. Islamic international terrorism appears to be a connecting thread for internal conflicts in Afghanistan, Pakistan, India (Kashmir), and Bangladesh in South Asia, and to a lesser degree in Indonesia and the Philippines in Southeast Asia. Although international connections are important and must be addressed, these conflicts are essentially grounded in local political and socioeconomic grievances: Without them the international dimension would be irrelevant. This is not intended to downplay the significance of international connections but to place them in proper perspective to highlight the salience of local and subregional dynamics that must be addressed in conflict management and resolution.

International Terrorism. Likewise terrorism, which has long been a concern for several Asian states, is rooted in local conditions. Terrorist methods have been employed by subnational groups in their struggle to gain autonomy or independence from the states in which they were located. In some cases these groups had the support of similar groups in neighboring countries and at times were supported and used by certain neighboring states. The international connections of these groups, especially to the Middle East and Pakistan, were highlighted and became more evident after 9/11. International nonstate actors and their causes are important in establishing regional and global networks, but to be successful they must connect with local groups, their causes, and objectives.

Since South Asia adjoins Southwest Asia and is close to the Middle East, terrorism is a major concern in this subregion, with the nexus of the Taliban, Al-Qaeda, and Pakistan as the central focus. When it was in power in Afghanistan, the Taliban provided a safe haven for Al-Qaeda, which is believed to be seeking weapons of mass destruction. Pakistan had supported the Taliban regime as a way of influencing developments in neighboring Afghanistan and to secure strategic depth in the event of a war with India. Although dislodged and disrupted, the Taliban and Al-Qaeda appear to be regrouping in Afghanistan and along the ungoverned Afghanistan-Pakistan border. Islamabad has since joined the war on terrorism, but it also sees militancy and terror as a useful instrument of policy in its conflict with New Delhi. India has borne the brunt of militant insurgent movements and terrorism in South Asia. Cross-border terrorist activities have reached deep into India, raising the potential for major armed hostilities between India and Pakistan. Confronted with terrorist attacks in its heartland and in the areas bordering Afghanistan, Islamabad now appears to be reconsidering its approach to militant and terrorist movements with sanctuary in its territory.

In Southeast Asia there is an international dimension to terrorism, but the terrorist threats in the Philippines and Thailand are linked to separatist struggles waged by minority communities. In Indonesia, Singapore, and Malaysia, the concern is with the regional Jemaah Islamiya (JI), which, according to terrorism experts, seeks to establish Islamic states and an Islamic caliphate in maritime Southeast Asia (Abuza 2003; Vaughn et al. 2005). At present, however, JI appears to be in disarray. Although the nature, intensity, and purposes of the terrorist threat may vary, it is perceived as a significant threat by several Asian governments. Some states have jumped on the bandwagon to serve their parochial political interests. Sri Lanka, for example, seeks to deal with the ethnic minority problem under the label of terrorism. China brands Uyghur resistance movements as terrorists, while the Philippines seeks to label the Moro Islamic Liberation Front that is seeking autonomy for the Muslims as a terrorist group.

Although nonstate transnational actors have always existed, certain contemporary actors (such as Al-Qaeda and JI) and the challenge they pose for national and international security is specific to the contemporary era. These actors not only challenge the very foundation of a system based on sovereign states but, in addition, their nonterritorial organization and activities, their attempt to acquire sophisticated and highly destructive weapons, and their use of high-technology communications and information methods make it exceedingly difficult for states to detect, deter, and defeat them.[2] The threats posed by such organizations are likely to continue for some time, but on their own they are unlikely to have systemic implications. The greater danger lies in the possibility that radical Islamic groups may acquire or seize state power in majority Muslim countries like Pakistan, Bangladesh, or Indonesia. Such developments would have subregional implications in South and Southeast Asia and connect these subregions more closely to the Middle East.

A related concern is the threat of nuclear terrorism. In Asia, the concerns center largely on Pakistan and North Korea and to a much smaller degree on India. In the case of Pakistan, the international concern centers on the unstable nature of the Musharraf regime and the fear that in the event of political instability its nuclear weapons and facilities may come under the control of Islamic extremist political parties or military elements sympathetic to the anti-West, anti-India, anti-Israel causes of radical Islamic groups; or that radical Islamic groups on their own or in collusion with military elements could take control of certain nuclear facilities (Basrur and Rizvi 2003). In India the concern is with possible terrorist attacks on nuclear facilities or that terrorists may target nuclear weapons in storage or in transit. India and Pakistan (the latter with U.S. assistance) appear to have taken a series of measures to reduce their exposure by safeguarding nuclear facilities and securing command and control arrangements. In the case of North Korea, as discussed earlier, the concern is that Pyongyang may aid or sell nuclear technology to terrorist groups.

Concern about illicit trafficking of nuclear and other radioactive material, though traditionally directed at the former Soviet states, has become an important issue in Asia, especially in relation to South and Southeast Asia (Prosser 2004). Of particular concern is the proliferation network of A. Q. Khan, which is believed to have done enormous damage to international peace and stability and to the nonproliferation regime (Albright and Henderson 2005). It is believed that without assistance from this network Iran would not have been able to develop a uranium enrichment capability. There is also suspicion that the network may have helped Al-Qaeda obtain nuclear secrets before the fall of the Taliban regime.[3] Revelations of the A. Q. Khan proliferation network and of trade in nuclear weapon-related dual-use technologies have highlighted issues relating to nuclear safety and security. Clearly there are regional and global dimensions that must be addressed. At the same time, conflict management, including settlement, hinges on addressing the core local and subregional issues. This is evident, for example, in the effort to deal with the North Korean problem through the Six-Party Talks.

Territorial Disputes. Asia is witness to numerous territorial disputes on land and at sea (Blanchard 2003; Fravel 2005; Wang 2003). Nearly every country has had a border dispute with its neighbor(s), and several still continue to do so. China, India, Russia, and Japan have long-standing territorial disputes with each other. The disputes between China and India and between China and Vietnam led to major wars. The territorial dispute between China and the Soviet Union resulted in a military clash in 1968. Most territorial disputes have their origins in ill-defined boundaries by colonial powers or in the contestation of colonial demarcations. Maritime territorial disputes are relatively recent, with their origins in the interpretation and implementation of the Law of the Sea Treaty regime and in competing historical claims. Some of these disputes in the East and South China Seas have resulted in occasional military clashes. The territorial conflicts on land and at sea were not deeply enmeshed in the Cold War strategic dynamic. Settlement in some cases and continuation of others demonstrate the importance of domestic and bilateral dynamics.[4] In the present context, territorial disputes other than those considered crucial for state identity and sovereignty appear unlikely to result in major wars. In certain cases, as for example between China and India, conflicting parties have entered into bilateral negotiations to manage and possibly resolve their dispute; in some other cases (between Malaysia and Indonesia, and between Malaysia and Singapore) certain territorial disputes have been submitted for international adjudication.

Identity and Sovereignty Conflicts. Of the continuing security challenges in Asia, the long-standing identity and sovereignty conflicts involving Taiwan, Korea, and Kashmir are the most significant from a regional perspective. During the Cold War these conflicts, especially those across the Taiwan Strait and on the Korean peninsula, were deeply enmeshed in the Soviet-American confrontation. Over time the nature of these conflicts has been transformed and their dynamics have become largely regional and local.

Regionalization and Localization. Beginning in the late 1980s the conflict between the KMT and the CCP over the right to rule China was transformed into a conflict between China and Taiwan over the identity and sovereignty of Taiwan. Asserting that Taiwan is a part of China, Beijing claims sovereignty over that island state. Its goal is to unify Taiwan with China if necessary through the use of force. With the transfer of KMT leadership to native Taiwanese leaders and democratization, both major Taiwan political parties (the Democratic Progressive Party [DPP] and the KMT) have rejected unification but are split on the issue of independence. The survival of Taiwan as a de facto sovereign state rests on the security guarantee of the United States that was initially given in the context of the Cold War. After the normalization of U.S. relations with China in 1979, that security guarantee became implicit but was demonstrated when the need arose. Washington adheres to a one-China policy; it is firmly opposed to unilateral change in Taiwan's status or status change through the use of force.

The Korean conflict was produced and deeply embedded in the structure of the Cold War. Since then it has undergone two transformations. The termination of the Cold War completed the localization of the conflict, making the North-South dimension more pronounced. Chinese and Russian support for North Korea, especially the likelihood of their military intervention in support of Pyongyang, declined dramatically. Washington continues to be committed to the security of South Korea, but its commitment is not linked to larger strategic concerns. A further transformation of the conflict resulted from the isolation of North Korea, its weaknesses as a state, its collapsing economy, and Washington's characterization of North Korea as a "rogue state." The focus of the conflict shifted to the survival of the North Korean regime and its nuclear weapon program. Although the nuclear problem has commanded much attention in recent times, settlement of the Korean conflict will have to address the North-South and the DPRK-U.S. dimensions of the conflict, as well as the survival of the Kim Jong Il regime and prevention of economic collapse in North Korea.

The dynamics of the Kashmir conflict have always been local. The Cold War did not transform the conflict as it did the Taiwan Strait and Korean conflicts. The Cold War did, however, enable Pakistan to mobilize massive military aid and diplomatic support from the United States and China. Likewise, the termination of the Cold War did not have a significant impact on the nature of the conflict, but it did affect external support for Pakistan, especially from the United States. While the conflict itself has altered little, there have been important changes in actors, mode of pursuing the struggle, and in the armaments of the conflicting parties. The emergence of militant movements against India with sanctuaries in Pakistan, especially those that seek independence from both India and Pakistan, complicates bilateral relations and a future settlement. These militant movements could be spoilers in the ongoing peace dialogue. Guerrilla war and terrorism, with the support of Pakistan, have become the primary means of waging the struggle over

Kashmir and the broader struggle against India. Over the years, India and Pakistan have become nuclear powers, with Pakistan threatening to use nuclear weapons should India undertake conventional military operations against Pakistan.

Conflict Escalation and Peaceful Settlement. Notwithstanding the transformation in dynamics, all three conflicts continue to manifest themselves in large-scale confrontational military deployment. Despite periodic dialogues among conflicting parties, they have defied settlement. Although they appear stable and under control, these conflicts are crisis prone; overt hostility cannot be ruled out. Should such a crisis escalate and develop into a full-scale war, it would affect regional security and stability. Peaceful settlement would also have regional security implications. This is especially the case with the conflict across the Taiwan Strait.

Should China initiate hostilities without provocation, the United States and possibly Japan would almost certainly become involved.[5] The threat and use of nuclear weapons may feature in the escalation of hostilities. A war would also create a firm line of enmity, with implications for the entire region. Sino-American and Sino-Japanese relations would spiral downward, making the United States-Japan security treaty an instrument to contain China, whose international image would be tarnished. There would be serious domestic political repercussions in China, especially if it initiated hostilities and suffered a reversal. Involvement in overt hostilities would have a dramatic impact on Japanese domestic politics as well. The U.S. reputation as a reliable security partner and its security engagement in Asia would be tested. In the lead-up to overt hostilities, should it perceive erosion in the commitment of Washington to its survival, the Taiwanese government could attempt a nuclear option as it did earlier. Though Beijing would almost certainly respond to Taiwan's bid for a nuclear option, the nature of that response and the U.S. reaction to Taiwan's quest for nuclear weapons and to Beijing's response are all in the realm of conjecture. In the event of hostilities, other regional states would be forced to take sides, and the region could become polarized.

A peaceful settlement would also have far-reaching consequences, although the implications would hinge on the type of settlement reached: unification with China, a confederal arrangement, or an independent Taiwan. An amicable settlement would remove a contentious issue in U.S.-China relations, making for greater cooperation and stability between the two countries and in East Asia. However, it is unlikely to eliminate U.S. anxieties about a rising China and vice versa. With the Taiwan issue settled, China's military development would require a new rationale, raising questions about the new focus of Chinese military development and its use of military power. The purpose and nature of the U.S. security commitment and military presence in Asia might also be up for debate in U.S. domestic politics and in the region, with the distinct possibility that it could undergo retrenchment.

Likewise, escalation and resolution of the conflicts on the Korean peninsula and over Kashmir would have wider implications but more limited than the Taiwan conflict. Should North Korea start a war, the United States and possibly Japan would come to the aid of South Korea. China, Russia, and other regional states are unlikely to become involved militarily. Although such a war may be limited, it would be devastating for the two Koreas and strain if not antagonize Sino-American and Sino-Japanese relations. Peaceful conflict resolution would also set in train developments that could have strategic consequences in Northeast Asia, for the U.S.-South Korea alliance, and the U.S. security role in that subregion. Even if the alliance continues, U.S. military presence and commitment would likely be scaled back substantially. There is also the possibility of strategic realignment of South Korea with China (Chung 2005). The future of North Korea's nuclear weapon program and Pyongyang's relations with China and South Korea in the event of a settlement are difficult to predict. Retrenchment of the U.S. security commitment and its military presence in South Korea, and closer relations between South Korea and China, might cause anxiety in Japan, but the implications drawn by Tokyo are likely contingent on the state of Sino-Japanese and Sino-American relations.

On the India-Pakistan conflict over Kashmir, it is unlikely that any outside power or regional state would intervene militarily, especially as both protagonists are now nuclear weapon states. Escalation, if it occurs, would be vertical to the nuclear level. International concern would focus on preventing such escalation. Although rather unlikely, a Kashmir settlement would remove a contentious issue in India-Pakistan relations, but it would not end Islamabad's aspiration to be an equal of India. Internal and external balancing (including in the nuclear arena) with external assistance from China and the Islamic world would continue to be a feature of Pakistan's policy. However, this would not preclude cooperation with India. A settlement in Kashmir would transform the bilateral relationship from one of pure enmity to one with mixed motives and payoffs; the combination of amity and enmity would make possible both cooperation and competition. This could augur well for cooperation in South Asia.

A Complex and Changing Strategic Landscape

The preceding discussion highlighted the contemporary security concerns—a mixture of traditional and nontraditional challenges. The Asian security landscape is likely to further alter. As indicated in earlier discussion, regional security dynamics could be affected by regime change in key countries such as China, Indonesia, and Pakistan. Significant change would also flow from escalation or resolution of the three key regional conflicts (Taiwan, Korea, and Kashmir). Significant regional level systemic changes are likely to flow from the rise of Asian powers and from the economic dynamism and growing economic interdependence among them. The rise of Asian powers is likely to affect system structure and increase the salience of strategic competition, while growing economic interdependence is likely to make for a more complex strategic environment in which lines of amity and enmity are less clear-cut.

Rise of Asian Powers

Over the next two decades, the continued rise of Asian powers is likely to gradually alter system structure away from unipolarity toward bipolarity or multipolarity, or some combination of them. A new unipolar system with China at the center is unlikely in that time frame. As the rise of China would pose a significant challenge to the U.S.-dominated security order in Asia, Sino-American relations would become the primary security dynamic with regionwide implications. Sino-Japanese and Sino-Indian relations could also become more consequential. A net effect would be greater strategic competition and new alignments among major powers or extensions of existing ones. Both developments would broaden the boundaries of the Asian security region. This outlook is premised on two conditions. One is that the economic growth of Asian powers will continue. The second condition is that the United States will continue to be engaged in Asia. It is possible to envisage scenarios (internal socio-political upheavals, severe economic setbacks, and involvement in war) that could curtail or derail Asian economic growth. The prediction in the 1980s that Japan would become number one failed to materialize.[6] The present assessment appears to be that Asian economies, including China, may suffer reversals (like the 1997–98 Asian financial crisis or the decade-long stagnation in Japan) but their fundamentals support continued economic growth (Asian Development Bank 2007; World Bank 2007). The pace, however, may slow as their economic base becomes bigger. Similarly the U.S. military presence and security role may alter but the United States is unlikely to disengage from Asia, which will remain important to its security and prosperity.

Gradual Transition from Unipolarity

In earlier discussion, I posited that global unipolarity also pervades Asia and that none of the Asian powers are presently in a position to compete with the United States. The strong alliance relationship between the United States and Japan, which still has the world's second largest economy, makes it even more difficult for China to compete with the dominant position of the United States in Asia. At the same time, the economic and diplomatic power of China has increased. Together with Russia, at times with the support of certain European powers, and through its position and influence in global and regional organizations, China has attempted to constrain the effects of American dominance. This has been referred to as "soft balancing."[7] However, China and other countries

TABLE 1-1

Projected GDPs, Per Capita Income, and Growth Rates

	2005	2015	2025	2040
	PROJECTED GDP (US$ BN)			
United States	12,416	14,786	18,340	27,229
China	2,243	4,754	10,213	26,439
Japan	4,533	4,858	5,567	6,039
India	805	1,411	3,174	12,367
Russia	764	1,232	2,264	4,467
	PROJECTED PER CAPITA (US$)[a]			
United States	43,560	45,835	52,450	69,431
China	1,740	3,428	7,051	18,209
Japan	38,950	38,626	46,391	55,721
India	730	1,149	2,331	8,124
Russia	4,470	8,736	16,652	35,314
	PROJECTED GROWTH RATE[b]			
United States	3	2.1	2.4	2.6
China	10	5.2	4.2	3.7
Japan	3	1.3	1.0	0.7
India	9	5.8	5.8	5.8
Russia	6	3.5	3.6	2.4

SOURCES: Data (except 2005) is drawn from Dominic Wilson and Roopa Purushothoman, *Dreaming with BRICs: The Path to 2050,* Goldman Sachs Global Economics Paper No: 99. Data is based on 2003 US dollars. 2005 data is drawn from World Bank World Development Indicators available at: www.worldbank.org

[a]2005 World Bank data on GNI per capita

[b]as a percentage of year on year

have not attempted a counter-balancing coalition; even if it tries, China will not succeed in constructing an Asian coalition against the United States.

Over time, China's own power is likely to increase substantially with consequences for the regional structure. China is expected to become the world's second largest economy by about 2015 and challenge the United States for the lead by about 2040 (Wilson and Purushothaman 2003; also see Table 1-1). China's growing importance in the global and regional economies would enable it to structure them in ways that increase its influence. Beijing would be able to devote even more resources to research and development and to military modernization. It is not unreasonable to expect China's growing economic power to translate into hard and soft power as well as structural power. In about two decades, China's comprehensive power would become structurally significant, diluting American dominance and influence in Asia. Chinese power would be even more consequential if the U.S.-Japan alliance were to loosen or end. With erosion or termination of that alliance, it would be difficult for the United States to maintain military dominance in Asia. However, a normal and autonomous Japan and a growing India would also constrain China, preventing the domination of Asia by a single power and trend the region in the direction of a multipolar system. It is highly likely that the distribution of power in Asia will alter, but it would be in a gradual fashion and defy neat classification. In about two decades from now, the unipolar features of the Asian security system would significantly diminish; features of bipolarity and multipolarity would become more prominent. Competing quests for wealth, power, status, and influence between rising Asian powers and the predominant United States and among the Asian powers themselves would make strategic competition a more significant feature of the Asian security landscape.

Sino-American Relations: Central Regional Security Dynamic

America's preponderant power and the public goods it provides are widely acknowledged in Asia. Its security roles include creating a stable balance of power through its interaction with the major Asian powers (anchoring Japan and encouraging it to become a full security partner, engaging and balancing China to make it a responsible stakeholder, and promoting and integrating India as an important power); reassuring and controlling allies (Japan, South Korea, and Taiwan); deterring aggression and defusing conflicts across the Taiwan Strait and on the Korean peninsula; defusing and preventing escalation of the India-Pakistan conflict; securing sea lines of communication; countering proliferation of WMD; and combating terrorism. Japan, Australia, Taiwan, and many ASEAN countries have actively sought and support U.S. security commitments in Asia. At the same time, America's unparalleled military power—so visibly demonstrated in the first Iraq war, Kosovo, Afghanistan, and the invasion phase of the second Iraq war—has touched raw nerves, creating apprehensions even in China and Russia. Generally, U.S. predominance and its deep involvement in Asia, which now extend to South, Southwest, and Central Asia, have both positive and negative security implications for a wide range of countries. All major Asian powers seek cordial relations with the United States, although mistrust, apprehension, and dissatisfaction also characterize specific bilateral relations.

Dissatisfaction with American dominance is perhaps most evident in China. Beijing's concern with such dominance is twofold. One, it perceives American hegemony and its vastly superior military power as having negative consequences for China's security—on internal stability, its goal of unifying Taiwan with the PRC, and the effectiveness of its strategic deterrent. Two, it perceives the American system of alliances, especially the strengthening of the U.S.-Japan security treaty and the idea of a democratic coalition among the United States, Japan, India, and Australia as working against its own interest, further widening the gap between the United States and China and enhancing the position of its Asian neighbors (Japan and India). Washington's de facto policy of multiple centers of power in Asia works against the opportunity for Beijing to become the primary Asian pole.

There are competing views on the implications of a rising China for the United States.[8] Some argue that gains for China in Asia have not necessarily been at the expense of the United States (Sutter 2005, 2006). Others posit that China is a revisionist state that cannot be socialized. It is already a threat or will become one soon (Elwell, Labonte, and Morrison 2006; Mearsheimer 2001; Menges 2005).[9] Concerned about the uncertainty that surrounds the future behavior of China and concerned about preserving its primacy, Washington has responded to the rise of China with a mix of policies encapsulated in terms like "responsible stakeholder" (Zoellick 2005) and "favorable balance of power" (National Security Strategy 2002, 2006).[10] These policies seek to engage, socialize, restrain, hedge, and balance China with the goal of making it an economic partner in an international system underpinned by the values advanced by Washington. Presently there is no clear trend in U.S.-China relations. Neither partnership nor conflict is inevitable (Friedberg 2005). The relationship may well continue to exhibit mixed features for a considerable time until China becomes a truly comprehensive power and strong enough to pose a major systemic challenge to the United States.

Although China may not rival the United States for some time to come, Sino-American relations are already an important driver of security in Asia. The conflicting Taiwan policies of the two countries underlie the most serious security issue in Asia. The growing power and influence of China and the U.S. response to these developments have contributed among others to a stronger U.S.-Japan security alliance, closer U.S.-India relations, strategic partnership between China and Russia, and China's policy to diversify and improve relations with major powers. Beijing has sought to strengthen its position and influence in Asia through a series of measures including active diplomacy (so-called charm offensive), providing support for countries like North Korea and Burma that have been castigated by the United States, a higher profile in regional multilateral arrangements, advocacy of Asia-only regional organizations that would effectively exclude the United States, condemnation of U.S.-led alliances as remnants of the Cold War, Japanese participation in them as inimical to Asian regionalism, and active pursuit of China-centered economic arrangements.[11] China is also upgrading its military capability, including modernizing its nuclear arsenal to ensure a robust deterrent force against the United States.

The importance of Sino-American relations for regional security is almost certain to grow. Should the United States forge a strategic condominium with China, Beijing would become regionally more influential. Its need to forge strategic partnerships with Russia and Europe, and accommodate other Asian powers, would be a lesser priority. Japan and India would have less flexibility and may have to come to terms with China on its terms. Though not impossible, the circumstances that would impel a strategic condominium (as opposed to ad hoc or issue-specific cooperation) between the predominant power and a fast-rising power are difficult to imagine.

A confrontational situation is less difficult to envisage. China sees the United States as its principal security concern and has instituted measures to reduce and counter that concern.[12] Certain quarters in Washington already perceive a rising China as an economic challenge and possibly a military threat. The 2006 Quadrennial Defense Review, for example, states: "Of the major and emerging powers, China has the greatest potential to compete militarily with the United States and field disruptive military technologies that could over time offset traditional U.S. military advantages absent U.S. counter strategies" (Office of the Secretary of Defense 2006b: 29). An open Sino-American confrontation would create a clear line of enmity that would certainly bring the present quiet strategic competition to the fore. In that situation, Japan may seek to ally even more closely with the United States and be inclined to engage more in balancing behavior than in reaching accommodation with China. The positions of India and Russia in the eventuality of a Sino-American confrontation are more difficult to predict. It is possible India may lean toward the United States, and Russia may move closer to China. Much will hinge on their state of relations with the United States and China and their interests at stake.

At the same time, it is important to recognize that there are very few situations that could lead to a strategic confrontation between the United States and China. Conflict over Taiwan is an obvious situation; severe economic recession and simultaneous disputes on several fronts may be another. Even in these cases there are checks, balances, and cushions to resolve or manage disputes and prevent an inexorable slide toward confrontation. Strategic condominium and confrontation are extreme and unlikely scenarios. More likely is a relationship characterized by cooperation and competition but with competition for relative power and influence becoming more pronounced. That competition can significantly affect the pattern of relations among Asian powers.

Sino-Japanese Relations: Competing Aspirations

For the first time in history, Northeast Asia is home to two major powers—China and Japan—that are distrustful of each other and have competing international aspirations and visions of regional order. Despite strong economic relations, political and security relations between the two countries have soured since the late 1990s (Ming Wan 2006). China is unwilling to accept Japan as an equal. Beijing uses its power and influence to compete with and marginalize Tokyo's regional initiatives, deploys the history card to cast Japan in an unfavorable light, and depicts Japan's close relations with the United States as inimical to Asian regionalism. Yet Beijing recognizes that denying Tokyo its "proper" place and role risks adversarial relations with that country, which would push Japan further into the embrace of the United States, widen the power gap between the United States and itself, and entrench the United States in Asia. Isolation and estrangement could also impel Tokyo to seek security partnerships with other countries such as India and Australia and seriously explore the nuclear option. Although Japan is still unlikely to acquire nuclear weapons in the foreseeable future, it is no longer taboo to speak about amending the constitution or to discuss nuclear issues (Hughes 2007).

Apprehensive of the rapid growth in Chinese power and influence, Tokyo does not want to be dominated by Beijing. It aspires to a status and role befitting its economic and technological power. In East Asia, Japan seeks to order the region on the basis of certain values that include democracy, human rights, and market economic principles, and to broaden the membership of Asian regional organizations to include India, Australia, and the United States. The implicit intention is to dilute the power and influence of China. The growing perception of threat from a China that is deemed to be seeking hegemony in Asia and the North Korean missile and nuclear tests have helped strengthen the Japanese conservative elite, which is spearheading the quest for a larger international political and security role.

The United States, especially the administration of George W. Bush, has supported Japan's quest for a larger international role to create a favorable balance of power in Asia (Armitage and Nye 2000, 2007; National Security Strategy 2002, 2006). Except for a brief period in the early 1990s, Tokyo has all along viewed the security treaty with the United States as the cornerstone of its security policy. Growing concern about a rising and nationalist China, as well as North Korea, has renewed emphasis on the U.S.-Japan security treaty. Despite Japanese concerns of entrapment and a desire for greater autonomy, the U.S.-Japan security treaty is likely to endure and become more equal. Tokyo is also likely to deepen security relations with Australia, forge strategic relations with India, and reach out to countries in Southeast Asia.

Although there are fundamental differences, it is not certain that Sino-Japanese animosity will result in rivalry and confrontation. Some have argued that Sino-Japanese relations are heading toward "a period of dangerous rivalry," but others posit the "emergence of a new equilibrium . . . based on common interests, on frankness, and mutual respect and understanding" as more likely (Mochizuki 2005). Still others posit that Japan may engage in closer collaboration with China as both share common interests (Pyle 2007: 337–38). Richard Samuels (2007) posits that Japan would opt for a strategy that is "not too dependent on the United States or too vulnerable to China." A likely scenario is that Japan's relations with China would be characterized by cooperation and competition, and through incremental steps Japan would emerge as a comprehensive power with consequence for the balance of power in Asia.[13] The competitive dimension of Sino-Japanese relations for status and leadership in East Asia and the world, rising nationalism in both countries, and their lingering suspicions of each other grounded in contradictory readings of history give rise to a security dynamic that is consequential not only for East Asia but for the broader region.

Sino-Indian Relations: Quiet Competition, Growing Relevance

As two large countries sharing a common but disputed border over which they went to war in 1962, China and India could be viewed as rivals in a struggle for security, wealth, and status (Tellis 2004).[14] China has a border dispute with India, has been concerned about possible Indian support for Tibetan resistance, and views India as a potential rival for power and influence in Asia. Though not explicitly stated, Beijing's India strategy appears designed to bolster Pakistan, with the purpose of containing India, and taking advantage of India's troubled relations with its neighbors to limit New Delhi's regional influence. For New Delhi, China has been a direct security concern since the eruption of the border dispute in the late 1950s and especially after the 1962 war. Equally worrisome has been the de facto China-Pakistan alliance that enables Pakistan to engage in open confrontation with India. Indian perception of China as a security threat has waxed and waned, but a consensus "moderate-realist" view appears to have emerged. That view seeks to resolve differences and invigorate economic relations with China but at the same time be vigilant and develop China-related military capabilities (Hoffmann 2004).

The underlying mistrust between the two countries has contributed to what has been termed "quiet competition" (Frazier 2004). The dramatic increase in China's power and influence in the region has caused envy and apprehension but has also been a stimulant and model for India. India's sustained economic growth at higher rates since 1991, its move to overt nuclear weapon state status after 1998, and the burgeoning U.S.-India relationship, along with international recognition of India as a major power, are beginning to alter the image of India in China. In recent years, the two countries have engaged in high-level exchanges and political dialogue to resolve the border dispute, promote bilateral trade and investment, and downplay differences.

Direct consequences of the earlier enmity between the two countries are the Sino-Pakistani strategic alignment and the actual or perceived Chinese intrusion into the Indian sphere of influence. During the Cold War, the implications of this dynamic were largely confined to South Asia, although it did play into the Sino-Soviet conflict and Soviet-American confrontation. The growing economic and military reach of India into Southwest and Southeast Asia, China's growing reach into nearly all of Asia, and American and Japanese concerns with China are broadening the relevance of India and the state of the Sino-Indian relationship. Washington seeks to help India become a great power. India, too, sees benefit in building better relations with the United States. Beginning in the second term of the Clinton administration, U.S.-India relations have steadily improved, with the Bush administration broadening cooperation to include the strategic arena. The burgeoning U.S.-India relations coupled with India's growing power and a foreign policy that emphasizes improved relations with all major powers have increased the profile of India in the region. Observing the improvement in U.S.-India relations, and in pursuit of its own foreign policy and security objectives, Japan has begun to build strategic understanding and relations with India. Southeast Asian countries, for their part, increasingly view India as one moderating factor in managing the growing power and influence of China.

India does not perceive itself as part of an effort to contain China, and it is unlikely that the two countries will engage in overt hostilities over their border dispute. However, as in Sino-Japanese relations, suspicions and fundamental differences remain. These will sustain the "quiet competition." It is unclear as to what developments or circumstances would lead to open rivalry and confrontation. As with the Sino-Japanese relationship, the future state of Sino-Indian relations will hinge on domestic developments in both countries, how they work out their border dispute and other differences, how they adjust to each other's quest for greater international status and role in the region and the world, and their relationship with other major powers, especially the United States.

Quiet Competition, Strategic Flux, and Uncertainty

From the preceding discussion it is evident that the sustained rise of Asian powers would have implications for system structure and security dynamics in Asia. Competing interests deriving from positional considerations and competing visions for organizing the region, as well as historically grounded suspicion make for apprehension and mistrust in almost all significant bilateral relationships. At the same time despite perceptions of long-range threats and rivalries, there is as yet no firm basis for the development of strategic fault lines comparable to the Soviet-American confrontation or the Sino-Soviet conflict during the Cold War. Except for the U.S.-Japan security alliance, there is no other firm line of amity. All other major power bilateral relationships have elements of cooperation, competition, and conflict.

Quiet strategic competition is already visible in Sino-American, Sino-Indian, and Sino-Japanese relations. As China continues growing its power and influence, Sino-American relations are likely to become more competitive. At the same time there are few scenarios that could lead to open strategic confrontation between the two countries. Both countries, however, will seek to quietly restructure regional relationships and institutions (realist, liberal, and sociological) to enhance their own power and influence and constrain that of the other. This is also likely to be the case in Sino-Indian relations and in Sino-Japanese relations.

It is difficult to define the "eventual" configuration of major power relations with certainty. Many outcomes are possible. One is Sino-American ideological and military confrontation that leads to an alliance of democracies (United States, Japan, Australia, and India), with China and Russia drawing closer. This will be an extension of the present quiet competition scenario. For such a pattern of relations to materialize, all three bilateral relationships discussed in this section would have to be in a downward spiral with India willing to join (de facto or de jure) the U.S.-led alliance system. Despite the rhetoric of the Bush administration, ideology is not the driving force in U.S. policy toward Asia. For its part, China is not committed to an ideology or vision that that would mobilize broad support in Asia in a confrontation with the United States. Further, except perhaps the conflict across the Taiwan Strait, there is little possibility of direct military confrontation between them. Other plausible outcomes include an alignment of China, Russia, and India against the United States and Japan or a balance-of-power system directed at China or the United States. The developments that would trigger the formation of such systems remain distant and unclear. It is possible to conjure up further outcomes, including a concert of major powers, a United States-Japan-China triangle, a United States-China-India triangle, and so forth, but none of these would have a self-sustaining dynamic that could form the basis for durable regional strategic formation.

An informal, loose balance-of-power system in which strategic competition becomes more prominent, but still below the surface and not specifically directed at any particular state, and with the implicit purpose of preventing domination of Asia by any one power appears a more likely outcome. The United States will remain a central player in that system, but American dominance will be reduced. China's power and influence will increase significantly, and the power and influence of Japan, India, and Russia would also increase. Such a system will prevent American and Chinese hegemony and enhance the flexibility and leverage of Japan and India. Whatever the outcome, it appears likely that strategic competition would become a more significant feature, and Sino-American interaction will be the primary security dynamic in Asia that interconnects other major powers.

A main conclusion to draw is that strategic relations among the major powers in the Asian security region are in a state of flux and likely to be so for a considerable time. Making for strategic uncertainty, such a situation encourages a tendency to seek security through multiple strategies that emphasize engagement, cooperation, and competition (internal and external balancing including hedging) to guard against unanticipated developments. In this context, major powers are likely to develop military capabilities, including nuclear arsenals with multiple purposes to avoid undesirable outcomes and protect their long-range strategic autonomy as well as to deal with specific immediate threats, contingencies, and policy priorities. Military capabilities and strategies will have to deal with an array of long- and short-range security concerns.

Economic Overlay and Complex Interdependence

Strategic interaction among major powers will also be influenced by the high priority accorded to economic growth and development in Asian countries, their economic dynamism, and growing economic interdependence among them and with the rest of the world. Although the implications of economic dynamism and interdependence are not straightforward, the net effect would be to produce a more complicated strategic picture in which traditional security interests are tempered by the priority accorded to economic growth. The intersection of economic and traditional security interests would make for less clear and crosscutting lines of amity and enmity. The deep interest in a stable environment increases the incentives for states to avoid strategic confrontation and war. States may still seek to alter the status quo in their favor but through political, economic, and diplomatic means with military force held in the background. Strategic competition will remain below the surface.

By affecting state strength and capacity, and by affecting patterns of trade, financial flows, production, and related issues, economic power can mitigate or reinforce security concerns. As observed earlier, sustained economic growth in large countries is a key driver of structural change in Asia. Sustained growth will also provide Asian countries with resources to build strong military capabilities and capacity in other areas. Their economic power (foreign aid, loans, investment by sovereign wealth funds, etc.) and other means could be deployed to competitively pursue foreign and security policy goals, including milieu goals. They could also be deployed to promote cooperation and build a regional community.

It has been argued that economic interdependence can decrease or at least reduce the incentives for conflict (McMillan 1997). Several propositions have been advanced in support of this argument. One is that the growing salience of capital as a factor of production and its increasing mobility decreases the incentives for conquest of territory and increases interest in peace and good government (Hirschman 1977). Second, it is argued that a high level of commercial interaction produces peace because it is in the self-enlightened interest of affected states. Economic disruption because of war would be costly to all parties (Rosecrance 1986). Third, the principles, norms, rules, procedures, and organizations established to facilitate smooth economic interaction also foster rule-governed behavior in other areas, advancing stability and predictability. A domestic-level argument is that international trade would bring about a redistribution of domestic political power in favor of those who benefit from international commerce and work against those who rely on military power and war for their influence (Solingen 1998). The redistribution of power also empowers actors and issues that could make the political system more open, accountable, and democratic. Here the economic interdependence pathway to peace merges with democratic peace or republican liberalism.

Those who counterargue that the benefits of economic interdependence may not be equally shared contest the argument that economic interdependence can reduce conflict and contribute to peace (Waltz 1979). Because of the inequality and dependency it creates, increased economic interaction may actually increase the potential for conflict. Another counterargument is that there is no connection between commercial activity that is conducted by individuals and corporations, and matters of war and peace that are the preserve of the state. Considerations of politics and power trump commercial matters when it comes to certain core issues like territory, national identity, and sovereignty. In these situations, even high levels of economic specialization and interdependence have not prevented international military conflict. In certain cases, political and strategic considerations have prevented mutually beneficial economic interaction.

Evidence can be found in Asia for the competing propositions. Economic growth and national modernization are very high priorities for nearly all Asian states. Their own growth as well as that of other countries in the region, the aspiration to become a developed country quickly, and the belief that economic growth holds the key to greater international position and influence as well as to address domestic challenges to sustain regime and government legitimacy all interact to produce an addiction to growth and a virtuous cycle. The high priority accorded to economic growth through participation in the global economy strongly argues for a stable international environment. It competes with and tempers traditional security priorities even in acute situations like that across the Taiwan Strait.

Economic interaction among major powers has grown despite strategic suspicion, competition, and military tension. Bilateral economic relations between the United States and China have burgeoned (from US$4.9 billion in 1980 to US$289 billion in 2005); the two countries are highly interdependent (in 2006 China was the second largest trading partner for the United States, and the latter was the top trading partner for China). Likewise, trade between India and China is increasing dramatically (though from a small base). Despite deep suspicion and competition for status and influence, the high level of economic interdependence between China and Japan continues. On the other hand, strategic considerations have obstructed otherwise mutually beneficial economic relations between Pakistan and India. A high level of economic interdependence has not prevented a rapid deterioration of political and strategic relations between Japan and China or transformed or resolved the conflict between China and Taiwan. However, economic consideration has been a significant factor in stabilizing the conflict across the Taiwan Strait. And economic incentives are a key component of the effort to resolve the North Korean nuclear problem and integrate North Korea into the international community.

Economic growth can reinforce as well as temper strategic competition among major powers. Economic interdependence has produced cooperation, competition, and tension in bilateral relations among them. This is evident in the benefits and tensions arising from the high level of economic interaction between the United States and China. It is not possible to evaluate the competing arguments with evidence from Asia in an overview chapter. However, it is not unreasonable to assert that the high priority accorded to economic development creates a vested interest in peace and stability. Increasing economic interdependence can create alternative lines of interaction and institutions that may modify or mitigate traditional security concerns and lines of enmity and foster rule-governed behavior that enhances predictability and stability. Generally, economic dynamism and growing economic interdependence make for a more complex strategic picture than painted by traditional security concerns. They have and are likely to further contribute to the development of a complex interdependence situation in Asia, which simultaneously supports cooperation, competition, and conflict. A complex interdependence situation increases the cost and decreases the incentives for overt use of force to resolve differences and disputes.

Evolutionary and Peaceful Systemic Change

Upon the termination of the Cold War, several analysts deploying the general theories of neorealism and neoliberalism, drawing on Europe's history, and emphasizing the institutional weaknesses and security challenges confronting Asia envisioned a dangerous region in which rivalry, power balancing, and conflict would be endemic (Buzan and Segal 1994; Friedberg 1993–94). Continuing this line of argument and positing the relatively peaceful 1990s as an anomaly, John Mearsheimer (2001) argues that the benign power structure (a consequence of inertia and low cost) and relative peace in Northeast Asia are not sustainable. Positing one decade of experience as too short, he argues that the 1990's decade is not a good indicator of the future. Continued U.S. involvement in Northeast Asia in his view is the key to peace and security in Northeast Asia. That would be contingent upon whether there will be a potential regional hegemon that the United States must help contain. If China does not become a hegemon, he asserts the United States would pull out. With Japan replacing the United States, the Northeast Asia system would become less stable due to more intense security competition linked to problems associated with Japan. If China does become a potential hegemon, Northeast Asia's multipolar system would become unbalanced, and the United States would retain forces to contain China. He advocates a shift in U.S. strategy from engagement to containment and a policy that would prevent China's economic growth.

Resting on a thin and contestable empirical base, such analysis suffers shortcomings in logic and prescription. The system in Northeast Asia in the 1990s was not multipolar. Counting Russia as a pole in Northeast Asia in the 1990s is highly questionable. The United States clearly was the predominant power. Incomplete unipolarity or hegemony would be a more accurate description and analytically useful conception (Mastanduno 2003). The contention that the United States would pull out if China does not become a potential hegemon is not supported by two decades of post-Cold War experience. Further, would it not be in the U.S. interest to stay and sustain a favorable balance of power that serves its purpose in an important region than simply relinquish a favorable position because there is no one to contain? Great powers do not only balance or contain another great power. They also pursue milieu goals (constructing social, political, security, and economic arrangements and institutions) to entrench their dominant position, enhance their authority, and advance their national interests. What would it take for China to be considered a potential hegemon? How long will this take? What happens till then? If it takes several decades for China to become a hegemon, would the United States pull out and then return to contain a hegemonic China? On policy prescription, is it within the power of the United States to start and stop China's economic growth? Can the United States slow China's economic growth without undermining the global economic system, which underpins its own power and influence? What would be the consequence of a protectionist world that could result from such a policy? Though simple and attractive, analysis and prescription based solely on a theory of offensive realism suffers serious shortcomings, is dangerous, and could be self-fulfilling.

Contrary to the "ripe for rivalry thesis," I had argued earlier that Asia has enjoyed relative peace and a high level of prosperity since the late 1970s (Alagappa 2003a, 2003b). The long peace in Asia started in 1979 well before the termination of the Cold War. Despite periodic political and economic crises and setbacks, and military tensions and clashes, there has not been a major war in Asia since 1979. The 1999 Kargil conflict came close, but that conflict was deliberately limited in purpose, geography, and military action. The long peace in Asia is now almost three decades old and cannot be considered an anomaly. The U.S. contribution to peace and security in Asia is certainly important, but it is not the only factor. Peace, security, and prosperity in Asia in the last three decades rested on several other pillars as well, including the consolidation of Asian countries as modern states, their increased capacity to defend themselves, increased ability to partake in regional and global arrangements in rule making and implementation, growing acceptance in Asia of the political status quo, and deep interest in a wide range of Asian countries in preserving peace and stability (Alagappa 2003b). Asia has been transformed from a region of turmoil and numerous hot wars (many of which were waged by or with the support of external powers) to a relatively peaceful and prosperous region that has become a core world region.

The critical question is will this continue in light of the anticipated systemic change (change in the distribution of power as well as interaction change) anticipated from the rise of Asian powers? Much will hinge on the nature and pace of change. I argue that systemic change in Asia will be incremental, evolutionary, and relatively peaceful; revolutionary change through hegemonic war is unlikely.[15] Several reasons underlie my claim. First, increase in the power of the Asian countries including China will be gradual and likely to suffer reversals. There is no guarantee that China will realize its potential or that the United States will irreversibly decline or disengage from Asia. Although China's military power is increasing, it has limited regional force projection capability and has no significant global military capability. It appears unlikely to come close to matching that of the United States in the next two decades (Shambaugh 2005a). Second, although China may seek to alter the status quo to better serve its interests and enhance its influence, the disjuncture between power, prestige, and rules is not severe. An ascending China feels constrained by U.S. predominance, but it is also a beneficiary of the present international system. China does not want to be seen as a revisionist power, and Chinese behavior does not meet the definition of a revisionist power (Johnston 2003). The Chinese authorities, through the strategy of "peaceful rise," seek to cooperate with the United States and other major powers in addressing certain common international problems (Goldstein 2005). Such cooperation has helped keep China's economic development on track, enhanced Beijing's economic and diplomatic power and influence in Asia and the world, and helps constrain the United States. Third, except for the Taiwan situation, there is no issue that can make for a serious confrontation between the United States and China. Fourth, Beijing suffers a legitimacy deficit in the region that flows from its behavior in the early phase of the Cold War and from uncertainty as to how an ascendant China would use its newfound power. Although it has been successful in its policy of good neighborliness, it still has a long way to go in developing a strong claim to legitimacy for international governance. Finally, the Chinese approach to international governance is still reactive and pragmatic. Beijing has yet to fully develop ideas, values, and mechanisms that can harmonize its interests with that of other Asian powers and build a common worldview to organize the region on the basis of a common vision. These considerations imply that change will be incremental and relatively peaceful though not tension-free. As later discussion will show, circumscription of the role of force and the increasing salience of military force in the deterrence, defense, and assurance roles further underscore my claim that system or systemic change through major war is unlikely in Asia.

Success in peaceful change, however, hinges on the ability of the rising power to bring pressure on the dominant power, the willingness of the dominant power to make concessions, and the ability of the two countries to resolve and harmonize differences in values and interests (Carr 1951). Through policies of engagement, successive U.S. administrations have sought to accommodate and integrate China into the international system; and China is becoming a key member of the international community in the economic arena and in several other areas, including arms control regimes (Kent 2007; Medeiros 2007). It is keen to be seen as a responsible power. However, there are also areas of serious disagreement especially in the political and security arenas. Except for the Taiwan situation, the differences are not so fundamental as to lead to major war. In a situation of incremental change, differences and disputes among major powers are likely to be resolved through bargaining, coercive diplomacy, and in rare cases through limited war. Full-scale war is highly costly and unlikely.

The Changing Role of Force in Asia

Military power is widely viewed as an important national asset and a key instrument of policy in the Asian security region. By devoting a substantial share of state revenue to defense, nearly all countries seek to develop credible military forces to ensure national security and, in the case of major states, to shape the regional security environment in line with their policy priorities. Ongoing and anticipated changes in the strategic environment and in military technology are stimulating modernization of military forces and development of new military capabilities, including in the nuclear arena. At the same time, the role of force in Asian international politics is becoming circumscribed and changing, with deterrence, defense, and assurance functions assuming greater salience.

Salience of Military Power

Nearly every country in the Asian security region devotes a significant percentage of government revenue to modernizing and developing its military capabilities. See Table 1-2 for an overview of defense expenditures by countries in the Asian security region. Table 1-3 provides details of the fifteen major defense spenders in the world. The United States accounts for about 46 percent of total world spending on defense, and that exceeds the combined total of the next fourteen countries on the list. With high rates of economic growth, Asian countries, especially the larger ones, are also able to allocate more resources to defense.

Military modernization programs are underway in all major states. Seeking to maintain an armed force without peer, the United States is transforming its military to meet four primary challenges: irregular challenges (defeating terrorist networks), catastrophic challenges (preventing acquisition or use of WMD and defending the homeland), disruptive challenges (shaping choices of countries at strategic crossroads), and traditional interstate security challenges (National Defense

TABLE 1–2

Defense Expenditures in the Asian Security Region (1995–2005)
(in billion US$ at constant 2003 prices and exchange rates, for calendar years if not stated otherwise)

Country	1995		2000		2005	
	Expenditure	% GDP	Expenditure	% GDP	Expenditure	% GDP
United States[a]	357.382	3.8	342.172	3.1	504.638	4.1
Russia[b]	21.700	4.4	19.100	3.7	31.100	4.1
China[c]	15.000	1.8	23.800	2.0	44.300	2.0
India	12.550	2.7	17.697	3.1	22.273	2.8
Japan	42.471	1.0	43.802	1.0	44.165	1.0
North Korea[d]	5.232	25.2	2.049	12.7	n.a.	n.a.
South Korea	15.476	2.8	16.652	2.5	20.333	2.6
Mongolia	0.020	1.6	0.028	2.4	0.030	1.6
Taiwan	9.062	3.8	7.389	2.4	7.352	2.2
Burma (Myanmar)[e]	n.a.	n.a.	n.a.	n.a.	n.a.	n.a.
Malaysia	2.055	2.8	1.677	1.7	3.120	2.4
Thailand	3.240	2.3	1.982	1.4	2.018	1.1
Vietnam[f]	0.91	4.3	2.303	7.3	n.a.	n.a.
Indonesia	2.613	1.6	2.242	1.0	3.410	1.2
Philippines	0.885	1.4	0.853	1.1	0.865	0.9
Singapore	3.378	4.4	4.634	4.7	5.468	4.7
Bangladesh	0.554	1.3	0.675	1.3	0.669	1.0
Nepal	0.049	0.8	0.063	0.9	0.175	2.1
Pakistan	3.435	5.3	3.320	3.7	4.534	3.5
Sri Lanka	0.863	5.3	0.904	4.5	0.612	2.6
Iran	2.351	2.4	6.695	5.4	9.057	5.8
Israel[g]	7.996	8.6	9.553	8.0	12.522	9.7

SOURCE: Expenditure data from *The SIPRI Military Expenditure Database 2007* available at: http://first.sipri.org/non_first/milex.php. Some data are from *The Military Balance* (London: Brassey's for the International Institute for Strategic Studies (IISS), 1996/97 and 2002/2003).
Where IISS data were used, the figures are expressed in constant U.S. dollars of the year.

[a]Figures for the United States are for financial years rather than calendar years.

[b]Figures for Russia are estimated total military expenditures.

[c]Figures for China are estimated total military expenditures.

[d]Figures for North Korea are from *The Military Balance 1996/97* and *2002/2003*.

[e]Figures for Burma are not represented in constant U.S. dollar terms because of the extreme variation in stated exchange rates between the kyat and the U.S. dollar.

[f]Figures for Vietnam are from *The Military Balance 1996/97* and *2002/2003*.

[g]Figures for Israel include military aid from the United States of US$2 billion annually.

Strategy 2005; Quadrennial Defense Review 2006). Since the early 1990s Beijing has accelerated defense modernization. In addition to building military capability focused on the Taiwan conflict, China is developing a strong modern navy to secure sea lines of communications and to project power, and it is developing its nuclear arsenal and space capabilities to enhance the effectiveness of its strategic deterrent (Shambaugh 2005a). India's military modernization is aimed at restoring conventional superiority over Pakistan, building a strategic deterrent capability against China, and building a regional force projection capability in support of its major power aspiration (Gill 2005). Japan's military modernization is designed to support a more proactive international role, including an expanded military

TABLE 1-3
Major Military Spender Countries in 2006
(US$ at constant 2005 prices and exchange rates)

Military expenditure in MER dollar terms						Military expenditure in PPP dollar terms[a]		
Rank	Country	Spending ($ billion)	Spending per capita ($)	World share (%)		Rank	Country	Spending ($ billion)
				Spending	Population			
1	United States	528.7	1,756	46	5	1	United States	528.7
2	Britain	59.2	990	5	1	2	China	[188.2]
3	France	53.1	875	5	1	3	India	114.3
4	China	[49.5]	[37]	[4]	20	4	Russia	[82.8]
5	Japan	43.7	341	4	2	5	Britain	51.4
Subtotal top 5		*734.2*		*63*	*29*	*Subtotal top 5*		*965.5*
6	Germany	37.0	447	3	1	6	France	46.6
7	Russia	[34.7]	[244]	[3]	2	7	Saudi Arabia[b,c]	36.4
8	Italy	29.9	514	3	1	8	Japan	35.2
9	Saudi Arabia[b,c]	29.0	1,152	3	-	9	Brazil	32.0
10	India	23.9	21	2	17	10	Germany	31.2
Subtotal top 10		*888.7*		*77*	*50*	*Subtotal top 10*		*1,147.0*
11	South Korea	21.9	455	2	1	11	South Korea	30.1
12	Australia[c]	13.8	676	1	—	12	Iran[b]	28.6
13	Canada[c]	13.5	414	1	—	13	Italy	28.6
14	Brazil	13.4	71	1	3	14	Turkey	20.2
15	Spain	12.3	284	1	1	15	Pakistan	15.6
Subtotal top 15		*963.7*		*83*	*56*	*Subtotal top 15*		*1,270.2*
World		*1,158*	177	*100*	*100*	*World*		..

SOURCE: Stockholm International Peace Research Institute, *SIPRI Yearbook 2007*.
MER = market exchange rate; PPP = purchasing power parity; [ ] = Estimated figure

[a] The figures in PPP dollar terms are converted at PPP rates (for 2005), calculated by the World Bank, based on comparisons of gross national product.

[b] Data for Iran and Saudi Arabia include expenditure for public order and safety and might be slight overestimates.

[c] The populations of Australia, Canada and Saudi Arabia each constitute less than 0.5% of the total world population.

role in the region and beyond (Hughes 2005). Modernization would increase the strategic military capabilities of these countries, although the Asian countries also face technological, organizational, and human resource challenges in successfully implementing modernization programs.

National military assets figure prominently in the conflicts across the Taiwan Strait, on the Korean peninsula, and over Kashmir. In Asia, force is an option as well in the numerous border and other territorial disputes on land and at sea. Naval and air intrusions into disputed territories at sea and military responses to such intrusions have occurred in recent times even among major states (China and Japan). And both government and insurgent forces in domestic conflicts in China, India, Pakistan, Indonesia, Burma, Thailand, Philippines, Sri Lanka, and until recently Nepal deploy military force routinely and at times massively.

In addition to immediate security concerns, military modernization and development of new capabilities are also driven by considerations relating to the balance of power in the region. To preserve its dominant position, Washington seeks to maintain a military force without peer. China is increasing its military power and reach with a view to enhancing its national power and position in Asia and to alter the regional balance of power in its favor (Shambaugh 2005a). Likewise, military modernization and development in India are driven not only by the ongoing conflict with Pakistan but also by balance-of-power and strategic autonomy considerations related to China (Gill 2005). Japan's move to become a normal state and to strengthen its military capability and the alliance with the United States is driven both by immediate concerns as well as to prevent Chinese dominance in the region (Hughes 2005).

Lack of International Regulation

Collective management of force is not a viable option in the Asian security region at present. Zealously guarding their sovereignty, the United States and the Asian powers do not accept constraints on their autonomy. There is no North Atlantic Treaty Organization (NATO)-like collective defense organization in Asia. The United States presents its bilateral military alliances in the region as a public good for regional peace and security. The primary purpose of that alliance system, however, is to serve U.S. national interests and those of its allies. Non-allies that feel threatened by the United States do not see the alliance system as a public good. Ad hoc concerts may form from time to time to manage specific issues. There are few bilateral and multilateral arms control measures restricting the possession and use of force in the region. Those that exist are designed primarily to build confidence or prevent accidental outbreaks of hostilities rather than to limit or regulate the use of force. Most Asian countries also score poorly on issues of accountability and transparency. There is no regional mechanism to advance these concerns. Military power in Asia remains very much a national asset that suffers little in the form of international regulation of its possession, deployment, and use.

Circumscription of Force

Despite this, the role of force in Asian international politics is becoming more limited due to a number of developments. First, the traditional need for force to protect the territorial integrity of states has declined in importance. With few exceptions (Taiwan, North Korea, and South Korea) state survival is not problematic. The Asian political map is for the most part internationally accepted, although some boundaries are still in dispute. Such disputes are being settled through negotiations or shelved in the interest of promoting better bilateral relations (Wang 2003).

Second, the political, diplomatic, strategic, military, and economic cost of using force has increased dramatically. Over the past several decades, a normative framework has developed in Asia that delegitimizes the use of force to invade and occupy another country or to annex territory that is internationally recognized as belonging to another state. The use of force to invade and occupy another country or to annex territory will incur high costs. For example, if China were to invade Taiwan without serious provocation, it can expect civil and military resistance in Taiwan, U.S. military intervention, international condemnation, and a setback to its image as a responsible power. Such action would also incur huge economic costs resulting from international and domestic disruptions. Unless military action were swift and surgical, it would also result in substantial physical damage that would only increase as Asian countries continued to modernize and urbanize. Further, military action that is not successful can have negative domestic political consequences as well.

Third, most Asian countries benefit from participation in the regional and global capitalist marketplace. The 1997–98 financial crisis sensitized Asian countries to the vagaries and negative consequences of globalization but did not turn them away from liberalization and participation in the global economy. Preserving international stability has become a key goal of major powers. Economic growth, modernization, and growing economic interdependence have increased the cost of the force option and restrained the behavior of states even when major political issues are at stake, as for example in cross-Strait relations. Economic interdependence does not close the force option in all cases, but the high costs of economic disruption can restrain military action. Further, force is no longer relevant for the attainment of economic goals such as access to resources, labor, and markets. Energy security, for example, is sought through the market, national stockpiling, and sourcing arrangements.

Finally, resolution of existing disputes through the use of force is not practical. Except for the United States, none of the Asian states can marshal the necessary military power to impose a settlement by force. The experience in Iraq and Afghanistan suggests that even the United States suffers limitations and that the use of force carries much risk. These considerations explain the reluctance of the United States to undertake preventive action against North Korea, the reluctance of China to carry out its threat of using force to unify Taiwan with the PRC, and the continuing stalemate in the India-Pakistan conflict over Kashmir. Force may still be used in these cases, but the attendant strategic, political, diplomatic, and economic costs and risks are high.

Thus, despite the many conflicts, substantial increases in defense expenditures, and the acquisition of more lethal capabilities, there has not been a full-scale war in Asia since 1979. The 1999 Kargil conflict came close, but India scrupulously limited the war initiated by Pakistan to territory occupied by Pakistani troops on the Indian side of the line of control. Over the past two decades, resort to the use of force in the Asian security region has been limited to border clashes, militant insurgencies, and occasional clashes at sea where the danger of escalation is low.

Force has also been used in a few cases in the coercive diplomacy role—as in the PRC's attempt to influence Taiwan's presidential election in 1996 and Pakistan's attempt to coerce India to the negotiating table on the Kashmir issue.

Deterrence, Defense, and Assurance to the Fore

The primary mission of the armed forces in most Asian countries is the protection of territorial integrity and populations from external threats, not military aggression and conquest. Deterrence and defense are the primary roles in carrying out the protection mission. Even in the most serious regional conflict across the Taiwan Strait the primary role of force from China's perspective is to dissuade Taiwan from declaring independence and to deter the United States from intervening in the event of hostilities. From the perspective of the United States, the purpose is to dissuade China and deter its forceful absorption of Taiwan, and, within limits, assure and control Taiwan. On the Korean peninsula, force is most relevant in the defense and deterrence functions. And in the India-Pakistan conflict, with growing recognition of the limitations of the offensive role of force including coercive diplomacy, deterrence appears to be becoming more important.

Assurance of allies is an important function of military power. A primary role of American alliances and forward deployment in Asia is to assure allies (Japan, Australia, South Korea, and Taiwan) and prevent them from pursuing undesired capabilities or engaging in undesired actions. Only the United States has deployed force in preventive and intervention roles to dislodge unacceptable regimes, to stop gross violation of human rights, or to prevent the acquisition of WMD. Asian countries do not support, or only reluctantly support, such actions. Even the United States has been reluctant since the Vietnam War to engage in such military action in Asia proper. Evidence over the last three decades supports the contention that the role of military force in Asian international politics is becoming more limited and that deterrence, defense, and assurance functions are becoming more prominent. How would nuclear weapons and ballistic missiles, and the introduction of BMD, affect this trend? These and related questions are investigated in the country chapters in Part II of this study.

Notes

1. The ensuing discussion of the colonial and Cold War eras is drawn from Alagappa (1998).

2. On the use of the Internet by terrorist groups, see Lim 2005.

3. For details about the Khan network, see Carnegie Endowment for International Peace, "A. Q. Khan Nuclear Chronology," *Issue Brief* 8 (8), September 7, 2005.

4. Fravel (2005) argues that regime insecurity best explains China's many compromises in its territorial disputes.

5. On possible scenarios and implications of violent resolution or irresolution of the Taiwan conflict for China and the United States, see Cliff and Shlapak (2007).

6. See, for example, Vogel (1979).

7. On soft balancing, see Paul (2006).

8. See, for example, Sutter (2005); Lampton (2005); and Elwell, Labonte, and Morrison (2006).

9. For an assessment of the China threat, see Ross (2005).

10. The "responsible stakeholder" phrase was used by Deputy Secretary of State Robert B. Zoellick (see Zoellick 2005).

11. On China's regional strategy see Zhang and Tang (2005).

12. See Chapter 5 by Chu and Rong this volume.

13. A revolutionary change in Japan's military capability and international security role, however, appears unlikely. See Mochizuki (2005).

14. Some argue that it is a one-sided rivalry since China matters far more for India than vice versa, and India on its own is not taken seriously by China (Shirk 2004). Others counter that Chinese indifference to India is feigned and that Beijing has a deliberate strategy that seeks indirectly to limit Indian influence to South Asia (Tellis 2004).

15. On incremental and revolutionary change, see Gilpin 1981.

References

Abuza, Zachary. 2003. *Militant Islam in Southeast Asia: Crucible of Terror.* Boulder, Co: Lynne Rienner.

Acharya, Amitav. 2003. "Regional Institutions and Asian Security Order: Norms, Power, and Prospects for Peaceful Change." In *Asian Security Order: Instrumental and Normative Features,* ed. Muthiah Alagappa. Stanford, Calif.: Stanford University Press.

Alagappa, Muthiah. 1998. "International Politics in Asia: The Historical Context." In *Asian Security Practice: Material and Ideational Influences,* ed. Muthiah Alagappa. Stanford, Calif.: Stanford University Press.

———. 2003a. "Introduction: Predictability and Stability Despite Challenges." In *Asian Security Order: Instrumental and Normative Features,* ed. Muthiah Alagappa. Stanford, Calif.: Stanford University Press.

———. 2003b. "Managing Asian Security: Competition, Cooperation and Evolutionary Change." In *Asian Security Order: Instrumental and Normative Features,* ed. Muthiah Alagappa. Stanford, Calif.: Stanford University Press.

Albright, David, and Corey Henderson. 2005. "Unraveling the A. Q. Khan and Future Proliferation Networks." *Washington Quarterly* 28 (2): 111–28.

Armitage, Richard L., and Joseph S. Nye. 2000. *The United States and Japan: Advancing toward a Mature Partnership.* Washington, D.C.: National Defense University.

———. 2007. *The U.S.-Japan Alliance: Getting Asia Right through 2020.* Washington, D.C.: Center for Strategic and International Studies.

Asian Development Bank. 2007. *Asian Development Outlook 2007.* Manila: Asian Development Bank.

Basrur, Rajesh M., and Hasan-Askari Rizvi. 2003. *Nuclear Terrorism and South Asia.* Cooperative Monitoring Center Occasional Paper 25. Sandia National Laboratories.

Blanchard, Jean-Marc F. 2003. "Maritime Issues in Asia: The Problem of Adolescence." In *Asian Security Order: Instrumental and Normative Features,* ed. Muthiah Alagappa. Stanford, Calif.: Stanford University Press.

Buzan, Barry, and Gerald Segal. 1994. "Rethinking East Asian Security." *Survival* 36, 2: 3–21.

Carr, Edward Hallet. 1951. *The Twenty-Year's Crisis, 1919–1939: An Introduction to the Study of International Relations.* New York: Harper & Row.

Chung, Jae Ho. 2005. "China's Ascendancy and the Korean Peninsula: From Interest Reevaluation to Strategic Realignment." In *Power Shift: China and Asia's New Dynamic,* ed. David Shambaugh. Berkeley: University of California Press.

Cliff, Roger, and David A. Shlapak. 2007. *U.S.-China Relations After Resolution of Taiwan's Status.* Santa Monica, Calif.: RAND Corporation.

Elwell, Craig K., Marc Labonte, and Wayne M. Morrison. 2006. *Is China a Threat to the U.S. Economy?* CRS report for the Congress. Washington, D.C.: Congressional Research Service.

Fravel, Taylor M. 2005. "Regime Insecurity and International Cooperation: Explaining China's Compromises in Territorial Disputes. *International Security* 30, 2: 46–83.

Frazier, Mark W. 2004. "Quiet Competition and the Future of Sino-Indian Relations." In *The India-China Relationship: What the United States Needs to Know,* ed. Francine R. Frankel and Harry Harding. New York: Columbia University Press.

Freidberg, Aaron L. 1993–94. "Ripe for Rivalry: Prospects for peace in Multipolar Asia." *International Security* 18, 3: 5–33.

———. 2005. "The Future of U.S.-China Relations: Is Conflict Inevitable?" *International Security* 30 (2): 7–45.

Gill, John H. 2005. "India and Pakistan: A Shift in Military Calculus?" In *Strategic Asia 2005–6: Military Modernization in an Era of Uncertainty,* ed. Ashley Tellis. Seattle, Wash.: National Bureau of Asian Research.

Gilpin, Robert. 1981. *War and Change in World Politics.* Cambridge: Cambridge University Press.

Gilpin, Robert. 1987. *The Political Economy of International Relations.* Princeton, N.J.: Princeton University Press.

Goldstein, Avery. 2000. *Deterrence and Security in the Twenty-first Century: China, Britain, France, and the Enduring Legacy of the Nuclear Revolution.* Stanford, Calif.: Stanford University Press.

———. 2005. *Rising to the Challenge: China's Grand Strategy and International Security.* Stanford, Calif.: Stanford University Press.

Hirschman, Albert O. 1977. *The Passions and the Interests.* Princeton, N.J.: Princeton University Press.

Hoffmann, Steven A. 2004. "Perception and China Policy in India." In *The India-China Relationship: What the United States Needs to Know,* ed. Francine R. Frankel and Harry Harding. New York: Columbia University Press.

Hughes, Christopher W. 2005. "Japanese Military Modernization: In Search of a 'Normal' Security Role." In *Strategic Asia 2005–6: Military Modernization in an Era of Uncertainty,* ed. Ashley Tellis. Seattle, Wash.: National Bureau of Asian Research.

Hughes, Llewelyn. 2007. "Why Japan Will Not Go Nuclear (Yet): International and Domestic Constraints on the Nuclearization of Japan." *International Security,* 31, 4: 67–96.

Johnston, Alastair Iain. 2003. "Is China a Status Quo Power? *International Security* 27, 4: 5–56.

Jones, David Martin, and Michael L. R. Smith. 2007. "Making Process, Not Progress: ASEAN and the Evolving East Asian Regional Order," *International Security,* 30, 1: 148–84.

Jones, Rodney W., and Sumit Ganguly. 2000. "Debating Delhi's Nuclear Decision." Correspondence in *International Security* 24, 4: 181–89.

Kang, David. C. 2003. "Getting Asia Wrong: The Need for New Analytical Frameworks." *International Security* 27 (4): 57–85.

Katzenstein, Peter J., and Takashi Shiraishi, eds. 1996. *Network Power: Japan and Asia.* Ithaca, N.Y.: Cornell University Press.

Kent, Ann. 2007. *Beyond Compliance: China, International Organizations, and Global Security.* Stanford, Calif.: Stanford University Press.

Lampton, David M. 2005. "China's Rise in Asia Need Not Be at America's Expense." In *Power Shift: China and Asia's New Dynamic,* ed. David Shambaugh. Berkeley: University of California Press.

Ledyard, Gary. 1983. "Yin and Yang in the China-Manchuria-Korea Triangle." In *China Among Equals: The Middle Kingdom and Its Neighbors, Tenth-Fourteenth Centuries,* ed. Morris Rossabi. Berkeley: University of California Press.

Lim, Merlyna. 2005. *Islamic Radicalism and Anti-Americanism in Indonesia: The Role of the Internet.* Policy Studies 18. Washington, D.C.: East-West Center Washington.

Mastanduno, Michael. 2003. "Incomplete Hegemony: The United States and Security Order in Asia." In *Asian Security Order: Instrumental and Normative Features,* ed. Muthiah Alagappa. Stanford, Calif.: Stanford University Press.

McMillan, Susan M. 1997. "Interdependence and Conflict." In *Mershon International Studies Review* 41, 1: 33–58.

Mearsheimer, John J. 2001. *The Tragedy of Great Powers.* New York: W. W. Norton & Company Inc.

Medeiros, Evan S. 2007. *Reluctant Restraint: The Evolution of China's Nonproliferation Policies and Practices.* Stanford, Calif.: Stanford University Press.

Menges, Constantine C. 2005. *China: The Gathering Threat.* Nashville, Tenn: Nelson Current.

Ming Wan. 2006. *Sino-Japanese Relations: Interaction, Logic, and Transformation.* Stanford, Calif.: Stanford University Press.

Mitchell, Derek J. 2004. "Taiwan's Hsin Chu Program: Deterrence, Abandonment, and Honor." In *The Nuclear Tipping Point: Why States Reconsider Their Nuclear Choices,* ed. Kurt M. Campbell, Robert J. Einhorn, and Mitchell B. Reiss. Washington, D.C.: Brookings Institution Press.

Mochizuki, Mike M. 2005. "China-Japan Relations: Downward Spiral or New Equilibrium." In *Power Shift: China and Asia's New Dynamic,* ed. David Shambaugh. Berkeley: University of California Press.

National Security Strategy of the United States of America. 2002, 2006. Washington, D.C.: The White House. Available at http://www.whitehouse.gov/nsc/nss.pdf.

National Defense Strategy 2005. Washington, D.C.: U.S. Department of Defense. Available at http://www.defenselink.mil/news/Mar2005/d20050318nds1.pdf.

Office of the Secretary of Defense. 2006. *Annual Report to the Congress: Military Power of the People's Republic of China 2006.* Washington, D.C. Available at http://www.defenselink.mil/pubs/pdfs/China%20Report%202006.pdf.

Paul, T. V. 2006. "Soft Balancing in the Age of U.S. Primacy." *International Security* 30, 1: 46–71.

Petri, Peter A. 2006. "Is East Asia Becoming More Interdependent?" Paper presented at the American Economic Association and American Committee for Asian Economic Studies. Boston, January 8.

Pollack, Jonathan D., and Mitchell B. Reiss. 2004. "South Korea: The Tyranny of Geography and Vexations of History." In *The Nuclear Tipping Point: Why States Reconsider Their Nuclear Choices,* ed. Kurt M. Campbell, Robert J. Einhorn, and Mitchell B. Reiss. Washington, D.C.: Brookings Institution Press.

Prosser, Andrew. 2004. "Nuclear Trafficking Routes: Dangerous Trends in Southeast Asia." Accessed from Center for Defense Information. http://www.cdi.org/PDFs/Traffickingsmuggling.pdf.

Pyle, Kenneth B. 2007. *Japan Rising: The Resurgence of Japanese Power and Purpose.* New York: Public Affairs.

Quadrennial Defense Review 2006. Washington, D.C. Available at http://www.defenselink.mil/qdr/report/Report20060203.pdf.

Rosecrance, Richard. 1986. *The Rise of the Trading State.* New York: Basic Books.

Ross, Robert S. 1999. "The Geography of the Peace: East Asia in the Twenty-first Century." In *International Security* 23 (4): 81–118.

Ross, Robert S. 2003. "The U.S.-China Peace: Great Power Politics, Spheres of Influence, and the Peace of East Asia." In *Journal of East Asian Studies* 3(3): 351–376.

Ross, Robert S. 2005. "Assessing the China Threat." *The National Interest,* Fall: 7.

Rossabi, Morris. 1983. "Introduction." In *China Among Equals: The Middle Kingdom and Its Neighbors, Tenth-Fourteenth Centuries,* ed. Morris Rossabi. Berkeley: University of California Press.

Samuels, Richard J. 2007. *Security Japan: Tokyo's Grand Strategy and the Future of East Asia.* Ithaca, N.Y.: Cornell University Press.

Shambaugh, David. 2005a. "China's Military Modernization: Making Steady and Surprising Progress" In *Strategic Asia 2005–6: Military Modernization in an Era of Uncertainty,* ed. Ashley Tellis. Seattle, Wash.: National Bureau of Asian Research.

Shambaugh, David, ed. 2005b. *Power Shift: China and Asia's New Dynamics.* Berkeley: University of California Press.

Shirk, Susan L. 2004. "One-Sided Rivalry: China's Perception and Policies toward India." In *The India-China Relationship: What the United States Needs to Know,* ed. Francine R. Frankel and Harry Harding. New York: Columbia University Press.

Solingen, Etel. 1998. *Regional Orders at Century's Dawn: Global and Domestic Influences on Grand Strategy.* Princeton, N. J.: Princeton University Press.

Sutter, Robert. 2005. "China's Regional Strategy and Why It May Not Be Good for America." In *Power Shift: China and Asia's New Dynamic,* ed. David Shambaugh. Berkeley: University of California Press.

———. 2006. *China's Rise: Implications for U.S. Leadership in Asia.* Policy Studies 21. Washington, D.C.: East-West Center Washington.

Tellis, Ashley. 2001. *India's Emerging Nuclear Posture: Between Recessed Deterrence and Ready Arsenal.* Santa Monica, Calif.: RAND.

———. 2004. "China and India in Asia." In *The India-China Relationship: What the United States Needs to Know,* ed. Francine R. Frankel and Harry Harding. New York: Columbia University Press.

Vaughn, Bruce, Emma Chanlett-Avery, Richard Cronin, Mary Manyin, and Larry Niksch. 2005. *Terrorism in Southeast Asia.* CRS report for Congress. Washington, D.C.: The Library of Congress.

Vogel, Ezra F. 1979. *Japan as Number One: Lessons for America.* Cambridge, Mass: Harvard University Press.

Waltz, Kenneth N. 1979. *Theory of International Politics.* New York: McGraw-Hill.

Wang, Jianwei. 2003. "Territorial Disputes and Asian Security: Sources, Management, and Prospects." In *Asian Security Order: Instrumental and Normative Features,* ed. Muthiah Alagappa. Stanford, Calif.: Stanford University Press.

Wilson, Dominic, and Roopa Purushothaman. 2003. *Dreaming With BRICs: The Path to 2050.* Goldman Sachs Global Economics Paper No. 99. New York: Goldman, Sachs & Co.

World Bank. 2007. *East Asia and Pacific Update: Will Resilience Overcome Risk?* Washington, D.C.: World Bank.

Yang, Lien-Shang. 1968. "Historical Notes on the Chinese World Order." In *The Chinese World Order: Traditional China's Foreign Relations,* ed. John K. Fairbank. Cambridge, Mass: Harvard University Press.

Zhang, Yunling, and Tang Shipping. 2005. "China's Regional Strategy." In *Power Shift: China and Asia's New Dynamic,* ed. David Shambaugh. Berkeley: University of California Press.

Zoellick, Robert E. 2005. "Whither China: From Membership to Responsibility?" Remarks to the National Committee on U.S.-China Relations, New York City, September 21.

2

Exploring Roles, Strategies, and Implications

Historical and Conceptual Perspectives

MUTHIAH ALAGAPPA

> Thus far the chief purpose of our military establishment has been to win wars. From now on its chief purpose must be to avert them. It can have almost no other useful purpose.
>
> *Bernard Brodie, 1946*

> The power to hurt is bargaining power. To exploit it is diplomacy—vicious diplomacy, but diplomacy.
>
> *Thomas Schelling, 1966*

The nuclear weapon has been referred to as the absolute or ultimate weapon because of the incomparable devastation packed by a nuclear warhead and the speed with which such devastation can be delivered.[1] Its advent was widely perceived as marking a new epoch in warfare, making for a revolution in thinking about war and in the relationship between war and politics with far-reaching implications for the role of force as an instrument of state policy and for the conduct of politics among nuclear weapon states (Brodie 1946, 1959, 1973; Jervis 1989; Schelling 1966). Military strategists, who tended to see the nuclear weapon in the traditional vein as a better and more effective bomb, contested the view that nuclear weapons brought about a paradigmatic change in thinking about war and politics (Friedberg 1982). Others, such as William Borden (1946), saw atomic weapons as revolutionizing strategy by elevating the tactical above the strategic; he asserted that "the key to victory lies in defeating hostile military forces," not in hitting cities and industrial centers to lay waste the war-making potential of a country. The tension between these competing viewpoints framed the many debates on U.S. nuclear strategy during the Cold War. American strategic doctrine as observed by Aaron Friedberg (1982) "always contained two strands." One was assured retaliation that emphasized countervalue deterrence. The second was the more traditional strand that focused on war outcomes should deterrence fail.

Nevertheless, the view that nuclear weapons had a transforming effect came to dominate strategic thinking especially in the civilian strategic community that became influential in the 1960s in framing U.S. nuclear strategy. Robert Jervis's (1989) central claim that nuclear weapons had dramatically altered statecraft, because force and the threat of force could not support foreign policy as they did in previous eras, reflected widespread thinking among civilian and military strategic thinkers. This chapter outlines the transforming logic of nuclear weapons and explores at a conceptual level the roles of nuclear weapons, the strategies for their employment, and their implications for international security to provide a historical and conceptual perspective for the investigation of these issues in the country and concluding chapters that follow.

Transforming Effect

Three characteristics of the nuclear weapon underlie its transforming or revolutionary effect: one is the speed and incomparable devastation; second is the lack of defense against a nuclear weapon; and third is its punitive character. As Bernard Brodie (1946, 1959) and Thomas Schelling (1966) pointed out graphically, what is new is not the quantum of damage itself but the speed, efficiency, and economy with which it can be delivered. Cities and strategic industrial assets could be destroyed and a country paralyzed rather quickly by a small number of nuclear bombs. Absolute damage became the primary consideration; relative damage, important in earlier times in the cost-benefit calculation of war, appeared less important, even irrelevant. The second key characteristic is that there is no significant defense against the missiles that carry nuclear warheads or against the devastation caused by nuclear weapons and their lingering effects. States possessing nuclear weapons can destroy each other (mutual kill) without victory in the battlefield. The state and society are highly vulnerable in a nuclear attack; protection of strategic assets and society becomes crucial but also highly difficult or impossible. The significance of nuclear weapons, as Brodie (1959: 173) asserted "depends above all on the possibility of defense against them in a strategic attack." Third, nuclear weapons are punitive in character (Schelling 1966: 33–34). Their significance lies in the power to hurt (kill hundreds of thousands of people and destroy strategic assets quickly), not in holding or taking ground or other assets of value. Taken together these characteristics have far-reaching implications for the purpose and employment of force as an instrument of state policy.

Limit War as an Instrument of Policy

Total war between nuclear weapon states can serve no conceivable political purpose. Victory in such a war would be meaningless, as both parties to the conflict would suffer irreparable damage; recovery would be slow and take many years or may be impossible. With no defense available, each would be able to inflict damage on the other. Mutual vulnerability (later associated with the possession of mutual second-strike capability) implied that no nuclear weapon state could impose its will on another through total war. This underscored Brodie's famous assertion that the chief purpose of military establishments is no longer to win wars but to prevent (deter) them (1946: 76). The impossibility of military victory in total war led some, including Brodie for a brief period, to assert that nuclear weapons had invalidated Clausewitz's famous dictum that war is a continuation of policy by other means.[2]

The view that war had ceased to be a rational instrument of policy among nuclear weapon states was challenged on two grounds. First, although total war could no longer be a rational instrument, it was argued that limited war using conventional weapons could still be waged and serves that function. The idea of limited war later extended to include limited nuclear war to serve intrawar deterrence and war fighting functions in a strategy of conflict escalation. Limited wars were seen as more likely and having greater consequences than before (Kissinger 1957). Still the potential for escalation of limited war to total war among nuclear weapon states induced caution and set limits to the role of war as an instrument of policy among nuclear weapon states (Jervis 1989: 19–22).

The second challenge came from those who posited that although military victory was impossible in a nuclear war, nuclear weapons can serve important political ends (Schelling 1966; Kahn 1961). They argued that the threat of punishment and the manipulation of that risk had political-diplomatic value and should be exploited. Even exemplary forcible action, they argued, may have to be contemplated to demonstrate resolve and the threat of more pain to come. Utility can be derived from the threatened use of nuclear weapons to protect the nuclear weapon state's homeland, that of its allies, as well as to protect other vital interests and the international status quo. Others argued that limited nuclear war is a viable nuclear strategy that with appropriate diplomacy provides a means to escape the "sterility of the quest for absolute peace . . . and . . . of the search for absolute victory" (Kissinger 1957). Because of their limited or lack of utility in a military sense and the political utility derived from their threatened use, nuclear weapons came to be seen essentially as a political rather than a military weapon.

Threat of Punishment to the Fore

The punitive character of nuclear weapons and the lack of defense against nuclear weapons shifted the emphasis in the role of force in policy and strategy from actual use to threatened use (Schelling 1966). The devastating consequences rendered the rational use of nuclear weapons unthinkable, but the threat of devastating punishment became highly potent and became the mainstay of policy and strategy in the nuclear era. The salience of force shifted from use on the battlefield to coercive threat to inflict unacceptable damage and pain.[3] This shift has several important implications.

First, it elevates the salience of deterrence and downgrades that of defense and offense. The destructive power of nuclear weapons is of little use in defense (holding ground and defeating an attacking enemy, denying assets of value to the enemy) or in offense (attacking and defeating an enemy in the battlefield to acquire assets of value—land, population, resources, etc.). Its primary role is to deter attack by threatening devastating consequences. This elevates deterrence from a way station to war in the conventional era to the centerpiece of strategy in the nuclear era (Freedman 1983, 2004). During the Cold War, nuclear deterrence became the cornerstone of national security strategy and international politics. The lack of defense against nuclear weapons and possession of mutual second-strike capability—the ability to inflict absolute pain and extinction on each other regardless of who strikes first—decouples deterrence from defense.[4] Nuclear weapons make for a sharp distinction between "deterrence by denial" and "deterrence by punishment" (Snyder 1961: 8–9, 14–16). Nuclear weapons reduce the potency of the former and dramatically elevate the importance of the latter. Deterrence is the central function of nuclear weapons and has come to exclusively mean deterrence by threat of punishment.

Second, the shift to the threatened use of force focuses attention on the adversary's intentions. Traditional military strategy focused almost exclusively on capability. A certain level of capability to carry out the articulated threat still remains crucial in the nuclear era; however, the significance of superiority beyond a certain level of retaliatory capability is much less important, possibly even irrelevant. The credibility of a nuclear threat depends not only on capability but also on influencing an adversary's perception and intention (Schelling 1966: 35). Issues relating to the credibility of threat including the "art of commitment" and "manipulation of risk" become highly important.

Finally, the threat of punishment has connected violence and diplomacy in novel ways that is vividly captured in the "diplomacy of violence" phrase coined by Schelling (1966). Diplomacy was always connected to the possible use of violence as demonstrated by phrases such as *gunboat diplomacy* and *coercive diplomacy*. However, diplomacy and force were distinct instruments that were considered alternatives, with force used when diplomacy failed. In the nuclear era, the threat and use of violence itself can be seen as an instrument of diplomacy. The danger and threat of nuclear war could be exploited as an important technique of influence, bargaining, and intimidation.

Nuclear Weapon Roles

Discussion of the roles of nuclear weapons must begin with Clausewitz's central insight that "war is a continuation of political intercourse, with the addition of other means," and that its purpose and conduct must be influenced by the political objective (1976: 605–10). Rather than negate Clausewitz's insight, the immense destruction potential of nuclear weapons highlights the importance of discussing the purposes, roles, and limitations of these ultimate weapons in relation to desired political objectives and the prevailing political-strategic context. Even total war must be part of policy. A criticism leveled against "second-wave" strategic analysts was that their thinking was largely apolitical and abstract (Trachtenberg 1989). Abstract thinking is important for conceptualization and theorizing, but such thinking must be infused with political considerations when contemplating the role of nuclear weapons as an instrument of policy.

States resort to the threat and use of force for three basic political ends: to preserve their existence, to enhance state power to achieve national foreign policy goals including that of shaping the international environment (milieu goals), and to maintain international order.[5] In an anarchic system, survival is precarious and highly contingent and is the basic goal of states. State survival entails protecting territorial integrity, preserving internal sovereignty (compulsory internal jurisdiction), and preserving international sovereignty (independence and autonomy in decision making). Informed by zero-sum distributional consequences, security is a scarce value, and the quest for it through competitive armament creates a security dilemma (Herz 1950; Jervis 1978). Pursuit of foreign policy objectives, including shaping the international environment, may require both preserving and altering the status quo, including protecting allies and friends, securing access to vital resources, denying them to adversaries, and prevailing in regional conflicts. The third goal of maintaining international order, which overlaps with shaping the international environment, includes domination (power and authority) to ensure a certain type of order and the construction of domestic regimes and international organizations in support of that order.[6] Traditionally, military force has been assigned a primary role in the pursuit of all three goals. What is the role of the immense destructive power of nuclear weapons in the pursuit of these three basic goals?

As observed earlier, the punitive character of nuclear weapons and the lack of defense against them elevate deterrence and downgrade offense and defense. The primary function of nuclear weapons is to ensure survival and preserve the status quo by deterring aggression (deterrence) and compelling an adversary not to embark on or to undo a transgression that seeks change in the status quo (compellence). The threat of punishment, the danger of escalation to nuclear war, and the exemplary use of force may be exploited in an offensive role to compel or prevent a change in the status quo (coercive diplomacy or limited war), or to destroy an enemy's strategic assets (counterforce). The counterforce role can also serve a damage limitation function and be viewed as defensive. These roles are elaborated below.

Deterrence

Although deterrence has been employed in many ways (as a concept, a theory, and a strategy), my concern here is with the function of deterrence in a political-security role to deter aggression by threatening unacceptable punishment. Deterrence has a status quo orientation. The threat intent in deterrence is to keep the enemy from starting something. Types of deterrence may be distinguished on the basis of the referent unit for protection (who is to be protected), against what threats, and how deterrence is to be prosecuted. On who is to be protected, two types of deterrence may be identified. One is *basic* or *central deterrence,* which is the protection of the nuclear state's homeland by deterring outright military attack through threat of unacceptable consequences (Freedman 2004). The second is *extended deterrence.* This refers to the extension of the deterrence function of a state's nuclear arsenal to protect the homeland of an ally. Extended deterrence could also be applied more broadly to the protection of a nuclear weapon state's vital interests (maintaining a sphere of influence, protecting sea lines of communications) that lie outside the territory of an ally.

The question of what is to be deterred is more complicated. In the early years of the Cold War, it was believed that nuclear weapons could deter a wide range of threats, including direct nuclear attack, large-scale conventional attack, limited conventional attack and intrusion, low-intensity war, and biological and chemical attack. Progressively, however, it became clear, especially with the development of parity and mutual second-strike capabilities, that nuclear weapons could deter only a narrow range of threats and that other deterrents were essential to cope with lesser threats and plug the widening gap in deterrence policy (Huntington 1982; Kauffman 1956). The how question relates to strategy and is discussed later.

Finally, although it has to be in place and working all the time, deterrence may be general or immediate (Morgan 2003). The difference between the two is in the intensity of the threat and the readiness to execute the threat. Immediate deterrence is a crisis situation in which war is distinctly possible; general deterrence is "far less intense and anxious because the attack to be forestalled is still hypothetical" (Morgan 2003: 9). Nevertheless, general deterrence is a situation in which an opponent would consider attacking if a suitable occasion arose, but does not proceed beyond preliminary consideration of this option in light of the threat of retaliation posed by the other party (Morgan 2003: 80). In general deterrence, "an actor maintains a broad military capability and issues broad threats of punitive response" to prevent anyone from thinking seriously about attacking. In immediate deterrence, an actor has developed specific capabilities and issues threats to an opponent who is preparing to attack.

Compellence

In contrast to deterrence, which is passive, compellence is an irrevocable commitment to action that can only cease when the adversary complies with a demand.[7] The threat of nuclear punishment is deployed to change the behavior of a state by affecting its cost-benefit calculus, usually to compel an enemy to stop or undo a certain course of action that he is embarked on (Schelling 1966: 69–78). A compellence threat involves initiation of a commitment or action and a clear deadline by which the adversary must respond. Should the opponent fail to comply, the initiator must be committed to carry through the stated action if the threat is to be credible.

Coercive Diplomacy

Alexander George defines coercive diplomacy broadly to include both defensive and offensive use of force.[8] However, most Western analysts focus on the defensive role of coercive diplomacy—"efforts to persuade an opponent to stop and/or undo an action he is already embarked upon" (George 2004: 71). The defense orientation of coercive diplomacy in the literature privileges the status quo and may be a function of viewing it essentially through the lens of U.S. policy in the Cold War (Freedman 2004: 109–10). In this study, coercive diplomacy is defined broadly to also include the use of coercion (including exploitation of the danger of escalation to nuclear war) to bring about change in the status quo, to compel changes in the policies of an adversary, or to support other foreign policy objectives. Treating the risk of nuclear war as a shield, a state may pursue political objectives including intimidation and blackmail or compelling another state to negotiate on a particular issue by engaging in lower-level violence (conventional or low-intensity war) and threatening nuclear war. The threat and use of violence become infused with diplomacy.

Counterforce Role

In the counterforce role, nuclear weapons would be used to destroy or drastically impair an opponent's strategic force and other key military targets (such as massed troop formations, large military complexes, hardened military installations, and communication centers). Nuclear weapons may be used in a counterforce role for deterrence, damage limitation, and in support of an assertive foreign policy (Glaser and Fetter 2005). By denying a survivable retaliatory capability, counterforce capabilities can enhance deterrence. In the event deterrence fails, such capabilities (especially a second strike) can limit damage to a state's own assets and society by destroying enemy strategic assets. An ability to destroy enemy strategic assets would liberate foreign policy from the constraints arising from enemy possession of nuclear weapons. Although the benefits of counterforce against the Soviet Union were ambiguous, it is argued that these benefits are more certain and useful for a country like the United States facing small nuclear powers (Buchan et al. 2003: 41–43). The 2002 Nuclear Posture Review (NPR) identifies counterforce as a key role for nuclear weapons. Together with ballistic missile defense (BMD), it is seen as "bringing into better balance U.S. stakes and risks in a regional confrontation and thus reinforcing the credibility of U.S. guarantees designed to deter attacks on allies and friends" (2002 NPR: 14, quoted in Glaser and Fetter 2005: 108). The distinction in the use of the counterforce role in deterrence and damage limitation lies in the purpose rather than in the nature of military action. It is thus subject to misperception. Glaser and Fetter argue that the counterforce role has limited deterrence value for a country that already has a strong second-strike capability and that it could be counterproductive in the conduct of foreign policy relating to regional conflicts. They see the chief value of the counterforce role in damage limitation.

Preserving Strategic Autonomy

A nuclear weapon state could coerce and constrain the policy choices of a nonnuclear weapon state (either ally or foe) or could compel it into submission in certain conflict situations. To avoid such situations and to preserve autonomy in international relations, states may view nuclear weapons (their own or those of an ally) as vital to their national security and as a backstop to their foreign policy. A primary concern of a nonnuclear weapon state is avoiding blackmail by a nuclear weapon state in an adversarial situation. Although some nuclear weapon states have articulated a no-first-use (NFU) policy and pledged that they will not employ nuclear weapons against nonnuclear weapon states, those who could be on the receiving end do not take such pledges seriously. Forging an alliance with a substantial nuclear weapon state can alleviate this concern, although that arrangement may also constrain freedom of action.

Power and Prestige

Military power has always been an index of national power and prestige. Seen as the ultimate weapon, the possession of nuclear force may confer international power and status (membership in an exclusive club and big-power status) or enhance a state's international prestige (authority and legitimacy) (Gilpin 1981). Often Western analysts, especially in the arms control community, deprecate this role by assigning it a negative connotation in regard to nuclear weapon states and aspirants from the developing world. However, it is undeniable that countries such as the former Soviet Union, Britain, and France also viewed possession of nuclear weapons as necessary indicators of their international power and prestige. It is possible to argue that nuclear weapons no longer serve this function in the post-Cold War world in which the significance of military power including nuclear weapons is declining relative to other indexes of power (Paul 1998).

Relationship to Conventional Capabilities

The connection between nuclear and conventional forces is important in understanding the contemporary roles of nuclear weapons and their significance in the overall national security policy of a state. As noted in the Introduction chapter, states that possess nuclear weapons are also modernizing their conventional military capabilities. The United States, for example, seeks to reduce its reliance on nuclear weapon capabilities by developing ballistic missile defense and more lethal conventional capabilities that can perform missions that were previously assigned to nuclear weapons. The old nuclear strategic triad is only one leg in Washington's new triad envisaged in the 2002 NPR. However, the United States also contemplates modern nuclear weapon capabilities for certain military purposes such as earth penetration. Russia, on the other hand, in light of its weaknesses in conventional capabilities, emphasizes the centrality of nuclear weapons for its international security. For most other nuclear weapon states and their allies, conventional capability is the more relevant means to deal with the immediate security challenges confronting them. Nuclear weapons serve other functions. The division of labor between the two capabilities, how they reinforce or constrain each other, and their respective weight in national security policy are important issues to investigate.

Redressing conventional power imbalance in a relatively cheap way is at times advanced as a separate purpose of nuclear weapons. During the Cold War, nuclear weapons were perceived by China as a cost-effective way to deter the vastly stronger United States and Soviet Union (Goldstein 2000). And American policy makers sought to counter Soviet conventional superiority in Europe and North Korean conventional superiority on the Korean peninsula with the deployment of tactical and intermediate range nuclear weapons. The purpose, however, was still deterrence. Compensating for weakness in conventional military capability is not a separate purpose in itself, but a means to an end—deterrence.

Apart from their role in dealing with certain security challenges for which nuclear weapons would not be relevant, conventional capabilities could be employed in conjunction with nuclear weapons in three ways. One conventional military force may be deployed to prevent a fait accompli by a blitzkrieg-type attack by the adversary and enhance the effectiveness of extended nuclear deterrence.[9] This was the purpose of conventional forces in Europe and South Korea during the Cold War. The deployment of U.S. conventional forces in these theaters also served as a visible symbol of U.S. commitment and a trip-wire function to trigger stronger reaction including nuclear retaliation. Second, and this is linked to the first point, for situations in which nuclear threats seem disproportional, the threat of conventional retaliation provides a credible alternative, preventing the stark choice between all and nothing. Conventional capability may be incorporated into escalation and war-fighting strategies. Third, conventional forces could be employed in a coercive diplomacy role, including limited war to pursue certain political objectives based on the assumption that the fear of escalation to nuclear war would deter large-scale conventional retaliation. Limited war in the shadow of the nuclear umbrella was and is envisaged in this context.

Nuclear Strategies

Connecting ends-and-means strategy formulates how military force will be employed in the pursuit of desired political outcomes. Correctly formulated, it can function as a force multiplier (Betts 2000). Some have questioned the utility of strategy. Criticisms include the absence of criteria for selecting a strategy, the difficulty of prediction in light of the complexity and contingency of war, difficulties communicating across cultures, and implementation problems. Often strategies are developed in an ad hoc manner and in hindsight to rationalize or provide an intellectual framework for a situation that already exists. Even if strategy is driven by specific purposes, the purposes themselves may not be clear, and there may be multiple and conflicting objectives. Further, there may be a wide gap between declaratory strategy, actual capability, and behavior in a crisis situation. In light of these problems, it could be argued that strategy cannot be meaningful. However, discussion of strategy is still necessary and useful because it provides the rationale for meaningful use of violence and threat of it as an instrument of state policy, and it indicates the international orientation and overall military posture of a state. Other states infer intent from the orientation of a state's strategy and behavior (Posen 1984). Strategies also affect the quality of international life, with consequences for security interaction, the nature and intensity of the security dilemma, and the type of security order.

Military strategy in the prenuclear era emphasized the achievement of political goals by winning wars. With the advent of nuclear weapons, as noted earlier, the emphasis in strategy shifted from the physical use of force to the threat and exemplary use of force to achieve political and military objectives. This shift underpins Brodie's claim that nuclear weapons revolutionized military strategy. Thomas Schelling (1966: 1–34) extends this further by arguing that the growing centrality of power to hurt without "collapsing [the enemy's] military force," implies that military strategy is no longer about winning wars but about the "art of coercion, of intimidation and deterrence," and "of manipulating risk" to achieve certain political outcomes.

Drawing on the Cold War experience but also on recent scholarship, this section outlines the main nuclear strategies and their key elements. The selection of specific roles and strategies would be a function of the political objectives of the state, its political-strategic position in the international system, and its satisfaction or dissatisfaction with it. A revisionist state seeking to bring about change in the international system would most likely emphasize offense-oriented roles and strategies. By contrast, a state that is concerned about its own survival or satisfied with the status quo is likely to emphasize deterrence and defensive roles and strategies (Posen 1984).

Strategies of Deterrence

Nuclear deterrence seeks to prevent enemy aggression by threatening awful consequences usually labeled as unacceptable damage. For a strategy of deterrence to be effective, a state must commit to a political outcome that is vital, threaten unacceptable damage if that outcome is jeopardized, have the capability to inflict such damage, and communicate the seriousness of its intention through a clear policy, firm commitment, and a reputation for carrying out commitments (Morgan 2003: 13–19; Schelling 1966: 35–91). Nuclear deterrence thinking has gone through different phases, and there has been a proliferation of adjectives to convey specific situations or orientations.[10] Some of these, such as *existential deterrence, recessed deterrence, opaque deterrence,* and *mutual assured destruction* (MAD), are situations or conditions, not strategies. Here, I discuss three primary strategies of basic or central deterrence—massive retaliation, assured retaliation, and minimum deterrence—and the strategy of extended deterrence. At base, all three basic deterrence strategies are similar in that they rely on the threat of punishment. They differ on the retaliatory capability (and by extension the size of the nuclear arsenal) required to deter, the degree of desired certainty, and the threats to be deterred or contingencies to be covered.

Massive Retaliation. First articulated in 1954 after the Korean War, this strategy was taken to imply that communist or communist-inspired aggression anywhere in the world would result in massive retaliation by the United States.[11] The threat of massive retaliation was considered important to supplement local ground defense and avoid worldwide commitment of U.S. ground forces and to reduce the cost of defense. It was also seen as providing flexibility in decision making because it allowed the United States to decide when and how to respond (Kauffman 1956). This strategy, which sought to maximize the utility of the special asset of the United States, was controversial from the outset.

Formulated in the context of American nuclear superiority, the United States clearly had the requisite capability to carry out the strategy of massive retaliation. However, the strategy was deemed not credible on several counts, most importantly on the proportionality of response to threat (Kauffman 1956). It was considered credible only in regard to a very narrow range of contingencies, including the use of nuclear weapons by communist powers and direct attacks on the United

States and its key allies in Western Europe. The idea of a single deterrent to cope with a wide range of threats appears to have been a nonstarter from the outset.

Assured Retaliation. The strategy of assured retaliation (also known as assured destruction) was derived from a critique of the strategy of massive retaliation and in light of Soviet advances in strategic arms that supposedly neutralized American nuclear superiority.[12] The assured retaliation strategy seeks to deter a deliberate nuclear attack "by maintaining at all times a clear and unmistakable ability to inflict an unacceptable degree of damage upon any [and all] aggressors—even after absorbing a first strike" (Enthoven and Smith 1971, quoted in Freedman 1983: 246). The emphasis in this strategy is on surviving a first strike with the capability to execute a retaliatory threat to inflict unacceptable damage (countervalue targeting to destroy cities and populations). A secure second-strike capability is essential for an effective assured retaliation strategy. During the Cold War, this translated into a requirement for a large nuclear arsenal; a strategic triad of land, air, and sea assets; force protection; and sophisticated command, control, communications, and intelligence arrangements. The strategy was seen as credible against nuclear threats to the United States but less so in regard to key allies in Europe and Asia. Conventional military force, tactical nuclear weapons, and intermediate range missiles were deemed essential to shore up the deterrence commitment to allies. Along with damage limitation and conventional defense, assured retaliation formed a part of the U.S. flexible response policy that was designed to provide policy makers with options in dealing with different contingencies.

With advances in Soviet nuclear capability, a situation of MAD became a reality. As Jervis (1989) points out, MAD was not a strategy but a fact: a condition that developed as a consequence of the ease of countervalue retaliation (as opposed to counterforce damage limitation) and the development of secure second-strike capabilities by both superpowers. Though not preferred, vulnerability to mutual retaliation came to be seen as essential for the stability of deterrence. It is important to distinguish between MAD and assured retaliation. Although the end of the Cold War has undermined the MAD situation, the strategy of assured retaliation continues to be relevant for and among countries that possess the capability to retaliate after suffering a first strike.

Minimum Deterrence. The strategy of minimum deterrence rests on the belief that only a small nuclear force is required to deter nuclear and full-scale conventional attack. Absolute rather than relative level of damage is what matters, and nuclear balance and deployment are not as critical as they are in the strategy of assured retaliation. Nuclear threats are considered highly effective. The risk that nuclear weapons would be used either in retaliation or in the escalation of a conventional war, and the high level of absolute damage (countervalue) that can be caused even by a small number of nuclear weapons, lies at the heart of minimum deterrence

(Basrur 2006; Freedman 1983). A minimum deterrent force may deter nuclear and full-scale conventional attack. It may also have some limited utility in the following roles: compellence, coercive diplomacy, and protecting and enhancing foreign and strategic policy autonomy. Though the strategy of minimum deterrence appears cost-effective and attractive, it is seriously underdeveloped. What constitutes a minimum and how does one arrive at that figure? What are the survivability requirements necessary to reduce an adversary's temptation to strike first and one's own temptation to launch on warning? What sorts of deployment and command and control arrangements are required? Is minimum deterrence more suited for general deterrence than for immediate deterrence? Is countervalue targeting acceptable, especially in democratic states? These questions require investigation.

A subset of minimum deterrence is existential deterrence. Initially articulated in the context of the huge American and Soviet stockpile of nuclear weapons in relation to Europe, the idea of existential deterrence is rooted in the belief that the very existence of a nuclear weapon stockpile would create considerable caution in relations among nuclear weapon states (Bundy 1983, 1984, 2004). Existential deterrence rests on the fear of uncertainty about what could happen, not on specific force structure or doctrine, or what has been declared as policy. It is not affected by changes in the balance of power except those that "might truly challenge the overall survivability of the forces on either side" (Bundy 1983: 9). Existential deterrence deters impersonally; no provocative threat is required; and it deters both sides simultaneously. Seen in this manner, existential deterrence is more a condition or outcome than a strategy.

The idea of existential deterrence appears to have been adapted to the present period as a basic deterrence strategy for states with opaque, small, or nascent nuclear forces with the purpose of inducing caution and deterring large-scale conventional or nuclear attack by posing the danger of nuclear escalation and retaliation. In this conception, existential deterrence requires only the capability to carry out a simple, undifferentiated countervalue strike. A very small nuclear force would be sufficient for this purpose. For states that have not declared their nuclear weapon capabilities (India and Pakistan before 1998 and Israel), nuclear deterrence rests primarily on the perceived existence of nuclear capability than on declared intention or on relative capabilities (Hagerty 1998: 3). Existential deterrence would have no other purpose than protection of the homeland, although it could provide a certain measure of freedom in foreign policy and help mitigate the negative consequences of imbalance in conventional capability. Conceived in this manner, existential deterrence overlaps minimum deterrence and is likely to be the strategy of a weak or isolated state. Although presented as separate strategies, existential deterrence, minimum deterrence, and assured retaliation can form part of a continuum, with the first two as way stations on the path to assured retaliation.

Extended Deterrence. The strategy of extended nuclear deterrence broadens the deterrence function of a nuclear arsenal to protect the homeland of an allied state against attack. The strategy usually suffers two credibility problems. One arises when the home territory of the deterring state is vulnerable to nuclear attack. Would a nuclear weapon state risk nuclear war to counter a threat to an ally if its own home territory were vulnerable to nuclear attack? This question was at the heart of the extended deterrence problem in Cold War Western Europe. The greater the vulnerability of the nuclear weapon state's homeland to nuclear attack, the less credible would be its extended deterrence commitment. The second credibility problem arises if the nuclear threat appears out of proportion to the threat confronting an ally. Nuclear threats can deter only a narrow range of threats. Deterring nuclear threat will be more credible; deterring limited conventional attack, low-intensity aggression, and chemical and biological attack by threatening nuclear retaliation is less credible.

In both situations, the concern is how to make the extended deterrence commitment credible. Measures to make extended deterrence commitments credible include clear articulation of commitment, stationing troops and tactical nuclear weapons in allied countries, developing an ally's conventional capability to prevent a fait accompli, integrating that capability with one's own to demonstrate escalation potential, developing and deploying BMD to protect the strategic assets of the nuclear weapon state and that of its ally, and demonstrating resolve through regular exercises and development of reputation.

Strategies of Offense

Offensive strategies exploit the threat value of nuclear weapons, the risk of nuclear war, and the use of force in an exemplary or controlled manner as a means of bargaining to achieve certain political outcomes. These include rolling back infringements of the status quo, preventing or bringing about change in the status quo, calibrating means and ends in the pursuit of limited political objectives without resorting to general war, and demonstrating political resolve to foe and friend.

Compellence. Although it relies on the threat of punishment as well, compellence—unlike deterrence—demands change. The purpose of compellence is to demand compliance with a political demand and involves inducing action (acquiescence, retreat, or collaboration) through threat of punishment or exemplary use of force to indicate that more pain is in store if the adversary does not comply. A compellent threat may be designed to intentionally involve some loss of control. Schelling labeled this "threats that leave something to chance." Citing the Cuban missile crisis, he posits that this kind of threat "is more impersonal, more external to the participants [and] the threat becomes part of the environment rather than a test of will between adversaries. The adversary may find it easier—less costly in prestige or self-respect—to back away from a risky situation . . . than from a threat that is backed exclusively by . . . resolve and determination" (Schelling 1966: 121n). Unlike deterrence, compellence strategies must be designed for specific situations as they develop.

A compellent strategy must have a definite objective, have a deadline that is near-term but allows sufficient time for the adversary to act, ensure that the threat will not be carried out if the adversary acts accordingly, and provide a reasonable exit for the adversary. To be effective, a compellent strategy must have a high probability that the threat will be executed if the adversary does not meet the demand.

Controlled Escalation and Limited War. Though these two strategies are often discussed separately, they have common premises and overlapping features of deterrence and compellence. Limited war and controlled escalation strategies assume that deterrence of general nuclear war would continue to operate even after lower-level conflict has been deliberately waged. By calibrating ends and means and relying on intrawar deterrence, strategies of controlled escalation and limited war seek comparative advantage in a conflict by escalating the means and level of violence, crossing limits that previously constrained both sides, and threatening even greater risk and damage (Freedman 1983: 210–11). Controlled escalation and limited war presume a process of bargaining, concession, or further escalation based on deliberate decisions by belligerents. To be successful, these strategies require clear identification of interests and threats, calibrated responses, clear communication, implementation monitoring, and an exit strategy. These stringent requirements are not easily met, and the strategies could have unintended and opposing effects as demonstrated by the experience in the Vietnam War in which a strategy of controlled escalation was deliberately applied (Gaddis 2004).

Strategies of Defense

Counterforce is the only defensive role of nuclear weapons. If deterrence fails, nuclear weapons can be used to limit damage by destroying the enemy's strategic assets. Defense in a nuclear context, however, also includes BMD and conventional defense. As with offense, there is no specific defense strategy. Depending on the threat and desired comprehensiveness, strategies of defense may be developed around one or more of three elements: counterforce damage limitation, conventional defense, and defense against missile attacks. In light of earlier discussion, the consideration of counterforce and conventional defense in this subsection is brief.

Counterforce Damage Limitation. The purpose of a counterforce damage limitation strategy is to destroy the opponent's nuclear assets, other weapons of mass destruction, and command and control facilities through a first strike (preventive or preemptive), or second strike (retaliatory action) to reduce the damage from attacks by such weapons. A successful damage limitation strategy can prevent enemy attacks on cities and its own strategic assets; hence it can be enormously useful. Glaser and Fetter (2005) argue that a first-strike strategy risks precipitating early launch by the enemy and undermining deterrence. A strategy that relies on retaliatory action does not undermine deterrence; targeting surviving nuclear forces avoids unnecessary use of nuclear weapons and prevents a large retaliatory strike by the enemy. A damage limitation strategy may be limited or comprehensive; the latter may include invasion to gain control of the enemy's strategic assets.

Although more useful than the counterforce role in deterrence or in increasing the leeway for foreign policy, the damage limitation counterforce strategy is not without drawbacks. A first-strike strategy can bring about an unnecessary nuclear war. A counterforce strategy that emphasizes prevention and preemption could also provide an incentive for target states to launch first, making for an unstable crisis situation. With a second-strike strategy there is no certainty that it can destroy desired enemy targets. Some analysts claim that the costs outweigh the benefits and that a counterforce strategy can be destabilizing (Glaser and Fetter 2005). Still others argue that counterforce missions and roles might work in the contemporary context against fledgling nuclear powers (Buchan et al. 2003: 41–43). However, as with BMD, the advantage of counterforce is likely to be temporary and uncertain; over time the target country could presumably develop more survivable nuclear forces. In any case, attacking an adversary's nuclear forces with nuclear or conventional forces is a serious matter that most likely would result in a retaliatory strike. It carries much risk, is likely to undermine the taboo against the use of nuclear weapons, and could have negative political and military ramifications.

Conventional Defense. The purpose of a conventional defense is to deny victory to the enemy if deterrence fails and to provide credible options in responding to enemy attack. The defense force must be able to stop and defeat limited conventional intrusion as well as large-scale conventional attack, especially of the blitzkrieg type, on home territory or that of allies. It also must have the capability to launch a counteroffensive to destroy and limit enemy capability or to regain lost value (such as territory). As indicated in earlier discussion, in a nuclear setting the size, purpose, and role of conventional forces and the strategy for their employment would necessarily be linked to and vary with nuclear policy and strategy.

Ballistic Missile Defense. In the defense role, the purpose of BMD is to destroy enemy missiles to defeat an enemy attack, and to protect and limit damage to a state's own strategic assets. BMD may also enhance deterrence by protecting strategic assets to secure the second-strike capability. The capability to reduce the vulnerability of the nuclear weapon state to nuclear attack and the capability to protect strategic assets deployed overseas could also enhance the effectiveness of extended deterrence. BMD may also be a key component of an offensive strategy. With an effective defense shield, a state would be less deterred and may seriously contemplate attacks on other countries.

BMD may comprise boost phase, midcourse, and terminal interceptors. And it may be limited and tactical or comprehensive and strategic. It may be designed to protect specific strategic assets, civilian populations, or both against a specific threat or a wide array of threats. The 1972 Anti-Ballistic Missile (ABM) Treaty, for example, specifically allowed the deployment of BMD for force protection in two sites. The Clinton administration pursued a limited ground-based midcourse system designed to defend "the territory of the United States against limited ballistic missile attack (whether accidental, unauthorized, or deliberate)."[13] North Korea was the country of most concern. Vide the 2002 NPR, the Bush administration proposed the development of an integrated, layered missile defense system with boost, midcourse, and terminal components. The idea is that if one layer of interceptors misses the target the next will have a second shot (Coyle 2006). Although public pronouncements still cite rogue states as the target, such a comprehensive system would appear to have broader ramifications as well. The United States and its allies (Japan, Taiwan, and North Atlantic Treaty Organization [NATO] member states) are also investing heavily in theater or tactical missile defense.

From the foregoing discussion of roles and strategies for the employment of nuclear weapons, it is evident that strategies of deterrence are better grounded and developed than offensive and defensive strategies. Though intellectually attractive, there are practical limits to exploiting the threat potential of nuclear weapons for offensive purposes. This situation could alter dramatically if defense against ballistic missiles became effective. For the present, technological and other hurdles suggest that defense against nuclear threats is likely to be limited and rather easily countered. In this context, deterrence appears likely to continue to be the dominant purpose and strategy for the employment of nuclear weapons.

Security Implications

Robert Jervis (1989: 23–45) identified several far-reaching security implications of mutual vulnerability arising from the possession of mutual second-strike capability: the impossibility of military victory and the perpetuation of peace, preservation of the status quo and the absence of peaceful change, stability and infrequent crises, high effectiveness of threats and the importance of commitments and compromise, the salience of nuclear danger as opposed to the military balance, and a tenuous link between military balance and political outcomes. He concluded that evidence from the Cold War period generally confirms these propositions. The issue is whether these implications continue to be valid in the contemporary strategic environment. Taking into account the differences between the Cold War and the contemporary strategic situations, this section develops an overview for exploring the security implications of nuclear weapons and strategies in the present period. Specifically it addresses the impact of nuclear weapons on distribution of power and alliance arrangements, bilateral and regional security dynamics, peace and stability, and dispute resolution.

Structural Consequences

The structural effects of nuclear weapons may be explored by investigating the implications of nuclear weapons for the balance of power, the balancing behavior of states, and the salience of alliance arrangements.

Power Balance. The term *balance of power* has many meanings.[14] The focus here is on the impact of nuclear weapons on the distribution of power, which realists posit determines the material structure of the international system, with consequences for state behavior and system stability. A second focus is the imperative of balancing in an anarchic system and the associated realist claim that weak states balance strong ones through internal generation of power or through alliance formation.

On the distribution of power, a key question is what constitutes a pole. Although it is difficult to compute the power of nations and rank them, Hans Morgenthau and Kenneth Waltz assert that the rank of a state and whether it constitutes a pole depends on how well it scores on all dimensions of power, not just one dimension or sector. Morgenthau identifies geography, natural resources, industrial capacity, military preparedness, population, national character, national morale, quality of diplomacy, and quality of government as key elements of national power (1978: 117–55). Size of population and territory, resource endowment, economic capability, military strength, political stability, and competence are the key attributes of power identified by Waltz (1979: 131). International influence as a pole, however, depends not only on material capabilities; it is also contingent on certain nonmaterial qualities such as vision, policy, and political will to translate brute power into authority and influence over other states in the system.

Nuclear weapons may modify the military balance of power, but on their own they are unlikely to affect the overall distribution of power in the system. Nuclear weapons can affect the military balance by reducing or negating the potency of imbalance in conventional military capabilities. A small nuclear force can deter large-scale conventional and nuclear attacks by countries that are much stronger. This consideration underlies the claim that nuclear weapons, or more specifically the "balance of terror," equalize imbalances in military power. However, the equalizing effect operates only against specific adversaries and contingencies; it is not fungible like the defensive balance that is based on conventional military capability.[15] The military balance canceling effect of nuclear weapons does not alter the distribution of power at the system level unless nuclear weapon capability is combined with other attributes of power. In the post-World War II era, for example, nuclear weapons sharpened the already existing bipolarity. They did not create it. China became a nuclear weapon state in 1964 but did not figure significantly in the regional balance of power until well into the 1980s after it had become politically more stable, its economy began growing rapidly, and resources were available to modernize its military. Though Russia continues to have a formidable nuclear weapon capability, it is not considered a superpower or a pole today. Until its recent economic resurgence, Russia was not even taken seriously as a regional power in Asia. For change in the distribution of power, concurrent growth is required in several key attributes of power, and the state concerned should be willing to exercise that power in pursuit of a particular vision. Nuclear weapon capability adds to national military power, but by itself does not alter the ranking of a state or the distribution of power in the system.

Balancing Behavior. As with the distribution of power, nuclear weapons need not have a significant impact on the imperative of balancing in an anarchic international system. They may make internal balancing more possible and desirable than external balancing, but do not obviate the need for external balancing. Internal balancing is more possible and preferable for several reasons. First, even small nuclear forces can deter aggression (conventional and nuclear) by much stronger countries. Because it is easier to exploit the danger of nuclear war and to sustain a retaliatory force than to ensure a successful disarming first strike or an effective defense against nuclear weapons, superior nuclear capability (advantage in the ability to inflict retaliatory damage) is less likely to affect political outcomes when vital interests are at stake. Nuclear weapons can reduce the fear of abandonment, eliminate the concern about the commitment credibility of a nuclear weapon ally, and make states more self-reliant in ensuring their survival. Second, nuclear weapons do not add up in the same way as conventional capability and are much less fungible; that is, potency ceases to increase with numbers beyond a certain point (unlike with conventional weapons). Destructive power beyond a certain level (when parties to a conflict have a secure second-strike capability that can inflict unacceptable damage) is politically and strategically irrelevant. Third, alliances among nuclear weapon states may also complicate and limit the flexibility in nuclear planning by smaller states (a version of the fear of entrapment). However, the decision of a state to forego external balancing depends on its nuclear capability and the security contingencies it has to cover. A nascent nuclear weapon state that still has not developed a reliable retaliatory capability would find it useful to ally with a nuclear weapon state that can extend the deterrence function of its nuclear arsenal. Broader political and economic considerations may also make for alliances among nuclear weapon states. Nuclear Britain continued the alliance relationship with the United States, France developed its own nuclear force and pulled out of nuclear NATO but remained a member of NATO, and China strategically aligned with the United States until the early 1980s.

Salience of Alliances. Balance of power informed by consideration of threat provides the rationale for alliance formation (Walt 1987). Alliances and alignments combine the power of states to confront a powerful adversary. They may also serve broader functions that go beyond purely military considerations. As observed earlier, nuclear weapons could reduce the salience of allies in military balancing because they make internal balancing more possible and attractive in certain situations. However, this consideration does not make alliances irrelevant. Although allies could not affect the strategic balance, alliances were considered important during the Cold War. Allied countries, especially large ones such as Japan and several NATO countries, did matter in many other attributes of power. Alliances not only extend the power and influence of the dominant partner; they can assist in the construction of a preferred order, allow for shared responsibilities, and balance the conventional military capability of an aspiring hegemon.

For nonnuclear weapon states, alliance with a nuclear weapon state that can provide security support or a guarantee makes eminent security sense, although the credibility issue can argue against relying on the nuclear guarantee of another state when that state itself is vulnerable to nuclear attack. Through a nuclear guarantee, the nuclear weapon state can discourage nuclear proliferation and also influence allies. Smaller countries obtain voice opportunities through alliances, which could also be a means for constraining the alliance lead power. For these and other reasons, alliances were important during the Cold War. Would alliances among nuclear weapon states and between nuclear and nonnuclear weapon states continue to be important in the contemporary unipolar world? This question is explored in Chapter 18, with specific reference to the U.S.-centered alliance system in Asia. It will also be useful to explore if and how the development of nuclear weapon capability by Pakistan has affected the China-Pakistan strategic alignment and Pakistan's security relationship with the United States.

Security Interaction Consequences

A key consequence of the transforming effect of nuclear weapons is the elevation of deterrence to center stage in national security policy and the relative decline in the salience of defense and offense. How this affects security interaction may be investigated by exploring its consequences for regional peace and stability and dispute resolution.

Cold War Experience: Relative Peace and Strategic Stability. The impossibility of military victory in a total war in a situation of mutual vulnerability has been cited as a cause of the unprecedented "long peace" between the two superpowers since 1945

(Jervis 1989: 23–24). Although other reasons (bipolarity, political and economic modernization, and satisfaction of the two superpowers with the status quo) may also have contributed to the long peace, it is unclear if they, on their own, can account for the Soviet-American peace.[16] It is difficult to apportion responsibility, but it is unlikely that mutual vulnerability was unimportant. It is more likely that the different factors reinforced each other.

Jervis argues that nuclear weapons enhanced stability because they favor preservation of the status quo. Traditionally the threat and use of military force have been deployed along with other instruments to alter the status quo through war. Because of the mutual vulnerability of the two superpowers, nuclear weapons were more relevant during the Cold War in the deterrence role than in the coercive diplomacy or forcible use roles. Further, the state protecting a firmly entrenched status quo through deterrence enjoys certain bargaining advantages. Jervis (1989: 29–35) argues that the status quo country has a higher stake and therefore higher resolve in defending it; and the country seeking to alter the status quo bears the onus of moving first, knowing full well that its action could cause a conflict to escalate to a full-scale war. The status quo advantage applied in the prenuclear era as well. Nuclear weapons have magnified the effect. A firmly established status quo in the nuclear era favors the state practicing deterrence and is difficult to alter.

Crisis should also be infrequent in a condition of mutual, secure second-strike capability and when the status quo is firm (Jervis 1989: 35–38). Prenuclear causes of crisis, such as adventures in the expectation of victory and defection by significant allies that could change the distribution of power, are not valid in a situation of mutual vulnerability where security is provided by secure second-strike capability. The Cuban missile crisis occurred when the Soviets were weak and still seeking parity. Although there were conflicts on the periphery since then, they did not generate a crisis between the superpowers. As long as both sides were satisfied with the status quo, generating a crisis to gain something was not attractive enough to outweigh the costs. Should a crisis occur in the nuclear era, it will not be due to misreading enemy military strength as in the past; it will be based on the importance of the issue at stake, each state's willingness to run risks, and judgment of each other's resolve. Mutual vulnerability and the desire to avoid undesirable outcomes also provided incentives for Soviet-American cooperation. Such cooperation was designed to strengthen strategic stability and reduce the risk of unintended war.

However, it was feared that stability at the strategic level would make it safe to engage in lower-level violence. The stability-instability paradox rested on the belief that the mutual possession of second-strike capability lowers the probability that conventional wars will escalate to the nuclear level.[17] The low likelihood of escalation (termed *strategic stability*) makes conventional war less dangerous, opening up space for limited war and other lower levels of violence in the pursuit of political goals. However, as Jervis notes, because escalation can occur, mutual second-strike capability does not make the world safe for major provocations and limited wars. A requirement of U.S. strategy during the Cold War was to set in train a process that reconnected nuclear retaliation to conventional aggression. Despite fear of a Soviet blitzkrieg-type attack in Europe, the two superpowers studiously avoided conventional conflict with each other, fearing that such conflicts could escalate to the nuclear level.

Relevance for the Contemporary Era. The claim that nuclear weapons contribute to peace and strategic stability is grounded almost exclusively in the Cold War context of the two superpowers' mutual vulnerability. Would nuclear weapons have a similar effect in the contemporary nuclear context? There are two issues to consider here. One relates to the condition of asymmetry and the small size of the nuclear force of many states in the Asian security region. Can small nuclear forces deter each other, and can they deter stronger nuclear powers? Can stability be achieved with small nuclear forces? Would the risk of escalation to nuclear war make conventional war and low-intensity violence more likely among newer nuclear weapon states and undermine stability? The second issue relates to deterrence dominance. Does the development of missile defense in combination with a nuclear counterforce role undermine deterrence dominance and increase the space for offense by states with such capabilities?

Small Nuclear Forces and Deterrence. The premise that nuclear danger induces uncertainty and caution among nuclear weapon states underscores the thinking that small nuclear forces can deter aggressive action by other small nuclear powers as well as those by superior ones. Bundy (2004) argued that it did not take a huge stockpile of nuclear weapons or an assured destruction capability to deter even a formidable adversary like the Soviet Union. The strategies of minimum and existential deterrence rely on this premise. Kenneth Waltz (1995) forcefully makes the case that small nuclear forces can deter each other and also deter stronger nuclear powers. Arguing that a low probability of destructive attack is sufficient for deterrence, he posits that the requirements of effective deterrence—second-strike capability, avoiding launch on warning and on false signals, and effective command and control arrangements—can be satisfied by new nuclear weapon states with small nuclear forces and that nuclear threat by weaker countries is highly credible. What counts is not the balance of force but the balance of resolve, which hinges on the issue at stake (defense of the homeland for the weaker states) and the fear that aggressive action will invite nuclear retaliation.

This line of thinking is countered by those who argue that the requirements of stable deterrence cannot be satisfied by the new nuclear weapon states because military officers view preventive war in a positive light and are not interested in constructing invulnerable strategic forces; they also argue that the nuclear arsenals of the newer nuclear weapon states are more prone to accidental and unauthorized use (Sagan 1995). A critical difference (not just between Waltz and Sagan, but between Waltz and his other critics as well) centers on the requirement of a secure second-strike capability. For assured retaliationists, effective deterrence entails certainty of retaliation and the capability to inflict a level of damage that is defined as unacceptable. For Waltz, the uncertainty and risk of nuclear war, and the perception that even a few bombs can inflict a high level of damage, are sufficient for deterrence to be effective. Even a slight chance that a provocation could lead to nuclear war is sufficient to deter all but the most highly motivated adversary (Bundy 1983). Robert Powell (2003: 101) argues that resolve is the key issue. When the balance of resolve favors a small nuclear power, it can deter a larger nuclear power. Even when the balance of resolve is ambiguous, if the smaller state is willing to run a higher risk, it can deter the larger nuclear power.

Small Nuclear Forces, Peace, and Stability. Building on the argument that small nuclear forces can deter like forces and even superior ones, Waltz posits that the spread of nuclear weapons to more states is not destabilizing. It can advance peace, security, and stability (Waltz 1995). He supports this assertion with these points: Nuclear weapons help ensure the security of states in an international system based on self-help; small nuclear forces will not affect the strategic balance; nuclear weapons reduce the chance of war by making miscalculation difficult and increasing the cost of war; and new nuclear weapon states will feel the same constraints that have been experienced by the older ones. The combination of nuclear deterrence and conventional defense eliminated war among advanced states in their core area of interest, but the proliferation of conventional weapons has sustained and possibly increased the incidence of wars on the periphery, making violence the privilege of the strong against the weak and among the weak and the poor. The gradual spread of nuclear weapons, according to Waltz, will decrease the incidence of war among the new states as well.

Analysts who argue that organizational pathologies, technological shortcomings, geographic proximity, intense disputes and distrust, and small nuclear arsenals increase volatility in the already conflict-prone regions contest such reassuring analysis (Feaver 1992/3, 1993; Sagan 1994, 1995). Some take this critique a step further by claiming that, instead of inducing caution and reducing the incidence of conventional war, the danger of nuclear war can make conflict among newer nuclear weapon states more likely (Kapur 2006: 10). Rather than restrain behavior, the introduction of nuclear danger makes the world a more violent place. Earlier, Jervis argued that the advantage favoring the status quo in the nuclear era may not hold when the status quo is ambiguous or when a revisionist state has the power to implement its threats with little cost or danger, has high resolve, and sees the domestic or international situation as precarious enough to merit great risk and cost (Jervis 1989: 32–34). Along these lines but in a more detailed fashion, in the context of new nuclear powers and drawing on Pakistan's behavior in the conflict over Kashmir in the post-1990 period (de facto and overt nuclear periods), Paul Kapur (2006: 42–43) argues that nuclear weapons may provide incentives for a weaker, revisionist state to engage in limited conventional military action to alter the status quo. Such a state would not engage in aggressive behavior in a conventional world because it would most likely result in failure.

In a nuclear world, the stronger state is inhibited from employing its full military might against a weaker state because of the fear of escalation to nuclear war. This risk of escalation emboldens a highly motivated weaker state to behave aggressively. Kapur advances two reasons why a weak, revisionist state might engage in conventional aggression (2006: 45). First, conventional military aggression can forcefully alter the territorial status quo while the nuclear weapons of the weaker state deter full-scale conventional retaliation by the stronger adversary. Second, conventional military action can trigger a highly visible international crisis, which can be used by the weaker state to seek favorable international diplomatic intervention and an outcome favorable to itself.

That nuclear weapons enable weaker states to punch above their weight is difficult to refute. Kapur's line of argument is not without merit, but it can be rebutted on several counts. One, behaving aggressively carries high costs—although escalation concerns may reduce the military cost, the political, diplomatic, and economic costs can be considerable. Repeated adventurism is counterproductive. Second, it is unlikely that such aggressive behavior could in fact bring about meaningful change in the status quo. If the stakes are high enough, the stronger status quo party will resort to full-scale conventional retaliation. The onus of escalating to the nuclear level then shifts to the conventionally weaker, revisionist state that initiated the crisis. Third, there is no certainty that international diplomatic intervention would favor the revisionist state. It could work against it. The net effect could still favor the status quo state. Finally, it is possible to argue that, as in the Cuban missile crisis, a long view of the 1999 and 2002 crises in South Asia would demonstrate the limited utility of nuclear weapons in altering the status quo through force and the danger of such behavior and thus constrain future action by the affected states. I will further develop this argument in Chapter 18.

Is Deterrence Dominance Eroding? The assertions that small nuclear forces can deter other nuclear weapon states, including those with much stronger nuclear arsenals, and that they can contribute to peace, security, and stability are based on the premise that nuclear weapons favor deterrence dominance. However, if defense against nuclear weapons becomes effective, the assumption of mutual vulnerability would not hold, deterrence dominance would be undermined, and the relationship between force and statecraft among nuclear weapon states would undergo substantial change. As Waltz states, the logic of strategic defense is that of conventional weaponry. It reintroduces the defense/offense race (Waltz 2004). If all sides have impregnable defenses, according to Waltz, the world has been made safe for World War III. Effective ballistic missile defense and the development of a nuclear counterforce capability would undermine deterrence dominance and the stability that is based on it. Growing possibility and effectiveness of offense increases the prospects for opportunistic expansionism, the incentive to strike first, and arms racing. Increasing effectiveness of defense against nuclear threats introduced many uncertainties.

Currently, only the United States and its allies are actively pursuing a missile defense capability with the stated purpose of defending against threats posed by rogue states, increasing the credibility of extended deterrence, and reducing the incentive for proliferation by U.S. allies. Through its new triad, Washington is seeking to reduce its reliance on nuclear weapons but increase their tactical role. Should all these efforts succeed, the vulnerability of the United States to attack by other nuclear weapon states would decline, allowing it greater freedom to engage in offensive operations (preventive, preemptive, and limited war) against them. To be operationally meaningful, however, U.S. vulnerability must decline greatly, possibly to zero before decision makers can have sufficient confidence to employ offensive and defensive strategies.

At the same time, even a marginal increase in effectiveness would create concern in target countries about the effectiveness of their strategic deterrent. They may seek better force protection, build additional missiles and decoys, and develop other countermeasures such as multiple warhead missiles to overwhelm and penetrate the U.S. defense system, and in a crisis situation they may attack the defense system to limit its effectiveness or destroy it. They might also engage in the development of their own missile defense systems. Probably only Russia and China have the capability to move in these directions. Other target states would likely disperse and hide their nuclear arsenals to create uncertainty in the minds of U.S. decision makers as to whether they can destroy the entire arsenal of those states in a first strike. In light of continuing technological limitations reflected in the partial success of tests and limited deployment, and the relative ease with which a retaliatory capability can be sustained, it appears that deterrence dominance would continue to prevail. Uncertainty and the danger of nuclear war are likely to create cautious relations among nuclear weapon states, although they may not prevent all violence.

Nuclear Superiority. Unless defense becomes more effective, superiority in nuclear capability may not confer military or diplomatic advantage on strong nuclear weapon states in their interaction with lesser nuclear weapon states. During the Cold War, although superiority in numbers appears to have been a consideration in the strategies of the two superpowers at certain points in time, it does not appear to have been consequential, especially after both had developed secure second-strike capabilities. One lesson of the Cold War was that political outcomes had little or no connection to the strategic balance. Differences in capability did not seem to have affected the security behavior of lesser nuclear weapon states. The security relationships of these states were shaped in large measure by the dispute at stake and the resolve of the conflicting parties as the Soviet Union discovered in the military clashes with China in 1969. However, the certainty of massive retaliation by a more powerful adversary when provoked can be expected to limit the range of goals and options available to a smaller nuclear weapon state and restrain its behavior.

Nuclear weapons do not seem to have conferred any definite advantage to nuclear weapon states in their dealings with nonnuclear weapon states. The huge American nuclear arsenal, for example, did not deter North Vietnam. For a number of reasons, the United States was constrained in using its nuclear capability. Bundy (2004) disputes the claim that the threat of nuclear war had any impact on the 1953 Korean armistice agreement or the 1946 Soviet withdrawal from Iran. He argues that since the 1958 Taiwan crisis pertaining to the offshore islands, nuclear threats have not featured in regional conflicts and that possession of nuclear capability did not confer diplomatic and military advantage, as nonnuclear weapon states were not deterred. Vietnam invaded Cambodia, which was supported by China; and China attacked Vietnam, which was backed by the Soviet Union.

Nuclear Weapons and Resolution of Disputes

Although nuclear weapons contributed to Soviet-American peace and strategic stability, they did not bring about resolution of disputes or prevent all forms of violence. Some, including Jervis, identify this as a weakness of deterrence theorizing, which focused almost exclusively on threats and demonstrating resolve in a conflict situation. It did not focus on rewards or compromise to ease tensions and bring about conflict settlement. Nuclear weapons also prevented the traditional use of military force along with other instruments of policy to resolve disputes on the battlefield. Consequently, the security interaction of the two superpowers remained "frozen," preventing the resolution of disputes through peaceful means or through the use of force, as would have happened in the prenuclear era (Jervis 1989: 29–32). The absence of change is also attributed to the bargaining advantages enjoyed by the side defending a firmly established status quo.

However, to argue that nuclearization or mutual vulnerability prevents the resolution of disputes is to conflate cause and symptom. Nuclear weapons are not the cause of political disputes. Although nuclear weapons may have negated conflict resolution through the use of force, conflicts could still have been addressed peacefully through negotiations and other means as long as the parties were amenable to bridging differences through compromise. The Cold War came to a peaceful end despite the situation of mutual vulnerability. Domestic political change in the Soviet Union was a principal factor in terminating the Cold War.

The debates over the implications of nuclear weapons—deterrence effectiveness of small nuclear forces and their contribution to peace and stability—are grounded largely in abstract reasoning, the Cold War experience, or refutation of that experience. More empirical work is required to develop and substantiate claims. This, however, is made difficult because the effectiveness of deterrence and its contribution to stability are not easy to demonstrate; because of limited real-world cases and experience; the tendency to downplay the significance and role of nuclear weapons; and the high confidentiality and lack of transparency in Asian countries on matters associated with nuclear weapon capabilities, strategies, interaction, and outcomes. Nevertheless, more empirical work is becoming available especially on the India-Pakistan relationship during the crises at the turn of the twenty-first century. This book seeks to contribute to this by making it possible to advance stronger empirically grounded statements on the purposes and roles of national nuclear forces and to offer broad observations on their implications for regional security dynamics, peace, stability, and conflict resolution.

Notes

1. *The Absolute Weapon* is the title of the book by Bernard Brodie and others (1946) that examines the implications of atomic power for world order.

2. Cited in Trachtenberg (1989: 304). It should be noted here that Brodie subsequently changed his view. He wrote an introductory essay titled "The Continuing Relevance of 'On War'" for the publication of Clausewitz's "On War" in English (Brodie 1976). See also Brodie (1973, Chap. 9).

3. Schelling (1966: 7) posits that the distinction between use and threat of force does not effectively capture the change brought about by nuclear weapons.

4. Forces and weapon systems developed for deterrence were no longer useful in defense in the sense that they could not guarantee that a nuclear-armed state could not retaliate and inflict unimaginable devastation. Nuclear weapons also negated the potential for war mobilization that was important in earlier periods. Nuclear war would be fought and decided with the arsenal in place. See Brodie (1946: 88–90). Urban-industrial centers continued to be important targets, however, not because of their economic and war potential, but as hostages in coercive warfare.

5. The discussion of political ends draws on the realist paradigm, which assigns state violence a central role in these quests.

6. On international order, see Alagappa 2003.

7. Thomas Schelling introduced the term *compellence* (Schelling 1966).

8. George and Simon (1994) first employed the term *coercive diplomacy* in 1970. George (2004) distinguishes coercive diplomacy from compellence.

9. On conventional deterrence, see Mearsheimer (1983) and Huntington (1982).

10. On the waves or evolution of deterrence thinking, see Jervis (1979), Freedman (1983), and Morgan (2003). Freedman (2004) documents the rise and decline of deterrence.

11. The discussion of the strategy of massive retaliation draws on Dulles (1954), Kauffman (1956), and Freedman (1983).

12. Because the term *assured retaliation* was perceived as bland, the strategy was labeled as "assured destruction" in order to convey the intentional nature of the retaliatory threat and to highlight the harsh consequences that would follow. The new label was also intended to convey an image of toughness to the American right (Freedman 1983: 246). However, the term *assured retaliation* is more accurate as a concept and strategy.

13. National Missile Defense Act of 1999, quoted in Glaser and Fetter (2001: 46).

14. On the many meanings of balance of power see Claude (1962), Haas (1953), Morgenthau (1978), and Sheehan (1996).

15. On balance of terror, deterrent balance, and defensive balance, see Snyder (1961: 43–44).

16. On alternative explanations for the long peace, see Mueller (1988) and Waltz (1979).

17. On the stability-instability paradox, see Snyder (1961) and Jervis (1989: 19–22).

References

Alagappa, Muthiah. 2003. "The Study of International Order: An Analytical Framework." In *Asian Security Order: Instrumental and Normative Features,* ed. Muthiah Alagappa. Stanford, Calif.: Stanford University Press.

Basrur, Rajesh M. 2006. *Minimum Deterrence and India's Nuclear Security.* Stanford, Calif.: Stanford University Press.

Betts, Richard. 2000. "Is Strategy an Illusion? *International Security* 25 (2): 5–50.

Borden, William L. 1946. *There Will Be No Time: The Revolution in Strategy.* New York: Macmillan.

Brodie, Bernard. 1946. "War in the Atomic Age'" and "Implications for Military Policy." In *The Absolute Weapon: Atomic Power and World Order,* Frederick S. Dunn, Bernard Brodie, Arnold Wolfers, Percy E. Corbett, and William T. R. Fox. New York: Harcourt, Brace.

———. 1959. *Strategy in the Missile Age.* Princeton, N.J.: Princeton University Press.

———. 1973. *War and Politics.* London: Cassell.

———. 1976. "The Continuing Relevance of 'On War.'" Introductory essay to Carl Von Clausewitz, *On War.* Edited and Translated by Michael Howard and Peter Paret. Princeton, N.J.: Princeton University Press.

Buchan, Glenn C., David Matonick, Calvin Shipbaugh, and Richard Mesic. 2003. *Future Roles of U.S. Nuclear Forces.* Santa Monica, Calif.: RAND.

Bundy, McGeorge. 1983. "The Bishops and the Bomb." *New York Review of Books* 30 (10): 3–8.

———. 1984. "Existential Deterrence and Its Consequences." In *The Security Gamble: Deterrence Dilemmas in the Nuclear Age,* ed. Douglas MacLean. Totowa, N.J.: Rowman & Allanheld.

———. 2004. "The Unimpressive Record of Atomic Diplomacy." In *The Use of Force: Military Power and International Politics,* ed. Robert J. Art and Kenneth N. Waltz. Boulder, Colo.: Rowman & Littlefield.

Claude, I. 1962. *Power and International Relations.* New York: Random House.

Clausewitz, Carl von. 1976. *On War.* Edited and translated by Michael Howard and Peter Paret. Princeton, N.J.: Princeton University Press.

Coyle, Philip. 2006. *The Limits and Liabilities of Missile Defense.* Washington, D.C.: Center for Defense Information. Available online at www.Ciaonet.org.proxyau.wrlc.org/wps/cdi022.html.

Dulles, John Foster. 1954. "Policy for Security and Peace." *Foreign Affairs* 32 (3): 353–64.

Enthoven, Alain C., and Wayne K. Smith. 1971. *How Much Is Enough? Shaping the Defense Program, 1961–1969.* New York: Harper and Row.

Feaver, Peter. 1992/3. "Command and Control in Emerging Nuclear Nations." *International Security* 17 (3): 160–87.

———. 1993. "Proliferation Optimism and Theories of Nuclear Operations." *Security Studies* 2 (3/4): 159–91.

Freedman, Lawrence. 1983. *The Evolution of Nuclear Strategy.* New York: St. Martin's Press.

———. 2004. *Deterrence.* Malden, Mass.: Polity.

Friedberg, Aaron L. 1982. "The Evolution of U.S. Strategic 'Doctrine'—1945–1981." In *The Strategic Imperative: New Policies for American Security,* ed. Samuel P. Huntington. Cambridge, Mass.: Ballinger.

Gaddis, John Lewis. 2004. "Implementing Flexible Response: Vietnam as a Test Case." In *The Use of Force: Military Power and International Politics,* ed. Robert J. Art and Kenneth N. Waltz. New York: Rowman & Littlefield.

George, Alexander L. 2004. "Coercive Diplomacy." In *The Use for Force,* ed. Robert J. Art and Kenneth N. Waltz. New York: Rowman & Littlefield.

George, Alexander L., and William E. Simons, eds. 1994. *The Limits of Coercive Diplomacy.* Boulder, Colo.: Westview.

Gilpin, Robert. 1981. *War and Change in World Politics.* Cambridge: Cambridge University Press.

Glaser, Charles L., and Steve Fetter. 2001. "National Missile Defense and the Future of U.S. Nuclear Weapons Policy." *International Security* 26 (1): 40–92.

———. 2005. "Counterforce Revisited: Assessing the Nuclear Posture Review's New Missions." *International Security* 30 (2): 84–126.

Goldstein, Avery. 2000. *Deterrence and Security in the 21st Century.* Stanford, Calif.: Stanford University Press.

Haas, Ernst B. 1953. "The Balance of Power: Prescription, Concept, or Propaganda?" *World Politics* 5 (4): 442–77.

Hagerty, Devin T. 1998. *The Consequences of Nuclear Proliferation: Lessons from South Asia.* Cambridge, Mass: MIT Press.

Hertz, John. 1950. "Idealist Internationalism and the Security Dilemma." In *World Politics,* 2 (January 1950): 157–80.

Huntington, Samuel P. 1982. "The Renewal of Strategy." In *The Strategic Imperative: New Policies for American Security,* ed. Samuel P. Huntington. Cambridge, Mass.: Ballinger.

Jervis, Robert. 1978. "Cooperation under Anarchy." *World Politics* 30 (2): 167–214.

———. 1979. "Deterrence Theory Revisited." *World Politics* 31 (2): 289–324.

———. 1989. *The Meaning of the Nuclear Revolution: Statecraft and the Prospect of Armageddon.* Ithaca, N.Y.: Cornell University Press.

Kahn, Herman. 1961. *On Thermonuclear War.* Princeton, N.J.: Princeton University Press.

Kapur, S. Paul. 2006. *Dangerous Deterrent: Nuclear Weapons Proliferation and Conflict in South Asia.* Stanford, Calif.: Stanford University Press.

Kauffman, William W. 1956. "The Requirements of Deterrence." In *Military Policy and National Security,* ed. William W. Kauffman. Princeton, N.J.: Princeton University Press.

Kissinger, Henry A. 1957. *Nuclear Weapons and Foreign Policy.* New York: Harper Brothers.

Mearsheimer, John. 1983. *Conventional Deterrence.* Ithaca, N.Y.: Cornell University Press.

Morgan, Patrick M. 2003. *Deterrence Now.* Cambridge, U.K.: Cambridge University Press.

Morgenthau. Hans J. 1978. *Politics among Nations: The Struggle for Power and Peace.* New York: Alfred A. Knopf.

Mueller, John. 1988. "The Essential Irrelevance of Nuclear Weapons: Stability in the Postwar World." *International Security* 13 (2): 55–79.

Paul, T. V. 1998. "Power, Influence, and Nuclear Weapons." In *The Absolute Weapon Revisited: Nuclear Arms and the Emerging International Order,* T. V. Paul, Richard J. Harknett, and James J. Wirtz, eds. Ann Arbor: The University of Michigan Press.

Posen, Barry R. 1984. *The Sources of Military Doctrine: France, Britain and Germany between World Wars.* Ithaca, N.Y.: Cornell University Press.

Powell, Robert. 2003. "Nuclear Deterrence Theory, Nuclear Proliferation, and National Missile Defense." *International Security* 27 (4): 86–118.

Sagan, Scott D. 1994. "The Perils of Proliferation: Organization Theory, Deterrence Theory, and the Spread of Nuclear Weapons." *International Security* 18 (4): 66–107.

———. 1995. "More Will Be Worse." In *The Spread of Nuclear Weapons: A Debate,* ed. Scott D. Sagan and Kenneth Waltz. New York: W. W. Norton.

Schelling, Thomas C. 1960. *The Strategy of Conflict.* New York: Oxford University Press.

———. 1966. *Arms and Influence.* New Haven, Conn.: Yale University Press.

———. 2006. "Nuclear Deterrence for the Future." *Issues in Science and Technology* 23 (1): 50–52.

Sheehan, Michael. 1996. *The Balance of Power: History and Theories.* New York: Routledge.

Snyder, Glenn H. 1961. *Deterrence and Defense: Toward a Theory of National Security.* Westport, Conn.: Greenwood Press.

Trachtenberg, Marc. 1989. "Strategic Thought in America, 1952–1966." *Political Science Quarterly* 104 (2): 301–34.

Walt, Stephen. 1987. *The Origins of Alliances.* Ithaca, N.Y.: Cornell University Press.

Waltz, Kenneth. 1979. *Theory of International Politics.* New York: Random House.

———. 1995. "More May Be Better." In *The Spread of Nuclear Weapons: A Debate,* ed. Scott D. Sagan and Kenneth Waltz. New York: W. W. Norton.

———. 2004. "Nuclear Myths and Political Realities." In *The Use of Force: Military Power and International Politics,* ed. Robert J. Art and Kenneth N. Waltz. Boulder, Colo.: Rowman & Littlefield.

PART II

National Nuclear Policies and Strategies

3

United States
Nuclear Policy at a Crossroads

JAMES J. WIRTZ

Describing U.S. nuclear doctrine is no small task. National approaches to nuclear matters can be divided into several components, which are not always well synchronized. Most analysts focus on declaratory policy—that is, public statements made by officials and officers about the role played by nuclear weapons in U.S. defense strategy and how they might be used preemptively in battle or in retaliation if deterrence should fail. Of course, this declaratory policy might have little to do with actual employment policy, classified plans that assign specific weapons to specific targets. One might discuss procurement and deployment policy by describing what weapons are being developed by the U.S. government, the systems used to deliver them, and where they are deployed. In fact, the best way to assess a state's true intentions might be to discover how leaders spend limited resources, because such expenditures provide the basis of a reliable guide to what leaders believe is important (Jervis 1970). Another way to describe a policy might be to identify its strategic impact. In other words, how does U.S. nuclear policy interact with the policies of other nuclear and nonnuclear states in Asia to produce a military balance that fosters peace or acrimony? Because this interaction itself is beyond the control of any one country, the effects of a state's nuclear policy and doctrine might be quite unintended. Policy makers might also be relatively unaware of underlying trends in technology or politics that are slowly transforming nuclear force postures and the strategic nuclear balance. Official characterizations of nuclear doctrine and policy might thus be a poor guide to understanding strategic reality.

A state's overall nuclear policy and doctrine also reflects its military strategy. Deterrence, for example, dominated U.S. nuclear doctrine during the Cold War.

A policy based on deterrence reflects the idea that other states are not necessarily hell-bent on aggression. Because of the anarchical international environment and because of their inherent right to self-help, however, others are driven to seize available opportunities to strengthen their position against potential rivals. Therefore, if one wants peace, one must prepare for war, to reduce the benefits and increase the potential costs rivals face when they contemplate some opportunistic act of aggression. Deterrence theorists recognize the security dilemma—the fact that actions taken to increase the security of one state tend to decrease the security of other states—as a source of tension, but most believe that the risk of opportunistic aggression is greater than the dangers of inadvertent escalation or an "action-reaction" arms race (Herz 1950: 157–80). Deterrence is the preferred nuclear weapon doctrine of most officials because it allows them to avoid war by threatening potential opponents with devastating destruction under extreme circumstances. American declaratory doctrine states that U.S. nuclear weapons are intended to deter the use of nuclear weapons against the United States, its forces overseas, and its friends and allies. American declaratory policy regarding the use of nuclear weapons in response to an attack by chemical or biological weapons is far more ambiguous, although during crises officials sometimes make veiled threats that U.S. nuclear weapons are available for more than retaliation in kind.

Nuclear doctrine also might be based on preventive war (i.e., initiating war on one's own terms to maximize advantages and minimize costs and risks) or preemption (i.e., beating to the punch an opponent that is about to attack). These "war in sight" strategies could require the complete integration of conventional and nuclear forces for battlefield use. Often, policy makers see war in sight when they encounter revolutionary or millenarian governments or individuals or syndicates that appear willing to behave aggressively to achieve their objectives. Politics, negotiation, and deterrence become difficult under these circumstances, because both parties in a conflict actually see each other, not politics or policy differences per se, as the basis of the threat itself (Kissinger 1977: 11–50; Walt 1996). Although much concern about deterring terrorist groups or biological weapon attacks focuses on technical issues (e.g., terrorist attacks might lack a return address, making retaliation impossible), it is dangerous to try to deter opponents who view war as profoundly desirable. When opponents see war, even nuclear war, as a way to achieve their objectives, preventive war and preemption become salient because they provide the side initiating a war with the opportunity to minimize the costs of battle after a political decision has been made that a conflict is inevitable. In addition, several scholars have recently focused on the inherent obstacles encountered in the effort to undertake a policy of deterrence: deterrence can fail catastrophically, and a policy of deterrence is unlikely to prevent terrorist syndicates or superempowered individuals from launching mass casualty attacks (Payne and Walton 2002). Although some observers have not given up hope that terrorists can be deterred, most scholars and officials believe that, under certain circumstances, preventive war and preemption might be the only realistic way of dealing with actors that are relatively immune to deterrent threats (Dunn 2005).

Officials who embrace disarmament as the centerpiece of defense policy take to heart the security dilemma. Because protestations of benign or defensive intent on the part of others cannot be taken at face value, because it is often difficult or even impossible to tell offensive weapons and doctrines from defensive ones, and because it is hard to estimate whether offensive or defensive strategies enjoy battlefield dominance, policy makers often use worst-case planning to respond to changes in other states' military capability (Jervis 1978). Because international relations are fundamentally anarchic, and states reserve the right to use force for self-help, policy makers are caught in a vicious spiral of armament and tension, in which the tyranny of small decisions yields suboptimal outcomes—that is, arms races and war. For those who identify the security dilemma as the primary cause of war and instability, disarmament offers the best way to eliminate arms races and war. Because weapons themselves are responsible for the fear and hostility that breeds conflict, if one state begins to reduce and eliminate its weaponry, other states will soon follow suit. This is the central point made by recent disarmament advocates: "There is no legitimate purpose for nuclear weapons aside from deterring their use, an aim that would be more safely and effectively carried out through total elimination of the weapons" (Feiveson 1999: 288).

Today, U.S. nuclear doctrine seems to comprise a strange mix of deterrent, war-in-sight, and disarmament policies (Wirtz 2005: 383–95). Officials talk about the importance of nuclear deterrence in U.S. foreign and defense policy, but the George W. Bush administration abandoned deterrence in favor of preventive war to forever prevent Saddam Hussein from obtaining nuclear, chemical, and biological weapons. Paradoxically, the Bush administration's efforts to create a modern nuclear force capable of executing deterrence by denial strategies has failed to muster congressional support. The administration's effort to update U.S. nuclear doctrine and capability, reflected in the 2001 Nuclear Posture Review (NPR), has failed to generate much academic, military, or even political attention beyond a few obligatory denunciations by the international disarmament community. The Bush administration has even failed to obtain funding to support a *study* of the desirability of producing new earth-penetrating nuclear warheads designed to hold at risk deeply buried underground targets, which are often used as storage facilities for chemical, biological, and nuclear weapons or command and control complexes. Officials at U.S. nuclear weapons laboratories also warn that the U.S. nuclear arsenal will eventually reach the end of its practical life expectancy, creating a need for a reliable new nuclear warhead that is designed to withstand long-term storage, not optimized to produce maximum yield at minimum weight. Although many observers mistakenly believe that little has changed in

U.S. nuclear doctrine and force structure since the end of the Cold War, disarmament has become the dominant enduring theme in U.S. nuclear policy since the early 1990s. If current trends continue, it is likely that nuclear weapons will play an increasingly modest role in U.S. foreign and defense policy. There are signs of this reduced reliance on nuclear weapons even in the new capabilities being added to the U.S. strategic deterrent: Trident submarines are being converted to carry conventional cruise missiles and special forces personnel. On the remaining Trident submarines, there are plans to remove nuclear warheads from two missiles so that they can be replaced with conventional munitions (Woolf 2006).

To support this characterization of U.S. nuclear policy, this chapter first traces the evolution of U.S. nuclear doctrine and force posture since the end of the Cold War, describing the slow but steady reduction in the number and importance of nuclear weapons in U.S. defense planning. It identifies the nuclear test moratorium as a long-term disarmament effort, which also restricts the ability of other nuclear powers to maintain a nuclear arsenal. The chapter concludes by offering some observations about the nature of the strategic nuclear balance in Asia, the likely U.S. response to current and potential challenges in Asia, and the prospects for the status quo in the years ahead.

Do U.S. Nuclear Weapons Have a Future?

Although disarmament advocates continuously decry the continued existence of nuclear arsenals everywhere and even the most modest efforts to modernize nuclear forces, Democratic and Republican administrations have reduced the size, readiness, and reliance on U.S. nuclear forces in ways that were barely imaginable only twenty years ago. Bureaucratic reorganization and reform, procurement and modernization programs, and even the missions assigned to deployed military units have changed in ways that deemphasize the role of U.S. nuclear forces in military operations and planning. The George W. Bush administration devised a new vision to update U.S. nuclear force planning, to modernize nuclear weapons, and to deploy active defenses, but these initiatives have generated minimal congressional or public interest and support. Those involved in the U.S. nuclear weapons program today are clearly engaged in a tertiary defense program. Curtis LeMay is rolling in his grave.

Cutting the Arsenal after the Cold War

The "turning away" from maintaining a Cold War–sized nuclear arsenal, a phenomenon described by some observers as nuclear marginalization (Baylis 2000; Cambone and Garity 1994/95; Freedman 1994/95), began in the early 1990s. The military buildup undertaken by the Reagan administration during the 1980s had just peaked, supplying the U.S. strategic deterrent with an array of the latest warheads and delivery systems that optimized stealth and prompt hard-target kill capability. U.S. nuclear forces were optimized for the countervailing strategy; they were increasingly configured to match the Soviet Union's apparent ability to engage the United States in a counterforce duel in the event of Armageddon. Nuclear-tipped air-launched cruise missiles extended the life of the aging B-52 bomber force by turning it into an effective standoff bomber, while improving the "footprint" of penetrating bombers by allowing them to strike targets at great ranges. Sea-launched cruise missiles turned every attack submarine and surface combatant into a potential nuclear strike platform, bolstering the U.S. nuclear reserve force and greatly complicating Soviet efforts to create an effective preemptive attack. The highly secret stealth B-2 bomber and F-117 strike fighter threatened to make Soviet air defenses obsolete. Modern Trident ballistic missile submarines were entering the fleet at a fast rate, and these submarines were being upgraded with the highly accurate D-5 missile that carried light, high-yield, multiple independently targetable reentry vehicles (MIRVs). The MX intercontinental ballistic missile (ICBM), which possessed greater throw weight and higher yield and better accuracy MIRVs than the Minuteman III ICBM, had entered into service, giving the United States a system that approximated the capability of the Soviet SS-18 missile. The United States was also moving forward with its Strategic Defense Initiative (SDI). Even though the program yielded few tangible results, it did lead some observers to believe that the United States was about to marry this surge in prompt hard-target kill capability generated by its new strategic systems with active defenses in an effort to pursue a concerted damage limitation strategy.

By 1989 it was increasingly clear that the Cold War was ending and that a diminishing political risk of nuclear war no longer justified the military and technological risks undertaken to keep thousands of nuclear weapons on day alert. Operational plans and day-alert operations changed first. In May 1991 the George H. W. Bush administration finished a review of nuclear targeting policy. Headed by General Lee Butler, United States Air Force, the review eliminated targets in Eastern Europe and former Soviet republics from U.S. nuclear war plans (Mlyn 1998). In September 1991, the president announced a series of unilateral initiatives. Short-range tactical nuclear weapons and artillery shells were removed from Europe and placed into storage in the United States. The president also called for a halt to routine deployment of tactical nuclear weapons on board U.S. Navy warships. The U.S. nuclear bomber force was also taken off day alert (the United States had maintained about 40 bombers on strip alert, armed and ready to respond to tactical warning of attack). The president also ordered that the 450 Minuteman II single-warhead ICBMs that were scheduled for elimination under the Strategic Arms Reduction Treaty (START I) be taken off alert "immediately." He also announced that the United States would cease combat patrols of the

10 Poseidon submarines scheduled for elimination under START I. These initiatives demonstrated that the United States now considered the risk entailed by forward deploying nuclear forces was greater than the evaporating threats that they were intended to deter and that Cold War alert and force levels were no longer justified. Most important, President Bush canceled the existing force modernization and procurement projects that were under way. MX Rail-Garrison, a program to increase the survivability of the Peacekeeper ICBM by flushing it onto the civilian railroad network in times of crisis, was canceled. The mobile Midgetman ICBM program was canceled. SRAM-II, a new version of the ultimate defense suppression weapon, was terminated, and B-2 bomber procurement was capped (Powaski 2000). In effect, the 1991 unilateral initiatives signaled that the Reagan buildup was the last wave of Cold War nuclear competition. The wave had crested. From this point onward, U.S. force structure would be based on "surplus" nuclear weapons and delivery systems left over from the Cold War.

Arms control also accelerated in the 1990s as improving Russian-American relations allowed rapid negotiation of a series of agreements that helped to order the drawdown of forces. START I, signed in 1991, entailed about a 40 percent reduction in the number of "accountable" (operational) warheads to 6,000. START II, signed in 1993, called for another 50 percent reduction in operational nuclear warheads and for the end of MIRVed ICBMs, a step that improved crisis stability by increasing the survivability of Russian and American ICBM forces. START II also meant the end of the MX missile—the last of which was taken out of service in 2005. START II was superseded by the 2002 Moscow Treaty, which limits U.S. operational warheads to 1,700–2,200 by the end of 2012. The 1994 Moscow Declaration also reduced the risk of catastrophic accidents among remaining nuclear forces on day alert by calling for the detargeting of strategic forces, and Cooperative Threat Reduction Programs provided vital assistance to members of the former Soviet Union to secure their surplus nuclear weapons and materials.

Although these unilateral and bilateral arms control initiatives will ultimately lead to about an 80 percent reduction in the number of operational warheads deployed by the United States (see Figure 3-1), a remarkable change in strategic posture by any standard, two further changes have received less attention. First, the transformation of the Strategic Air Command to U.S. Strategic Command (STRATCOM) in 1992 facilitated the consolidation of nuclear forces and a change in attitude toward maintaining a force structure exclusively for deterrent purposes. The services now had less interest in maintaining their nuclear force structure as officers at STRATCOM began to focus on "strategic" deterrence and on exploring various confidence-building measures with their Russian counterparts. Forces that traditionally were held in reserve as a strategic deterrent now were employed in conventional war-fighting roles. The U.S. Army, which spent most of the Cold War deterring attacks along the inter-German border and the 38th parallel, has

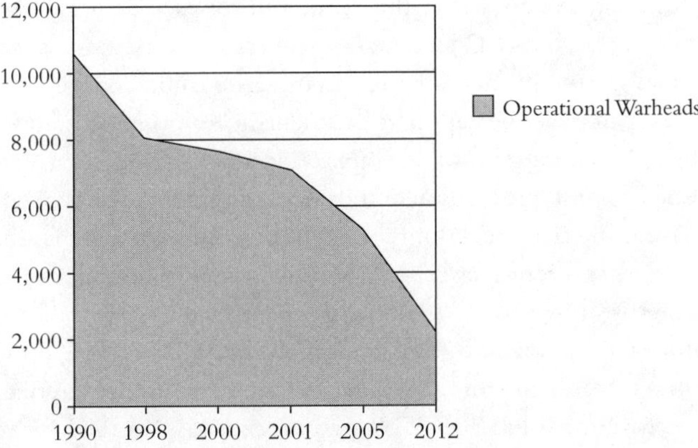

FIG 3-1. The Drawdown of U.S. Strategic Nuclear Warheads, 1990–2012.

been fully engaged in high-intensity conventional combat, counterinsurgency, and peacekeeping operations since the early 1990s. Air tankers, which are critical to executing long-range nuclear air strikes, are completely engaged in support of conventional forces and operations. The B-2 bomber, designed for a one-way mission to Armageddon, now routinely flies conventional bombing runs; the B-1 bomber has lost its nuclear mission; and advanced strategic reconnaissance vehicles (e.g., Global Hawk) apparently are employed exclusively in support of the war on terrorism. Today there are plans to convert SSBNs (nuclear-powered submarines that carry ballistic missiles tipped with nuclear warheads) to carry cruise missiles armed with conventional weapons and for Trident SSBNs to carry conventionally armed ballistic missiles. The distinction between U.S. deterrent and warfighting forces and commands, which was maintained during most of the Cold War, collapsed from the top down. This collapse had a major impact on the willingness of military officers to make nuclear weapons the focus of their career. Why choose a career path that offered only shrinking opportunities for advancement? A shrinking force and command infrastructure implies a shrinking opportunity for promotion to senior rank.

Second, and most important, the 1996 Comprehensive Test Ban Treaty (CTBT), which codified an emerging nuclear test moratorium among the existing nuclear powers, is the most important international agreement to emerge in the euphoria that followed the end of the Cold War. It is important because it is a disarmament treaty, whose effects, while not irreversible, are cumulative and extraordinarily expensive to counteract over time. According to the Union of Concerned Scientists: "Without testing, the five original and two newly declared nuclear weapon states will be less confident about any new types of nuclear weapons they develop. Thus, a test ban will effectively limit future weapon-development activities. However, exactly where that limit falls for each nuclear state is an issue of some debate" (Union of Concerned Scientists n.d.). Because nuclear physics and weapon design and production are "living arts," much of the weapon development process can never be captured in blueprints or other written instructions, but has to be passed along through an apprentice system. Since the end of testing means the end of bomb production and design, the living art has been effectively terminated, meaning that much knowledge will be lost when the last experienced bomb designer passes from the scene (Commission on Maintaining United States Weapons Expertise 1999).

Despite the fact that the U.S. Senate failed to ratify the CTBT on October 13, 1999, the United States and all other nuclear powers continue to adhere to a nuclear test moratorium. What the CTBT guaranteed was that the U.S. nuclear policy would focus on devising ways to extend the service life of existing warheads and delivery systems as long as possible by getting the most out of Cold War surplus weapons and infrastructure. Nuclear force modernization and procurement programs had for all intents and purposes ended with the collapse of the Soviet Union.

The 2001 NPR: Reversing the Trend?

In contrast to the George H. W. Bush administration's unilateral nuclear initiatives, or the Clinton administration's decision to sign the CTBT, U.S. nuclear policy documents produced in the first decade after the Cold War offered little departure from traditional approaches to nuclear doctrine. The 1991 Base Force Review, the 1993 Bottom-Up Review, and the 1997 Quadrennial Defense Review were "budget drills" intended to support planned force structure and to protect parochial interests while securing a "peace dividend." The 1994 Nuclear Posture Review (NPR) also was criticized for a lack of originality and for failing to do little more than rationalize decisions undertaken in support of START II (National Institute for Public Policy 2003). None of these reviews offered a significant departure from the U.S. approach to deterrence or nuclear weapons. The 2001 NPR undertaken by the George W. Bush administration would break this pattern.

The 2001 NPR, in conjunction with the 2001 decision to abandon the ABM Treaty, marked the first significant effort to transform U.S. strategic doctrine in a decade (Wirtz and Larsen 2005). Although critics had much to say about both initiatives, they reflected an effort to transform Russian-American strategic relations toward cooperation by reducing the role played by nuclear deterrence between the former Cold War adversaries. Administration officials even announced publicly their willingness to cut the U.S. nuclear arsenal unilaterally because they believed that arms control negotiations were not justified by any underlying hostility in Russian-American relations. Bush administration spokespersons stated that countries enjoying friendly relations could coordinate a nuclear drawdown without what they considered to be the risk of acrimony created by formal negotiations. In a sense they were correct: START I and II were providing more of a floor than a ceiling on Russian and American nuclear force deployments.

The 2002 Moscow Treaty on Strategic Offensive Reductions facilitates the transformation of U.S. strategic forces by reducing the number of legacy systems that will remain operational. By 2007 the United States had deployed 3,800 nuclear warheads on the way to deploying between 1,700 and 2,200 by the end of 2012. The planned "legacy triad" will eventually consist of 14 Trident SSBNs, 500 single-warhead Minuteman III ICBMs, 76 B-52H bombers armed with cruise missiles and gravity bombs, and 21 B-2s armed with gravity bombs. Four Trident submarines and 18 B-52Hs will soon be retired. The last MX ICBM was deactivated from operational service in 2005, and U.S. bomber forces no longer stand on day alert. These force reductions also simplify nuclear stockpile life extension plans: only three warhead refurbishment programs—the W80 cruise missile warhead, the W76 SLBM warhead, and the B61 bomb—will be undertaken by 2010.

The NPR, however, also called for the transformation of the U.S. nuclear deterrent to a *strategic* deterrent of conventional and nuclear offensive forces to meet the challenge created by the proliferation of chemical, biological, and nuclear weapons, more advanced delivery systems, and deeply buried and hardened underground targets, which are often used as weapons storage sites and command and control complexes. To create this strategic deterrent, the NPR calls for the creation of a "new triad" of (1) nonnuclear and nuclear strike capabilities, including systems for command and control; (2) active and passive defenses, including ballistic missile defenses; and (3) research and development (R&D) and the industrial infrastructure needed to develop, build, and maintain nuclear offensive forces and defensive systems. Administration officials hoped that the new triad would eventually provide policy makers with a range of strike capabilities to bolster deterrence by creating options other than what they consider to be the incredible threat of retaliation with high-yield nuclear weapons to less-than-catastrophic provocation. The new triad would also provide strike options to hold at risk emerging target structures associated with the proliferation of weapons of mass destruction, creating an ability to engage in preventive or preemptive strikes to bolster counterproliferation policies. The fundamental goal of the 2001 NPR was to create a strategic deterrent containing options for a wide variety of circumstances, not to preserve a Cold War force structure optimized to guarantee a secure, second-strike capability against Russia.

The first real step toward making the NPR a reality came with the passage of the FY2004 National Defense Authorization Act, which repealed Section 3136 of Public Law 103-160, the so-called PLYWD (precision low-yield weapons design, pronounced "plywood") amendment. The 1994 PLYWD restriction prohibited the secretary of energy from conducting research and development to produce new, low-yield nuclear weapons. The Bush administration moved quickly to launch an R&D program to investigate future applications for low-yield nuclear weapons. It requested US$7.5 million from Congress to continue assessing the feasibility and cost of a robust nuclear earth penetrator (RNEP) and US$6 million to begin other advanced concepts work to determine whether existing nuclear warheads could be adapted—without nuclear testing—to hold at risk deeply buried targets. The RNEP program was in reality "an engineering study of the feasibility, design definition, and cost of two [nuclear] candidate weapons for conversion to RNEP" (Medalia 2005).

On June 16, 2004, however, the RNEP program was effectively terminated when the Energy and Water Development Subcommittee of the House Appropriations Committee approved the FY2005 Energy and Water Appropriations Bill and failed to include funding for RNEP or advanced concepts work. The way the committee explained its decision highlights the fundamental ambivalence generated by any discussion of nuclear modernization issues in the United States today:

> The Committee continues to oppose the diversion of resources and intellectual capital away from the most serious issues that confront the management of the nation's nuclear deterrent . . . [T]he Committee's priorities are maintaining our Nation's nuclear deterrent in a safe and secure condition and maintaining our Nation's integrity in the international effort to halt the proliferation of weapons of mass destruction. The [Energy] Department's obsession with launching a new round of nuclear weapons development runs counter to those priorities. The Committee directs the NNSA [National Nuclear Security Administration] to focus wholly on its primary mission of maintaining the safety, security, and viability of the existing stockpile. (U.S. Congress 2004)

The Bush administration subsequently shifted its nuclear force modernization priorities.

In May 2005, senior administrators at Lawrence Livermore, Los Alamos, and Sandia National Laboratories issued a white paper titled "Sustaining the Nuclear Enterprise—a New Approach" (Goodwin, Tarantino, and Woodward 2005). Although officials have emphasized that the U.S. Stockpile Stewardship Program is working, the weapons currently in the U.S. nuclear arsenal were not designed to remain in service for many decades: all of the weapons in the current arsenal will probably have to be retired within two to three decades. In response, the Bush administration called for funding in FY2007 budget requests for a reliable replacement warhead (RRW) optimized for safe and reliable storage over a service lifetime of decades (Wirtz 2006). According to Ambassador Linton Brooks, "the RRW would relax Cold War design constraints that maximized yield to weight ratios and thereby allow us to design replacement components that are easier to manufacture, are safer and more secure, eliminate environmentally dangerous materials, and increase design margins, thus ensuring long-term confidence in reliability and a correspondingly reduced chance we will ever need to resort to nuclear testing" (Brooks 2006). The switch from RNEP to RRW demonstrates that there simply is no political support in the United States for undertaking a significant military modernization of the U.S. nuclear arsenal. Bush administration officials consider no news about the U.S. nuclear arsenal to be politically beneficial: administration officials chose not to highlight the decision to accelerate warhead dismantlement to cut the overall size of the nuclear stockpile (Anonymous 2006).

In 2005, John Harvey, policy planning director of the NNSA, summarized the state of U.S. nuclear forces and policy as follows:

1. Nuclear forces, after the Cold War, have been rightly deemphasized under the NPR.
2. They no longer compel the same attention from senior military or civilian Department of Defense officials, or from Congress for that matter (despite the controversy over RNEP).
3. The military career path for the nuclear mission has serious shortfalls.
4. The bipartisan consensus we had during the Cold War has evaporated.
5. We have not designed or developed a new warhead in 20 years—as a result some key capabilities the nation has asked us to maintain are in jeopardy.
6. We stopped testing nukes in 1992. (Harvey 2005)

Harvey's points are critical because they reflect the impact of the nuclear test moratorium, the end of the Cold War, and the general loss of political or military urgency behind maintaining a highly robust nuclear capability. If current trends continue, the U.S. nuclear arsenal will continue to shrink in size and importance in U.S. military strategy. Congressional Research Reports on the subject of U.S. nuclear forces have confirmed this trend. No replacement strategic systems are scheduled to enter service before 2018, and the U.S. ICBM and bomber forces are likely to face additional cuts in the not-too-distant future. The Navy's Trident ballistic missile submarines recently have had their initial thirty-year operational lifetimes extended to at least forty-two years. At the moment, the Navy can delay planning for a replacement of the Trident submarine to 2016 (Woolf 2006, 2007).

The Nuclear Balance in Asia

There is an anomaly today in terms of a divergence between the policies of established and emerging nuclear powers. Because of the CTBT and generally benign relations among the great powers, the nuclear force structure and related industrial base of Britain, France, Russia, the United States, and China are in stasis, if not a slow and steady decline. The United States has undertaken only modest missile defense deployments, and the U.S. Congress has ended the Bush administration's nascent effort to marry the revolution in precision global-strike capabilities with boutique nuclear weapons optimized to hold hardened targets at risk while producing minimal collateral damage (Müller 2000). French politicians have recently reemphasized that their nuclear force can be used to respond to less than existential threats to France, and Russian military figures have noted that they are determined to maintain a modern and secure nuclear capability within the limits of the Moscow Treaty. But there is little evidence that these states consider nuclear weapons to be much more than a necessary evil. Nuclear weapons remain a part of the defense policies and strategies of these five nuclear states, but they are shrinking in number and are an aging asset. Some observers have called this a situation of partial marginalization of nuclear weapons. The importance of nuclear weapons is fading in the strategic policies of some governments, although there is little official support for the abolition of nuclear weapons or the complete abandonment of nuclear deterrence.

The situation among the great powers (for lack of a better term), however, is not mirrored in the policies of other emerging nuclear states. India and Pakistan are on the verge of a nuclear arms race; nuclear weapons have come to dominate their military competition. Iran is flaunting its obligations under the Non-Proliferation Treaty and antagonizing the entire international community by combining provocative and irresponsible rhetoric with a credible effort to create a nuclear arsenal. North Korea continues to be a wild card in Northeast Asia: the decision to test a nuclear weapon in October 2006 sparked reactions across all of Asia and in the United States, and it is still too early to tell if the test will prompt a new round of proliferation in Asia or a nuclear arms race. The possibility that nonstate actors could acquire a nuclear or radiological weapon also threatens to upset the relatively benign political and military balance in Asia.

The nuclear balance in Asia thus reflects multiple influences and serves several purposes. For China, Russia, the United States, and Japan, the nuclear test moratorium and the CTBT have cooled nuclear ambitions in the region and reduced the likelihood that a nuclear arms race might be produced as an inadvertent by-product of one state's decision to modernize or rapidly increase its nuclear arsenal. Because there is little overt political animosity driving relations among most of these countries, the extremely modest growth or even decline in nuclear capabilities is reflected in the moderate behavior among these states. All concerned wish to avoid a full-blown nuclear arms race, and the stasis and decline of nuclear capabilities in the region matches the relatively benign political environment.

Despite the gradual reduction in its nuclear capabilities, the United States still asserts its traditional deterrent threats against attacks on its allies and forces in the region. U.S. extended deterrence plays a positive role in Asia by reassuring South Korea and Japan that they can rely on the U.S. nuclear umbrella, reducing pressures to acquire nuclear weapons in response to Pyongyang's acquisition of a limited nuclear arsenal. As the U.S. arsenal shrinks, U.S. and Japanese ballistic missile defenses might become more important, raising the possibility that allies might transition from deterrence to defense against small missile threats. In that sense, missile defense is positive because it reflects a minimal response to a potential North Korean threat and it reduces pressure on Japanese and American policy makers to respond to North Korean nuclear developments with nuclear acquisition or modernization programs.

U.S. nuclear deterrent capabilities also backstop U.S. conventional forces in the region in at least one other important way. While the majority of U.S. conventional military capability has been engaged in the Middle East since the end of the Cold War, the U.S. nuclear arsenal remains a credible deterrent commitment to allies in the region. Without a robust nuclear capability, allies might become increasingly concerned that the United States will be unable to reinforce the region with conventional forces in a crisis, leading them either to strengthen their conventional capabilities or to contemplate developing their own nuclear arsenal. The credibility of U.S. nuclear deterrent threats might actually increase when its conventional forces are heavily engaged elsewhere because its conventional options in a second major contingency would be limited.

There is little talk of preventive war or preemption in U.S. nuclear policy toward Asia, with the exception that precipitous action on the part of North Korea or Iran could prompt a U.S. effort to eliminate nascent nuclear threats. Some observers have incorrectly suggested that the United States has a deliberate policy of nuclear predominance, but the reality is that the United States has simply managed the nuclear drawdown to retain a capable, albeit shrinking, force structure (Lieber and Press 2006). The United States retains escalation dominance over all other states in Asia, but this capability is not seen as a wasting asset or as an advantage that must be exploited for short-term political benefit. U.S. nuclear superiority plays only a modest role in the politics of the Pacific Rim because relatively benign political relations have failed to make this superiority a highly salient issue. If the nuclear balance became a salient concern during a crisis, however, potential antagonists might find themselves confronting concerns about crisis stability—that is, the incentives of states to be the first to use nuclear weapons.

Potential Nuclear Policies: Can Current Trends Be Reversed?

There are no military or political developments on the strategic horizon that threaten to reverse current U.S. attitudes toward nuclear weapons, but it is possible to identify potential developments that could lead U.S. officials to reinvigorate their strategic nuclear weapon programs. Some trends seem to continue indefinitely: the number of people relying on horses for everyday transportation has steadily declined over the past several centuries. But the stasis and even decline in the nuclear arsenals of the established nuclear powers is a relatively recent phenomenon. For the next several decades it will remain possible to restart nuclear weapon programs quickly. From an American perspective, what could prompt U.S. policy makers to start a significant nuclear buildup?

The Korean Issue. The North Korean nuclear test in October 2006 placed U.S. nuclear strategy in the Pacific Rim in a new context. Although the Six-Party Talks seem to be producing positive results (at this writing in the spring of 2008), pessimism and optimism about containing the North Korean nuclear weapons program are cyclical. The North Korean nuclear test, however, underscored the importance of U.S. extended deterrence in Asia. Japanese officials liken the North Korean test to the Cuban missile crisis, using the analogy to emphasize the gravity and proximity of the nuclear threat to their homeland. The analogy also raises the idea that the current state of affairs is intolerable to the Japanese people, highlighting the possibility that if the crisis is not resolved peacefully it could end in a Japanese decision to procure nuclear weapons or even go to war (*Gulf Times* 2006). There are a host of actions that North Korea might undertake that would greatly exacerbate the strategic situation in North Asia: carrying out a series of nuclear tests, ballistic missile tests, conventional aggression, or even actual use of nuclear weapons in a demonstration shot along the demilitarized zone or a limited nuclear attack in response to some real or imagined provocation. A sustained and successful North Korean nuclear weapon program would likely make policy makers along the entire Pacific Rim reexamine their strategic assumptions and programs.

Under these circumstances, American policy makers could offer allies in Seoul and Tokyo a combination of improved missile defenses, improved conventional counterforce capabilities, and renewed promises of extended deterrence to diminish the perception of threat from Pyongyang and to reduce local incentives to acquire nuclear weapons. It is impossible to tell whether such reassurances would work in the face of the ongoing nuclear drawdown in the United States and the ongoing process of nuclear marginalization. U.S. allies in the region—Japan, South Korea, Taiwan, and even Australia—would have to believe that ballistic missile defenses and advanced conventional precision strike capabilities are sufficient to deter a nuclear armed North Korea. Supporters of nuclear nonproliferation efforts might also decry U.S. efforts to reinvigorate its nuclear weapon programs, pointing to the fact that U.S. nuclear force modernization would send the wrong signal to friend and foe alike about the perceived efficacy of nuclear weapons. Nevertheless, a growing North Korean nuclear arsenal could force U.S. policy makers to take significant steps to modernize their strategic nuclear forces. U.S. policy makers could decide to develop nuclear weapons tailored to Korean war-fighting contingencies in response to improved North Korean capabilities. They also might want to demonstrate to allies in the region that the United States retains a modern, reliable, and usable nuclear deterrent, prompting a swift return to nuclear force modernization. At a minimum, nuclear force modernization could be viewed as a necessary element to strengthen deterrent threats in the face of a significant North Korean nuclear challenge to U.S. allies and forces in North Asia.

China, the Wild Card. For decades, U.S. analysts have disagreed about the future of China and whether Beijing intends to somehow challenge the United States directly as a global military power. Some believe that China will become a more democratic, and wealthier, regional power. Others believe that Beijing will use its economic prosperity to fund a global military that will leapfrog "legacy" military systems by concentrating on new capabilities and styles of warfare that fully harness the information revolution. These concerns, however, have not coalesced into meaningful political or military action on the part of U.S. policy makers; the jury is still out when it comes to the future of China.

This situation could change quickly. Although it has not received much attention from scholars interested in political and strategic developments in Asia, U.S. space analysts have long debated the nature and extent of China's goals in space. On January 11, 2007, the Chinese launched an antisatellite (ASAT) weapon against one of their obsolete weather satellites. Not only did the ASAT destroy its target, it promptly terminated the U.S. debate about the future course and intentions of the Chinese space program. The Chinese ASAT now serves as the rallying point for those in the United States who want to accelerate U.S. military space programs (*Aviation Week* 2007). The decision to launch the ASAT might not have been particularly well thought out by officials in Beijing, or it might have been based on bureaucratic inertia or rivalry. But that launch was sufficient to create a significant shift in the political and strategic debate about the future of the U.S. space program. Those critical of the further weaponization of space cannot point to Chinese restraint, or a potential Chinese response, as a reason to limit U.S. military space programs.

It is within the realm of possibility that if Chinese officials decide to reinvigorate their nuclear weapon program U.S. officials would, at a minimum, be forced to reevaluate the assumptions that drive U.S. strategic nuclear policy. The emerging U.S. strategic nuclear force policy, based on the procurement of relatively low numbers of "safe" warheads deployed in ways that secure them against the terrorist menace or the possibility of inadvertent or accidental nuclear use, might appear inadequate or inappropriate in the face of a rapid surge in the quality or quantity of China's strategic nuclear arsenal. Chinese nuclear tests, a successful series of long-range ballistic missile tests, or evidence of some kind of new weapon or technological breakthrough could force U.S. policy makers to jumpstart their own nuclear programs. The Sino-American nuclear balance is stable and relatively inconsequential for relations between the two countries, but the balance could quickly become politically and militarily salient if subjected to significant insult.

Systemic Effects. Analysts have long recognized that nuclear arsenals, doctrines, and command and early warning systems can form tightly interconnected networks that can produce system effects (Bracken 1983). Such effects can defeat purposive policy because military action or policy change can produce unintended and unanticipated consequences (Jervis 1997; Perrow 1984). Tightly connected networks can produce cascade effects, as relatively minor changes in one part of a system lead to increasingly negative consequences for all of the parties involved.

Several dangerous cascade effects come to mind when contemplating the nuclear balance in Asia. For instance, an increase in U.S. strategic forces and missile defenses along the Pacific Rim carries with it greater risk of inadvertent escalation or even accidental war, especially in a crisis in the Taiwan Strait, on the Korean peninsula, or in some military encounter between Chinese, Japanese, or even Russian maritime or air forces. In other words, if the tempo or scale of military operations in the region were to accelerate in response to North Korean actions or some other strategic development, an inadvertent military encounter among third parties would become a distinct possibility. Threats or actions undertaken for purposes of deterrence might be misperceived by the targets of deterrence or by third parties, leading to competing military alerts or even war. Any sort of military encounter in the region thus becomes worrisome because the great powers in the region have relatively little experience in multilateral crisis diplomacy: the strategic setting in Asia has been mercifully calm for several decades. A crisis in the region could offer a crash course for all concerned in the military doctrines and strategic expectations and objectives of the major actors in the region.

Because great powers are involved, relatively inconsequential problems might quickly create changes in strategic policies across the globe, leading to changes in force structure or doctrine that have a negative (and potentially unintended and unanticipated) impact on bilateral nuclear relationships. An India-Pakistan war, a preventive strike against Iran's nascent nuclear arsenal, or a terrorist attack involving a nuclear weapon or radiological device could cause one or more of the existing nuclear weapon states to reevaluate its force structure or doctrine, leading to cascade effects. Any use of a nuclear weapon on the planet would in all likelihood cause at least one of the great powers to reinvigorate its nuclear programs by testing nuclear weapons or modernizing its nuclear forces, which would create incentives for other states to modernize their arsenals. Aggressive counterproliferation policies could force other states to strengthen their arsenals. The great powers might be forced to respond to this vertical proliferation.

A system perspective suggests that U.S. nuclear doctrine and force posture can cause change on the global nuclear landscape or it can be shaped by strategic changes and events across the world. Regardless of whether the United States initiates or responds to change, however, a shift in U.S. nuclear policy is likely to produce change in other nuclear-armed states. But it remains unclear whether the international nuclear balance is highly resilient to change. So far, the North Korean nuclear test has not provided a sufficient military or political rationale to reverse the great powers' nuclear programs. Whether a great power could undertake a similar initiative without creating cascade effects remains to be seen.

The Hopeless Search for Consistency

Because nuclear weapon policy is a second-order concern to the George W. Bush administration, and is likely to remain of only secondary importance to future administrations, consistency will not emerge in the U.S. approach to a variety of issues that are related to nuclear weapons. For example, the U.S. supports the nonproliferation regime, but it often places other important objectives ahead of the goal of stopping or rolling back the spread of nuclear weapons at all costs. The United States has agreed to assist India with its civilian nuclear program in exchange for India's agreement to operate its civilian nuclear industry under international safeguards. India would then have access to international supplies of nuclear fuel for its commercial reactors, although critics charge that the agreement will allow India to divert its dwindling supplies of indigenous uranium to its nuclear weapon program (Vandehei and Linzer 2006). From the U.S. perspective, however, the agreement serves nonproliferation goals by moving India toward de facto compliance with the nonproliferation regime while also creating the basis for an Indo-American strategic partnership in Asia. From the Bush administration's perspective, the agreement also builds economic and diplomatic ties with an emerging democracy in Asia, a state that will be a natural ally of the United States in the years ahead.

Washington's attitude toward Islamabad also reflects a similar pragmatism. As a key ally in the global war on terrorism, Pakistan has been left to its own devices in dealing locally with revelations about A. Q. Khan and his clandestine nuclear technology suppliers network. Given U.S. nonproliferation initiatives like the Proliferation Security Initiative, which is designed to deter, detect, and dismantle trade in nuclear materials and dual-use technologies, one might have expected a stronger U.S. response to information that Pakistan's nuclear weapon program had been hijacked by a group of individuals simply to make money. The fact that Pakistan plays a critical part in the hunt for Al-Qaeda, and that President Pervez Musharraf is under pressure from local fundamentalists, creates an urgency to bolster the regime in Pakistan. For the moment, there is little interest in adopting a policy of quid pro quo toward Pakistan to gain adherence to global proliferation norms or to integrate Pakistan's nuclear weapon program into the international safeguards regime. The decision has apparently been reached that the prospects of nuclear surety and security are better under the current regime than what might follow.

In comparison to Washington's approach to Pakistan, the Bush administration has taken a harsh attitude toward the regime in Tehran. Here the calculations are different. There is greater concern that a nuclear-armed Iran might either deliberately or inadvertently supply terrorist organizations with either nuclear weapons or radiological materials, which might be incorporated into a "dirty bomb." There also is a concern that a nuclear-armed Iran might set off a sustained round of proliferation in the Middle East as America's allies in the region (Turkey, Saudi Arabia, and Egypt) develop a nuclear response to a "Shi'a" bomb. Washington also believes that, unlike in Pakistan, regime change in Iran might actually produce a more benign state of affairs, especially if a disgruntled Iranian middle class is allowed to express its preferences in the formation of a replacement government.

The fact that Iran's nuclear ambition raises alarm in Washington about nuclear terrorism should not be dismissed as a matter of propaganda. The Bush administration has highlighted the prospect of nuclear terrorism as the critical homeland security threat facing the United States. It is difficult to plan for this type of "doomsday scenario," which is often described as the detonation of a 10-kiloton weapon in a major urban area. Observers debate the likelihood that such an attack might take place or even whether it is possible to mitigate the death and destruction that would follow such an attack. At the moment, however, it is not clear that the political will exists to increase domestic surveillance sufficiently to reduce the prospect that nuclear terrorism would actually succeed.

Conclusion

Because of the enormous arsenals they created during the Cold War, the United States and Russia remain the greatest nuclear powers in the Pacific Rim. Nevertheless, nuclear disarmament appears to be the dominant trend in their nuclear policies, a trend that has so far lasted for about a quarter of a century. Russia and the United States will reduce the number of strategic weapons they deploy by about 80 percent from Cold War levels and have engaged in only modest force modernization. Admittedly, the rhetoric emanating from Moscow and Washington sometimes fails to match these procurement and arms control realities: Moscow and Washington continue to emphasize the role of nuclear weapons in their deterrence strategies. Moscow also has announced a few programs intended to replace aging nuclear delivery systems, although it is difficult to assess how many of these programs will actually be undertaken. At least in the United States, however, the process of nuclear marginalization is gaining momentum. For instance, the National Nuclear Security Administration announced that, in FY2007, it had achieved a 146 percent increase in the number of dismantled nuclear warheads compared to the previous fiscal year (*Arms Control Today* 2007). The Bush administration's plan to revitalize the U.S. nuclear arsenal to meet emerging threats seems to have generated no congressional support. The U.S. House Appropriations Energy and Water Committee "zeroed out" funding for the RRW program from the Department of Energy's FY2008 budget request, while former Senator Sam Nunn has suggested that Senate ratification of the CTBT should precede any decision to move ahead on the RRW (Pincus 2007).

The marginalization of nuclear weapons in U.S. defense policy is a robust trend. Indian and Pakistani nuclear tests had little effect on U.S. nuclear force deployments. North Korean nuclear programs have little effect on U.S. nuclear doctrine, although the North Korean missile tests increased the attractiveness of the deployment of U.S. missile defenses along the Pacific Rim, and the North Korean nuclear tests will increase U.S. and allied attention to extended deterrence in Asia. The 9/11 terrorist attacks and the global war on terror also had little effect on U.S. nuclear policy, although the attacks did raise the specter of terrorist acquisition and use of weapons of mass destruction (WMD). Because prevention, not retaliation, is seen as the preferred way to defeat the terrorist threat, the threat that terrorists might acquire WMD has created little pressure to revitalize the U.S. nuclear force structure or industrial infrastructure. It remains to be seen how the nuclear program and rhetoric emanating from Tehran will affect attitudes toward relying on Cold War surplus as the basis for the U.S. nuclear deterrent. So far, however, the North Korean nuclear test has not reversed the long-term trends in U.S. nuclear policy.

Several key nuclear issues face the next American administration. One involves how Russia and the United States might coordinate further force reductions and modernization efforts after the Moscow Treaty expires in 2012. Formal arms control might indeed be a type of diplomacy better suited to more adversarial relationships, but Washington and Moscow should maintain a strategic dialogue to keep each other abreast of their nuclear policies. Another is to determine what, if any, response should be made to Chinese nuclear weapon modernization, especially if China engages in a rapid expansion of its arsenal. How will the attitudes of Asian leaders toward nuclear weapons be affected if the Sino-American nuclear balance becomes an increasingly salient issue in Asian strategic calculations? Will the marginalization of U.S. nuclear forces continue if U.S. nuclear superiority vis-à-vis China begins to wane? Policy makers also will face the ongoing problem of preventing or at least delaying the proliferation of nuclear weapons and associated delivery systems to regional powers (e.g., North Korea, Iran). They might confront the possibility of "second order effects" (allied acquisition of nuclear arsenals), if proliferation creates doubts about the credibility of the U.S. nuclear umbrella. Proliferation also raises the specter of terrorist acquisition of WMD and the concomitant need for the United States to lead the international community to prevent nonstate actors from acquiring extremely hazardous materials and lethal weapons.

The turning away from nuclear weapons is not an irreversible trend. It is easy to imagine that significant setbacks among any of these issues might prompt a future administration to engage in a determined modernization of the U.S. nuclear arsenal. The 2001 NPR raised the possibility that nuclear weapons might again play an increasing role in U.S. defense policy, a response that was prompted by what appeared to be a spike in chemical, biological, and nuclear weapon proliferation. The Bush administration demonstrated a willingness to reassess the role nuclear weapons play in U.S. defense strategy in response to what they perceived as a changing threat environment, reducing the role played by nuclear deterrence in the Russian-American strategic relationship, and looking for ways to increase the role of nuclear deterrence in other emerging relationships. They suggested the possibility of marrying smaller nuclear weapons to long-range precision-guided delivery systems to make U.S. nuclear weapons better suited to hold at risk hardened underground targets or other targets associated with weapons of mass destruction. They believe that by increasing the utility of these new nuclear weapons to service emerging target sets, they can increase the effectiveness of U.S. deterrent threats in a growing number of diverse contingencies.

The U.S. Congress ended the debate about the desirability of the RNEP by failing to fund preliminary research on the utility of these weapons, and it appears that the RRW could meet the same fate. But the NPR demonstrates that the U.S. government also can choose to revitalize its nuclear arsenal in response to a changing threat environment. What sort of development might reverse the global trend among the United States and the other great powers toward nuclear marginalization? So far, the post-Cold War reduction in U.S. and Russian nuclear forces has withstood a good deal of free riding. Beijing's January 2007 ASAT test is just the most recent political-military challenge to the global nuclear order. But few if any trends continue indefinitely in world politics. The fact that nuclear stasis is the policy that holds sway in the United States today will be a controversial finding for some, but an alternative nuclear reality has been articulated in the NPR that many will find highly undesirable when compared with today's status quo. The United States could marry an array of modern nuclear warheads onto the latest precision-guided delivery systems and fully integrate these weapons into its conventional force structure to deter and defeat opponents armed with WMD. There is virtually no *political* support in the United States to undertake this kind of conventionalization of nuclear weapons and doctrine (Wirtz 1998). Nevertheless,

NPR advocates fully expect that Tehran, Pyongyang, or entrepreneurs like A. Q. Khan will soon provide some compelling evidence—in the form of a political insult or, even worse, a nuclear or radiological incident—that nuclear weapons should remain a crucial element of U.S. defense policy.

References

Anonymous. 2006. Interview with senior administration official, February.

Arms Control Today. 2007. "Panel Questions Warhead Concept Plausibility" November. Available at http://www.armscontrol.org/act/2007_11/PanelQuestions.asp.

Aviation Week. 2007. "Kyl Calls for Bigger Space Budgets," March 9. Available at http://www.aviationweek/com/aw/generic/story_channel.jsp?channel=space&id=news/ky1%20Calls%20For%20Bigger%20Space%20Budgets.

Baylis, John. 2000. "Nuclear Weapons, Prudence, and Morality: The Search for a 'Third Way.'" In *Alternative Nuclear Futures,* ed. John Baylis and Robert O'Neill. Oxford: Oxford University Press.

Bracken, Paul. 1983. *The Command and Control of Nuclear Forces*. New Haven, Conn.: Yale University Press.

Brooks, Linton F. 2006. Statement of Ambassador Under Secretary for Nuclear Security and Administrator, National Nuclear Security Administration, U.S. Department of Energy Before the House Armed Services Committee, Subcommittee on Strategic Forces March 1.

Cambone, Stephen A., and Patrick J. Garity. 1994/95. "The Future of U.S. Nuclear Policy." *Survival* 36 (4): 73–95.

Commission on Maintaining United States Weapons Expertise. 1999. Report to Congress and the Secretary of Energy, March 1. Available at http://www.fas.org/nuke/guide/usa/doctrine/doe/chilesrpt.pdf.

Dunn, Lewis A. 2005. *Can al Qaeda Be Deterred from Using Nuclear Weapons?* Center for the Study of Weapons of Mass Destruction, Occasional Paper 3. Washington, D.C.: National Defense University.

Feiveson, Harold, ed. 1999. *The Nuclear Turning Point*. Washington, D.C.: Brookings Institution.

Freedman, Lawrence. 1994/95. "Great Powers, Vital Interests and Nuclear Weapons." *Survival* 36 (4): 35–52.

Goodwin, Bruce T., Frederick A. Tarantino, and John B. Woodward. 2005. "Sustaining the Nuclear Enterprise—a New Approach." Lawrence Livermore, Los Alamos, and Sandia National Laboratories. UCRL-AR-212442; LAUR-05-3830; and SAND2005-3384, May 20.

Gulf Times. 2006. "Japanese Official Likens Threat to Cuban Crisis." November 2. Available at http://www.gulftimes.com/site/topics/article.asp?cu_no=2&item_no=115465&version=1&template_id=45&parent_id=25.

Harvey, John R. 2005. "Moving the Nuclear Weapons Program to DoD?" Address to the Federation of American Scientists' 60th Anniversary Celebration, November 30.

Herz, John. 1950. "Idealist Internationalism and the Security Dilemma." *World Politics* 2 (January): 157–80.

Jervis, Robert. 1970. *The Logic of Images in International Relations.* Princeton, N.J.: Princeton University Press.

———. 1978. "Cooperation under the Security Dilemma." *World Politics* 30 (January): 167–86.

———. 1997. *System Effects: Complexity in Political and Social Life* Princeton, N.J.: Princeton University Press.

Kissinger, Henry. 1977. *American Foreign Policy.* New York: W. W. Norton.

Lieber, Keir A., and Darly G. Press. 2006. "The End of MAD? The Nuclear Dimension of U.S. Primacy," *International Security* 30 (4): 7–44.

Medalia, Jonathan. 2005. *Robust Nuclear Earth Penetrator Budget Request and Plan, FY2005-FY2009.* CRS Report for Congress, Order Code RL323347, January 10. Washington, D.C.: Congressional Research Service.

Mlyn, Eric. 1998. "U.S. Nuclear Policy and the End of the Cold War." In *The Absolute Weapon Revisited: Nuclear Arms and the Emerging International Order,* ed. T. V. Paul, Richard Harknett, and James Wirtz. Ann Arbor: University of Michigan Press.

Müller, Harald. 2000. "Nuclear Disarmament: The Case for Incrementalism, In *Alternative Nuclear Futures,* ed. John Baylis and Robert O'Neill. Oxford: Oxford University Press.

National Institute for Public Policy. 2003. "Strategic Offensive Forces and the Nuclear Posture Review's 'New Triad.'" Fairfax, Va.: National Institute for Public Policy.

Payne, Keith, and C. Dale Walton. 2002. "Deterrence in the Post-Cold War World." In *Strategy in the Contemporary World,* ed. John Baylis, James Wirtz, Colin Gray, and Eliot Cohen. Oxford: Oxford University Press.

Perrow, Charles. 1984. *Normal Accidents.* New York: Basic Books.

Pincus, Walter. 2007. "Congress Skeptical of Warhead Plan," *Washington Post,* April 22. Available at http://www.washingtonpost.com/wp-dyn/content/ article/2007/04/21/AR2007042101000.html.

Powaski, Ronald. 2000. *Return to Armageddon.* Oxford: Oxford University Press.

Union of Concerned Scientists. N.d. Backgrounder, CTBT and Proliferation. Available at http://www.ucsusa.org/global_security/nuclear_weapons/page.cfm?pageID=1040.

U.S. Congress, House Committee on Appropriations. 2004. Energy and Water Development Appropriations Bill. 2005 H. Rept. 108-554, 1108th Cong., 2nd sess., June. Washington: GPO.

Vandehei, Jim, and Dafna Linzer. 2006. "U.S., India Reach Deal on Nuclear Cooperation: With Fuel Imports Allowed, Arms Program Could Grow." *Washington Post,* March 3. Available at http://washingtonpost.com/wpdyn/content/article/2006/03/02/AR2006030200183.html.

Walt, Stephen. 1996. *Revolution and War.* Ithaca, N.Y.: Cornell University Press.

Wirtz, James J. 1998. "Beyond Bipolarity: Prospects for Stability after the Cold War. In *The Absolute Weapon Revisited: Nuclear Arms and the Emerging International Order,* ed. T. V. Paul, Richard Harknett, and James Wirtz. Ann Arbor: University of Michigan Press.

———. 2005. "Disarmament, Deterrence, and Denial." *Comparative Strategy* 24 (5): 383–95.

———. 2006. "Do U.S. Nuclear Weapons Have a Future?" *Strategic Insights* 5 (3). Available at http://www.ccc.nps.navy.mil/si/2006/Mar/wirtzMar06.asp.

Wirtz, James J., and Jeffrey Larsen, eds. 2005. *Nuclear Transformation: The New U.S. Nuclear Doctrine.* London: Palgrave Macmillan.

Woolf, Amy F. 2006. "U.S. Strategic Nuclear Forces: Background, Developments, and Issues." CRS Report for Congress, RL 22640, September 8. Washington, D.C.: Congressional Research Service.

———. 2007. "U.S. Strategic Nuclear Forces: Background, Developments, and Issues." CRS Report for Congress, RL 33640, January 12. Washington, D.C.: Congressional Research Service.

4

Russia

"New" Inconsistent Nuclear Thinking and Policy

YURY FEDOROV

There is growing evidence that nuclear weapons play an increasingly important role in Russia's strategic thinking and policy. At the end of 2007, President Putin said that "increasing combat readiness of our strategic nuclear forces is one of our biggest tasks."[1] This assertion reflects the intellectual mainstream thinking in Russian military, political, and bureaucratic elites. They consider nuclear weapons to be the main foundation of national security and a tool to ensure Russian interests and international influence. Consequently, Moscow invests substantial resources to maintain its nuclear arsenal (which degrades nevertheless) and to develop new strategic nuclear missiles and submarines. Many believe this emphasis is at the expense of modernizing Russia's conventional forces.

The emphasis on nuclear weapons raises the following questions. What are the roots of Russia's nuclear policy? Is the force posture adequate for the nation's security needs? What are the possible consequences of Russia's nuclear policy for national and international security, including the strategic situation in Asia?

Nuclear Weapons in Russia's "Grand Strategy"

Principal strategic decisions in Russia are made by the president and a small circle of confidants consisting mainly of a few leading figures from the national security sector. This group is under constant pressure from lobbies within the armed forces, the military-industrial complex, and top bureaucratic echelons competing for budget funds and bureaucratic influence. Within this coterie, the "nuclear" and "missile" lobbies that arose in the last decades of the former Soviet Union have considerable influence. They are in fact a large fellowship of chief military scientists, masters of design bureaus and industry, as well as generals involved in the development, production, and exploitation of nuclear weapons and their delivery. Many of them dream about restoring, perhaps in a new form, the collapsed empire in which they enjoyed privileged positions, controlled enormous resources, and influenced national decision making. Russia's status as a great power, they insist, is much more important than human rights, freedom, and people's well-being. This status, according to them, depends on military might, the core of which is nuclear weapons.

The present role of nuclear weapons in Russia's "grand strategy" is based, first of all, on its national self-identification as an important center of power and threat perceptions among ruling groups, as well as on the deficiency of Russia's conventional forces. Nuclear weapons are seen as the only means to compensate for the growing gap in nonnuclear forces between Russia and technologically advanced countries, especially the United States.

Nuclear Weapons and Russia's Self-Identification

After the fall of the Soviet Union, two opposite national self-identifications have emerged within Russian ruling circles. Segments of Russia's political, military, and bureaucratic milieus and academia, today relatively small ones, accept that Russia is no longer a global superpower but a "normal" regional power and that the prospects for "large wars" with North Atlantic Treaty Organization (NATO) member states in Europe, with the United States, and with Japan in Northeast Asia have disappeared. This "pragmatic" school sees the security challenges for Russia mainly as results of instabilities and low-intensity conflicts in nearby regions and hypothetically China's northward expansion. This self-perception assumes that the military machine inherited from the Soviet Union should be radically restructured; instead of a huge army and navy designed for continentwide land operations and large naval battles, Russia needs relatively small but modern mobile forces able to fight effectively in local wars (including counterguerrilla warfare) and to conduct peace missions outside of Russia. Also, Russia does not need a massive nuclear arsenal for a "large" nuclear exchange with the United States, as it had during the Cold War. Nuclear weapons are seen as the ultimate security guarantee in the event of dangerous yet unpredictable international developments, including possible Chinese expansionism.

This view is typical not only of so-called pro-Western intellectuals, as many believe, but is also supported by some military commanders and security officers who, from their experience in actual conflicts, are aware of the deteriorating capacity of Russian conventional forces. They understand that the future of the Russian armed forces depends both on nuclear weapons and increasingly on the ability to neutralize "new threats," including local conflicts and terrorism.

However, this view is alien to most other segments of the Russian elite. In part, this is a legacy of the Soviet past. It also results from an inability to understand deep changes in the global strategic environment after 1991, as well as the international policy motivations in the West. It is produced by deep yet naïve ambitions among ruling groups to be masters of a global power, not of a large but regional state. For these groups, nuclear weapons are not only Russia's main military asset but also both a symbol and proof of national stature, a principal resource of international influence and means of protecting national interests. These views were conceptualized in the mid-1990s by the former chief of Russian intelligence and foreign minister Eugeny Primakov in his theory of a "multipolar world." In that framework, Russia was "an influential centre of a multipolar world," the core of which consisted of the United States, the European Union, China, Japan, and a few emerging "centres of power." The only justification for including Russia on a list of "influential centres" of the international system was its nuclear arsenal. In 1996, Igor Ivanov, then deputy foreign minister and Primakov's close lieutenant, wrote that one of the main tasks of Russia's foreign policy was "retention and strengthening of the role of Russia as an important centre in the emerging multipolar world . . . An efficient Russian economy, as well as a convincing Russian military power, and most of all a sufficient strategic nuclear arsenal, are necessary for strengthening the foundations of a multipolar world" (Ivanov 1996, my translation).[2]

During Putin's presidency, Russia's self-identification changed at least twice. After becoming president and until approximately 2004, Putin realized that Russia was not a great power and that his practical aim should be to transform it into a "normal" European power, an equal member of the Western community of nations, but not to seek an elusive position as "an influential centre of a multipolar world," whatever that might mean. In this phase, Putin's foreign and security policies resulted from a realistic assessment of Russia's weaknesses and skepticism about ideological mantras. His principal goal was to increase Russia's competitiveness and to integrate the country into the globalizing world community to prevent Russia's final degradation.

> We must melt the ice of distrust that built up over the 80 years of confrontation between the Soviet Union and the rest of the world . . . And our aim is to make Russia a full-fledged and equal member of today's international community . . . If we all the time refer to our thousand-year history and speak about our rich natural resources and how clever we are, and rest on these laurels, we shall decay finally. We are to be competitive in all spheres . . . This is exactly our basic national idea today.[3]

Until the middle of the present decade, Putin had not formulated clearly his vision of the function of nuclear weapons. It is probable that he did not consider nuclear might to be able to compensate for Russia's military, economic, and political weakness. In 2001–02 he partially supported the plan developed by the then head of the Russian General Staff, Anatoly Kvashnin, to decrease the number of nuclear weapons and to redirect funding toward strengthening Russia's conventional forces.

Beginning in 2007, Russia's national self-identification changed. Economic growth fueled by huge oil and gas export earnings, combined with the marginalization of the opposition, suggests to the Russian elite that the period of decay and retreat is over. Instead of a country in crisis that seeks to increase its competitiveness and integrate itself into the world community, today Russia is envisaged by the Kremlin and the political class to be an "energy superpower" with its own "ideological project" formulated in language such as "real sovereignty" and "sovereign democracy" that has to be protected by military force, mainly by nuclear weapons. Vice Prime Minister Sergey Ivanov, known to be close to Putin, has formulated this vision quite clearly:

> Today, Russia has returned itself in full measure to the status of great power, exercising global responsibility for the situation in the world and for the future of human civilization . . . By proclaiming its own ideological project, Russia has entered into a brutal and uncompromised competitive struggle . . . The fate of Russia as a sovereign state depends on its ability to respond adequately to pressure from outside as well as direct aggression . . . Because of existing geopolitical risks we rely on the development and deployment of new generations of strategic armaments that are able to eliminate the aggressor by retaliatory strike or that can be launched under attack in any situation.[4]

Thus, in the second half of this decade Russia's top echelon has returned to the perception of Russia as a great power, this time involved in an "ideological competition," which in fact implies a political-ideological confrontation with the West. The theory of "real sovereignty" insists that instead of integrating itself into a globalizing international system Russia should stay outside of globalization and strive to maximize its independence. Andrey Kokoshin, a leading ideologue and military expert in the pro-Putin United Russia party has written: "The cornerstone of national defence that will ensure real sovereignty of the country should remain independent national forces and means of nuclear deterrence supplemented by a system of 'non-nuclear deterrence'" (Kokoshin 2006: 103).

Nuclear weapons are seen today as a major factor in and a prerequisite for Russia's "real sovereignty." They will guarantee its independence, deter "ideological competitors," and make Russia a great power once again.

Nuclear Weapons and Threat Perceptions

Threat perception is the other key factor in determining nuclear policy. The question, "Who are Russia's enemies and what sources of military threat to it exist after the end of the Cold War?" was posed just after the demise of the Soviet Union and since then has been under intense discussion. Different political forces and interest groups in Russia have different lists of actual and potential enemies. Some believe that the West is neither an enemy nor a threat to Russia but a partner in fighting Islamic terrorism and radicalism. Others are sure that the United

States is an imminent rival. Serious debates are going on in Russian policy making and academic communities over whether China is a "strategic partner" or a future enemy.

No official Russian document has referred directly to any particular state or group of states as an actual or prospective military adversary. Yet analysis of these documents, as well as the writings of high military commanders and political figures, allows one to conclude that Russian elites see three types of actual and potential adversaries:

- the West, the United States and NATO, and pro-Western groups and forces in the newly independent states;
- radical Islamic and other extremist groups and forces; and
- China.

The West. Since 1996, when Eugeny Primakov became the foreign minister and Colonel-General Igor Rodionov was appointed defense minister, the idea of predestined confrontation between Russia and the West dominated official Russian political thinking. For instance, "The Concept of National Security of the Russian Federation," the principal official document approved at the end of 1997, stated:

> The threat to Russian national security in the military field is posed by the retention or creation by large powers (or by their coalitions) of powerful groupings of armed forces in the regions neighbouring Russia . . . NATO's eastward enlargement and its emergence as the dominant military-political force in Europe create the threat of a new division of the continent that is extremely dangerous because of the existence of the mobile strike groupings of forces and nuclear weaponry in Europe, and because of the insufficiency of the multilateral mechanisms of peacekeeping."[5]

The "powerful groupings of armed forces in the regions neighbouring Russia" might belong not only to NATO but to China too. Yet the mention of NATO's eastward expansion and its military domination in Europe made clear that it was the West that was considered Russia's primary external threat. The U.S. plans to build a missile defense system were interpreted as a manifestation of hostile intentions. The proposed U.S. ballistic missile defense (BMD) system, insisted the chorus of Russian military and academic experts, was designed to neutralize the Russian strategic missile force and thus ensure American military dominance over Russia.

Since 9/11, international terrorism and nuclear proliferation were outlined as the main threat to Russia's security, while the West was portrayed as Russia's partner in the global antiterrorist coalition. War between Russia and NATO or Russia and the United States has been declared unthinkable. "The Declaration of a New Relationship between the United States and the Russian Federation" of May 24, 2002, said:

> We are entering a new strategic relationship. The era in which the United States and Russia saw each other as an enemy or strategic threat has ended. We are partners and we will cooperate to advance stability, security, and economic integration, and to jointly counter global challenges and to help to resolve regional conflicts . . . The United States and Russia will intensify joint efforts to confront the new global challenges of the twenty-first century, including combating the closely linked threats of international terrorism and the proliferation of weapons of mass destruction and their means of delivery.[6]

This strategic philosophy was frequently articulated by President Putin and some high-ranking Russian officials. In particular, in September 2002 Sergey Ivanov declared:

> Nobody expects a full-scale nuclear war; nobody expects a war similar to the Great Patriotic War now. Today, local conflicts, borderline conflicts, combating terrorism are more and more acute points of the agenda . . . Believe me, the things that were thought over in the Soviet Union (the USSR against NATO, tank hordes), now can appear in delirium only.[7]

Yet the majority of the military commanders, captains of the military-industrial complex, and academics did not recognize a confrontation with NATO as a product of delirium. If they had, their very raison d'etre would have been called into question. Because of this, the new strategic philosophy was not supported by an appropriate reformulation of Russia's official doctrines. Also, the president himself was not really persistent in supporting these views. Putin has not abrogated principal documents he personally approved in the first half of 2000.

Three key documents were "The Military Doctrine of the Russian Federation," "The Concept of National Security of the Russian Federation," and "The Foreign Policy Concept of the Russian Federation." Having been developed at the end of the 1990s, they presented in aggregate the quintessence of strategic thinking typical of military commanders, the Ministry of Foreign Affairs, and other Russian government agencies at that time. On the one hand, "The Military Doctrine" characterized the emerging global strategic situation by reducing the danger of a large-scale war, including nuclear war. It highlighted a surge in national, ethnic, and religious extremism; activation of separatism; expansion of local wars and armed conflicts; rise of a regional arms race; proliferation of weapons of mass destruction and means of their delivery; and intensification of the information war.[8] On the other hand, these documents pointed to "the West" as a basic threat to Russia. In a long list of military threats to the country, the doctrine mentioned attempts by certain states to reduce the role of existing institutions in maintaining international security, in particular the United Nations and the Organization for Security and Co-operation in Europe (OSCE), and the consolidation of military-political coalitions, in particular NATO's eastward expansion.

There were no doubts that only the United States was able and inclined to reduce the role of the United Nations and to consolidate hostile military coalitions. What is more, "The Foreign Policy Concept" pointed out that increasing influence of the United States in global politics (it was called the formation of "a unipolar world") was a source of threat for Russia. Having reproduced the basic thoughts of "Primakovian" strategic philosophy, the "Concept" said: "The tendency to seek the creation of a unipolar world structure based on the USA's economic and power domination is strengthening. Western institutions and forums of limited membership will become the main bodies deciding principal issues of international security, a role the Security Council of the United Nations is easing."[9]

This strategic thinking was characterized also by persistent great power ambitions increasingly removed from Russia's true weight in the world arena. National security was perceived as international influence and maintenance of great power status. "External forces" were accused of undermining Russia's international stature by ousting it from its traditional zones of interest: "Threats to the national security of the Russian Federation in the international sphere are resulting from attempts by other states to prevent the strengthening of Russia as one of the influential centres of a multipolar world, to prevent achievement of its national interests, and to weaken its positions in Europe, the Middle East, Transcaucasia, Central Asia, and the Pacific region."[10]

The Russian military command and like-minded political elite opposed strategic partnership with the West mainly because it would facilitate military reform, including structural transformation of the armed forces and defense industry, and massive shake-up among their cohort. Three basic arguments have been developed to discredit partnership with the West. Integration into a globalizing world results in "a limited sovereignty" legitimizing intervention into Russian internal affairs; the old theory of a "war for resources" has been reanimated; and it was said that global strategic conditions had become progressively less predictable.

These arguments inform the current Russian strategic philosophy. It insists that in the foreseeable future global demand for hydrocarbons will outstrip supply. The growing gap between energy demand and supply leads to "wars for energy resources," in both the literal and the figurative senses of the term, with a view to establishing military and political control over the regions with key reserves of hydrocarbons and over routes of their transportation. Russia, it is argued, should capitalize on its unique position as one of the world's major energy-exporting countries. This would give Moscow a powerful tool of political influence in Europe and the so-called Near Abroad. Yet at the same time, Russia should protect its energy reserves from encroachments by the main energy-importing countries, including the United States, Europe, and perhaps China by developing powerful armed forces, mainly its nuclear arsenal.

The other key element of Russian official thinking today is the belief that "nobody likes a strong Russia." The restoration of Russia's economic might and political stability has fueled hostile attitudes in other countries as Russia would become an effective competitor. For instance, Sergey Ivanov has included Russia's partners from the "community of democratic states who are worried by an independent, strong, self-confident Russia that has a developed economy and a clear political position" in the list of current adversaries alongside international terrorists and other radical elements sharing "man-hating ideas."[11]

Since Putin's speech in Munich in 2007, Russia's foreign policy has acquired a defiant anti-Western character. Along with increasingly hostile anti-Western rhetoric coming from the top of the Russian hierarchy, Moscow has suspended the Conventional Armed Forces in Europe (CFE) Treaty and threatens to deploy nuclear weapons in Byelorussia and Kaliningrad and to withdraw from the Intermediate Range Nuclear Forces (INF) Treaty. The latter most probably will ignite a new missile crisis in Europe like that of the 1970s and 1980s. These moves are justified by Russian politicians as responses to the Western military buildup near Russia's borders, albeit this buildup exists in the minds of the Russian military only.

Thus, the West is seen in Moscow today as an ideological and military rival that is concerned about Russia's newly acquired might and independent political strategy and is intent on encroaching on its oil and gas resources. To defend itself and ensure its independence, Russia needs effective armed forces, especially nuclear weapons.

China. Russian perceptions of China are controversial and complicated; the vision of China as a strategic partner is combined with a view of it as a potential threat. In the second half of the 1990s, Moscow hoped to compensate for the degradation of its economic and military might by forging an effective "strategic partnership" with China. Today, Russia's agenda includes intensification of political consultations, the formulation of common approaches to acute international problems, and other forms of political cooperation with Beijing. It seems Moscow not only has in mind the coordination of the two countries' foreign policies but also is looking for an informal political-military alliance directed against the United States and destructive Islamic forces in Central Asia. The Shanghai Cooperation Organization is seen as a core element of this alliance, which should institutionalize multifaceted Russia-China cooperation in military and security areas. Commenting on the Russo-Chinese joint military exercise "Peace Mission 2005" Sergey Ivanov wrote: "These exercises were based on the similar tasks and missions of the Russian and Chinese armies. This similarity is rooted in both states' desire to guarantee national and regional stability."[12]

The idea of a Russo-Chinese coalition is not a new one. It is rooted in the Soviet-Chinese alliance of the early 1950s and was resurrected by Eugeny Primakov in the middle of the 1990s. It is based on the premise that Russia's and China's interests in minimizing American influence are much more important for both countries than their divergent interests in Central Asia and in the Far East. Also, Moscow believes that developing a strategic partnership with China strengthens its position against the West. Beijing is believed to be interested in playing the "Russia card" to improve its position against the United States.

But a formal or informal alliance between Russia and China is wishful thinking. China's strategy excludes military alliances with any country. Economic and normal political relations with the United States are much more important for China than a partnership with Russia because of the huge volume of trade between the two, and China's interest in acquiring new technologies and investments from the United States. Beijing would not sacrifice its own interests in the event of a conflict between Russia and the West. And, despite the diplomatic rhetoric about a "strategic partnership," Beijing understands that Russia is turning into a "petro-state" whose capacity to develop and use high technologies is degrading and that it is not capable of preventing the demographic crisis that affects especially the eastern parts of that country.

The notion of a Russo-Chinese political-military coalition is combined with the Russian strategic perception of China as a potential military threat that can be deterred only by nuclear weapons. This has not been mentioned in official documents but is discussed among certain segments of the elite. The then head of the Center for Military-Political Studies of the General Staff of the Russian Armed Forces, Lieutenant-General Vladimir Ostankov, wrote in 2005:

> The rise of the PRC's military and economic power and its population growth demand huge resources. As other areas of the world rich in natural resource are already divided, it is only logical that the vector of the Chinese expansion will be directed toward nearby areas of Russia (Siberia and the Far East), Kazakhstan, and other countries of Central Asia . . . Despite a current stable relationship between the Russian Federation and the PRC, old suspicions about large-scale armed non-nuclear conflict between the two countries have not disappeared . . . Prevention of such conflict by political methods only . . . or by conventional forces may be inefficient. Because of the Chinese factor, Russia's policy is to be founded on nuclear weapons and presumes strategic cooperation with the West. (Ostankov 2005: 7)

Actually, many in Russia worry that the demographic imbalance between the Russian Far East and the Chinese northeastern provinces may lead to massive Chinese expansion into Russian Siberia. This strengthens concerns about the superiority of Chinese armed forces deployed in two northern military regions, Beijing and Shenyang, over the Russian army in eastern Siberia and the Russian Far East. Also, a competition between Russia and China for the energy resources of Central Asia and the Caspian region seems increasingly probable. And the fact that something very big, powerful, and unpredictable is growing close to the Russian

TABLE 4-1

Schools of Thought on Russia's Status and Military Position

Pragmatic school	Primakov school	Putin-I (after 9/11)	Putin-II (since 2005)
	CONCEPTUALIZATION OF RUSSIA		
"Normal" regional power	A great power; one of the influential centers of the "multipolar world"	A European country and equal member of the Western community of nations	A rising "energy superpower" restoring its might after the period of "Yeltsin's decay"
	KEY THREATS TO RUSSIA		
Local conflicts, separatism, irredentism, irresponsible regimes nearby; Iran, North Korea, and China as potential threats	The U.S policy of global domination; Western intrigue in the "near abroad" aimed at ousting Russia from its "natural" zone of influence	Terrorism; Islamic extremism; WMD proliferation; transnational crime	Globalization threatening Russia's "real sovereignty"; A West that is afraid of Russia's newly gained might; China as a latent rival and potential enemy; Islamic terrorism
	FUNCTION OF NUCLEAR WEAPONS		
Deterrence of China; ultimate guarantee of security in the event of unpredictable yet highly dangerous international development	A symbol of Russia's "grandeur"; a principal resource of Russia's influence; to compensate for the degradation of conventional forces; deterrence of the United States	Ultimate guarantee of security	Deterrence of possible encroachments on Russian energy resources; principal guarantee of Russia's "real sovereignty"

Far East more and more disturbs Russian elites and public opinion. The evolution of Russian perceptions of the role and function of nuclear weapons is summarized in Table 4-1.

The principal function of Russia's nuclear weapons today is deterrence of the West and China. Nuclear weapons are seen also as a symbol and proof of the nation's great power status and, together with oil and gas resources, a principal source of Russia's international influence.

Nuclear Weapons as Compensation for Conventional Arms Deficiency

The growing role of nuclear weapons in Russia's strategy is based on the fundamental fact that its conventional armed forces are degrading, that Russia is not able to master the "revolution in military affairs," and that it will be incapable of ensuring the national security in the foreseeable future without nuclear weapons. Colonel-General Victor Yesin, then the head of the Military Department of the

Security Council of Russia, said in early 2000: "In a large-scale war Russia will never (and this is scientifically forecast, whatever its economic growth is) be able to resist organizations such as NATO with conventional weapons only. It will not be able to repel massive conventional aggression by this bloc. This accounts for our focus on using nuclear weapons to ensure Russia's security against external threats" (Yesin 2000: 33).

Russia's conventional forces are inferior to NATO troops in Europe and to Chinese, American, and Japanese forces in the Far East. For instance, the Russian military has stationed huge numbers of heavy armaments in military districts in Siberia and the Russian Far East (about 7,000 main battle tanks, 10,000 armored combat vehicles, and more than 6,000 artillery pieces). Yet these armaments are largely useless, as there are not enough personnel to operate them. Russia has approximately 126,000 personnel in the Russian Far East and Siberia, whereas China has 550,000 in the Shenyang and Beijing military regions (International Institute for Strategic Studies [IISS] 2006: 160–61, 266). A realistic assessment would be that due to the degradation of Russia's armed forces since 1991 and the modernization of China's armed forces, battle efficiency and the quality of the forces and equipment of the Russian and Chinese troops are approximately equal. However, as China has more troops in the region than Russia, it could be argued that Russian military potential in Northeast Asia is substantially inferior. The Russian Pacific fleet has lost a substantial share of its former battle capabilities, in many respects yielding to the American Pacific fleet and the Chinese, Japanese, and South Korean navies (see Table 4-2).

Presently there is no threat of armed conflict between Russia and any Northeast Asian country. Yet an official Russian document predicts that large-scale naval landing operations against Russia in the Far East will include air, space, sea, and land components. It says that the efficiency of an antilanding defense of the Russian Far East will depend on the ability of the troops to act autonomously, and the document pays special attention to the deficit in transport communications between the Far East and the European part of Russia which can negatively affect Russia's combat capabilities (Ministry of Defense of the Russian Federation 2003: 30).

The Russian military command sees the United States and perhaps Japan as Russia's potential enemies in Northeast Asia because no other state in the region has large-scale landing capabilities with massive air and space components. Russia has no means, other than nuclear weapons, to prevent such landing operations, in particular because of the difficulty of transporting troops, military equipment, and armaments from the central areas of Russia. Also, as mentioned by Lieutenant-General Ostankov, armed conflict with China is not excluded. It most probably would be in the form of large-scale operations of land forces in which Russia would use nuclear weapons.

TABLE 4-2

Naval Forces in the Pacific

	Russia (Pacific Fleet)	China	Japan Korea	South	United States (Pacific Fleet)
Aircraft carrier group	—	—	—	—	5
Cruisers	1	—	—	—	13
Large antisubmarine ships	4	—	—	—	—
Destroyers	4–5	27	51	6	24
Frigates	2	44	4	9	15
Corvettes	—	—	—	28	—
Patrol and coastal combatants	30	254	9	75	?[a]
Mine warfare	8	69	31	15	2
Amphibious	4	76	3	10	3
Logistics and support	57	163	28	14	8
Strategic submarines	4–6	1	—	—	8
Tactical submarines, nuclear	11–12	5	—	—	24
Tactical submarines, nonnuclear	8–9	51	18	20	?[a]

SOURCES: IISS (2006: 43, 163, 267, 274, 279); Barabanov (2006); Ilya Kramnik, "The Great Ocean Fleet" (http://www.lenta.ru/articles/2006/08/24/pacific/index.htm) (in Russian).

NOTE: [a]No data is available.

The deficiency of Russia's conventional forces has resulted in some similarities between Russia's strategy today and NATO's strategy during the Cold War. Lawrence Freedman has correctly written:

> The logical counter-strategy to this growing U.S., and more generally Western conventional strength is not to fight on their terms but to rely on more irregular methods: from terrorism to weapons of mass destruction. This was the logic, at least as far as nuclear weapons were concerned, followed by NATO, when confronted with what is supposed to be overwhelming Warsaw Pact conventional superiority during the Cold War. The Alliance refused to rule out the first use of nuclear weapons. So it is that the prospect of Russian conventional inferiority has now stimulated a greater readiness in Russia to rely on nuclear threats. (Freedman 1999: 31)

Also, NATO's strategy included flexible response and gradual escalation from conventional fighting up to total nuclear "exchange" between the United States and the Soviet Union, the risk of which was seen as the ultimate means of preventing a Soviet attack on Europe. The principal task of Russian nuclear doctrine is to develop a scheme for using nuclear weapons that enables Russia's armed forces to deter or stop an attack by superior conventional forces and at the same time avoid escalation into total nuclear exchange.

Russia's Nuclear Strategy

Unlike the Cold War notion of deterrence, which focused on full-scale strategic nuclear attack, in the 1990s the Russian military saw the main threat to

Russia's national security coming from attack by conventional high-technology precision weapons, mainly of the type used in Kosovo. The outlook for Russia's nuclear strategy was described by well-known Russian military expert, Alexei Arbatov, then deputy head of the parliamentary committee for the armed forces as follows:

> Russia's principal strategic mission is to exclude the possibility that selective air and rocket strikes by NATO would go unpunished for some protracted period of time . . . Russian selective strikes using tactical nuclear weapons would be justified . . . In this case the other side would be challenged by an awful dilemma: either to stop the aggression and recognize its defeat, or to respond with a nuclear strike, which would be followed by an escalation to strategic nuclear exchange with catastrophic consequences for all countries. Lacking anything better, Russia sees this strategy as reasonable. (Arbatov 1999: 370–71)

This vision reflected Russia's actual nuclear planning, presuming that Russia should be able to use nuclear weapons first, wage limited nuclear war with either tactical or strategic nuclear weapons, and deter a large-scale "disarming" and "decapitating" nuclear attack by threatening to strike back (the "classic" deterrence model).

First Use of Nuclear Weapons

The previous Soviet commitment to not use nuclear weapons first was factually denounced by "The Basic Provisions of the Military Doctrine of the Russian Federation" approved by Boris Yeltsin in November 1993. It stated that Russia:

> will not employ its nuclear weapons against any state party to the Treaty on the Non-proliferation of Nuclear weapons . . . which does not possess nuclear weapons except in the case of: (a) an armed attack against the Russian Federation, its territory, armed forces, other troops or its allies by any state that is connected by an alliance agreement with a state that does possess nuclear weapons; (b) joint actions by such a state with a state possessing nuclear weapons in the carrying out or in support of any invasion or armed attack on the Russian Federation, its territory, armed forces, other troops, or its allies.[13]

In other words, Russia may use nuclear force first against any Non-Proliferation Treaty (NPT) member state that is a U.S. ally, if that state is in armed conflict with Russia or its allies. Strictly speaking, this formulation presumed that Russia could use nuclear weapons in any armed clash between Russian allies such as Byelorussia and Armenia and neighboring NATO member states.

Unclear Nuclear Threshold

The doctrinal documents approved in the first half of 2000 confirmed Russia's willingness to use nuclear weapons first, although these documents were not clear when describing a key element of a nuclear strategy: the "nuclear threshold." For instance, the National Security Concept said that Russia might use "all means available to it, including nuclear weapons, if it is necessary to repel the armed aggression and if all other crisis management measures have been exhausted or turned out to be inefficient." The Military Doctrine stated that "The Russian Federation keeps the right to use nuclear weapons in response to the use of nuclear weapons or other WMD against Russia or its allies, as well as in response to the large-scale conventional aggression in situations critical for the Russian national security."[14] These documents do not define key terms, such as "situation critical for the national security," and do not identify any criteria for efficiency or inefficiency of "crisis management measures." This enables Russia to regard such measures as "exhausted" or "inefficient" and/or consider a situation as "critical for national security" at almost any stage of a military confrontation. It seems that the lack of definite language and well-defined criteria of the nuclear threshold is by design. Such ambiguity and uncertainty, it is believed, increase the value of a nuclear deterrent because a potential aggressor does not know what particular action would provoke a highly dangerous nuclear response.

Extended Deterrence

The documents mentioned above and other doctrinal documents presume that Russia would use its nuclear weapons if one of its allies (such as Byelorussia or Armenia) were under WMD attack or the target of a large-scale conventional aggression. For Russia, a strategy of extended deterrence means that it should risk its own existence to stop or prevent attacks in Byelorussia, Armenia, or some other remote post-Soviet space. Military conflict between Russia and NATO over Byelorussia is impossible. NATO member states will not risk a war in Europe to restore democracy or even stop massive violation of human rights in Byelorussia, and Russian leaders will not risk the existence of their country to save the current dictatorial regime in Minsk. The threat to deploy nuclear weapons in Byelorussia as well as the regular military exercises of Russian and Byelorussian armies, including use of nuclear weapons, are manifestations of Moscow's irritation with NATO's eastward enlargement and with U.S. plans to establish antiballistic missile facilities in Poland and the Czech Republic, rather than genuine training for future combat operations.

Yet there may be dangerous developments in the South Caucasus. In the event of a new Armenian-Azerbaijani war over Nagorno-Karabakh, Russian troops stationed in Armenia might be taken hostage if Turkey were involved in the war on the Azeri side. Lack of land communications with troops in Armenia would prevent Moscow from supporting them effectively; the dilemma would be whether to allow its military contingent in the South Caucasus to be defeated or to threaten the use of nuclear weapons to stop Turkish forces. The latter situation would initiate a conflict having unpredictable consequences with a NATO member state.

"Nuclear Deescalation" Through Limited Use of Nuclear Weapons

Russia's position on limited nuclear war was stated in the report "The Priority Tasks of Development of the Armed Forces of the Russian Federation" presented by the Ministry of Defense in October 2003. In particular, it postulated "nuclear deescalation" of a conflict if conventional deterrence fails as the principal mission for Russian nuclear weapons. "Nuclear deescalation" scenarios have been part of large-scale command and staff exercises in Russia since 1999. The scenarios posit the southern part of the Baltic region, including Byelorussia, the Kaliningrad area, and some of the new Baltic states as the most probable area of military conflict between Russia and NATO.

Deescalation is the principal innovation of Russia's official strategic thinking in the first decade of the twenty-first century. Deescalation refers to Russia's ability to inflict precisely calculated damage—"pre-set damage"—on an attacker to convince it that using conventional military force (precise air and missile strikes) against Russia would be irrational. "The Priority Tasks" defines "pre-set damage" as "damage, subjectively unacceptable to the enemy, which exceeds the benefits the aggressor expects to gain as a result of the use of military force" (Ministry of Defense of the Russian Federation 2003: 43). This may mean that "pre-set damage" should be enough to stop a conventional attack (most probably this is the meaning of the term *subjectively unacceptable*) yet at the same time should not provoke NATO's nuclear response. To put it differently, the Russian military believes that first limited use of nuclear weapons would not automatically escalate to a large-scale nuclear war. This is the most dubious element of the "nuclear deescalation" theory.

"Demonstrative Nuclear Strikes"

Russian nuclear strategy presumes that limited use of nuclear weapons may take the form of a "demonstrative nuclear strike" against targets located in unpopulated areas of enemy territory. By this tactic, Russian military and civilian strategists hope to convince adversaries of Moscow's determination to use nuclear weapons and at the same time not to provoke automatic massive nuclear retaliation.

For instance, according to the scenario played out in the exercise "The West-99" in June 1999 immediately after the war in Yugoslavia, NATO forces launched massive nonnuclear air and missile strikes against Byelorussia and Kaliningrad. The Russian-Byelorussian forces could not stop the escalation or repel the aggression. Russia decided to make a demonstrative limited nuclear strike using strategic bombers against some targets in remote northern areas of North America.[15]

But a demonstrative strike is only one of a few possible first uses of Russian nuclear weapons. Russian mass media revealed that during command and staff exercises in early autumn 2002 Russian strategic nuclear forces imitated not a demonstrative but a massive nuclear strike[16] to "prevent an escalation of military aggression against Russia, including by use of nuclear weapons."[17] If this is true, then the Russian military is in fact planning the first full-scale use of nuclear weapons, which almost automatically invites a nuclear response and thus "total" nuclear war.

Tactical Nuclear Weapons

Although very little is known about Russian tactical nuclear weapons, their role could be great because they were designed specifically for geographically limited nuclear war. A number of Russian analysts have insisted that tactical nuclear weapons deter regional powers such as Iran and Turkey from expanding into the former Soviet Union. Some have proposed to deploy tactical nuclear weapons in Byelorussia, Kaliningrad, and other areas close to Poland and other new NATO member states as a response to the deployment of U.S. BMD facilities in Poland and the Czech Republic.

A Russian official document on national strategy published in June 1996 stated: "The Russian Federation is consistently putting into practice the policy of nuclear deterrence. The maintenance of the Russian Federation's nuclear potential at the global level (Strategic Nuclear Forces), as well as at sufficient regional and local levels (operational-tactical and tactical nuclear weapons) . . . is playing the key role in the realization of this policy."[18] This statement was accompanied by a number of writings by high-ranking military officers and academics who endorsed the significance of tactical nuclear weapons for Russia's security mostly because of its weak conventional forces. The then State Military Inspector Andrey Kokoshin wrote in August 1996: "Not only strategic nuclear forces, but also operative tactical forces and tactical nuclear weapons, are an important component of the nuclear deterrence forces. In the current circumstances, when there is no ability to build up general-purpose forces powerful enough . . . the nuclear shield plays a more important role than other military means of preventing aggression."[19]

The scenario of the Russo-Byelorussian military exercise "The Union's Security—2004" in June 2004 included the use of tactical nuclear weapons against superior foreign forces invading the territory of the Russo-Byelorussian "union state." In 2006, during Russo-Byelorussian joint military exercises, Byelorussian President Alexander Lukashenko announced that tactical nuclear weapons could be used in the event of threat to the "union state."[20]

Thus Russian nuclear doctrine presumes that Russia will use nuclear weapons first in the form of a demonstrative strike with a few strategic weapons or a number of tactical armaments. This should force an enemy to stop armed hostilities or risk nuclear escalation at the regional level since full-scale nuclear exchange would be blocked by the prospect of an inevitable retaliatory strike inflicting some "pre-set damage." The question is whether Russia has enough nuclear weapons to implement such a strategy.

Russia's Nuclear Force Posture

Just before the demise of the Soviet Union, its strategic assets were about the same size as the U.S. strategic nuclear arsenal. But the principal defect of the Soviet nuclear assets was that they included too many types of intercontinental ballistic missiles (ICBMs) and nuclear submarines armed with ballistic missiles (strategic submarine ballistic nuclear [SSBN] and sea-launched ballistic missiles [SLBMs]). In 1990 the Soviet Strategic Rocket Force was armed with seven types of ICBMs; and the Soviet navy was armed with seven types of SSBNs, six of which had been equipped with their own specific types of SLBM (U.S. Department of State 1991). This force structure was the result of a policy motivated mainly by technological factors, not by economic or military considerations. It led to a cost-is-no-object approach and to large-scale overspending of material and financial resources, as well as to substantial difficulties in the maintenance and exploitation of strategic forces. After the demise of the Soviet Union, this strategic force structure produced additional problems for the Russian military command and political leadership because of the radical reduction of resources allocated to maintaining and developing strategic forces.

Since the fall of the Soviet Union and up to January 31, 2006, the total number of Russian strategic nuclear warheads decreased by a factor of approximately 2.3; the number of ICBMs has been reduced by a factor of 2.5 and, the SLBMs by a factor of 2.7. Reduction of other elements of the strategic triad were less dramatic. Air-based strategic warheads were reduced by a factor of 1.4 (see Table 4-3).[21]

The principal reductions in the former Soviet strategic forces resulted from decommissioning and eliminating nuclear weapons in Ukraine and Kazakhstan. Also, about 400 outmoded ICBMs, 37 out-of-date submarines, and about 60 heavy bombers that were not equipped with air-launched cruise missiles (ALCMs) were decommissioned and eliminated.

TABLE 4-3

Elements of Russia's Strategic Triad, 1990 and 2006

	1990			2006		
	Airplanes	Missiles	Warheads	Airplanes	Missiles	Warheads
Land-based	no	1,398	6,612	no	557	2,183
Sea-based	no	940	2,804	no	292	1,592
Air-based	162	no	855	78	no	624
TOTAL	162	2,338	10,271	78	849	4,399

SOURCES: http://www.state.gov/www/global/armsfactsheet/wmd/nuclear/start1/strtdata/html; http://www.state.gov/documents/organizations/64162.pdf.

By the end of the 1990s, Russia's leadership was to make the principal decisions about the future profile of the national strategic forces. It was a subject of controversy in Russia's top echelons, fueled by competition for government funding. Russia had no resources to maintain its diverse nuclear forces and the Kremlin had to decide which systems would be developed and which would not. In 2002 the principal directives on development of Russia's strategic nuclear force were approved. The total number of strategic warheads Russia can have at the beginning of the next decade has been appointed within the limits of the Strategic Offensive Reductions Treaty—that is, between 1,700 and 2,200 pieces. It also was decided that maintenance of the land-based MIRVed (multiple independently targetable reentry vehicle) ICBMs would be a high priority for the Russian military command and that the life expectancy of these missiles would be increased by as much as possible. Speaking on December 15, 2002, the commander in chief of the Strategic Rocket Force (SRF), Colonel-General Nikolay Solovtzov, revealed the possibility of equipping the most modern Russian ICBMs, Topol-Ms, with three warheads. "The Priority Tasks" reveals that by 2007–08 the SRF will consist of ten divisions (reduced from the current eighteen). These divisions will consist primarily of old-type ICBMs, whose service lives will be extended; gradually these ICBMs will be replaced with "prospective missile complexes."[22] These decisions meant a radical reformulation of the previous concept of the development of the SRF. Previously, it was taken as an axiom that, because of a number of serious technical reasons, prolonging the life of existing ICBMs would be impossible or highly risky. The reason for the policy change was that by 2005 the lion's share of strategic warheads had been deployed on old MIRVed ICBMs commissioned before the fall of the Soviet Union. The oldest of them are an earlier version of the SS-18 commissioned in 1979–83 and the SS-19 commissioned in 1980–84 (Podvig 1998: 190–91, 194). At the same time, the deployment rate of the Topol-M is quite low; during the 1997–2005 period an average of four to six were produced each year (see Figure 4-1).

If that deployment rate continues over the next ten years, then by the middle of the next decade Russia may have approximately 100 modern missiles. Also, the manufacturing cost of the Topol-M is growing. Over the past few years it has increased by a factor of 3.[23] Thus, the extension of the service life of the old ICBMs was seen as the only way to avoid the radical and fast decrease in Russia's strategic armaments. As for the technical possibility of prolonging the service life of Russian MIRVed ICBMs to twenty-five to thirty years, neither advocates nor opponents of this policy provide any concrete data that would allow making an independent assessment. Today, the only thing that can be said is that this decision is sometimes criticized in the mass media.

As of 2005, Russia's sea-based strategic forces had about 1,000 operational warheads stationed on thirteen SSBNs. Two critical factors will determine the future

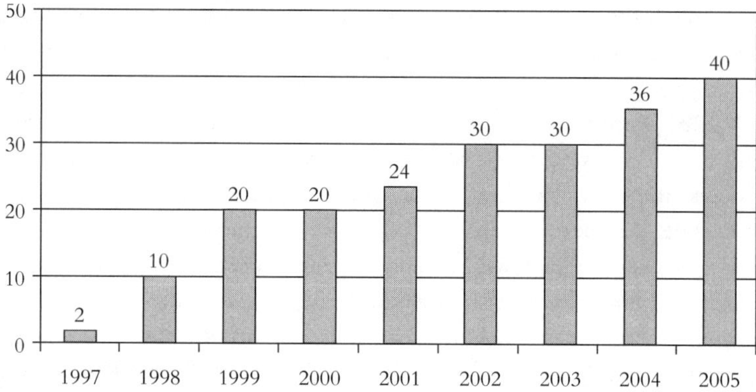

FIG. 4-1. Topol-M Deployment, 1997-2005.
Source: U.S. Department of State 1991; START Aggregate Numbers of Strategic Offensive Arms. (http://www.state.gov/t/ac/rls/fs/54166.htm); "START Aggregate Numbers of Strategic Offensive Arms, April 1, 2004." (http://www.state.gov/t/ac/rfs/fs/2004/30816.html); "START Aggregate Numbers of Strategic Offensive Arms, April 1, 2003." (http://www.state.gov/t/ac/rfs/fs/2003/18973.html); "START Aggregate Numbers of Strategic Offensive Arms, October 1, 2002." (http://www.state.gov/t/ac/rfs/fs/9075.htm); "START Aggregate Numbers of Strategic Offensive Arms, April 1, 2001." (http://www.state.gov/t/ac/rfs/fs/7394.htm); "START I Aggregate Numbers of Strategic Offensive Arms, October 1, 2000." (http://www.state.gov/www/global/arms/factsheet/wmd/nuclear/start1/startagr.htm); Ivan Safronov, "Russia Has More 'Topols,'" Kommersant, December 27, 2000 (in Russian); Ivan Safronov and Konstantin Laptev, "The Government Has Modernized the Defense Order," Kommersant, December 26, 2003 (in Russian); http://www.rambler.ru/db/news/msq.html?mid=5108513&s=10337 (in Russian).

development of Russia's strategic naval force: (1) regularity of maintenance and repair services, and (2) development of a new missile to be deployed on new SSBNs of the "Borey" type and on one or two older submarines of the Typhoon type (if they are not decommissioned). Most probably by the end of the present decade, the Russian Strategic Naval Force will consist of six Delta IV-class submarines armed with a new highly modified version of the SS-N-23 SLBM,[24] few if any Typhoons, and some new SSBNs of the Borey class. Current plans call for building six of these submarines.[25] Three of them are planned to be built before 2010.[26] Yet the very slow pace of building the first one, the *Yury Dolgoruky* (its construction began in 1996 and it is not yet in active service) raises some doubts that these plans will be fulfilled.

As for Russia's strategic aviation, "The Priority Tasks" emphasized the need to modernize the Blackjack (Tu-160) heavy bombers, which should be able to carry new high-precision cruise missiles for both nuclear and conventional missions, as well as gravity bombs, and fulfill a variety of battle missions (Ministry of Defense of the Russian Federation 2003: 44).

A lack of clarity about the life expectancy of Russian MIRVed ICBMs, as well as uncertainty about resources to be allocated for the production of new ICBMs and the maintenance of older SSBNs, makes it difficult to reach conclusions about the prospects for Russia's strategic forces. There are, however, a few assessments of Russia's evolving nuclear posture over the next ten to fifteen years. Each is based on a particular set of assumptions with regard to funding of repair and maintenance and producing new ballistic and cruise missiles and submarines.

One of the most detailed outlines of Russia's future nuclear force has been presented by the adviser to the commander of Russia's SRF, Colonel-General Victor Yesin, former head of the Military Department of the Security Council of Russia. In 2012, he said that Russia's strategic arsenal will consist of approximately 1,900 deployed warheads. Its structure will change significantly from the current one. About 35 percent of warheads will be deployed on SS-18, SS-25, and SS-27 (Topol-M) ICBMs; 38 percent of warheads will be stationed on SSBNs and the rest on heavy bombers.[27] As for Russian substrategic nuclear weapons, Yesin said that Russia plans to decrease its tactical stockpile to no more than 3,000 weapons in the future. Of these, 60 percent will be air-based systems, 30 percent will be sea-based systems, and 10 percent will be surface-based systems. In addition to the current 200 short-range SS-21 missiles (IISS 2003: 90), about 100 new Iskander tactical missiles with a maxium range of 300 kilometers are planned to be produced and deployed.[28]

There are also much more pessimistic assessments of the future of Russia's missile assets. Yury Maslyukov, former vice prime minister in the Primakov government and also a former head of the Soviet military-industrial complex, has written that by the beginning of the next decade the Russian strategic force will be one-eighth or one-tenth of the size it was at the beginning of this current decade. According to him, Russia will have 100 to 120 ICBM Topol-Ms, 2 to 3 SSBNs with about 200 to 250 warheads, and 100 to 120 ALCMs deployed on heavy Blackjack bombers (Tu-160).[29]

Thus, the numerical strength of the Russian nuclear force at the beginning of the next decade is assessed to be between 400 and 1,900 strategic warheads and up to 3,000 substrategic weapons. In the first case, one may suggest that the Russia-U.S. nuclear balance will be highly asymmetrical, and Russian nuclear strategy in relation to the United States may be based on the use-first-or-lose principle and thus become a destabilizing factor. At the same time, Russia will be able to wage large-scale substrategic nuclear war and retain reliable second-strike deterrent potential vis-à-vis China. Yet if Russia has about 1,900 nuclear warheads deployed on relatively survivable delivery vehicles, it will have second-strike deterrent capability vis-à-vis the United States.

Russia and Nuclear Proliferation in Asia

Officially Moscow regards nuclear proliferation along with international terrorism as threats to Russia's security. It is concerned about the prospect of emerging nuclear weapon states under extremist regimes close to Russia's borders. Russia does not want to be within striking distance of Iranian or North Korean nuclear-tipped missiles. Yet Russia's practical stance toward the Iranian and North Korean nuclear programs is controversial.

It has avoided taking strong measures to compel Iran and North Korea to stop their nuclear programs. Moscow insists that its efforts should be political and diplomatic only; it opposes effective sanctions against proliferating states and is in favor of developing peaceful atomic energy in these countries; and it strives to avoid military action against them. Russia's nonproliferation policy is similar in some ways to the former Soviet Union's approach to Iraqi nuclear efforts at the beginning of the 1980s. The Soviet and Russian diplomat Oleg Grinevsky described Soviet Foreign Minister Andrei Gromyko's reaction to Saddam Hussein's nuclear activities in this way:

> Development of nuclear weapons, if of course Saddam Hussein is able to do this, will change the Middle East conflict significantly, Gromyko said to his trusted subordinates. Yet . . . is this really dangerous for us? Can we imagine the circumstances under which an Iraqi atomic bomb threatens us? I do not see such a situation. But for Americans and for Israel, which is an American ally, it will generate a strong headache. The Middle East conflict will flare up with new strength and they will be on their knees begging us to help them to settle it. (Grinevsky 2002: 99–100)

Iran

Russia's approach to the Iran nuclear issue may be described briefly as "three no's": no to an Iran with nuclear weapons; no to a military option; and no to a political solution of the problem. To put it differently, Moscow would like to freeze the current status quo. Russia certainly wants to prevent Iran from having nuclear weapons. A nuclear Iran would result in a dramatic and mostly undesirable change in the strategic environment near Russia's southern borders and in the areas of the Southern Caucasus and Central Asia that are regarded in Moscow as zones of its exclusive influence and vital interest. In particular, a nuclear Iran may become a large-scale source of tension and also may encroach on Russian positions and interests in the southern provinces of the former Soviet Union. This could explain Russian reluctance to supply Iran with fuel for the Bushehr reactor under the pretext of an unsettled payment issue. This explains also President Putin's commitment to stop nuclear cooperation with Iran if the latter refuses to cooperate with the international community. In June 2004 at the G8 Summit, Putin announced: "Russia will stop work at Bushehr if Iran ignores the international community's demands to make its nuclear programs transparent and to expand its cooperation with the IAEA."[30] A year later, in April 2005, President Putin, speaking in Israel, confirmed that Iran "should cease developing full nuclear fuel cycle technologies and stop impeding all international monitoring of its nuclear facilities."[31]

Yet Moscow does not want to see a political solution of the Iranian nuclear problem. Any settlement of this problem seems possible only if, instead of the current extremist regime, a moderate, pro-Western political and economic group were to take office in Iran. If that were to happen, the Iran-U.S. relationship would change radically; and Iran might become an American partner. This is not what Moscow wants. In October 2004 the following comments were printed in *Nezavisimaya gazeta,* the Russian newspaper that is often used by those close to the Kremlin to reveal the regime's true interests and ambitions:

> Westernization of Iran will mean an inevitable and unambiguous turn of the whole of Central Asia towards the West; for Russia this means a final loss of all levers of control over the former Soviet Central Asian republics it has today. A shortage of current Western economic and hence political influence upon this region results from natural (geographical) reasons: Central Asia is isolated from the outer world by a barrier of states either unstable (Afghanistan) or disloyal to America (Iran, China). A "renewed" Iran will rise for the states of this region as a kind of a "window to the West," providing the attractive prospect of free exports of Central Asian energy resources to global markets via the Mediterranean, Turkey or, if necessary, to the southern seas.[32]

Also, if this problem is settled politically, Russia will not be able to use it as a bargaining chip in its relationship with the West. The logic of Russia's position is not particularly sophisticated. It believes that Iran's nuclear program creates more problems and headaches for Israel and the United States than for Russia. It offers Russia scope for manipulating these concerns and for positioning itself as an intermediary between the United States and Iran—although neither country accepts Russia in such a capacity. By modifying, albeit insignificantly, its position toward the Iranian nuclear program Moscow tries to gain some concessions from the West. Also, the Kremlin may feel more secure if American political and military resources are focused on Iran and not on areas that Moscow considers its principal zones of interests, such as the Ukraine, the Caspian, Central Asia, and other newly independent states. And last, tensions caused by Iran's nuclear efforts are stimulating high oil and gas prices, which favor a Russian economy highly dependent on hydrocarbon exports. Seen in this light, Moscow's veto of effective sanctions against Tehran may be motivated by concerns that such sanctions could in the long term result in a pro-Western political solution of the problem.

At the same time, Moscow is doing everything it can to prevent the United States from taking a military option. If a military operation were to prove successful, then a pro-American leadership may take power in Iran, which Moscow would regard as a foreign policy defeat. If the United States and Israel succeeded in destroying Iran's nuclear capability but were unable to establish effective control over the country, then an abyss of chaos, Islamic extremism, and instability would open up on Russia's borders. This would also not be good for Russia. Finally, if Iran were broken up into separate parts along ethnic lines a powerful Azerbaijan could appear, fundamentally altering the balance of power in the region to the detriment of Russia.

Thus Russia's approach toward the Iranian nuclear problem, combined with hints that Moscow may effectively help the West to settle that problem "in exchange" for Western recognition of Russia's exclusive interests in the post-Soviet Union space, is one of the few Russian trump cards in its complicated game with the West. It may produce some tactical gains. Yet the longer Moscow plays this game the deeper may be the trap for Russian foreign policy: it will be challenged either by a nuclear armed Iran or by the consequences of a military operation against Tehran.

North Korea and Potential "Nuclear Dominos" in East Asia

North Korea timed its missile and nuclear tests in Autumn 2006 perfectly. The United States remains stuck in a hopeless "bellum omnia contra omnes" in Iraq. Taliban activities in southern Afghanistan call into question both stability in the heart of Eurasia and the future of NATO, and Iran has ignored attempts by the Group of Six to find a compromise solution to its nuclear issue and has demonstrated its ability to weather international sanctions. In this context the United States has no political resources and not enough political will to respond to the North Korean nuclear test with a "nuclear castration strike."

There are different explanations of the North Korean nuclear test. But it seems that North Korea has stepped over a kind of "red line." Of special importance, Pyongyang disregarded the opinion, strategic interests, and position of its closest political and ideological ally, China, which supplies North Korea with vital economic aid. However, Beijing does not support regime change or collapse in North Korea, which most likely would entail an armed intervention by South Korea and the United States. This would not serve Chinese interests. At the same time the Chinese government has been alarmed by the prospect that North Korean actions could have a "nuclear domino" effect on the region and possibly result in strengthening the U.S. and Japanese military potentials in the area. Given these circumstances, Beijing's efforts were directed at mitigating the situation. An active Chinese position, including most probably strong pressure upon the North Korean leadership, as well as American flexibility, resulted in the February 13, 2007, agreement on "initial actions for the implementation of the Joint Statement" of September 19, 2005. That joint statement was based on the understanding that North Korea would freeze its nuclear program in exchange for provision of energy and official direct negotiations between North Korea and the United States. That agreement has mitigated the strategic situation in Northeast Asia, yet one of the most crucial issues—how many nuclear explosive devices North Korea has and how and when they will be destroyed—has not been addressed.

Both the North Korean nuclear test and the agreement of February 13, 2007, were bad news for Russia. They confirmed that the Russian strategy of capitalizing on North Korean nuclear ambitions has helped Pyongyang to develop its nuclear program and avoid international sanctions. They discredit the basic foundation of Moscow's policy on the Korean nuclear issue, which presumed that Pyongyang is motivated by rational considerations, and that North Korea's "legitimate" security concerns should be taken into account. Further, the agreement of February 13, 2007, has been achieved mainly due to Beijing's active efforts and U.S. flexibility, not due to Russian mediation. It has demonstrated that Moscow's role and influence on the Korean peninsula and in the wider regional strategic context is minimal.

Conclusion

While the role of nuclear weapons in Western security thinking is more modest than it was during the Cold War, Russian strategic thinking and policy are evolving in a different direction. Nuclear deterrence may turn out to be essential to Russia in a "worst case scenario" in its relationship with China. Yet a "revolution in military affairs" is devaluing the potential use of nuclear weapons in "major regular wars." Nuclear armaments are not effective in "major irregular wars," like those currently being waged in Iraq, Afghanistan, and Chechnya. At the same time, current nuclear weapon programs consume a lot of financial, intellectual, and material resources vitally needed to reform and modernize Russia's conventional forces. In turn, weak conventional forces will fuel the "nuclearization" of Russia's military strategy and its orientation toward first use of nuclear weapons.

Also, a strategy that allows first use of nuclear weapons, even in the form of a demonstrative strike, is highly destabilizing. For a potential victim of the demonstrative strike, it produces an unacceptable threat partly because it is unknown beforehand whether this strike will be targeted at unpopulated areas or key cities. On the one hand, it may persuade Russia's potential adversary not to use force against Russia. But, on the other hand, it may stimulate a potential victim of a demonstrative strike to eliminate a threat of such strike once and forever by using nuclear weapons first in a disarming strike. This radically decreases crisis stability and substantially enhances the risk of massive nuclear conflict. Russia's nuclear strategy may become a highly destabilizing factor in Northeast Asia in the event that its military situation in the region deteriorates.

Notes

1. President Vladimir Putin. Opening remarks at the meeting with the Armed Forces senior command, November 20, 2007, Defense Ministry, Moscow. Available at http://www.presidentkremlin.ru/eng/text/speeches/2007/11/20/1356_type82912type82913_151712.shtml (in English, official translation).

2. Unless stated otherwise, all translations are mine.

3. Vladimir Putin's answers to questions at a meeting with campaign supporters, February 12, 2004. Available at http://www.putin2004.ru/english/authorized/402D7D27.

4. Sergey Ivanov, "The Triad of National Values," *Izvestiya*, July 13, 2006. Available at http://www.mil.ru/847/1291/12671/index.shtml?id=14769 (in Russian).

5. "The National Security Concept of the Russian Federation," *Krasnaya Zvezda*, December 27, 1997 (in Russian).

6. Joint Declaration on a New Relationship between the United States and the Russian Federation, May 24, 2002. Available at http://moscow.usembassy/gov/bilateral/jointstatement.php?recordid=13.

7. Sergey Ivanov, "The USSR against NATO: A Product of Delirium," *Kommersant Vlast*, September 23–29, 2002, pp. 27, 29 (in Russian).

8. "The Military Doctrine of the Russian Federation." Available at www.mid.ru.

9. "The Foreign Policy Concept of the Russian Federation." Available at www.mid.ru.

10. "The National Security Concept of the Russian Federation." Available at www.mid.ru.

11. Sergey Ivanov, "The Triad of National Values," *Izvestiya*, July 13, 2006. Available at http://www.mil.ru/847/1291/12671/index.shtml?id=14769 (in Russian).

12. Available at http://www.rian.ru/world/foreign_russia/20060316/44393277.html (in Russian).

13. "The Basic Provisions of the Military Doctrine of the Russian Federation," *Krasnaya Zvezda*, Special Appendix, November 19, 1993, p. 2 (in Russian).

14. "The Concept of National Security of the Russian Federation." Available at www.mid.ru; "The Military Doctrine of the Russian Federation," *Nezavisimaya Gazeta*, April 22, 2000, p. 5 (in Russian).

15. Sergey Sokut, "A Balkan Scenario Has Been Stopped," *Nezavisimaya Gazeta*, June 24, 1999 (in Russian).

16. Sergey Sokut, "Through Nuclear Sight," *Nezavisimoye Voennoye Obozreniye,* October 18–24, 2002, p. 6 (in Russian).

17. Dmitry Litovkin, "The Military Have Rehearsed the Preventive Strike," *Izvestiya*, October 13, 2002 (in Russian).

18. "Address of the President of the Russian Federation to the Federal Assembly on the National Security," Moscow, 1996, p. 24 (in Russian).

19. Andrey Kokoshin, "What Army Do We Need?" *Segodnya*, August 7, 1996 (in Russian).

20. Victor Myasnikov, Vladimir Ivanov, and Anton Khodasevich, "Lukashenko Presses Nuclear Button," *Nezavisimaya Gazeta*, June 26, 2006. Available at http://www.ng.ru/68920 (in Russian).

21. In fact, the total number of Russian strategic weapons was substantially lower because about one-third of SSBNs were nonoperational, yet technically they have not met the terms of decommissioned platforms as it was defined by the START-I Treaty.

22. Sergey Sokut, "Nuclear-Missile Circling," *Nezavisimoye Voennoye Obozreniye*, January 24, 2003. Available at http://nvo.ng.ru/concepts/2003-01-24/4_defense.html (in Russian); START Aggregate Numbers of Strategic Offensive Arms. Available at http://www.state.gov/t/ac/rls/fs/54166.htm; Ministry of Defense of the Russian Federation 2002: 44.

23. Vladimir Mukhin, "The State Defense Order Will Be Approved till the End of the Year," *Nezavisimoye Voennoye Obozreniye*, December 25, 2003–January 15, 2004, p. 2 (in Russian).

24. Vladimir Gundarov, "Country's Nuclear Trident," *Krasnaya Zvezda*, August 14, 2004 (in Russian).

25. "Nuclear Fleet Is Growing," *Nezavisimoye Voennoye Obozreniye*, August 20–26, 2004, p. 3 (in Russian).

26. Vladimir Gundarov, "The Punishing Mace That Is the *Dmitry Donskoy*," *Krasnaya Zvezda*, September 25, 2004 (in Russian).

27. Victor Yesin, presentation at the Carnegie Endowment for International Peace, meeting with experts of the Institute for Applied International Research (IAIR), Moscow. February 6, 2003. Available at http://www.carnegieendowment.org/events/index.cfm?fa=eventDetail&id=583.

28. *Nezavisimoye Voennoye Obozreniye*, November 14–20, 2003, p. 6 (in Russian).

29. Yury Maslyukov, "A Right to Retaliate," *Voenno-Promishlennii Kurier*, October 22–28, 2003 (in Russian).

30. Available at http://www.president.kremlin.ru/eng/speeches/2004/06/11/14_0172690.shtml.

31. Available that http://top.rbc.ru/indexshtml?/news/daythemes/2005/04/28 (in Russian).

32. Viktoriya Panfilova, "Moskve mozhet dorogo oboitis yadernaya programma Tegerana" ("Moscow may pay a lot for Tehran's nuclear programme"), "Diplomaticheskii kurier," *Nezavisimaya Gazeta*, Oct. 11, 2004, p. 12.

References

Arbatov, Alexei. 1999. *Security: Russia's Choice.* Moscow: EPI-Tzentr (in Russian).

Barabanov, Mikhail. 2006. "It Is Time to Raise Questions about the Priority of the Development of the Pacific Fleet," *Voenno-Promishlennii Kurier,* August 30–September 5, 2006. Available at 9Hhttp://www.vpk-news.ru/article.asp?pr_sign=archive.2006.149.articles.army_02) (in Russian).

Freedman, Lawrence. 1999. "The New Great Power Politics." In *Russia and the West: The Twenty-first Century Security Environment,* ed. Alexei G. Arbatov, Karl Kaiser, and Robert Legvold. Armonk, N.Y.: M. E. Sharpe.

Grinevsky, Oleg. 2002. *Scenario for a Third World War.* Moscow: Olma Press (in Russian).

———. 2004. *The Turning Point: From Brezhnev to Gorbachev.* Moscow: Olma Press (in Russian).

International Institute for Strategic Studies (IISS). 2003. *The Military Balance, 2003–2004.* Oxford: Oxford University Press.

———. 2006. *The Military Balance, 2006.* Available at http://www.sinodefense.com/army/orbat/beijingmr.asp; http://www.sinodefense.com/army/orbat/shenyangmr.asp.

Ivanov, Igor. 1996. "The Factors of Power." *Krasnaya Zvezda,* November 11 (in Russian).

Kokoshin, Andrey. 2006. "Real Sovereignty and Sovereign Democracy." In *Sovereignty,* ed. Nikita Garadja. Moscow: Evropa (in Russian).

Ministry of Defense of the Russian Federation. 2003. "Priority Tasks of the Development of the Armed Forces of the Russian Federation." October. Moscow: Author.

Ostankov, Vladimir. 2005. "Geopolitical Problems and Their Possible Solution in the Context of Russian Security." *Military Thought* 1 (in Russian).

Podvig, P. L. 1998. *Strategic Armaments of Russia* [Strategicheskoye Yadernoye Vooruzheniye Rossii]. Moscow: Izdat (in Russian).

Sokut, Sergey. 2002. "Through Nuclear Sight." *Nezavisimoye Voennoye Obozreniye,* October 18–24 (in Russian).

U.S. Department of State. 1991. "START: Data Base." Fact Sheet, August 1, 1991. Available at http://www.state.gov/www/global/armsfactsheet/wmd/nuclear/start1/strtdata/html.

Yesin, Victor. 2000. Interview in *Yaderny Kontrol* 6 (2) (in Russian).

5

China
Dynamic Minimum Deterrence

CHU SHULONG AND RONG YU

Nuclear weapons play a limited but important strategic role in China's foreign and security policies. In addition to symbolizing China's prestige and international status as a great power, the primary role of Chinese nuclear weapons is deterrence of stronger powers like the United States and Russia. Despite its strong military capability, Russia is not considered a security threat. It is considered a power in decline, and there are no serious disputes between China and Russia. The principal security concern is the United States, which could confront China over Taiwan or seek to contain China's rising power and influence. Beijing relies on its conventional capability to deal with most other security threats.

China's minimum deterrence nuclear strategy is focused primarily on deterring the United States from intervening in a conflict across the Taiwan Strait and preventing an American attack on Chinese soil. The Chinese understanding and practice of the strategy of minimum deterrence is dynamic—its features are continually adjusted to meet the changing strategic environment and threat. In light of the vastly superior American nuclear capability, the U.S. emphasis on preemption and prevention in its national security strategy, and development of a ballistic missile defense (BMD) system, China is diversifying, modernizing, and strengthening its nuclear force posture, with some Chinese analysts reexamining the Chinese commitment to a no-first-use (NFU) policy. Although China can devote increasing resources, it is unlikely to develop a large nuclear arsenal to compete with the United States or to dramatically alter its nuclear strategy. That would undermine its strategy of peaceful rise. Beijing does not seek to become a strong world military power on par with the United States. Nevertheless Beijing is not likely to stand still. It would develop its nuclear force posture to maintain a strong deterrent capability against the United States and to protect its interests in a changing security environment. The pace of nuclear modernization could accelerate if there is a rapid deterioration in China's relations with the United States and Japan.

China's Security Environment in the Twenty-First Century

With the beginning of the twenty-first century, there is broad consensus among Chinese leaders, strategists, officials, and experts that China's security environment is more favorable and secure than it has been, since the founding of the People's Republic of China in 1949, though it has never been completely free from security concerns. A 2006 Chinese government white paper describes the country's current security environment as follows:

> China's overall security environment remains sound. China is committed to building a moderately prosperous society in an all-round way and a socialist harmonious society, and it enjoys steady economic growth, political stability, ethnic harmony and social progress. Its overall national strength has considerably increased, as has its international standing and influence. China's practical cooperation with major countries continues to grow, its friendly relations with its neighboring countries have developed steadily, and it is forging strong ties with other developing countries. This has given rise to a new relationship of mutual benefit and win-win between China and other countries. The Chinese government has taken a number of significant measures to improve relations across the Taiwan Straits, thus promoting cross-Straits relations toward peace and stability. (Information Office of the State Council of the People's Republic of China 2006)

Today, although there are long-range apprehensions, no country in the world claims China as its enemy. China has established and normalized diplomatic relations with all countries in Asia and the world, except for twenty-five small states that recognize Taiwan. China's economic ties with other economies are set to grow stronger in the future. Its role and influence in Asia and in the world are growing as its economy and power continue to rise.

However, looking ten to twenty years or longer into the future, Chinese leaders, strategists, officials, and scholars have expressed concern about the uncertainties or developments that could threaten China's national security: "China's security still faces challenges that must not be neglected. The growing interconnections between domestic and international factors and interconnected traditional and nontraditional factors have made maintaining national security a more challenging task. The struggle to oppose and contain the separatist forces for 'Taiwan independence' and their activities remains a hard one" (Information Office of the State Council of the People's Republic of China 2006).

Security Challenges

The security threats of concern to Beijing are Taiwan independence, a Sino-American conflict, the "three forces," and a militarized Japan.

Taiwan's Independence. The most serious threat facing the People's Republic of China now and in the future is the independence of Taiwan. Taiwan's independence threatens China's sovereignty, its territorial integrity, and its national unity, which are central to the national security of all nations. Taiwan's independence may also encourage separatist movements in other parts of China, such as Tibet and Xinjiang. Movement toward the independence of Taiwan would not only lead to a serious war across the Taiwan Strait, but also very likely between China and the United States and possibly Japan as well. Taiwan's independence also poses an economic threat to the rise of China, because a war would halt China's process of modernization, at least for a few years or perhaps for a few decades. Taiwan would seem to be the only issue that could stop the economic boom and prosperity of China in the early decades of the twenty-first century.

Sino-American Conflict. The United States is the only country that China may have a major war or military conflict with in the foreseeable future. Either a cold war or a hot war is probable in two possible situations.

One situation is the eruption of the Taiwan crisis. Under the Taiwan Relations Act, the United States is committed to "protect" Taiwan in a military conflict with China. Thus a war or military clash between the two sides of the Taiwan Strait could develop into a war or conflict between the United States and China.

The second possibility is a confrontation between China and the United States if a rising China decides to challenge America's role in Asia and in the world or if the United States adopted a comprehensive containment strategy toward a stronger China. Then Sino-U.S. relations in the twenty-first century would resemble the U.S.-Soviet Union rivalry during the Cold War.

The "Three Forces." Since the mid-1990s, the Chinese government has defined the "three forces" as a major threat to China, including to its regime. The three forces are separationists, extremists, and terrorists.

Separationist forces consist of Taiwan's independence movement and separatist organizations and activities in Xinjiang and Tibet. These challenges are the top three threats to China's stability. With the Soviet Union no longer a threat, the major security threat to China comes from inside, not outside, the country. This is the fundamental difference between the Cold War and post-Cold War eras. Separationist forces are perceived as extremist, ethnic, and religious groups that threaten China's security and national unity.

Inside and outside China over the past decade, separationists and extremists have used terrorist methods to pursue their goals. So China shares a common concern with the international community about terror and the war on terrorism. The major terrorist groups targeting China come from many of the same areas that produce other international terrorists—that is, Central, South, and Western Asia. The "three forces" are not only a long-term threat to China in the post-Cold

War era. They may become more serious to China in the near term, including when China hosts the 2008 Olympic Games in Beijing.

A Nationalistic and Militarized Japan. Among China's neighbors, Russia, Japan, and India are major powers that have the potential or capability to pose a threat to China. However, Russia is much weaker than its predecessor, the Soviet Union. Even though its military is still stronger than China's, its economy and comprehensive power are falling behind. Furthermore, Russia does not have the incentive to enter into conflict with China. These two countries are no longer engaged in bitter ideological rivalry. All their territorial disputes have been resolved.

India is rising and will become much more powerful. However, for most Chinese, India is geographically distant. As the two countries are determined to resolve or settle their territorial disputes in the short term, conflicts between China and India are unlikely in the foreseeable future. Besides, India is unlikely to become stronger than China in the near term; therefore, China does not worry about an "India threat" even if bilateral relations are not particularly cordial.

The only neighbor that China is concerned about is Japan. Until now Japan has had neither the intention nor the capacity to pose a major threat to China. However, Beijing is worried about the direction of Japanese politics. Many Chinese interpret the rise of the right wing in Japanese politics, the rising nationalism in Japanese society, the move by Japan to change its pacifist constitution, and the dispatch of the Self Defense Forces abroad as evidence that, decades after it became a global economic power, Japan is now on the road to becoming a political and military power as well. Combined with Japan's economic and technological capabilities and its disputes with China over history, territory (the Diaoyu Islands), and resources (in the East China Sea), many in China believe Japan will eventually pose a great security threat to China.

However, the Chinese leadership and serious scholars have not been so pessimistic. They believe that as long as Japan remains within the framework of the U.S.-Japan security alliance, it is not likely to increase its military forces and transform its force posture dramatically. It does not need to do so, and the United States would not allow this to happen. Therefore, although Japan may pose a security problem for China, especially related to its military capability and activity, it is not likely to become a significant threat to China in the near future.

The Role of Nuclear Weapons: The Strategic Forces Counter the Stronger Powers

The primary role of nuclear weapons in China has been defined as deterring other countries from using or threatening nuclear weapons against China (Information Office of the State Council of the People's Republic of China 2006). Nuclear weapons have little role to play in China's security and foreign policies with most other countries. Considering China's force structure, this is not difficult to understand. As China has been a major conventional power, it does not need nuclear weapons to deter or fight with most of the other countries in Asia and around the world. In the four decades since it acquired nuclear weapons in 1964, China has not sought to use them in military conflicts or war with countries such as Vietnam (1979) or against the Philippines in the South China Sea (1998). China's conventional capability is more than adequate in a war situation with these countries.

China's nuclear weapons are targeted primarily against countries that are stronger than China: the United States and Russia. The function of China's nuclear weapons is to deter these two countries from using their nuclear or conventional forces and to deter other countries from using nuclear weapons against China. General Jing Zhiyuan, the commander of China's Strategic Forces, and General Peng Xiaofeng, the political commissar, wrote in June 2006 that "the function of China's strategic forces is to serve as the major strategic force to protect the nation, contain the use of nuclear weapons against China by its enemies, and take the task of nuclear retaliation when China is attacked by nuclear weapons" (Jing and Peng 2006: 15, our translation).

The deterrent nature of China's nuclear force is evident in its foreign and security policies of the past forty years. Unlike the United States and the former Soviet Union, China has not seriously sought to offensively use its nuclear weapons for two reasons. First, China would be less vulnerable than other countries in the event of a nuclear war. As had been argued by Chinese military thinkers decades ago, use of strategic nuclear weapons would be most effective on countries with concentrated mass population and industry, while tactical nuclear weapons would be most effective when used against a highly concentrated military buildup (Su 1950: 59). China is a developing country with a massive population scattered across a vast territory. Destruction of Beijing, or even Shanghai, would not shatter the country's will and capacity to fight to the end. Once heavily concentrated to the 500 miles along its eastern coastal line, China's national goal of "the Great Development of the West" is now in a certain sense carrying on China's past efforts of the "third line construction," which, while spreading wealth, industry, and population to its vast western area, also helps to alleviate the risks posed by concentrated wealth, industry, and population. For another, China's conventional force, although not the most advanced, is the largest in terms of manpower, which would be hard to obliterate or even cripple by battlefield-class nuclear weapons. Long accustomed to and trained to fight in adverse situations, the Chinese army is renowned and respected for being able to withstand great losses and still be operational. These existential factors alone would make a potential aggressor think twice before launching or threatening a nuclear attack on China.

The second major reason for China to rely on deterrence is the so-called defensive nature of China's nuclear strategy. Because China has never considered invading the United States or the Soviet Union/Russia, and has not fought a war on their soil, any major war with the superpowers would be on Chinese soil or nearby. In such a circumstance, China would enjoy the advantage of large territory and population, which would allow it to engage in a protracted "people's war" without using nuclear weapons. With the advent of modern military technology, there is also the possibility that other powers don't plan on invasion and occupation, but instead engage in limited strikes with power-projection forces. Limited strikes, though, simply would not be enough to bring such a vast country as China to its knees. One might ask: if seventy-eight days of air strikes against a small European country like the former Yugoslavia had almost emptied the American inventory of cruise missiles, who could afford the amount of missiles it would require for any power to bring down China?

With the demise of the Soviet Union and the settlement of territorial disputes, China does not consider Russia to be a threat, even though the Russian military, including its strategic force, is still strong. The only target of China's nuclear weapons now and in the future is the United States. Chinese leaders and the general public believe that the dispute over Taiwan or the rise of China may eventually lead to a war or a major military conflict between the United States and China. Thus China has to maintain its nuclear weapons and has to keep its deterrence capability in order to deter the United States from attacking China and to retaliate if deterrence fails.

China understands that its future lies in economic and technological development, and perhaps also in "soft power," but certainly not in military power alone. The war in Iraq has taught the United States, China, and the rest of the world that military power alone, even that of the strongest country, can do little in the twenty-first century. The Chinese national goal is to become an economic superpower and a rich country, not a military superpower. There are speculations that in twenty-five to thirty years, China will become economically stronger and start to shift its preference more to the military side. However, even in that case, taking into consideration China's basic underlying rationale regarding its nuclear weapons, China will not heavily invest in a nuclear arsenal that it considers unusable.

China's Nuclear Strategy and Force Posture: "Minimum Deterrence"?

China has all along adhered to a strategy that may be labeled as minimum deterrence. However, as circumstances are always changing, the content, quantity, quality, and structure of *minimum deterrence* also must change. In the early decades of the twenty-first century, China will continue to adjust certain features of its "minimum deterrence" strategy, even if the label itself does not change.

Since the role of nuclear weapons has been and will continue to be limited and partial, Chinese leaders and strategists believe that the country does not need a large nuclear arsenal comparable to that of the United States or Russia; they adhere to the belief that it is not necessary to be able to destroy the enemy a hundred times if you can destroy it once.

The Chinese government has seldom provided a clear definition of its nuclear strategy, which is a constant source of debate among China scholars. Some even believed China did not have a nuclear strategy and only managed with what it could get technologically (Lin 1988: 46). Most Chinese scholars argue that China has a "minimum deterrence" strategy, and many Western scholars agree (see, e.g., Gill, Mulvenon, and Stokes 2001: 516; Li Bin 2001). Others, however, disagree. Alastair Iain Johnston believes China is transitioning from a "minimal nuclear deterrence" to a "limited nuclear deterrence" strategy (Johnston 1996: 5–42). Lin Chong-Pin argues for a "unique nuclear strategy" derived from China's strategic culture, which does not belong to any Western category, though he believes it is more akin to a war-fighting strategy (Lin 1988: 139–71). Some Chinese scholars reject the terminology of deterrence, believing it connotes aggressiveness, which is unsuitable to describe China's purely defensive nuclear strategy (Goldstein 2000: 120). These arguments deserve more discussion.

Chinese leaders, political and military, have often used the term *deterrence* to describe the *function* of China's nuclear weapons, even if they never clearly state that China's nuclear *strategy* is deterrence. The word *deterrence* appears on numerous occasions in speeches and domestic documents by Chinese military and government leaders. In 1988, "deterrence" first appeared in a Central Military Commission (CMC) document on China's new-era military strategy. In the same year, another document issued by the CMC more specifically called for "an emphasis on the deterrence role of the armed forces," and "fostering deterrence with Chinese characteristics" (Wu 1999: 206). Another sign that the term *deterrence* has been accepted is its wide use by the research and educational institutions attached to the People's Liberation Army (PLA). In recent years, three textbooks sharing the title *Strategic Studies* have been published: one was compiled by the then deputy chairman of China's Military Academy (CMA) General Gao Rui, another by Wang Wenrong of the Strategic Teaching Section of the Chinese National Defense University, and the third was authored collectively by the Strategic Studies Department of the CMA. Major General Peng Guangqian of the CMA Strategic Studies Department also compiled a book titled *Brief Introduction to Military Strategies.* In all of the above-mentioned books, the importance of nuclear deterrence was discussed in great detail.[1] A more comprehensive analysis of China's nuclear deterrence thoughts can be found in *Trends in International Nuclear Strategic Thought,* whose chief editor is Professor Wu Tianfu of the Strategic Teaching Section of the Second Artillery Command Institute of the PLA (Wu 1999: 201–23).

In 1997, President Jiang Zemin set out in a speech a fifty-year, three-step national defense and military modernization plan, which, among other things, called for enhancing the "nuclear deterrence capability" (Central Party School of China's Communist Party 1997). On March 11, 2006, when addressing the Fourth Session of the Tenth National People's Congress, President Hu Jintao told the PLA's delegation that during the forthcoming Eleventh Five-Year Plan, China would realize the first of the three steps set out by Jiang (Sun 2006). Obviously, for these directives to be executed, China has to have a nuclear strategy.

General Jing Zhiyuan, the commander of China's Strategic Forces, and General Peng Xiaofeng, the political commissar of the forces, wrote in June 2006 that the Chinese strategic force is "the central part of our country's strategic deterrence forces" (Jing and Peng 2006: 15). *China's National Defense in 2006* states the country's nuclear strategy as follows:

> China's nuclear strategy is subject to the state's nuclear policy and military strategy. Its fundamental goal is to deter other countries from using or threatening to use nuclear weapons against China. China remains firmly committed to the policy of no first use of nuclear weapons at any time and under any circumstances. It unconditionally undertakes not to use or threaten to use nuclear weapons against nonnuclear-weapon states or nuclear-weapon-free zones, and stands for the comprehensive prohibition and complete elimination of nuclear weapons. China upholds the principles of counter-attack in self-defense and limited development of nuclear weapons, and aims at building a lean and effective nuclear force capable of meeting national security needs. It endeavors to ensure the security and reliability of its nuclear weapons and maintains a credible nuclear deterrent force. China's nuclear force is under the direct command of the Central Military Commission (CMC). China exercises great restraint in developing its nuclear force. It has never entered into and will never enter into a nuclear arms race with any other country. (Information Office of the State Council of the People's Republic of China 2006)

It is clear that China has pursued and is likely to maintain a "minimum deterrence" nuclear strategy. However, it is less clear exactly what "minimum" means and requires. *Minimum* is a relative term, meaning different things to different people; and it means different things to the same people and countries at different times and in different conditions. What is minimum for one country may not be the minimum for others.

Looking at the mission of China's nuclear force and the capability required to fulfill the minimum deterrence strategy, the strategy can be seen as a "large-scale minimum" strategy or a "limited deterrence" strategy. The Chinese "minimum" is not a matter of number, but a matter of capability. And the "minimum deterrence" nuclear strategy is to have and maintain the "minimum capability" to deter stronger powers from using nuclear and large-scale conventional forces against China. And since "minimum deterrence" refers to a capability of deterrence, retaliation, and actual "second strike capability" in any situation and at any time, then the strategy itself must be dynamic. Because the forces and conditions that the strategy deals with are always changing, the strategy itself has to change in some ways all the time.

In 1964, one Chinese nuclear weapon might have been sufficient to serve the purpose of "minimum deterrence." And in the 1990s when there was no missile defense, 200–400 strategic weapons might have been required to serve the goal. But in the early decades of the twenty-first century, as the United States develops and deploys missile defense systems, the current quantity, quality, and structure of China's strategic force may not be sufficient to fulfill the mission of "minimum deterrence." Thus the "minimum" is likely to increase, although it may not reach the level of the strategic forces of the superpowers.

Therefore, the real meaning of the Chinese "minimum deterrence" is the minimum required to deter stronger powers; it is a "minimum" relative to the strategic forces of stronger powers such as the United States and Russia.

Force Posture

A more suitable indicator of minimum nuclear deterrence strategy is force posture and structure. China has maintained a relatively small but diversified nuclear arsenal. According to John Wilson Lewis and Xue Litai, after China embarked upon its nuclear project in 1955, Mao Zedong had said in various speeches that China "should have some nuclear weapons, but . . . less and better nuclear weapons," which not only became the comprehensive guideline for the nuclear program, but also delineated the boundary of China's future nuclear development (Lewis and Xue 1994: 232). Echoing Mao's thoughts, Deng Xiaoping said years later, "We will develop a few more nuclear weapons, but [our nuclear arsenal] will be limited anyway" (Wu 1999: 207).

China has developed strategic nuclear forces made up of land-based missiles, submarine-launched missiles, and bombers. Within this triad, China also has developed weapons of different ranges, capabilities, and survivability (Zhu et al. 2005: 131). According to Avery Goldstein, China maintains its nuclear deterrence with a small but diversified nuclear arsenal because it believes that the nuclear revolution makes it difficult for an adversary to ascertain the strength of China's military forces and the circumstances under which they might be used (Goldstein 2001: 124, 129, 133, 135–36). Among the three legs of China's nuclear triad, by far the strongest is land-based nuclear missiles. The other two legs are relatively less developed and less reliable. China's H-6 aircraft, which formed the core of the strategic bomber fleets, has become obsolete; China's strategic missile submarine has a very long development phase. Although the West believes nuclear missile submarines are the most survivable leg of the nuclear triad, China seems to have less confidence in that and has been slow in developing and manufacturing strategic nuclear missile submarines.

The other evidence of the relatively minimalist nature of China's nuclear strategy is the fact that China has no tactical nuclear weapons. The existence of tactical nuclear weapons is an important indicator of a war-fighting nuclear strategy in which the country is prepared to use nuclear weapons in a deliberate escalation strategy, which in turn requires the deployment of a large quantity of nuclear weapons of all yields and ranges. The allegation that China had tactical nuclear weapons was widespread during the 1980s.[2] However, concrete evidence is lacking, leading scholars to agree that China currently does not have deployed tactical nuclear weapons.[3] Indeed, recent outside assessments of China's nuclear weapons capability, such as *Proliferation: Threat and Response* by the U.S. Defense Intelligence Agency (2001) and *Chinese Military Power* by the U.S. Department of Defense (2000, 2002, 2003, 2004, 2006), do not mention possible Chinese possession of tactical nuclear weapons except for theater ballistic missiles like the CSS-5 (Lewis 2004: 51). To the contrary, *Chinese Military Power* specifically identifies China's short-range ballistic missile (SRBM) force as conventionally armed (U.S. Department of Defense 2005: 29).

Because of the secrecy surrounding its nuclear arsenal, speculations about the size of China's nuclear stockpile vary. A generally accepted estimate is that China has up to 400 weapons (Norris and Kristensen 2003: 77–80). According to a Chinese government fact sheet, however, "among the nuclear-weapon states, China . . . possesses the smallest nuclear arsenal" (Lewis 2005: 52). The statement implies that China possesses fewer than 200 nuclear weapons, the size of the British nuclear arsenal. The limited nature of China's nuclear force is manifest not only in its size, but also in that China could have developed more nuclear weapons but has chosen not to do so. China could have stepped up its nuclear modernization in the 1980s, but chose instead to invest more in its economic development and continue its nuclear modernization at a measured pace (Li Bin 2001). According to one estimate, it even allowed its nuclear weapons stockpile to shrink from about 150 to 70 in the 1980s, illustrating its reserved approach to nuclear weapons (Lewis 2004: 77).

According to Li Bin, China's current nuclear policy is beginning the third stage of its development. In the first stage, from 1964 until 1980, when China acquired the capability of launching intercontinental ballistic missiles (ICBMs), it had only a symbolic or existential nuclear deterrence. In the second stage, from 1980 until now, the Chinese nuclear deterrence has been based on the quantitative ambiguity of its nuclear force. Today Chinese nuclear development is about to enter a third stage, in which China will have credible and visible minimum nuclear deterrence. Li argued that "China will most probably maintain the policy of quantitative ambiguity as a way of protecting its nuclear deterrence until it has built up a survivable nuclear retaliatory force that relies on geographical ambiguity instead" (Li Bin 2003: 52).

Looking at the longer-term trend, China seems willing to maintain its minimum deterrence nuclear strategy and relatively limited force posture required by the strategy. However, the meaning and conditions of both the strategy and the posture are changing. Externally, the United States and others are always changing the quantity and quality of their strategic forces; missile defense is increasingly becoming a reality in the military world; and new members are joining the "nuclear club." Second, internally, China's economic position is becoming stronger, and its technology is more able to contribute to defense modernization. Therefore, although the minimum deterrence strategy label may not change, its form and content are likely to alter. Forty years ago, a nuclear warhead might have been the "minimum" needed for deterrence; now 200 may be needed. And in the future, 300 or 400 may be necessary to maintain a "minimal" capability to serve the purpose of minimum deterrence.

Future Trajectory

There has been considerable debate over China's nuclear future within China's strategic community. One school, citing the security dilemma theory, claims China is heading for an inevitable showdown with the United States, however much China shows its goodwill. Just as the U.S. BMD system is seen as detrimental to China's interests, likewise, the intention of China to increase its own security by strengthening its defense forces will be seen as a challenge to the huge advantage enjoyed by U.S. forces, which will in turn accelerate the U.S. quest for better defensive and offensive weapons. In the end, both countries will pay heavily for the arms race. According to that school, the rule of the game is simple and crude: those who comply will pay heavy costs, but those who fail to comply will drop out of the international order. It is therefore necessary for China to seek a "symmetric deterrence" with the United States, in which China has a credible second-strike capability against the United States. For China to achieve a credible second-strike capability, it is argued that it must have a much larger and technologically improved nuclear arsenal, which should be comparable to that of the United States (see, e.g., Zhang 2002).

The second school, calling for an "asymmetric nuclear deterrence," believes it is best for China to avoid a nuclear arms race with the United States while maintaining minimal nuclear forces. Taking a constructivist or "deterrence optimist" view, they believe security dilemmas mostly arise out of a sense of mutual distrust and suspicion between states. If countries can build confidence among themselves, they can avoid the security dilemma and a consequent arms race. In addition, missile defense systems cost huge sums to develop, but the penetration aids for missiles are much cheaper and easier to achieve. Therefore, in the case of China, their prescription is that China should stick to its minimum deterrence strategy and only upgrade its nuclear arsenal or increase its size modestly, the aim of which is to preserve credible minimum deterrence against nuclear powers or potential nuclear weapon states.[4]

While it may still be too early to predict the trajectory of China's nuclear strategy, there are some indications of its direction. In recent Chinese official publications, including PLA media such as the *PLA Daily,* there have been unprecedented extensive reports on otherwise behind-the-scenes strategic nuclear forces (see, e.g., Gao 2006; Jing and Peng 2006; *Liberation Army Daily* 2006; Wang 2006; Xu 2006). From June through August 2006, a wealth of reports appeared on the achievements of China's nuclear modernization, including the advances made in range, accuracy, command and control, and rapid response capabilities of China's nuclear forces. From these reports, we are able to make an informed guess about China's plans for its nuclear arsenal.

First, China has increased the number of its nuclear weapons. According to recent reports, China's missile engineering units are engaged in extensive construction projects in the mountain areas, the quantity of which over the past four years equals that of the previous thirty years combined. By implication, China has built many missile silos and is building more, suggesting either that it is increasing the number of its nuclear missiles or that it is building more decoy missile bastions.

Second, China's nuclear weapons will be increasingly mobile. According to reports, the mobility of China's nuclear forces has been dramatically improved. The Second Artillery is now both road mobile and rail mobile. In addition, China has enhanced the training of its nuclear forces, enabling them to fight under all weather conditions.

Third, to improve the survivability of its nuclear weapons, China has shortened the time required to prepare for a missile launch to "several times faster than before" (Xu 2006), which has been achieved by adopting new training plans. China has also found ways to actively defend the missile silos. In addition, China has focused on preparation for complex electromagnetic environments. The accuracy of China's nuclear missiles has also been improved substantially, marking a historic leap forward in the operational capability of the strategic nuclear forces.

These reports are a summary of China's nuclear modernization efforts. In revealing these efforts, China hopes to convince observers of the credibility of its nuclear deterrence without actually providing numbers. China seems to imply that its nuclear arsenal is competent, both quantitatively and qualitatively. At the very least, these reports show what the Chinese military believe would be necessary to maintain a credible nuclear deterrence and indicate what steps they have taken or intend to take.

Instead of following a strictly "symmetric deterrence" path or an "asymmetric deterrence" path as defined by Shi Yinhong (2002: 39–44), China is seeking to go somewhere in between. Trying to retain the credibility of its nuclear deterrent in the face of a BMD system, China may increase its nuclear arsenal until it is beyond doubt that it is large enough. China will also try to make its deterrent more credible by improving the accuracy of its missiles. The survivability of its nuclear arsenal will also be improved by high mobility, active defense, and shortened launch time.

BMD Countermeasures

The Chinese media have also openly discussed possible countermeasures against the U.S. missile defense system. One newspaper article published in 2001 listed ten technical methods of penetrating the nuclear missile defense (NMD) system (Chang 2001). Approximately two months later, after the reported successful fourth test of the NMD system, another *PLA Daily* article reported seven "new breakthroughs" in countermeasures (Zhou, Dong, and Zhao 2001). Indeed, according to one report, China has already enhanced the prelaunch survivability of its nuclear weapons by "shifting to solid propellants; improving C4ISR (command, control, communications, computers, intelligence, surveillance, and reconnaissance); using camouflaged, hardened silos; and developing road-, rail-, and barge-mobile ICBMs. Possible sub-elements of this process could include increasing missile accuracy, developing a robust submarine-launched second strike, and even ultimately replacing Russia as the 'second nuclear power'" (Erickson 2005: 77). In addition, to increase survivability, China's strategic triad will lean more toward the development of surface-launched ballistic missiles (SLBMs) and land-mobile ICBMs. In particular, China is rapidly improving its submarine force, which will allow it both to better control its vast maritime periphery and to create a more effective platform for nuclear deterrence (Erickson 2005: 77).

Postlaunch countermeasures, which include counterintercept measures and penetration aids, can be combined to increase their effectiveness. In addition, China has mastered the cold-launch technique, which slightly delays detection of a launch and thereby reduces the time available to the boost-phase BMD systems to launch an interceptor.[5] Chinese testing and modeling indicate that the trajectory of the DF-31 could be reduced from 330 miles to 60 miles (Stokes 2002: 133), which would increase reentry speed. Infrared stealth, on the other hand, "can be implemented by several means, such as using low emissivity coatings or a cooled shroud" (He and Qiu 2003), while fast-burning motors shorten the duration of the boost phase. The huge size of China also makes it extremely difficult for a boost-phase intercept system to defend against missiles launched "because of the difficulty of getting American interceptor platforms close enough to launch sites in the interiors of these large continental powers" (Sessler et al. 2000: xxi).

Increasing the size of China's nuclear arsenal, though not as openly exalted as the former option, is certainly on the agenda. According to Li Bin:

> Although the costs could be large, the buildup option cannot be ruled out. The reason for this is that the buildup option is so mathematically simple to understand and so certain to work. So, in the Chinese debate this idea would easily win some support from nontechnical people. Another advantage is that the buildup would be visible to the outside and would therefore help discourage any first strike against China. (2001: 9)

A Chinese missile buildup would facilitate, among other things, wartime launch of strikes incorporating various types of missiles in synchronized launches from a wide range of azimuths in order to supress active missile defenses and associated battle management systems.

The unclassified version of the U.S. National Intelligence Council's December 2001 report estimates that "Chinese ballistic missile forces will increase several-fold by 2015" and that by that year "Beijing's . . . ICBM force deployed primarily against the United States . . . will number around 75 to 100 warheads" (National Intelligence Council 2001). Chinese scholar Shen Dingli, on the other hand, projects that "a nine-fold increase in Chinese ICBMs capable of hitting U.S. targets would defeat even a BMD system with a 90 percent interception rate, and at the manageable cost of several billion dollars over one or two decades" (Urayama 2004). It has also been suggested that China make the size of its nuclear arsenal proportionate to the projected size of the U.S. missile defense (see, e.g., Li 2001; Manning, Montaperto, and Roberts 2000; Saunders and Yuan 2000; Tompkins 2003).

As China's military develops and becomes stronger, it would increase its nuclear force quantitatively and qualitatively. However, because of its "minimum deterrence" strategy, the Chinese do not want to vastly increase the number of nuclear weapons. They seem certain that having a reliable "second strike" capability is good enough to retaliate against a superpower's first-strike attack.

NFU: Real or Not?

A key and unique element of China's nuclear doctrine has been its NFU policy. Since its first nuclear test in 1964, China has undertaken to "never at any time or under any circumstances be the first to use nuclear weapons." This pledge has been reiterated and sustained over time and later expanded to include a positive security assurance and a negative security assurance to the states that do not possess nuclear weapons.[6]

That China pledged not to be the first to use nuclear weapons when it first came into possession of them can be understood from various angles. First, as described earlier in this chapter, the Chinese leadership decided that nuclear weapons would not be used; rather, they are tokens of major power and weapons of last resort. Second, first use of China's nascent nuclear capability was not credible and would only invite much greater retaliation (see, e.g., Chen et al. 1969: 167). Third, China has ample confidence in its conventional forces. Back in the 1950s, China had fought against the United States in Korea and did not lose the war. China's conventional capability was further reinforced by a military strategy stressing a People's War, which would immerse the adversary in a sea of people's mass resistance. Fighting a stronger adversary on Chinese territory as its scenario, this military strategy contemplates the reliance on the organization of China's huge population and leaves the inferiority of weapons as a secondary consideration.

However, especially in recent years with the deterioration of relations across the Taiwan Strait, this pledge has often been eyed with suspicion. Two anecdotes are illustrative and deserve close examination.

First, as reported in the *Washington Post* in 1998 (Gellman 1998), Ambassador Chas Freeman told National Security Adviser Anthony Lake in January 1996 that a Chinese senior official had made implicit nuclear threats to trade Los Angeles for Taiwan. The newspaper also reported that Freeman's interlocutor had been Lieutenant-General Xiong Guangkai, deputy chief of the general staff of the Chinese military. The news made headlines and spread and has been cited numerous times as evidence of a "China threat."

What was not cited, though, was Freeman's personal clarification of the origin and the true meaning of the famous "Los Angeles" quote on April 30, 1999. According to Freeman, the statement had come out "in garbled form" in the report. "It was made toward the end of a five-hour argument in October 1995, over what the probable effect would be of the military maneuvers the CMC had authorized in the Taiwan Straits . . . It was the position of the Chinese military officers . . . that there would be no American military reaction. At the end of the very heated argument, one of them said, 'And finally, you do not have the strategic leverage that you had in the 1950's when you threatened nuclear strikes on us. You were able to do that because we could not hit back then. But if you hit us now, we can hit back. So you will not make those threats. In the end you care more about Los Angeles than you do about Taipei.'" Freeman emphatically pointed out that "the statement is in a deterrent context and it is consistent with no first use. It is not a threat to bomb Los Angeles" (Cirincione 2001). In addition, Freeman never named Lieutenant-General Xiong as the Chinese official.

Second, and to make matters worse, in 2005, Major-General Zhu Chenghu, the dean of the Defense College at China's National Defense University, was reported to again tread on sensitive nerves over the possibility of a nuclear exchange between China and the United States. The *Financial Times* reported on July 14, 2005 that Zhu claimed "China is prepared to use nuclear weapons against the U.S. if it is attacked by Washington during a confrontation over Taiwan. We . . . will prepare ourselves for the destruction of all of the cities east of Xian. Of course the

Americans will have to be prepared that hundreds . . . of cities will be destroyed by the Chinese" (Alden 2005).

The report attracted much attention, having appeared during the sensitive weeks before the Pentagon released its annual Chinese Military Power report to the U.S. Congress. It also attracted much interest because it contradicted China's proclaimed NFU nuclear policy. U.S. Department of State spokesperson Sean McCormack called these remarks "highly irresponsible" and expressed the hope that they did not represent the views of the Chinese leadership.[7] Though the same news story recorded toward the end of the report Zhu's disclaimer that "his views did not represent official Chinese policy and he did not anticipate war with the U.S.,"[8] and Chinese Foreign Minister Li Zhaoxing specifically clarified China's continued commitment to its NFU nuclear stance,[9] skepticism hovers over China's NFU policy.[10]

Of these two anecdotes, the first is a result of miscommunication, while the latter ostensibly only reflects the personal opinion of a scholar in uniform. However, it is suspected that these incidents were not purely accidental and may reflect the PLA's thinking and planning.[11] The question arises as to how committed China is to its NFU nuclear policy, which might merit from a brief analysis.

Even without these incidents, China's NFU policy has been under much suspicion. Many Americans believe that NFU is highly symbolic, lacks real substance, is not verifiable, and can easily be changed (Pollack 1995: 159). According to this logic, when faced with adverse situations or a crisis in which the strategic gains of breaking the NFU pledge are higher than abiding by it, China will have an incentive to break its promise.

A more in-depth analysis shows that the only plausible scenario that would cause China to abandon its NFU policy is a showdown with the United States over Taiwan. The two parties have clear knowledge of each other's nuclear forces; therefore, how the scenario evolves will depend on how each views the other's will and intention, as well as the interplay of factors such as strategic reality, international norms, and recent history.

To date, the United States has remained somewhat ambiguous about whether it will rush to Taiwan's aid in the event of a war, emphasizing its interest in preserving the status quo and warning of a unilateral change of situation on either side of the Taiwan Strait.[12] The aim of Beijing in the game between China and the United States over the Taiwan issue has been to deter the United States from military interference in China's internal affairs, and the best way to achieve this aim is to make full preparations for an armed conflict. Therefore, to make China's war efforts credible, China has kept the modernization of its conventional forces going at a fast pace, focusing on improving and acquiring weapon systems that will allow it to gain a decisive conventional advantage over Taiwan forces and to pose a credible threat to U.S. forces in a standoff over Taiwan. Allegedly, the number of SRBMs deployed by the PLA against Taiwan, with current estimates at over 700, is growing at a rate of 100 annually (Lieggi 2005). China has also increased its focus on improving its fighter aircraft and antiship weapons. In addition, China's naval assets are an important part of the military modernization—with military plans to improve its submarine fleet and acquire and deploy Russian-made destroyers. China's military analysts have also been searching for innovative ways of conducting asymmetric warfare (see Qiao and Wang 1999). These combined efforts and the PLA war preparation supported by successive yearly increases in defense spending of about 15 percent since the mid-1990s, will soon be sufficient to induce caution in the United States before it interferes with China's reunification.

In the meantime, it is undeniable that the conventional buildup falls into the category of deterrence by denial, which could be escalation prone. Logically, as both sides try to gain the upper hand and deter the other side, a dangerous arms race will be initiated, increasing the risks of an unintended escalation of crisis. China is clear-eyed about the unprecedented superiority of the U.S. military capabilities and the U.S. inclination to make preemptive attacks (Cui 2004). The Bush administration's report *The National Security Strategy of the United States of America* in 2002 made explicit that the United States has adopted a policy of preemption, stating that the United States must act against emerging threats "before they are fully formed" (White House 2002: 2). Considering the great uncertainty regarding the scenario of a Taiwan Strait war, China's adherence to the NFU nuclear policy seems to be a safeguard against a sharp escalation into nuclear exchange between China and the United States. Indeed, if China gave up its NFU policy, instead of buying strategic advantage, the risk of a preemptive U.S. attack would dramatically increase; by retaining it, China's nuclear weapons will play their deterrent role more fully.

Hard evidence of China's seriousness about NFU was provided by the border disputes with the Soviet Union in 1969 and the early 1970s. Though those large-scale and costly military disputes were highly dangerous, China did not consider using nuclear weapons first to deter a large Soviet invasion.

China's Nuclear Arms Control, Disarmament, and Nonproliferation Policies

China's position and action toward arms control, disarmament, and especially nonproliferation have changed dramatically since the mid-1990s. China, in the words of Americans and others, has shifted from being "part of the problem" to "part of the solution." The year 2006 saw China becoming a force in the global efforts against the proliferation of weapons of mass destruction (WMD), such as in North Korea and Iran. Looking into the future, as long as China continues to be an integral part of global economic and security systems, and as long as its relations with the United States and other Western countries are normal, it will remain committed to the global nonproliferation regime.

Consistent with its general judgment that nuclear weapons should not be used, China committed itself to complete prohibition and thorough destruction of nuclear weapons even before it came into possession of nuclear weapons. Its stance on arms control, disarmament, and nonproliferation, however, has undergone dramatic changes over the decades.

From 1949 to the late 1970s, driven by a desire to gain international prestige and overcome its "hundred years of humiliation," China was adamant about its national security choices and generally stood outside of international institutions. During that period, China's relations with the two superpowers were also in turmoil, fostering a besieged mind-set among Chinese leaders. Suspicion and distrust of international arms control regimes led China to denounce the 1963 Treaty Banning Nuclear Weapon Tests in the Atmosphere, in Outer Space and Under Water on the ground that it was discriminatory and with the purpose of securing the monopoly of the superpowers over nuclear weapons. China had accompanied its first nuclear test with a renewed call for a world summit conference on radical nuclear disarmament, which was disregarded. During those years, as a revisionist power, China refused to be bound by the international regime, while trying to pursue its own agenda in nuclear weapon development. Significantly, even the 1968 nuclear Non-Proliferation Treaty (NPT), which acknowledged China's legitimate status as a nuclear weapon state, was rejected on the grounds that it discriminated against mononuclear states. In the meantime, China had been proactive in the promotion of nonnuclear zones (Li 2001: 60–63).

During the years from 1980 through 1990, China entered into partial cooperation with and participation in the international nuclear arms control regime, but it never fully joined the regime or implemented international treaties and regulations on nonproliferation. In fact, the starting point can be traced to 1978, when China joined the U.N. Special Disarmament Convention (Pan 1996: 419). By 1980, China had begun talking about its opposition to nuclear proliferation (*Compilation of Conference Documents of Chinese Delegation to the United Nations [1980.1–6]* 1981: 239). In 1984, Prime Minister Zhao Ziyang said when addressing the National People's Congress that "though China did not join in the discriminatory Nuclear Nonproliferation Treaty, it does not promote, pursue, or help other countries with their nuclear weapons program" ("Government Performance Report" 1984). During these years, China had retrieved its U.N. Security Council permanent membership and gradually joined the mainstream international community. Its domestic politics had regained stability after the turmoil of the radical leftist fervor of the late 1960s and early 1970s, contributing to its self-identification as a supporter of the status quo.

Since 1991, China has slowly and gradually embraced the international nuclear arms control regime. Its participation in the existing regimes coincides with the end of the Cold War, which signaled the end of the bipolar strategic structure. The first several years of the last decade of the twentieth century was also an era of breakthroughs in international arms control and disarmament, with the United States and Russia engaging in deep cuts of deployed strategic nuclear weapons. Encouraged by these positive developments in the international situation, China envisioned the advent of a multilateral world in which China would be an indispensable party. It was during this period that China began allowing its foreign policy mission to have an impact on its nuclear weapons. Indeed, China's participation in almost all of the international institutions and its conformity to international norms have sometimes come at the expense of China's nuclear capabilities (Johnston 2003: 12–25). In March 1992, the Chinese government signed the NPT. Since then, China has joined a series of international arms control regimes, including the Comprehensive Test Ban Treaty (CTBT) and the Nuclear Suppliers Group, and has also willingly complied with the requirements of the Missile Technology Control Regime (Information Office of the State Council of the People's Republic of China 2005). And since the middle of the 1990s, China has taken a more serious approach to nonproliferation.

Recent years have seen multiple setbacks for the international arms control and nonproliferation regimes. The United States, fueled with a unilateralist thrust, has abandoned the Anti-Ballistic Missile (ABM) Treaty. It also declined to ratify the CTBT and began the deployment of a U.S. BMD system and renewed its interest in new earth-penetration nuclear bombs (Pincus 2001). On the other hand, there have been additions to the number of nuclear states, the most noteworthy of which are India, Pakistan, North Korea, and perhaps Iran, spreading seeds of further nuclear proliferation. To Chinese nonproliferation experts, the most recent blow to the arms control regime is the nuclear technology-sharing agreement between India and the United States (the Global Security Network 2006), which sets a negative example for the proliferators and exhibits a U.S. double standard on nuclear proliferation, which is detrimental to the viability of the regime. The North Korea and Iran nuclear crises are other hot issues that threaten the nuclear nonproliferation regime.

China's participation in global arms control and nonproliferation regimes is the primary constraint on Chinese nuclear behavior. China has taken a generally active position on nuclear arms control since the 1990s and now supports most international nuclear arms control regimes. If China wants to engage in a large-scale nuclear expansion quantitatively or qualitatively, it will first have to free itself from various arms control commitments. The CTBT forbids signatory countries to conduct nuclear tests. In 1996, China signed the CTBT and has since stopped nuclear tests. Even after the U.S. Congress refused to ratify it in 2004 and caused considerable concern in international society, China showed consistent support for this regime. As such it cannot possibly start to design new nuclear weapons according to theories different from what it has already mastered. In addition, China has in principle agreed to hold talks on the Fissile Material Cutoff Treaty (FMCT), which would limit its capacity to produce more fissile material. This treaty, if agreed to, would severely constrain China's capacity to produce more nuclear weapons. Even before the negotiation of FMCT, China has kept a moratorium on fissile material production since 1990. That China is willing to commit itself to these treaties, even in the face of the United States backing out of the ABM Treaty and abandoning the CTBT, as well as the Indian and Pakistani nuclear tests, has significant implications. By taking this stance within the present context, China shows its willingness to take risks in national security in order to help ease the nuclear arms race and hence the possibility of a nuclear disaster. In the meantime, its plutonium in storage is estimated to be one to three tons (Wright et al. 1996), which, even if China decides to turn all the stored fissile material into nuclear weapons, translates into an additional 200 to 600 nuclear weapons at most.

In these early years of the twenty-first century, China has taken a more active stance on nonproliferation and is becoming a major player in the regional and global nonproliferation regime. China advocates nuclear arms control, disarmament, and a nonproliferation regime; it believes in diplomatic solutions to the nuclear crises in North Korea and Iran; and it maintains a responsible position to nuclear weapons by itself. The Chinese position is a corollary of its strategic security calculation. A rapidly developing China is seeking to minimize the skepticism and unease with which the established powers and its neighbors view it. It is therefore in China's interest to defend international norms and to practice multilateralism. In addition, China has come to understand the reality of its security environment. Chinese scholars have realized that China is already surrounded by legitimate and unrecognized nuclear states, including Russia, the United States, India, Pakistan, and North Korea.[13] Japan, which does not have nuclear weapons but does have a large plutonium stockpile and the necessary technology and industrial capability, is also a latent nuclear power. Iran, though not a direct neighbor, is in its near vicinity. With the complicated relations and instabilities among these countries with diverse interests, this region poses the world's biggest nuclear risk. Nuclear proliferation is obviously not in China's interest, nor is sharp confrontation. This explains China's active attitude toward the North Korean and Iranian nuclear crises. China has organized and hosted five rounds of the Six-Party Talks and will continue to provide diplomatic channels for the peaceful solution of the North Korean nuclear issue. Iran's case is no less complicated, since the Middle East region harbors the world's largest known oil reserve. China's rapidly developing economy hungers for petroleum, whose price hinges on the stability of the region, which partly explains China's stance on the issue. Therefore, China's action in implementing U.N. sanctions against North Korea and Iran will continue to be a key and at the same time a difficult part of international negotiations over nonproliferation.

Conclusion

China is on the road to becoming a much more powerful state, if not a comprehensive superpower, in the early decades of the twenty-first century. At the same time, its major goal of national reunification is under increasing challenge from the Taiwanese secessionists, which could lead to a grave crisis involving an armed confrontation with the United States. Torn between conflicting demands, China sees its nuclear deterrent forces as a long-lasting important strategic stabilizer to deter attack from stronger powers.

Under the pressure of U.S. BMD systems, China is seeking to maintain the deterrent value of its nuclear weapons by modernizing and enlarging its nuclear arsenal. Its current efforts, which remain primarily focused on improving the survivability and mobility of existing strategic nuclear forces, can be satisfactorily explained by a desire to develop and maintain a "credible" minimum nuclear deterrent force by 2010 (see Saunders 2005; Saunders and Yuan 2000). Indeed, even today China may have only around 200 nuclear weapons. A more aggressive nuclear strategy certainly would not have allowed this to happen. There is no evidence that China is seeking a change from its "minimum deterrence" strategy to a "limited nuclear deterrence" strategy.

China is changing and rising. At the same time China's nuclear force, strategy, and doctrine are relatively stable or changing within a larger stable framework. China will continue to increase the quality and quantity of its nuclear and strategic forces, but gradually rather than dramatically.

One of the biggest challenges to China and all of Asia is the long-term goal, size, and strategic intention of the Chinese military modernization, including its strategic force. There is uncertainty about the role of China's nuclear force in the country's foreign and security policies over the longer term. If China continues to focus on economic and internal development, then its leadership and people will spend less energy dealing with the outside world. But if China's focus is instead on achieving greater world power and on pride and "responsibility," or "nationalism," then China will find that it needs more nuclear weapons and other strategic forces. And if China's strategy is to challenge the United States and seek a greater international role, or if the United States adopts a comprehensive containment strategy toward China, then the country is likely to use those strategic forces to serve these purposes. Currently there is no indication that China will go in that direction, but the possibility cannot be ruled out in the longer-term future of the twenty-first century.

If China modernizes its strategic military forces gradually, it will not change the balance of power and stability in Asia, although it will still cause concern among the other great powers. But if China increases its military forces dramatically over the short term, that would change the balance of power and stability in Asia and cause a dramatic response from other powers. In any case, China and its military modernization is a dynamic factor in twenty-first-century Asia. Any act of military modernization will be watched carefully by other countries and have a great impact on regional peace and security. Therefore, China has an ongoing challenge in the twenty-first century to settle on the goals and mission of its military modernization and to make them transparent to other countries in Asia and the rest of the world.

If China "rises peacefully," with a limited, modest, and reasonable defensive strategic force and strategy, then it will be a stabilizing factor to other countries. But if China does not rise peacefully, engages in large-scale military modernization, becomes a super military and nuclear power, and adopts an aggressive military and foreign strategy, it will alarm the other nations of the world and perhaps lead to an arms race, a new cold war, confrontation, and instability. Therefore, for the peace and development of China and other countries in Asia and in the world, it is important for China to "rise peacefully" in its defense modernization process and in its foreign strategy and relations. If that happens, the twenty-first century might be both an "Asian century" and a peaceful century.

Notes

1. China's Military Academy (1987: 94–95, 114–15); Peng and Wang (1989: 168–69); Wang Wenrong (1999: 357–58) Strategic Studies Department of China's Military Academy (1999: 230, 234).

2. See, for example, Lin (1988: 95-131). His argument that China had tactical nuclear weapons, however, seemed to rely on circumstantial evidence.

3. Defense Intelligence Agency and Army Foreign Science and Technology Center, *A Guide to Foreign Tactical Nuclear Weapon Systems under the Control of Ground Force Commanders*, DST-1040S-541-87 (September 1987), p. 79; Lewis (2004: 49–51).

4. Arguments in this vein may be found in Shi (2002).

5. It has been reported that China cold-launched the JL-1 solid-propellant SLBM and that China conducted a cold-launch test on the new DF-31 ICBM in December 1998. Available at http://www.globalsecurity.org/wmd/world/china/jl-1.htm and http://www.globalsecurity.org/wmd/world/china/df-31.htm.

6. See, for example, white papers on China's national defense released by Information Office of the State Council of the People's Republic of China, namely, *China's National Defense in 2000, 2002, 2004*, as well as the white paper *China's Contribution to Nuclear Disarmament* issued by the Ministry of Foreign Affairs, People's Republic of China on July 29, 1996.

7. Sean McCormack, "State Department Daily Press Briefing," July 15, 2005. Available at http://www.state.gov/r/pa/prs/dpb/2005/49692.htm.

8. Alexandra Harney et al., "Top Chinese General Warns U.S. over Attack," *Financial Times*, July 14, 2005. Available at http://news.ft.com/cms/s/28cfe55a-f4a7-11d9-9dd1-00000e2511c8.html; "PLA General Zhu Chenghu Claims Nuclear Remarks 'Quoted out of Context,'" *Hong Kong Ta Kung Pao*, July 17, 2005.

9. "Foreign Minister Says China's 'No First Use' Nuclear Stance Unchanged," *BBC Monitoring International Reports*, July 21, 2005.

10. Danny Gittings, "General Zhu Goes Ballistic," *Wall Street Journal*, July 18, 2005, p. 13; Lieggi (2005).

11. Max Boot, "China's Stealth War on the U.S.," *Los Angeles Times*, July 20, 2005; "HK Paper: PLA General's Remarks on Using Nuclear Weapons Shows PLA's Bottom-Line," *Hong Kong Sing Tao Jih Pao*, July 20, 2005; John Tkacik, "U.S. State Department Condemns Threats by PLA General Zhu Chenghu," *Taipei Times*, July 17, 2005; "PRC Scholar: Zhu Chenghu Remarks Represent View of Most Chinese," *Hong Kong Hsin Pao* (Hong Kong Economic Journal), July 16, 2005; "Beijing Scholar Says PLA General's Nuke Remarks Represent PLA Stand," *Hong Kong Ming Pao*, July 16, 2005; Danny Gittings, "General Zhu Goes Ballistic."

12. See, for example, a press briefing by Scott McClellan, the White House press secretary, on February 27, 2006. Available at http://www.whitehouse.gov/news/releases/2006/02/20060227-1.html.

13. *Liaowang Oriental Weekly Online*, "PLA Officers and Arms Control Experts Discuss China's Nuclear Policy for the New Era," August 9, 2005.

References

Alden, Edward. 2005. "Top Chinese general warns US over attack," *Financial Times*, July 14. Available at http://news.ft.com/cms/s/28cfe55a-f4a7-11d9-9dd1-00000e2511c8.html.

Central Party School of China's Communist Party. 1999. *Compilation of Five Contemporary Manuscripts*. Available at http://qpdx.vicp.net/wgdd/d9.htm.

Chang, Tian. 2001. "Many Ways to penetrate NMD," *National Defense Newspaper*. May 15, p. 8.

Chen Yi, Ye Jianying, Xu Xiangqian, and Nie Rongzhen. 1969. *Report to the Central Committee: A Preliminary Evaluation of the War Situation* (July 11). In Chen Jian and David L. Wilson, trans., 1996, "All under the Heaven Is Great Chaos: Beijing, the Sino-Soviet Border Clashes, and the Turn toward Sino-American Rapprochement, 1968–69, *Cold War International History Project Bulletin* 11: 166–68.

China's Military Academy, ed. 1987. *Strategic Studies*. Beijing: Military Sciences Press.

Cirincione, Joseph. 2001. "Did China Threaten to Bomb Los Angeles?" *Carnegie Proliferation Brief* 4(4). Available at http://www.carnegieendowment.org/publications/index.cfm?fa=view&id=651.

Compilation of Conference Documents of Chinese Delegation to the United Nations (1980.1–6). 1981. Beijing: World Knowledge Press.

Cui Zhiyuan. 2004. "The Western Humanistic Tradition: Neoconservatism and the Bush Principle." *Journal of SJTU (Philosophy and Social Sciences)* 12 (1): 5–10.

Erickson, Andrew S. 2005. "China's BMD Countermeasures: Breaching America's Great Wall in Space?" In *China's Nuclear Force Modernization,* ed. Lyle J. Goldstein and Andrew S. Erickson, pp. 65–91. Newport, R.I.: Naval War College Press.

Gao, Zhiwen. 2006. "Engineering Units in Second Artillery Have Accomplished Workload in Recent 4 Years the Amount of the Past 30 Years Combined." *Liberation Army Daily,* July 9. Available at http://jczs.news.sina.com.cn/2006-07-09/0721382334.html.

Gellman, Barton. 1998. "U.S. and China Nearly Came to Blows in 1996." *Washington Post,* June 21, p. A1.

Gill, Bates, James Mulvenon, and Mark Stokes. 2001. "The Chinese Second Artillery Corps: Transition to Credible Deterrence." In *The People's Liberation Army as an Organization,* ed. James C. Mulvenon and Andrew N. D. Yang, Reference Volume 1.0, pp. 510–86. Santa Monica, Calif.: Rand.

Global Security Network. 2006. "U.S, India Continue Work on Nuclear Agreement." February 27. Available at http://actnow.saferworld.org/ctt.asp?u=4124394&l=117842.

Goldstein, Avery. 2000. *Deterrence and Security in the 21st Century.* Stanford, Calif.: Stanford University Press.

"Government Performance Report (on the Second Session of the Sixth National People's Congress, May 15, 1984)." 1984. *People's Daily Online.* Available at http://www.people.com.cn/zgrdxw/zlk/rd/6jie/newfiles/b1090.html.

He Yingbo, and Qiu Yong. 2003. "THAAD-Like High Altitude Theater Missile Defense: Strategic Defense Capability and Certain Countermeasures Analysis." *Science and Global Security* 11 (2–3): 151–202.

Information Office of the State Council of the People's Republic of China. 2005. China's Endeavors for Arms Control, Disarmament and Non-Proliferation. *China Daily Online.* Available at http://www.chinadaily.com.cn/english/doc/2005-09/01/content_474248.htm.

———. 2006. "China's National Defense in 2006." *China Daily,* December 29.

Jing Zhiyuan, and Peng Xiaofeng. 2006. "Faithfully Fulfilling the Historical Role of the Strategic Missile Forces—In Commemoration of the 40th Anniversary of the Second Artillery." *Qiu Shi Magazine* 12: 14–16.

Johnston, Alastair Iain. 1995. "China's New 'Old Thinking': The Concept of Limited Deterrence," *International Security,* 20(3): 5–42.

———. 2003. "Is China a Status Quo Power?" *International Security* 27 (4): 5–56.

Lewis, Jeffrey. 2004. "The Minimum Means of Reprisal: China's Search for Security in the Nuclear Age." PhD diss., University of Maryland.

———. 2005. "The Ambiguous Arsenal." *Bulletin of the Atomic Scientists* 61 (3): 52–59.

Lewis, John Wilson, and Xue Litai. 1994. *China's Strategic Seapower.* Stanford, Calif.: Stanford University Press.

Liberation Army Daily. 2006. "The Launch Time for Multiple Types of Missiles in Second Artillery Has Been Considerably Shortened." August 24. Available at http://jczs.news.sina.com.cn/2006-08-24/0916392518.html.

Li Bin. 2001. "The Impact of U.S. NMD on Chinese Nuclear Modernization." Available at http://www.pugwash.org/.

———. 2003. "China and Nuclear Transparency." In *Transparency in Nuclear Warheads and Materials: The Political and Technical Dimensions,* ed. Nicholas Zarimpas, pp. 50–57. Oxford: Oxford University Press.

Li, Shaojun. 2001. "China and Nuclear Nonproliferation Regime." *World Economy and Politics* 10: 60–63.

Lieggi, Stephanie. 2005. "Going beyond the Stir: The Strategic Realities of China's No-First-Use Policy." Monterey Institute of International Studies. Available at http://www.nti.org/e_research/e3_70.html#fn2.

Lin, Chong-Pin. 1988. *China's Nuclear Weapons Strategy: Tradition within Evolution*. Lexington, Mass.: Lexington Books.

Manning, Robert A., Ronald Montaperto, and Brad Roberts. 2000. *China, Nuclear Weapons, and Arms Control: A Preliminary Assessment*. New York: Council on Foreign Relations.

McCormack, Sean. 2005. State Department Daily Press Briefing. Available at http://www.state.gov/r/pa/prs/dpb/2005/49692.htm.

Ministry of Foreign Affairs of the People's Republic of China. 1996. *China's Contribution to Nuclear Disarmament*. Available at http://www.china.org.cn/e-caijun/e-caijun.htm.

National Intelligence Council. 2001. Foreign Missile Developments and the Ballistic Missile Threat through 2015. Available at www.cia.gov/nic/PDF_GIF_otherprod/missilethreat2001.pdf.

Norris, Robert S., and Hans M. Kristensen. 2003. "Chinese Nuclear Forces." *Bulletin of the Atomic Scientists* 59 (6): 77–80.

Pan Zhenqiang, ed. 1996. *International Disarmament and Arms Control*. Beijing: National Defense University Press.

Peng Guangqian and Wang Guangxu, eds. 1989. *Brief Introduction to Military Strategies*. Beijing: PLA Press.

Pincus, Walter. 2001. "U.S. Studies Developing New Nuclear Bomb." *Washington Post*, April 15. Avalable at http://www.commondreams.org/headlines01/0415-04.htm.

Pollack, Jonathan D. 1995. The Future of China's Nuclear Weapons Policy. In *Strategic Views from the Second Tier: The Nuclear Weapons Policies of France, Britain, and China*, ed. John C. Hopkins and Weixing Hu, pp. 157–65. New Brunswick, N.J.: Transaction.

Qiao, Liang, and Wang Xianghui. 1999. *War with No Limits: Scenario of War and War-Planning in the Globalized Era by Two Air Force Senior Colonels*. Beijing: PLA Arts Press.

Saunders, Phillip. 2005. *China's Strategic Force Modernization*. Available at http://www.ndu.edu/inss/Repository/INSS_Proceedings/Chinese_Military_Seminar_jan05/China_Force_Mod_Saunders_012005.pdf.

Saunders, Philip, and Jing-dong Yuan. 2000. "China's Strategic Force Modernization: Issues and Implications for the United States." In *Proliferation Challenges and Nonproliferation Opportunities for New Administrations*, ed. Michael Barletta. Occasional Paper 4, pp. 40–46. Monterey, Calif.: Center for Nonproliferation Studies, Monterey Institute of International Studies.

Sessler, Andrew M., et al. 2000. *Countermeasures: A Technical Evaluation of the Operational Effectiveness of the Planned U.S. National Missile Defense System*. Cambridge, Mass.: Union of Concerned Scientists and MIT Security Studies Program.

Shi, Yinhong. 2002. "The U.S. National Defense System and China's Response." *Pacific Journal* 4: 39–44.

Stokes, Mark A. 2002. "Chinese Ballistic Missile Forces in the Age of Global Missile Defense: Challenges and Responses. In *China's Growing Military Power: Perspectives on*

Security, Ballistic Missiles, and Conventional Capabilities, ed. Andrew Scobell and Larry M. Wortzel, pp. 107–67. Carlisle, Penn.: Strategic Studies Institute.

Strategic Studies Department of China's Military Academy, ed. 1999. *Strategic Studies.* Beijing: Military Sciences Press.

Su, Yu. 1950. "Major and Minor Battlefields and Modern Warfare." In *Selected Writings of Su Yu (1949.10–1984.1),* ed. Editing Panel for Selected Writings of Su Yu, p. 59. Beijing: Military Sciences Press.

Sun, Chongfeng. 2006. "Hu Jintao: Recognize the International Strategic Situation & Speed Up Military Preparation." Sina News Center. Available at http://news.sina.com.cn/c/2006-03-11/20159326423.shtml.

Tkacik, John. 2005. "U.S. State Department Condemns Threats by PLA General Zhu Chenghu." *Taipei Times,* July 17.

Tompkins, Joanne. 2003. "How U.S. Strategic Policy Is Changing China's Nuclear Plans." *Arms Control Today* 33 (1): 11–15.

Urayama, Kori. 2004. "China Debates Missile Defense." *Survival* 46 (2): 123–42.

U.S. Department of Defense. 2000. *Chinese Military Power.* Annual Report on the Military Power of the People's Republic of China, Report to Congress Pursuant to the FY2000 National Defense Authorization Act. Washington, D.C.: Department of Defense.

———. 2002. *Chinese Military Power.* Annual Report on the Military Power of the People's Republic of China, Report to Congress Pursuant to the FY2000 National Defense Authorization Act. Washington, D.C.: Department of Defense.

———. 2003. *Chinese Military Power.* Annual Report on the Military Power of the People's Republic of China, Report to Congress Pursuant to the FY2000 National Defense Authorization Act. Washington, D.C.: Department of Defense.

———. 2004. *Chinese Military Power.* Annual Report on the Military Power of the People's Republic of China, Report to Congress Pursuant to the FY2000 National Defense Authorization Act. Washington, D.C.: Department of Defense.

———. 2005. *Chinese Military Power.* Annual Report on the Military Power of the People's Republic Of China, Report to Congress Pursuant to the FY2000 National Defense Authorization Act. Washington, D.C.: Department of Defense.

———. 2006. *Chinese Military Power.* Annual Report on the Military Power of the People's Republic of China, Report to Congress Pursuant to the FY2000 National Defense Authorization Act. Washington, D.C.: Department of Defense.

Wang Wenrong, ed. 1999. *Strategic Studies.* Beijing: National Defense University Press.

Wang, Yongxiao. 2006. "Drastic Changes in the Shape of New PLA Nuclear Missiles, Making It Capable of Strategic Counterattack under All Weather Conditions." *China News Week* July 19. Available at http://mil.news.sohu.com/20060719/n244329697.shtml.

White House. 2002. *The National Security Strategy of the United States of America.* Washington, D.C.

Wright, David et al. 1996. "Estimating China's Stockpile of Fissile Materials for Weapons." Draft, Union of Concerned Scientists Technical Working Paper. Washington, D.C. (April 1996).

Wu, Tianfu, ed. 1999. *Trends in International Nuclear Strategic Thought.* Beijing: Junshi Yiwen Press.

Xu, Lin. 2006. "China Deploys New Intercontinental Nuclear Missiles, Decreasing the Chances of a U.S. Attack." *Global Daily,* July 24. Available at http://mil.news.sohu.com/20060724/n244408714.shtml.

Zhang, Ruizhuang. 2002. "Respond with Caution vs. Self-Disarm." *International Economics & Politics* 1: 68–72.

Zhou, Xi, Dong Chun, and Zhao Weidong. 2001. "New Penetration Technological Breakthroughs in NMD Countermeasures." *PLA Daily Online.* Available at http://www.pladaily.com.cn/item/nmd/content/backsoft11974366-nmd.htm.

Zhu, Mingquan, Wu Chunsi, and Su Changhe. 2005. *Deterrence and Stability: Sino-American Nuclear Relationship.* Beijing: Shishi Press.

6

India

The Logic of Assured Retaliation

RAJESH RAJAGOPALAN

When India decided to become an overt nuclear weapon state with its 1998 nuclear tests, it settled a long debate about whether nuclear weapons were necessary for Indian security. But the question about how nuclear weapons fit within Indian security policy and strategy remained. In the decade since the 1998 tests, India has built a fairly modest nuclear arsenal, surprising those who expected India to engage in a nuclear arms race with Pakistan and China, and frustrating sections of the Indian strategic community who have advocated a more dynamic Indian nuclear weapon program and posture. This slow pace raises questions about the role and purpose of nuclear weapons in Indian security policy, which appear to be far more limited than those of most other nuclear powers.

In this chapter, I first outline the logic of India's nuclear strategy, which I characterize as "assured retaliation," and then its consequences for India's security and regional stability. I argue that nuclear weapons play a vital but limited role in Indian security policy—deterring nuclear attacks from Pakistan and China—and that this is unlikely to change over the next decade. It is a vital role because both China and Pakistan are armed with nuclear weapons for which there is no nonnuclear riposte.

Nuclear weapons play only a limited role in Indian security policy, however, because India has sufficient conventional military strength to deal with nonnuclear threats from any of its neighbors, including China, without recourse to nuclear weapons. It is possible to imagine conditions under which this situation might change, but such changes are unlikely in the next several years. Rather than being restrained by moralism, a frequent charge (Karnad 2002), the shape of India's nuclear strategy reflects the limitations of nuclear weapons for dealing with many of the security challenges that it faces.

Nuclearization has had important consequences for India's security, and Indian security managers are still struggling to cope with them. The central problem that India faces is that nuclear weapons have reduced India's conventional military options, especially in dealing with Pakistan. Recognizing this, India's military has sought to find ways to bring its superior conventional strength to bear on Pakistan without provoking nuclear escalation, though, I argue, these efforts have not yet been successful.

This chapter is divided into six sections. In the first four sections, I present my argument about the logic of India's nuclear strategy. Understanding this logic requires an examination of the security context within which Indian strategy has to operate. In the first section I illuminate the Indian security environment and describe how it reduces the tasks required of India's nuclear forces. The argument is carried forward in the second section, where I explain how these limited tasks serve to shrink the role that nuclear weapons play in India's security and foreign policy. The third section outlines the purposes of India's nuclear forces, these primarily being to deter Pakistani and Chinese nuclear forces. In the fourth section, I argue why it is more appropriate to characterize India's nuclear doctrine as assured retaliation rather than minimum deterrence, outlining the capabilities that India has developed to meet the requirements of this strategy and the limitation of these capabilities. In the fifth section I examine the consequences of the U.S.-India nuclear deal and arms control measures on these capabilities. In the final section, I look at the impact of nuclearization on India's conventional military options, on India's national security management, and on regional stability.

India's Security Environment

Three broad sets of conditions—the political environment and India's relations with the major powers, the balance of military power in India's neighborhood, and internal security threats—determine India's security environment.[1]

The Political Environment

The evolution of the post-Cold War international system, especially over the past decade, has been largely favorable to India.[2] India's relations with the United States changed dramatically for the better during the presidency of George W. Bush, capped by the U.S.-India nuclear deal of July 2005 (Mohan 2006; Tellis 2006). Though there is some domestic political disquiet over the emerging shape of the U.S.-India relationship, primarily from communist parties who are partners in the ruling coalition in New Delhi, these worries are about the increasing closeness of the ties, a far cry from the Cold War era when India worried about an adversarial Washington.[3] India also enjoys good relations with other major powers: India's relations with its traditional ally Russia continues to be good, and

India's relations with Japan have also improved significantly in the past few years (Naidu 2005). But the rise of China, the other Asian power, complicates India's security environment. Though Sino-Indian relations have improved in recent years, China is seen as a competitor for influence in Asia and beyond (Mohan 2007). But outside of the China issue, the broad political environment that India sees is a comfortable one.

The Balance of Power in India's Neighborhood

A perusal of India's annual defense reports would suggest that India faces constant danger. But this is an inaccurate picture. India is the largest and most powerful nation in the South Asian region, and its spectacular economic growth since the 1990s has only increased the existing absolute power gap between India and the rest of the region. Among India's neighbors, only China is more powerful and has the potential to be a significant military threat. India and China also have an unresolved border dispute that goes back to the 1950s. The two countries fought a brief border war in 1962, which China won decisively. Despite the dispute, the Sino-Indian border is relatively quiet, and it appears unlikely there will be any military confrontation as a consequence of the border problem in the immediate future.

But as China rises, India does have other security concerns about China. Indian strategists worry about the need to balance China (Chellaney 2006). But there is no necessary correlation between China's absolute power differential with India and the balance of military power between the two countries, which is much more favorable to India today.[4] Though Chinese forces should be expected to modernize in the coming years, the geographic disadvantages and associated logistical problems that China faces on its border with India are unlikely to be entirely overcome. China is improving its logistical capabilities on the border—and India is responding to these changes—but this is unlikely to dramatically increase the potency of China's conventional military threat to India (Joseph 2006).

India's concerns about China are related to two issues: the imbalance in the Chinese and Indian nuclear capabilities and the strategic collusion between China and Pakistan. India's 3,500-kilometer range Agni-3, the only missile with a capability to target much of China, is still under development and will not be fielded for some time.[5] The second concern is China's arms supplies to Pakistan. Though China's policy has become more evenhanded on India-Pakistan disputes, China has continued its robust military assistance to Pakistan (Garver 2004).

Within the South Asian region, the power asymmetry in India's favor is a source of both comfort and insecurity. It is a comfort because that superiority allows India to be confident of defeating any regional (specifically Pakistani) military challenges; but that very superiority, by frightening Pakistan, ensures that Pakistan will continue to seek a balance that necessitates Indian vigilance and produces Indian insecurity, a classic illustration of the security dilemma (Herz

1950). There are several disputes between India and Pakistan including Sir Creek, the Wullar barrage, and the Siachen glacier. But the most serious of these disputes is about Kashmir: two of the three wars that India and Pakistan fought were over this territory, and the rebellion in the Indian-controlled Kashmir that began in the late 1980s has further exacerbated tensions between the two countries. But a more basic cause for conflict between the two countries is the gross imbalance of power in favor of India. Since the 1940s, Pakistan has pursued both internal and external balancing strategies, devoting, proportionately, about twice as much of its national wealth to defense as India, and seeking alliances with stronger extra-regional powers such as the United States and China (Rajagopalan 2004). Despite these efforts, India's military capabilities are greater than those of Pakistan. But if India holds the edge in conventional military forces, that is partly negated by Pakistan's possession of nuclear weapons. What this means is not that the conventional imbalance is completely irrelevant, only that Pakistan can take comfort that its nuclear weapons can prevent India from using its superior conventional military forces offensively. But should Pakistan attempt to go on the offensive against India, India's superiority in conventional military forces (detailed below) would become immediately relevant. As in the case of the Sino-Indian dyad, despite India's conventional military superiority, Pakistan's nuclear weapons complicate India's security calculus.

Internal Security Challenges

The "million mutinies" that rack the Indian body politic are another important element in India's security environment. These rebellions divert Indian military forces, particularly the army, from their traditional responsibilities of protecting the country from external threats and present serious challenges to their readiness for conventional military operations. Nevertheless, none of these are currently serious enough to threaten India's integrity.

Overall, then, India's security environment presents a complicated picture. A comparison of India's situation with that of its two potential adversaries, China and Pakistan, illustrates this well.[6] China worries about a potential clash with the United States, a country with far stronger conventional and nuclear power. Pakistan sees itself as facing an existential threat from a far-stronger India. Though India faces a number of security threats, it is well placed to counter most, save nuclear ones, where it faces a very capable Pakistan and a superior Chinese nuclear force.

National Security, Foreign Policy, and Indian Nuclear Weapons

Given the picture just described, what role do nuclear weapons play in India's security and foreign policies? A very limited one. Nuclear weapons are seen to have little direct utility in conventional wars and even lesser in subconventional wars. The primary role for India's nuclear weapons is deterrence of Chinese and Pakistani nuclear arsenals. Nuclear weapons do play a role in Indian foreign policy, but, I argue, in a manner unlike the traditional conception among scholars of that role.

Nuclear Weapons and Territorial Defense

India faces two challenges in defending its territorial integrity: internal secessionist movements and external military threats. Nuclear weapons have little relevance for the first challenge and only a limited role in the second. On the other hand, nuclear weapons have complicated the conventional military balance between India and Pakistan.

India has faced a large number of secessionist insurgencies in the past half century. Though a good part of Indian military and paramilitary forces are engaged in putting down these insurrections, India's strategy for dealing with such movements has usually involved a mix of political concessions and military force, with an emphasis on the political. Military force has also been used, and used extensively, though it has been limited in intensity. This is the consequence of an Indian consensus that there is no military solution to an insurgency, a consensus that includes the Indian army. Given the extraordinary restrictions on the use of even conventional military force, it is reasonable to assert that India sees little by way of a role for nuclear weapons in such internal wars.

Nuclear weapons do play a limited deterrent role in India's defense against external military threats, but not against conventional threats. Their role is limited to deterring the use or threat of use of nuclear weapons against itself. But given the threat of escalation, nuclear weapons could also reduce the possibility of any war from breaking out.

As noted earlier, the chief reason why India sees little use for nuclear weapons in a conventional war is that it is fairly confident of its conventional military capability against both Pakistan and China. India has overwhelming conventional military superiority over Pakistan, at least in a bean count of major indices.[7] India spends about fives times as much as Pakistan on defense, has an army that is twice as large, with twice as many tanks. The Indian navy has twice as many submarines and seven times as many main surface combatants as the Pakistani navy. And India's air force has almost three times as many combat aircraft as that of Pakistan. India was also the developing world's largest arms importer in 1997–2004, signing agreements to purchase more than US$15 billion in weaponry (Grimmet 2005: 50).

India's superiority over Pakistan needs to be kept in perspective: India faces a two-front problem because a good part of its conventional military forces have to face China also. Moreover, a large fraction (as much as one-third, by some estimates) of the infantry strength of the Indian army is deployed for counter-insurgency operations. But even with such diffusion, Indian conventional forces are capable enough to obviate the need to resort to nuclear weapons in a conflict. But the earlier caveat needs to be noted again: India's superiority in conventional military forces is relevant only if India is attacked. India's conventional superiority gives it no offensive options, because Pakistan's nuclear capability will negate such options. India's conventional superiority is also not of much use in dealing with subconventional military threats posed by Pakistan, such as its support for terrorist groups operating in India.

Nuclear Weapons and India's Global Ambition

India's enduring desire to play a larger role in global affairs needs little elaboration. New Delhi's long-running and still unfruitful campaign to become a permanent member of the U.N. Security Council is but one indicator of this desire. But until the late 1990s, India's economic weakness, its interminable internal conflicts, and the incessant squabbling with its smaller neighbors, especially Pakistan, ensured that India's voice was largely confined to South Asia. But a decade and a half of rapid economic growth has placed India on a trajectory toward its long-desired role as a key player in regional and global affairs.

Nuclear weapons had a small but vital role to play in this transformation of India's fortune, but not in the manner usually conceptualized in academic literature. It is common to see India's pursuit of nuclear weapons as motivated, at least partly, by its desire for great-power status (Perkovich 1999: 448–50). But it would be difficult to argue that nuclear testing was the sole reason for New Delhi's increasing prominence, if only because India's nuclearization coincided with a period of rapid Indian economic growth. But India's demonstrated nuclear prowess was at least one factor in this transformation.

India's nuclear weapon capability also plays an increasingly significant, if unusual, role in its growing global profile. India's handling of its nuclear capability has become a means of demonstrating its international good citizenship—its ability to be a responsible global player. This was an unexpected by-product of the 1998 nuclear tests—and even more so of the A. Q. Khan episode,[8] which threw into sharp relief the difference between Indian and Pakistani nuclear behavior—rather than something that was consciously sought before the test, or an explanation for the tests. For India to be a global player, it was vital for New Delhi to change its status from a nuclear pariah that violated global nuclear nonproliferation norms, to reach an understanding with that same regime, without fundamentally compromising its nuclear capability (Mohan 2006: 219–20). The challenge, then, was to find areas of common interest on which to build such an understanding.

Though New Delhi has been a consistent and vociferous critic of the nuclear Non-Proliferation Treaty, its primary objection to the nuclear nonproliferation regime was that it was discriminatory in the manner that the regime treated the balance of obligations between nuclear and nonnuclear states. Unlike some of the other nuclear weapon powers, however, India has not been accused of attempting to spread nuclear weapon technology for strategic, economic, or ideological purposes.

But India's record on nonproliferation was by itself insufficient to reach an understanding with the global nuclear order, or more specifically, the United States, which leads that order. New Delhi also needed to reach an understanding on a number of other issues, including its nuclear doctrine, force posture, nuclear testing, and export controls, which were seen as critical for India to be accepted as a "responsible" nuclear actor, and thus as a world player. The U.S.-India dialogue, which started in late 1998, was the vehicle that India used to convince Washington of India's credentials. Paradoxically, therefore, nuclearization opened the doors for India to demonstrate its "responsible actor" credentials.

The Purpose of India's Nuclear Weapons

If nuclear weapons play only a limited role in India's security and foreign policy, what then is the purpose of India's nuclear forces? I suggest that they serve only to deter nuclear threats, specifically nuclear threats from China and Pakistan.

Deterring Pakistan

Deterring a nuclear Pakistan remains the central purpose of India's nuclear forces. It was Pakistan's development of its nuclear weapon capability that forced India to begin building a nuclear arsenal in the late 1980s (Deshmukh 2004: 171). Pakistan's nuclear threat stems primarily from its nuclear capability, but is exacerbated by that country's first-use nuclear doctrine.

Unlike Pakistan's perception of India, or even American and Soviet perceptions of their nuclear relationship during the Cold War, India does not see Pakistan as presenting an existential threat. There is little fear that a Pakistani nuclear strike would lead to state or societal demise, and thus there is little concern about issues such as civil defense. The fear, rather, is of a limited Pakistani nuclear strike aimed at New Delhi, in particular, which could affect India's retaliatory capability by targeting the Indian political and military leadership. Though other intermediate threats, such as limited attacks on other important Indian civilian or military centers are possible, they do not appear to have been considered, possibly because cost considerations limit Indian response to the most serious threats. In response to such perceptions, nuclear shelters have been built in New Delhi to protect the leadership, alternate command centers have been built outside the city, and alternate command authorities have been designated to take over in case of a successful decapitation strike (Government of India 2003; Mohan 1999; Nandy 2003). India's interest in missile defense is yet another response to this concern.

Another source of danger from Pakistan is what is perceived as Pakistan's secret chemical weapon program. Because India has eliminated its chemical weapon program by joining the Chemical Weapons Convention (CWC), India is seen as being vulnerable to an attack by Pakistan's chemical weapons, which is odd because Pakistan is also a CWC member. One goal of the Indian nuclear deterrent is to remove this particular vulnerability, though, as I note later, this complicates India's no-first-use (NFU) posture.[9]

Deterring China

Indian nuclear forces are also meant to deter a nuclear attack from China. Though China is a far more capable nuclear adversary than Pakistan, India is less concerned about a Chinese nuclear attack than about one from Pakistan. This is a function of at least two factors: China is seen as a relatively more responsible and predictable actor, and China's NFU doctrine, which is similar to India's, is seen as reducing the risk of a Chinese attack. Since India is unlikely to attack China with nuclear weapons first, the logic goes, it is unlikely that China will attack India with nuclear weapons. This, of course, presumes that China's NFU pledge is not a ruse. Sino-Indian relations have also improved, and though the border dispute is yet to be resolved, it has none of the tension of the India-Pakistan border dispute. Nevertheless, India does worry about the accretion of China's nuclear capability.

Despite China's greater nuclear capability, India's view of the nature of the Chinese nuclear threat is not very different from that of the Pakistani nuclear threat: Chinese nuclear weapon use is likely to be a limited one, not an existential threat. But New Delhi has not yet built sufficient capability to deter even this limited threat. Changes in Chinese thinking about deterrence, including Chinese conceptions of nuclear war fighting and the utility of tactical nuclear weapons, have made little impact on Indian strategic thinking or on Indian nuclear strategy.

Indian Nuclear Capabilities and Posture

The limited purpose of India's nuclear forces—as a deterrent against Chinese and Pakistani threats and use of nuclear weapons against India—has conditioned India's nuclear strategy and posture. In this section, I examine India's conception of its nuclear strategy and the development of its nuclear capabilities to match that conception.

The Evolution of the Nuclear Strategy

The changes that have taken place in India's nuclear strategy since 1998 suggest the difficulties that India is facing in grappling with the problems of nuclear deterrence. The doctrine has evolved in a slightly more muscular direction, responding to both a changing security context and domestic pressures.

The main elements of India's nuclear strategy—the NFU policy with a survivable minimum deterrent force—were established in a series of statements and documents submitted in the Indian parliament by the government's senior leaders in the months following the May 1998 nuclear tests (Government of India 1998; Vajpayee 1998). By the time the National Security Advisory Board (NSAB), a semiofficial group of nongovernmental experts set up to review security policies, produced its draft nuclear doctrine in August 1999, these elements of the Indian doctrine had been stated and restated so many times that all the NSAB could add were a few comments about force structure (a triad) and command and control arrangements (National Security Advisory Board 1999). Nevertheless, the government refused to make the doctrine official policy. Three years later, it published its own "official" doctrine in the form of a press statement that reiterated many of the basic elements of the NSAB's draft doctrine, though it left out any mention of a nuclear triad (Government of India 2003). Along with the new doctrine, the government announced the establishment of India's Strategic Forces Command (SFC).

But there were at least two critical changes in the official doctrine as stated in 2003. The doctrine now talks of retaliation being "massive," a characterization that was absent from previous statements. That term had been used only once earlier, when Vajpayee commented that Indian retaliation to a nuclear attack would be massive (*Dawn* 2000). It is possible that this was simply an elaboration, but it is also likely that in the aftermath of the Kargil War and the full-scale mobilizations of 2001–02, New Delhi felt the need to warn Pakistan that India had the resolve to use its nuclear deterrent. There has been no further elaboration of this statement or any explanation of this change. On the one hand, it is possible that those who framed the statement did not recognize the significance of the formulation or its conceptual underpinning in nuclear strategic thought.[10] On the other hand, a couple of weeks after the new formulation was published, Indian Defense Minister George Fernandes did warn Pakistan that it would be "erased from the world map" if it used nuclear weapons against India—as good an operational definition of massive retaliation as any (Rediff.com 2003). It is quite possible that Fernandes's statement was simply nuclear braggadocio, but the timing does suggest something more than coincidence.

The second change in the doctrine was an expansion of the conditions under which India would use nuclear weapons. Until this point, the Indian position had been that India would only use nuclear weapons in retaliation against a nuclear attack. But the newly released doctrine stated that India would, in the event of a "major" attack against India or on Indian forces "anywhere" by biological or chemical weapons, "retain the option of retaliating with nuclear weapons" (Government of India 2003). Again there was little explanation of this change. In interviews, former senior officials gave at least two different reasons for the change:

one, that since India had given up its right to build chemical and biological weapons, using nuclear weapons was the only choice left to respond to an attack by such weapons (Senior Official 2006a); and two, the government was expanding the conditions under which nuclear weapons use would be considered, at least partly to respond to domestic critics of India's NFU policy, including within the NSAB (Senior Official 2006b).

There was at least one other change. In January 2003, according to Tellis (2006: 144), the Indian government formally informed the United States that it had decided to integrate missile defense into its nuclear posture, though this was not mentioned in the doctrine. The explanation appears to be that the publicly stated nuclear doctrine mentioned only a few details of what is said to be a much larger and complex doctrine.[11]

India's Nuclear Strategy

India's nuclear strategy is difficult to characterize. The Indian government, as well as scholars, usually portrays it as "minimum deterrence" (Basrur 2006). But minimum deterrence is more a force posture than a strategy. In terms of the categorization used in this volume, moreover, India's nuclear strategy has moved in the direction of "assured destruction" (see Alagappa, Chapter 2 in this volume). But assured destruction is usually associated with nuclear forces and strategies of the kind that the two superpowers deployed during the Cold War. These include very large nuclear forces capable of causing unacceptable damage, hair-trigger alerts, and a capacity for nuclear war fighting. India's nuclear strategy does not include most of these elements, save for an emphasis on causing unacceptable damage through massive retaliation. Massive retaliation, again, has to be seen in the context of India's relatively small nuclear arsenal rather than as a nuclear strategy that aims at the annihilation of the adversary. Thus, India's nuclear strategy cannot be characterized as one of assured destruction either. One intermediate position is Johnston's argument about limited deterrence (Johnston 1995/96). But this does not fit India either because Johnston's notion of limited deterrence includes war-fighting elements as well as a counterforce strategy, which are absent in the Indian case. The Indian view of deterrence includes disparate elements that are better described as "assured retaliation," which, as Alagappa notes in Chapter 2, was the term that was dropped in favor of "assured destruction" by U.S. officials. This captures the major elements of India's nuclear strategy: not using nuclear weapons first, and emphasizing survival and retaliation.

Below, I outline the elements of India's assured retaliation strategy. But before doing so, two caveats must be noted. First, the Indian government continues to characterize its nuclear doctrine as one of "credible minimum deterrence." *Minimum* here has certain political value because it invokes the idea of India's limited goals and responsible attitude, which New Delhi would like to project to the world. For this reason, officially, India is likely to continue calling its nuclear doctrine "credible minimum deterrence."

Second, as I characterize it, assured retaliation shares many of the characteristics of minimum deterrence. But the distinction between the two is more than a matter of semantics. Assured retaliation differs from minimum deterrence in two crucial ways. First, it reflects more accurately the dynamic nature of India's nuclear strategy. Of course, dynamism in terms of the growth of the arsenal can be explained within the logic of minimum deterrence. After all, the growth of India's arsenal has been very measured, and minimum deterrence does envisage the need for some retaliatory capability, a goal that India has yet to reach, especially with regard to China (see below). Rather than numbers, dynamism here refers to India's attitude toward nuclear weapons. As narrated above, India has expanded both the quantum of nuclear force it might use in retaliation ("massive") and the conditions under which that retaliation might take place, which now includes also nonnuclear contingencies. These changes may reflect declaratory policy more than operational ones, but they nevertheless reflect changes in Indian thinking that are difficult to encompass within the idea of minimum deterrence.

Second, risk plays an important role in at least some conceptions of minimum deterrence. As Basrur points out, "minimum deterrence rests on the risks one's weapons pose to an adversary, not on one's assurance that the weapons will be efficient, credible, or invulnerable" (Basrur 2006: 47). But the emphasis of India's nuclear strategy is less on risk and more on credibility. Indeed, Indian officials routinely characterize India's nuclear strategy as "credible" minimum deterrence, rather than simply as minimum deterrence. As Basrur (2006: 48) notes, this could lead to an open-ended conception of deterrence. The point, of course, is that given that Indian thinking does emphasize these elements, it is difficult to characterize India's nuclear strategy as minimum deterrence.

Three elements make up India's "assured retaliation" deterrence strategy: first, India will only retaliate against a nuclear (or a chemical/biological) weapon attack; second, Indian retaliation will be certain ("assured"); and finally, it will be massive and designed to inflict damage unacceptable to the enemy. This deterrence strategy is tied to a nuclear force structure that is designed to be small (minimum) but undefined, which would be able to survive an enemy first strike through mobility and dispersal, and whose deterrent capability will be based on the certainty rather than the instantaneity of the response.

The first element of the assured retaliation strategy is the NFU pledge, which emphasizes pure retaliation. This policy can be traced to India's view of nuclear weapons as political rather than purely military weapons. Nuclear weapons are useful as a "currency of power" and for deterrence—the diplomacy of force—rather than in actual combat. As Tellis (2001: 280–95) notes, there are a number of reasons for this view: the idealist-liberal political culture; the nature of Indian civil-military relations, which emphasizes very strict political control over the military; and finally, the costs of building a large nuclear arsenal. Nevertheless, because NFU is a purely declaratory policy, it is difficult to state with certainty that India will not violate it if the need arises.

Indeed, India's NFU pledge is no longer a "pure" NFU: what India says it will retaliate against has changed from just a nuclear attack to an attack with any weapon of mass destruction (WMD). This opens up at least the theoretical possibility that India could use nuclear weapons first, albeit as a retaliation for use of chemical or biological weapons against it. There is also an expanding spatial dimension to this pure retaliation strategy because India claims it will retaliate not only to a direct attack on its territory but also to attacks on Indian forces anywhere. Such contradictions raise credibility issues about India's declared policy and thus ill-serve Indian strategy. In addition, such modifications raise the risks associated with what Sagan (2000) has called the "commitment trap," that decision makers might be trapped by peacetime declarations into using nuclear weapons where they might otherwise not want to.

The second element of the assured retaliation strategy is the certainty of retaliation. The Indian view of assured retaliation is slightly different from the traditional conception of assured retaliation that emphasizes having a substantial second-strike capability that can be deployed either in a launch-on-warning profile or at least in a launch-under-attack profile. In the Indian conception, assured retaliation does mean having second-strike capability, but this includes mainly forces that will ride out and survive a first attack and retaliate later. It specifically does not mean either launch on warning or launch under attack. Indian officials such as Jaswant Singh have explicitly ruled out the need to have any instantaneous response to a nuclear attack, though this is a declaratory policy that might not tie Indian hands in an actual crisis (Mohan 1999). The emphasis, then, is on ensuring that there will be a certain nuclear retaliation, even if this retaliation is not instantaneous.

The third element of the assured retaliation strategy is also the most problematic: that any retaliation will be massive. The original Indian view was simply that retaliation had to hold out the promise of "unacceptable damage," but more recently this has been taken to mean that retaliation must be massive. Such a posture will have little credibility because it is unlikely that Pakistan's (or China's) leadership will believe that they should expect a full-scale countervalue counterattack even in response to a single demonstration attack, say on the forward elements of an attacking Indian armored column. If an adversary did find it credible, another scenario would present itself: such an Indian posture would force an adversary to consider a full-scale first strike rather than a limited demonstration strike because the adversary would have little incentive to keep a first attack limited if it expected a massive retaliation even in response to a limited demonstration strike. For an adversary, launching a large-scale first attack might be more rational than a limited attack or a demonstration strike against India, because India's massive retaliation might destroy any remaining capacity for a further response. In other words, the adversary would find itself in a strategic "use-it-or-lose-it" dilemma. Given these complications, a likely explanation for the assertion about massive retaliation is that it was an ad hoc modification, brought about by the need to demonstrate resolve in the aftermath of the just-concluded Operation Parakram experience, rather than a serious or considered doctrinal change.

Indian strategists have disagreed with certain elements of the Indian strategy, in particular the NFU pledge. Indeed, in early 2003, the NSAB, composed of civilian strategists, asked the government to withdraw the NFU pledge (Roy-Chaudhury 2004). Others have called for a far more capable nuclear force that could deter both China and the United States (Chellaney 1999; Karnad 2002). But there is little indication of any rapid changes in India's official nuclear posture. Given the relatively limited purposes that Indian nuclear forces serve, it is unlikely that such changes will happen in the immediate future.

Indian Nuclear Capabilities

Indian officials are cagey about a number of the doctrine's operational details. For example, there has been no clarification of critical terms such as *credible minimum deterrent.* One reason for the reticence about issues such as the size of the nuclear arsenal is to leave the government enough elbow room for future contingencies. Similarly, it is not clear what "retaliation . . . will be massive and designed to inflict unacceptable damage" means. This makes it difficult to come to clear judgments about whether Indian capabilities meet the requirements of Indian nuclear strategy. Nevertheless, the assured retaliation strategy has the following two basic requirements: (1) Indian nuclear delivery capability must survive a nuclear attack. (2) Indian command and control facilities must be capable of maintaining themselves and retaliating in the aftermath of a nuclear attack.

Whether Indian capabilities are sufficient for these two tasks will, obviously, depend on the kind of nuclear attack that takes place. Several types of nuclear attacks can be visualized, in a spectrum from a demonstration strike—for example, by Pakistan, on an Indian armored spearhead—to a full-scale nuclear attack. Neither China nor Pakistan has the capability to launch a full-scale counterforce first strike—which would require intelligence capabilities and missile accuracy that neither is thought to have—and this eventuality is thus not considered here. I also assume that if Indian capabilities were sufficient to meet a full-scale nuclear attack, they should be sufficient to meet all other lesser contingencies.

Because neither Pakistan nor China has the capability to launch a counterforce first strike, the threat to the assured retaliation strategy would arise from the possibility of a decapitation strike, a nuclear strike that targets the "head," India's political and military leadership in New Delhi. But the requirements of meeting such an attack depend not so much on the ability of India's nuclear force to retaliate as on India's ability to protect the Nuclear Command Authority (NCA) through a variety of means, including missile defense and a robust, hardened, command and control system that can function after such a strike (Kumar 2006). A secondary requirement of assured retaliation strategy is having nuclear forces that can perform the task of launching such an attack. In short, India requires the following capabilities to satisfy the requirements of its strategy: a sufficiently large nuclear weapon capability (warheads and fissile material), a sufficient number of delivery vehicles, a robust command and control system, and passive and active defense systems for protecting the leadership. I examine India's capabilities in each of these areas in the following paragraphs. Given the secrecy that surrounds India's strategic programs, my conclusions are necessarily tentative.

Warheads and Fissile Material. India is estimated to have anywhere between 65 and 110 weapons, based on calculations of India's possible weapons-grade plutonium stocks (Albright 2005). How many of these have actually been fashioned into weapons remains in doubt, however. Other estimates are roughly comparable (Cirincione, Wolfsthal, and Rajkumar 2005: 221). The slow accretion of India's fissile material stocks should continue to increase Indian warhead potential. It should be noted that this calculation does not take into account India's much larger stocks (reportedly about ten tons, sufficient for about 1,000 warheads) of reactor-grade plutonium (Ramachandran 2006). These capabilities—even if India's stocks of reactor-grade plutonium are excluded—would be sufficient for the purposes of massive retaliation, since a nuclear attack by even a few dozen nuclear warheads would cause destruction adequate to be characterized as "massive" even to China.

Delivery Vehicles. As with fissile material, India's current delivery capabilities are not known with any degree of certainty. India has tested three different indigenously designed nuclear-capable ballistic missile systems—Prithvi (1 & 2), Agni-1, and Agni-2—several times (International Institute of Strategic Studies [IISS] 2005: 229). The Agni-1 and Agni-2 have apparently been accepted for induction, but it is unclear if they have already been inducted or how many (Ministry of Defense 2005: 105). All of these are delivery vehicles that can primarily only target Pakistan. The Prithvi and Agni-1 appear to have been designed explicitly with Pakistan as the target. The 2,000-kilometer range Agni-2 cannot target large parts of China. Even the Agni-3, a longer-range missile, might not have sufficient range to target all of China from southern India, which would require a missile with a 6,000-kilometer range, about twice the reported range of the Agni-3.

India also has a number of combat aircraft that can carry nuclear payloads, including the Jaguar, the Mirage 2000, Mig-27s and 29s, and the SU-30. But it is unclear which, if any, of these aircraft are currently deployed for such missions.

Though these combat aircraft might be sufficient to target Pakistan, they have inadequate range to be used as delivery platforms against China.

The Indian navy has at least one ship-based missile in development, the Dhanush, a naval variant of the Prithvi missile. But the Dhanush has the same weakness that other Prithvi missiles have: a short range. The navy is also thought to be developing a nuclear-powered missile submarine under the Advanced Technology Vessel (ATV) project, as well as a missile that could be deployed on the ATV called the Sagarika, though the government has denied it is developing any such missile (Rajya Sabha 2006).

Indian delivery capabilities appear sufficient to match the requirements of Indian nuclear strategy against Pakistan but are insufficient to match the requirements of the strategy against China. Until the Agni-3 is deployed, India's deterrent capability against China will be severely limited.

Command and Control System. India's nuclear command and control system is a highly "assertive" one. Nuclear weapons and their use are controlled by the NCA, which comprises the Political and Executive Councils. Only the Political Council, chaired by the prime minister, can authorize the use of nuclear weapons; the Executive Council, headed by the national security advisor, "provides inputs for decision making by the Nuclear Command Authority and executes the directives given to it by the Political Council" (Government of India 2003). The composition of these councils has not been formally revealed, but the Political Council is thought to comprise the Cabinet Committee on Security, while the Executive Council includes top civil servants and the military chiefs (Mohan 2003). For the system to operate effectively in a nuclear environment, a number of weaknesses, especially with regard to the communications infrastructure and limitations of the command arrangements for nuclear weapons, will need to be addressed (Kumar 2006: 30–32). It is unclear whether this has happened. Given the emphasis in the Indian strategy on survival—an absolutely minimum requirement for an assured retaliation posture—any weakness in India's command and control system would present a serious problem.

Passive Defenses: Bunkers and Alternate Command Centers. The emphasis on riding out an enemy nuclear attack and retaliating subsequently requires defensive capabilities to ensure the survival of the political and military leadership. India has built bunkers for top decision makers within the South Bloc, the complex of government offices that houses the prime minister's office, as well as alternate command centers outside Delhi, and possibly even decided on alternate chains of command if the top political leadership is eliminated (Mohan 2003; Nandy 2003). Details about these arrangements are understandably sketchy and insufficient to make judgments about the adequacy of these efforts or their weaknesses.

Active Defenses: Missiles. Missile defense, though not absolutely necessary to Indian deterrent capabilities, can supplement passive defense measures and enhance the survivability of the NCA and India's nuclear forces. Though India has been pursuing a missile defense system since the mid-1990s, it was only in 2005 that the government officially admitted that it was considering the purchase of such systems. Replying to a question, Pranab Mukerjee, the Indian defense minister, stated that India had received briefings about the Patriot system—though he clarified that it "was not a commercial offer"—and that manufacturers from Israel and Russia had also made such briefings earlier in 2003 (Rajya Sabha 2005). In late 2006, India conducted a missile defense test with an indigenously built system, suggesting that India is continuing to explore the indigenous route too. Interviews with several former senior officials and decision makers suggest that India is still at an exploratory stage and that no decision on acquisition has been made. India, then, is unlikely to acquire a missile defense system for some time to come.

To summarize, India has adequate deterrent capability against Pakistan. But it has some ways to go before it develops a full deterrent capability against China, even by the limited requirements of its assured retaliation strategy. Therefore, Indian capabilities, especially its long-range delivery capabilities, can be expected to grow—albeit slowly—over the next decade.

Nuclear Weapons and Conventional Forces and War

Nuclear weapons have had a significant effect on the conventional military balance between India and Pakistan. The fear of escalation has reduced conventional military options for both countries. In this section, I focus on how nuclear weapons affected Indian conventional military options during the Kargil War in 1999 and Operation Parakram in 2001–02 and on Indian thinking about the conventional war options in light of these crises.

The Kargil War

It seems clear that India limited its conventional military options during the Kargil War, restricting operations to its side of the Line of Control (LoC) between India and Pakistan, even prohibiting its air force from crossing the LoC. Though senior Indian leaders and officials more than once reiterated that they retained the option of crossing the LoC if needed, they never actually did so (Goldberg 1999). Nuclear escalation might have been a factor, though no explicit nuclear threat was made by either side. The most serious claim about the nuclear impact was made by American officials, who maintained that they had detected Pakistani missile movements. But Indian officials, publicly and in private, have disputed the claim.

Even if no explicit nuclear threat was made, neither side could ignore the presence of nuclear weapons. India's decision not to cross the LoC is the best evidence of the restraint imposed by the presence of nuclear weapons, though it must be noted that several other factors, such as the progress Indian forces made on the ground and the favorable international support India was receiving, were also factors in India's restraint. Nevertheless, the fear of escalation does appear to be one of the self-imposed restraints on the use of conventional military force. A comparison is illustrative: in 1965, when Pakistan used irregular forces to launch attacks, India showed little restraint in its response, sending its army to attack across the border.

But this self-control also had limits: India showed little restraint in the use of military forces on its side of the border, even as it took steps to ensure that it did not cross the LoC. Pakistan protested when India began to use its air force, claiming that it was an escalation, but India refused to accept that characterization and continued to use air power on its side of the border. Similarly, Indian restraint did not prevent the navy from threatening a blockade of Karachi.

Though India achieved its basic objectives in the Kargil War, it would be fair to conclude that both the political and the military leadership in New Delhi felt the need for more options in dealing with Pakistan. There had been little consideration, before Kargil, of the constraints that India would face in using its conventional military forces. Almost by default, it was assumed that, with nuclearization, India did not have to worry about the possibility of another war with Pakistan. One consequence of the Kargil War was that Indian decision makers began discussing conventional military options, especially the "limited war" option (discussed below). These debates were given further impetus by the terrorist attack on the Indian parliament in December 2001 and the resulting military mobilization.

Operation Parakram

Much more so than in Kargil, India's inability to go to war in the aftermath of the attack on the Indian parliament indicated the extent to which India's conventional military options had been constrained by nuclearization. Despite the vast military mobilization that India ordered, Indian actions and speech were extremely cautious. There were only a few isolated nuclear threats, and some statements not meant as nuclear threats were misinterpreted as such (such as Army Chief Padmanabhan's statement on January 11, 2002, that anyone launching a nuclear attack on India would be severely punished). Additional indicators of India's restraint included the postponement of a scheduled Agni-1 missile test and downplaying Pakistan's shooting down of Indian spy drones (Rajagopalan 2005).

The Parakram experience demonstrated that the limits imposed during Kargil remained in place: India could use force in any manner on its side of the border but could not cross the border. If Kargil represented one type of force—direct fire, Parakram defined a second type of force—demonstrative. Without any viable targets for direct fire, Operation Parakram had to limit itself to demonstrative force. But as the Parakram experience showed, demonstrative force has severe limits.

From New Delhi's perspective, unlike Kargil, Operation Parakram did not end satisfactorily. Despite post-Kargil discussions about limited war, it was clear that New Delhi had not found any satisfactory answer to the problem of bringing to bear its superior conventional military might on Pakistan. Coercive diplomacy, if it was indeed that, appeared more the consequence of the lack of any conventional military options than a deliberate and considered choice. Though the inadequacy of the army's mobilization process is usually blamed for the lack of this military option, it is unclear whether faster mobilization would have provided India any more alternatives. The central problem for India in the Parakram crisis was that New Delhi did not understand how constraining nuclear weapons were. Faster mobilization would not have resolved that problem.

Conventional Forces and Nuclear War

The limitations imposed by nuclearization on the use of force are also visible in the public discussion in New Delhi about the possibility of fighting a limited war under nuclear conditions (Mohan 2000). Both Army Chief General V. P. Malik and Indian Defense Minister George Fernandes asserted that there was space between a subconventional war and a full-scale nuclear war for a limited conventional war even in a nuclear environment. The argument was that Pakistan was unlikely to reach for its nuclear weapons at the first sight of Indian troops crossing the border, and the nuclear threshold would be crossed only if India captured large chunks of Pakistan's territory or destroyed substantial parts of the Pakistan army or its nuclear capability. This was the gap that India could exploit by using conventional military force in a manner that would keep it below this threshold but would nevertheless be sufficiently painful to punish Pakistan for its intransigence.

Such ideas have found few takers in India's officialdom. There is little indication that they were supported by even the former coalition government of the National Democratic Alliance, and there has been little subsequent discussion of this proposal. The threat of nuclear escalation was too serious to countenance such views.

The Indian army's interest in developing the so-called Cold Start doctrine in the aftermath of the Parakram crisis is another indication of the Indian effort to overcome the limits imposed by nuclearization and the limitations of that effort (Swami 2004; *Telegraph* 2006). One of the significant problems that the Indian army encountered during Operation Parakram was that full mobilization of forces took about three weeks, by which time international concerns about the possibility of a nuclear war between India and Pakistan had led to considerable pressure on New Delhi. Cold Start envisages a rapid offensive with forces that are already available near the front, without waiting for the mobilization to be complete, thus giving New Delhi greater freedom to use its conventional forces. The military objectives would also be different: instead of conducting one or two deep thrusts into Pakistani territory, which was the traditional Indian army strategy, Cold Start envisages shallow thrusts designed to capture smaller chunks of territory with many separate, simultaneous offensives by forces already near the border. If implemented successfully, the Cold Start doctrine would permit India "to conduct a limited war without provoking the threat of a Pakistani nuclear response" (Ashraf 2004: 58). Though parts of this doctrine have been tested in several exercises by the Indian army since 2004, it is unclear whether it has been fully implemented. Implementing this doctrine would require a significant strengthening of Indian forces at the border and a political commitment from the Indian civilian leadership to permit the army to wage such a war. There is little to indicate that either of these has happened. There is a more fundamental problem too: any successful Indian conventional offensive is likely to increase the chances that Pakistan might resort to nuclear weapon use, even if Indian objectives are limited to seizing relatively small areas of Pakistan's territory. Whether it is possible to think in terms of a conventional military victory in a nuclearized environment is left unaddressed by this doctrine.

These issues highlight the complexities India faces in bringing to bear its conventional military power when fighting under nuclear conditions. And New Delhi has yet to resolve them.[12] If India were to become embroiled in another war with Pakistan, dilemmas such as these would likely continue to limit India's conventional military options.

India and the Global Nuclear Regime

Multilateral and bilateral nuclear arrangements have the potential to affect India's nuclear weapon posture. Two issues are examined below: the nuclear deal between the United States and India and the impact of arms control policies.

The U.S.-India Nuclear Deal

In the U.S.-India nuclear deal, India has agreed to sign the Additional Protocol of the International Atomic Energy Agency (IAEA) with regard to its civilian nuclear facilities and to put under IAEA safeguards fourteen of its twenty-two thermal power reactors that are currently in operation or under construction, as well as all future *civilian* nuclear reactors.[13] The agreement represented a middle path between international nuclear safeguard norms, which called for full-scope safeguards (safeguards on all nuclear facilities) in exchange for nuclear cooperation, and India's traditional partial safeguards approach (under which India was only willing to accept safeguards on nuclear facilities or material that came from foreign suppliers). India agreed to put under safeguard many plants and facilities that were not foreign sourced, but insisted on leaving aside a significant number of facilities in the interest of its future strategic needs, including its fast-breeder research reactors. The deal has been severely criticized within India on several counts (Shourie 2006). Nevertheless, the only element of the agreement that could affect the Indian weapon program is a limitation on nuclear testing, which New Delhi has repeatedly insisted it will not accept (Press Trust of India 2007). Overall, then, the nuclear deal should have little direct effect on India's nuclear weapon capability and posture.

Arms Control Policies

As with the nuclear deal, New Delhi is unlikely to accept changes that have the potential to constrain its strategic capabilities in the future. For example, it has been lukewarm toward the Fissile Material Cutoff Treaty (FMCT), maintaining that its scope must be limited to future production (and not extended to existing stocks, as some states, including Pakistan, wanted) and that any such treaty must be verifiable (Ministry of External Affairs 2006a). Similarly, India has refused to accept any limitations on its right to test, arguing that its nuclear test moratorium is voluntary.

More broadly, India has taken the domestically unpopular position of voting against Iran in the IAEA. The prime minister, in response to a debate in the lower house of the Indian parliament, pointed out that though Iran has the right to develop peaceful uses of nuclear energy, it also has obligations and responsibilities (Ministry of External Affairs 2006b). India also opposed North Korea's decision to conduct a nuclear test in October 2006, pointing not only to its consequences for regional stability but also to the dangers of clandestine proliferation (Ministry of External Affairs 2006c). Both positions appear at least partly determined by the desire to demonstrate India's nonproliferation credentials.

Implications for National and Regional Security

A decade after the nuclear tests of 1998, what have been the consequences of nuclearization? First, I examine the impact of nuclearization on Indian security management. I then focus on regional issues, in particular on two sets of arguments about the impact of nuclear weapons on South Asian stability.

Nuclear Weapons and India's National Security

As both the Kargil War and Operation Parakram demonstrated, India's conventional war options have been severely constrained by nuclearization. The fear of escalation, or "instability" at the nuclear level, may have been critical (Kapur 2005). But against this disadvantage must be balanced at least four benefits. First, nuclearization froze the possibility of forcible changes of territory, something that is to India's advantage, as in maintaining the status quo in the region. Second, nuclearization provides Pakistan with a means to overcome the disadvantages of its weakness and insecurity in relation to India, and this should eventually reduce Pakistan's insecurity vis-à-vis India and the consequent balancing efforts against India. Admittedly, this transformation has not yet taken place. Third, overt nuclearization permitted India to begin the process of closing the nuclear deterrence gap between itself and China, partly by demonstrating India's deterrence capability and partly by allowing India to openly develop other elements of its strategic force. Finally, India's nuclear capability is at least partly responsible for India's greater prominence in world affairs.

The Stability-Instability Paradox

The stability-instability paradox suggests that stability at the strategic level creates instability at lower levels of conflict by inducing states to take risks at the subconventional levels. Originally credited to Glenn Snyder (Snyder 1965), the thesis has been widely used in the South Asian context to suggest that nuclearization has led to instability.[14] The logic of the argument is as follows: in a nuclearized South Asia, Pakistan is free to engage in subconventional conflicts (Kargil) or support local insurgencies (Kashmir), creating instability at that level, because India cannot bring its greater conventional forces to bear without risking escalation to the nuclear level. Kapur has modified this thesis somewhat, arguing that it is *instability* at the strategic level, rather than stability, that heightens the risk of escalation and thus constrains India (Kapur 2005).

Snyder's argument cannot be fully explicated here, but it dealt primarily with the relationship between nuclear and conventional levels of conflict, *not,* as it is usually represented when the paradox is applied to South Asia, between nuclear and subconventional levels of conflict. Even with regard to this relationship, Snyder suggested that the relationship has both negative and positive effects. Though a completely stable nuclear relationship can lead to conventional war because the fear of escalation is diluted (thus creating the negative effect, instability at lower levels of conflict), the threat of gradual escalation to the nuclear level can also ensure overall stability (Snyder 1965: 199).

Applying the stability-instability paradox in South Asia is problematic. The assumption behind such arguments is that Pakistan's involvement with subnational insurgencies in India, particularly Kashmir, was the direct result of the nuclearization of the region. This ignores much of the history of Pakistan's involvement in previous subnational conflicts in India, including in Punjab in the 1980s, in Kashmir in 1965, and in the northeast since the 1950s. It is possible that nuclearization made Pakistan relatively more comfortable with taking risks in Kashmir, but to suggest that nuclearization led to Pakistan's involvement would be mistaken. A simple counterfactual point can illustrate this: even if Pakistan did not have nuclear weapons, it is inconceivable that it would have stood aside when the

Kashmiri rebellion began in the late 1980s. Pakistan's involvement in Kashmir cannot be traced to the operation of the stability-instability paradox, and instability in South Asia cannot be traced to nuclearization.

Nuclear Dangers in South Asia

There has been a continuing debate about the consequences of the spread of nuclear weapons on regional stability. Proliferation optimists argue that nuclear weapons have a stabilizing effect on regional conflict; pessimists suggest that nuclear weapons are particularly dangerous in the hands of third world nations (Sagan and Waltz 2003). Though the possession of nuclear weapons automatically involves dangers for any state, pessimists argue that some of these dangers are greater when third world countries possess them. For third world nuclear powers in general, and India and Pakistan in particular, the following dangers are usually cited: the inadequacy of command and control arrangements, the uncertainty of civil-military relations, the proximity of adversaries, and the possibility of nuclear weapon theft or unauthorized use.

How realistic are these concerns? Though these dangers cannot be ruled out—they exist with all nuclear forces—the doctrine and posture that India and Pakistan have adopted reduce these risks. For example, nuclear weapons are kept "de-mated" in both India and Pakistan.[15] In India, the components of the weapon are believed to be held with three different agencies: the Department of Atomic Energy holds the radioactive core, the Defense Research and Development Organization has custody of the firing assemblies, and delivery vehicles are with the armed forces (Pandit 2002). Moreover, neither India nor Pakistan has adopted a "delegative" command and control system—where authority to use nuclear weapons is delegated to lower levels of the military command—opting instead for "assertive" systems that emphasize central control over nuclear weapons.[16] Such a posture greatly decreases the risks of nuclear accidents, theft of nuclear weapons, and the possibility of unauthorized use.

Indian and Pakistani nuclear doctrines also reduce the likelihood of nuclear weapons use. India's "retaliation-only" doctrine is generally considered safer than Pakistan's doctrine, which allows for the possibility of first use of nuclear weapons in response to a threatening Indian conventional military advance. But even Pakistan's doctrine, as I noted earlier, is not a first-strike doctrine: it can be more accurately termed a "first-use-but-last-resort" doctrine. In addition, both the Kargil War and Operation Parakram demonstrated that both Indian and Pakistani leaders behave very carefully during crises. Both sides showed a willingness to minimize losses rather than gamble on escalation (Rajagopalan 2005). In summary, the dangers associated with nuclearization in South Asia are far fewer than are indicated on the pessimist's charge sheet.

Conclusion

The measured pace of India's nuclear weapon program is noteworthy. Despite citing China as the reason for its nuclear tests in 1998, India has yet to build up a sufficient deterrent capability against China. Until now, India has focused on building up its forces against Pakistan. Now that New Delhi has built an adequate deterrent against Pakistan, over the next decade it should be expected to pay greater attention to the need to build a deterrent against China. But this process is likely to be as unhurried as it has been over the past decade.

This unhurried pace is the consequence of India's relatively advantageous security context and the limited role that nuclear weapons play in India's security policy. India sees nuclear weapons primarily as tools for deterring nuclear attack. It does not exhibit any intense security concerns, partly because the power imbalance in its favor within the region ensures that no regional adversary can launch a successful offensive against India. Pakistan's nuclear weapons cannot compensate for its conventional weakness if it were to launch an attack on India. But Pakistan's nuclear weapons can deter India from using its conventional superiority to threaten Pakistan. This is not a big concern for India given that it is the status quo power in the region, except in one respect: as the Operation Parakram experience demonstrated, Pakistan's nuclear capability limits India's conventional military options in dealing with Pakistan's subconventional threats. Even though India enjoys no conventional superiority over China, India's military strength at the Sino-Indian border is considerable and unlikely to change immediately. Though these circumstances do not preclude security threats, the point is that these are security concerns for which nuclear weapons provide no good answers.

Dramatic changes in these conditions could, of course, alter India's approach to nuclear weapons. Should India's relative advantage in conventional military capabilities change, it could call into question the utility of a retaliation-only nuclear strategy. Such a change could take place either because India weakens severely or because the conventional military muscle of potential adversaries such as Pakistan or China (at the Sino-Indian border) advances impressively relative to India. Such a large reversal of fortune is unlikely over the next several years, though it cannot be ruled out in the long term. There is another possibility, too: Sino-Pakistani collusion until now has not included a joint military thrust against India, but should such a remote possibility arise, India might find itself pressed in a two-front pincer, testing India's retaliation-only nuclear strategy.

The improbability of these scenarios is also reflected in the arguments of those Indian strategists who call for a larger nuclear arsenal. Those arguments are framed not on the basis of any immediate threats to India that nuclear weapons can counter, but in the language of the presumed but dubious political benefits of having a larger nuclear arsenal (Karnad 2002). Such arguments find little resonance in the prudent corridors of power in New Delhi, another condition that is unlikely to change. Limited needs are likely to continue determining India's "assured retaliation" nuclear strategy for some time to come.

Notes

1. For an analysis based on similar categories but focused more on nuclear threats, see Tellis (2001: 20–115).

2. For a positive assessment of India's position in the early post-Cold War period, see Gordon (1995). For more skeptical views, see Thornton (1992).

3. Some Indian strategists also worry about the need to balance the United States. See Chellaney (1999) and Karnad (2002: 483).

4. See, for example Zhang (1999: 45). Pillsbury (2000) argues that Chinese analysts see India as superior to China in some areas, such as naval power, but not in the overall balance. Karnad (2002: 360–61, especially n. 236) notes an assessment made by a former Indian army officer that China would have difficulty even fighting a conventional war with India.

5. The Agni-3 has been tested twice, but it is expected to undergo several more tests before it is deployed.

6. See Chapter 5 on China and Chapter 7 on Pakistan in this volume.

7. The following comparative military strength data, unless otherwise noted, are from IISS 2005.

8. Dr. Abdul Qadeer Khan, one of the leading figures in Pakistan's nuclear weapon program, was responsible for setting up an illegal international network trading in nuclear and missile technology.

9. This observation is based on interviews with several senior Indian officers and, in particular, a senior decision maker closely associated with India's strategic programs.

10. Interviews with high-ranking former Indian officials led me to suspect that this was the case. But one former official stated that this formulation, even though not well thought out, reflected a sentiment against notions such as proportionate response.

11. This is based on interviews with two former high-ranking officials in the National Security Council Secretariat and the Strategic Forces Command, September–October 2006.

12. Jervis (1984) highlights many similar dilemmas that faced U.S. nuclear strategy.

13. India reserved the right to decide which of the future reactors will be designated as civilian (Government of India 2006).

14. See Ganguly (1995: 326). For a counterpoint, see Sahni (2007).

15. See also Chapter 7 on Pakistan in this volume.

16. On the command and control challenges of assertive and delegative systems, see Feaver (1992–93).

References

Albright, David. 2005. "India's Military Plutonium Inventory, End 2004." Available at http://www.isis-online.org/global_stocks/end2003/india_military_plutonium.pdf.

Ashraf, Air Commodore Tariq M. 2004. "Doctrinal Reawakening of the Indian Armed Forces." *Military Review* 84 (6): 53–62.

Basrur, Rajesh. 2006. *Minimum Deterrence and India's Nuclear Security.* Stanford, Calif.: Stanford University Press.

Chellaney, Brahma. 1999. "Value of Power," *Hindustan Times,* May 19.

———. 2006. "Mastering Martial Arts," *Hindustan Times,* November 27.

Cirincione, Joseph, Jon Wolfsthal, and Miriam Rajkumar. 2005. *Deadly Arsenals: Nuclear, Biological and Chemical Threats.* 2nd edition. Washington, D.C.: Carnegie Endowment for International Peace.

Dawn. 2000. "Nuclear Attack: Vajpayee Threatens Retaliation," February 7.

Deshmukh, B. G. 2004. *From Poona to the Prime Minister's Office: A Cabinet Secretary Looks Back.* New Delhi: HarperCollins.

Feaver, Peter, D. 1992–93. "Command and Control in Emerging Nuclear Nations." *International Security* 17 (3): 160–87.

Ganguly, Sumit. 1995. "India-Pakistan Nuclear Issues and the Stability-Instability Paradox." *Studies in Conflict and Terrorism* 18 (4): 325–34.

Garver, John. 2004. "China's Kashmir Policies." *India Review* 3 (1): 1–24.

Goldberg, Suzanne. 1999. "'Barbarism' Insult Fired at Pakistan," *The Guardian,* June 12. Available at http://www.guardian.co.uk/international/story/0,3604,292479,00.html.

Gordon, Sandy. 1995. "South Asia after the Cold War: Winners and Losers." *Asian Survey* 35 (10): 879–95.

Government of India. 1998. "Paper Laid on the Table of the House on *The Evolution of India's Nuclear Policy.*" Available at http://www.indianembassy.org/pic/nuclearpolicy.htm.

——— 2003. "Press Release of the Cabinet Committee on Security on Operationalization of India's Nuclear Doctrine (04.01.03)." In *Security and Diplomacy: Essential Documents,* ed. Arvind Gupta, Mukul Chaturvedi, and Akshay Joshi, pp. 19–20. New Delhi: National Security Council Secretariat/Manas Publications.

———. 2006. "Implementation of the U.S.-India Joint Statement of July 18, 2005: India's Separation Plan." Tabled in the Indian Parliament on May 11, 2006. Available at http://meaindia.nic.in/treatiesagreement/2006/11ta1105200601.pdf.

Grimmet, Richard F. 2005. *Conventional Arms Transfers to Developing Nations, 1997–2004.* Washington, D.C.: Congressional Research Service.

Herz, John H. 1950. "Idealist Internationalism and the Security Dilemma." *World Politics* 2 (2): 157–80.

International Institute of Strategic Studies (IISS). 2005. *The Military Balance, 2005–2006.* London: Author.

Jervis, Robert. 1984. *The Illogic of American Nuclear Strategy.* Ithaca, N.Y.: Cornell University Press.

Johnston, Alastair Iain. 1995/96. "China's New 'Old Thinking': The Concept of Limited Deterrence." *International Security* 20 (3): 5–42.

Joseph, Josy. 2006. "Coming Soon: Roads Along Chinese Border," *DNA: Daily News and Analysis,* May 9.

Kapur, S. Paul. 2005. "India and Pakistan's Unstable Peace: Why Nuclear South Asia Is Not Like Cold War Europe." *International Security* 30 (2): 127–52.

Karnad, Bharat. 2002. *Nuclear Weapons and Indian Security: The Realist Foundations of Strategy.* New Delhi: Macmillan.

Kumar, Rakesh. 2006. *Indian Nuclear Command and Control Dilemma.* Monterey, Calif.: Naval Postgraduate School.

Ministry of Defense. 2005. *Annual Report 2004–2005.* New Delhi: Ministry of Defense, Government of India.

Ministry of External Affairs. 2006a. "Statement Made by Jayant Prasad, Permanent Representative of India to the Conference on Disarmament, Geneva." Available at http://meaindia.nic.in/speech/2006/05/17da01.htm.

Ministry of External Affairs. 2006b. "Reply by Dr. Manmohan Singh to the Lok Sabha Debate on India's Vote at the IAEA on Iran's Nuclear Programme." Available at http://meaindia.nic.in/speech/2006/03/06ss01.htm.

Ministry of External Affairs. 2006c. "Remarks by Official Spokesperson on the reported nuclear test by DPRK." Available at http://meaindia.nic.in/pressbriefing/2006/10/09pb01.htm.

Mohan, C. Raja. 1999. "India Not to Engage in Nuclear Arms Race: Jaswant," *The Hindu,* November 29.

——— 2000. "Fernandes Unveils Limited War Doctrine." *The Hindu,* January 25.

——— 2003. "Nuclear Command System Credible: India," *The Hindu,* January 7.

——— 2006. *Impossible Allies: Nuclear India, United States and the Global Order.* New Delhi: India Research Press.

——— 2007. "Beijing Is Testing Strategic Waters in India's Backyard," *Indian Express,* January 30.

Naidu, G.V.C. 2005. "India-Japan Relations: Towards a Strategic Partnership." *China Report* 41: 327–30.

Nandy, Chandan. 2003. "Two Nuclear Bunkers to Shield Union Cabinet," *Hindustan Times,* September 21.

National Security Advisory Board. 1999. *Draft Report of the National Security Advisory Board on Indian Nuclear Doctrine.* New Delhi: Author.

Pandit, Rajat. 2002. "India All Set to Set Up Nuclear Forces Command," *Times of India,* December 30. Available at http://timesofindia.indiatimes.com/articleshow/32896380.cms.

Perkovich, George. 1999. *India's Nuclear Bomb: The Impact on Global Proliferation.* New Delhi: Oxford University Press.

Pillsbury, Michael. 2000. *China Debates the Future Security Environment.* Washington, D.C.: National Defense University Press. Available at http://www.ndu.edu/inss/books/books%20-%202000/China%20Debates%20Future%20Sec%20Environ%20Jan%202000/pills2.htm.

Press Trust of India. 2007. "India Not to Accept Any Legal Binding," *Indian Express,* January 13.

Rajagopalan, Rajesh. 2004. "Neorealist Theory and the India-Pakistan Conflict." In *International Relations in India: Theorising the Region and the Nation,* ed. Kanti Bajpai and Siddharth Mallavarapu, pp. 142–72. New Delhi: Orient Longman.

——— 2005. *Second Strike: Arguments about Nuclear War in South Asia.* New Delhi: Penguin.

Rajya Sabha. 2005. Unstarred Question no. 5150, May 11, 2005 (Ministry of Defense, Department of Defense Research and Development), "Patriot Missile." Available at http://164.100.24.219/rsq/quest.asp?qref=100889.

——— 2006. Unstarred Question no. 937, August 2, 2006 (Ministry of Defense, Department of Defense Research and Development), "Development and Trials of Missiles." Available at http://164.100.24.219/rsq/quest.asp?qref=116889.

Ramachandran R. 2006. "India and Talks on the Nuclear Issue," *The Hindu,* January 23.

Rediff.com. (2003). "Pakistan Would Be Erased If It Uses Nukes: Fernandes," rediff.com, January 27, 2003. Available at http://www.rediff.com/news/2003/jan/27fer.htm.

Roy-Chaudhury, Rahul. 2004. *Nuclear Doctrine, Declaratory Policy and Escalation Control.* Washington, D.C.: Stimson Center. Available at http://www.stimson.org/pub.cfm?id=105#.

Sagan, Scott D. 2000. "The Commitment Trap: Why the United States Should Not Use Nuclear Threats to Deter Biological and Chemical Weapons Attack." *International Security* 24 (4): 85–115.

Sagan, Scott D., and Kenneth N. Waltz. 2003. *The Spread of Nuclear Weapons: A Debate Renewed.* New York: W. W. Norton.

Sahni, Varun. 2007. "India-Pakistan Crises and the Stability-Instability Paradox: A Less Than Perfect Explanation." In *The India-Pakistan Nuclear Relationship: Theories of Deterrence and International Relations,* ed. Easwaran Sridharan, pp. 185–207. New Delhi: Routledge.

Senior Official. 2006a. Interview with a former senior official in the National Security Council Secretariat, Government of India.

Senior Official. 2006b. Interview with a former senior official in the Strategic Forces Command, India.

Shourie, Arun. 2006. "The Way Out," *Indian Express,* December 23. Available at http://www.indianexpress.com/story/19185.html.

Snyder, Glenn H. 1965. "The Balance of Power and the Balance of Terror." In *The Balance of Power,* ed. Paul Seabury, pp. 185–201. Scranton, Penn.: Chandler.

Swami, Praveen. 2004. "Gen. Padmanabhan Mulls Over Lessons of Operation Parakram," *The Hindu,* February 6.

Telegraph. 2006. "Cold Start, Quick Thrust," May 17. Available at http://www.telegraphindia.com/1060517/asp/nation/story_6233011.asp.

Tellis, Ashley. 2001. *India's Emerging Nuclear Posture: Between Recessed Deterrent and Ready Arsenal.* New Delhi: Oxford University Press.

——— 2006. "The Evolution of U.S.-Indian Ties: Missile Defense in an Emerging Strategic Relationship." *International Security* 30 (4): 113–51.

Thornton, Thomas P. 1992. "India Adrift: The Search for Moorings in a New World Order." *Asian Survey* 32 (12): 1063–77.

Vajpayee, Atal Bihari. 1998. "PM's Statement in Parliament on 'Bilateral Talks with the United States,'" December 15.

Zhang, Ming. 1999. *China's Changing Nuclear Posture: Reactions to the South Asian Nuclear Tests.* Washington, D.C.: Carnegie Endowment for International Peace.

7

Pakistan

The Dilemma of Nuclear Deterrence

FEROZ HASSAN KHAN AND PETER R. LAVOY

Pakistan's quest to acquire nuclear weapons arose from an urgent need to deter political coercion or outright military attack by its powerful rival India, especially when Pakistan could no longer count on an offsetting security relationship with the United States. Pakistan's initial concept of deterrence was vague: little thought was given to how the nuclear-use option would prevent another war with India after the 1971 loss of East Pakistan or even after India's nuclear test in 1974 turned that option into an imperative. Now, after possessing a nuclear force for over two decades, Pakistan's defense planners have worked out a comprehensive set of policies and procedures to manage nuclear weapons during times of peace, crisis, and war. However, the security landscape around Pakistan is changing fast. The transformative shifts in the international and regional environments have created new defense predicaments and imperatives for Pakistan as it expands its nuclear arsenal and refines its nuclear strategy.

This chapter has three themes, each pertaining to a particular security problem Pakistan faced, the strategic response it devised to address the problem, and the consequences of that strategic behavior. The first theme, which could be called the tragic dilemma of nuclear deterrence, explains how Pakistan's compulsion to acquire nuclear weapons was rooted in its perception of an existential threat and also how the emergent nuclear rivalry with India has created new forms of mistrust and animosity between the two neighbors. On the one hand, nuclear weapons are seen in Islamabad as the only reliable means of preventing India from acting on its presumed desire to undo Pakistan's sovereignty and territorial integrity. On the other hand, the growing capability to annihilate one another makes each side permanently insecure and ever suspicious of the other's motives and capabilities.

The second theme attests to a classic security dilemma. Pakistan's nuclear doctrine, force posture, and capability requirements are the direct outcomes of India's growing military, technological, and industrial advantages; but in turn they unintentionally push India to seek new advantages. Pakistan's policy makers are aware that an arms race with India will further widen the economic and military imbalance. Thus Pakistan says little about its nuclear doctrine so as not to provoke India or reveal information about actual nuclear employment plans. During peacetime, Pakistan keeps its nuclear warheads and delivery systems in an unassembled state to minimize the provocation to India and to reduce the risk of accidental or unauthorized launch. In addition, while Pakistani planners view their nuclear arsenal as a deterrent to Indian aggression, a robust conventional war-fighting capability is deemed necessary to allow nuclear forces to operate deep in the background of political-military conduct. In response, Indian defense planners are engaged in a wide array of efforts to modernize and expand their conventional and strategic capabilities to neutralize the gains that Pakistan has achieved. India hopes that by increasing its military power Pakistan will take decisive action to prevent militants organized in its territory from conducting terrorist attacks against India.

The third theme relates to the costs and consequences of Pakistan's nuclear quest. Because Islamabad placed such a high premium on overcoming the myriad nonproliferation pressures and constraints that stood in the way of its acquisition of nuclear weapons and missiles, it developed a highly secretive and personalized decision-making system that gave extraordinary autonomy to the heads of the Pakistan Atomic Energy Commission (PAEC) and the Khan Research Laboratories (KRL). Instead of creating a nuclear oversight and regulatory apparatus, Islamabad actually instituted policies and procedures to prevent outsiders—including some from within the Pakistan government and armed forces—from prying into the affairs of the PAEC and the KRL. This system enabled Pakistan to field a nuclear deterrent quickly, cheaply, and secretly. But it also allowed KRL director Abdul Qadeer Khan to turn his clandestine nuclear import network into an unsanctioned export business for personal profit (International Institute for Strategic Studies [IISS] 2007: 15–91). After Khan's proliferation activities became public, it became imperative for the government to reorganize the nuclear structure and institute effective command and control arrangements—a task made all the more urgent after the 9/11 terrorist attacks in the United States and the two military crises with India (International Institute for Strategic Studies [IISS] 2007: 93–118).

This chapter begins with a discussion of Pakistan's grand strategy, its threat perceptions, and the role of nuclear weapons in the country's security strategy. The ensuing section analyzes Pakistan's nuclear doctrine, likely employment policies, force posture, and projected force requirements. The third section discusses the evolving command and control structure for the management of Pakistan's nuclear arsenal in times of peace, crisis, and war. The final section examines the implications of Pakistan's nuclear strategy for security interdependence, regional stability, and system management. The chapter ends with a discussion of future challenges that Pakistan is likely to confront in view of emerging regional and international trends, most notably the rise of India as a major power and a strategic partner of the United States, an emerging nuclear Iran, and shifting power balance in Asia.

Grand Strategy

Pakistan's development of an operational nuclear deterrent in the late 1990s and into the 2000s is an outcome of competing threat analyses and conceptions about national security that were constructed, articulated, and defended by Pakistan's politicians, scientists, and military leaders over a four-decade period. Ever since Pakistan's independence in 1947, Indian leaders expressed skepticism that the new Muslim nation could survive with the meager political and economic infrastructure it inherited from Britain (Uz-Zaman 1969).[1] National survival continues to be the primary concern of all Pakistani policy makers. Until recently, when internal threats to Pakistan became a paramount concern, Pakistan's leaders insisted that India was the primary security threat.

During the 1950s and 1960s, Pakistan's defense planners believed that the best way to counter the Indian military buildup was through conventional military preparedness and alliance with the United States (P. I. Cheema 1990: 145–61). When it became clear that India was readying its nuclear option after China's first nuclear test in 1964, Pakistani elites, led by Zulfiqar Ali Bhutto, tried to persuade the government to start a nuclear bomb program. Pakistan's military leader at the time, General Ayub Khan, however, chose to stay the course of conventional defense and alliance as the surest response to India's mounting military capability. This strategy collapsed after the 1965 and 1971 wars. The United States embargoed military supplies to Pakistan (and India) in 1965, and Pakistan's allies were unable to prevent its dismemberment in 1971. The once ignored bomb lobby stood vindicated when Zulfiqar Ali Bhutto came to power. He initiated the nuclear weapon program in January 1972.

Threat Perceptions

Pakistan faces a four-dimensional threat. First and foremost is the prospect of major conventional war with India that potentially could turn nuclear. Second, Pakistan's western border has been volatile. Tensions there could expand into a wider insurgency if not handled with prudence and care. Third is the possible emergence of a nuclear-armed Iran and the possible negative security dynamic in the Persian Gulf. At present Pakistan's relations with Iran are good. However, Pakistan is also a major non-North Atlantic Treaty Organization (NATO) ally of the United States. Depending on how the situation evolves in that region, a nuclear-armed Iran will have significant security implications for Pakistan. Fourth, Pakistan's armed forces could be entangled in domestic political violence in a major internal security situation with or without the involvement of external powers. Restive tribes in the Pakistan-Afghanistan frontier region, and in Baluchistan, combined with simmering unrest in the Sindh province, make Pakistan prone to internal disorder and exploitation by hostile countries.

The India Threat. At the core of Pakistan's national identity and strategic culture is India's threat to Pakistan's survival. Since the early 1970s, Pakistan's leaders have consistently seen nuclear weapons as crucial to deterring the existential threat from India, which they believe is real. India's military force posture, geographic location, and modernization reaffirm Pakistan's threat perceptions—as does the long history of violence between the two neighbors.

India and Pakistan fought three major wars between 1948 and 1971. The two Kashmir wars in 1948 and 1965 underscored Pakistan's strategic vulnerability. It realized that India had no intention of allowing Kashmir to become part of Pakistan. Lacking military strength, Pakistan sought to enlist tribal Pashtuns in the liberation of Kashmir. That effort failed, and the ensuing war in 1947–48 ended in stalemate. The second war in 1965 was based on the notion that Pakistan could create and exploit a window of opportunity to improve its position in Kashmir. Pakistan's plan to incite insurgency (Operation Gibraltar), followed by the use of limited conventional force to capture key areas of southern Kashmir and cut off the northern part of Kashmir (Operation Grand Slam), was not successful. Instead, India counterattacked across the international border mainly in Punjab, threatening Lahore, thereby escalating the conflict. This was the first war that expanded outside the confines of Kashmir and threatened Pakistan's communication lines and cities.

The war in 1971 was not related to Kashmir but stemmed from a secession movement in East Pakistan that was actively abetted by India. Indian intervention in blitzkrieg-type operations following nine months of insurgency and civil war ended in the defeat of Pakistan. With the transformation of East Pakistan into independent Bangladesh, Indians claimed that the two-nation theory was dead, reinforcing Pakistani perceptions that the war was more about humiliating Pakistan than liberating Muslim Bengalis (Kux 2001: 206). Pakistan became more convinced that India had not reconciled with its separate existence and that New Delhi would exploit any opportunity that arose. Nuclear weapons came to be seen by the new Pakistan leadership as the only reliable guarantee of state survival.

Pakistan's Troubled Western Borderlands. The border with Afghanistan has been volatile and disputed since 1893 when Britain established the Durand Line, a 1,600-mile border between Pakistan and Afghanistan spanning a mountainous, porous, and unsettled area. That frontier region has featured insurgencies involving alienated tribes that take great pride in their autonomy and are extremely hard to handle. Afghanistan has never accepted this border. Its irredentist claims, supported by India, fan Pashtun nationalism, which from time to time produces calls for an independent Pashtunistan. After the Soviet withdrawal from Afghanistan, Pakistan executed a forward policy in the 1990s to support sympathetic tribes, Pashtun nationalists, and eventually the Taliban with the aim of installing a friendly government in Kabul. As President Pervez Musharraf explains, Pakistan supported the Taliban for strategic reasons: "If we had broken with them, that would have created a new enemy on our Western border, or a vacuum of power there into which might have stepped the Northern Alliance, comprising anti-Pakistan elements. The Northern Alliance was supported by Russia, India, and Iran" (Musharraf 2006: 203).

Mixed into the deck of volatile, religious, and nationalist Pashtuns are tribal militants and suspected Al-Qaeda terrorists. Since 9/11, Pakistani military operations in the western borderlands have involved intelligence-gathering missions, Special Forces operations, infantry assaults, and precision strikes from the air and ground. Nuclear weapons do not play any role in deterring or coercing the forces operating in the tribal areas of Pakistan. However, this border region presents a major security concern, especially if India steps up its activity there. That could ultimately threaten the Pakistani state and lead to the use of nuclear weapons against India.

The Prospect of a Nuclear-Armed Iran. A third security concern stems from the prospect of a nuclear-armed Iran. Although Iran poses no direct threat to Pakistan, relations have been strained over three major issues in the recent past. First, Islamabad's close relationship with the Arab countries, most notably Saudi Arabia, fanned the rise of Sunni fundamentalism in Pakistan. Iran's promotion of Shiite ideology has led to sectarian problems within Pakistan. A nuclear Iran is likely to be more assertive in pushing its ideology within the Shia population, leading to further sectarian violence and crossborder tension. Second, Iran and Pakistan compete for influence over Afghanistan. In the 1990s, Iran supported the Northern Alliance against the Pakistan- and Saudi-backed Taliban. Third, India has courted Iran closely for the past few years, which has troubled Pakistan. A hostile Iran working in concert with India (for example, allowing India land and air space) can cause instability and pose a second-front threat to Pakistan. This concern now has an economic dimension. Iran and Pakistan are competing over the outlet of Central Asian energy and access to the Arabian Sea.

Internal Instability. The fourth threat is the prospect of serious domestic instability. Pakistan has a history of ethnolinguistic subnationalism in its smaller provinces, often leading to intermittent insurgencies. The country's original two wings, East and West Pakistan, were separated in 1971. Since then Pakistan has existed with Punjab at the core. The other provinces on the periphery have often struggled for more autonomy and greater control over their resources. Pakistan's military and bureaucratic elites mostly hail from Punjab and are imbued with memories of foreign involvement in its internal political problems. These include India's support for the creation of Bangladesh, Soviet support for the Baluch insurgency in the 1970s, and India's alleged assistance to Sindhi nationalists against the government of Zia ul-Haq (Weaver 2002: 72–73). Lately, Pakistan has alleged Indian involvement in Baluchistan's tribal instability (Rubin and Siddique 2006: 176). Pakistan's defense planners fear that India's role in internal unrest could again be a precursor to Indian military intervention, making a linkage between domestic unrest and the nuclear deterrent.

Fear of Preventive Strikes. Since the advent of Pakistan's nuclear weapon program, Pakistani officials have feared military attacks against their nuclear production facilities and their concealed weapons stockpile. This fear arose in the 1970s when Washington blocked Pakistan's attempt to acquire nuclear reprocessing technology from Europe. Islamabad believes that the Nuclear Suppliers Group was created to target Pakistan. In 1979, after President Jimmy Carter enacted nonproliferation sanctions against Pakistan, Islamabad feared U.S. sabotage or air attack on the uranium enrichment facility at Kahuta. In response, perimeter security and air defenses were tightened around the nuclear facility. These fears were rekindled after Israel's successful attack on Iraq's Osirak reactor in June 1981.

In the mid-1980s, during a particularly tense period with India—when the Indian army attacked the Golden Temple in Amritsar to quash the Sikh insurgency and simultaneously occupied the Siachen glacier in the disputed northern areas of Kashmir—concern arose over possible Indian air attacks on Kahuta. In 1986–87 during the Brasstacks crisis, renewed Pakistani fears of a preventive strike against Kahuta triggered serious alarms. Pakistan's defense planners feared that Indian Army Chief General Sundarji was planning a preventive war in the shadow of military exercises with the intention of establishing a war situation, which could be used as a pretext to neutralize Pakistan's nuclear program (Sagan and Waltz 2003: 92–95). The crisis subsided after President Zia ul-Haq visited India for a cricket match.

During the Kashmir uprising in early 1990, Pakistani intelligence warned of a possible joint Israeli-Indian attack against Pakistan's nuclear facilities. On this occasion, the Pakistan leadership of President Ghulam Ishaq Khan, Prime Minister Benazir Bhutto, and Army Chief General Aslam Beg signaled that Pakistan would attack India's key nuclear facilities if Kahuta were struck. Concerns again surfaced in Pakistan about a joint attack by India and Israel on Pakistan's nuclear test site after the 1998 Indian nuclear tests. This fear was stimulated in part by the aggressive rhetoric of the ruling party in India, the Bharatiya Janata Party, and also by intelligence reports of an Israeli aircraft at an Indian air base (Rizvi 2001: 943–55).

In the wake of 9/11, Washington's urgent response to wipe out Al-Qaeda and the Taliban regime in Afghanistan created new fears in Islamabad about military strikes against Pakistan's nuclear arsenal by the United States, acting alone or possibly in coordination with India. In a statement announcing Pakistan's withdrawal of support for the Taliban and its full cooperation with the U.S.-led war on terrorism, Musharraf cited the protection of the country's strategic assets as a key reason for this policy reversal: "The security of our strategic assets would be jeopardized. We did not want to lose or damage the military parity that we had achieved with India by becoming a nuclear weapon state. It is no secret that the United States has never been comfortable with a Muslim country acquiring nuclear weapons, and the Americans undoubtedly would have taken the opportunity of an invasion to destroy such weapons. And India, needless to say, would have loved to assist the United States to the hilt" (Musharraf 2006: 202). Less than a year later, fears of an attack resurfaced during the 2002 military standoff with India. This time, however, Pakistan countermobilized with conventional forces and went into full operational alert. Though the entire national security apparatus was on high alert, there is no report that nuclear weapons were mated with delivery systems during the crisis.

Now that India and the United States appear to be forging a strategic partnership, there is renewed fear in Pakistan of a joint U.S.-India attack—even though there is no evidence that either the United States or India has full knowledge of Pakistan's deployed nuclear weapons or that they have ever discussed joint military action against Pakistan. In response to the U.S.-India civil nuclear cooperation accord, Pakistan's National Command Authority (NCA) publicly resolved that any deal that could shift the nuclear balance would force Pakistan to reassess its minimum nuclear deterrence requirements (Lavoy 2007). The implication of this announcement is that Pakistan would increase its fissile material production and nuclear force goals to match an expansion in India's nuclear force potential. This complicates the regional security dilemma and has made Pakistan's proposal of a strategic restraint regime with India an unlikely prospect.

The Role of Nuclear Weapons in Pakistan's Security Strategy

The main role of nuclear weapons in Pakistan's security strategy is to deter India and to counter the military imbalance. Pakistan relies on its standing professional armed forces to fight India in the context of geographic and strategic vulnerabilities. At one level, Pakistan matches India's force modernization by acquiring comparable weapons, equipment, and training, as well as by placing a premium on operational readiness. At another level, Pakistan engages in external balancing through strategic alliances with the United States and China, to a limited extent through international institutions (the United Nations), and at times through organizational arbitrations (World Bank). However, these strategies have proven insufficient. Nuclear weapons are deemed necessary to ensure crisis stability and strategic independence. Pakistan wants sufficient nuclear forces for a second-strike capability, reliable and reasonably accurate delivery means to ensure counterforce as well as countervalue targeting options, and robust command and control systems to survive sustained military strikes. These are all Pakistan's requirements for a strategy of minimum deterrence against a larger, wealthier, and conventionally powerful adversary.

Since the nuclear tests of 1998, four interrelated strategic concepts—coercive diplomacy, hot pursuit, Cold Start, and limited war under the nuclear umbrella—have gained traction in India to justify the legitimacy of conventional war under the nuclear shadow (Basrur 2005). The injection of nuclear weapons into South Asia's strategic equation has left the region prone to military crises—five have occurred since the mid-1980s when rudimentary nuclear capabilities were achieved—but armed conflict has become far too costly for Indian and Pakistani leaders to contemplate except in the most dire circumstances. Nuclear weapons so far have provided the ultimate security that Pakistan has sought, lending credence to Kenneth Waltz's argument about the stabilizing effect of nuclear weapons (Sagan and Waltz 2003: 3–45).

Many Indians believe that Pakistan has tried to leverage nuclear force to wrest control over Kashmir. In particular, Pakistan's failed attempt to extend the Kashmir Line of Control (LoC) near the town of Kargil within a year of the May 1998 nuclear tests is often cited as evidence of the stability-instability paradox. Pakistan did attempt to loosen India's grip over Kashmir when both sides had nuclear weapons in the 1990s. But a historical perspective shows that this has been Pakistan's objective since 1948—both before and after Islamabad had nuclear weapons (Schofield 2003; Swami 2006). The 1999 Kargil operation took place *despite* the presence of nuclear forces, not because of it. Pakistan's Kargil plan was launched with utter neglect of the effect of the nuclear dynamic on India, the United States, and virtually the rest of the world. Moreover, even if veiled nuclear threats were issued to liberate Kashmir, the outcome of Kargil proved this strategy to be counterproductive. Far from loosening India's grip, Kargil significantly tightened its hold over Kashmir and gave it greater international legitimacy. On balance, it can be said that Pakistan's nuclear arsenal influenced India to the extent that general war was ruled out. Nuclear weapons provide powerful incentives for both countries to resolve bilateral disputes peacefully. The same pressure has forced three U.S. presidents to intervene in South Asian crises to restrain India and Pakistan from fighting (Nayak 2002: 2).

Political Roles of Nuclear Weapons

Nuclear weapons have brought few political benefits for Pakistan. Unlike India, whose ascent to major power status has been assisted by a nuclear weapon capability, Pakistan's nuclear might has not created much global influence. In fact, it highlighted Pakistan's other weaknesses in civil-military relations, the rise of extremism, and revelations of proliferation. Regardless of these and other shortcomings, however, China, the United States, and Pakistan's neighbors have had to contend with a new nuclear power.

China. China is the only major power that sees the utility of a nuclear Pakistan as a balancer against India. China's public position is to not support nuclear proliferation, but the unspoken reality of its preference is well known. A nuclear Pakistan is important to China in the long run as a hedge against the growing U.S.-India strategic relationship and in the context of increased U.S. presence in South Asia in the post-9/11 period. Pakistan has worked hard to sustain its partnerships with both the United States and China and to promote itself as a relevant power on the global stage. Nuclear weapons, in this scheme, have both positive and negative leverage, and Pakistan does not hesitate to play the high-stakes power game in Asia.

Regional Neighbors. Relations with Afghanistan are tense again. As the Afghan war continues, the Pakistan army faces a real prospect of military force engagement with local tribal groups and a resurgent Taliban, the Afghan National Army, and possibly even NATO or U.S. forces in pursuit of militants inside Pakistan's tribal regions. If the insurgency succeeds in widening the fissure between Pakistan and Western forces, the tribal areas could become a major area of conflict. Under these circumstances, the nuclear dimension could come into play because NATO powers are operating against the territory of another nuclear power; but it is hard to anticipate just what kind of impact nuclear weapons would have. As an ally of the Western powers since its inception, it is highly unlikely that Pakistan would come into direct conflict with U.S. forces either independently or in Afghanistan. However, this possibility cannot be ruled out in the long term, given the volatility of the situation along the western border.

In the mid-1980s, Iran sought nuclear technology from Pakistan. Because Islamabad rejected these overtures, permitting only standard nuclear energy training, Iran secretly contacted the A. Q. Khan network in Dubai (International Institute for Strategic Studies [IISS] 2007: 67–71). Far from being grateful for the "Islamic brotherhood," Iran has ridiculed A. Q. Khan's contribution to its nuclear program and disputed the quality of equipment provided by the network. Whether or not Iran succeeds in obtaining nuclear weapons, Pakistan's nuclear arsenal will influence Iranian policy choices in any regional conflict, including one between Pakistan and India. Pakistan's fear is that India is courting Iran to join its encirclement strategy. The two countries do cooperate on some issues, especially on Afghanistan. Within South Asia, both India and Pakistan compete for influence. A nuclear Pakistan has little pull on any of the South Asian Association for Regional Cooperation countries. Nor do Pakistan's nonnuclear regional neighbors fear nuclear coercion from Pakistan. At best, some countries seek peaceful nuclear energy training from Pakistan's Atomic Energy Commission in Islamabad. Several regional countries also receive conventional military training, supplies, trade, and commerce.

Muslim Countries. Muslim nations make up the next group of states that could be influenced by Pakistan's nuclear program. Ever since Zulfiqar Ali Bhutto introduced the notion of an "Islamic bomb" in the late 1970s, Pakistan has been suspected of sharing nuclear technology with other Muslim countries, most notably Saudi Arabia. Pakistan and Saudi Arabia have very close military and intelligence ties, including a formal defense agreement under which up to an infantry division of Pakistani forces could be sent to augment the Saudi armed forces. Saudi Arabia also is believed to have provided generous financial support to Pakistan that helped to sustain the nuclear program during the 1990s when Pakistan was under Western nonproliferation sanctions. Saudi Defense Minister Sultan bin Abdulaziz reportedly visited KRL in May 1999 and again in August 2002. If this were true, he would be the only foreign official to have visited a strategic facility in Pakistan. However, there is no evidence of any nuclear-related agreement between Pakistan and Saudi Arabia (IISS 2007: 83).

The idea of providing extended deterrence to Muslim countries has been raised by some retired Pakistani military officers and by Pakistan's religious opposition parties, such as Jamaat-i-Islami (JI) (Hashmi 2004: 341). To date, no serious planning has occurred in Pakistan that would indicate that the myth of Islamic nuclear influence has taken hold or that the government is thinking about extending deterrence or proliferating nuclear weapons to profit from their value as an ideological weapon. That said, the rhetoric that Pakistan was the first Muslim country to acquire nuclear weapons remains popular in the domestic political culture of Pakistan.

Western Powers. Despite close military relations between Washington and Islamabad, they never saw eye-to-eye on the nuclear issue, and this remains a controversial dimension of the U.S.-Pakistan partnership. Rather than providing any positive leverage with the West, Pakistan's nuclear arsenal causes great concern. The Western world reacted aggressively to the post-9/11 environment and the A. Q. Khan revelations. Only Pakistan's role in the global war on terror and its nuclear weapon capability allowed it to escape from deeper crisis and opprobrium.

Today, Western countries are deeply concerned about the prospect of Pakistan losing control over its nuclear capabilities, especially the prospect that weapons or fissile material could fall into the hands of terrorists or extremist Islamic groups.

Nuclear Doctrine and Force Posture

Pakistan's deterrence strategy revolves around three key elements: an ambiguous doctrine of minimum deterrence, survivable strategic forces, and a robust strategic command and control. Pakistan has announced a minimum nuclear deterrence doctrine to deter and balance against a stronger adversary without provoking New Delhi to take precipitous military action and the United States to apply excessive nonproliferation pressures. As part of this strategy, Pakistan relies on a robust conventional fighting force to meet a wide range of conventional and subconventional threats to national security and to raise as high as possible the threshold of possible nuclear use. It also seeks to maintain a sufficient stockpile of nuclear weapons and delivery systems to ensure a second-strike capability. Despite the "minimum" claim, the quantity and quality of the arsenal required to meet this challenge can evolve according to Pakistan's perception of the adversary's offensive and defensive capabilities. Second, Pakistan places a premium on a survivable strategic force to withstand local sabotage and conventional military attacks and possibly also to absorb a nuclear strike. Finally, Islamabad seeks a completely renovated strategic command and control apparatus to ensure assertive control over the weapons stockpile during a range of strategic conditions—from a peacetime recessed state to an operationally deployed ready-to-launch status within the short time span that South Asian military crises take to develop.

Nuclear Doctrine

Pakistan's strategic doctrine has evolved over several decades, but a thoroughly considered and planned nuclear deterrence strategy took shape only after the country conducted its first nuclear explosive tests in May 1998. At that time, the armed forces had no real nuclear employment doctrine, and command and control over the nuclear arsenal and delivery systems had not been carefully organized or tested in field exercises (Z. I. Cheema 2000: 159). After the 1998 nuclear tests and the creation in 1999 of a dedicated nuclear organization—the Strategic Plans Division (SPD)—Pakistani strategists recognized that premising national security on nuclear weapons required a multitude of new undertakings related to doctrine, force structure, delivery systems, and the vetting and training of specialized personnel assigned to strategic force responsibilities. Despite statements by officials alluding to situations in which nuclear weapons might be used, Pakistan's use doctrine is deliberately undeclared and ambiguous, even though nuclear forces presumably have been integrated into operational war-fighting plans. Every civilian and military leader since Zulfiqar Ali Bhutto has defended the country's right to acquire nuclear weapons, but the precise role of this capability beyond providing a "nuclear deterrent" against Indian conventional or nuclear attacks has intentionally not been clarified.[2]

After its own nuclear test series, India quickly declared a draft doctrine in August 1999. Pakistan did the opposite. Rather than declaring an official nuclear-use doctrine, it formulated the basic contours of its doctrinal concept through periodic statements by leaders and officials, with only a hint of how and under what circumstances nuclear weapons would be used. Lieutenant-General Khalid Kidwai, SPD director general, remarked that Pakistan would not publicize a nuclear doctrine because ambiguity and secrecy about nuclear capabilities and operations enhance the deterrent effect (Cotta-Ramusino and Martellini 2002). India has a doctrine of conducting a limited conventional war based on a belief that it can accurately determine Pakistan's nuclear threshold and make space for limited conventional war by controlling escalation (Raghavan 2002: 84). Pakistan believes that ruling out the use of nuclear force in response to conventional attack or articulating nuclear red lines would reduce the power of its nuclear deterrent to such an extent that India would feel free to use its huge conventional military might in a wide range of circumstances. This fear has led Pakistan to reject a no-first-use assurance and declare only the basic logic of its nuclear-use policy, leaving India and the rest of the world to calculate the risks.

At the peak of an intense military standoff with India, President Pervez Musharraf made the most authoritative Pakistani statement about nuclear use: "If Pakistan is threatened with extinction, then the pressure of our countrymen would be so big that this option, too, would have to be considered" (Boyes 2002). In a rare interview conducted during the same crisis, SPD Director General Kidwai provided more information about the circumstances in which nuclear use might be considered: "In case deterrence fails, nuclear weapons will be used if: (1) India attacks Pakistan and conquers a large part of its territory (space threshold); (2) India destroys a large part either of its land or air forces (military threshold); (3) India proceeds to the economic strangling of Pakistan (economic strangling); (4) India pushes Pakistan into political destabilization or creates a large-scale internal subversion in Pakistan (domestic destabilization)" (Cotta-Ramusino and Martellini 2002).

Kidwai's first two thresholds are understandable; however, the other two points are offshoots of steps India might take as preludes to a conventional war. "Economic strangulation" implies an Indian naval blockade or possibly the placement of Indian dams on rivers to either dry up or flood Pakistan's Punjab plains. "Domestic destabilization" refers to memories of India's assistance to the Mukti Bahini guerrillas that led to the separation of East Pakistan in 1971. Since then, Pakistan has continued to be apprehensive about Indian support for militants in the volatile Pakistani provinces of Sindh, Baluchistan, and the Northwest Frontier Province. Although nuclear weapons have no apparent role in these two scenarios (though a naval blockade could be perceived as an act of war), the prospect of an Indian-sponsored internal crisis in conjunction with conventional force posturing is an enduring concern for Pakistan's security planners.

The geographical disadvantage and conventional force imbalance limit Pakistan's defense options. Pakistani officials emphasize that effective deterrence is based on a clearly communicated capability and willingness to use nuclear weapons, as well as a robust conventional military posture. In their view, one is ineffective without the other. From this logic, if India attacks, Pakistan would counterattack with conventional forces, each side would inflict damage on the other, and India would refrain from escalating the conflict out of fear of Pakistan's nuclear response. The widespread belief that Pakistan's nuclear capability is required to augment its conventional military deterrence of India is reinforced by the common perception in Pakistan that its nuclear capability deterred attacks by India on at least six occasions: in 1984–85, 1986–87, 1990, 1998, and 1999 (Shahi, Khan, and Sattar 1999). Similar claims appeared in the Pakistani media that Pakistan "deterred" Indian plans to attack in the early winter and summer of 2002 (*Daily Times* 2002: 11). This interpretation gained greater credibility in light of President Musharraf's statement, in December 2002, that war with India was averted because of his repeated warnings that if Indian forces crossed the border Pakistan's response would not be confined to conventional warfare.[3]

Conventional Forces and Strategic Deterrence

Pakistan's conventional armed forces are viewed as the first line of defense against an Indian conventional military attack and the backbone of the country's overall deterrence posture. Strategic deterrence is believed to depend on a robust conventional military capability that can deter an attack, make adversaries' offensive plans costly, and counterattack against incoming forces. Pakistan's nuclear weapons are intended to limit the scope and duration of an Indian conventional military attack should conventional deterrence fail and to inflict unacceptable damage on India's military and industrial infrastructure should Pakistan's conventional armed forces become overwhelmed.

Significant portions of Pakistan's land forces have been deployed along the LoC in Kashmir since 1948. However, the majority of armed forces is not deployed and carries out training for war in peacetime garrisons that are carefully selected with the proximity of the operational areas in mind. Since the mid-1980s, a series of crises—Siachen glacier (1984), Brasstacks (1986–87), and a Kashmir uprising (1990)—have prompted numerous force deployments and alerts. Following the 2002 crisis, the Indian army's adoption of a Cold Start doctrine of limited war, which calls for rapid attacks within hours against Pakistani military targets, has created new challenges for Pakistan's strategic planners. The time frame for crisis escalation could become so compressed that Pakistani planners would feel compelled to cross the threshold of nuclear use much earlier than contemplated in the past. Anticipation of this condition could cause Pakistan to change its nuclear force posture from the present nondeployed status to a near-alert hair-trigger deployment (Khan 2005).

Pakistan's operational planning for conventional war fighting probably does not involve the use of tactical nuclear weapons (Cotta-Ramusino and Martellini 2002). Corps and division commanders do not command any nuclear forces. These are organized in service strategic commands and are centrally managed by unified civil-military control under the NCA. Pakistan's conventional military plans do not rely on the use of nuclear weapons, but emphasize fighting conventional battles based on traditional principles of terrain, tactics, and conventional firepower. Since the late-1980s, Pakistan's leaders, starting with General Mirza Aslam Beg, embraced an operational concept referred to as "riposte," which was tested in 1989–90 in "Exercise Zarb-i-Momin" (Cloughley 1999: 307–09). This concept came about in response to offensive concepts developed by Beg's Indian counterpart, General K. Sundarji, famously known for the provocative Brasstacks military exercise. In 1986–87, a crisis ensued when Sundarji planned a military exercise close to the border, complete with full complements of live ammunition and logistical support. Fearing the worst, Pakistan retaliated by counterdeploying military forces. Some analysts believe that Sundarji was planning to trigger a war in the process (Perkovich 1999: 280; Sagan and Waltz 2003: 94–95).

The 2001–02 military crises revealed Pakistan's strategic orientation. Shortly after the December 13, 2001, terrorist strike against the Indian parliament, India mobilized its armed forces close to the Pakistan border. Pakistan countermobilized immediately by putting its own armed forces on the border, bringing the two neighbors into an intense confrontation. Geography and short distances to the battlefield helped Pakistan's military planners reach their designated strike positions more quickly than their opposite numbers, thus eliminating the element of surprise and nullifying any advantage that India might have had by striking across the border first. The crisis peaked in May 2002 when another terrorist incident upped the ante, and the Pakistani leadership received tactical intelligence that India once again was preparing to attack in early June 2002. Pakistan's military command was instructed to counterattack immediately should India cross the international border or the Kashmir LoC. This message was conveyed on open wireless communication in the hope that it would be intercepted by India.[4]

President Musharraf acknowledges this strategy in his memoir: "We went through a period of extreme tension throughout 2002, when Indian troops amassed on our borders during a hair-trigger, eyeball-to-eyeball confrontation.

We responded by moving all our forces forward. The standoff lasted ten months. Then the Indians blinked and quite ignominiously agreed to a mutual withdrawal of forces" (Musharraf 2006: 301). By demonstrating its readiness to use conventional military force in response to any Indian provocation, Pakistan hoped then, and still hopes today, to compensate for India's advantages in conventional troop numbers and equipment quality with demonstrations of resolve and the willingness to run greater military risks.

Nuclear Weapon Stockpile and Delivery Systems

India and Pakistan each claim minimum deterrence policies; but in South Asia minimum deterrence does not call for a finite ceiling on the development of nuclear weapons and delivery systems. As defined in India's 1999 draft doctrine, minimum deterrence is a dynamic concept that changes with the evolving threat environment. The "minimum" label has more to do with Indian and Pakistani desires not to provoke nuclear-armed adversaries (China and India, respectively) or the United States and other nonproliferation stalwarts. It does not mean set limits on fissile material inventories or force structures. Pakistan likely calculates its strategic force requirements in terms of what it needs to survive an Indian attack and destroy significant Indian military and industrial targets. This includes a sufficiently large weapons stockpile to ensure dispersal to multiple launch sites and the capacity to launch nuclear weapons even after suffering an Indian nuclear attack (Yusuf 2005). As India's technological capabilities increase and new conventional and war-fighting doctrines emerge (e.g., Cold Start), Pakistan would seek to improve the number, range, accuracy, and miniaturization of its warheads, as well as its command and control systems. Gradually, it may shift from a simple countervalue retaliation strategy to a combination of counterforce and countercontrol targeting.

According to public estimates of Pakistan's fissile material stockpile at the end of 2006, Islamabad has amassed between 30 and 85 kilograms of weapon-grade plutonium from its Khushab research reactor and between 1,300 and 1,700 kilograms of highly enriched uranium (HEU) from the Kahuta gas centrifuge facility. The output of the Khushab reactor is estimated to be between 10 and 15 kilograms of plutonium per year, and Pakistan reportedly is constructing another such reactor (Khushab-2), which is expected to have a similar capacity. Unconfirmed reports discuss a commercial-scale reprocessing facility at Chashma, which will likely double or triple Pakistan's plutonium-producing capacity in a decade or so (Albright and Brannan 2007). The Kahuta centrifuge plant is able to produce about 100 kilograms of HEU each year. To date, there is no indication that another HEU facility is being planned or constructed in Pakistan. Based on the assumption that 5 to 7 kilograms of plutonium are required to make one warhead

TABLE 7-1.
Estimates of Pakistan's Fissile Material and Nuclear Weapons, End of 2006

	Low	Medium	High
Weapon-grade plutonium (kg)	30	55	85
Weapon-grade uranium (kg)	1,300	1,500	1,700
Number of weapons	70	90	115

and 20 to 25 kilograms of HEU are needed to produce a bomb, by the end of 2006 Pakistan could have accumulated enough fissile material to manufacture between 70 and 115 nuclear weapons (Institute for Science and International Security [ISIS] 2005).[5] A mid-range estimate based on these figures would mean that Pakistan could have an arsenal of about 90 weapons (see Table 7-1).

Details about the deployment of Pakistan's nuclear weapon systems during peacetime are not known, but it is generally believed that nuclear weapons are not mated with delivery systems. Nuclear warheads and missile delivery systems are believed to be stored in secure locations, separate from one another—possibly not too far apart—and are mated only when a command order is given. Delivery aircraft are spread over the country's ten major air bases or forward operating air bases. Since 2000, Pakistan has started to set up strategic forces in all three services, two of which (land and air) are presently operational.

Pakistan relies on a combination of aircraft and ballistic missiles for nuclear delivery missions. Two aircraft in its inventory, the U.S.-supplied F-16 Fighting Falcon multirole fighter and the French Mirage 5PA, are particularly well suited to this role. Pakistan has about 50 Mirage 5s and 35 1980s-vintage F-16s. At the end of 2006 the United States agreed to provide midlife upgrades for Pakistan's existing F-16 aircraft and to transfer another eighteen F-16s to the Pakistan air force (Grevatt 2007).

In the 1990s, nonproliferation sanctions curtailed Pakistan's ability to modernize its air force. In response, Islamabad aggressively sought to procure technology and parts for a variety of ballistic missiles. Today, Pakistan possesses a missile force comprising road- and rail-mobile solid-fuel missiles (Abdali, Ghaznavi, and Shaheen 1 and 2) as its mainstay, and the less accurate liquid-fuel missiles (Ghauri 1 and 2) for long-range strikes against population centers deep in India. Pakistan is also working on a ground-launched cruise missile, called the Babur, which was tested first in August 2005 and again in March 2006. Table 7-2 lists the main air and missile delivery systems in Pakistan's inventory.[6]

Pakistan does not openly discuss its nuclear targeting policy. India's proximity, however, exposes it to both Pakistani aircraft and short- and long-range ballistic missiles. Pakistan can place major Indian industrial centers, military-industrial complexes, and defense facilities at risk. Nearly three-fourths of Indian armed forces, including air and army bases, are deployed against Pakistan, placing them

TABLE 7-2.
Pakistan's Nuclear Delivery Systems

Aircraft/Missile	Range	Source	Status
F-16 A/B	925 km	United States	35 planes in inventory
Mirage 5 PA	1,300 km	France	50 planes in inventory
Hatf $_1$	80–100 km	Indigenous	In service since mid-1990s
Hatf $_2$ (Abdali)	180 km	Indigenous/China	Tested in May 2002, in service
Hatf $_3$ (Ghaznavi)	300 km	Indigenous/China	M-11, tested May 2002, in service
Hatf $_4$ (Shaheen 1)	600–800 km	Indigenous/China	First tested October 2002, in service
Hatf $_5$ (Ghauri 1)	1,300–1,500 km	Indigenous/DPRK	Nodong, tested May 2002, in service
Hatf $_5$ (Ghauri 2)	2,000 km	Indigenous/DPRK	Nodong, tested April 2002, in development
Hatf $_6$ (Shaheen 2)	2,000–2,500 km	Indigenous/China	First tested March 2004, in development
Hatf $_7$ (Babur)	500 km GLCM	Indigenous/China?	First tested August 2005, in development

within range.[7] After three wars and numerous military crises, the deployment patterns of the Indian armed forces are well known to Pakistan's defense planners.

There is considerable ambiguity regarding the type of warheads that each system can carry. Fighter planes, bombers, and ballistic missiles can carry both conventional and nuclear warheads, and given Pakistan's doctrine of ambiguity there is no way to distinguish which missile system or aircraft is nuclear tipped. This confusion and uncertainty about warheads makes the possibility of waging a conventional war highly destabilizing. Should a conventional war break out, almost all Indian air force bases and army concentration centers would risk attack by Pakistan with multiple delivery means.

Force Posture

Pakistan's nuclear force posture is based on the government's calculations about regional developments, strategic alignment, and threat perception. Pakistan's nuclear force was recessed until the late 1990s: the program was dormant, opaque, and nonweaponized, but had the capacity to be rapidly weaponized and deployed on short notice. The delivery systems, particularly those using solid-fuel missile technology, remained under the PAEC, which had created research and development organizations for special projects. The liquid-fuel technology systems were under the KRL. After the establishment of the SPD in 1999, Pakistan created new military units exclusively for nuclear operations. These included the creation of strategic force commands in all three services. Subsequently, the warheads and the delivery means were handed over to units and brigades under the strategic force commands. Even though the strategic forces are in place and carry out their peacetime training on missiles, they are not believed to have live mated nuclear weapons on any of their delivery systems.

From the outset, Pakistan planned to base its deterrence on a relatively small and nonthreatening nuclear force comprising a small number of aircraft-delivered weapons and a combination of liquid- and solid-fuel ballistic missiles. However, a series of crises from 1999 through 2002 prompted Pakistan to shift to a larger, more sophisticated, and more operationally oriented nuclear force posture, but one still based on a dyad of land- and air-based forces. Over the next four to five years, Pakistan is likely to maintain a nondeployed force posture, with its missiles and warheads stored in separate locations. At the same time, Pakistan is likely to improve its command and control system by integrating real-time information inputs, radar-based early warning systems, and redundant and reliable communications systems for the strategic forces.

A dramatic deterioration in the security situation may well propel Islamabad to shift to a more operationally oriented force posture. The impetus for change would likely be external factors, such as an expanded U.S.-Indian strategic partnership or a weapons buildup by India in reaction to the modernization of Chinese armed forces (Winner and Yoshihara 2001: 48). Such a posture would feature a large number of ballistic missiles. Fighter aircraft for tactical as well as strategic delivery, probably produced jointly by China and Pakistan, also would play a major delivery role. In addition, Pakistan might field highly accurate shorter-range missiles to deliver miniaturized warheads for greater counterforce targeting against India's conventional forces, command and control centers, and launch sites.

Such an operationally oriented force posture would likely be based on a triad, which would include a naval leg. Research and development for the naval nuclear option already has begun. Pakistan tested a cruise missile (Hatf 7, or Babur) in August 2005. It is likely that a sea-based submarine-launched cruise missile would be deployed in the near future. Further, since defense cooperation between Pakistan and China remains a secret, it is unclear whether those two countries would develop joint maritime strategies in the Indian Ocean. Pakistan is unlikely to develop a power projection capability. Its sea-based strategic force eventually could provide the assured second-strike capability against targets deep on the Indian peninsula.

Two factors are likely to affect Pakistan's force posture in the future. The first is the sophistication India's air force can achieve through new platforms and upgrades that will affect Pakistan's survivability measures. Second is the degree of improvement and lethality of India's air defenses, particularly if India deploys ballistic missile defenses, which will force Pakistan to reassess its targeting requirements. The introduction of these technologies is likely to tilt the offense-defense balance in ways that will force Islamabad to seek countervailing strategies.

In the short term, Pakistan is unlikely to lower the threshold for nuclear weapon use. It has worked hard to increase the robustness of its conventional fighting capability in order to keep the nuclear threshold as high as possible. As its nuclear delivery capacity improves—especially the range and accuracy of its missile inventory—Pakistan likely will continue to target major Indian industrial cities using its strategic assets, most notably its short-range ballistic missiles, in conventional roles to offset India's air superiority. Using ballistic missiles that can carry nuclear or conventional warheads would create greater instability, as neither India nor Pakistan can determine which missile is nuclear tipped. This could precipitate a nuclear exchange on false warning in the fog of war. In the long run, Islamabad might seek relatively greater sophistication in forces that might reach beyond the Indian subcontinent into areas of the Persian Gulf and Middle East—provided there is an emerging threat from these areas.

Pakistan's force posture is tied to India's decisions on the overall peace and security architecture of the region. If India and Pakistan work toward conflict resolution and enter into a formal arms control agreement, Pakistan's nuclear forces are likely to remain unmated. If there is no negotiated peace or prospect of conflict resolution between the two countries, Pakistan's force posture will increasingly focus on operational readiness. A more robust Pakistani nuclear posture in reaction to India's force modernization will make crisis stability elusive.

Command and Control and Strategic Stability

After the 1998 nuclear tests, Islamabad placed a premium on creating a robust command and control system. The nuclear program had been spread among three separate organizations. PAEC controlled the front end of the fuel cycle that produced yellow cake and hexafluoride gas. KRL converted the hexafluoride gas into enriched uranium. And the National Defense Complex was responsible for the metallization and preparation of warheads. But no structured command system was put in place until President Musharraf took control. Further, Pakistan's three strategic priorities—integration of conventional and nuclear forces, a deterrence strategy of limited flexible response, and survivable nuclear forces—necessitated the creation of a robust nuclear command and control apparatus. Finally, stable and secure command and control was judged to be an essential component in ensuring strategic stability.

In February 2000, President Musharraf formally established Pakistan's NCA. The NCA operates much like the decision-making body that earlier was responsible for national security affairs: the Defense Cabinet Committee. The NCA is sited in the Joint Services Headquarters and has a new secretariat, the SPD. The SPD supports each of the two main elements of the NCA. The Employment Control Committee (ECC), the country's top decision-making group, provides policy direction and has the authority over the strategic forces. It is chaired by the president and includes the prime minister (who is vice chairman) and key cabinet ministers. The second, subordinate committee is the Developmental Control Committee, which comprises military and scientific elements. It is tasked with optimizing the technical and financial efficiency of the entire program to implement the strategic force goals set by the ECC.

The command and control system Pakistan has adopted does not resemble the elaborate architectures of the United States and Soviet Union during the Cold War. Pakistan faces a much different security predicament, holds different views on the role of nuclear weapons during conflict, and has fewer resources to devote to either nuclear competition with India or its command and control apparatus. Pakistan gradually has disclosed the basic features of its nuclear command and control organization (see Associated Press of Pakistan 2000; Pakistan Ministry of Foreign Affairs 2000).

For new nuclear powers, concerns and expectations about command and control of nuclear weapons are often mixed with broader concerns about the safety, security, survivability, and stewardship of nuclear weapons and sensitive material under conditions of peace, crisis, and war. The safety requirements include measures to prevent nuclear weapon accidents and to ensure they perform as intended. Security involves physical custody and control practices to prevent theft, sabotage, unauthorized access, tampering, and use of nuclear forces and materials. Survivability is essential for assured retaliation against the adversary, inflicting unacceptable damage in a timely manner. The survival of Pakistan's strategic forces requires a carefully planned configuration of the command, control, communications, and intelligence systems combined with the surveillance and reconnaissance system.

As the weaker state in an asymmetric environment, Pakistan faces inherent tensions and contradictory command and control dilemmas. Fear that communications might be disrupted or collapse in a conventional war provides an incentive to predelegate in an extreme situation of war. Such a scenario might well lead to inadvertent use of nuclear weapons during a conventional war. It then would become difficult to calculate escalation control thresholds and to anticipate red lines. For these reasons, conventional war between two nuclear-armed neighbors is inherently dangerous. This condition was recognized in early 1963, when Morton H. Halperin concluded that a limited war in a nuclear environment would almost certainly expand and that attempts to limit escalation, guided by the anticipation of an adversary's response and prediction of that adversary's reactions, are certain to be wrong (Halperin 1963: 2).

Implications for Regional Stability

The introduction of nuclear weapons in South Asia not only created a dangerous new security dilemma, it also gave birth to new strategic concepts that were largely unknown or untested during the Cold War. Four distinct strategic "realities" have emerged with the rise of regional nuclear forces. First, although asymmetric military strategies have existed in South Asia since Pakistan's independence in 1947 and the subsequent wars with India in 1947–48, 1965, and 1971, Pakistan has continued this tradition in defense planning despite the presence of weapons of mass destruction on both sides of the border. In this respect, Pakistan's defense planners may overestimate the value of nuclear deterrence. Second, in order to counter Pakistan's asymmetric strategies, Indian defense planners have tried to find space to wage limited conventional war on India's own terms—something that the Cold War belligerents discussed but never fully implemented. Third is the South Asian notion of escalation control or escalation control denial. Strategies on both sides are based on the belief that the adversary will be forced to change its security policies because each assumes that it will be able to retain escalation control or deny it to the adversary in a military crisis. Fourth, each side pursues a strategy of brinkmanship. Because of the growing realization that war is suicidal, and thus infeasible, the threat of force might produce political dividends either by forcing the other side to yield or by inducing the intervention of a greater power to resolve issues in its favor. None of these strategies is conducive to regional stability.

Conventional wisdom holds that the display of nuclear weapon capabilities by India and Pakistan in 1998 ought to have raised caution and restraint in bilateral relations. But the true understanding of nuclear revolution is always a delayed phenomenon (Jervis 1989: 1–45; Lavoy 1998: 260–371). Two recent major crises—Kargil in 1999 and the military standoff in 2001–02—and two earlier ones in the covert nuclear days—Brasstacks in 1986–87 and the 1990 Kashmir crisis—indicate that nuclear weapons did not bring about an era of détente in the region (Feinstein 2002: 3–4). Indeed, they exacerbated the intensity of regional crises: in each successive crisis the probability of deterrence failure was higher than before. Nevertheless, South Asia has remained free of total war since the advent of nuclear weapons, and even though crises peaked, they did not spiral out of control—a state Ashley Tellis calls "ugly stability" (Tellis 1997).

The Cold War concept of the stability-instability paradox is applicable in a nuanced manner. Nuclear forces have prevented war at the nuclear level, but have paved the way for low-level military activity. India and Pakistan have severely tested each other's patience threshold, even though they have maintained a high degree of nuclear discipline in all of the recent crises. These strategic competitors largely disagree about the locus of instability in the region. India accuses Pakistan of creating nuclear dangers by supporting infiltration of Indian-administered Kashmir and political instability in other parts of India. Pakistan in turn charges that India raises nuclear risk by repeatedly flexing its conventional military muscles on any pretext, thus leaving Pakistan with fewer defense options.

In addition, Pakistan believes that India's acquisition of destabilizing technologies (air force platform upgrades, space programs, and ballistic missile defenses), along with threats to undertake punitive hot pursuit and limited war, are designed to undermine Pakistan's deterrence. According to Pakistani military planners,

India's constant testing of Pakistan's determination and resolve pushes it into a corner. Pakistan is forced to choose between lowering the nuclear threshold and matching Indian provocations with conventional force. Ironically, this dilemma contributes to Pakistan's reliance on asymmetric strategies. After all, insurgencies in Kashmir have occupied large numbers of Indian conventional forces that would otherwise be menacing Pakistan with even more strength and vigor.

Pakistan's strategy of supporting insurgency against its larger, nuclear-armed neighbor is a dangerous one. Nuclear and revolutionary warfare strategies have existed simultaneously for the past sixty years, but the Cold War belligerents quickly learned to temper their revolutionary zeal in the interest of strategic stability. The situation may be more complicated in South Asia because of the proximity of the two adversaries and the intensity of bilateral disputes, animosity, and mistrust. Renewal of Pakistan's support for Kashmiri insurgents could well trigger a conventional military response by India. The seemingly unshakable confidence of Pakistani strategists that conventional war will be deterred by nuclear weapons may be on solid theoretical and empirical ground, but the very success of this strategy to date has pushed India to develop new strategies for its conventional forces, such as the Indian army's Cold Start doctrine (Haider 2003: 142; Yusuf 2005). Further, Pakistan's efforts to bring India to the negotiation table are also flawed, especially owing to the systemic changes after 9/11, which provide zero international tolerance for terrorism. India finds itself on the moral high ground in responding to terror-type tactics by insurgents. Conversely, Pakistan has lost moral standing by supporting what it believes is the just cause of Kashmiri freedom. That policy isolates Pakistan and raises the danger of domestic instability through backlash and radicalism within Pakistan.

Pakistan's strategy of offsetting India's conventional force superiority by relying on nuclear deterrence is analogous to the NATO strategy of countering superior Soviet conventional forces in Europe. As was true of NATO, Pakistan lacks strategic depth, and its major communications centers are vulnerable to enemy attack. However, there is a critical difference between the NATO and Pakistani positions. Strategically and technically, Pakistan does not have NATO's ability to assess threats in real time. The close proximity and potential for rapid deployment of nuclear forces in a sudden crisis makes the risk of escalation as high, if not higher, in South Asia (Quinlan 2001: 150). Pakistan also is likely to react more quickly than NATO to false warnings and fears of preventive strikes because NATO has multiple means of verifying threats before responding. For its part, India has repeatedly attempted to intimidate Pakistan through conventional force deployments, threats, and coercion against an insecure nuclear-armed neighbor, rather than focusing on conflict resolution. Pakistan is thus left with few choices but to keep its nuclear options open and ambiguous.

India and Pakistan probably will continue to assume that they can retain escalation control as crises escalate to total war. India's plan to wage a conventional war and keep it limited is based on the assumption that it can terminate a war at will. But it is dangerous to assume that it is possible to control escalation in a conventional war when nuclear weapons loom in the background. Both Pakistan and India have therefore designed their brinkmanship strategies to garner outside intervention (primarily from the United States) to help terminate the conflict or push their respective interests forward (Limaye 2003: 159). Nuclear weapons have created a curious dilemma for stability in the region by making states independent in their brinkmanship actions yet still dependent on outside powers to diffuse tension in times of extreme crisis (Khan 2003: 15–19).

Future Challenges

The future is likely to bring several difficult challenges for Pakistan and its nuclear strategy. Pakistan faced shocks at four different times over the past three decades that fundamentally altered its security environment: the 1971 war over East Pakistan and the 1974 nuclear explosion by India; the 1979 Soviet invasion of Afghanistan and the revolution in Iran; the 1990 Kashmir crisis and U.S. withdrawal from the region; and finally, the 9/11 terrorist attacks in the United States and the 2001–02 military crisis with India. Each of these events enabled powerful lobbies to institutionalize the role of nuclear weapons in Pakistan's security policy and to become more influential in Pakistan's national security organizations and political culture. Even sanctions and international isolation did not alter this course. The popular appeal of nuclear weapons caused fence-sitters to join the bandwagon. As a result, there now exists a near absolute consensus on the importance of nuclear weapons for Pakistan's security in the Pakistani polity. This consensus is likely to create an intense interest in modernizing and expanding the nuclear force in response to new security trends and shocks.

What role nuclear weapons play in Pakistan's policy and in its regional and international engagements in the context of the evolving Asian power balance will depend primarily on four developments: first, how the war on terrorism proceeds and the role Pakistan plays in it; second, how regional dynamics affect conflict resolution and the regional power balance between India and Pakistan; third, how the United States acts in Asia (particularly with respect to China and India) and toward the Islamic world (particularly with respect to Iran); and fourth, Pakistan's own domestic political development under, or after, military rule. For now Pakistan's strategy is to revive itself economically, which is at the core of President Musharraf's vision. In the near term Pakistan will grapple with the inherent tension over its requirement to match external developments against the exigencies of domestic prosperity. Pakistan's desire to match developments in India is easily predictable. Pakistan's response in the medium to long term to the rise of India will affect major reconfigurations in regional alliances and the Asian power balance.

Notes

The authors wish to thank Adam Radin for valuable research assistance. The views expressed are the authors' alone; they do not represent the positions of the Naval Postgraduate School, the U.S. Department of Defense, or any other organization.

1. At the time of partition, even the British viceroy considered the division of India as temporary, "like pitching a tent or a nissun hut" (Uz-Zaman 1969).

2. Written shortly after the 1965 war with India, Bhutto's *The Myth of Independence* contains the rationale for a Pakistani "nuclear deterrent," which continues today as state policy. See Bhutto (1969: 153).

3. Musharraf told an army corps gathering in Karachi that he was prepared to take severe measures at the height of the 2002 crisis: "In my meetings with various world leaders, I conveyed my personal message to Indian Prime Minister Vajpayee that the moment Indian forces cross the Line of Control and the international border, then they should not expect a conventional war from Pakistan." Musharraf added: "I believe my message was effectively conveyed to Mr. Vajpayee" (*The News International* 2002).

4. Authors' conversations with senior Pakistan military officers, June 2006.

5. A separate study by a team of Indian and Pakistani analysts puts Pakistan's plutonium inventory slightly higher (90 kilograms) and its HEU holding slightly lower (1,300 kilograms). See Mian et al. (2006).

6. Information contained in the table is from various sources, including *Jane's Sentinel Security Assessment* (2006) and *Jane's World Air Forces* (2006), both subscription websites.

7. India has twelve corps, nine of which are deployed against Pakistan. Two-thirds of India's air force and navy are poised or operationally active on the India-Pakistan border. For details see ISIS (2005: 223–58).

References

Albright, David, and Paul Brannan. 2007. "Chashma Nuclear Site in Pakistan with Possible Reprocessing Plant." Institute for Science and International Security website, January 18. Available at http://www.isis-online.org/publications/southasia/chashma.pdf.

Associated Press of Pakistan. 2000. "National Command Authority Established," February 3. http://www.fas.org/news/pakistan/2000/000203-pak-app1.htm.

Basrur, Rajesh M. 2005. "Coercive Diplomacy in a Nuclear Environment: The December 13 Crisis." In *Prospects for Peace in South Asia,* ed. Rafiq Dossani and Henry S. Rowen. Stanford, CA: Stanford University Press.

Bhutto, Zulfikar Ali. 1969. *The Myth of Independence.* Karachi: Oxford University Press.

Boyes, Roger. 2002. "Musharraf Warns India He May Use Nuclear Weapons." *Times Online,* April 8. Available at www.thetimes.co.uk/article/0,,3-260481,00.html.

Cheema, Pervez Iqbal. 1990. *Pakistan's Defense Policy 1947–58.* New York: St. Martin's.

Cheema, Zafar Iqbal. 2000. "Pakistan's Nuclear Use Doctrine and Command and Control." In *Planning the Unthinkable: How New Powers Will Use Nuclear, Biological, and*

Chemical Weapons, ed. Peter R. Lavoy, Scott D. Sagan, and James Wirtz. Ithaca, N.Y.: Cornell University Press.

Cloughley, Brian. 1999. *A History of Pakistan Army: Wars and Resurrections.* New York: Oxford University Press.

Cotta-Ramusino, Paolo, and Maurizio Martellini. 2002. "Nuclear Safety, Nuclear Stability and Nuclear Strategy in Pakistan." Concise Report of a Visit by Landau Network-Centro Volta, January 21. Available at http://lxmi.mi.infn.it/~landnet. The Draft Report of National Security Advisory Board on Indian Nuclear Doctrine can be found at http://www.meadev.nic.in/govt/indnucld.htm.

Daily Times (Lahore). 2002. "Are Pakistani Nukes More Effective Than Indian?" Available at http://www.dailytimes.com.pk/print.asp?page=story_13-12-2002_pg1_11.

Feinstein, Lee. 2002. "Avoiding Another Close Call in South Asia." *Arms Control Today* (July/August): 3–4.

Grevatt, John. 2007. "USAF Awards Lockheed Martin Pakistan's F-16 Upgrade." *Jane's Defence Industry,* January 1.

Haider, Ejaz. 2003. "Managing Nuclear Weapons in South Asia: In Search of a Model." In *India's Nuclear Fantasies: Costs and Ethics,* ed. M. V. Ramana and C. Rammanohar Reddy. Hyderabad, India: Orient Longman.

Halperin, Morton H. 1963. *Limited War in the Nuclear Age.* New York: John Wiley & Sons.

Hashmi, Sohail H. 2004. "Islamic Ethics and Weapons of Mass Destruction: An Argument for Nonproliferation." In *Ethics and Weapons of Mass Destruction: Religious and Secular Perspectives,* ed. Sohail H. Hashmi and Steven P. Lee. New York: Cambridge University Press.

Institute for Science and International Security (ISIS). 2005. "Global Stocks of Nuclear Explosive Materials," July 12, revised September 7. Available at http://www.isis-online.org/global_stocks/end2003/tableofcontents.html.

International Institute for Strategic Studies (IISS). 2007. *Nuclear Black Markets: Pakistan, A. Q. Khan and the Rise of Proliferation Networks.* London: ISIS.

Jane's Sentinel Security Assessment: South Asia. 2006. "Pakistan: Armed Forces," November 22.

Jane's World Air Forces. 2006. "Pakistan: Air Force," November 28.

Jervis, Robert. 1989. *The Meaning of the Nuclear Revolution: Statecraft and the Prospect of Armageddon.* Ithaca, N.Y.: Cornell University Press.

Khan, Feroz Hassan. 2003. "The Dependence–Independence Paradox: Stability Challenges in South Asia." *Arms Control Today* 33 (8).

———. 2005. "Nuclear Command-and-Control in South Asia during Peace Crisis and War." *Contemporary South Asia* 14 (June): 163–74.

Kux, Dennis. 2001. *United States and Pakistan, 1947–2000: Disenchanted Allies.* Washington, D.C.: Woodrow Wilson Center.

Lavoy, Peter R. 1998. "South Asia's Nuclear Revolution: Has It Occurred Yet?" In *The Nuclear Non-Proliferation Regime: Prospects for the 21st Century,* ed. G. Raju and C. Thomas. New York: St. Martin's.

———. 2007. "Pakistan's Nuclear Posture: Security and Survivability." Nonproliferation Policy Education Center. Available at http://www.npec-web.org.

Limaye, Satu. 2003. "Mediating Kashmir: A Bridge Too Far." *Washington Quarterly* Winter 26(1): 159.

Mian, Zia, A. H. Nayyar, R. Rajaraman, and M. V. Ramana. 2006. "Fissile Materials in South Asia: The Implications of the U.S.-India Nuclear Deal." International Panel on Fissile Materials Research Report no. 1, September. Available at http://www.fissilematerials.org/ipfm/site_down/ipfmresearchreport01.pdf.

Musharraf, Pervez. 2006. *In the Line of Fire: A Memoir.* New York: Simon and Schuster.

Nayak, Polly. 2002. "Reducing Collateral Damage to Indo-Pakistani Relations from the War on Terrorism." Policy Brief 107. Washington, D.C.: Brookings Institution.

The News International. 2002. "India Was Warned of Unconventional War," December 31. Available at http://www.jang.com.pk/thenews/dec2002-daily/31-12-2002/main/main2.htm.

Pakistan Ministry of Foreign Affairs. 2000. "Organization of Pakistan's National Command Authority." Available at http://www.forisb.org/NCA.html.

Perkovich. 1999. *India's Nuclear Bomb: The Impact on global Proliferation.* Berkeley and Los Angeles: University of California Press.

Quinlan, Michael. 2001. "How Robust Is India-Pakistan Deterrence?" *Survival* 42 (4): 150.

Raghavan, V. R. 2002. "Limited War and Nuclear Escalation in South Asia." *Non-Proliferation Review* 8 (3): 84.

Rizvi, Hasan-Askari. 2001. "Pakistan's Nuclear Testing." *Asian Survey* 41 (6): 943–55.

Rubin, Barnett, and Abubakar Siddique. 2006. *Resolving the Pakistan-Afghanistan Stalemate.* Special Report 176. Washington, D.C.: United States Institute of Peace.

Sagan, Scott D., and Kenneth N. Waltz. 2003. *The Spread of Nuclear Weapons: A Debate Renewed.* New York: W. W. Norton.

Schofield, Victoria. 2003. *Kashmir in Conflict: India, Pakistan and the Unending War.* London: I. B. Tauris.

Shahi, Agha, Zulfiqar Ali Khan, and Abdul Sattar. 1999. "Securing Nuclear Peace." *News International,* October 5.

Swami, Praveen. 2006. *India, Pakistan, and the Secret Jihad: The Covert War in Kashmir, 1947–2004.* New Delhi: Routledge.

Tellis, Ashley. 1997. "Stability in South Asia." Documented Briefings for the U.S. Army, RAND.

Uz-Zaman, Waheed. 1969. *Towards Pakistan.* Lahore, Pakistan: Publishers United.

Weaver, Mary Anne. 2002. *Pakistan: In the Shadow of Jihad and Afghanistan.* New York: Farrar, Straus and Giroux.

Winner, Andrew C., and Toshi Yoshihara. 2001. *Nuclear Stability in South Asia.* Boston: Institute of Foreign Policy Analysis.

Yusuf, Moeed. 2005. "Nuclear Stabilization in South Asia." *South Asian Journal* (January/March). Available at http://www.southasianmedia.net/Magazine/Journal/7_nuclear_stabilisation.htm [January 27, 2007].

8

Israel
A Sui Generis Proliferator

AVNER COHEN

Israel is commonly viewed as the world's sixth nuclear power, the first and the only state in the Middle East to have acquired nuclear weapons. While exact figures are unknown, it is generally believed that the Israeli nuclear arsenal is significant in numbers and advanced in quality. Estimates of the Israeli nuclear arsenal vary, usually ranging from fewer than 100 up to 200 or more warheads (Cirincione et al. 2005; Hersh 1991; SIPRI 2006). Even by this modest estimate Israel appears to have a lead over both India and Pakistan in the strength of its nuclear arsenal.[1]

These estimates, however, ignore Israel's most distinct feature as a nuclear power: its commitment to caution and constraint as manifested in its unique code of nuclear conduct. To this day, two generations after Israel crossed the nuclear threshold, it has not acknowledged its nuclear status. This extraordinary conduct sets Israel apart from all other established nuclear weapon states. And Israel has never issued a membership claim to the nuclear club. And Israel has never issued an explicit nuclear threat. At home, Israeli military censors do not allow the media to refer factually to the nation's nuclear weapons; all reference to such nuclear weapons has to be attributed to "foreign sources." Nuclear caution—in the form of a strict policy and conduct of nuclear opacity—is probably Israel's most original contribution to the nuclear age. It complements the commitment to nuclear resolve.

The interaction between these two opposing forces—resolve and caution—has shaped the direction and character of Israel's nuclear policy throughout its history. It is the key to understanding the special purpose and role that nuclear weapons play in Israel's national security strategy, the way Israel has built its nuclear forces, and the nonproliferation diplomacy it has devised over the years. In all, this constitutes Israel's portrait as a sui generis case of proliferation.

In this chapter I elaborate, from a historical perspective, on Israel's nuclear policies and posture as that country confronts the new challenges of the early twenty-first century. Specifically, the chapter focuses on the following issues: Israel's fundamental nuclear dilemma, some of its key historical decisions, an appraisal of its current policy, and its looming challenges. I conclude with some reflections on the future.

I must add a note of scholarly caution about the limitations of academic research on this subject. Israel's unique nuclear condition directly affects the state of the research (Cohen 2005c; Dowty 1975, 2005).[2] Given the sketchy and unconfirmed public information that exists on the subject, the core facts in this chapter are inevitably tentative and partial, somewhat interpretive, and at times speculative. A great deal of the historical narrative I present here without additional citation and footnotes is based on my previous (and more detailed) historical accounts (Cohen 1998a, 1998b, 2000, 2003, 2005a, 2005b; Cohen and Burr 2006).

Israel's Fundamental Nuclear Dilemma

One way to conceptualize Israel's nuclear posture is as an ongoing effort to address one fundamental dilemma: whether, how, and to what extent nuclear weapons could serve or disserve Israel's pursuit of existential security. On this issue, Israel's nuclear pursuit has been driven by two opposing impulses or convictions: resolve and caution.

Israel's nuclear resolve is a commitment to develop and acquire the bomb in order to ensure the nation's existential security. This impulse has shaped the way Israel built its nuclear capabilities. The nuclear caution is manifest as a commitment to keep the Middle East free of nuclear weapons because nuclear weapons in enemy hands could pose a genuine existential threat to Israel. This imperative has inspired Israel's nonproliferation and counterproliferation policies (Cohen 1994). Inevitably, there is an intrinsic tension between resolve and caution.

Israel's response to this fundamental dilemma has been somewhat "schizophrenic"; that is, Israel has been trying to maintain both horns of the dilemma. This pattern started with David Ben-Gurion, Israel's first prime minister (1948–53, 1955–63), who initiated the nation's nuclear program in the 1950s, and it continues to this day. Israel's nuclear posture has been ambiguous because the nation has still not sealed its deal with the bomb in a straightforward way.

The Resolve Impulse

To highlight the continuity of the nuclear resolve, one must start with Ben-Gurion's worldview. Imbued with the Holocaust trauma, Ben-Gurion's geopolitical outlook was consumed by a deep existential anxiety about Israel's long-term survival. It stemmed from a sober view of the fundamentals of the Arab-Israeli conflict. Here are the basic features of Ben-Gurion's outlook as they came into being in the years after the 1948 war (Bar Zohar 1987; Ben-Gurion 1969, 1971; Mardor 1981; Shalom 2002).

- *Depth of the conflict.* The Arab-Israeli conflict runs deep—it is a conflict about land—and is not amenable to a quick diplomatic settlement. Hence, more rounds of the Arab-Israeli conflict are likely.
- *Unlikelihood of political settlement.* It would be difficult for the Arabs to accept the outcome of the 1948 war as final. Only when they are convinced that the post-1948 reality cannot be reversed by force could a lasting reconciliation of the conflict—peace—become possible. This is not likely to happen soon.
- *The Holocaust lesson.* The lesson of the Holocaust is that small Israel, lacking a formal alliance with an outside world power, must create its own existential national insurance policy for "a rainy day."
- *Concerns about a pan-Arab grand coalition.* The conventionally armed Israel Defense Forces (IDF) would encounter great difficulty in deterring a pan-Arab war coalition against Israel.
- *Unconventional deterrence.* Given the geopolitical asymmetries of the Arab-Israeli conflict, Israel may not be able to win a conventional arms race with the Arabs. Conventional weapons might not be sufficient to ensure an Israeli edge in deterrence or victory in war for the long run.
- *The "brain" factor.* Only reliance on the fruits of science and technology allows Israel to compensate for its geopolitical disadvantages—that is, its fundamental inferiority in manpower, land, and resources.

This outlook is the key to understanding the Ben-Gurionite origins of Israel's nuclear resolve. For a small nation born out of the ashes of the Holocaust, surrounded by neighbors committed to its destruction, and without a security alliance with any world power, the rationale for pursuing the bomb was obvious.[3] Only nuclear weapons could provide Israel with the existential insurance it needed. The notion of a national nuclear project was conceived as a way to provide future Israeli leaders an extra margin of existential security, a response against unexpected existential threats.

Ben-Gurion's geopolitical outlook was rooted in the historical reality of his time. However, a great deal of his outlook has survived the march of time. By and large, Israelis still see themselves facing existential threats (Arian 1995). Resolving the Palestinian-Israeli conflict—the core of the Arab-Israeli conflict—still looks elusive. And as long as the core issue remains unresolved, so will the larger Arab-Israeli conflict. Despite the peace agreements with Egypt and Jordan, most Israelis still view themselves as a nation under siege (Arian 1995).

The Holocaust as a national memory and a national commitment adds another key perspective to the existential rationale for Israel's nuclear project. With the Holocaust as its founding memory, the State of Israel was established on the pledge never to allow the Jewish people to suffer another Holocaust.[4] As long as Israel faces existential threats, Israel will feel the need to maintain capabilities of existential deterrence—that is, its nuclear capability.

More than half a century after the Holocaust, its impact on the Israeli mind remains as fresh and pervasive as ever. It is the most constitutive experience in Jewish history. For many Jews and non-Jews alike, it is the strongest moral and political justification for the existence of Israel as a Jewish state. Israel's commitment to "Never Again" is stronger now than ever before. The old concern over the formation of a grand Arab conventional war coalition against Israel barely exists anymore; it has been replaced by renewed talk about "wiping Israel off the map."

Six decades after the Holocaust and after the founding of the State of Israel, Israelis are still afflicted with a deep sense of existential anxiety about their place in the world. This existential anxiety may explain why contemporary Israelis view Ben-Gurion's decision to embark on Israel's nuclear project as the most fateful, wise, and praiseworthy set of decisions any Israeli prime minister has ever taken.[5]

The Caution Impulse

Israel's nuclear dilemma, however, has a nearly equal counterimpulse, a force toward nuclear caution. Just as the Holocaust trauma is the key to understanding Israel's nuclear resolve—believing that the capability to inflict the horror of Hiroshima would deter another Auschwitz—this trauma also constitutes the strongest argument *against* the introduction of nuclear weapons. Israel does not want to be responsible for another Auschwitz.

While Israel was seeking to establish a regional nuclear monopoly, it recognized that its own nuclear resolve could reverse itself and lead to a situation of nuclear parity. And that outcome could flip the entire strategic situation. Under nuclear parity, small Israel would be many times more vulnerable than its Arab neighbors to the awesome effects of nuclear weapons. A situation of existential security could very quickly turn into existential insecurity. It is the nuclear specter that causes the image of another Holocaust to loom large to the Jewish people. The conclusion is simple: Israel's interest is to make sure that nuclear weapons are not introduced into the Middle East.

This argument was articulated first in the early 1960s, soon after the nuclear project became known, by a small group of antinuclear intellectuals (Cohen 1998a: 142–46). They opposed nuclearization and argued that if Israel were to initiate a nuclear weapon project it would inevitably lead to a counterdevelopment on the other side, which would make Israel's security dramatically worse. A situation of mutual nuclear deterrence would clearly be to Israel's disadvantage. A small Israel would be much more vulnerable to nuclear weaponry than its Arab (or Persian) foes. From this perspective, Israel's nuclear ambition is self-defeating. The nation's true interest lies in nuclear disarmament—that is, a Middle East free of nuclear weapons.

This campaign never gained the momentum necessary to halt Israel's commitment to nuclear resolve. In the late 1960s, Israel "quietly" crossed the nuclear threshold and the small antinuclear movement disappeared from the public scene. The profound impact of the 1967 Six-Day War dramatically changed the political agenda in Israel; virtually no one had an interest in campaigning against nuclear weapons. But the argument in favor of caution did not fade away; it only changed form. As it turned out, the caution impulse continued to have an influence not only on Israel's diplomatic front but also on Israel's nuclear posture. The caution impulse has profoundly shaped the subtle and opaque way in which Israel deals with its nuclear monopoly.

Today, Iran is the state that challenges Israel's nuclear monopoly. Once again, Israelis have become aware how vulnerable their nation is to nuclear weapons. The old argument against nuclear deterrence from the early 1960s has returned with a vengeance: given the geopolitical asymmetry between Iran and Israel, small Israel is unquestionably much more vulnerable to a devastating nuclear attack than Iran. Israeli strategists have pointed out the difficulty to produce a stable mutual assured destruction (MAD) regime in the Middle East, given the basic geopolitical asymmetry between the parties (Evron 1994; Steinberg 2000).

The Israeli Synthesis: Nuclear Opacity

In responding to its fundamental nuclear dilemma, Israel chose a posture based on a certain compromise that includes elements of both resolve and caution. Ben-Gurion's modus operandi in initiating the project planted the seeds of the Israeli synthesis. He took decisive action on the side of technological resolve (he generally preferred action over inaction) but wrapped it with layers of caution and restraint. The scope of the Dimona project indicates how dedicated and ambitious the founding vision was (Pean 1991; Peres 1995). It included all the technological components required for a plutonium-based nuclear weapon infrastructure. The objective was to place Israel within reach of a complete nuclear option within a decade or so. The determination of the vision was manifest in the most important component of the Dimona project—the deep underground reprocessing plant dedicated to extracting weapon-grade plutonium (Hersh 1991; Pean 1991; Richelson 2005; *Sunday Times* 1986). Nothing could be more indicative of Israel's resolve than this supersecret facility.

Ben-Gurion's initiation decisions were the closest to a grand decision in favor of the bomb, and yet he was reluctant to present them in that light. He apparently presented the Dimona project to his close political associates as a prudent way to hedge against an uncertain future, as a way of building "options" and "infrastructure" for "future leaders," but not as an actual commitment to build the bomb, and certainly not as a commitment to move toward nuclear deterrence. As Shimon Peres (the nuclear project's chief executive officer) noted decades later, Ben-Gurion made decisions only about what was immediately necessary and kept all other issues deliberately vague and formally undecided. Technological resolve was moderated by political caution (Cohen 1998a; Peres 1995).

The conduct of his successor, Levi Eshkol (1963–69), reinforced this pattern even further. Eshkol did not touch the spirit of resolve that had already been infused into the project—that is, the ethos that the mission was to complete the research and development (R&D) phase *in full*. Like Ben-Gurion, Eshkol provided the funds required to complete the infrastructure but left the long-term (post-R&D) objectives vague and undecided. On the side of caution, he pledged that Israel would not be the first to introduce nuclear weapons to the region, and this pledge had one important implication. While Eshkol generally avoided providing political guidance to the project's leaders, there was one important exception: a full-yield test, which is the final act in the development process, was prohibited. On this key issue, political caution won out over technological resolve. This was necessary to maintain the credibility of his commitment to "nonintroduction" (Cohen 1998a: 231–34, 238).

By 1969, the United States realized that its efforts to halt Israel's nuclear development had failed. Israel's nuclear resolve had won, but it was recognized that this could not be publicly acknowledged: the Israeli bomb must remain invisible. This realization, on both sides, opened the door to a new set of nuclear understandings between the United States and Israel. Israel was committed not to test, not to advertise its capability, and not to threaten anybody. In plain language, the Israeli bomb had to remain invisible (Cohen and Burr 2006).

These nuclear understandings that were struck between the United States and Israel by President Richard Nixion and Prime Minister Golda Meir in September 1969 introduced nuclear opacity as a political modus vivendi under which the Israeli bomb would be tolerated by the United States as long as Israel did not acknowledge it in public. In retrospect, the 1969 deal laid the foundations for a unique, almost entirely tacit, code of conduct between the United States and Israel on the nuclear issue. The fundamentals of this code of conduct have survived to this day. Initially, the Israeli bomb was only tolerated but, over the decades, it became acceptable, maybe even quietly endorsed.

It was only in the mid-to-late 1970s, after the advent of the Non-Proliferation Treaty (NPT), that Israel found itself with a need to devise its own nonproliferation policy. Support for the cause of nonproliferation reflects Israel's fundamental commitment to nuclear caution. By that time Israel had already decided that NPT obligations were inconsistent with Israel's nuclear program (nuclear resolve), so Israel had to find another modality to demonstrate its commitment to nonproliferation. After internal deliberation, Israel decided to anchor its commitment to nonproliferation through a regional approach (as opposed to the universal approach of the NPT). Israel decided to commit itself to the vision of a nuclear weapon-free zone (NWFZ) but to link it to the demand for full and mutual political recognition of all the states in the Middle East.

This was a way to demonstrate that Israel was positively committed to the principles of nonproliferation, despite its specific opposition to the NPT. While the NPT is inconsistent with Israel's nuclear weapon program, Israel presented its official opposition to the NPT on the grounds of its inadequacy to address the security situation in the Middle East, in particular the lack of mutual recognition among the states in the region. In other words, only under conditions of peaceful coexistence—that is, after a formal peace had been achieved—could Israel conceive changing its NPT position.

Not only was the NWFZ approach proposed as an alternative to the NPT, but it allowed Israel to explain why it had to reject the NPT, at least for the time being, without openly acknowledging that it had a nuclear weapon program. A nation in conflict when its legitimacy is challenged by its neighbors and is exposed to existential threats cannot rely on the NPT system for its existential security. Notably, Israel defended its decision to stay outside the NPT system not in terms of its own national security requirements (the need to preserve elements of existential deterrence) but rather in terms of the deficiencies of the NPT safeguard system, which a hostile state could abuse to develop nuclear weapons.[6]

The cover of nuclear opacity allows quiet technological resolve to cohabit with a public commitment to nuclear caution. It allows Israel to design its own nonproliferation policy. Opacity permits Israel to keep invisible the tension between resolve and caution.

It is true that Israel's commitment to the NWFZ vision requires nothing immediate. Israel remains a free agent in its nuclear activities, as long as those activities are not visible or public. Still, it means that unlike all other nuclear weapon states, including present-day India and Pakistan, Israel has not made a *public* commitment to possess nuclear weapons. Israel has not legitimized nuclear weapons. This is not meaningless. While some would say that this is merely a matter of rhetoric, I believe that Israel's commitment to the vision of NWFZ reflects a commitment to nuclear caution. It is an affirmation of the principle that Israel has not sealed its bargain with the bomb as final, complete, or official. Israel has stubbornly avoided giving its bomb a seal of legitimacy, either at home (where the issue is taboo) or abroad (where it maintains its exceptionality stance).

Israel's nuclear resolve won the day, but that resolve remains wrapped in layer upon layer of political caution, operational restraint, and societal taboo and secrecy. Some of the Israeli nuclear inhibitions and hesitancy are politically motivated; they are rooted in the 1969 Nixon-Meir understanding and reflect an age-old Israeli realistic view that the "world"—not only the Arab world but even the United States—would not agree to grant Israel a nuclear status similar to, say, that of France. However, Israel's nuclear taboo—its societal and normative avoidance of the topic—cannot be reduced to tactics and convenience (Cohen 2005a).[7] The fact that even today—after four decades of nuclear possession and at a time when the old secret is no longer a secret—Israel is still so loyal to this taboo demonstrates its societal-cultural depth.

Resolve and caution are the two pillars of Israel's nuclear predicament. They are based on two sets of historical memories and lessons. Resolve rests on the lessons of Jewish history, in particular the Holocaust. Caution stems from historical insights about the nuclear age itself, particularly as applied to Israel's unique geopolitical position. Ultimately, both resolve and caution stem from the same site in the Israeli psyche, the vow "Never Again." If the resolve impulse manifests the recognition that the bomb is the only power that could provide Israel a measure of existential security, the caution impulse reflects the realization that nuclearization of the region could place Israel in a much worse existential situation.

Calibrating Resolve and Caution: Four Israeli Nuclear Dilemmas

Calibrating the balance between resolve and caution has been a continuous challenge for Israel's nuclear policy throughout its history. Addressing this challenge has determined the political, diplomatic, and operational parameters of Israel's nuclear posture. In the following sections, I elaborate, in a quasi-historical fashion, on four key related parameters of the Israeli nuclear posture.[8] Together, I believe, they present a portrait of Israel as a sui generis proliferator.

Nuclear Versus Conventional; Political Versus Military

After a nation embarks on a nuclear weapon program, it needs to define a role for nuclear weapons—and the nuclear program as a whole—within its overall national security posture, in particular to determine an adequate ratio between its conventional and nuclear commitments. While Israel was decisive on the issue of the nuclear infrastructure, it was hesitant, slow, and tentative on the question of designing a balance between its conventional and nuclear commitments. Its leadership wanted a nuclear infrastructure, a bomb "option," but was less clear initially about its concrete parameters.

Israel started to think about these matters in the early 1960s. Two schools of thought emerged. One advocated the notion that the IDF should be reorganized to focus on deterrence and achieving "decisive victory" by relying on the anticipated scientific and technological achievements of the 1970s. This school argued that only advanced technological weaponry could provide Israel with the kind of deterrence it needed for the long run without getting caught in an increasingly hopeless conventional arms race that would drain the Israeli economy and tempt the Arabs to prolong the conflict. In the absence of an external security guarantee, the bomb should be Israel's only independent security guarantee. The advocates of this view called it "the doctrine of self-reliance," an Israeli version of the French notion of force de frappe (Cohen 1998a: 149; Evron 1994).

The other school invoked an attitude of skepticism, even opposition, toward nuclear weapons. It carried the message of nuclear caution. Its leaders advocated strengthening the IDF as a strong and modern *conventional* army. They rejected the three fundamental presumptions of the nuclear advocates, questioning the inevitability of the spread of nuclear weapons, dismissing the pessimism underlying the view that the bomb was the only solution for Israel's long-term security, and more important, raising serious doubts about the applicability of nuclear deterrence to the context of the Middle East. Significantly, the conventionalist school maintained that an Israeli nuclear monopoly would be short lived and inevitably replaced by a nuclearized Middle East. They believed that the Soviets would not allow Israel to maintain a nuclear monopoly in the region. Given the geopolitical and demographic asymmetries of the Arab-Israeli conflict, Israel's national interest was at odds with the nuclearization of the conflict. Investment in a dedicated nuclear weapon program would only weaken the IDF and might encourage the Arabs to wage a preventive war.

According to Israeli lore, Ben-Gurion was reluctant to make a doctrinal decision on the debate. He thought that the debate was premature, theoretical, unnecessary, and counterproductive. Instead, he made smaller incremental decisions, endorsing elements of each school's agenda: resolve and caution. On the side of resolve, Ben-Gurion authorized a ballistic missile project (to be pursued in collaboration with the French contractor Marcel Dassault). This decision, which was made when the future of the nuclear project was still uncertain and years before Israel made a formal commitment on nuclear weapons, strengthened the commitment to nuclear resolve. The costly missile project made little sense in a nonnuclear context. On the side of caution, Ben-Gurion rejected the proposal (made by Shimon Peres) that Israel should take concrete action to join the nuclear club. It is also believed that Ben-Gurion turned down the proposal to put more funds into the nuclear project at the expense of the conventional army. On the contrary, he authorized establishing another regular armored brigade in the IDF. Most significant, he decided to maintain the IDF as a conventional army with a doctrine based on conventional warfare (Cohen 1998a: 150–51; Evron 1994).

In retrospect, these decisions left a lasting legacy. Ben-Gurion's reluctance to make a cardinal decision, and his focus instead on smaller, more specific decisions, without changing the conventional orientation of the IDF, set the stage for the approach that would constitute the Israeli idea of a proper ratio between the conventional and the nuclear. Those decisions were derived from the proposition that while Israel must develop and maintain an operational nuclear force for "a rainy day," its overall military posture must remain conventional, not nuclear, *as long as the military threats that Israel faces remained conventional.* The nuclear program was to be treated as an "extra" for unique situations of existential threat. It also affirmed the notion that Israel's self-interest was not to nuclearize the region. This cautious view still shapes the fundamentals of Israeli nuclear thinking (Ne'eman 1986).

A related feature of this legacy is the notion that the nuclear project must be run and controlled strictly by civilian-scientific authority, not as a military project under military responsibility and custodianship. It was apparently an arrangement favored by all. Just as the army generals had a skeptical view of the supersecret project and no real interest in running it, so the nuclear project's leaders did not see themselves as working on a military project and had little interest in reporting to the military. Neither side considered the project's ultimate products—if those products were ever produced—as just another military weapons system. Strict budgetary separation was maintained between the nuclear project and the rest of the defense establishment (Cohen 1998a).

Over time, a great deal of quiet consensus has been built into and reinforced by the decision-making process. It created a strong element of continuity. This consensus is based on the proposition that the role of the nuclear dimension in Israel's national security posture should be narrow and distinct. The main strategic purpose of the nuclear program is to provide the nation with credible deterrence against *existential* threats: that is, those that would endanger the very existence of the state. In fact, it is believed that the Israeli bomb has credibility only on the existential level in the eyes of Israel's potential enemies. Both sides know that Israel would never resort to nuclear weapons in situations short of existential last resort. Having the bomb is about knowing that Israel possesses the ultimate weapon for use in the most unlikely moments of "last resort." It is not about fighting a war.

Viewed in this way, the proper context in which to understand the role of Israel's nuclear program is political (and psychological), *not* military. That is, the Israeli bomb is about providing the nation's political leaders a sense of existential security in an uncertain world; it is about the ability to project an existential statement to the world; it is about Israel's oath, "Never Again." Conversely, it is *not* about providing another advanced weapon system to the IDF; it is not about Israel's military doctrine.

This does not mean that Israel's nuclear program lacks any military meaning. Without operational credibility—and credibility requires the capability and the will to use it—the bomb would lack most of its political credibility. It does mean that the nuclear program should be relatively small, insulated from the mainstream military, and not too costly, and that its liaison with the military must be limited and strict. By and large, it is a political matter, not a military one.

Post-R&D and Post-NPT Dilemmas

Another (but related) cycle of decisions with far-reaching consequences that a nation that embarks on a nuclear path must address concerns the post-R&D phase of the nuclear program. In the late 1960s, Israel had to make some new decisions about the depth and substance of its nuclear commitment beyond the R&D stage.

In the experience of previous nuclear weapon states, a full-yield nuclear test signified crossing the weapons threshold and transitioning from the R&D phase to the production and deployment phase. It also was a political act of public acknowledgment. None of the five de jure members of the nuclear club considered skipping the test; nor did they consider forgoing the production and deployment mode. Technologically, Israel could have joined the nuclear club in the late 1960s and become the sixth nuclear state, but, politically and strategically, it was not in a position to take that path. Unlike France and China, the last two additions to the nuclear club, Israel was highly unsure and tentative about its long-term nuclear intentions.

Israel's nuclear program faced a dilemma. On the side of resolve, it was inconceivable to bring to a halt the nuclear project at that critical juncture. The rationale of the project was always to develop an *operational* capability available for the existential moment of last resort. Freezing the program in a nondeployable mode was unthinkable to the project's leaders. It was obvious to them that Israel must retain a real nuclear option, not something virtual and amorphous. But on the side of caution, Israel was still pledging "nonintroduction," that it would not be the first to introduce nuclear weapons to the region.

It turned out that the post-R&D dilemma coincided with the political dilemma that the NPT presented to Israel. While from today's perspective Israel's decision to not sign the NPT looks sensible and obvious, it was not so in 1968–69. At that time Israel was unsure, even deeply divided, about the fundamental parameters of its nuclear future. Israel was committed to having some form of a nuclear option, but it lacked clarity as to what that option should look like, and whether—and how—it could be compatible with the NPT. It was feared that the United States would force Israel to sign the NPT (Cohen 2007; Cohen and Burr 2006).

Both issues were ultimately resolved through the Nixon-Meir deal in 1969. In the wake of the deal, in February 1970, Israel formally informed the United States of its decision not to join the NPT (Cohen and Burr 2006). On the matter of the NPT, resolve trumped caution. The United States tolerated the Israeli decision, accepting Israel as a nonsignatory state to the NPT, and allowed the nuclear issue to vanish almost entirely from the bilateral agenda.

Looking back, one sees that the opacity deal determined a great deal of the operational parameters of Israel's nuclear conduct. Israel went forward with its deployment mode, but did so in a most cautious manner that conformed with the basic requirements of the 1969 deal. The deal also put to rest another nuclear dilemma that Israel would otherwise have had to confront: whether to disclose publicly the nation's nuclear status. The deal reinforced the view that Israel must keep all its nuclear-related activities classified, sealed under total secrecy. This generated far-reaching ramifications for domestic nuclear discourse that have lasted to this day.[9]

If Israel's decision not to join the NPT highlights its commitment to nuclear resolve, its subsequent advocacy of the regional NWFZ vision was an indication of its commitment to nuclear caution. Less than two years after the Egyptian-Israeli peace treaty was signed in 1978, Israel joined at the United Nations the Egyptian-Iranian proposal for an NWFZ in the region. However, it insisted that negotiations for such an arrangement can begin only after Israel is recognized by all the region's states and after a regional peace is established (Feldman 1997; Landau 2006).

The Use Issue

A nation that develops and acquires nuclear weapons must inevitably address the use issue: the circumstances in which nuclear weapons could be used. In the mid-to-late 1960s Israeli defense intellectuals started to translate the intuitive idea of "last resort" into a concrete nuclear use doctrine. These efforts produced the first articulation of strategic "red lines" that, if crossed, could trigger the use of nuclear weapons. Specifically, four distinct strategic scenarios were identified at that time that could invoke such use: (1) a successful Arab military penetration into populated areas within Israel's post-1949 borders; (2) the destruction of the Israeli air force; (3) the exposure of Israeli cities to massive and devastating air attack or to possible chemical or biological attack; and (4) the use of nuclear weapons against Israeli territory. Each of these scenarios was defined as an existential threat to the State of Israel against which the nation could defend itself by no other means than nuclear weapons, which it would be politically and morally justified in using. It was also evident that all of these scenarios were extremely improbable (Cohen 1998a: 237).

Already in the mid-to-late 1960s it was evident that finding a sensible use for nuclear weapons in the Arab-Israeli theater would be highly problematic. At that time some thought that halting a massive troop invasion would be a justified "last resort" use of nuclear weapons. But it became apparent that to use a nuclear bomb *after* a massive Arab army had penetrated Israel's borders would be too late to be militarily effective and perhaps utterly useless because of the proximity of Israeli troops (or citizens). Conversely, using nuclear weapons to preempt Arab army troops on their way to the border was deemed too early a use—that is, politically unacceptable. Israeli strategists encountered a problem similar to the one that North Atlantic Treaty Organization (NATO) member state planners had been grappling with throughout much of the Cold War: the difficulty of defining the proper moment—militarily and politically—that nuclear weapons can be used effectively to stop a conventionally superior enemy attack (Cohen 1998a: 237; Ne'eman 1986).

Another realization that emerged through those discussions was the deficiency of nuclear ambiguity for deterrence purposes. How could Israel effectively deter if it could never acknowledge possessing the nuclear bomb? It also became evident that it would be politically impossible for Israel to resort to nuclear weapons without an explicit warning, and this could render the very idea of the bomb as a "last resort" impractical. So the Israeli doctrine considers a "demonstration" use an act that must precede real use (Cohen 1998a).

More than four decades have passed since Israel began struggling with the dilemmas of nuclear use. In that period, Israel had three occasions to think about those issues in the context of actual wars—the Six-Day War (1967), the Yom Kippur War (1973), and the First Gulf War (1991). It appears that each war made it clearer how *almost* impossible it is that Israel could find itself in circumstances that would compel a resort to nuclear weapons. All of these events revealed that, short of a direct nuclear attack, it is *almost* inconceivable that Israel would use nuclear weapons to defend itself against existential threats (Cohen 2000). Yet even if nuclear weapons are unusable as military weapons, Israeli leaders found that nuclear dispositions could play an important role in persuading and deterring action by both friend and foe.

Advanced Weaponry and Arsenal Size

Another dilemma that all nuclear weapon states must grapple with involves posture and arsenal design: how big and how advanced the nuclear component should be. We know that all the first five nuclear weapon states moved on to develop advanced nuclear weaponry, in particular thermonuclear weapons, within a decade or so. All, except China, also developed tactical nuclear weapons.

Israel's nuclear secrecy makes it difficult to assess, let alone to determine, how Israel has dealt with its posture design dilemmas. My explications here are educated guesses. There are indirect indications, including the Vanunu revelations (Barnaby 1989; Hersh 1991; Inbar 1999; *Sunday Times* 1986) that after the 1973 war Israel decided to commit itself to more advanced nuclear weaponry. This should not be viewed as a great surprise. Indeed, it is consistent with Israel's decision in the mid-to-late 1970s to develop a longer range and more accurate intermediate missile to replace its French-based Jericho I. According to news reports, Israel tested the 1,500-mile Jericho II in the late 1980s and moved into deployment mode around the early 1990s (Cirincione et al. 2005; SIPRI 2006). This manifests Israel's commitment to nuclear resolve.

Despite some claims (e.g., Hersh 1991) that Israel produced, and even possibly deployed, tactical nuclear weapons, it appears that while Israel may have completed the R&D required for such weaponry it ultimately decided against the production and deployment of tactical nuclear weapons. If true, that decision demonstrates Israel's view that nuclear weapons have a distinct and very limited existential deterrence role in its national security posture.

Finally, there is a relatively high degree of uncertainty about the size of the Israeli arsenal. Following the Vanunu revelations, it became common to claim that Israel might have 100 to 200 nuclear weapons. In his *Samson Option,* Seymour Hersh refers to some 300 or even more Israeli weapons, both tactical and strategic (Hersh 1991). More recent estimates, based on leaks attributed to the U.S. intelligence community, refer to a much smaller and stable arsenal, perhaps in the neighborhood of 100 weapons, possibly even fewer than that (Cirincione et al. 2005).

If these claims are true, on matters of advanced weaponry and arsenal size Israel ended up crafting its own careful balance between resolve and caution. On the side of resolve, Israel did not freeze its nuclear development. On the contrary, Israel has moved since the 1970s to advance its weaponry. Given that Israel has some serious limitations on its nuclear R&D, in particular its inability to test, one must assume that Israeli technological resolve found smart ways to compensate for those limitations that would guarantee the safety and reliability of Israeli weapons.

At the same time, these actions highlight Israel's commitment to caution. If it is true that Israel decided not to produce and deploy tactical nuclear weapons, and also kept the size of its arsenal relatively small, this indicates that, unlike most other nuclear nations, Israel treats its nuclear arsenal in merely existential terms. If correct, these decisions are in line with earlier Israeli nuclear decisions, the fundamental decision to maintain the conventional orientation of the Israeli army as well as the related requirements intrinsic to the regime of opacity.

Since the early 1980s (and possibly earlier), the Israeli navy (with the support of other governmental agencies) has promoted the idea that Israel should build a small fleet of modern conventional (diesel) submarines for "strategic purposes," an Israeli euphemism for a sea-launched nuclear capability. After complex negotiations, when a deal was almost signed with a German shipyard in early 1990, it was vetoed by the chief of staff, General Barak, owing to cost considerations (Cirincione et al. 2005; Cohen 2005a).

But after the First Gulf War in 1991, in the wake of Iraq's Scud missile attack against Israel, Israel's strategic picture changed fundamentally. Sometime after the war, Israel reversed its earlier decision and decided to establish a sea-based strategic arm. Israel accepted the offer of the German government to finance the purchase of two large diesel submarines and to share equally the cost of the third (as compensation for the role that German industry played in the development of Iraq's unconventional weaponry). The strategic developments throughout the 1990s, in both Iraq and Iran, compounded by the failure of all Western intelligence to detect the full scope of Iraq's nuclear program, were critical in the Israeli decision to boost Israel's strategic capabilities. Nuclear resolve took the lead. It is presumed that the sea-based strategic arm has a second-strike nuclear component (Cirincione et al. 2005).

By July 2000, Israel completed taking delivery of all three Dolphin-class submarines it had ordered after the First Gulf War at the Thyssen-Nordseewerke shipyard in Kiel, Germany. In doing so, it is assumed Israel has moved significantly toward acquiring a survivable second-strike nuclear capability. By all indications, Israel is now on the way to finalizing the restructuring of its nuclear forces into a triad form. It is also presumed that in recent years Israel has significantly modernized its strategic command and control systems. These are probably the most important strategic developments in Israel.

Initially a fleet of three submarines was believed the minimum Israel needed to have a deployment at sea of one nuclear-armed submarine at all times. In 2006 Israel placed an order in Germany for two more submarines. A survivable deterrent fleet of five is now perceived essential because of Israel's unique geopolitical and demographic vulnerability to nuclear attack, and one that no potential nuclear enemy of Israel could ignore.

Israel's Nuclear Opacity: A Political Appraisal

In retrospect, the 1969 Nixon-Meir opacity deal was a fateful event in Israel's nuclear history, maybe second only to Ben-Gurion's initiation decision. After a stormy decade in which Israel's nuclear program had been a continuous source of irritation and friction in the relations between Israel and the United States, the understanding allowed the United States to tolerate Israel's de facto nuclear status. More significantly, it removed a thorny issue in their bilateral relations. After the bargain, Israel was effectively left alone on the nuclear issue, as long as it kept its part of the deal.

Over time, the Nixon-Meir understanding evolved into a working arrangement under which the United States provided Israel diplomatic cover whenever Israel's nuclear program was under attack in international forums, in particular at the United Nations and the International Atomic Energy Agency (IAEA). To put it bluntly, without active and ongoing U.S. support the 1969 deal would not have been as successful as it has been. Endorsement by the United States helped influence other Western nations' attitudes toward the Israeli bomb.

But the benefits to Israel from its policy of nuclear opacity go beyond Israeli-U.S. relations or even relations between Israel and the NPT regime. To make an objective appraisal of the benefits to Israel of its posture of nuclear opacity, one has to examine the effects and consequences of the policy through a number of parameters.

Existential Deterrence

Under opacity Israel has been in possession of nuclear weapons for some two generations, but in a uniquely unacknowledged manner. Israel's possession of a nuclear deterrent is known by both friends and foes alike, yet Israel has never issued an explicit nuclear threat to any country, including Iran. In this way Israel has been able to extract the benefits of maintaining an *existential* nuclear deterrence posture, but without the need even to acknowledge nuclear possession, let alone to issue an explicit nuclear threat. A case in point was the effective way Israel used its nuclear deterrence posture in the First Gulf War (Feldman 1991).[10]

Freedom of Action

Ultimately, under the veneer of opacity, Israel's nuclear program—the nation's commitment to nuclear resolve—has enjoyed remarkable freedom of action. Total secrecy has served as an extraordinary shield; it insulated the program from the outside world. Nobody—either at home or abroad—could intervene because nobody knew clearly what was going on inside. And even when the veneer seemed to be shattered briefly, as it was with the infamous Vanunu revelations in 1986 (*Sunday Times* 1986), it became evident that the international system had no interest in delving too deeply into the secrets of the Israeli nuclear program. The United States' endorsement influenced other Western nations to treat Israel as a sui generis case. Given estimates about the Israeli arsenal and its advanced nature, it could be argued that under opacity Israel's commitment to nuclear resolve has been even better served than under a declared posture. For all practical purposes, the opaque Israeli nuclear program has probably had more freedom of action than a more visible program would have.[11]

The Vanunu revelations may also illustrate this point (*Sunday Times* 1986). On its face, they highlight how mature and advanced the Israeli nuclear program is; they show the remarkable freedom of action that Israel enjoys in this area. However, the limited political reaction they invoked also indicates the lack of political interest on the part of the international community in meddling in Israel's nuclear affairs. Except Norway (where the opposition forced the government to take action on the issue of heavy water that Norway had supplied to Israel in the late 1950s), no Western government made a political issue out of those revelations. Even the official Arab response was relatively mute and restrained.

Regional Stability and Peace

Against the concern that the advent of Israeli nuclear weapons would further polarize and destabilize the Arab-Israeli conflict, the political reality of Israel's nuclear deterrence under opacity was probably more benign than anyone expected. While it is difficult to measure in precise empirical terms the political effect of nuclear opacity, most Israeli analysts believe that Israeli nuclear deterrence under opacity has contributed to regional stability (Cohen 1992; Evron 1994, 1998; Schiff 2000a, 2000b; Steinberg 2000). It contributed to lowering the intensity of the Arab-Israeli conflict, and in some important cases it even contributed to achieving peace.

A brief historical review highlights this line of thinking. When Ben-Gurion initiated the nuclear project in the late 1950s he did so against the background of pan-Arab discourse about the "destruction of Israel and Zionism." The Arab defeat in the 1967 Six-Day War started the curve of decline of that pan-Arab rhetoric. The 1973 Yom Kippur War, which took place under the shadow of the Israeli bomb, stimulated two related developments. First, Arab discourse about the "destruction of Israel" declined further. Second, it gave impetus to the view that the nuclear age can no longer tolerate total wars. Less then five years later, Egypt's President Anwar Sadat visited Jerusalem and vowed "no more war." It turned out that the 1973 Yom Kippur War was the last great Arab-Israeli war involving major armies in battle. The Egyptian-Israeli 1978 peace treaty was signed under the shadow of the opaque Israeli bomb.[12] Various comments made by President Sadat during his 1977 visit to Jerusalem implied that the bomb played some role in both the fading away of Arab discourse about the destruction of Israel and Egypt's (and subsequently other Arab states') acceptance of Israel as an ineradicable entity in the Middle East. Many Israelis view Israel's invisible bomb as a "quiet" anchor of the Egyptian-Israeli peace.

By and large, the presence of a benign Israeli bomb not only has been grudgingly accepted by the Arab world, including Egypt; it has also quietly contributed to the notion that Israel is a fact in the Middle East that Arabs must accept and learn to reckon with. The Saudi peace plan that calls for a two-state solution in resolving the Palestinian-Israeli conflict based on the 1948 borders and in return full recognition of Israel by the Arab world highlights the enormous change that has taken place in the Arab world toward Israel. Many Israelis believe that the presence of the "invisible" Israeli bomb has contributed significantly to this development.

Impact on Hostile Proliferation

The most serious concern in the 1960s was that the Israeli nuclear project would stir up a dangerous regional nuclear arms race. This was the fear underlying the impulse for nuclear caution. However, the regional consequences of the Israeli nuclear bomb under opacity proved to be more benign than had been feared. It turned out that under opacity Israel was able to maintain a benign monopoly.

The record here is mixed, ambiguous, and ultimately incomplete. On four occasions Israel faced the emergence of hostile nuclear programs—Egypt in the 1960s, Iraq in the 1970s and 1980s, Libya in the 1990s, and today the most difficult case, Iran. In the first three instances, owing to a combination of both luck and policy, the hostile proliferators ultimately failed to reach their objectives. Israel's own opacity policy has probably been a moderating force, but surely it was not formidable enough to prevent cases of hostile proliferation.

Nuclear Secrecy and Democracy

I have written extensively elsewhere about the negative nondemocratic domestic aspects of Israel's nuclear opacity (Cohen 2005a, 2005c; also Maoz 2003, 2006). My comments here are brief and descriptive. While Israelis recognize that the policy of opacity is at odds with the normative principles of liberal democracy—built on secrecy, it stands in tension with the democratic values of open debate, the public's right to know, accountability, and governmental transparency—they support the continuation of the policy. The Israeli citizenry accepts that the far-reaching national security value of the policy, in particular its existential benefits, outweigh its democratic deficiencies. When survival is at stake, in the view of the citizenry, the requirements of national security are more important than democratic principles. The result is that the nuclear issue is treated as a national taboo, and the citizenry endorses this societal attitude (Cohen 2005a).

If this is the case with the citizenry, the national security establishment overwhelmingly supports the continuation of the policy (Schiff 2000a, 2000b, 2001). In addition to the many international benefits, the policy provides extraordinary bureaucratic benefits. Most important, it provides the bureaucracy with the convenience of acting out of sight of the public eye, in a culture of secrecy with little transparency. It allows the bureaucracy to be kept both insulated and isolated (Maoz 2003).

In sum, Israel's policy of nuclear opacity is viewed by Israeli policy makers and the public alike as a remarkable national success story. Probably no other government policy in Israel has enjoyed such strong popular consensus and support as the policy of nuclear opacity. It is viewed by Israelis as a "smart" way to live with nuclear weapons, to extract the benefits of existential deterrence, but without paying the "dues" that other nuclear weapon states have to pay. It would be fair to say that Israelis—the public and its elected officials—have fallen in love with the posture (Schiff 2000a, 2001).

The New Challenges: Iran and Beyond

Israel's nuclear policy, especially its loyalty to opacity, has been dominated by a strong element of continuity. All other nuclear nations—with the possible exception of South Africa—advertise their nuclear weapon status. It took India and Pakistan years to resolve their deal with the bomb, but both nations decided in 1998 to make overt their nuclear weapon status. Israel has taken a different and sui generis path. Since the 1960s, all Israeli prime ministers have firmly adhered to a policy of restraint and have kept a low nuclear profile. Despite Israel's undeniable nuclear resolve, no Israeli government has seriously considered changing, or even modifying, the policy of opacity. All have complied with the Nixon-Meir understanding that the Israeli bomb should remain invisible. Israel has never sought legitimacy—at home or abroad—for its "bomb in the basement." This has made Israel, at least thus far, a special kind of proliferator.

The strong instinct of Israeli policy makers, both elected and senior professionals, is to sustain the continuity rather than pursue change. If the policy of opacity has been so successful, why change it? Continuity is known, familiar, and proven, while change is unknown and full of risks. But things are not as they used to be. While the imperative for continuity remains strong, there is also a fundamental and growing recognition that the nation's way of doing business on the nuclear issue is facing new and difficult challenges that ultimately may lead to fundamental changes in Israel's nuclear policy and posture. Those concerns have evolved gradually, but Iran's nuclear ambitions give the issue a sense of urgency.

By the end of the first decade of the twenty-first century, Israel's nuclear policy and posture will be at a crossroads. There are strong indications that a new nuclear order is looming on the horizon, in the region and possibly beyond it, which may force Israel to rethink the fundamentals of its own nuclear future. As of this writing, these developments are far from being conclusive, mature, or exhaustive—it is all a work in progress—but they are already forcing Israel to rethink and adapt; and it is possible that Israel will have to adopt a completely new outlook and posture.

The Iranian Nuclear Threat

First and foremost among the new challenges is the advent of Iran as a nuclear power that soon could pose a direct existential threat to Israel. Whether the Israeli posture of nuclear deterrence will remain in its opaque and undeclared mode depends, to a large extent, on the developments on the Iranian nuclear scene. The closer Iran gets to the bomb, or to the technical ability to produce a bomb, the more likely it is that Israel would find itself compelled to change some of its fundamental parameters. The advent of a nuclear Iran has the potential to profoundly affect Israel's thinking on the nuclear question, especially its opaque nuclear posture.

From an Israeli perspective, the existential threat posed by the Iranian nuclear situation lies in the link between two critical elements: (1) Iran's determined and vigorous pursuit of nuclear weapon capability, and (2) the extreme hostility of the Iranian regime toward Israel. It is this link between extreme ideological hostility and nuclear weapons that elevates the concern over the Iranian nuclear problem to an existential threat.

On the question of Iran's nuclear pursuit, Israel has a high degree of confidence that Iran's intentions and aspirations are directed toward nuclear weapons, or at least an advanced nuclear weapon "option"—that is, the technical industrial capability to produce them quickly. According to Israeli assessments, the grandiose Iranian civil nuclear program is a cover for a determined Iranian effort to develop nuclear weapons. Such assessments are based on analysis of multiple and independent sources of evidence, both open and classified. Prime Minister Ehud Olmert expressed the Israeli official position on this in a public speech on the Iranian nuclear threat in early January 2007: "For many long years, we have followed Iran's efforts to acquire nuclear weapons, in the guise of a civilian nuclear program. They are working through secret channels in a number of sites spread out across Iran. In the past few years, we have been witness to especially intense Iranian activity on two tracks—the overt and the covert" (Olmert 2007).

There is abundant evidence of the Iranian regime's extreme hostility toward Israel. Such hostility toward Israel has characterized the Iranian regime for some time, but it became more prominent after the election of Mahmoud Ahmadinejad as the president of Iran in 2005 (Chubin 2006). In highly publicized statements President Ahmadinejad has denied the occurrence of the Holocaust, questioned the legitimacy of Israel as a state, and, most disturbingly, repeatedly expressed a desire that Israel be "wiped off the map."[13]

The Israeli public—both leadership and citizenry—listens carefully to those statements. This extreme rhetoric is taken in Israel as more than outrageous but meaningless talk by an irresponsible leader. It is viewed as a true expression of the Iranian regime's desire to see the end of Israel. From a historical perspective, this is a return to the pan-Arab discourse about the destruction of the Zionist entity—a discourse that hardly exists anymore in the Sunni Arab world (some would argue due, in part, to the existence of the Israeli bomb). However, Iran's nuclear ambition makes the new statements more ominous than their precursors. The difference between the anti-Israeli rhetoric of Ben-Gurion's era and today's is that now, for the first time, such threats are voiced by a president of a state that is pursuing the nuclear route.

Furthermore, President Ahmadinejad's rhetoric is made against the background of growing Iranian involvement in other parts of the Middle East, in particular through the Hezbollah in Lebanon and in the Palestinian territories. Iran's activities in the Middle East, particularly its involvement in the Palestinian-Israeli conflict, are aimed at instigating regional instability and are driven by its pursuit of Shiite hegemonic aspirations in the Middle East.[14]

The Public Impact on Israel: The Politics of Nuclear Fear

A new generation of Israelis is reminded once again—what previous generations of Israelis had recognized in theory but tended to dismiss as unreal—of the existential vulnerability of Israel to nuclear threat. They are reminded that one bomb could cast a grave shadow on the future of Israel (Morris 2007). The old argument from the early 1960s about the fragility and instability of nuclear deterrence has resurfaced with a vengeance. It has opened the door to a new nuclear politics of fear.

Israel's nuclear deterrent is a well-established reality, and Iran's nuclear pursuit is still uncertain, so one might expect Israelis to feel both confident and secure. But this is not so. Israel's nuclear deterrence provides only limited peace of mind to Israelis. Sociologically speaking, the Iranian nuclear effort has elevated the collective sense of existential anxiety in Israel to new heights. A poll published in Israel in September 2006 found that 79 percent of Israeli Jews believed Iran posed a genuine threat to Israel's existence. Another poll, published two months later, found that 66 percent of Israeli Jews were convinced Iran would develop a nuclear weapon and try to use it against Israel.[15] A new politics of fear has introduced a burst of anxiety as if the nation is on the eve of another Holocaust.[16] A number of prominent Israelis have called on the international community to treat President Ahmadinejad as another Hitler.[17] After the Holocaust, it is said, Israeli leaders cannot ignore such threats.

Not many nations in today's world have an existential anxiety about their future. Israel is among the very few, perhaps the only one. An array of respectable national sources of information and opinion—politicians, parliamentarians, academics, and columnists—have all contributed to this new politics of fear based on an imminent reality of the Iranian nuclear threat.[18]

It is in response to this new politics of fear that Prime Minister Olmert delivered a sober message in January 2007, combining both resolve and caution. While a nuclear Iran could become an existential danger to Israel, that danger is not there yet, he said: "As serious as the Iranian threat is, the threat of nuclear attack on Israel is by no means imminent." Olmert referred somewhat obliquely to the time dimension of the Iranian threat: "At this stage, there is still time, while not unlimited, to stop Iran's intention of becoming a nuclear power which threatens its adversaries, first and foremost Israel. We are not complacent, we cannot be complacent, and we are responding to the Iranian threats with the necessary seriousness" (Olmert 2007).[19] Prime Minister Olmert made it clear that during that window of time Israel's strong preference is to reach a solution (elsewhere he used the word *compromise*) through diplomatic means. Olmert did not elaborate on what would constitute a solution that would address Israeli concerns—that is, the minimum requirements on which there can be no compromise—but he did make clear that the general principle is that "Iran cannot be allowed to acquire nuclear weapons or the material to produce them" (Olmert 2007).

From an Israeli national security perspective, the existential threat issue does not lie merely in the possibility that Iran would attack Israel with nuclear weapons. Israelis do acknowledge that Iran is very unlikely to attack Israel out of the blue with nuclear weapons and that Iran is fully aware of the catastrophic consequences to Iran of such a demonic act. To drop a bomb on Israel would be insane and unthinkable. (But rational or not, nuclear nightmares do not leave citizenry and leaders calm.) Still, the existential issue manifests itself on two other fronts. The first is the inherent danger involved in the formation of a nuclear balance of terror between Iran and Israel, given the Iranian regime's hostility toward Israel and the lack of communication between the two states.[20] Israelis do not want to live under a MAD regime with Iran.

The second is the impact that a balance of terror might have on Israel's citizens and their social psyche. Some Israeli public figures who push the politics of nuclear fear, such as Deputy Minister of Defense Ephraim Sneh, have made the point that Iran might be able to "wipe the Zionist state off the map" without actually dropping a bomb. The mere existence of the Iranian nuclear bomb, or the fear that Iran has the bomb, they argue, might lead Israelis to leave Israel for a friendlier place where their very existence is not threatened. After the Holocaust, Sneh argues, Jews would have no stomach to live in the shadow of an Iranian bomb, another Holocaust. Those who had the means would leave. Few Israelis would dismiss this way of thinking as too far-fetched.

Closing Reflections

As of this writing, the Iranian nuclear situation is fluid and highly uncertain even to speculate about how it will work itself out. But whatever the outcome, it will certainly have an enormous impact on Israel's nuclear policies of resolve and caution. Whether the future will be on the side of continuity or change depends on the outcome of that challenge and Israel's response to it.

In the following list, I identify some of the conceptual issues that Israeli decision makers will have to grapple with in the coming years. The issues are conceptually distinct, but they are also interconnected. I highlight these issues by presenting them as questions.

- *Success or failure in halting Iran.* Can the international community succeed in denying the Iranian bomb? Could a working compromise be worked out? If so, what would be its political and technical parameters?

- *Preventive military action against Iran.* At the end of the window, whatever the outcome may be, Israel would be required to decide whether it could live with a nuclear Iran. In particular, Israel would have to decide whether to take preventive action. Israel would have to make a fundamental strategic choice between prevention and deterrence. This dilemma would test Israel's commitment to the 1981 "Begin doctrine": the commitment to take preventive action, including military action, against any hostile neighbor in proximity to the bomb. Whatever action Israel takes or decides not to take would have far-reaching consequences for the region and for Israel itself.
- *The disclosure dilemma: if, when, and how.* Should Israel keep its nuclear opacity policy or should it move to a declared nuclear deterrence posture? What would trigger such a dramatic change? Would Israel conduct a nuclear test? It is nearly certain, according to Israeli conventional wisdom, that an Iranian nuclear test would require Israel to follow suit. But the situation would be more ambiguous if Iran were perceived to have acquired the bomb opaquely, without officially acknowledging it, and from within the NPT. One thing is clear, once Israel removed its layers of opacity, it would no longer be a *benign proliferator* as we know it now. Israel and Iran would be more like India and Pakistan.
- *Upgrading Israel's nuclear deterrence posture.* What operational steps would Israel have to take to retain a robust and credible deterrent against a nuclear Iran? Should Israel develop and announce a second-strike nuclear capability? Will Israel imitate the U.S. triad, as India does? What would be the implications of these developments on Israel's nuclear infrastructure? What would be the implications of such a transformation on the command and control systems?
- *Arms control and disarmament.* If the rivalry between Iran and Israel moved further toward the nuclear level, would the two countries be more likely to establish a dialogue to avoid inadvertent or accidental use? What types of arms control dialogue could be developed among Israel and other nuclear powers in the Middle East? Would the dangers of a nuclear Middle East renew political efforts to establish direct dialogue? What about the cause of disarmament and an NWFZ?

Although the future is uncertain, one thing is evident: the challenge is enormous. Israel is already in the midst of transforming itself for a new strategic era, but so far it has not firmly sealed its bargain with the bomb. The Israeli nuclear case is sui generis, both domestically and internationally. But could Israel transform its strategic posture much further without changing its long-standing sui generis character? Will this legacy continue? Part of the uncertainty is how Israel's historical commitment to those two opposing forces—resolve and caution—will play out.

Notes

The author wishes to express his intellectual gratitude to all the contributors to this project who provided helpful comments on two earlier drafts that were presented in workshops in Washington, D.C., and Singapore. Special thanks to Muthiah Alagappa and Shlomo Brom for their most helpful insights.

1. SIPRI Yearbook 2006, for example, ranks Israel as the fourth nuclear nation in the world in terms of its deployed weapons in active service, just below France but above the United Kingdom and China. The two recently declared nuclear weapon states, India and Pakistan, lag behind Israel in the SIPRI ranking.

2. Most scholars who worked on the subject acknowledge these methodological difficulties. In a recent article Alan Dowty made the following comment: "Israel's nuclear weapon program, including both actual weapon production and defense policies governing their deployment and possible use, is extremely problematic as a subject for academic research. The reasons for this, according to conventional wisdom, are too obvious to require comment and too sensitive to allow it" (Dowty 2005: 3).

3. Ben-Gurion never acknowledged publicly that the nuclear project was about security, so it is impossible also to find direct public statements that link the nuclear project with the Holocaust. Yet, behind the veil, those links do exist. Ben-Gurion's correspondence with President Kennedy in the period 1962–63, especially in response to Kennedy's nuclear pressure, are replete of reference to the Holocaust (Cohen 1998a: 9–16, 120, 122).

4. Once again, due to Israel's taboo over nuclear talk, it is nearly impossible to demonstrate a straightforward and public linkage between the Holocaust and Israel's nuclear commitment. If the entire nuclear issue is unacknowledged in public, how can it be linked to the Holocaust? Yet, beyond the nuclear mist, the commitment to "Never Again" has become more apparent as a younger generation of Israelis has developed a tradition of pilgrimage to the primary Holocaust site. A few years ago the government of Poland allowed Israeli advanced F-15I to fly over Auschwitz as a symbolic gesture to the memory of the Holocaust. The official IDF web site makes a long reference to the "Never Again" speech that IDF Chief of Staff Lieutenant-General Gabi Ashkenazi delivered to his general staff at the Hall of Names at *Yad Vashem* in Jerusalem in the 2007 Holocaust Memorial Day ceremony. "We are gathered here," continued Lieutenant-General Ashkenazi, "the members of the general staff and I, in order to declare that this will never happen again . . . Almost every soldier of the IDF visited and was involved in the programs in museums such as *Yad Veshem* in order to remember and learn from the Holocaust." Available at http://dover.idf.il/IDF/English/News/holiday/2007/april/1501.htm.

5. In a nonscientific survey conducted in 2000 by Israel's leading newspaper *Yediot Achronot,* most respondents ranked Ben-Gurion's decision to initiate the nuclear project as Israel's "best" and most fateful decision any Israel leader has ever made.

6. This was an "excuse" for the real reasons Israel had to stay away from the NPT. The real Israeli issue was not that the regime was deficient, but that the NPT was inconsistent with Israel's nuclear weapon program. Signing the NPT would have meant either giving

up a great deal of the nuclear program or engaging in a major scheme of deception and concealment. In any case, Israel's nuclear deterrence would have been reduced substantially. Israel did not want to be a recognized nonnuclear weapon state. Even if the NPT/IAEA system had been much stronger, Israel still would not have signed it. However, Israel was proved correct about the dangerous weaknesses of the safeguard system. As the Iraqi case proved twice and as the Iranian case is believed to demonstrate, the NPT safeguard system, even after the reform it has endured, cannot provide real assurance to states that are under existential threat.

7. Usually the term *nuclear taboo* is used by scholars (such as Nina Tannenwald or T. V. Paul) to refer to the normative prohibition against use. Here (and elsewhere, Cohen 2005a) I use the term in reference to a societal inhibition to speak about or even to acknowledge the possession of nuclear weapons.

8. Some words of academic caution are required. The account I present here is my own reconstruction. While I believe that it accurately reflects the essence of real decisions that Israel has made on its nuclear path, it should not be viewed as historical evidence by rigid historical standards. The actual history of such decisions is inevitably messier and more complex than any researcher's conceptual construct, but in the Israeli case the primary historical evidence is simply unavailable. Virtually none of Israel's decisions were made public. Hence my reconstruction is filled in at times by educated guesses. My goal here is not to describe history for its own sake, but rather to highlight some aspects of the portrait of Israel as a benign proliferator.

9. Subsequently, it was decided that the Israeli press would be allowed to refer to Israel's nuclear capability as a "nuclear option" or "nuclear capability," keeping the words "bomb" and "nuclear weapons" out of the public discourse. This is still the practice of Israeli military censors today (Cohen 2005c).

10. While it is difficult to discern the specific effects of nuclear deterrence—in part, because Israel has not faced (at least since the 1973 war) real situations of existential threat—it is widely believed that Israel's nuclear deterrence helped persuade Saddam Hussein in 1991 to limit his missile attacks against Israel to conventional weapons (Feldman 1991). I should also note, however, that the case is far from being empirically or methodologically clear. Not only is it difficult to "observe" the specific effects of nuclear deterrence under opacity, but in this particular case the epistemic difficulties are compounded by the difficulty of discerning between the effects of U.S. and Israeli deterrence; both countries threatened Saddam with horrific consequences if he used unconventional weaponry.

11. It could even be argued that Israel has effectively enjoyed more freedom of action and lack of interference in its nuclear affairs than any de jure members of the nuclear club (with the possible exception of China and maybe also France). Those states, since their nuclear weapon programs were on the table, had to deal with some pressure at home (in the case of the democratic nuclear states) or some international treaties and norms. Israel, on the other hand, not only avoided making any formal obligations in the nuclear field but was "allowed" to keep its nuclear activities virtually "off limits" to any diplomatic discussion with any other state or international body. For all practical purposes, with the tacit support of the United States, the Israeli nuclear program has been treated as de facto "off limits," at least in terms of information.

12. Initially, Egypt insisted during the *peace process* that the peace treaty include a clause requiring Israel to join the NPT, but when Israel (and the United States) made it clear that

this would be a nonstarter for Israel, Egypt agreed to overlook the Israeli nuclear issue (Quandt 1986).

13. President Ahmadinejad has also raised international outrage by making many similar statements. His assertion that Israel should be "wiped off the map" was a slogan used often by the father of the 1979 revolution, Ayatollah Ruhollah Khomeini. On October 19, 2006, President Ahmadinejad talked again about the Holocaust, saying: "Even if we assume that six million Jews were killed in World War II, how come you don't have sympathy for the other 54 million who were killed, too? It is not even clear who counted those you have sympathy for." He said Israel has effectively held European countries hostage for what happened during World War II.

14. This point was central in Prime Minister Ehud Olmert's Herzelya speech in January 2007: "The Iran of today, whose leadership is motivated by religious fanaticism and ideological extremism, has chosen a policy of confrontation with us and threatens to wipe Israel off the map of nations. It supports terror and undermines stability in the region. The Iranian regime, in its aspiration to regional hegemony, bears responsibility for the riots perpetrated by the Hezbollah today to bring down the Lebanese government" (Olmert 2007).

15. Cam Simpson, "Israeli Citizens Struggle Amid Iran's Nuclear Vow," *Wall Street Journal,* December 22, 2006, A3.

16. The weekly magazine of the Israeli daily newspaper *Ha'aretz* indulged those fears with a five-page feature in which the editors posed the following question to prominent cultural figures: What would you do if you knew there were only two months left before Mr. Ahmadinejad dropped his atomic bomb?

17. Yossi Melamn, "Peres: Israel Has No Intention of Attacking Iran," *Ha'aretz,* October 21, 2006. Available at http://www.haaretz.com/hasen/spages/777440.html.

18. In 2007, for example, a respected Israeli historian, Benny Morris, published an editorial in English and German in which he explicitly invoked the fear that Israel is approaching a second Holocaust (Morris 2007).

19. Analytically, Iran would become an existential threat to Israel only once it masters the technology to produce significant quantities of weapon-grade fissile material. It is not the building of the bomb itself, but the technology of producing the fissile material that makes Iran an "existential threat."

20. Cam Simpson, "Israeli Citizens Struggle."

References and Selected Bibliography

Arian, Asher. 1995. *Security Threatened: Surveying Israeli Opinion on Peace and War.* New York: Cambridge University Press.

Barnaby, Frank. 1989. *The Invisible Bomb.* London: I. B. Tauris.

Bar Zohar, Michael. 1987. *Ben-Gurion.* 3 vols. Tel Aviv: Zmora-Bitan.

Ben-Gurion, David. 1969. *The Renewed State of Israel.* Tel Aviv: Am Oved (in Hebrew).

———. 1971. *Uniqueness and Mission.* Tel Aviv: Ma'archot (in Hebrew).

Cirincione, Joseph, et al. 2005. *Deadly Arsenals.* Washington, D.C.: Carnegie Endowment for International Peace.

Cohen, Avner. 1992. "Patterns of Nuclear Opacity in the Middle East: Understanding the Past, Implications for the Future." In *Aurora Papers 16: Regional Approaches to Curbing Nuclear Proliferation in the Middle East and South Asia,* ed. Tariq Rauf. Ottawa: Canadian Center for Global Security.

———. 1994. "The Lessons of Osiraq and the American Counterproliferation Debate." In *International Perspectives on Counterproliferation,* ed. Mitchell Reiss and Harald Muller. Working paper 99. Washington, D.C.: Woodrow Wilson Center.

———. 1995. "The Nuclear Equation in a New Middle East." *Nonproliferation Review* 2 (2): 12–39.

———. 1998a. *Israel and the Bomb.* New York: Columbia University Press, 1998.

———. 1998b. "Israel and the Evolution of American Nonproliferation Policy: The Critical Decade" (1958–1968). *Nonproliferation Review* 5 (2): 1–19.

———. 2000. "Nuclear Arms in Crisis under Secrecy: Israel and the 1967 and 1973 Wars." In *Planning the Unthinkable: Military Doctrine for the Use of Weapons of Mass-Destruction,* ed. Peter R. Lavoy, Scott D. Sagan, and James J. Wirtz. Ithaca, N.Y.: Cornell University Press.

———. 2003. "The Last Nuclear Moment." *New York Times.* October 6, A17.

———. 2005a. *The Last Taboo.* Tel Aviv: Kinneret Zmora Bitan (in Hebrew).

———. 2005b. "Before the Non-Proliferation Norm: Israel's Nuclear History." *Current History* 104 (681): 169–75.

———. 2005c. "Nuclear Opacity and the Question of the Boundaries of Information in a Democratic Governance." *Politica* (special issue edited by Gad Barzilai and Shimon Shitrit on National Security and the Freedom of Expression) 13 (Winter): 33–52 (in Hebrew).

———. 2007. "Crossing the Threshold: The Untold Nuclear Dimension of the 1967 Arab-Israeli War and Its Contemporary Lessons." *Arms Control Today* 37 (5): 12–16.

Cohen, Avner, and William Burr. 2006. "Israel Crosses the Threshold." *Bulletin of the Atomic Scientists* 62 (3): 22–80.

Chubin, Shahram. 2006. *Iran's Nuclear Ambitions.* Washington, D.C.: Carnegie Endowment for International Peace.

Dowty, Alan. 1975. "Israel's Nuclear Policy." *M'dina, Mimshal, V'yahasim Benleumiim* 7 (Spring): 5–27 (Hebrew).

———. 2005. "The Enigma of Opacity: Israel's Nuclear Weapons Program as a Field of Study," *Israel Studies Forum* 20:2 (Winter, 2005): 3–21.

Evron, Yair. 1994. *Israel's Nuclear Dilemma.* Ithaca, N.Y.: Cornell University Press.

———. 1998. *Weapons of Mass Destruction in the Middle East.* Washington, D.C.: Stimson Center.

Feldman, Shai. 1991. "Israeli Deterrence: The Test of the Gulf War." In *War in the Gulf: Implications for Israel,* ed. Joseph Alpher. Tel Aviv: Jaffee Center for Strategic Studies (in Hebrew).

———. 1997. *Nuclear Weapons and Arms Control in the Middle East.* Cambridge, Mass.: MIT Press.

Hersh, Seymour. 1991. *The Samson Option.* New York: Random House.

Inbar, Ephraim. 1999. *Rabin and Israel's National Security.* Baltimore: Johns Hopkins University Press.

Landau, Emily B. 2006. *Arms Control in the Middle East.* Brighton, UK: Sussex Academic Press.

Maoz, Ze'ev. 2003. "The Mixed Blessing of Israel's Nuclear Policy." *International Security* 27 (3): 44–77.

———. 2006. *Defending the Holy Land.* Ann Arbor: University of Michigan Press.

Mardor, Munya. 1981. *Rafael.* Tel Aviv: Ministry of Defense Press.

Morris, Benny. 2007. "This Holocaust Will Be Different." *Jerusalem Post,* January 18. Available at www.jpost.com/servlet/Satellite?cid=1167467762531&pagename=JPost%2FJPArticle%2FshowFull.

Ne'eman, Yuval. 1986. "Israel and Nuclear Deterrence." *Ma'archot* 308: 19–21 (in Hebrew).

Olmert, Ehud. 2007. Herzelya Speech, January 7. Available at http://www.pmo.gov.il/NR/rdonlyres/6ED362EF-3FD1-44FB-A918-D78E2683C5E4/0/herENG240107.doc.

Pean, Pierre. 1991. *Les Deux Bombes.* Paris: Fayard.

Peres, Shimon. 1995. *Battling for Peace.* New York: Random House.

Quandt, William B. 1986. *Camp David: Peacemaking and Politics.* Washington, D.C.: Brookings Institution Press.

Richelson, Jeffrey T. 2005. *Spying on the Bomb.* New York: Norton.

Schiff, Ze'ev. 2000a. "Nuclear Opacity: For How Long." *Ha'aretz,* August 24.

———. 2000b. "Why There Is No Nuclear Debate." *Ha'aretz,* March 29.

———. 2001. "Comments on the Balance of National Strength and Security." In *The Balance of National Strength and Security,* ed. Uzi Arad. Tel Aviv: Yediot Achronot Press (in Hebrew).

Shalom, Zaki. 2002. *David Ben-Gurion, the State of Israel and the Arab World, 1949–56.* Sussex: Sussex Academic Press.

SIPRI. 2006. *Yearbook 2006: Armaments, Disarmament and International Security.* Cambridge: Cambridge University Press.

Steinberg, Gerald. 2000. "Parameters of Stable Deterrence in a Proliferated Middle East." *Non-Proliferation Review* 7 (3): 43–60.

Sunday Times (London). 1986. "Revealed: The Secrets of Israel's Nuclear Arsenals." October 5.

9

North Korea

Existential Deterrence and Diplomatic Leverage

JOHN S. PARK AND DONG SUN LEE

Most of the contemporaneous analyses of the North Korean nuclear crisis are inadequate in explaining Pyongyang's nuclear policy. Two patterns are common in explanations of North Korea's nuclear policy. The first is an overreliance on what a rational state actor would do or not do. North Korean actions that run counter to these prescriptions are declared to be reckless. The second pattern overemphasizes the sui generis nature of the North Korean state and its nuclear proliferation activity. A consequence of adhering to this viewpoint is the inability to apply lessons learned from dealing with other nuclear proliferants. Pursuing either approach results in a lopsided appraisal that diminishes the opportunity to assess nuances in Pyongyang's nuclear policy.

In this chapter, we seek to provide a comprehensive and balanced enquiry into the core areas of Pyongyang's nuclear policy. First, we address the primary purpose of North Korea's nuclear weapon program and against this background explore the main applications of the nuclear policy. Next, we examine the foundations of North Korea's nuclear policy—*songun* politics and *juche* ideology—and the manner in which Pyongyang has employed them in the development of its nuclear capability and doctrine. Then, we analyze the regional impact of North Korea's nuclear policy. Finally, we suggest some implications.

The central argument of this chapter is that while North Korea's primary purpose in developing nuclear weapons and missile delivery systems is deterrence, Pyongyang has leveraged its weapon program in a concerted manner to secure long-sought diplomatic relations with Washington and much-needed economic development assistance.

Overview

Washington's open threats to use nuclear weapons to end the deadlock during the Korean War and its subsequent postwar deployment of advanced tactical nuclear weapon systems in South Korea imbued North Korea with a deep sense of vulnerability to U.S. attack. Given the close proximity of massive North Korean troop concentration along the inter-Korean border, quantitative superiority in conventional forces largely provided North Korea with a deterrent capability. However, as its economic and military situation worsened with the collapse of the Soviet bloc trading system and the end of military aid in the early 1990s, North Korea's conventional military superiority began to be overshadowed by the rapid improvement of South Korea's armed forces.

While the precise moment of Pyongyang's decision to launch a nuclear weapon program is unknown, activity in this area accelerated during the period of Seoul's full implementation of its *nordpolitik* or northern policy, whereby South Korea notably established diplomatic relations with Moscow and Beijing. Commencing in the late 1980s and growing in the early 1990s, North Korea intensified efforts to increase production of weapon-grade plutonium. During a period of intensifying economic and diplomatic isolation, North Korea's rapid nuclear weapon development activity provided a critical element of existential deterrence against the perceived intense U.S. threat. That deterrent enabled North Korea to restore a semblance of balance on the peninsula after the enormous effectiveness of Seoul's northern policy that initially skewed inter-Korean power dynamics heavily in South Korea's favor.

Lacking its former Soviet and Chinese patrons and its preferential trade terms with Eastern European countries, Pyongyang also began leveraging different aspects of its nuclear weapon program to explore and secure diplomatic, economic, and energy concessions. This effort culminated in the 1994 U.S.-North Korea Agreed Framework. Pyongyang has continued the practice of leveraging its nuclear weapon program to seek a package deal through the Six-Party Talks. Despite key multilateral agreements facilitated by the Talks—*The Joint Statement* (September 19, 2005), *Initial Actions for the Implementation of the Joint Statement* (February 13, 2007), and *Second-Phase Actions for the Implementation of the Joint Statement* (October 3, 2007)—doubts linger as to whether Pyongyang will give up its entire nuclear weapon capability in return for promised concessions.

To facilitate a comprehensive examination of North Korea's nuclear policy, we draw insights from two main sources: (1) U.S.-Democratic People's Republic of Korea (DPRK) Track II meetings and (2) research interviews with government policy advisers from each of the Six-Party Talks member states working to resolve the North Korean nuclear problem.[1]

North Korea's Nuclear Arsenal and Policy

Defying U.N. Security Council warnings, North Korea conducted an underground nuclear test on October 9, 2006. While it was much smaller than tests carried out by previous nuclear club aspirants, the explosive yield of the North Korean test had a far greater political, rather than technical, importance. By demonstrating the possession of a nuclear deterrent capability to defend itself from the United States, Pyongyang's assertiveness in its dealings with Washington grew significantly. From Pyongyang's perspective, the attainment of "a powerful, self-reliant defense capability" was the culmination of a concerted effort to effectively counter Washington's "hostile policy" (Korean Central News Agency [KCNA] 2006b).

The Primary Purpose of the Nuclear Deterrent

To North Korea, the potency of Washington's hostile policy has been underscored by the overwhelming U.S. nuclear arsenal. The origins of this policy are rooted in the embryonic North Korean state's formative experiences with U.S. nuclear threats made during the Korean War. Pyongyang's response to those threats sheds light on how a deeply ingrained sense of insecurity became a core part of the reclusive regime's view of its place and relations with the international community. North Korea has all along existed on the periphery of this community.

At the height of the Korean War, faced with the seemingly endless onslaught of Chinese volunteer forces, General Douglas MacArthur sought to deploy atomic weapons as part of a strategy to push the Chinese out of the Korean peninsula (Oberdorfer 1997: 252). In early 1953, newly elected President Dwight Eisenhower threatened atomic attack to end the deadlock that had continued for more than two years after Kim Il Sung's invasion of the South (Weathersby 1993: 425–58, 1995–96: 30–34, 1998: 90–115). Eisenhower and his close advisers would later claim that the armistice North Korea and China concluded in 1953 with the U.N. Command—under the leadership of the United States—had been largely secured by the American nuclear threat (Cumings 1992: 16–17).

Open debate in the U.S. Congress about using the atomic bomb during the Korean War is believed to have constituted a strong formative experience for Kim Il Sung.[2] The resulting sense of insecurity was exacerbated after the war when the United States began assembling complete nuclear weapon systems in South Korea. These deployments were intended to deter another North Korean attack on South Korea (Norris, Arkin, and Burr 1999: 26–35).[3] According to declassified documents, Washington violated armistice provisions that proscribed the introduction of new armaments onto the Korean peninsula by deploying nuclear-tipped 280-millimeter artillery shells in South Korea (Mazarr 1997: 20–21). In 1957, U.S.

forces were augmented with sixty nuclear bombs stored at Kunsan Air Base near Seoul (An 1992: 676).

Previously classified reports reveal that Washington deployed additional nuclear weapon systems in South Korea over the next several years. In the late 1960s, U.S. forces in South Korea acquired atomic demolition munitions, essentially nuclear land mines designed to slow a North Korean armored advance. Nuclear-tipped Nike Hercules antiaircraft missiles were also sent to South Korea (Hayes 1991: 34). These deployments formed an extensive and growing nuclear arsenal aimed directly at North Korea.

The psychological impact of Korean War-era U.S. nuclear threats combined with the physical deployment of U.S. nuclear weapons on South Korean soil elicited a strong response from Kim Il Sung. Referring to the threat posed by America's nuclear armaments to the survival of the Workers' Paradise, Kim reportedly began exploring prospects for a North Korean nuclear program.[4] From the North Korean perspective, a major compounding impetus for such a program was the nuclear threat emanating from South Korea. With the U.S. nuclear deterrent already arrayed against it, revelations in the mid-1970s about South Korea's nuclear weapon program magnified Pyongyang's sense of insecurity (Song 1991: 474).

North Korea's insecurity was exacerbated by the increased isolation it experienced as a direct result of Seoul's highly effective northern policy. In the late 1980s and early 1990s, Seoul embarked on a campaign to establish diplomatic relations with Pyongyang's core allies—China, the Soviet Union, and the Soviet bloc countries—through massive trade incentives. Seoul swiftly attained the dominant position in inter-Korean relations by securing these countries' de facto recognition of South Korea's superior economic and political power on the peninsula. Although South Korea sought to deploy this increased political capital to establish détente with Pyongyang, in practice, the enormous success of this policy meant that North Korea's initial experience in the post-Cold War period was traumatic (Park 2006: 31). The intense betrayal that North Korea felt following Beijing's and Moscow's normalization of ties with its rival sparked the beginning of the most isolated period in North Korea's short history. Building a nuclear weapon capability provided North Korea a path to restore some security and diplomatic balance on the peninsula.

Following the 9/11 terrorist attacks in the United States, North Korea's persistence on this path and the U.S. allegation in October 2002 of a clandestine uranium enrichment program in that country rapidly raised tensions between Pyongyang and Washington. North Korea felt the full impact of an intensified U.S. *hostile* policy in the form of Washington's post-9/11 security policy, laid out by President George W. Bush in his 2002 State of the Union address. Labeled a member of the "axis of evil" in that landmark speech, North Korea was censured for its tyrannical leadership and destabilizing nuclear ambition.[5] By including

North Korea, along with Iraq and Iran, in the axis of evil, Bush had, in practice, discredited South Korea's proengagement efforts, which constituted the core of its sunshine policy.

Moreover, by labeling North Korea an enemy of the United States, the carefully implemented regional confidence and trust-building process that had been put into place under the auspices of the 1994 Agreed Framework and the Korean Peninsula Energy Development Organization was nullified. It has been asserted that Kim Jong Il, having initially responded to Seoul's and Washington's engagement overtures, began to seriously rethink the promises that had been made in the 1994 nuclear accord.[6]

Kim Jong Il's paranoia was compounded by the events that began to unfold in mid-2002. From the North Korean perspective, President Bush's campaign to oust Saddam Hussein in Iraq bore a striking similarity to Kim's predicament. After meeting with senior leaders in Pyongyang, Donald Gregg, a former U.S. ambassador to Seoul, stated, "the predominant fear there is that North Korea is next" (U.S. Senate 2003).

A major theme in this period was the consistent Bush administration stance of refusing to enter into substantive negotiations with the Kim Jong Il regime until the confirmation of complete, verifiable, irreversible disarmament (CVID) in North Korea. Pyongyang had insisted on the precise opposite—that is, negotiations first, CVID later. Although the North Koreans and Americans held talks in a trilateral venue hosted by the Chinese in late April 2003 to end the nuclear deadlock, an analysis of the official North Korean and U.S. statements reveals that the above policy stance remained largely unchanged (Sanger 2003b). While the trilateral meeting and the subsequent rounds of Six-Party Talks were greeted as signs of progress in the nuclear crisis, North Korea analysts at the time expected the talks to "devolve into a long, arduous process with no certainty of success" (Kirk 2003).

In Track II meetings, North Korean diplomats expressed frustration with the early rounds of the Talks. Citing the Bush administration's overriding insistence on CVID before engaging in substantive negotiations, the North Koreans felt that their security concerns were not being adequately addressed. They believed that if they were to completely dismantle their nuclear program before the conclusion of a comprehensive deal, U.S. security assurances would be insufficient during the intervening period of vulnerability. On a stand-alone basis—rather than as an integral part of a comprehensive, step-by-step package—security assurances were viewed as just a piece of paper. In the search for security, it was argued that a nuclear deterrent would be much more effective in satisfying this purpose.

The Main Application of North Korea's Nuclear Policy

While the primary purpose of its nuclear arsenal is deterrence, North Korea has derived much utility from leveraging it in negotiations. Based on its negotiating stance in the 1994 nuclear crisis and in periodic rounds of the Six-Party Talks, it can be argued that North Korea has used its nuclear program to expand its bargaining power to secure important concessions. Although much attention has been drawn to North Korea's demands for energy and economic development aid, a long-running theme has been Pyongyang's desire to normalize relations with Washington. This core objective is in line with North Korea's efforts to formalize a peaceful coexistence with the United States on its terms. Should normalization and peaceful coexistence be achieved, a major justification for a nuclear deterrent would diminish. How has North Korea executed its bargaining tactics to pursue these diplomatic and security goals? As seen in the multilateral meetings in Beijing, Pyongyang closely assesses the existing divisions among the other Six-Party Talks participants as well as the state of the international community to meticulously calibrate and effectively execute its bargaining ploys.

Widening divisions between and among its adversaries to create opportunities to win future concessions is a long-practiced North Korean tactic. Continuing with "bad behavior" such as nuclear proliferation activity enables North Korea to offer to cease such behavior in return for much larger concessions than it has received in the past. While Washington has been vehemently opposed to "rewarding bad behavior," Beijing and Seoul have subsumed their current North Korea policy efforts in a longer-term pragmatic approach to foster momentum toward full implementation of Six-Party Talks-facilitated agreements. While anger and condemnation bind Washington, Beijing, Seoul, Moscow, and Tokyo in the aftermath of events such as North Korea's nuclear test, this cohesion weakens as divergent national interests and priorities reemerge (Park 2005: 75–87).

In this context, Pyongyang has been able to use its nuclear policy in two specific ways to great effect: first, to widen the gap in the U.S.-Republic of Korea (ROK) alliance; and second, to contribute to rising friction between Beijing and Tokyo. After each Pyongyang act of brinkmanship, Washington seeks to enlist its South Korean ally to increase pressure on Pyongyang. Intent on continuing the normalization of inter-Korean relations to achieve a gradual reunification on the peninsula, Seoul has been careful in avoiding the full adoption of a U.S. policy that would disrupt that process.[7] From Washington's perspective, such behavior raises questions about the priorities of its ally and the necessity of a military alliance.

In Japan, North Korean acts of nuclear defiance foster more support among Japanese for conservative political factions that stress the need for preemptive military capabilities and fundamental change to the pacifist constitution.[8] These reactions, in turn, evoke memories in China of the atrocities committed by a militaristic Japan during World War II. History constitutes a raw nerve that North Korea seeks to exploit.

In both situations, Pyongyang has used a carefully calibrated nuclear policy to increase opportunities to extract concessions. As a wedge is driven deeper into the U.S.-ROK alliance, Pyongyang is able to gradually entice its southern brethren to sign additional inter-Korean cooperation pacts that call for Seoul to provide more economic aid and assistance to North Korea. In a similar manner, growing tensions between Beijing and Tokyo allow Pyongyang to align itself more closely with Beijing and Seoul in terms of the common experience of Japanese wartime occupation. A heightened sense of community is achieved among these three countries through the evocation of historical wrongs that have yet to be fully addressed by Tokyo.

The Role of *Songun* Politics and *Juche* Ideology in North Korea's Nuclear Policy

The meticulous craftsmanship that Pyongyang applies to using its nuclear policy to drive wedges between adversaries is also evident in the formulation of the solid foundation in which its nuclear policy is anchored. The key enablers of North Korea's nuclear policy are *songun* (military-first) politics and *juche* ideology (policy of self-reliance). Because the development of a nuclear deterrent entails enormous resource commitment for an aid-dependent state, *songun* politics enables the Kim Jong Il leadership to ensure that the military receives required materiel. Given the primacy of attaining a nuclear deterrent in *songun* politics, advancement of this goal brings great prestige and influence to the Kim Jong Il leadership. This in turn ensures the continuation and strengthening of the symbiotic relationship between Kim Jong Il and the Korean People's Army. That is a testament to the foresight of Kim Jong Il's father, the "Great Leader."

Cognizant that his son did not possess his charisma and anti-Japanese guerrilla credentials, Kim Il Sung sought to closely pair the military with his son, and his son with the military, at an early stage. By appointing the "Dear Leader" as the chairman of the National Defense Commission in 1993, the elder Kim made certain that rather than an individual leading the country, a system would. Indeed, the binding of Kim Jong Il to the military ensured that the leadership would be dependent on the management and maintenance of this system, thereby boosting prospects for the regime's survival.[9] Kim Jong Il's implementation of *songun* politics in the mid-1990s formalized a process that his father had initiated.

Songun politics has been coupled with the *juche* ideology,[10] which instills a fierce sense of nationalism in North Korea. The *juche* ideology serves as a powerful political binding force that enables the leadership to justify the collective sacrifice of the North Korean people. By collectively channeling the privation required to concentrate scarce resources towards the advancement of the indigenous nuclear program, *juche* serves a critical purpose as the foundation for the regime and allows *songun* politics to be effectively implemented.

As with the relationship between Kim Jong Il and the military, a symbiotic relationship exists between *songun* and *juche*. The one provides meaning to the other. *Songun* politics on its own would likely prove to be unsustainable because the military-first policy imposes massive economic hardship on the people. Likewise, in the aftermath of devastating floods in the mid-1990s and the demise of relationships with communist patrons following the end of the Cold War, the *juche* ideology was largely bankrupt in practice in terms of facilitating economic self-sufficiency. However, *songun* politics and *juche* ideology together provide the Kim Jong Il regime with a state structure that allows it to configure and implement its nuclear policy.

North Korea's Nuclear Capability and Doctrine

The potency of Pyongyang's nuclear policy is directly linked to a credible nuclear capability and doctrine. Given minimal available information, it is difficult to judge whether North Korea currently has or plans to build deliverable nuclear weapons. However, there is a reasonable chance that Pyongyang already possesses or is close to possessing an operational nuclear arsenal. It seems to have the technical capability as well as the political motive to do so.

What is certain is North Korea's ability to manufacture nuclear explosives. The partially successful nuclear test in October 2006 demonstrates that Pyongyang has the necessary technical and material resources, including weapon design expertise and fissile material.[11] Its nuclear devices, however, may not be sophisticated in comparison with those possessed by the established nuclear weapon states. According to expert estimates and media reports, the yield of the 2006 nuclear explosion amounted to less than 1 kiloton, falling far short of Pyongyang's apparent aim of 4 kilotons. (The scale of other states' maiden tests ranges between 9 and 60 kilotons.) This estimate implies that North Korea's weapon design and manufacturing have much room for improvement (Squassoni 2006). The underground test, while not a total success, would nevertheless provide its scientists and engineers with useful test data for making refinements. There is also a possibility that Pyongyang will conduct additional nuclear tests if the Six-Party Talks stall and thereby leap forward in its technical expertise (Karl 2007).

While North Korea's nuclear explosive-building capabilities are primitive, they can still produce significant military benefits. It is estimated that a 1-kiloton bomb, which amounts to a small tactical warhead, "could kill people in an area of about one square mile and partially destroy a much larger area" (Sessler et al. 2000). This is a significant, if limited, military threat, particularly given the high population density of Seoul and Tokyo. According to census statistics, in 2005, 42,334 persons per square mile resided in Seoul, compared to 14,864 in Tokyo (National Statistical Office 2007; Tokyo Metropolitan Government 2007a). In

TABLE 9-1.
Estimates of North Korea's Nuclear Capacity

Source of estimate	Plutonium inventory (kg)	Weapon equivalents (number)	Current plutonium production capacity (kg/yr): 5 MW(e) reactor
Siegfried Hecker (November 15, 2006)	40–50[a]	6–8	6
Congressional Research Service (October 18, 2006)	N/A	8–10	6
Institute for Science and International Security (June 26, 2006)	20–53	4–13	N/A

SOURCES: Hecker (2006); Squassoni (2006); Albright and Brannan (2006).
[a]Hecker estimates that the maiden nuclear test consumed approximately 6 kg.

addition, North Korea has an indigenous infrastructure to further increase its weapon production capacity. It possesses a considerable stockpile of fissile material, which was derived from domestic production and possibly foreign sources (Niksch 2006: 14). Table 9-1 presents key authoritative estimates of North Korea's nuclear capacity.

Importantly, North Korea's nuclear stockpile could expand further unless its fissile material production is checked through diplomatic or military means. It is estimated that the 5-megawatt electric (MW[e]) reactor at Yongbyon, when operated, produces up to 6 kilograms of plutonium per year (Hecker 2006), roughly sufficient for one nuclear weapon. If Pyongyang resumes construction of the 50 MW(e) reactor, 60 kilograms of plutonium could be produced annually upon completion in several years. The 200 MW(e) reactor located at Taechon, if completed, could generate up to 200 kilograms of plutonium. North Korea also has other facilities that combine to constitute a full plutonium cycle, including a uranium mine, a fuel fabrication plant, and a reprocessing laboratory, which separates weapon-grade plutonium from spent fuel (International Institute for Strategic Studies [IISS] 2004: 32).

Besides the ability to produce plutonium, North Korea possesses equipment that could be used as a component of a program capable of producing highly enriched uranium (HEU). North Korea reportedly received assistance from Pakistani nuclear scientist A. Q. Khan in procuring essential components such as centrifuges as early as 1996 (Niksch 2006: 11). Pyongyang, according to U.S. officials, admitted to having such a program in October 2002, but subsequently denied its existence. In November 2002, the Central Intelligence Agency estimated that the enrichment facilities could have been operational by as early as 2005, annually producing enough HEU for two or more weapons (IISS 2004: 42). While doubts have emerged over the program's progress over the past few years, most U.S. intelligence agencies still accept its existence with modest conviction (Sanger and Broad 2007). For example, Joseph DeTrani, a longtime intelligence official, testified to the U.S. Senate in March 2007 that "we still have confidence that the program is in existence—at the mid-confidence level."

North Korea has also developed delivery systems that could potentially carry its warheads to regional targets. Nearly half a century after initiating its missile development program with technical assistance from the former Soviet Union and China, North Korea has an indigenous infrastructure with an extensive capacity for research, development, testing, and production. It also exports technology and material for hard currency.

Its single-stage, medium-range Nodong missile—with a range of 1,000–1,300 kilometers and a payload of 700–1,000 kilograms—could accommodate a simple fission-type warhead. However, there is no confirmation that Pyongyang has deployed any reliable nuclear-armed missile (IISS 2004). Pyongyang has yet to demonstrate the capability to craft a nuclear warhead small enough to fit onto a missile or the ability to build a reentry vehicle (Center for Nonproliferation Studies [CNS] 2006: 2). The Nodong, nevertheless, is the sole potentially nuclear-capable missile operationally deployed in the North Korean arsenal. (The smaller, short-range Hwasong and Scud missiles are probably unable to deliver a nuclear payload.) Since the first test in May 1993, between twelve and thirty-six Nodong missiles reportedly have been deployed (Federation of American Scientists [FAS] 2007). They are designed for delivery from mobile launchers and are capable of reaching targets in Japan, as well as in South Korea.

At present, no operational North Korean missile can deliver nuclear weapons to U.S. territories. However, the long-range, multiple-stage Taepodong missile with such potential is currently under development. The Taepodong-1 missile was test fired with mixed success on August 31, 1998, with an estimated range of 2,896 kilometers and a payload of 700–1,000 kilograms (FAS 2007). The advanced Taepodong-2 missile is believed to have intercontinental range. However, a test flight on July 5, 2006, failed, indicating that efforts to develop an intercontinental ballistic missile still face significant technical obstacles. North Korea is also reportedly developing a land-based mobile Taepodong-X with a range of up to 4,000 kilometers, which appears to be based on the Soviet SS-N-6 submarine-launched missile (CNS 2006: 2).

Given its nascent nuclear-weapon capability, North Korea, like other new members of the nuclear club, will likely adopt a doctrine of minimum deterrence. Such a doctrine is predicated on the maintenance of a relatively modest arsenal—in both quantity and quality—and assumes that even a small risk of unacceptable nuclear retaliation suffices to deter an adversary. This minimalist doctrine is particularly suitable for Pyongyang because of its limited nuclear material and technical capacity. A more expansive limited deterrence, to say nothing of a maximalist assured retaliation strategy, is simply beyond Pyongyang's reach at the moment. It will not be able to build a sizable and sophisticated triad in the foreseeable future.

Although there is no intelligence that directly confirms this assessment of North Korea's nuclear doctrine, Pyongyang's statements are largely consistent with it. Pyongyang boasts of its "nuclear deterrent" despite the fact that it is estimated to have produced enough plutonium for roughly a dozen weapons at most and possesses no reliable means with which to hit U.S. cities. Vice Foreign Minister Kim Gye Gwan's assertion during an ABC News interview in June 2005 that North Korea has "enough nuclear bombs to defend against a U.S. attack" appears to support the assessment that Pyongyang is employing a minimalist doctrine (Squassoni 2006: 4). If North Korea has adopted a more demanding doctrine, Kim's confidence makes little sense in light of its small arsenal.

While declaring and demonstrating its nuclear power status, Pyongyang also has promulgated a general policy of no first use. In October 2006, North Korea officially announced that it "will never use nuclear weapons first" (KCNA 2006a). Although this declared policy might partly seek to reassure the concerned states of its nonaggressive intent and thereby reduce international pressure, the policy may also reflect its genuine preference, stemming from strategic realities. The United States has massive retaliatory capability against a North Korean nuclear attack, so Pyongyang has a compelling incentive not to cross the nuclear threshold first under most circumstances. North Korea, which possesses a robust conventional deterrent, also need not threaten a nuclear first strike in order to deter a conventional attack. Therefore, Pyongyang will probably want to adhere to its no-first-use policy except in extreme situations (e.g., a U.S. invasion). A North Korean nuclear first attack against the United States and its key allies is highly improbable, although Pyongyang might threaten such an attack in an effort to extort concessions from nonnuclear states such as South Korea and Japan.

The Regional Impact of North Korea's Nuclear Policy

Pyongyang's nuclear weapon development itself does not markedly affect the risk of war on the peninsula. However, it tends to breed dissension and sharpen cleavages among major states in the region.

The Risk of War on the Korean Peninsula

Deployable North Korean nuclear armaments would decrease the likelihood of a U.S. preventive war on the peninsula.[12] Preventive war—military action to stop adversaries from increasing military capabilities—tends to be a risky endeavor, as demonstrated by the long history of failed attempts and the ongoing ordeal in Iraq

(Lee 2008). Democratic governments usually face daunting challenges in selling such a war to their publics—unless a swift and cheap victory is anticipated (Levy and Gochal 2001; Schweller 1992). Such a victory is a remote possibility, however, when target states are nuclear armed, because the prospect of nuclear retaliation adds to the associated risks. For this reason, there is no historical case of a preventive war against a nuclear-capable state, although some states have seriously considered it.

While North Korea's nuclear arsenal has captured the headlines, the North Korean military does not need it to inflict unacceptable damage to the United States and its allies in the event of a U.S. invasion (Lee 2006). When Pyongyang was believed to possess a meager arsenal—comprising only one or possibly two untested nuclear devices and no effective long-range missiles—military experts still calculated that a major war on the Korean peninsula would cost the United States approximately 80,000 to 100,000 casualties and US$100 billion (Oberdorfer 2001). When damage to other countries was also considered, the estimated cost of such a war increased to as high as "one million casualties and one trillion dollars in estimated industrial damage and lost business" (Cha and Kang 2003). Another estimate calculated that a second Korean War would entail destruction costing "more than $60 billion and result in 3 million casualties, including 52,000 U.S. military casualties" (Cha and Kang 2003).

The prospect of such a costly conventional war clearly suffices to deter the United States (Lee 2006). The U.S. government could not persuade its public to approve such a war. In December 2006, when the number of combat deaths in Iraq surpassed 3,000 and the cost of that war exceeded US$350 billion, 61 percent of Americans surveyed said that the war had not been worth fighting (ABC News/*Washington Post* Poll 2006; Associated Press 2007a). In light of such sensitivity to war costs, few if any presidents would be able to sell the U.S. public on an obviously more expensive war on the Korean peninsula—unless North Korea were to directly attack the United States or its key allies first or to transfer nuclear weapons to terrorist organizations. A public opinion poll confirmed this point: Even before the test that demonstrated North Korea's nuclear capability, 62 percent of Americans opposed military action against North Korea in the absence of grave provocation (Balz and Morin 2005; Gallup Poll 2005).

Policy makers have recognized the political constraint in using military force against Pyongyang. "I am not saying we don't have military options," one of President George W. Bush's most senior advisers reportedly admitted in an interview. "I am just saying we don't have good ones" (Sanger 2003a). Similarly, former U.S. Defense Secretary William Perry stated in a 1999 report on North Korean policy that "the prospect of such a destructive war is a powerful deterrent to precipitous U.S. or allied action" (Perry 1999). In the face of such a political constraint, the Clinton and Bush administrations have understandably backed away from the use of force. A North Korean nuclear arsenal would add one further constraint, but there already are enough hurdles to dissuade a preventive war.

The possibility of a *preemptive* war, on the other hand, looms larger as Pyongyang develops nuclear weapons. Preemption entails attacking an adversary first in anticipation of an imminent aggression by that adversary (Schelling 1966). Such a war is likely when antagonists perceive strong incentives to strike first—in other words, when absorbing an enemy's first blow carries high cost and risk, while an early action has a reasonable chance to spoil such a disastrous attack.

North Korea's nuclear armaments can put the United States in such a precarious situation. Unless forestalled, a North Korean nuclear attack against major cities in the region could inflict considerable damage directly on civilian populations and regional economies. As noted earlier, high population densities in Seoul and Tokyo mean that even a small-scale attack can produce large civilian casualties. The economic consequences of an attack might also be severe due to the high geographical concentrations of economic activities in South Korea and Japan. For example, the gross regional domestic product (GRDP) of Seoul accounted for 22.8 percent and adjacent Gyeonggi province amounted to 19.9 percent, respectively, of South Korea's national total in 2004 (National Statistical Office 2005). Tokyo's GRDP accounted for a similarly large fraction of Japan's national production—16.4 percent in 2002 (Tokyo Metropolitan Government 2007b). On the other hand, the United States has sophisticated conventional and nuclear weaponry that could destroy much if not all of Pyongyang's small, rudimentary nuclear force as long as the precise locations of North Korea's underground storage and launch sites could be confirmed; the U.S. missile defense system can probably cope with the remainder with reasonable confidence.

If the United States were certain that its robust retaliatory capability would deter a nuclear attack by Pyongyang, it could conclude that a preemptive attack is unnecessary. However, Washington seems to have little confidence in deterrence. At the 2002 graduation exercise of the U.S. Military Academy, President Bush categorically stated that "containment is not possible when unbalanced dictators with weapons of mass destruction can deliver those weapons on missiles or secretly provide them to terrorist allies" (Bush 2002b). Also, Washington cannot completely trust that its rudimentary missile defense system is capable of fending off all incoming nuclear weapons by itself. In the midst of an acute crisis and with no fool-proof alternatives available to them, American policy makers might be tempted to launch a preemptive strike against North Korean nuclear and missile facilities, if they detect Pyongyang raising the readiness of its nuclear forces and anticipate an impending nuclear attack (Kim 2006).

For its part, Pyongyang also has an incentive to preempt in a desperate situation. Pyongyang views its nuclear arsenal as a valuable yet vulnerable strategic asset. In its pursuit of a nuclear capability, the Kim Jong Il regime has diverted scarce resources from North Korea's ailing economy and has not hesitated to risk a confrontation with the United States as well as with major regional powers—including its Chinese patron. This fact reveals the significant strategic (and perhaps political) value Pyongyang attaches to a nuclear deterrent. However, this prized asset is potentially vulnerable to an enemy attack—particularly a nuclear one. The liquid-fuel missiles in the North Korean inventory—the probable delivery vehicles for its nuclear weapons—can be located during their rather lengthy launch preparation and destroyed on the ground. Also, the size of the North Korean arsenal is so small that even a partially successful attack against it could reduce its nuclear capability drastically. Although U.S. intelligence presently seems deficient with regard to the location of North Korea's nuclear force, Pyongyang cannot rely on the continuation of this deficiency.

North Korean leaders would thus be susceptible to a "use-it-or-lose-it" mindset if they anticipate an impending disarming offensive as a prelude to an invasion. A desperate North Korean attack to preempt U.S. action would aim to either increase casualties up front and coerce the United States to abandon its plan of attack, or achieve battlefield advantages (e.g., delay U.S. reinforcements). Although the effectiveness of such an attack is moot, the Kim Jong Il regime will not give up any potential advantage in an existential conflict. Even if Pyongyang initially decides not to preempt, it will probably take precautionary measures—such as placing its nuclear forces on high alert or dispersing them to reduce their vulnerability. Washington may, in turn, mistake these extraordinary moves for harbingers of an imminent attack and take provocative countermeasures, thereby amplifying incentives for a North Korean preemptive attack.

In an acute crisis, such fears and temptations on both sides could possibly interact to trigger an armed conflict that neither side wants. As noted earlier, Pyongyang's nuclear arsenal poses a considerable potential threat to Washington and its allies. In a crisis situation, the U.S. military would likely raise its operational preparedness for a possible preemptive attack as it did in 1994 (Kim 2006). The United States might strengthen surveillance efforts to locate and track North Korea's nuclear forces or reinforce U.S. offensive strike capabilities. Pyongyang, in turn, might mistake such precautionary measures for actual first-strike preparation. Such misperception is a real possibility, given North Korea's limited intelligence gathering capability.

Two other factors could also negatively color Pyongyang's interpretation of U.S. action and further increase the chances of misjudgment and overreaction: first, Washington's doctrine of preemption, and second, North Korea's abiding perception that the United States is hostile, a perception ingrained by decades of confrontation. Consequently, North Korean leaders might be tempted to use their valuable nuclear weapons for fear of losing them to a U.S. disarming strike.

This temptation will be especially powerful if Pyongyang views such a strike by Washington as a prelude to a full-scale invasion.

While an inadvertent nuclear escalation is a significant potential threat, it does not justify an alarmist view. The potential danger of an unwanted nuclear conflict will eventually breed caution on both sides and reduce the odds of its realization (Jervis 1989). The United States will likely avoid applying provocative military and economic pressures for fear of a crisis spiraling out of control into a nuclear exchange. In fact, Clinton administration officials feared this possibility of inadvertent escalation and therefore hesitated to resort to limited use of force or economic sanctions—even when Kim Jong Il was suspected of having only one or possibly two nuclear devices of unproven potency. Since Pyongyang attained a greater retaliatory capability following its nuclear test, preemption carries higher risks. Should Pyongyang's retaliatory capability grow, the possibility of U.S. preemption will further decrease.

For its part, Pyongyang will avoid overly provocative brinkmanship tactics and participate in negotiations—at least until it moves out of a period of vulnerability when it is not yet able to deploy a secure nuclear force capable of hitting major U.S. urban-industrial targets (CNS 2006: 11). A preemptive strike will be Pyongyang's last resort in any case, because such a strike would provoke a massive retaliation by Washington. Although the possibility of a preemptive war cannot be altogether dismissed, history tells us that states rarely have launched preemptive attacks because these actions carry considerable political costs of appearing to be an aggressor (Reiter 1995). Given the nuclear taboo, nuclear preemption will have a far greater political backlash; so there has been no such attack.

Relations Among Major States

Against this background of strategic stability on the peninsula, North Korea's overt nuclear armaments have sharpened cleavages among major powers. In the aftermath of North Korea's October 2006 nuclear test, the U.N. Security Council passed a unanimous sanctions resolution rebuking Pyongyang for defying the international community. While there was momentary unity among the other five members of the Six-Party Talks in condemning North Korea's nuclear defiance, Pyongyang's nuclear policy has succeeded in exploiting the fundamental rifts between two blocs—Beijing, Seoul, and Moscow on one side, and Washington and Tokyo on the other.[13]

The continuation of economic engagement along the Sino-North Korean border and between the two Koreas, along with the deepening two-bloc configuration, reveals why Security Council sanctions have come to comprise a collection of words rather than actions. The combination of U.S. Treasury financial regulatory measures and the Security Council sanctions resolutions exacerbated the situation for North Korea, but not to the point where Pyongyang was forced to fully and immediately denuclearize.[14]

As the pressure increased on Pyongyang, the resulting strain was essentially borne by Beijing and Seoul. Pyongyang used its nuclear policy to further divide Seoul and Washington, as the louder calls of the United States for South Korean cooperation in applying greater pressure on North Korea through sanctions were gradually side stepped. Washington's insistence that Beijing join the Proliferation Security Initiative and inspect North Korean vessels suspected of carrying weapons of mass destruction-related material was similarly set aside. The South Korean and Chinese positions enabled North Korea to avoid the full impact of Washington-led punitive and enforcement measures. In practice, stability in the region has been buttressed by ongoing economic engagement of North Korea by Seoul and Beijing. Occurring under the surface of the Six-Party Talks process, incremental regional economic integration has provided a modicum, though significant amount, of stability.

Why would Beijing and Seoul continue with their respective versions of economic engagement even after North Korea's nuclear test? That is the key to understanding why North Korea's nuclear policy, which focuses on manipulating the divergent national interests of the core negotiating countries, has been effective. The nuclear policy's efficacy, in turn, reveals why there is a low probability that sanctions will achieve the stated goal of denuclearization. North Korea has become intricately intertwined with the domestic priorities of both China and South Korea, driving and limiting their respective policies toward North Korea.

For China, the primacy of *xiaokang,* or reaching internal economic development goals, is central to its government policies. Focused on bringing the majority of the Chinese population into the middle class, the Chinese Communist Party leadership views the attainment of a US$3,000 per capita gross domestic product by 2020 as the primary means of doing so (Jiang 2002). The leadership deems three major components to be essential to realize this goal: (1) ensuring a stable political and security environment on its borders; (2) securing access to international markets by integrating China further into the global political and economic order through active participation in multilateral fora and organizations; and (3) fostering comprehensive and deep relations with Washington to reduce the need for excessive competition in military spending.[15]

For South Korea, the engagement policy has been the designated means through which the two Koreas will gradually realize a peaceful reunification. Having closely studied the German reunification model, Seoul is extremely reluctant to shoulder the tremendous economic burden of suddenly absorbing the failed state of North Korea. Seeking to moderate Pyongyang's nuclear brinkmanship behavior through some form of an engagement policy will remain an integral part of Seoul's preferred policy path.

Overall, China and South Korea believe that their medium and long-term prosperity is tied to opening up North Korea and integrating it into a regional economic system. Both seek to avoid potentially destabilizing policies that could increase the chance of regime collapse in North Korea. The regional integration of North Korea is believed to hold the key to securing stability and peaceful coexistence. The hope in Seoul and Beijing is that this will eventually foster the development of a regional engine of economic growth. That critical point is not fully understood or appreciated outside of Northeast Asia.

Even in the aftermath of North Korea's nuclear test, these economic engagement policies, especially South Korea's, were not terminated. Clearly, both China and South Korea were angered by North Korea's October 9, 2006, act of defiance as it disrupted their carefully laid regional plans. Following the nuclear test, however, the debate within the South Korean government was not about whether to end its sunshine policy, as would be expected from Washington, but rather how to continue pursuing it in a manner whereby Seoul could have more influence over Pyongyang's behavior—particularly in avoiding another test.

As ways to increase its political influence were explored, Seoul announced that its Kaesong Industrial Complex and Kumkang Mountain tourism project in North Korea would move forward (Roh 2006a). This is because a majority (67.1 percent) of the South Korean public opposes an end to these inter-Korean cooperative projects (*Hankook Ilbo* 2006).

If successfully implemented, the Six-Party Talks agreements could eventually facilitate complete nuclear dismantlement of North Korea. Should this materialize, many experts and political leaders hope that the establishment of a regional cooperative security regime could be realized based on the Six-Party Talks process. However, the obstacles to attaining nuclear dismantlement and launching a regional security organization are formidable. North Korea has become adept at widening the policy differences among the countries in the Six-Party Talks. Although the same policy issues appear on each country's list, each one prioritizes the issues differently. With Beijing, Seoul, and Moscow eager to move ahead with internally driven regional economic development plans, and Washington and Tokyo focused on strict adherence to nuclear disarmament, Pyongyang has ample opportunity to exploit differences in each bloc's policy priorities.

Such dissension among major powers, however, does not guarantee North Korea's survival. Although international sanctions would not cause the collapse of the North Korean regime in the short run, its nuclear weapon program might undermine its long-term survival.[16] Unless Pyongyang moves to abandon its nuclear program completely, the international community is unlikely to expand its currently marginal economic interaction with North Korea. Insofar as the international crisis continues to prevent a more permanent stable external environment from taking root, far-reaching internal reforms would not be forthcoming.

Consequently, chronic economic difficulties and food shortages would persist in North Korea.

These hardships would cause the Kim Jong Il regime to remain unstable and insecure and could lead to its gradual disintegration. North Korea might be able to mitigate these problems if a heightened sense of security resulting from its nuclear arsenal led to a substantial reduction of conventional forces and a redistribution of resources into the civilian economy. In January 2007, Pyongyang vowed to set production of food and consumer goods as top priorities, since its nuclear armaments presumably have provided a self-reliant "war deterrent" (*Rodong Sinmun* 2007). With the military-first politics still firmly in place, however, it is doubtful that North Korea can make substantial and sustainable moves in this direction.

Implications of North Korea's Nuclear Proliferation for the Northeast Asian Region

The primary purpose of North Korea's nuclear policy has been to develop a deterrent to counter the hostile policy of the United States. To increase opportunities for extracting concessions from key members of the Six-Party Talks, Pyongyang has also carefully calibrated its nuclear policy as an effective tool in conducting its diplomatic stratagems. After the October 2006 nuclear test, North Korea's nuclear behavior was viewed with great apprehension because of a perceived increase in the likelihood of regional nuclear proliferation.

Despite concerns about falling atomic dominos in the region (Associated Press 2006), a North Korean nuclear arsenal is unlikely to spur countries like South Korea and Japan to go nuclear in the short run. There are several major reasons for this restraint. One is that the U.S. nuclear umbrella reassures these regional allies. Although Kim Jong Il tends to be overconfident and risk acceptant, U.S. nuclear superiority is too obvious for him to overlook. Washington currently possesses thousands of sophisticated nuclear weapons and an array of advanced delivery vehicles. Tokyo does not want to undercut this robust protection by pursuing a less potent indigenous arsenal in opposition to Washington's policy of global nonproliferation. The versatile U.S. alliance also can protect a wide range of Japanese security interests such as sea lanes, while an indigenous arsenal can only ensure territorial integrity. For these very reasons, the Japanese government decided against a nuclear option in the wake of China's maiden nuclear test in 1964. Thus, in the immediate aftermath of the North Korean nuclear test, the then Japanese Foreign Minister Aso Taro was quick to reassure U.S. Secretary of State Condoleezza Rice that Japan was "absolutely not considering" nuclear development, receiving a strong reconfirmation of the U.S. nuclear commitment to Japan in return (Pinkston and Sakurai 2006). The Roh Moo Hyun government also thought that the nuclear test could not destroy the balance of power buttressed by the U.S.

military alliance as well as the qualitatively superior South Korean military and that an independent arsenal was therefore unnecessary (Roh 2006b).

Another brake against a nuclear domino effect is missile defense technology, which provides an apparent alternative to an indigenous nuclear deterrent. Since the North Korean missile and nuclear tests in 2006, Japan has augmented its programs to develop a next-generation missile defense system jointly with the United States and to deploy current-technology interceptors, including Patriot Advanced Capability (PAC)-3 systems and sea-based SM-3 platforms (Associated Press 2007b). Tokyo views missile defense as the least politically burdensome countermeasure to North Korea's nuclear weapons. Although the development of missile defense has drawn protests from Beijing, possible alternatives (such as the acquisition of a nuclear deterrent or a preemptive strike capability) would meet even stronger opposition from Japan's neighbors as well as the Japanese public. In a July 2006 poll of Japanese citizens, 48.8 percent of respondents disapproved of an offensive strike capability, while 40.6 percent acknowledged its necessity for national security (Pinkston and Sakurai 2006). Facing similar if lesser political constraints, Seoul also has decided to pursue a missile defense capability instead of a nuclear arsenal, establishing a missile defense command and allocating an emergency budget for procurement of the Patriot missile system and control equipment. Unlike Japan, however, South Korea is building an independent system out of concern that cooperation with the United States would elicit a negative reaction from China.

Diplomacy presents another appealing alternative to developing a nuclear deterrent against North Korea. Many South Koreans and (to a lesser extent) many Japanese still believe that it is possible to find a diplomatic way of disarming North Korea. Former South Korean President Roh Moo Hyun is a notable example. He has argued that the North Korean nuclear program—despite the nuclear test—remains numerous steps away from producing a significant operational arsenal. He has also argued that the program poses a long-term rather than an immediate threat, allowing the international community adequate time to seek and implement a negotiated solution (Roh 2006c).

Roh's optimistic assessment is hardly unique. In a public opinion poll, 33.7 percent of South Koreans responded that North Korea would eventually abandon its nuclear program (*Hankook Ilbo* 2006). Kim Dae Jung—a highly influential former president—shares such an optimistic outlook and supports a continued diplomatic effort (*Yonhap News* 2006b). Japanese elites, though less sanguine about the prospect for diplomacy, similarly view the window of opportunity as not yet closed, since Pyongyang will probably still need years to acquire the capability of manufacturing effective nuclear weapons and mating them with reliable missiles (Hughes 2007). These elites understand that developing nuclear armaments will undercut their diplomatic strategy by undermining the nonproliferation regime and eliminating their leverage on China to put pressure on North Korea.

Finally, some normative considerations stop nuclear dominos from falling. The atomic bombings of Hiroshima and Nagasaki in 1945 created a lingering aversion to nuclear weapons in Japanese society. This nuclear taboo has found firm expression in the widely accepted principles in Japan of not possessing, producing, or allowing nuclear weapons. A nationwide survey of Japanese conducted in November 2006 (shortly after the North Korean nuclear test) reported that 80 percent of respondents either supported or somewhat supported upholding the Three Non-Nuclear Principles despite the shock of the test (*Yomiuri Shimbun* 2006). Such public sentiment is an important political obstacle on the path to a nuclear-armed Japan, although there are some signs of its gradual erosion and possibilities of political manipulation (Berger 1993).

While North Korean nuclear weapon production is not likely to produce a regional nuclear chain reaction, the development could exacerbate the security dilemma among the region's major powers and thereby destabilize regional international relations. The North Korean nuclear threat is strengthening the U.S. alliance with Japan in a manner that has significant implications for regional stability. Washington has reaffirmed its nuclear commitment to Tokyo, and these allies are cooperating more extensively in the field of missile defense.

Also, Japan is considering improving its surveillance and long-range precision-strike capabilities, which could provide Tokyo with an offensive option of preemption. There have been some indications that Japan is interested in acquiring such a capability. In July 2006, for instance, the then Japanese Prime Minister Abe Shinzo said: "If we accept that there is no other option to prevent an attack . . . there is the view that attacking the launch base of the guided missiles is within the constitutional right of self-defense" (Yamaguchi 2006). In August 2006, the Subcommittee on Defense Policies in Japan's Liberal Democratic Party debated whether a military capability to strike "a foreign enemy base" is necessary (Pinkston and Sakurai 2006). There also has been discussion in Japan on preparing a constitutional basis for expanded military activities, including "collective self-defense."

While these measures are designed primarily for self-defense, they are raising significant concerns in Beijing, which regards them as potentially detrimental to its security interests. China suspects that the strengthened cooperation between Washington and Tokyo might be an attempt to contain its growing power and influence, and that the two allies' development of a missile defense might be aimed at undermining China's nuclear deterrent (Friedberg 2005). Chinese officials are particularly concerned that the joint missile defense system might be extended to include Taiwan, neutralizing their coercive capabilities and facilitating the island's formal independence (*China's National Defense* 2006; Cody 2006).

If Japan (which occupied parts of Chinese territory between 1931 and 1945) acquired any offensive capability, Beijing also would suspect that Japan aggressively intended to expand its influence at China's expense in order to dominate East Asia (Blanchard 2006). A Chinese Foreign Ministry spokesman strongly criticized high-level Japanese politicians' consideration of a preemptive strike as "extremely irresponsible" (*Yonhap News* 2006a). In response to the increasing military capabilities of its potential adversaries, China will likely expand its own nuclear arsenal to maintain an effective deterrent against the United States (and Japan) and augment its missile and submarine capabilities to restrain Taiwan.

The United States and Japan might, in turn, interpret these Chinese moves as an aggressive attempt at blackmail aimed at subjugating Taiwan—and therefore take countermeasures, such as an increase of their missile defense capabilities. Moreover, Taiwan may also strengthen its own military capabilities—for example, by acquiring ballistic missiles and missile defense systems—to offset China's augmented offensive capability. These reactions could further reinforce China's suspicions about the two allies' intention and strengthen its effort to expand its military power. In the midst of this arms buildup, mutual suspicion and tension would further grow, and the region would become unstable.

This potential danger, however, does not warrant an alarmist reading of the North Korean nuclear situation. China presently sets economic development as its top priority and tries hard to avoid an open conflict with its major trading partners and investors. The United States does not want to confront China militarily because it faces more pressing security challenges such as the wars in Iraq and Afghanistan, terrorism, and nuclear proliferation. Also, Japan needs a stable relationship with China to resuscitate its economy fully and to disarm North Korea peacefully. These powerful politico-economic incentives for cooperative relations will reduce, at least for the near future, the potential danger that North Korean nuclear armament will spur an intense arms race as well as spiraling conflicts.

Conclusion

This chapter has advanced a two-part argument regarding North Korea's nuclear policy. First, North Korea embarked on building a nuclear arsenal to have a deterrent capability sufficient to counter Washington's hostile policy. Second, while the primary purpose of its nuclear program is deterrence, Pyongyang has effectively leveraged different facets of it to pursue key policy goals such as normalizing ties with Washington and securing economic assistance.

In an effort to maximize its gains, Pyongyang has become adept at further dividing its regional negotiating partners by calibrating its nuclear policy to widen differences and disagreements. For example, when progress is made with the denuclearization process, Pyongyang increases pressure on Washington to remove

North Korea from the U.S. State Department's State Sponsors of Terrorism List. Pyongyang seeks such a measure in order to access funds and loans from major international financial institutions like the World Bank. However, given the lack of progress on the issue of Japanese citizens abducted by North Korea from 1977 to 1983, Tokyo is adamant about keeping North Korea on the State Department's Terrorism List until the abductee issue has been satisfactorily resolved. By making the next step in denuclearization contingent on removal from the Terrorism List, Pyongyang puts Washington in the precarious position of having to choose between accelerating denuclearization work or standing united with its Japanese ally.

This second component of North Korea's nuclear policy—leveraging the nuclear program for concessions—raises important questions about the quandary that emerges for Pyongyang. If North Korea's primary purpose is deterrence, the facilitation of peaceful coexistence and full diplomatic normalization with Washington could constitute security developments sufficient for Pyongyang to dismantle its nuclear weapon capability. However, this process will take time, with setbacks and disputes along the way.

As Pyongyang becomes more adept at and dependent on applying its nuclear policy to divide adversaries and create opportunities for itself to secure important short-term tactical concessions, diplomatic relations and peaceful coexistence with Washington are effectively pushed further out of reach. It is unlikely that Pyongyang will seek to completely abandon the divisive tactic that has proven to be so fruitful. The other five countries in the Six-Party Talks will need to more closely coordinate policy and maintain a common position. This undertaking is daunting, as there is no precedent of a sustained and united group dealing with North Korea.

Notes

1. Starting in the fall of 2002, North Korea policy analysts at the John F. Kennedy School of Government's Belfer Center for Science and International Affairs launched a series of Track II meetings with senior DPRK diplomats and U.S. Senate officials to discuss the nuclear issue. The DPRK officials were from the DPRK Permanent Mission to the United Nations and the Foreign Ministry's Institute for Peace and Disarmament. The U.S. Senate officials were from the Senate Foreign Relations Committee and the Senate Armed Services Committee.

Significant points drawn from these Track II meetings will be augmented by key findings from off-the-record interviews and meetings conducted with Six-Party Talks member states' government policy advisers in Beijing, Washington, Seoul, and Tokyo. Sessions were held with government policy advisers from the following organizations: the U.S. Department of State; the Political Affairs Section of the U.S. Embassy in Beijing; the People's Republic of China (PRC) Foreign Ministry's North America Division; the Communist Party of China's International Department; the PRC Central Party School; the PRC Ministry of State Security; the Political Affairs Section of the Embassy of the

Republic of Korea (ROK) in Washington, D.C.; the ROK Foreign Ministry's North Korea Task Force; the Japanese Foreign Ministry's North America Desk; and the Political Affairs Section at the Russian Embassy in Beijing. In addition to these sources, our analysis draws on publicly available information, including North Korean official statements, news reports, and authoritative independent studies.

2. Interviews with PRC government policy advisers in Beijing, August 2–6, 2004.

3. Released under the U.S. Freedom of Information Act, the U.S. Defense Department's "History of the Custody and Deployment of Nuclear Weapons: July 1945 through September 1977," reveals the early and widespread deployment of U.S. nuclear weapons around the world. The initial idea was to preposition nuclear bomb components so that the U.S. military could rapidly assemble them in the event of an all-out conflict with the Soviet Union. Complete weapon systems were eventually deployed in a host of locations—South Korea, Japan, the Philippines, Morocco, France, and most of the NATO countries in the West (Norris, Arkin, and Burr 1999: 26–35).

4. Interviews with Political Affairs official in Russian Embassy in Beijing, August 5–6, 2004.

5. "North Korea is a regime arming [itself] with missiles and weapons of mass destruction, while starving its citizens . . . States like these, and their terrorist allies, constitute an axis of evil, arming to threaten the peace of the world . . . They could attack our allies or attempt to blackmail the United States" (Bush 2002a).

6. "A hedging strategy probably appeared thoroughly justified to Pyongyang. North Korea had concerns from the very beginning that relations with the United States might sour. Those concerns were reflected in the 1994 agreement, structured at Pyongyang's insistence so that it would not have to give up the plutonium-based nuclear program until near the end of a long process during which the Korean Peninsula Energy Development Organization would build two new nuclear reactors and provide yearly shipments of heavy-fuel oil" (Wit 2003: 6–10).

7. Interviews with South Korean government policy advisers in Seoul, June 22–23, 2006.

8. Interviews with Japanese government policy advisers in Tokyo, August 12–15, 2004.

9. Interviews with PRC government policy advisers in Beijing, August 2–6, 2004.

10. "Juche is the North Korean doctrine of 'self-reliance' that Kim Il Sung built into the dominant political credo of his totalitarian state" (Wit, Poneman, and Gallucci 2004: 25). "While the term juche is commonly translated from the Korean language as 'self-reliance,' it does not lend itself to any single, precise definition. Depending on the context in which it is used it can mean national identity, self-reliance, national pride or national assertiveness. The four guiding principles of juche are autonomy or identity in ideology, independence in politics, self-sufficiency in economy, and reliance on Korea's own forces in national defence" (Kwon 2005). Though there was a period of solid industrial output in the second half of the 1960s, juche's achievements were extolled in later years to an extent that bordered on myth.

11. North Korea first announced that it had developed nuclear weapons on February 10, 2005. According to defectors, including Hwang Chang Yop, former secretary of the Korean Workers' Party, North Korea may have had a (latent) nuclear capability since the

early 1990s. Similarly, U.S. intelligence estimates posit that Pyongyang, before 1992, may have produced "enough plutonium for one or possibly two nuclear weapons" (8–12 kilograms) from the 5 MW(e) reactor and the IRT-2000 research reactor IISS 2004: 47.

12. The following discussion is partly drawn from Lee 2007.

13. The two-bloc configuration in the Six-Party Talks can be clearly seen in Beijing, Seoul, Pyongyang, and Moscow's insistence on applying a version of the Ukrainian model's step-by-step approach to resolving the nuclear crisis, and Washington and Tokyo's strong preference for the Libyan model's completion of nuclear disarmament prior to the provision of security, diplomatic, and economic concessions.

In a similar pattern, Washington's concern about the increased likelihood of nuclear terrorism due to increased plutonium production in North Korea is strongly supported by Tokyo. Washington specifically asserts that with the growing North Korean stockpile of weapon-grade plutonium, there is a greater chance of this material getting into the hands of terrorists who, in turn, would use it in a dirty bomb attack in the United States. While sympathetic to this concern, Beijing, Seoul, and Moscow—citing the lack of evidence that North Korea has engaged in nuclear terrorism or smuggling—view a country like Pakistan as a more likely source of fissile material for a terrorist attack due to chronic command and control issues and political instability there.

To allay U.S. concerns about North Korea's involvement in nuclear terrorism, President Hu Jintao sent a personal letter to Kim Jong Il early in the Six-Party Talks process via the Chinese Communist Party-Korean Workers' Party channel, warning about the dire consequences of engaging in the sale of nuclear material. Interviews with PRC, ROK, DPRK, U.S., Russian, and Japanese government policy advisers, August 2–15, 2004, and June 22–23, 2006.

14. The nuclear agreement signed in Beijing on February 13, 2007, constitutes an important, though very early, step toward realizing North Korea's nuclear disarmament. North Korea's actual signing of the agreement was more likely the result of the Bush administration's intent to realize a foreign policy achievement by offering Pyongyang enticements than it was the sole outcome of intense pressure applied through the Treasury Department's financial regulatory actions.

15. Interviews with PRC government policy advisers in Beijing, August 2–6, 2004.

16. Interviews with U.S. government officials in Washington, D.C., February 23, 2007.

References

ABC News/*Washington Post* Poll. 2006. December 7–11.

Albright, David, and Paul Brannan. 2006. *The North Korean Plutonium Stock Mid-2006.* Washington, D.C.: Institute for Science and International Security.

An, Tai Sung. 1992. "The Rise and Decline of North Korea's Nuclear Weapons Programme." *Korea and World Affairs* (Winter).

Associated Press. 2006. "North Korea Nuke Test Fans Fears of East Asian Nuclear Arms Race," October 8.

———. 2007a. "U.S. Sustains 3,000th Fatality in Iraq," January 1.

———. 2007b. "Japanese Missiles," March 30.

Balz, Dan, and Richard Morin. 2005. "Two Years after Invasion, Poll Data Mixed." *Washington Post,* March 16.

Berger, Thomas U. 1993. "From Sword to Chrysanthemum: Japan's Culture of Anti-Militarism." *International Security* 17 (4): 119–150.

Blanchard, Ben. 2006. "China Defends Military Rise, Says Faces Threats." *Reuters,* December 29.

Bush, George W. 2002a. State of the Union Address. Washington, D.C., January 29.

———. 2002b. Graduation Exercise Address. West Point, N.Y.: United States Military Academy, June 1.

Center for Nonproliferation Studies (CNS). 2006. "Special Report on North Korean Ballistic Missile Capabilities." Monterey, Calif.: Monterey Institute of International Studies.

Cha, Victor D., and David C. Kang. 2003. *Nuclear North Korea: A Debate on Engagement Strategies.* New York: Columbia University Press.

China's National Defense in 2006. 2006. Beijing: Information Office of the State Council.

Chosun Ilbo. 2007. Interview with Japanese Defense Minister Fumio Kyuma. January 23.

Cody, Edward. 2006. "China Defends Military Program." *Washington Post,* December 29.

Cumings, Bruce. 1992. "Spring Thaw for Korea's Cold War?" *Bulletin of the Atomic Scientists* 48 (3): 14–23.

Federation of American Scientists (FAS). 2007. "WMD around the World: Missiles." Available at www.fas.org/nuke/guide/dprk/missile/index.html [January 9, 2007].

Friedberg, Aaron L. 2005. "The Future of US-China Relations: Is Conflict Inevitable?" *International Security* 30 (2): 7–45.

Gallup Poll. 2005. February 25–27. The poll sought the American public's overall opinions on a possible use of force against Iran, Syria, and North Korea, as well as on other political issues including social security. Available at www.usatoday.com/news/polls/tables/live/2005-02-28-poll.htm.

Hankook Ilbo. 2006. "Bukhaek Jeonmang" (Outlook on North Korean nuclear development), December 18.

Hayes, Peter. 1991. *Pacific Powderkeg: American Nuclear Dilemmas in Korea.* Lexington: Lexington Books.

Hecker, Siegfried S. 2006. *Report on North Korean Nuclear Program.* Stanford, Calif.: Center for International Security and Cooperation.

Hughes, Christopher W. 2007. "North Korea's Nuclear Weapons: Implications for the Nuclear Ambitions of Japan, South Korea, and Taiwan." *Asia Policy* 3: 75–104.

International Institute for Strategic Studies (IISS). 2004. *North Korea's Weapons Programmes.* London: IISS.

Jervis, Robert. 1989. *The Meaning of the Nuclear Revolution: Statecraft and the Prospect of Armageddon.* Ithaca, N.Y.: Cornell University Press.

Jiang Zemin. 2002. Speech at Chinese Communist Party's 16th National Congress, Beijing, November 8–14.

Karl, Jonathan. 2007. "North Korea Prepping Nuclear Weapons Test." ABC News, January 4.

Kim, Jungsup. 2006. "The Security Dilemma: Nuclear and Missile Crisis on the Korean Peninsula." *Korean Journal of Defense Analysis* 18 (3): 89–106.

Kirk, Don. 2003. "North Korea Touts Nuclear Capability Before U.S. Talks." *International Herald Tribune,* April 19.

Korean Central News Agency (KCNA). 2006a. "DPRK Foreign Ministry Clarifies Stand on New Measure to Bolster War Deterrent," October 3.

———. 2006b. "U.S. and S. Korean Bellicose Forces' Moves for Nuclear War against DPRK Blasted," October 27. Available at http://www.kcna.co.jp/item/2006/200610/news10/28.htm.

Kwon, Soyoung. 2005. "Survival of the North Korean Regime and Changing Legitimation Modes." Paper presented at Stanford-Cornell University Joint Workshop on North Korea, Palo Alto, California, April 11.

Lee, Dong Sun, 2006. "US Preventive War against North Korea," *Asian Security* 2 (1): 1–23.

———. 2007. "A Nuclear North Korea and the Stability of East Asia: A Tsunami on the Horizon?" *Australian Journal of International Affairs* 61 (4): 436–54.

———. 2008. *Power Shifts, Strategy, and War: Declining States and International Conflict.* London: Routledge, 2008.

Levy, Jack S., and Joseph R. Gochal. 2001. "Democracy and Preventive War: Israel and the 1956 Sinai Campaign." *Security Studies* 11 (2): 1–49.

Mazarr, Michael J. 1997. *North Korea and the Bomb: A Case Study in Nonproliferation.* Basingstoke, U.K.: Macmillan.

National Statistical Office. 2005. "Gross Regional Domestic Product." Available at kosis.nso.go.kr/cgi-bin/sws_999.cgi [June 6, 2007].

———. 2007. "Population Density." Available at kosis.nso.go.kr/Magazine/NEW/PR/pr01.pdf [August 17, 2007].

"New U.S. Land Mine Policy." 1996. Statement by President Bill Clinton, Washington, D.C., May 16. Available at www.defenselink.mil/Speeches/Speech.aspx?SpeechID=982.

Niksch, Larry A. 2006. *North Korea's Nuclear Weapons Program.* Washington, D.C.: Congressional Research Service.

Norris, Robert S., William M. Arkin, and William Burr. 1999. "Where They Were." *Bulletin of the Atomic Scientists* 55 (6): 26–35.

Oberdorfer, Don. 1997. *The Two Koreas: A Contemporary History.* New York: Basic Books.

———. 2001. *The Two Koreas: A Contemporary History.* Rev. ed. New York: Basic Books.

Park, John S. 2005. "Inside Multilateralism: The Six-Party Talks." *Washington Quarterly* 28 (4): 75–91.

———. 2006. "How China Can Bring Sunshine to Korea." *Far Eastern Economic Review* 169 (5): 29–31.

Perry, William J. 1999. *Review of United States Policy toward North Korea: Findings and Recommendations.* Washington, D.C.: U.S. Department of State. Available at http://www.state.gov/www/regions/eap/991012_northkorea_rpt.html.

Pinkston, Daniel A., and Kazutaka Sakurai. 2006. "Japan Debates Preparing for Future Preemptive Strikes against North Korea." *The Korean Journal of Defense Analysis* 18 (4): 95–121.

Reiter, Dan. 1995. "Exploding the Powder Keg Myth: Preemptive Wars Almost Never Happen." *International Security* 20 (2): 5–34.

Rodong Sinmun (North Korea). 2007. New Year's Statement, January 1.

Roh Moo-hyun. 2006a. Remarks to the National Assembly. Seoul, November 6.

———. 2006b. Remarks on November 11, released by the ROK office of the President.

———. 2006c. Press Briefing on October 9.

Sanger David E. 2003a. "President Makes Case That North Korea Is No Iraq." *New York Times,* January 1.

———. 2003b. "Bush Takes No-Budge Stand in Talks with North Korea." *New York Times,* April 17.

Sanger, David E., and William J. Broad. 2007. "U.S. Had Doubts on North Korean Uranium Drive." *New York Times,* February 28.

Schelling, Thomas C. 1966. *Arms and Influence.* New Haven, Conn.: Yale University Press.

Schweller, Randall L. 1992. "Domestic Structure and Preventive War: Are Democracies More Pacific?" *World Politics* 44 (2): 235–69.

Sessler, Andrew M., et al. 2000. *Countermeasures: A Technical Evaluation of the Operational Effectiveness of the Planned U.S. National Missile Defense System.* Cambridge, Mass.: Union of Concerned Scientists.

Squassoni, Sharon. 2006. *North Korea's Nuclear Weapons: Latest Developments.* Washington, D.C.: Congressional Research Service.

Song, Young Sun. 1991. "The Korean Nuclear Issue." *Korea and World Affairs* 15 (3): 471–93.

Tokyo Metropolitan Government. 2007a. "Tokyo's Geography, History, and Population." Available at www.metro.tokyo.jp/ENGLISH/PROFILE/overview03.htm [Aug. 17, 2007].

———. 2007b. "Statistics." Available at www.metro.tokyo.jp/ENGLISH/PROFILE/appendix2.htm [June 6, 2007].

U.S. Senate. 2003. "Testimony of Donald P. Gregg, Former U.S. Ambassador to South Korea." Hearing before the Senate Committee on Foreign Relations, February 4. Washington, D.C.: U.S. Government Printing Office.

Weathersby, Kathryn. 1993. "The Soviet Role in the Early Phase of the Korean War: New Documentary Evidence." *Journal of American-East Asian Relations* 2 (4): 425–58.

———. 1995–1996. "New Russian Documents on the Korean War." *Cold War International History Project Bulletin* 6–7: 30–84.

———. 1998. "Stalin, Mao and the End of the Korean War." In *Brothers in Arms: The Rise and Fall of the Sino-Soviet Alliance, 1945–1963,* ed. Odd Arne Westad. Stanford, Calif.: Stanford University Press.

Wit, Joel S. 2003. "A Strategy for Defusing the North Korean Nuclear Crisis." *Arms Control Today* (January/February): 6–10.

Wit, Joel S., Daniel B. Poneman, and Robert L. Gallucci. 2004. *Going Critical: The First North Korean Nuclear Crisis.* Washington, D.C.: Brookings Institution.

Yamaguchi, Mari. 2006. "Japan Considers Strike against N. Korea." Associated Press, July 10.

Yomiuri Shimbun. "Opinion Poll: Nuclear Weapons and North Korea," November 21, 2006.

Yonhap News. 2006a. "China criticizes Japan over Talk of Pre-emptive Strike on N. Korea." July 13.

———. 2006b. Interview with former president Kim Dae-jung, December 7.

10

Iran
The Nuclear Quandary

DEVIN T. HAGERTY

Barring a dramatic development such as a major preventive attack against Tehran's nuclear installations, Iran will probably become the world's tenth nuclear weapon state within the next decade. Owing in part to the opacity of the Iranian nuclear program, foreign assessments vary widely as to how soon Tehran is likely to achieve a fully operational nuclear weapon capability. Israeli military intelligence analysts estimate that Iran could deploy deliverable nuclear weapons as early as 2009 (Harel 2007), while some U.S. proliferation experts believe that Tehran will not cross that threshold until as late as 2015 (Associated Press 2007). The majority of forecasts put the relevant date sometime between 2009 and 2015, their variance depending mainly on the effectiveness of external sanctions against Iran, as well as Tehran's own proficiency at overcoming the remaining and not inconsiderable technical hurdles.[1]

Much of the literature on the Iranian nuclear program takes the form of policy-oriented discussion about how to prevent or inhibit its fruition. In turn, a substantial proportion of these prescriptive works are distinctly alarmist in tone or, at a minimum, normatively biased against Tehran's acquisition of nuclear weapons. In the United States especially, a certain breathless quality tends to pervade the writing on this subject, as evidenced by the common characterization of the issue as the "Iranian nuclear crisis." Although there is certainly some scope for this type of exigent analysis, its very urgency and its emphasis on the day-to-day tactical maneuvering in Beijing, Brussels, Moscow, New York, Tehran, Tokyo, Vienna, Washington, and other significant nodes of proliferation diplomacy generally lend it an all-too-brief shelf life. As a consequence, one finds disconcertingly little *strategic* analysis of this critical challenge, at least in the public domain.[2]

My aim in this chapter is to help fill this gap by analyzing the central elements of the Iranian nuclear quandary. In the first section—on Iran's Nuclear Policy—I briefly recount the evolution of Tehran's nuclear policy to date to provide a historical context for the subsequent analysis. The second section, on Iran's Grand Stategy, and the third, titled Nuclear Iran: Strategy and Doctrine, focus on the strategic dimensions of Iran's nuclear program. After encapsulating Iranian grand strategy, I consider the motives underlying Tehran's acquisition of nuclear weapon capabilities, the role those capabilities can be expected to play in the pursuit of Iran's objectives in world affairs, and the plausible operational aspects of Iran's nuclear arms, including the forces Tehran is likely to deploy and the doctrine that might eventually govern the use of those forces. The fourth section—Nuclear Iran: Implications for Regional and International Security—evaluates the potential consequences of a nuclear-armed Iran for the critical region stretching from the eastern shore of the Mediterranean to the Arabian Sea.

I make three central arguments: (1) Iran's quest for a nuclear weapon capability is intended primarily to ensure the country's security against attack, enhance the theocratic regime's legitimacy in the eyes of the Iranian people, and support Tehran's ambitions for great-power status in the Persian Gulf region and beyond; (2) Contrary to fears that Iranian leaders might go on the offense, launching nuclear missiles at Israel or U.S. forces in the Gulf region, Tehran will likely be deterred by Israel and the United States from doing so. Iran is likelier to pursue interlinked nuclear strategies of deterrence and what I term "asymmetric compellence," whereby Tehran's nuclear weapons deter attacks against its territory while simultaneously providing an umbrella of safety under which it can pursue unconventional compellent means—such as support for Hezbollah and Hamas operations against Israel, armed Shia militancy in nearby states, and perhaps terrorist attacks on Israeli and U.S. targets—to achieve its regional ends; (3) Although it would certainly lead countries such as Egypt, Saudi Arabia, and Turkey to consider responding in kind, Iran's acquisition of nuclear weapon capabilities is unlikely to spark a cascade of regional nuclear proliferation. U.S. military assistance and security guarantees are likely to appeal more to these states than developing weapons that would make them a target of Iranian—and possibly Israeli—nuclear weapons.

The chapter is analytically framed by two distinct perspectives and a number of important assumptions. In the heart of the chapter, the second and third sections, the lens through which I examine the Iranian nuclear program is "inside-out," rather than "outside-in"; to put it differently, unlike the bulk of the extant literature, which is written from the vantage point of external actors seeking to influence Iran's nuclear calculations, the perspective adopted here is the view from Tehran. I seek to explain how Iranian decision makers define their vital interests, their national security goals, and their rightful place in the world, as well as the roles they envisage for nuclear weapon capabilities in pursuing their objectives. In the first and fourth sections, my standpoint is that of a disinterested strategic analyst; this is not a policy piece in the service of any particular country's interests.

Throughout the chapter, I assume that Iran will ultimately succeed in mastering the technology needed to assemble and use nuclear weapons, while leaving open the question of whether Tehran will overtly deploy a nuclear arsenal or instead content itself with nonweaponized nuclear capabilities. The nuclear era's history suggests to me that fearful, ambitious states that are determined to acquire nuclear weapon capabilities will eventually get them, but in individual cases there is not necessarily a predetermined endpoint of deployed, operational weapon systems. I also assume for analytical purposes that Iran is not concealing from interested intelligence agencies and International Atomic Energy Agency (IAEA) inspectors additional installations that can produce plutonium or highly enriched uranium (HEU). Given Iran's track record, however, this may be a faulty assumption, and the future discovery of now-secret facilities for making fissile material would dictate reconsideration of my conclusions. More broadly, it should be noted at the outset that the general dearth of reliable information on Iran's nuclear capabilities and intentions inevitably renders strategic analysis of its nuclear program more contingent than that of, say, China or India. Analytical modesty is the order of the day.

Iran's Nuclear Policy

The Iranian nuclear program began in 1957, when Washington and Tehran concluded a civil nuclear cooperation agreement as part of the U.S. "Atoms for Peace" program.[3] Iran and the United States planned to collaborate on civilian nuclear energy development, with Washington providing technical assistance and a small amount of enriched uranium. By 1967, U.S. aid had yielded Iran a small research reactor at Tehran University's new nuclear research center, which remains operational today. Iran signed the Treaty on the Non-Proliferation of Nuclear Weapons (NPT) in 1968 and ratified it in 1970. Four years later, Shah Mohammad Reza Pahlavi, the Nixon and Ford administrations' chief ally in the Persian Gulf region, unveiled plans for an extremely ambitious nuclear energy program. Guided by a new Atomic Energy Organization of Iran, Western firms would manufacture twenty-three nuclear power reactors over roughly twenty years.[4] The Shah also evinced an interest in nuclear weapons and set up a clandestine research group to explore their design and manufacture. As a result, when Ayatollah Ruhollah Khomeini's revolution toppled the Shah in 1979, the new Islamic Republic of Iran inherited "extensive nuclear hardware, materials, and technology." Although Khomeini ordered a halt to the nuclear program, which for the revolutionists symbolized Iran's toadying subjection to the West, limited nuclear training and experimentation continued at the Tehran Nuclear Research Center (Spector 1988: 411 [note 4], 219–20).

The Iran-Iraq war of 1980–88 rekindled Tehran's interest in nuclear weapons. During the fighting, Baghdad—supplied with arms and invaluable intelligence by the United States (Weiner 2007: 425) and the Sunni Arab monarchies—deployed chemical weapons against Iranian troops, rained Scud short-range ballistic missiles on populous Iranian cities, and repeatedly bombed the unfinished Bushehr nuclear installations (Jones and McDonough 1998: 255; McNaugher 1990; Spector 1988: 222, 412 [note 11]; Spector and McDonough 1995: 123). With Saddam Hussein resorting to every arrow in his quiver, the isolated theocracy resolved to resurrect the Bushehr project and, with China's help, began construction of a new nuclear research center at Isfahan.[5] More significantly, revolutionary Iran apparently embarked on its own secret nuclear weapon program in 1985 (Cirincione, Wolfsthal, and Rajkumar 2005: 298; Jones and McDonough 1998: 169). By this time, Tehran had also acquired Scud missiles and had begun to use them against Iraq. In 1987–88, North Korea sold Iran roughly 100 Scuds, which Tehran then began to produce indigenously (McNaugher 1990: 10 [note 19]). Right after the war, in which Iran suffered over one million casualties and at least 300,000 war deaths (GlobalSecurity.org 2007b), future president Akbar Hashemi-Rafsanjani rallied the elite Iranian Revolutionary Guards Corps (IRGC):

> With regard to chemical, bacteriological, and radiological weapons training, it was made very clear during the war that these weapons are very decisive. It was also made clear that the moral teachings of the world are not very effective when war reaches a serious stage and the world does not respect its own resolutions and closes its eyes to the violations and all the aggressions which are committed in the battle field.
>
> We should fully equip ourselves both in the offensive and defensive use of chemical, bacteriological, and radiological weapons. From now on you should make use of the opportunity and perform this task. (Jones and McDonough 1998: 120)

Iran's renewed pursuit of nuclear weapons was assisted by the A. Q. Khan nuclear supply network.[6] In 1986–87, the head of Islamabad's uranium enrichment program had brokered a secret deal between Pakistan and Iran, offering Tehran a "centrifuge enrichment 'starter kit.'"[7] Tehran's efforts to enrich uranium were "greatly accelerated in the 1990s after Iran gained access to centrifuge technology and material" from the Khan network.[8] This was only a part—albeit a crucial one—of Tehran's expansive global procurement effort, in which "Iran's critical nuclear materials, equipment, and technology have been acquired from foreign suppliers. The same is true for its missile capabilities" (Cirincione, Wolfsthal, and Rajkumar 2005: 299). Also in the 1990s, China continued as a major supplier of nuclear technology to Iran, and Russia began work on the damaged Bushehr plant (Spector and McDonough 1995: 119–20). Furthermore, Chinese, North Korean, and Russian missile technology transfers enabled Tehran to develop what the U.S. intelligence community today estimates to be the largest inventory of ballistic missiles in the Middle East.[9] Most worrisome for U.S. and Israeli defense officials has been the Iranian Shahab-III, a derivative of the North Korean Nodong medium-range ballistic missile (MRBM). First tested in 1998, the Shahab-III has a range of 1,300 kilometers and a payload of 760–1,158 kilograms, which puts Israel well within range of a potentially nuclear-capable Iranian missile.[10]

Secret Efforts Uncovered

In August 2002, a France-based Iranian dissident group accused Tehran of secretly building a uranium enrichment plant at Natanz and a heavy-water production facility at Arak, neither of which were previously known to the IAEA. Presented with incontrovertible evidence, Iran confirmed the allegation. Since then, nonproliferation experts have been particularly concerned with the Natanz complex, which houses a pilot fuel enrichment plant (PFEP) and a larger underground fuel enrichment plant (FEP). IAEA inspectors in spring 2003 found HEU particles in environmental samples taken from the Natanz PFEP *prior* to the introduction of uranium at the plant. "Iranian officials attributed the sample results to the contamination of imported centrifuge components, which were believed to have come from Pakistan. Iran had earlier denied importing any centrifuge components, but when confronted with the evidence changed its story" (Cirincione, Wolfsthal, and Rajkumar 2005: 300). Between 2003 and mid-2006, Tehran fitfully advanced its uranium-enrichment program, while sluggishly negotiating with Britain, France, and Germany (EU-3) and fending off the IAEA and the U.N. Security Council (Cirincione, Wolfsthal, and Rajkumar 2005: 300; Squassoni 2007: 3, 5). China, Russia, and the United States finally joined the EU-3 diplomatic effort in June 2006, with this "P5+1" team offering—if Iran would suspend uranium enrichment—to affirm Iran's right to peaceful nuclear energy, lend it assistance in building proliferation-safe light-water reactors, guarantee its supply of nuclear fuel, cease U.N. Security Council consideration of its prior NPT noncompliance, and allow it to join the World Trade Organization (Squassoni 2007: 6). Iran refused the offer, which remains on the table today. Faced with continued intransigence, the U.N. Security Council adopted modest sanctions against Iran in December 2006 and March 2007.

Iran plans ultimately to organize its Natanz centrifuges into "eighteen 164-machine cascades that operate together under a common control system to produce" low-enriched uranium (LEU). Eighteen such cascades will constitute a "module." The FEP "can hold about 17-18 modules, for a total of about 50,000 to 53,000 centrifuges."[11] In May 2007, IAEA inspectors "found that Iranian engineers were . . . using roughly 1,300 centrifuges and . . . producing fuel suitable for nuclear reactors" and "concluded that Iran appears to have solved most of its technological problems and is now beginning to enrich uranium on a far larger scale than before," with all the centrifuges "running smoothly."[12] Subsequently, a November IAEA report confirmed Tehran's claims that it was operating some 3,000 centrifuges at Natanz, albeit "well below their capacity." The report also said that because of restrictions placed on its inspectors, the IAEA's "knowledge about Iran's current nuclear program is diminishing" (Sciolino and Broad 2007; Wright 2007b)

As of fall 2007, Iran continues to press ahead with its uranium enrichment efforts at Natanz. But Iranian scientists still have to achieve their immediate goal, which is the installation and sustained operation of a "complete module, consisting of 18 cascades, or some 2,952 centrifuges that would operate in parallel, each producing" LEU (Albright, Shire, and Brannan 2007: 1–2). According to a credible assessment, once it has a "fully operational" module, "Iran would need approximately 6–12 months to produce enough highly enriched uranium for its first nuclear weapon;" alternatively, Tehran could hedge by continuing to produce LEU for potential later use in a "breakout" strategy (U.S. House 2007: 5). Iran apparently has no intention of buckling under U.S. or multilateral pressure to halt or temporarily suspend its program. President Mahmoud Ahmadinejad's statement on the eve of mid-July talks with IAEA officials in Tehran was representative of others routinely emanating from Iran's senior leadership: "The trend of installing centrifuges could be slowed down or gain momentum . . . but no-one should expect that we will give up our rights, and we will not halt the trend" (*Agence France-Presse* 2007).

Iran's Grand Strategy

Iran's grand strategy in the first decade of the twenty-first century represents a complex mixture of ambition and fear. Iran yearns to become a great power, at a minimum the strongest state in its immediate Persian Gulf region, and at a maximum a player of emerging global significance like China and India. This is an objective whose lineage runs from the Shah and his grandiose modernization plans of the 1960s and 1970s, through the revolutionary furor of the Khomeini period (1979–89), the postrevolutionary moderation of the Rafsanjani presidency (1989–97), and the abortive reformist interregnum of the Khatami years (1997–2005), right down to the present struggle for the soul of the Iranian polity. Although Tehran's grand-strategic means have shifted wildly over the past four decades—from trying to bandwagon with the United States under the Shah, to the Khomeinist revolt against the global powers-that-be, to a tentative postrevolutionary détente with the West, to the more confrontationist posturing of the Ahmadinejad era (2005–present)—the fundamental end has endured. In the eyes of Tehran's strategic elites, Iran today is the direct descendant of magnificent Islamic and pre-Islamic empires, a custodian of enormous energy wealth, and the overseer of the Strait of Hormuz, the world's most valuable strategic choke point.[13] They believe that Iran is a natural great power whose rightful status has been unjustly denied by imperialist and neocolonialist predators, often in league with Iran's own corrupt autocrats.[14]

Perceived Threats

Iran's ambition coexists uneasily with fear that is just as compelling for its leaders. Tehran has been remarkably isolated since 1979. Its only true allies in international affairs have been Syria and several nonstate actors, among them the terrorist groups Hezbollah and Hamas. Revolutionary Iran has consistently identified the United States and Israel as the country's—and the revolution's—main enemies.[15] According to the official line, America hijacked Iranian democracy in 1953 by ousting the popular prime minister, Muhammad Mossadeq, and restoring the despotic young Shah to his throne.[16] For the next twenty-five years, say the theocrats, the United States and Israel conspired with the Shah in suppressing the Iranian people and their Islamic faith, all in the guise of modernization—or, more accurately, westernization. In 1979, after the Shah was deposed and allowed into the United States for medical treatment, Khomeini's supporters sacked the U.S. Embassy in Tehran, igniting the 1979–81 hostage crisis.[17] When Saddam Hussein invaded Iran in 1980, in an effort to crush the revolution Tehran was trying to spread around the Middle East, Washington—from the standpoint of Iranian strategic elites—exacted its revenge against Iran by arming the Iraqi forces and providing Baghdad with intelligence on Iranian troop movements and battle plans. The U.S. and Iranian navies skirmished in 1987–88. In July 1988 the USS *Vincennes,* an Aegis cruiser, mistakenly shot down an Iranian passenger aircraft over the Persian Gulf.

Since the end of the Iran-Iraq war in 1988, Tehran has continued to portray the United States and Israel as the most dangerous threats to Iran and its ongoing revolution. Israel is regularly painted in harsh anti-Semitic and anti-Zionist terms as a country that cynically leveraged European and American guilt over the Holocaust to steal Muslim territory, brutalize the Palestinian people out of their homeland, and deny them their inherent right to statehood. Although Iran and Israel have never engaged directly in armed interstate conflict, Israel is the Middle East's only nuclear weapon state and is therefore considered an existential threat to Iran. Moreover, because postrevolutionary Iran has been unable to compete with U.S.-backed Israel in nuclear or conventional military terms, it has instead resorted to unconventional operations, arming and training Israel's most bitter enemies, foremost among them Hamas, Hezbollah, and the Palestinian Islamic Jihad. Iran's leaders also rail against Israel for its alleged role as Washington's regional deputy. While some observers would disagree, Christopher de Bellaigue goes as far as to argue that "Iran's enmity for Israel is based mainly on its view that Israel is an American proxy. It is inconceivable, Iranian officials believe, that Israel would commit its atrocities against the Palestinians without American approval" (2007: 113).

During various periods since 1988, Iran has received substantial military and nuclear assistance from China, Russia, and the A. Q. Khan network, but these have been fair-weather friends seeking commercial advantage, rather than allies who are willing and able to protect Tehran from U.S. and Israeli hostility. In the immediate aftermath of the Cold War, Washington began to identify Iran as one of a handful of "rogue states," along with Iraq, Libya, North Korea, and Syria. Rogue states were headed by dictators who burnished weapons of mass destruction, menaced their neighbors, supported terrorists networks, denied the human rights of their citizens, and generally refused to comply with the dictates of international regimes. For Washington and its allies, the best way to deal with rogue regimes was to seal them off from international society or, in cases of outright adventurism such as Iraq's 1990 invasion of Kuwait, to firmly repulse their aggression by force of arms.

The Great Satan Versus the Axis of Evil

The election of George W. Bush as U.S. president in 2000 only intensified Iranian fears. Unlike the Clinton administration, which had largely contented itself with a policy of "dual containment" (of Iraq and Iran) in the Persian Gulf region, senior Bush national security aides and their allies outside of government openly discussed the prospects for "regime change"—toppling or helping to topple authoritarian governments and replacing them with democracies more in step with U.S. interests. To the clerical leadership in Tehran, regime change would amount to nothing less than a reversal of the 1979 revolution. However, the 9/11 Al-Qaeda terrorist attacks in New York and Washington, D.C., and the subsequent U.S. invasion of Afghanistan in 2001, had the ironic effect of enabling official diplomatic cooperation between the United States and Iran. The two countries worked closely together at the December 2001 conference in Bonn, which produced agreement among the anti-Taliban political factions on a blueprint for Afghanistan's political future. According to the Bush administration's first envoy for Afghanistan after the 9/11 attacks, "the Iranian delegate . . . first insisted that the agreement include a commitment to hold democratic elections in Afghanistan. This same Iranian persuaded the Northern Alliance to make the essential concession that allowed the meeting to conclude successfully" (Dobbins 2007).

If policy makers in Tehran thought the Bonn process would mark the beginnings of a rapprochement with Washington, they soon discovered otherwise. One month later, in his January 2002 State of the Union address, after briefly discussing the threats posed by North Korea, Iran, and Iraq, President Bush argued that "states like these, and their terrorist allies, constitute an axis of evil, arming to threaten the peace of the world. By seeking weapons of mass destruction, these regimes pose a grave and growing danger. They could provide these arms to terrorists, giving them the means to match their hatred. They could attack our allies or attempt to blackmail the United States. In any of these cases, the price of indifference would be catastrophic" (White House 2002). Little more than a year later, U.S.-led forces invaded Iraq and ousted Saddam Hussein's dictatorship. Within nineteen months, the United States had forcibly unseated governments in two countries bordering Iran, precedents that, odious as those regimes were even to Tehran, caused severe trepidation in Iranian national security circles. The clerical leadership's concerns have eased to some extent, owing to the increasing difficulties experienced by U.S. and coalition forces in both Iraq and Afghanistan, but open U.S. discussion of policies aimed at crippling the Iranian theocracy have continued to stoke anxiety. By a wide margin, Tehran's top security priority today is to ensure its survival and perpetuate the revolution, in the face of what it perceives to be unremitting U.S. hostility.

Sunni Neighbors

Of second-order, but still substantial, concern for Iran's national security elites are several Sunni-majority neighbors: the six Gulf Cooperation Council (GCC) states,[18] led by Saudi Arabia, and Pakistan. While the centuries-old Shia-Sunni schism[19] provides ample historical backdrop for Tehran's checkered relations with the GCC, revolutionary Iran's more immediate grievances revolve around the GCC countries' support for Iraq in the 1980–88 war—which was itself largely a response to the Khomeini government's attempt to export its brand of Islamic revolution around the region. Although Tehran's backing of Shia dissidents in the GCC states tapered off during the Khatami presidency, the ever-present possibility of a reversal in policy casts a dark shadow over Iran-GCC relations, especially with several of the GCC states now embarked upon tentative, delicate efforts at political liberalization. Iran's nuclear progress, the 2003 U.S. removal of Saddam Hussein's regime—the primary "balancer" against Tehran in the Persian Gulf region—and the 2005 election of President Ahmadinejad have exacerbated the Gulf monarchs' nervousness regarding Iran's regional capabilities and intentions. These states have sought reassurance by solidifying their defense relationships with one another and, especially, with the United States.[20] Washington has designated Bahrain and Kuwait as "major non-NATO allies," the U.S. Navy's Fifth Fleet is based in Manama, and Qatar hosts the U.S. Central Command's (CENTCOM's) forward headquarters and a cutting-edge Combined Air Operations Center at the expansive Al Udeid Air Base.[21]

Although Iran's denunciations of the government in Riyadh for allowing "infidels" to pollute Islam's holy soil have been muted by the U.S. retrenchment from Saudi Arabia, Washington's muscular strategic presence in the other Gulf states raises considerable angst in Tehran. Aggressive sales of sophisticated U.S. weapon systems have served three purposes: cementing U.S.-GCC political ties, enhancing the interoperability of GCC military forces with each other and with CENTCOM, and sending a strong signal to Iran that Washington is firmly committed to ensuring the security of its regional allies. In July 2007, Washington disclosed a ramping up of its military assistance to the GCC governments. The details are yet to be negotiated, but sales of advanced weaponry totaling US$20 billion will reportedly include Joint Direct Attack Munitions (satellite-guided bombs), air-to-air missiles, fighter-aircraft upgrades, air and missile defense technology, and warships.[22] All in all, it would be difficult to overstate Iran's conventional military inferiority in comparison with its rivals in the immediate Persian Gulf region.

Pakistan is a Sunni-dominated country with which Iran historically has had a mixed relationship. Tehran's links with Islamabad were strong during the 1970s, as Zulfikar Ali Bhutto's government turned westward for succor after the Bangladesh debacle of 1971. Iran was one of several newly rich Middle Eastern petro-states with which Bhutto courted ties based on Islamic fraternity, military-to-military cooperation, and Pakistani labor flows, which pumped desperately needed cash remittances into Pakistan's staggering economy. Bhutto and the Shah also shared an interest in quelling Baluchi separatism; in 1977, the Pakistan Army used Iranian helicopter gunships and pilots to smash a four-year insurgency that both Tehran and Islamabad feared would develop into a full-blown movement for an independent Baluchistan.[23] However, Iran-Pakistan relations cooled after the Shia Bhutto was overthrown and hanged by Sunni General Mohammad Zia-ul-Haq, who ruled Pakistan from 1977 to 1988. The Shah distrusted Zia for his attempts to impose *Shariah* law—with enthusiastic Saudi ideological and financial backing. Iranian suspicions carried over into the post-1979 revolutionary period. During the Soviet occupation of Afghanistan from 1979 to 1989, Tehran and Islamabad both supported the Afghan resistance, but their largesse went to competing *mujahideen* factions, with Iran's going largely to Shia Hazaras and other non-Pashtuns, and Pakistan's to various Sunni Pashtun groups.

These divisions continued into the post-Soviet era, with the Pakistan Army's Inter-Services Intelligence branch essentially founding and sustaining the Wahhabist, Pashtun Taliban, and Iran aiding the opposition Northern Alliance, composed mainly of Tajiks, Uzbeks, and other non-Pashtuns. Tehran's low-grade rivalry with Islamabad intensified in 1998, when Pakistan conducted five nuclear explosive tests in Baluchistan, and Iran contemplated war against the Taliban after eleven Iranian diplomats were slain in Mazar-e-Sharif. In 2001, after 9/11,

Washington and Islamabad renewed their on-again off-again security entente, with the United States transferring billions of dollars in military assistance to Pakistan, its newly designated "non-NATO ally."

While Iran and Pakistan are not outright adversaries, their relations typically exhibit elements of conflict and cooperation. On the whole, however, they have more common than competing interests. This was demonstrated by the A. Q. Khan network's nuclear transfers to Tehran during the late 1980s and 1990s, which were supported by senior officials within Pakistan's national security apparatus (Corera 2006: 59–81). Indeed, those transfers continued even as Iran-Pakistan relations deteriorated during the Taliban's ascent to power in the 1990s. Today, Tehran and Islamabad have a joint stake in dousing separatist sentiment in Baluchistan and moving toward the successful completion of a natural gas pipeline running from Iran through Pakistan to India, a project that would yield substantial financial benefits for both Iran and Pakistan. More broadly, the two countries are hopeful that their observer status in the increasingly influential Shanghai Cooperation Organization will one day convert to full membership, creating a potential new bond between Tehran and Islamabad in what is shaping up to be a "unified energy infrastructure" connecting oil and gas producers and consumers in the Eurasian heartland (*Wall Street Journal Online* 2007). While it is relatively easy to imagine future wars between Iran and Israel, Iran and the United States, or Pakistan and India, it is difficult to envisage war between Iran and Pakistan. As Tehran and Islamabad both face long-standing enemies that are better armed in both nuclear and conventional terms, their nuclear planning is much more likely to focus on their traditional rivals than on one another. In sum, a nuclear-armed Iran is unlikely to exacerbate tensions between Islamabad and Tehran; indeed, it might reduce them by eliminating thoughts of war provoked by minor grievances.

Nuclear Iran: Strategy and Doctrine

Iranian national security officials are driven by the core belief that for Iran to achieve its grand-strategic ends, Tehran must at least master the complete nuclear fuel cycle. This stance is *nonnegotiable bedrock,* shared by every consequential actor in Iranian politics, although there may be scope for negotiating limitations on Iran's nuclear capabilities beyond this threshold. Apart from a brief period early in the revolution, all of Tehran's nuclear-diplomatic maneuvers over four decades—its resolute boasts, pledges of abstinence, global clandestine operations, bald-faced lies, enrichment suspensions and resumptions, dissembling obfuscations, and breached obligations—have been mere tactics, calculated to win the prize without suffering unacceptable cost.

Tehran's pursuit of nuclear weapon capability, like its grand strategy, is driven by both fear and ambition. First and foremost, Iran's strategic elites hope to ensure the security and survival of their state by making the costs of confrontation so high that the United States and its allies are dissuaded from invading Iran, reversing the revolution, or toppling the present regime. Their formative experiences give Iran's contemporary leaders—the so-called "war generation"—ample justification for fearing such aggression. In 1980, (Sunni) Iraq attacked Iran in an effort to squelch the (Shia) Islamic revolution. With the support of every interested party, Baghdad killed thousands of Iranians with ghastly chemical weapons and terrorized Iranian city dwellers with ballistic-missile strikes. In the wake of 9/11, the United States invaded two of Iran's neighbors in a year-and-a-half, setting precedents that inevitably unnerved Tehran. Iranian decision makers note the contrasting fates of the other two "axis-of-evil" members: nuclear-capable Kim Jong Il has successfully fended off U.S. aggression and preserved his totalitarian regime, while nuclear-bereft Saddam Hussein was humiliated twice on the battlefield and ultimately vanquished by the undeterred U.S. military machine.[24]

Iran's emerging nuclear capability also serves important domestic purposes. President Ahmadinejad's fiery rhetoric notwithstanding, "the Islamic revolution is today a spent force in Iran, and the Islamic Republic is a tired dictatorship facing pressures to change" (Nasr 2007: 212). In the theocrats' calculations, Iran's successes in the nuclear field, defying as they do the policies of the United States, the European Union, Israel, and the Gulf monarchies, serve to reawaken Iranian citizens' revolutionary fervor and to shore up the battered legitimacy of the radical conservatives aligned with Ahmadinejad. Although there is no way of knowing for sure, and some experts would disagree, Shahram Chubin goes as far as to say that "Iran's principal motive for developing nuclear technology appears to be domestic legitimation of the regime" (2006: 28).

In addition to quelling the anxieties of Iran's clerical establishment, the nuclear capability is viewed as promoting Tehran's ambitions for greater power and status, both in the Gulf region and more broadly. By building on its pivotal geostrategic position and its abundant natural-resource wealth, Iran hopes—like China and India before it—to become the predominant strategic player in its immediate neighborhood. Not unlike the late Shah, the theocrats see the mastery of the nuclear fuel cycle—and possibly a future nuclear arsenal—as critical elements of Iran's rise to regional and global prominence; they will buy the enhanced prestige sought by Iran in a world where great-power status is closely correlated with countries' nuclear prowess. As Iranian leaders look around the world, they observe that, with two exceptions, all of the current or aspiring great powers are nuclear armed. The outliers, Germany and Japan, have for historical reasons embraced near-pacifistic national security postures and enjoy ironclad security guarantees from the remaining superpower. Because Iran strives for regional preeminence and great-power standing, it unsurprisingly sees nuclear weapon capability to be a vital element in its power portfolio, necessary but not sufficient for enhanced international stature. The vehement resistance of outsiders, especially Israel and the United States, feeds into, substantiates, and intensifies Iran's nuclear resolve. From Tehran's perspective, acquiring nuclear weapons makes Washington fear you or respect you, but either way it takes you very, very seriously.

Nuclear Strategy

For policy makers and strategic analysts anticipating a nuclear-capable Tehran, several vital questions arise: Will the logic of the nuclear revolution extend to Iran? Will Iran, like its nuclear predecessors, evolve into a state that accepts that the primary value of nuclear weapons lies in their power to deter aggression? Or will Iran buck six decades of history and conceive new and potentially catastrophic uses for its nuclear capability?[25] Of the four possible roles for nuclear weapons—offense, defense, compellence, and deterrence—it seems most likely that Tehran will view its nuclear capability as providing some combination of deterrent and compellent strength. In the short-term future, say ten years, Iran's nuclear sophistication is not likely to yield it tactical nuclear weapons that can be used to defend Iranian territory against aggressors. Furthermore, while some fear that a nuclear-armed Iran might go on the offensive, launching ballistic missiles at Israel, U.S. forces in the Gulf region, or even—one day—the United States itself,[26] most analysts believe it is highly probable that Iran would instead be deterred by Israel and the United States from doing so (Cirincione 2007: 102–3; Pollack 2004: 384–85; Takeyh 2006: 140–46; Yaphe and Lutes 2005: 38–40). Tehran will be overwhelmingly outgunned by these adversaries' nuclear might. Given Iran's deep mistrust and suspicion of the United States and Israel, no Iranian leader can doubt that his country would be a charred, radioactive wasteland within an hour of launching nuclear missiles against them.

Some have argued that President Ahmadinejad's rhetoric denying the Holocaust and about "wiping Israel off the map" merits real concern over the possibility of nuclear weapons being under his control. Might it not be "rational" for an Iranian president like Ahmadinejad to commit the ultimate act of martyrdom by destroying Israel with nuclear weapons?[27] This scenario is alarmist. It is one thing for a fanatic to martyr himself; it is quite another for a leader to martyr an entire country, and perhaps his very civilization. Not only that, but Ahmadinejad is not a dictator with absolute authority. He holds one important post among several Tehran power centers, and his domestic rivals—reformers, pragmatists, *and* radical conservatives—have been discomfited by Ahmadinejad's vile bluster. Even if he were a lunatic, or if his brand of rationality implied a personal decision calculus in which national martyrdom promised greater benefits than costs, he lacks the authority to independently launch nuclear weapons. Critical Iranian security decisions are made by the Supreme Leader in close consultation with the Supreme

National Security Council (Takeyh 2007). Awful as it is, Ahmadinejad's vitriol is intended to boost his standing in a relentless competitive domestic political environment and among Muslims around the world. Overreacting to Ahmadinejad's provocations only serves his purposes.

Tehran is likelier to pursue interlinked nuclear strategies of deterrence and what might be called "asymmetric compellence." If we conceptualize the ladder of military force into three levels—nuclear, conventional, and unconventional—Iran is severely disadvantaged in conventional military terms relative to the United States, Israel, and the GCC states. Because of this pronounced inferiority, Iranian leaders will avoid direct conventional military confrontations with these countries, seeking rather to derive strategic leverage from Tehran's capabilities at the nuclear and unconventional levels. In such a strategy, Iran's nuclear weapons could serve as a deterrent to attacks against its territory, while simultaneously providing an umbrella of reassurance under which Tehran could more securely pursue unconventional compellent means, such as terrorist attacks or armed Shia militancy, to achieve its regional ends. Iran is already considered to have the world's largest, most capable network for supporting such operations, and it is difficult to see why a nuclear-deterrent capability would make it *less* likely to continue its unconventional aggression. On the other hand, if Iran can already exacerbate Israeli-Palestinian violence by aiding Hamas and the Palestinian Islamic Jihad, enable Hezbollah to fight Israeli forces to a draw in Lebanon in 2006, and arm Shia factions in Iraq and elsewhere, it is not apparent how a nuclear weapon capability would make it a significantly *more* capable supporter of these unconventional operations, apart from providing a measure of extra security against reprisals—reprisals that have not been ordered even in the absence of an Iranian nuclear deterrent. Indeed, an Iran that has surmounted considerable financial, diplomatic, and technological obstacles to achieve a nuclear weapon capability will also have very strong incentive not to give its adversaries additional justification for destroying it.

Nuclear Terrorism?

Would Iran transfer nuclear weapons or materials to terrorist allies for use against the United States, Israel, or American and Israeli targets around the world? On balance, probably not. While no Israeli or U.S. leader can in good conscience rule out this kind of nuclear leakage, especially given the history of the A. Q. Khan network and the ease with which it distributed nuclear technology and materials around the globe, Iran will have strong incentives not to diffuse its nuclear capabilities. Tehran is trying to turn itself into a regional and global power. Once it achieves a nuclear weapon capability, the imperative of protecting and sustaining that capability will likely push in the direction of careful nuclear stewardship. Notwithstanding its past deeds, Tehran is likely to portray itself to the world's nuclear establishment as a responsible nuclear power. Indeed, Iran's pragmatic conservatives are apt to argue that after several expensive, often frustrating decades of trying to develop nuclear weapons, leaking warheads or fissile materials to terrorists would represent a waste of precious time, effort, and resources.

Another important factor here is that Al-Qaeda, the terrorist network with the greatest likelihood of using nuclear technology to devastating effect, has had historically difficult relations with Tehran (Hastert 2007). Competitiveness, mutual mistrust, and Sunni-Shia animosities argue against sharing Iran's hard-won nuclear capability with Al-Qaeda. That having been said, certain elements within the radical-conservative camp of Iran's power structure could make the case that Iran is now in a position to be the hero, even the savior, of the Islamic world by doing catastrophic damage to Israel or the United States through its Hezbollah allies, while still maintaining enough plausible deniability of Iran's role to escape punishment. Which path Tehran chooses will rest on three factors: the outcome of the ongoing intense competition among Iran's conservative factions, the estimates of Iranian leaders about how easy it would be for Israel and the United States to credibly attribute to Iran responsibility for nuclear-terrorist attacks,[28] and how unambiguously the United States and Israel signal to Tehran that nuclear terrorist acts committed with transferred Iranian weapons or fissile material would eventuate in an appropriately ruinous nuclear response against Iran.[29]

Substate Threat?

Although this does not fall strictly within the category of state strategy, Iran's rivals will also be concerned about the potential for the unauthorized use of Iranian nuclear weapons. Security for Tehran's nuclear infrastructure rests with the IRGC, an elite military service and powerful support base for the radical-conservative camp spearheaded by President Ahmadinejad. The implications of IRGC authority in this context are both hopeful and worrisome. On the one hand, Iran's hard-won nuclear arsenal would be a source of intense institutional pride for the IRGC, which would have strong political and organizational incentives to exercise effective control over it. Given its two decades of experience overseeing nuclear security since the Khomeini regime had a change of heart about "Western" technology, the well-resourced IRGC is undoubtedly practiced at guarding against sabotage and preventing the theft of nuclear materials. Another source of confidence is that, unlike Pakistan, Iran does not—at least for now—confront the possibility of severe internal strife or state collapse. For all its divisions, Iran is a coherent, relatively unified country, where the state's authority is broader and deeper than it is in Pakistan.

On the other hand, Iran has a zealous Islamist praetorian guard whose ambitions and interests align very closely with the most radical rightist elements in the Iranian political system. The IRGC views itself as a vanguard force, the perpetuator and guardian of an Islamic revolution beset by apathy and moderation, especially among the roughly 60 percent of Iranians who are under thirty years old.[30] Today, the IRGC's ideology and aspirations parallel those of important segments of the country's political leadership, including the presidency; in five years, that may not be the case. The same quasi-democratic, populist impulse that brought Ahmadinejad to power in 2005 could easily veer in another direction. It is not impossible to imagine a future scenario in which IRGC forces—or renegade IRGC fanatics—attempt to commandeer Iranian fissile material or warheads for their own political purposes.

Nuclear Forces and Doctrine

Although Iran is often depicted as being on the "brink" of a nuclear weapon capability, its remaining tasks and potential obstacles are daunting.[31] As noted previously, to produce enough HEU for its first nuclear explosive device, Tehran must successfully run a fully operational centrifuge module for a sustained period of time, probably six to twelve months. Thereafter, note two experts:

> Warhead and bomb design are also major problems. It is one thing to create a nuclear device or even a bomb, and another to create a reliable and effective nuclear warhead. Such a device would have to be safe, reliable, and—for most uses that have predictable and controllable nuclear weapon effects—have arming and detonation that allow precise control of the height of burst. Even making a small, efficient bomb is still a state-of-the-art exercise in design, engineering, and manufacturing. A missile warhead requires far more skill. The leak of Chinese designs may help, as may other technology transfers, but Iran would want great assurance that such designs would function as planned. (Cordesman and Al-Rodhan 2006: 21)

The likeliest delivery systems for the earliest Iranian nuclear weapons are Tehran's 25–100 Shahab-III MRBMs. The missile systems and nuclear warheads would be under the command and control of the IRGC. The Shahab-III is mobile, but in addition to its Transport Erector Launcher, it "requires numerous launching support vehicles for propellant transport and loading and power." If in fact Iran received its weapon designs from the A. Q. Khan network, its warheads would fit the Shahab-III. However, Tehran still faces substantial "uncertainties in many aspects of developing, testing, and designing missiles and warheads, and will continue to do so until it has a comprehensive set of operational test data based on its missiles and the behavior of its warheads. Even then, there will probably be a significant risk that any given missile launch will be at least a partial failure, and could impact far from its target."[32]

To deter aggression, Iran must overcome enormous challenges to ensure the survivability of a small nuclear stockpile against Israeli and nearby U.S. forces.[33] Given the capabilities and limitations outlined above, the most realistic targets for nuclear-tipped Iranian missiles would be Israeli cities such as Tel Aviv and large U.S. naval formations in the waters of, or nearby, the Persian Gulf, such as an aircraft carrier strike group. Reliable, more precisely targeted counterforce or countercontrol options are likely to be out of Iran's reach for many years. Having learned from Israel's attack on Iraq's Osirak nuclear reactor in 1981, Tehran already has a great deal of experience in dispersing, burying, and hardening its nuclear installations, as well as in deceiving rival intelligence agencies. For deterrence purposes, it will need to build upon these practices by widely scattering and hiding its mobile Shahab-III systems and their warheads, protecting the MRBMs within hardened shelters, and devising enough convincing decoys and other evasions to create ambiguity among U.S. and Israeli planners about how redundant and dispersed Iran's nuclear weapons actually are. Israeli and U.S. theater missile-defense capabilities will further complicate Iranian calculations. Decision makers in Tehran will not be able to rely on a high percentage of their nuclear MRBMs destroying the intended targets if employed in retaliation for an attack on Iran.

Iran's policy makers will also have crucial decisions to make about the readiness and responsiveness of their nuclear forces. Taken together, the United States and Israel will have huge advantages in overall firepower, as well as in their vast array of distinctive capabilities to choose from. Conservative estimates put the number of Israeli nuclear weapons at between 100 and 250.[34] As for delivery systems, Israel is believed to deploy at least 50 Jericho IIs, an accurate, mobile MRBM with an approximate range of 1,500 kilometers and a reported payload of 1,000 kilograms. In all likelihood, it can also strike Iranian targets with nuclear-armed cruise missiles launched from its three Dolphin-class submarines. Furthermore, Israel possesses several advanced nuclear-capable aircraft, including the F-15I and F-16I. Both of these can be configured to deliver conventional laser-guided bombs and penetrating warheads (so-called "bunker busters") with pinpoint accuracy (Raas and Long 2007: 7–33). The U.S. nuclear arsenal, some of which would be targeted at Iranian nuclear weapons, delivery systems, and other critical military assets, includes gravity bombs and cruise missiles, deliverable by Dual-Capable Aircraft and long-range bombers; the Tomahawk Land Attack Missile/Nuclear, deliverable by attack submarines; submarine-launched ballistic-missiles; and intercontinental ballistic missiles (U.S. Joint Chiefs of Staff 2005). The United States also deploys a panoply of conventional military forces in the Persian Gulf region that could be brought to bear against Iranian nuclear targets. In addition to massive numerical and technological advantages, the U.S. military enjoys qualitative edges over Iran in real-time intelligence, adaptive planning, network and force integration, and escalation management.

All of these asymmetries mitigate against Tehran adopting a nuclear doctrine of no first use. It is likely that Iran, like the United States in Europe during the Cold War, would seek to build its deterrent credibility by publicly announcing that it reserves the right to respond to attack—nuclear or conventional—by resorting to the employment of nuclear weapons. For the same reasons, Tehran would resist embracing a ride-out-and-respond nuclear doctrine; with its adversaries enjoying such overwhelming military superiority across the board, Iran would not have the luxury of awaiting the outcome of major U.S. or Israeli aggression, assessing the damage, and then deciding upon the most appropriate response. This leaves Iranian decision makers with two doctrinal options: launch-on-warning (LOW) or prompt response. During a crisis, Iran's MRBMs would be unleashed either upon first warning of incoming strikes, or just at the moment of impact, when officials can be certain that an attack has actually transpired before responding. Even a prompt-response doctrine runs the risk of Iran's retaliatory forces being demolished in a first strike, but creative deception and dispersal would probably ensure that at least some Iranian MRBMs could respond.

Tehran's adoption of a LOW posture would raise serious concerns about the possible inadvertent launching of nuclear missiles as a regional crisis escalates. The most realistic scenario for inadvertent escalation is one in which severely stressed Iranian launch commanders release their MRBMs on the basis of information mistakenly suggesting that Israeli or U.S. nuclear weapons are headed in their direction. However, important factors also militate against such a "use-it-or-lose-it" scenario. Iran's MRBMs would have to be configured in a fully operational mode; preprogrammed to hit a particular, stationary, predetermined target; with the nuclear warhead reliably mated with a reliable missile. Additionally, for Iran's weapons to be that vulnerable, Tehran would have chosen to deploy a stationary, unconcealed missile system instead of a mobile system or multiple scattered systems incorporating decoys, topographical camouflage, and other types of deception. It defies reason to expect that the same Iranian decision makers who were wily enough to hide from the IAEA for years the construction of a mammoth uranium enrichment facility would be so unwise as to deploy such a vulnerable delivery system, especially one acquired at high cost in time and effort. But if they were, and if the Iranian missiles were targeted at Israel, in turn that country's small size, densely concentrated population, and early-detection capabilities suggest that in the absence of an extremely reliable missile defense system, Israel would itself be poised to react in a LOW or at least a prompt-response fashion. Although this scenario is possible, the probability that each of its elements would perfectly combine to cause an inadvertent nuclear exchange is low.

Nuclear Iran: Implications for Regional and International Security

Iran is an important, ambitious, and fearful state. Its leaders want to develop their country into a regional, and eventually global, great power, but at the same time they worry about the very survival of their regime. Looking outward from Tehran, they perceive a hostile U.S. military presence in neighboring Afghanistan, Iraq, Pakistan, and Turkey, as well as in the GCC states just across the Persian Gulf. Slightly further afield is America's close ally, Israel, the only nuclear weapon state in the Middle East, and a very capable one at that. Iran's government is developing its own nuclear weapon capability to perpetuate itself as an Islamic theocracy, to establish itself as the Gulf region's predominant power, to provide the foundation for a future great-power role, and—while seeking all of these objectives—to deter its adversaries from attacking Iran or otherwise thwarting its ambitions.

Tehran's quest for nuclear weapon capability is a grand-strategic pursuit that has remained essentially constant for more than three decades, irrespective of who has governed Iran. Despite the many crosscutting divisions in contemporary Iranian politics, every significant political actor shares the fundamental belief that nuclear weapons, or at least the capability to produce them, are crucial for Iran's return to international prominence. For Iran's political elites—and for many of its citizens—mastery of the complete nuclear fuel cycle has become nothing less than a symbol of national pride and sovereignty. Having said that, important decisions lie ahead for Tehran's strategic elites. It is far from clear that Iran has decided to become a declared nuclear weapon state. To do so, Tehran would have to make an outright break with its NPT obligations, which would undoubtedly invite harsh international criticism, diplomatic isolation, virtual economic strangulation, and possibly even the very military intervention that Iran's nuclear capability is intended to deter.

Assuming that Iran does ultimately leave the NPT, its acquisition of nuclear weapons would be a momentous development for regional international relations. As argued previously, Tehran is likely to be deterred from major aggression against its adversaries, either conventional or nuclear, by the prospect of swift, certain, and overwhelming retaliation by the United States or Israel. Having finally crossed the nuclear threshold at great cost and effort, no Iranian purpose would be served by going on the offensive in such a provocative way. The Islamic Republic's strategic behavior since the early 1990s suggests that Iran's theocrats are keenly aware of the steep costs they would pay for a return to the unbridled regional adventurism of the 1980s. As Ray Takeyh writes: "Despite continued revolutionary pronouncements, Iran has evolved from a revisionist state seeking to export its governing template to a rational state that bases its foreign policy on pragmatic calculations" (2006: 219). However, in carefully selected cases when it serves its purposes, Tehran *is* likely to continue its support for unconventional military operations by its allies, be they Shia insurgents in Iraq, Pakistan, or the GCC states; Hamas and other radical Palestinian factions; or Hezbollah terrorists in Lebanon and perhaps elsewhere. The possession of nuclear weapons is likely to make Iran's leaders more confident than they are today that such tactics are relatively cost free; decisions to ratchet them up or down in any given situation will depend on the Iranian political calculations of the day.

Would a nuclear-armed Iran instigate a flurry of destabilizing regional proliferation, or would the spread of nuclear weapons continue to be slow, sluggish, and manageable? Major Middle Eastern states like Saudi Arabia, Egypt, and Turkey would surely rethink their nuclear chastity. Given the rise of a nuclear Iran, their leaders would be derelict if they did not explore every option for addressing a markedly altered security picture. But it is hardly a foregone conclusion that they would rush to nuclearize. Egypt is barely a factor in Gulf geopolitics and would have little to fear from a nuclear Iran. Cairo would likely seek to deepen its already substantial security relationship with Washington, rather than embark upon an expensive nuclear project that would engender the opposition of Europe and the United States. While Turkey shares a border with Iran, their relations are generally sound. And Turkey's NATO status would go far to assuage any anxieties Ankara might have about Iranian nuclearization. Saudi Arabia, though an often bitter adversary of Iran's, has long been allied with the United States in everything but name, and Washington has an impressive record of defending it against external aggression. Furthermore, Riyadh's characteristic timorousness in regional security matters suggests that Saudi proponents of nuclearization might well be outmanned by opponents who fear that such a course would increase, rather than decrease, Iranian belligerence toward the kingdom.

In the final analysis, these states have long since accommodated themselves to the reality of a nuclear-armed Israel, in large part because they derive reassurance from their ties with the United States. A robust, Iranian-driven Shia revival—under Tehran's nuclear umbrella—might inspire a more hawkish reaction, but on balance, U.S. security guarantees are likely to limit the follow-on effects of Iran's nuclearization. The recently announced U.S. military aid increases, described earlier, are explicitly geared toward containing Iran, stiffening the spines of U.S. allies in the Persian Gulf, and demonstrating that Washington is engaged in the region for the long haul. In seeking congressional approval for the expanded arms sales to friendly governments, U.S. officials will undoubtedly argue, as they did with respect to Pakistan in the 1980s, that conventional military assistance to Egypt, Saudi Arabia, and the five smaller GCC states will give these countries the security reassurance they need to forswear the development of nuclear weapons in response to Iranian nuclearization.[35] *If* Iran leaves the NPT and goes overtly nuclear, and *if* its critical nuclear installations are not destroyed in U.S. or—more likely—Israeli preventive attacks, the most optimistic regional scenario is one in which Iran and Israel settle uneasily into a strategic equation of mutual nuclear deterrence, while the United States pointedly reaffirms its alliances with Israel and Turkey and undertakes to guarantee the security of its Sunni Arab allies as long as they refrain from pursuing nuclear weapons. Although the evolution of a regional security system along these lines is far from ideal, it bears comparison with other potential scenarios that may be far worse.

Notes

For their critical input, the author would like to thank Muthiah Alagappa, Avery Goldstein, Jim Hentz, Roy Meyers, Nicholas Miller, Patrick Morgan, and Geoffrey Vaughan.

1. See the discussion in Wolfsthal (2007: 22–26).

2. For noteworthy exceptions, see Clawson and Eisenstadt (2007), Schake (2007), Logan (2006), Sokolski and Clawson (2005), Yaphe and Lutes (2005), and Zaborski (2005).

3. For a lengthier history of Iran's nuclear progress, see Hagerty (2008). This section draws in part on that chapter.

4. In 1976, West Germany's Kraftwerk Union, a Siemens subsidiary, began building what was to be a nuclear power plant comprising two pressurized light-water reactors near Bushehr, on Iran's Persian Gulf coast. For a detailed timeline of the Iranian nuclear program, see Nuclear Threat Initiative (2007).

5. Tehran, noting Israel's devastating 1981 attack on Iraq's Osirak nuclear reactor, built parts of the Isfahan facility underground and has continued that practice with certain other nuclear installations.

6. Khan confirmed the Pakistan-Iran connection in February 2004. See *Economist.com* (2004). For detailed accounts, see Fitzpatrick (2007) and Corera (2006).

7. Tehran admitted this to IAEA officials in January 2005. Iran acknowledged in November 2005 that the Khan network also "supplied it with information on casting and machining parts of nuclear weapons." See Squassoni (2007: 2–3).

8. Cirincione, Wolfsthal, and Rajkumar (2005: 299). Another well-informed expert says that Khan "provided Iran the ability to build and operate gas centrifuges. Without their assistance, Iran would have likely been unable to develop a gas centrifuge program" (U.S. House 2007).

9. See Katzman (2007: 20), Spector and McDonough (1995: 120), and Jones and McDonough (1998: 54, 152). China curtailed its nuclear assistance to Iran in 1997, in order to realize the benefits of its 1995 nuclear cooperation accord with the United States. See Jones and McDonough (1998: 7, 50, 56, 169, 174, 176).

10. Cirincione (2002: 14, 15, 82, 94, 99). For a recent discussion of Israel's vulnerability to Iranian missiles armed with nuclear, biological, or chemical weapons, see Derfner (2007). The Shahab-III's reliability is a matter of vigorous debate. See Vick (2007).

11. U.S. House (2007: 3). Iran makes its own "P1" centrifuges, the ones now operating at Natanz. The A. Q. Khan network provided the designs for these centrifuges, hence the designation *P* for Pakistan.

12. Sanger (2007). This article quotes Mohamed ElBaradei, the IAEA director general, as saying: "We believe they pretty much have the knowledge about how to enrich . . .

From now on, it is simply a question of perfecting that knowledge . . . From a proliferation perspective, the fact of the matter is that one of the purposes of suspension—keeping them from getting the knowledge—has been overtaken by events." His remarks infuriated U.S. officials.

13. At its narrowest, the Strait is 34 miles (55 kilometers) wide. Oil tankers navigate inbound and outbound through two 2-mile-wide channels, separated by a 2-mile-wide buffer zone. Roughly 40 percent of all world-traded oil, including 75 percent of Japan's oil imports, flows through the Strait. U.S. energy analysts predict that oil exports transiting the Strait will double by 2020. (*Reuters Alert Net* 2007; U.S. Department of Energy 2007).

14. Iran is the world's eighteenth largest country and, after Saudi Arabia, the second largest in the Gulf region. It has the world's nineteenth largest population, and—with ten million more people than Iraq and Saudi Arabia combined—by far the region's largest population. Iran's gross domestic product (GDP) ranks twentieth in the world and first in the Gulf region, with second-place Saudi Arabia's GDP only 62 percent the size of Iran's. In the realm of strategic raw materials, Iran is the world's number three in proved oil reserves, second only to Saudi Arabia in the region, and number two in proved natural gas reserves, trailing only Russia. Iran's military spending ranks it second in the Gulf, trailing only Saudi Arabia's. Considering Iran's long head start in acquiring the capability to build nuclear weapons, definitively crossing the nuclear threshold would instantly vault it to marked military predominance vis-à-vis its immediate neighbors. For rankings, see U.S. Central Intelligence Agency (2007).

15. Of course, Baathist Iraq was also in this group. In the post-Baathist era, Iran is unlikely for many years to face a strong, hostile, fully sovereign adversary to its west.

16. For a concise historical account, see Keddie (2006: 123–31). Ray Takeyh points out that Iran's "mullahs preferred the deference of a conservative and uncertain monarch" to the "secular enterprise" of Mossadeq. "The Islamic Republic's perennial demand for an American apology over its complicity in the 1953 coup ought not to obscure the fact that the clerical community was either indifferent or actively conspired" against Mossadeq (Takeyh 2006: 91).

17. For a gripping, meticulously detailed narrative of the hostage ordeal, see Bowden (2006).

18. In addition to Saudi Arabia, these are Bahrain, Kuwait, Oman, Qatar, and the United Arab Emirates.

19. For background, see Nasr (2007).

20. At any given time, some 60,000 U.S. military personnel are stationed at U.S. military facilities in the Persian Gulf—40,000 ashore and 20,000 afloat (Knickmeyer 2007).

21. For an overview of the regional security balance, see Katzman (2006: 4–20). The GCC states alone now deploy some 300 F-15, F-16, and F/A-18 advanced U.S. warplanes, a stark contrast with Iran's 55 Russian MiG-29s and Su-24s (pp. 14–17). One report says that "nearly half of the U.S. Navy's 277 warships are stationed close to Iran" (Daragahi 2007).

22. See Cloud (2007) and Wright (2007a). Washington also announced that its military aid to Israel would increase to US$3 billion per year over the next ten years, up from its current US$2.4 billion. U.S. military aid to Egypt will continue at US$1.3 billion annually. All told, then, the United States plans to spend US$63 billion over the next decade bolstering its Middle Eastern allies' military capabilities, mainly owing to concerns about a rising Iran (*Economist* 2007a).

23. See GlobalSecurity.org (2007a). Baluchistan is rich in raw materials, especially natural gas.

24. Of course, this is not to say that Iran draws the correct lessons. On the Korean peninsula, Washington has been deterred at least as much by the fear of North Korea's conventional forces devastating Seoul than by Pyongyang's nascent nuclear capability.

25. For an analysis of these questions framed by the debate within the security studies community between "proliferation pessimists" and "deterrence optimists," see Hagerty (2008).

26. See *Economist* (2007b), "The Riddle of Iran" a fifteen-page special report.

27. Bernard Lewis (2006) writes: "There is a radical difference between the Islamic Republic of Iran and other governments with nuclear weapons. The difference is expressed in what can only be described as the apocalyptic worldview of Iran's present rulers. This worldview . . . , vividly expressed in speeches, articles, and even schoolbooks, clearly shape[s] the perception and therefore the policies of Ahmadinejad and his disciples." Regarding a nuclear-armed Iran, Lewis continues:

> A direct attack on the U.S., though possible, is less likely in the immediate future. Israel is a nearer and easier target, and Mr. Ahmadinejad has given indication of thinking along these lines. The Western observer would immediately think of two possible deterrents. The first is that an attack that wipes out Israel would almost certainly wipe out the Palestinians too. The second is that such an attack would evoke a devastating reprisal from Israel against Iran, since one may surely assume that the Israelis have made the necessary arrangements for a counterstrike even after a nuclear holocaust in Israel. The first of these possible deterrents might well be of concern to the Palestinians—but not apparently to their fanatical champions in the Iranian government. The second deterrent—the threat of direct retaliation on Iran—is, as noted, already weakened by the suicide or martyrdom complex that plagues parts of the Islamic world today, without parallel in other religions, or for that matter in the Islamic past. This complex has become even more important at the present day, because of this new apocalyptic vision.

28. For an analysis of the nuclear forensics involved, see Talmadge (2007).

29. Robert Gallucci (2006) has coined the term *expanded deterrence* to describe this challenge.

30. See *Boston Globe* (2007). Iran's youth unemployment rate is about 30 percent and rising, as the post-Iraq war baby boom reaches working age.

31. Given Iran's status as a prenuclear power and the tight secrecy with which it conceals its nuclear planning, this section is necessarily highly speculative. As Christopher de Bellaigue writes: "no outsider knows Iran's intentions, or how the country is changing as a result of international pressure and threats. Who can tell if Iran has a nuclear doctrine and, if so, what is written in it?" (2007: 187).

32. Cordesman and Al-Rodhan (2006: 3, 5, 13, 21–23). Tehran might eventually have other delivery options, such as the Ukrainian/Soviet-made Raduga KH-55 Granat cruise missile (with air, land, and ship capability) and aging ground-attack aircraft such as the Soviet Su-24MK, but at this point in time these are considered less certain and inferior alternatives to the Shahab-III. Also see GlobalSecurity.org (2007c). The analysis below

assumes the existence of perhaps dozens of nuclear warheads with only a Shahab-III delivery capability.

33. Iran is developing intercontinental ballistic missiles that might one day be targeted on the United States, but Washington estimates that these will not be ready until roughly 2015. See U.S. Senate (2005).

34. Unless otherwise noted, the data in this paragraph come from GlobalSecurity.org (2007d).

35. For a discussion of the Gulf monarchies' perceptions of this issue, see Russell (2005: 23–49).

References

Agence France-Presse. 2007. "Iran Will Not Halt Enrichment: Ahmadinejad." July 11. Available at http://www.france24.com/france24Public/en/news/world/20070711-Iran-IAEA-nuclear-atomic-watchdog.html [accessed July 19, 2007].

Albright, David, Jacqueline Shire, and Paul Brannan. 2007. "IAEA Safeguards Report on Iran: Iran Making Progress But Not Yet Reliably Operating an Enrichment Plant." Washington, D.C.: Institute for Science and International Security, May 25. Available at http://www.isis-online.org/publications/iran/IranSafeguards25May2007.pdf [accessed June 3, 2007].

Associated Press. 2007. "Pentagon Chief Urges Greater Pressure on Iran over Nuclear Arms." June 2. Available at http://www.iht.com/bin/print.php?id+5974177 [accessed June 2, 2007].

de Bellaigue, Christopher. 2007. *The Struggle for Iran.* New York: New York Review Books.

Boston Globe. 2007. "Iran's Youngsters." May 6.

Bowden, Mark. 2006. *Guests of the Ayatollah: The First Battle in America's War with Militant Islam.* New York: Grove Press.

Chubin, Shahram. 2006. *Iran's Nuclear Ambitions.* Washington, D.C.: Carnegie Endowment for International Peace.

Cirincione, Joseph. 2002. *Deadly Arsenals: Tracking Weapons of Mass Destruction.* Washington, D.C.: Carnegie Endowment for International Peace.

———. 2007. *Bomb Scare: The History and Future of Nuclear Weapons.* New York: Columbia University Press.

Cirincione, Joseph, Jon B. Wolfsthal, and Miriam Rajkumar. 2005. *Deadly Arsenals: Nuclear, Biological and Chemical Threats,* 2nd rev., exp. ed. Washington, D.C.: Carnegie Endowment for International Peace.

Clawson, Patrick, and Michael Eisenstadt, eds. 2007. *Deterring the Ayatollahs: Complications in Applying Cold War Strategy to Iran.* Policy Focus #72. Washington, D.C.: Washington Institute for Near East Policy. Available at http://www.washingtoninstitute.org/templateC04.php?CID=280 [accessed November 26, 2007].

Cloud, David S. 2007. "U.S. Set to Offer Huge Arms Deal to Saudi Arabia." *New York Times,* July 28.

Cordesman, Anthony H., and Khalid R. Al-Rodhan. 2006. "Iranian Nuclear Weapons? Iran's Missiles and Possible Delivery Systems." (working draft) Center for Strategic and International Studies, Washington, D.C.

Corera, Gordon. 2006. *Shopping for Bombs: Nuclear Proliferation, Global Insecurity, and the Rise and Fall of the A. Q. Khan Network.* New York: Oxford University Press.

Daragahi, Borzou. 2007. "U.S., Iran Do Persian Gulf Squeeze." *Los Angeles Times,* July 11.

Derfner, Larry. 2007. "Second Strike." *Jerusalem Post,* July 5. Available at http://www.jpost.com/servlet/Satellite?cid=1183459203248&pagename=JPost%2FJPArticle%2FShowFull [accessed July 18, 2007].

Dobbins, James. 2007. "How to Talk to Iran." *Washington Post,* July 22.

Economist. 2007a. "Arming Its Friends and Talking Peace." August 2.

———. 2007b. "The Riddle of Iran." July 21.

Economist.com. 2004. "Pakistan's Proliferator-in-Chief," February 5. Available at http://www.economist.com/agenda/displaystory.cfm?story_id=E1_NQDJGQP [accessed June 3, 2007].

Fitzpatrick, Mark, ed. 2007. *Nuclear Black Markets: Pakistan, A. Q. Khan and the Rise of Proliferation Networks: A Net Assessment.* London: International Institute of Strategic Studies.

Gallucci, Robert. 2006. "Averting Nuclear Catastrophe: Contemplating Extreme Responses to U.S. Vulnerability." *ANNALS of the American Academy of Political and Social Science* 607: 51–58.

GlobalSecurity.org. 2007a. "Baluchistan Insurgency." Available at http://www.globalsecurity.org/military/world/war/pakistan1.htm [accessed June 11, 2007].

———. 2007b. "Iran-Iraq War (1980–1988)." Available at http://www.globalsecurity.org/military/world/war/iran-iraq.htm [accessed July 9, 2007].

———. 2007c. "Iran's Air Force." Available at http://www.globalsecurity.org/military/world/iran/airforce.htm [accessed August 5, 2007].

———. 2007d. "Israel Special Weapons Guide." Available at http://www.globalsecurity.org/wmd/world/israel/index.html [accessed August 5, 2007].

Hagerty, Devin T. 2008. "The Implications of a Nuclear-Armed Iran in Light of South Asia's Nuclear Experience." In *Nuclear Deterrence in South Asia and Beyond,* ed. Sumit Ganguly and S. Paul Kapur. New York: Routledge.

Harel, Amos. 2007. "MI: Iran Will Cross Nuclear Threshold by 2009." *Haaretz,* July 11. Available at http://www.haaretz.com/hasen/spages/880731.html [accessed July 15, 2007].

Hastert, Paul. 2007. "Al Qaeda and Iran: Friends or Foes, or Somewhere in Between?" *Studies in Conflict and Terrorism* 30 (4): 327–36.

Jones, Rodney W., and Mark G. McDonough. 1998. *Tracking Nuclear Proliferation: A Guide in Maps and Charts, 1998.* Washington, D.C.: Carnegie Endowment for International Peace.

Katzman, Kenneth. 2006. "The Persian Gulf States: Issues for U.S. Policy." *CRS Report for Congress RL31533.* Washington, D.C.: Congressional Research Service.

———. 2007. "Iran: U.S. Concerns and Policy Responses." *CRS Report for Congress RL32048.* Washington, D.C.: Congressional Research Service.

Keddie, Nikki R. 2006. *Modern Iran: Roots and Results of Revolution.* New Haven, Conn.: Yale University Press.

Knickmeyer, Ellen. 2007. "Gulf States Buy Arms With Wary Eye on Iran." *Washington Post,* August 4.

Lewis, Bernard. 2006. "August 22: Does Iran Have Something in Store?" *Wall Street Journal,* August 8.

Logan, Justin. 2006. "The Bottom Line on Iran: The Costs and Benefits of Preventive War versus Deterrence." *Policy Analysis,* 583: 1–27.

McNaugher, Thomas L. 1990. "Ballistic Missiles and Chemical Weapons: The Legacy of the Iran-Iraq War." *International Security,* 15 (2): 5–34.

Nasr, Vali. 2007. *The Shia Revival: How Conflicts within Islam Will Shape the Future.* New York: W. W. Norton.

Nuclear Threat Initiative. 2007. "Iran Profile: Nuclear Chronology." Available at http://www.nti.org/e_research/profiles/Iran/index.html [accessed July 17, 2007].

Pollack, Kenneth M. 2004. *The Persian Puzzle: The Conflict Between Iran and America.* New York: Random House.

Raas, Whitney, and Austin Long. 2007. "Osirak Redux? Assessing Israeli Capabilities to Destroy Iranian Nuclear Facilities." *International Security* 31 (4): 7–33.

Reuters Alert Net. 2007. "Factbox: The Strait of Hormuz, Iran, and the Risk to Oil." March 27. Available at http://www.alertnet.org/thenews/newsdesk/L27344177.htm [accessed July 28, 2007].

Russell, Richard L. 2005. "Arab Security Responses to a Nuclear-Ready Iran." In *Getting Ready for a Nuclear-Ready Iran,* ed. Henry Sokolski and Patrick Clawson, 23–49. Carlisle, Penna.: U.S. Army War College Strategic Studies Institute.

Sanger, David E. 2007. "Inspectors Cite Big Gains by Iran on Nuclear Fuel." *New York Times,* May 15.

Schake, Kori. 2007. "Dealing with a Nuclear Iran." *Policy Review* 142. Available at http://www.hoover.org/publications/policyreview/6848072.html [accessed May 12, 2007].

Sciolino, Elaine, and William J. Broad. 2007. "Report Raises New Doubts on Iran Nuclear Program." *New York Times,* November 16.

Sokolski, Henry, and Patrick Clawson, eds. 2005. *Getting Ready for a Nuclear-Ready Iran.* Carlisle, Penna.: U.S. Army War College Strategic Studies Institute.

Spector, Leonard S. 1988. *The Undeclared Bomb: The Spread of Nuclear Weapons, 1987–1988.* Cambridge, Mass.: Ballinger.

Spector, Leonard S., and Mark G. McDonough. 1995. *Tracking Nuclear Proliferation: A Guide in Maps and Charts, 1995.* Washington, D.C.: Carnegie Endowment for International Peace.

Squassoni, Sharon. 2007. "Iran's Nuclear Program: Recent Developments." *CRS Report for Congress RS21592.* Washington, D.C.: Congressional Research Service.

Takeyh, Ray. 2006. *Hidden Iran: Paradox and Power in the Islamic Republic.* New York: Times Books.

———. 2007. "God's Will: Iran's Polity and the Challenges of the Future." Remarks made at the Faith Angle Conference, Pew Forum on Religion and Public Life, Key West, Florida, May 14. Available at http://www.eppc.org/programs/religionandmedia/publications/programID.37,pubID.2998/pub_detail.asp [accessed June 14, 2007].

Talmadge, Caitlin. 2007. "Deterring a Nuclear 9/11." *Washington Quarterly* 30 (2): 21–34.

U.S. Central Intelligence Agency. 2007. *World Factbook.* Available at https://www.cia.gov/library/publications/the-world-factbook/index.html [accessed November 26, 2007].

U.S. Department of Energy. 2007. Energy Information Administration. "Persian Gulf Oil and Gas Exports Fact Sheet." Available at http://www.eia.doe.gov/emeu/cabs/pgulf.html [accessed June 5, 2007].

U.S. House. 2007. Committee on Foreign Affairs. Subcommittees on Terrorism, Nonproliferation, and Trade and the Middle East and Asia. "Iran's Nuclear Program: Status and

Uncertainties." Testimony of David Albright, President, Institute for Science and International Security, March 15. Available at http://www.isis-online.org/publications/iran/AlbrightTestimony15March2007.pdf [accessed April 28, 2007].

U.S. Joint Chiefs of Staff. 2005. "Doctrine for Joint Nuclear Operations." Joint Publication 3-12. March 15. Available at http://www.nukestrat.com/us/jcs/jp3-12_05.htm [accessed August 4, 2007].

U.S. Senate. 2005. Committee on Armed Services. Statement of Vice Adm. Lowell E. Jacoby, Director, U.S. Defense Intelligence Agency, on "Current and Projected National Security Threats to the United States," March 17.

Vick, Charles P. 2007. "Shahab-3, 3A/Zelzal-3." GlobalSecurity.org, February 15. Available at http://www.globalsecurity.org/wmd/world/iran/shahab-3.htm [accessed July 18, 2007].

Wall Street Journal Online. 2007. "Central Asia Bloc Scorns U.S." August 17. Available at http://online.wsj.com/article/SB118728978238899955.html?mod=googlenews_wsj [accessed August 22, 2007].

Weiner, Tim. 2007. *Legacy of Ashes: The History of the CIA.* New York: Doubleday.

White House. 2002. "President Delivers State of the Union Address." Washington, D.C., January 29. Available at http://www.whitehouse.gov/news/releases/2002/01/20020129-11.html [accessed July 28, 2007].

Wolfsthal, Jon B. 2007. "Iran's Nuclear Trajectory to 2015." In *North Korea and Iran: Nuclear Futures and Regional Responses.* NBR Special Report No. 13. Seattle: National Bureau of Asian Research.

Wright, Robin. 2007a. "U.S. Plans New Arms Sales to Gulf Allies." *Washington Post,* July 28.

———. 2007b. "U.S. to Seek New Sanctions Against Iran." *Washington Post,* November 16.

Yaphe, Judith S., and Charles D. Lutes. 2005. *Reassessing the Implications of a Nuclear-Armed Iran.* McNair Paper No. 69. Washington, D.C.: National Defense University Institute for National Strategic Studies.

Zaborski, Jason. 2005. "Deterring a Nuclear Iran." *Washington Quarterly* 28 (3): 153–67.

11

Nuclear Terrorism
Prospects in Asia

S. PAUL KAPUR

Most discussions of the implications of nuclear weapons for international security focus on the behavior of nation-states. However, nuclear weapons also could affect the global security environment through nonstate actors such as terrorists. Analysts disagree about the likelihood of terrorist groups using nuclear weapons. According to many accounts, nuclear terrorism may be impossible to avoid. Graham Allison, for example, argues that "a betting person" would have to conclude that nuclear terrorism is "inevitable" (Allison 2004: 14–15). Other analysts disagree with these gloomy predictions. Robin M. Frost, for example, maintains that "the risk of nuclear terrorism . . . is overstated, and . . . popular wisdom on the topic is significantly flawed" (Frost 2005: 7). As we consider the impact of nuclear weapons on twenty-first-century Asia, it is important to assess the threat of nuclear terrorism in the region. Are terrorist groups likely to use nuclear weapons in Asia?

This chapter argues that the odds of nuclear terrorism[1] occurring in Asia are low; none of the leading Asian terrorist groups are likely to possess both the desire to launch nuclear attacks in the region and the material resources necessary to do so. The chapter proceeds in two parts. The first part develops a conceptual framework for thinking about nuclear terrorism generally. In this section, I discuss basic prerequisites for terrorist groups that may desire to engage in nuclear terrorism, explore the ways in which such groups could employ a nuclear capability, and suggest strategies that target states can adopt in response to a terrorist nuclear threat. The second part evaluates the nuclear threat that ten major Asian terrorist groups pose to the region in light of the framework developed earlier.

Requirements for Terrorists to Use Nuclear Weapons

Before a terrorist group can attempt to use nuclear weapons, it must meet two basic requirements. First, the group must decide that it wishes to engage in nuclear terrorism. Analysts and policy makers often assume that terrorist groups necessarily want to do so (Carter 2004; U.S. Government 2002). However, it is not clear that terrorist organizations would necessarily covet nuclear devices. Although analysts often characterize terrorism as an irrational activity (Laqeuer 1999: 4–5), extensive empirical evidence indicates that terrorist groups in fact behave rationally, adopting strategies designed to achieve particular ends (Crenshaw 1995: 4; Pape 2003: 344). Thus whether terrorists would use nuclear weapons is contingent on whether doing so is likely to further their goals.

Under what circumstances could nuclear weapons fail to promote terrorists' goals? For certain types of terrorist objectives, nuclear weapons could be too destructive. Large-scale devastation could negatively influence audiences important to the terrorist groups. Terrorists often rely on populations sympathetic to their cause for political, financial, and military support. The horrific destruction of a nuclear explosion could alienate segments of this audience. People who otherwise would sympathize with the terrorists may conclude that in using a nuclear device terrorists had gone too far and were no longer deserving of support.

The catastrophic effects of nuclear weapons could also damage or destroy the very thing that the terrorist group most values. For example, if a terrorist organization were struggling with another group for control of their common homeland, the use of nuclear weapons against the enemy group would devastate the terrorists' own home territory. Using nuclear weapons would be extremely counterproductive for the terrorists in this scenario.

It is thus not obvious that all terrorist groups would use nuclear weapons. Some groups would probably not. The propensity for nuclear acquisition and use by terrorist groups must be assessed on a case-by-case basis.

If a terrorist group's goal can be advanced by the use of nuclear weapons, it would still need to meet a second important requirement: it would need to acquire a nuclear capability in the first place. It could do so either by procuring an intact weapon or by producing one. Terrorists could procure an intact weapon in two different ways. First, a nuclear state could voluntarily transfer a weapon to terrorists for use against a designated enemy. This could enable the state to inflict massive damage on the enemy while maintaining deniability and potentially avoiding retaliation (Ferguson and Potter 2004: 55–57). This occurrence, however, is unlikely. In this "transfer" scenario, the nuclear state would lose control of the weapon in question, forcing it to place enormous trust in the terrorists' loyalty and judgment. It is doubtful that a nuclear state's leaders would be willing to trust a terrorist organization to this degree (Ferguson and Potter 2004: 57; Glaser and Fetter 2001: 55–56).

Terrorist groups could also acquire an intact weapon by stealing it from a nuclear state. This would be an extremely difficult feat even for sophisticated terrorist groups. Nuclear weapons are protected by the most robust security measures that nation-states can devise. Protective measures include programs to ensure the reliability of the personnel in charge of weapons; extensive physical barriers, including location in heavily guarded, often isolated military bases; electronic systems to prevent unauthorized weapons use; and storage of the fissile core separate from the rest of the weapon. According to Ferguson and Potter, in the absence of significant insider assistance, theft of a nuclear weapon by terrorists is probably better described as "the stuff of fiction than a practicable approach for a terrorist organization." Even in the event of inside help or major political unrest within a nuclear weapon state, terrorist theft of an intact nuclear device would be difficult and unlikely (Bunn, Holdren, and Wier 2002: 5; Ferguson and Potter 2004: 57–65, 119).

Given the difficulty of acquiring an intact weapon, terrorists are more likely to attempt to construct their own nuclear device. To do so, terrorists would need fissile material, either highly enriched uranium (HEU) or plutonium. Enriching uranium and reprocessing plutonium are sufficiently complex as to require national-level capabilities. This would probably prove impossible for nonstate actors. Terrorist organizations would therefore most likely acquire material that has already been refined to weapons grade (Ferguson and Potter 2004: 119–20; May, Davis, and Jeanloz 2006: 907). Since it is easier to construct a nuclear device with HEU than with plutonium, terrorists are likely to opt for HEU. Approximately 50–60 kilograms of HEU would be needed to make a relatively simple, gun-type nuclear device similar to the one that the United States dropped on Hiroshima (Allison 2004: 95–98; Bunn, Holdren, and Wier 2002: 5).[2]

Acquiring weapon-grade fissile material would not be easy, but the challenge would be less formidable than securing an intact weapon. This is true for three reasons. First, a great deal of fissile material—approximately 450 metric tons of plutonium and 1,700 tons of HEU—exists throughout the world. Second, because fissile material exists in bulk, it cannot be as easily inventoried as nuclear weapons, and is susceptible to small-scale thefts over time. Finally, the measures in place to ensure the physical security of fissile material are less robust than those currently protecting states' nuclear weapon arsenals (Ferguson and Potter 2004: 106–9).

What resources would terrorists need in order to acquire fissile material and construct a nuclear device? Peter D. Zimmerman and Jeffrey G. Lewis offer the most comprehensive available cost analysis for such a project. According to their itemized budget, terrorists could acquire a Hiroshima-type nuclear device for less than US$5.5 million, purchasing black-market HEU for roughly US$4 million and spending US$1.4 million on construction and transportation of the weapon (Zimmerman and Lewis 2006: 36).[3]

Zimmerman and Lewis probably underestimate the cost of acquiring a nuclear weapon. As they point out, there exists only one known instance of criminals obtaining a significant quantity of HEU. In that 1994 case, a team of Czech and Slovak smugglers attempted to sell HEU to undercover police in Prague for US$1,600 per gram. At that price, the roughly 50 kilograms of HEU needed to fashion a device similar to the Hiroshima bomb would have cost approximately US$80 million. The smugglers were acting as middlemen for the uranium's Russian suppliers, who were willing to sell the material for only US$800 per gram (Zimmerman and Lewis 2006: 38). However, even if the terrorists had been able to acquire the uranium at the suppliers' price, 50 kilograms of HEU would have cost US$40 million, far above Zimmerman and Lewis's cost estimate.[4] Thus, unless the Czech case is an outlier, we should conclude that terrorists will probably need at least several tens of millions of dollars in order to acquire a Hiroshima-type nuclear device.[5]

Potential Terrorist Strategies

Once terrorist groups have acquired a nuclear weapon, they will need to decide what to do with it. A number of different strategies would be open to them. Terrorists need not detonate a nuclear device to "use" it against a target country; they could potentially achieve coercive leverage based simply on the fact that they possess a nuclear weapon. I therefore group potential terrorist strategies into two broad categories: passive strategies, which do not involve the detonation of a nuclear device, and active strategies, which involve nuclear detonation.[6]

Terrorists could employ passive strategies to achieve deterrence against target countries, threatening to launch a nuclear attack if the targets take certain proscribed actions. Alternatively, terrorists could passively use nuclear weapons to compel target countries to deviate from the status quo, threatening to launch nuclear attacks unless the targets act in certain prescribed ways.[7] Active strategies may be employed in a number of different scenarios. First, terrorist groups might detonate a nuclear device at the beginning of a deterrent or compellent campaign to signal their capability. Second, they could detonate a nuclear weapon in the course of a deterrent or compellent campaign to punish a target state that has not complied with their demands. Finally, terrorist groups may explode a nuclear device not as part of a coercive strategy but simply to inflict damage on a target state. Terrorists could desire to damage a target state to exact revenge for some perceived misdeed, to trigger an expected apocalypse, or simply because they derive utility from causing large-scale death and destruction.

What strategies could target states adopt in order to protect themselves against this range of possible nuclear terrorism? Ideally, states would prevent terrorist groups from even trying to attack them with nuclear weapons. This would require potential target states to devise effective deterrent strategies. Most broadly, states could adopt two types of strategies: deterrence by denial and deterrence by punishment. Deterrence by denial would seek to dissuade terrorists from trying to launch a nuclear attack by convincing them that doing so is likely to be unsuccessful and therefore not worth the cost of the attempt. Deterrence by punishment would seek to dissuade terrorists by convincing them that the target state will retaliate, and the costs to the terrorists of this retaliation will outweigh the benefits of even a successful nuclear strike.[8]

Deterrence by denial would require target states to develop the ability to ensure that any attempted nuclear attack against them would be unsuccessful. Target states could do so either by thwarting an attack in progress or by derailing attempts to acquire a nuclear capability in the first place. Stopping an attack in progress would be highly challenging. Apprehending terrorists as they smuggled either nuclear materials or the components of a preexisting nuclear weapon into the target state would require effective policing of long borders and coastlines and monitoring the enormous volume of goods coming into the country through ports of entry. Once an assembled nuclear weapon was inside the target state, finding it before it was used would require highly accurate, real-time intelligence, which would be difficult to obtain (Allison 2004: 119–20). Terrorists could also attack the target state using a nuclear-armed boat or aircraft, rather than attempting to smuggle a nuclear device or nuclear materials into that state. In order to thwart such an attack, the target state would have to intercept the weapon before it reached its target. This again would require effective border and coastline defense.[9]

Preventing terrorist groups from acquiring a nuclear weapon capability would be somewhat easier. This could be done by ensuring that terrorists do not have access to nuclear materials. Keeping HEU and plutonium out of terrorists' hands would be difficult but not impossible. The international community knows the location of fissile material stockpiles around the world. Thus, cutting terrorist access to fissile materials does not require highly accurate intelligence or sophisticated technologies. What is required is the political will to devise and implement rigorous physical protection regimes for fissile material stockpiles. Some aspects of a robust physical protection regime would include enhanced screening and monitoring of personnel at nuclear facilities and fissile material storage sites; repair of crumbling security infrastructure such as fences, gates, walls, and doors; installation of electronic surveillance devices at storage locations; and independent audits of nuclear security measures (Allison 2004: 150). Implementing such a regime would significantly increase the difficulty of acquiring the ingredients necessary for terrorist groups to construct a nuclear device.[10]

Deterrence by punishment poses a set of difficulties quite different from those of deterrence by denial. The biggest problem associated with a punishment strategy is that terrorists are nonstate actors and often are prepared to die in pursuit of their objectives. Thus, a punishment campaign against nuclear terrorists would potentially be hobbled by two factors: (1) the target state would not know whom or what to punish, and (2) even lethal retaliation by the target state might not be sufficient to convince terrorists that the costs of launching a nuclear attack would outweigh the benefits of doing so.

Although these are serious problems, in certain cases they can be mitigated. A punishment strategy can be made effective through the targeting of third parties. For example, terrorist leaders who may personally welcome death may nonetheless fear the demise of their loved ones or the destruction of their homelands. States may be able to deter terrorists by threatening to punish such targets in the event of a nuclear attack. Also, terrorist groups may be supported by nation-states, which provide them with training, weapons, financial backing, and a territorial base. The leaders of these states may wish to support the terrorists, but may not be willing to face death or ouster in order to do so. In such scenarios, target countries can threaten to punish states that support nuclear terrorism. Such a threat could deter states from providing terrorists the aid necessary to launch nuclear attacks. Target countries can thus seek to achieve deterrence through third-party punishment strategies even where terrorist groups themselves are impervious to punishment.

Nuclear Terrorism in the Asian Security Region

What implications does the above discussion have for our assessment of the risks of nuclear terrorism in Asia? Are terrorist groups in Asia likely to use nuclear weapons, and in what ways might they do so? What strategies could regional states deploy against this danger? To answer these questions, I examine the ten Asian terrorist groups listed in the U.S. Department of State's report "Patterns of Global Terrorism 2003." While this list is not exhaustive, it is likely to include the most important and capable regional groups. To assess their propensity for nuclear terrorism, I consider the following questions.

1. Is this group likely to want to acquire and use a nuclear weapon if it could do so? In answering this question, I examine three factors. First, I assess the nature of the terrorist group's goals and determine whether they could plausibly be furthered through the use of nuclear weapons. Second, I determine the territorial relationship between the terrorist group's homeland and the group's likely targets. If the group's homeland is in or very near the vicinity of its likely targets, I assume that the group would be unlikely to engage in nuclear attacks, since it would not wish to destroy or damage its home territory.[11] Third, I assess the audiences that support the terrorists and determine whether nuclear use would be likely to alienate them.

2. If it used nuclear weapons, would the terrorist group or a patron state be vulnerable to retaliation by the target? If the group seeks goals related to the independence or well-being of a population in a particular territory, I assume that the target populations could punish that territory in retaliation for a nuclear attack.[12] This increases the likelihood that the terrorists could be deterred from attacking the target state with nuclear weapons. If the terrorist group is supported by a friendly nation-state, I assume that the supporting state could be targeted for attack and potentially deterred from supporting the terrorist group. This reduces the likelihood that the group would be able to engage in nuclear attacks.
3. Is the terrorist group likely to be able to acquire nuclear weapons? Here I focus on the terrorist group's financial resources. I assume that if the group has access to several tens of millions of dollars, it possesses the minimum resources needed to acquire a nuclear device.[13]
4. If the terrorist group were to employ nuclear weapons, would it do so actively or passively? If the group has apocalyptic or other primarily destructive goals, I assume that it could use a nuclear weapon actively, without warning, and without attempting to influence the behavior of the target state. If, however, the group has political or territorial goals beyond mere destruction, I assume that it would be likely to use nuclear weapons passively to achieve either deterrence or compellence.[14]

The section below applies this framework to the ten terrorist groups in the U.S. Department of State's report.[15]

Abu Sayyaf

The Abu Sayyaf Group (ASG) is a Muslim separatist organization operating in the southern Philippine provinces of Basilan, Sulu, and Tawi-Tawi. Its membership of 200 to 500 comprises several semiautonomous factions. The group split from the Moro National Liberation Front in the early 1990s. Since then, ASG has engaged in killings, kidnappings, and bombings. The group periodically claims that it seeks to establish an independent Islamic state in Western Mindanao and the Sulu Archipelago. However, the group is also motivated by the desire for financial gain. ASG generally finances its own operations, though it may receive aid from Islamic groups in the Middle East and South Asia (Jane's 2006b; U.S. Department of State 2004: 114–15).

ASG could use the threat of a nuclear attack to extort money from the Philippine government or to prevent the government from interfering in its activities. Nuclear terrorism could also garner useful publicity; the group has previously used high-visibility attacks in the Philippine capital of Manila to advertise its cause and to create an impression of strength (International Crisis Group 2005: 1).

ASG does not face major impediments to the use of nuclear weapons on the basis of proximity to target, audience alienation, or patron-state coercion. ASG's area of operation is not sufficiently close to Manila to prevent the group from using a nuclear weapon there. Because ASG is mostly self-funding, it does not need to worry that nuclear terrorism could alienate critical financial backers. External support for the group comes primarily from Islamic militants in the Middle East and South Asia, who would be unlikely to react negatively if ASG resorted to nuclear terror. And the group's relatively self-sufficient nature also means that it is not dependent on the support of a nation-state patron. Therefore, the Philippine government or its allies could not defend against ASG nuclear terrorism by threatening to punish a third-party patron state.

Would ASG be able to acquire nuclear weapons if it wished to do so? The likelihood of ASG acquiring nuclear weapons seems slight. With only 200 to 500 members, and the majority of its finances coming from ransom and extortion, it is doubtful that the group could muster the several tens of millions of dollars necessary to acquire fissile material and to construct a nuclear device. ASG may also lack the focus necessary to acquire nuclear weapons. During the late 1990s the group became a largely bandit organization, motivated by greed and governed by idiosyncratic leaders who employed haphazard strategies and enforced intermittent discipline (Abuza 2003: 189–90; Clark 2002; Gershman 2002; Rogers 2004). This trend appears to have been slowed or reversed after 2002 with the emergence of new leaders dedicated to Abu Sayyaf's separatist mission, and by ASG's establishment of closer ties with domestic separatist organizations such as the Moro Islamic Liberation Front and international terrorist groups such as Jemaah Islamiya. Still, ASG possesses limited command and control, discipline, or organizational unity (Abuza 2005; see also Kuppuswamy 2002a, 2002b).

If ASG were to use nuclear weapons against the Philippine government, what strategy would it most likely employ? The group's goals include the establishment of an independent Muslim state in the Sulu Archipelago and the extortion of monies from the victims of its kidnappings and other crimes. Both goals require the group's adversary to change its behavior, in one case withdrawing from the southern Philippines and in the other paying money to ASG. If ASG engaged in nuclear terrorism, it would therefore be likely to adopt a passive compellent strategy. ASG would threaten to use a nuclear device unless the Philippine government either withdrew from the Sulu Archipelago or paid the ASG a sufficient ransom.

However, despite its potential attraction, such a strategy could also inflict serious costs on ASG. To the extent that ASG seeks to establish the independence of the Sulu Archipelago, the group cares about the region. Government punishment of the area in retaliation for a nuclear attack could severely undermine ASG's goals and make nuclear terrorism undesirable to the group.[16] If ASG is motivated primarily by the desire for financial profit, it might be willing to risk government retaliation against the southern Philippines. However, in this scenario the group would be vulnerable to threats against its leaders and their families. The ASG leadership would probably be unwilling to sacrifice their lives, along with their loved ones, for mere financial gain.

Overall, the threat of nuclear terrorism from ASG seems low. In principle the group's goals could lend themselves well to nuclear compellent strategies, and it does not face a number of impediments to nuclear use. However, the group's concern for the well-being of the Sulu Archipelago, and for its leadership's survival, should reduce its willingness to invite punishment by the Philippine government. And its small size, limited finances, and lack of centralized discipline make it quite unlikely that ASG would be able to acquire a nuclear weapon in the first place.

Aum Shinrikyo

Aum Shinrikyo is a Japanese cult that was established in 1987 with the goal of taking over the world, starting with Japan. Eventually, the Aum came to stress the imminence of Armageddon, which it believed would be triggered when the United States attacked Japan and began World War III. Aum Shinrikyo was responsible for a series of chemical accidents and failed biological attacks in Japan, as well as a 1995 sarin gas attack on the Tokyo subway system. At the time of the Tokyo attack, the Aum possessed assets in the range of US$300 million to US$1 billion[17] and claimed a worldwide membership of 40,000. The Japanese government subsequently seized the group's assets and incarcerated its founder, Shoko Asahara. Asahara was sentenced to death in 2004. Current estimates of the Aum's size range from fewer than 1,000 to approximately 1,500 members. It generates funds by soliciting donations, organizing seminars, and selling literature and computers. The group is not known to receive any external assistance (Memorial Institute for the Prevention of Terrorism 2006; Rosenau 2001: 291; U.S. Department of State 2004: 117–18).[18]

Aum Shinrikyo would almost certainly wish to acquire and use nuclear weapons. Because the group believes that Armageddon is imminent, it would view widespread nuclear destruction as part of an inevitable apocalypse. Additionally, the Aum does not rely for support on any domestic or international audiences or patron states that might be vulnerable to retaliation and act as a check on its behavior. And as it does not seek the well-being of any particular population or territory, Aum Shinrikyo would not be deterred by threats to punish high-value targets.

If Aum Shinrikyo wished to engage in nuclear terrorism, would it be able to do so? During the 1990s, the group made serious but unsuccessful attempts both to develop and to purchase a nuclear weapon (Daly, Parachini, and Rosenau 2005: 10–20; see also Cameron 1999: 285–87). These failures occurred when Aum

Shinrikyo was at the height of its capabilities, with tens of thousands of members and hundreds of millions of dollars at its disposal (Rosenau 2001: 291). Now, with its vastly diminished size and funding, it is doubtful that the Aum would be able to secure nuclear materials and construct a nuclear device.

If Aum Shinrikyo were somehow able to acquire nuclear weapons, and sought to use them in a terrorist campaign, what strategy would the group employ? Aum Shinrikyo's millenarian philosophy seeks mass-casualty destruction. Thus the Aum would likely adopt an active strategy, attacking its targets without warning to maximize the destructive effect.

Overall, the threat of nuclear terrorism from Aum Shinrikyo is small. In principle, the group's millenarian philosophy and lack of external constraints could make it a strong candidate to engage in nuclear terrorism. However, even at its zenith, the Aum was unable to acquire a nuclear device. Now, with its vastly reduced size and resources, it is highly unlikely that the group would be able to do so.

Communist Party of the Philippines/New People's Army

The New People's Army (NPA) is the military faction of the Communist Party of the Philippines. The NPA, formed in 1969, seeks to overthrow the Philippine government through guerrilla warfare. The NPA has cells in Manila and other cities, but is primarily a rural organization, operating in Luzon, Visayas, and Mindanao. The NPA's operations have targeted Philippine security forces, politicians, judges, rival factions, and U.S. military personnel. The group numbers between 7,500 and 8,000 members, at least one-fifth of whom are under 18 years of age. The NPA receives the majority of its funding from supporters in the Philippines and in Europe, as well as from criminal activities such as extortion, kidnapping, and smuggling (Jane's 2006d; U.S. Department of State 2004: 118–19).

The NPA seems unlikely to want to acquire and use nuclear weapons, regardless of possible government threats of retaliation against the group or its supporters. The group rails against the injustice of what it describes as "semifeudal" and "semicolonial" sociopolitical conditions in the Philippines and seeks to replace the Philippine government with a Maoist regime (Communist Party of the Philippines 1994). Its specific agenda includes land reform, national industrialization, and wage increases (Communist Party of the Philippines 2001). The group thus cares about the well-being of Filipino workers and peasants and would probably not inflict long-term, mass-casualty damage on them by resorting to nuclear terrorism. Furthermore, the NPA relies for financial support on audiences in the Philippines and in Europe. These audiences might well view nuclear devastation as being incompatible with the goal of improving the lot of Filipino workers and peasants. Moreover, Philippines-based supporters might suffer personal harm if the NPA used a nuclear weapon in the country.

It is difficult to determine whether the NPA would be able to acquire a nuclear device if it decided to engage in nuclear terrorism. Although the group receives substantial overseas financial assistance, the amount of its external aid is unknown. The size of the NPA's membership is significant and is apparently growing. Thus while the NPA's status as a rural guerrilla group would seem to make its possession of sufficient resources to acquire nuclear weapons highly unlikely, the group's size and overseas support mean that the possibility cannot be completely discounted.

If the NPA sought to use nuclear weapons in a terrorist campaign, what strategy would it most likely employ? The group's goal would be to compel the government to relinquish control of some or all of the Philippines. Thus a passive compellence strategy, in which the NPA threatened to detonate a nuclear device unless the Philippine government made significant territorial concessions, would be the most appropriate approach. However, it is doubtful that such a strategy would be successful; the probability that the Philippine government would relinquish control over significant portions of its national territory upon being threatened with the detonation of one or two nuclear devices is very small.

Overall, the likelihood that the NPA would engage in nuclear terrorism seems low. Nuclear coercion would not be an appropriate strategy for the NPA to employ in pursuit of its goals. The group also faces a number of impediments to the use of nuclear weapons, including the problem of inflicting massive, long-term damage on a country that it wishes to control, and a high risk of alienating important audiences. Finally, as a rural guerrilla organization, the group probably lacks the resources necessary to acquire a nuclear weapon.

Harakat ul-Mujahidin

Harakat ul-Mujahidin (HUM) is a Pakistan-based militant organization that operates in Kashmir. It is the successor to Harakat ul-Ansar (HUA), which changed its name to Harakat ul-Mujahidin after the United States designated HUA as a terrorist organization in 1997. HUM seeks to wrest Jammu and Kashmir from Indian control and join the territory to Pakistan. The group's past operations include attacks on Indian troops and civilian targets in Kashmir and the hijacking of an Indian Airlines plane to Afghanistan in December 1999. The group's several hundred members include Pakistanis, Kashmiris, Afghans, and Arabs, some of whom are veterans of the Afghan war against the Soviet Union. HUM receives financial support from Saudi Arabia and other Persian Gulf states, as well as from individuals in Pakistan and Kashmir. It has also received extensive financial and military assistance from the Pakistani government (Jane's 2006f; Santhanam, Sreedhar, Saxena, and Manish 2003: 104–5; South Asia Terrorism Portal 2001a, 2001b; U.S. Department of State 2004: 120–21).

HUM has advocated the use of Pakistan's nuclear weapons against India (Jane's 2006f) and might wish to employ nuclear terrorism either to force an Indian withdrawal from Kashmir or simply to inflict damage on India. However, given HUM's dependence on Pakistan, it probably could not acquire and use a nuclear device without Pakistani support. The likelihood of Pakistan approving such a project is very small. Any attempted terrorist nuclear coercion of India would immediately be blamed on Pakistan, subjecting that country to intense diplomatic and conventional military pressure, as well as to threats of nuclear retaliation. Similarly, if a nuclear detonation occurred within India, the attack would undoubtedly be blamed on Pakistan, with potentially catastrophic results. Thus despite Pakistan's devotion to the Kashmir cause, it is highly unlikely that Islamabad would support a terrorist group such as HUM using nuclear weapons against India.[19]

This does not rule out the possibility of Islamist factions within Pakistan's military or intelligence services facilitating HUM's acquisition and use of a nuclear device without official government approval. The historical record suggests both that such Islamist factions could exist within Pakistan's military and that Pakistan's nuclear security regime may be unable to prevent unauthorized nuclear transfers. For example, in 1995 elements within the military planned to stage a coup that would have made Pakistan a Sunni state governed according to Islamic law (Jones 2002: 254–56). And the A. Q. Khan nuclear proliferation scandal, in which Pakistan's premier nuclear official supplied nuclear technology to countries including Iran and North Korea, demonstrated the woeful inadequacy of nuclear security in Pakistan (Braun and Chyba 2004: 15–18; Ferguson and Potter 2004: 57).

However, Pakistan has since instituted measures to improve nuclear security. In 2001, General Musharraf replaced several flag-rank officers whom he believed to be too closely allied with Islamist elements (Zubrzycki 2001). And Pakistan has undertaken a wide range of institutional reforms, including the creation of a National Command Authority, to increase the security of its nuclear weapons and fissile material (Federation of American Scientists 2000). The danger of unauthorized transfer of Pakistani nuclear weapons or materials to a group such as HUM, while real, would appear to be declining.

If HUM were able to acquire nuclear weapons and sought to use them in a terrorist campaign, what strategy would the group most likely employ? HUM's strategy would probably depend on the goals of the faction within the Pakistan security establishment that supports nuclear terrorism. If the faction's goal were simply to inflict damage on India, HUM would most likely adopt an active strategy, detonating a nuclear device in India without warning, in a manner calculated to maximize death and destruction. If the faction's goal were to coerce India into making concessions on Kashmir, then HUM would be more likely to adopt a passive compellent strategy, threatening to detonate a nuclear weapon unless India made significant territorial or political concessions.

Overall, the likelihood of nuclear terrorism by HUM appears low. The group faces serious impediments to nuclear use, including reliance on a patron state that would suffer significant diplomatic and military consequences if HUM engaged in such behavior. Although it is possible that factions within the Pakistani security apparatus could assist HUM in acquiring nuclear weapons or materials without authorization, the threat of such an occurrence will recede as Pakistan purges its security forces of radical elements and enhances its nuclear security regime.

Lashkar-e-Tayyiba

Lashkar-e-Tayyiba (LeT) is the militant wing of Markaz-ud-Dawa-wal-Irshad, a Pakistani religious organization. Based in the Pakistani cities of Muridke and Muzaffarabad, LeT engages in violent attacks on Indian military and civilian targets in Jammu and Kashmir. It seeks to oust India from Jammu and Kashmir and to Islamize the South Asian region. The Indian government has implicated LeT in a December 2001 attack on the Indian parliament in New Delhi. The group has several thousand members and receives financial support from the Pakistani community in the Persian Gulf and United Kingdom, as well as from Islamic nongovernmental organizations. LeT also receives extensive financial and military assistance from Pakistan security services (Jane's 2006c; Santhanam, Sreedhar, Saxena, and Manish 2003: 224–26; South Asia Terrorism Portal 2001e; U.S. Department of State 2004: 126–27).

The case of LeT is similar to that of HUM. The group might want to use nuclear weapons in an effort either to compel the Indians to withdraw from Jammu and Kashmir or simply to inflict damage on India. However, given its reliance on Pakistan, the group could probably not acquire and use a nuclear weapon without Islamabad's approval. Such approval would be highly unlikely, given the dangers to Pakistan that would result from a terrorist nuclear attack on India. As in the case of HUM, it is possible that individuals within the Pakistan security apparatus could facilitate LeT's acquisition and use of a nuclear weapon without official sanction. However, as noted above, improving Pakistani nuclear security is making such a possibility less likely. Overall, then, LeT is not a good candidate to engage in nuclear terrorism.

Jaish-e-Mohammed

Jaish-e-Mohammed (JEM) is another Pakistan-based terrorist organization that seeks to unite Kashmir with Pakistan. It also wishes to transform Pakistan into an Islamist state. The Indian government implicated the group in the December 2001 attack on the Indian parliament. JEM also initially claimed responsibility for an attack on the Jammu and Kashmir legislature in October 2001. The group is several hundred strong and receives extensive material and personnel support from other militant organizations such as HUM, as well as from the Pakistan security services (Jane's 2006e; Santhanam, Sreedhar, Saxena, and Manish 2003: 197–98, 200; South Asia Terrorism Portal 2001c; U.S. Department of State 2004: 123).

JEM is similar in important ways to HUM and LeT. Like those two groups, JEM could use nuclear weapons to compel India to withdraw from Jammu and Kashmir or to damage India. However, JEM, like the other two groups, relies heavily on Pakistan and probably could not acquire and use a nuclear weapon without Islamabad's approval. Such approval, as noted earlier, would be very unlikely. It is possible that individuals within the Pakistani security apparatus could facilitate JEM's acquisition and use of a nuclear weapon without official sanction. However, as noted above, improving nuclear security in Pakistan is making such a possibility less probable. Overall, then, JEM seems unlikely to engage in nuclear terrorism.

Lashkar-i-Jhangvi

Lashkar-i-Jhangvi (LiJ) is a small, Pakistan-based terrorist organization active in Punjab and Karachi. Numbering no more than a few hundred members, the group seeks to transform Pakistan into a Sunni Islamist state and to have the Shia declared as nonbelievers. It carries out attacks primarily against Pakistan's Shia community (Jane's 2006g; South Asia Terrorism Portal 2001d; U.S. Department of State 2004: 127). Nuclear weapons would not be a useful tool in LiJ's campaign of sectarian violence, regardless of the government's ability to retaliate against the group or its supporters. It is not possible for LiJ to use nuclear weapons to target only Pakistani Shiites; a nuclear explosion would kill a large number of Sunnis as well. Additionally, a nuclear detonation would devastate Lashkar-i-Jhangvi's home territory. Neither outcome would further LiJ's goals. Moreover, it is highly doubtful that such a small, provincial group would possess the resources necessary to acquire a nuclear weapon. Lashkar-i-Jhangvi thus would appear to be unlikely to engage in nuclear terrorism.

Jemaah Islamiya

Jemaah Islamiya (JI) is a predominantly Southeast Asian terrorist network with cells in Indonesia, Malaysia, the Philippines, southern Thailand, Pakistan, and other neighboring countries. The group seeks to create an Islamic state that would include Brunei, Indonesia, Malaysia, Singapore, the southern Philippines, and southern Thailand. JI has undertaken numerous attacks in Indonesia and the Philippines, including the Bali bombings of October 2002. Estimates of the group's membership vary from less than 500 to approximately 750 members. JI receives financial and logistical support from parties in the Middle East and South

Asia, including Al-Qaeda (Abuza 2003: 169; Jane's 2005b; U.S. Department of State 2004: 123–24).

It is possible that Jemaah Islamiya would attempt to acquire and use a nuclear device. The group could potentially use a nuclear weapon against parts of Thailand or the Philippines without inflicting undue damage on territories that it wishes to control. Also, the use of nuclear weapons might not alienate JI's Islamist, nonstate financial and logistical supporters in South Asia and the Middle East. Finally, JI does not rely for patronage on a nation-state that could be harmed if the group engaged in nuclear terrorism. Thus some of the impediments to the use of nuclear weapons that exist for other groups would not prevent JI from engaging in nuclear terrorism.

Despite this lack of impediments, it is not clear that nuclear terrorism would be an appropriate means for JI to achieve its political goals. It is unlikely that the Thai, Philippine, Malaysian, or Singaporean governments would relinquish control over significant portions of their national territories to avoid a threatened nuclear detonation. Further, the terrorists' threat to launch nuclear attacks in these countries would probably lack credibility; unless it restricted attacks to northern Thailand and the northern Philippines, JI would be threatening to devastate areas that it wants to control and about which it ostensibly cares.

Could JI acquire a nuclear device if it wanted to do so? The group is not particularly large and lacks the support of a nation-state patron. However, it does have access to a network of international financial and logistical support, the members of which include well-financed and organizationally sophisticated groups such as Al-Qaeda. Thus although the acquisition of nuclear weapons would pose enormous challenges, the possibility cannot be wholly ruled out.

If JI did decide to engage in nuclear terrorism, what sort of strategy would it likely adopt? The group would probably launch a passive compellent campaign, threatening to detonate a nuclear device in one or more of the target countries unless their governments made major territorial or political concessions. Target-state governments would face significant constraints in responding to such a compellent campaign, since punishing regions in which the group operates would mean attacking the governments' own territories. And target states would not be able to punish third countries, since JI does not rely on any patron state.

Overall, the threat of JI's engaging in nuclear terrorism appears to be low. The group does not face problems of audience alienation or patron-state vulnerability and could conceivably attack some targets without damaging the territory that it desires to control. However, the group is small and most likely lacks the resources to acquire nuclear weapons. More important, nuclear weapons are not a useful tool to achieve its political goals. The threatened detonation of one or two nuclear devices is unlikely to convince the governments of Malaysia, Thailand, the Philippines, or Singapore to relinquish control over their home territories.

And the threat to launch such nuclear attacks would lack credibility, as they could devastate areas that JI seeks to control. Thus the effort to acquire and use nuclear weapons would probably not be worth the effort for a group such as JI. It would be better off pursuing its goals using subconventional warfare.

Liberation Tigers of Tamil Elam

The Liberation Tigers of Tamil Elam (LTTE) seek to establish an independent Tamil state in Sri Lanka. The group combines guerrilla warfare with terrorist tactics such as bombings and political assassinations. LTTE members have historically been prolific suicide bombers. Their suicide operations have included the 1991 assassination of former Indian Prime Minister Rajiv Gandhi, who was responsible for India's intervention in Sri Lanka during the late 1980s. LTTE consists of approximately 8,000 to 10,000 armed combatants in Sri Lanka, where it controls most of the northern and eastern coastal regions. The group does not depend on a patron state, but rather receives financial, military, and propaganda support from an extensive network of overseas Tamil communities in Europe, North America, and Asia (Jane's 2006a; Pape 2003: 343; U.S. Department of State 2004: 128–29).

It is unlikely that LTTE would want to acquire and use nuclear weapons. The Tigers have been fighting the Sri Lankan government to establish an independent state on the island. Given Sri Lanka's confined geography, any use of nuclear weapons against the Sri Lankan government would also likely inflict significant damage on the areas that LTTE wants to rule. Might the Tigers use nuclear weapons against India, to prevent Indian involvement in the Sri Lankan conflict? India did intervene in Sri Lanka in 1987. However, India withdrew in 1990 after three years of costly and ineffectual operations (Ispahani 1992: 211–39). India shows no appetite for becoming militarily involved in Sri Lanka once again. Thus there would be little need for LTTE to use the threat of nuclear terrorism to deter an Indian intervention. Moreover, if the Tigers did use a nuclear device against India, they would be vulnerable to catastrophic Indian retaliation. Finally, the large-scale civilian casualties that would result from any use of nuclear weapons would run counter to stated LTTE policy; the Tigers have publicly eschewed attacks on civilian targets in an attempt to enhance their status as freedom fighters and avoid being branded as terrorists (Hoffman 2006: 144).

If the Tigers decided to pursue a policy of nuclear terrorism, they would be relatively well placed to acquire a nuclear device. LTTE can draw on extensive international financial support and a sophisticated logistical network. These capabilities have enabled LTTE to assemble "one of the best trained and equipped nonstate military forces in the world—complete with armored and artillery units . . . its own blue- and brown-water navies . . . [an] embryonic air capability . . . a commando and special reconnaissance force, many portable surface-to-air missiles, and . . . suicide attack units" (Hoffman 2006: 142). Additionally, the group controls territory in Sri

Lanka where it could work on constructing a weapon relatively unmolested. Thus while acquiring a nuclear device would undoubtedly be challenging, the LTTE would seem better equipped to do so than many other terrorist groups.

If LTTE did acquire a nuclear device and decided to undertake a campaign of nuclear terror, what type of strategy would it adopt? Against the Sri Lankan government, the group would probably engage in a passive compellent campaign, threatening to use a nuclear device unless the government made significant territorial and political concessions. Against the Indians, the Tigers would probably launch a passive deterrent campaign, threatening to detonate a nuclear device in India if that country intervened in Sri Lanka.

Overall, the threat of nuclear terrorism from LTTE appears to be low. The use of nuclear weapons against the Sri Lankan government would be counterproductive, as it would damage the Tigers' own home territory. Nuclear use against India would probably be unnecessary and would invite costly retaliation. And the massive civilian casualties resulting from any nuclear attack would run counter to stated Tiger policy and undermine its status as a liberation force. Thus despite their ferocity and extensive resources, the Tamil Tigers are not a likely candidate to engage in nuclear terror.

Al-Qaeda

Al-Qaeda seeks to expel Westerners and non-Muslims from Islamic countries and to establish an international Islamic caliphate. The group has carried out a number of deadly, high-profile operations, including the simultaneous bombings of the U.S. embassies in Kenya and Tanzania in 1998, the attack on USS *Cole* in 2000, and the attacks of 9/11 in 2001. Al-Qaeda was based in Afghanistan until coalition forces ousted the Taliban following the 9/11 attacks. The organization is now splintered into small groups in South and Southeast Asia and the Middle East. It has several thousand members. The group secures funds from an international network of front businesses, charitable organizations, and individual supporters (Jane's 2005a; U.S. Department of State 2004: 131–33).

Al-Qaeda has publicly announced its interest in nuclear weapons, calling for their use to defend Muslims against "Jews and crusaders" and to inflict maximum harm on the United States (Abu Ghaith 2002; Daly, Parachini, and Rosenau 2005: 25). However, any nuclear attack would probably occur in the United States, Europe, or Israel rather than in the Asian region. If Al-Qaeda's goal is to use nuclear weapons against Americans, "crusaders," and Jews, Asian states are not a logical target. Al-Qaeda's past operations in Asia have attacked specific Western interests, such as synagogues, hotels, or nightclubs, but have not attempted to inflict large-scale damage.

Al-Qaeda would seem to be in a strong position to acquire a nuclear weapon. The group has a large number of members and affiliates, a sophisticated financial and organizational network, and resources that may reach into the hundreds of millions of dollars (Abuza 2003: 170; Daly, Parachini, and Rosenau 2005: 28). It may also possess relevant scientific expertise (Albright and Higgins 2003; Bergen 2006: 340). And although the group lost its territorial base with the ouster of the Taliban from Afghanistan, the no-man's land between Pakistan and Afghanistan could offer it a place to develop a nuclear weapon capability in relative safety.

Despite these advantages, a number of the group's past attempts to acquire nuclear weapons or technologies apparently failed. For example, in the early 1990s, Al-Qaeda operatives purchased material they believed to be uranium stolen from Russia, but in fact it was low-grade reactor fuel of no weapons value. And documents captured in Afghanistan suggest that the group possessed little nuclear expertise or capability as of late 2001 (Cameron 1999: 289; Daly, Parachini, and Rosenau 2005: 31, 37–39). The loss of its Afghan base and the death or capture of many of its key leaders has degraded Al-Qaeda's coordination capabilities, and this may seriously hobble the group's efforts to acquire nuclear weapons in the future (Bergen 2006: 349; Jenkins 2002: 11–12).

Even if it were capable of obtaining a nuclear weapon, the likelihood of Al-Qaeda launching a nuclear terrorist campaign in Asia is low. Al-Qaeda's primary interest is not inflicting mass-casualty damage on Asian countries. Rather, it seeks to compel the United States and other Western powers to withdraw from Muslim states in the region and to kill as many Americans as possible. Given these goals, if Al-Qaeda were able to procure a nuclear device, the group, as mentioned previously, would be more likely to detonate it in the United States, Europe, or Israel than in Asia.

Policy Implications

The above analysis suggests that the likelihood of nuclear terrorism in Asia is low. Nonetheless, the effects of a nuclear attack, if it occurred, would be catastrophic. Thus despite its low probability of occurrence, the expected cost of a nuclear terrorist attack remains significant. In addition to the deterrent strategies outlined above, what policies can states adopt to minimize the likelihood of a nuclear terrorist attack?

First, states should identify which groups are likely to find nuclear terrorism attractive and focus their energies on thwarting the efforts of those organizations in particular. As we have seen, the number of groups in Asia for whom nuclear terrorism could be a useful strategy is small. Asian states should devote their energies especially to defeating those key groups, rather than assuming that all terrorist organizations in the region are likely to employ nuclear weapons and wasting resources by focusing on them equally.

Second, to retaliate against nuclear terrorists, states must be able to identify the source of a nuclear weapon in the wake of an attack. This process of nuclear attribution would use techniques ranging from satellite imagery to mass spectrometry to determine the sophistication of the nuclear device, the isotopics and efficiency of its fuel, and potentially the materials used to construct it. These factors, in turn, could enable investigators to identify the origin of the nuclear material and the actors behind the attack (Davis 2003; May, Davis, and Jeanloz 2006). Despite its importance, nuclear attribution remains a highly uncertain endeavor (Davis 2003). Thus it is not clear that states would currently be able to identify the source of nuclear material in the wake of its detonation. Given the importance of nuclear attribution for the credibility of deterrence, states should make the improvement of their nuclear forensic capabilities a high priority.

Third, Asian states need to realize that their own policies and actions can foster terrorism. India's heavy-handed policies in Kashmir, for example, helped spur the separatist movement responsible for terrorist violence in the region. Political solutions that incorporate the concerns of aggrieved groups may be the best insurance against nuclear terror (Pape 2003: 344, 357).[20] Despite the potential merits of such an approach, accommodation also has its dangers. If states appear overly conciliatory, terrorists may become emboldened to employ further violence against them. As Pape explains, terrorists undertake suicide attacks because they believe that such measures are effective; states have repeatedly made territorial concessions in the face of suicide terrorist campaigns (Pape 2003: 350). If this is correct, however, Pape's prescription that states should alter their foreign policies to avoid antagonizing terrorists may be self-defeating. By reinforcing the lesson that terrorism is effective, such an approach would probably invite more of it. This is not to argue that Asian states should needlessly adhere to policies that create resentment and spur regional violence. But states should recognize that they can also encourage violence if they are perceived to be surrendering in the face of terrorist threats. They will thus need to maintain a delicate balance between accommodation and perceived capitulation.

Notes

1. The United States Code defines terrorism as "premeditated, politically motivated violence perpetrated against noncombatant targets by subnational groups or clandestine agents," Title 22 United States Code sec. 2656f(d). I define nuclear terrorism as the detonation of a nuclear device in this manner. I do not include in my definition the detonation of a radiological device, or "dirty bomb," which would utilize a conventional explosive to disperse radioactive material. I exclude a radiological denotation because a nuclear explosion, while less likely to occur, would be far more destructive, potentially obliterating miles of infrastructure, killing hundreds of thousands of people, and wounding and sickening hundreds of thousands more (Allison 2004: 4–5; Ferguson and Potter 2004: 7, 265–67, 270–71; see also Falkenrath 1998: 48–50). Also, the technical requirements for construction of a dirty bomb differ substantially from those of an actual nuclear device.

Thus nuclear terrorism is qualitatively different from radiological terrorism and should be analyzed separately from it.

2. A "gun-type" weapon achieves detonation by firing an HEU projectile down a barrel into a hollowed uranium target. This was the design of the weapon used on Hiroshima during World War II and of the weapons that constituted South Africa's nuclear arsenal. A plutonium device, by contrast, requires the symmetrical implosion of its fissile core, triggered by the simultaneous detonation of high explosives around it. It would be more difficult for a terrorist group to design this type of weapon than a gun-type nuclear device.

3. Zimmerman and Lewis do not estimate the terrorist resources necessary for methods of HEU acquisition other than black-market purchase, such as theft by the terror group itself. Theft of HEU by terrorists could range from fairly cheap and easy to impractically expensive and difficult, depending on such factors as the target material's location, the possessor's internal and external security measures, and terrorists' level of insider access. In most cases, a terror group's surest means of acquiring fissile material would probably be to purchase it. This approach would afford terrorists access to a global fissile material market and would not require them to undertake risky and difficult theft operations potentially outside their area of expertise. I therefore judge terror groups' ability to acquire fissile material according to their ability to purchase HEU.

4. Note that even if we halve the amount of requisite fissile material, on the assumption that terrorists could be satisfied with a much smaller device, the cost of HEU would still be in the tens of millions of dollars.

5. Zimmerman and Lewis argue that a 1993 case in which Al-Qaeda operatives paid US$1.5 million for a cylinder of spurious HEU better indicates HEU's black-market cost than does the Czech case (Zimmerman and Lewis 2006: 38). However, this claim is dubious, since in the Al-Qaeda incident (1) the amount of HEU supposedly in the cylinder is unknown, and (2) the material was not genuine. We cannot, on the basis of an unknown quantity of spurious material, draw firm conclusions regarding the price of black-market HEU. Rather, we should assume that the Czech case, in which the price per unit of genuine HEU is known, offers a better indicator of HEU cost.

6. I borrow these categories from Schelling (1982: 65).

7. For an extensive discussion of the relationship between deterrence and compellence, see Schelling (1966: 69–91).

8. For a discussion of these types of deterrence see Jervis (1989: 8–13).

9. In theory, terrorists also could launch a nuclear-armed missile against a target state. However, such an attack is extremely unlikely, as it would require terrorists to infiltrate a nuclear state's strategic forces and to override procedures and mechanisms designed to prevent unauthorized launch.

10. The international community has made a number of multilateral efforts to keep nuclear weapons and materials away from nonstate actors. These include universal regimes such as United Nations Security Council Resolution 1540 and narrower collective initiatives such as the Proliferation Security Initiative. See http://www.proliferationsecurity.info/introduction.html; http://www.proliferationsecurity.info/introduction.html.

11. I make an exception if the group has apocalyptic goals, in which case it might be willing to devastate its homeland through a nuclear attack.

12. This ability might be reduced if the region in question is part of the target state's national territory.

13. As will become apparent below, the extent of terrorist groups' financial resources is often unknown. Therefore, in many cases one must make an educated guess as to whether a particular group is likely to have access to the requisite level of funding.

14. However, as noted above, terrorists could actively use a nuclear weapon as part of a primarily passive campaign, either to demonstrate capability or to punish noncompliance.

15. The brief sketches that follow do not purport to offer full discussions of the terrorist groups in question or of their propensity for nuclear terrorism. Rather, they illustrate the utility of my framework in assessing a group's propensity for nuclear terrorism.

16. Such threats might lack credibility, however, since the government would be loath to damage or destroy part of its national territory. Note that the Abu Sayyaf Group garners useful publicity when Philippine government responses appear heavy handed or anti-Muslim. See International Crisis Group (2005: 1).

17. The group amassed this fortune through member donations, tax-exempt businesses, and fraud and extortion (Falkenrath, Newman, and Thayer 1998: 19).

18. In 2000, under the leadership of Fumihiro Joyu, Aum Shinrikyo adopted the name Aleph and claimed to have renounced its violent goals. However, the extent to which the group has changed is unclear (Memorial Institute for the Prevention of Terrorism 2006). For the purposes of this discussion, I use Aum Shinrikyo's original name and assume that it adheres to its millenarian goals under Asahara.

19. It is possible that HUM could itself be deterred from nuclear use by Indian threats of retaliation against Pakistani Kashmir. However, given Pakistani Kashmir's proximity to Indian Kashmir, and India's claim to the entire Kashmir territory, Indian punishment options would probably be limited. Thus India's ability directly to deter Harakat ul-Mujahidin would seem to be considerably lower than its ability to deter Pakistan from supporting a HUM nuclear attack. Note that the same logic would apply to Lashkar-e-Tayyiba and Jaish-e-Mohammed, which are discussed below.

20. Pape also recommends such steps as the separation of rival ethnic populations and the strengthening of homeland security through the improvement of border controls.

References

Abu Ghaith, Suleiman. 2002. "In the Shadow of the Lances." Special Dispatch Series no. 338, June 12. Washington, D.C.: Middle East Media Research Institute.

Abuza, Zachary. 2003. "Funding Terrorism in Southeast Asia: The Financial Network of Al Qaeda and Jemaah Islamiya." *Contemporary Southeast Asia* 25 (2): 169–99.

———. 2005. "Balik-Terrorism: The Return of Abu Sayyaf," September. Carlisle, Penn.: U.S. Army War College Strategic Studies Institute.

Albright, David, and Holly Higgins. 2003. "A Bomb for the Ummah." *Bulletin of the Atomic Scientists* 59 (2): 49–55.

Allison, Graham. 2004. *Nuclear Terrorism: The Ultimate Preventable Catastrophe*. New York: Owl Books.

Bergen, Peter. 2006. *The Osama bin Laden I Know*. New York: Free Press.

Braun, Chaim, and Christopher F. Chyba. 2004. "Proliferation Rings: New Challenges to the Nuclear Nonproliferation Regime." *International Security* 29 (2): 5–49.

Bunn, Matthew, John P. Holdren, and Anthony Wier. 2002. "Securing Nuclear Weapons and Materials." Project on Managing the Atom, Harvard University, Cambridge, Mass., May.

Byman, Daniel. 2003. "Al-Qaeda as an Adversary: Do We Understand Our Enemy?" *World Politics* 56 (October): 139–63.

Cameron, Gavin. 1999. "Multi-track Microproliferation: Lessons from Aum Shinrikyo and Al Qaida." *Studies in Conflict and Terrorism* 22: 277–309.

Carter, Ashton B. 2004. "How to Counter WMD." *Foreign Affairs* (September/October): 72–85.

Castillo, Jasen J. 2003. "Nuclear Terrorism: Why Deterrence Still Matters." *Current History* (December): 426–31.

Clark, Emily. 2002. "In the Spotlight: Abu Sayyaf." Washington, D.C.: Center for Defense Information Terrorism Project, March 5.

Communist Party of the Philippines, Central Committee. 1994. "The New People's Army of the Communist Party of the Philippines Celebrates its 25th Year of Heroic Struggle for National and Social Liberation," March 29. Available at http://www.philippinerevolution.org/cgi-bin/statements/statements.pl?author=cc;date=940329;language=eng.

———. 2001. "On the Vital Issues Concerning the Current Struggle of Filipino Workers for a P125 Wage Increase," September 12. Available at http://www.philippinerevolution.org/cgi-bin/abshow/abshow.pl?year=2001;month=09;day=12;edition=eng;article=01.

Crenshaw, Martha. 1995. "Thoughts on Relating Terrorism to Historical Contexts." In *Terrorism in Context*, ed. Martha Crenshaw. University Park, Penn.: Pennsylvania State University Press.

Daly, Sarah, John Parachini, and William Rosenau. 2005. *Aum Shinrikyo, Al Qaeda, and the Kinshasha Reactor: Implications of Three Case Studies for Combating Nuclear Terrorism*. Santa Monica, Calif.: RAND.

Davis, Jay. 2003. "The Attribution of WMD Events." *Journal of Homeland Security* (April 2003). Available at www.homelandsecurity.org/journal/Articles/Davis.html.

Falkenrath, Richard A. 1998. "Confronting Nuclear, Biological and Chemical Terrorism." *Survival* 40 (3): 43–65.

Falkenrath, Richard A., Robert D. Newman, and Bradley A. Thayer. 1998. *America's Achilles' Heel: Nuclear, Biological, and Chemical Terrorism and Covert Attack*. Cambridge, Mass.: MIT Press.

Federation of American Scientists. 2000. "National Command Authority." Available at http://www.fas.org/nuke/guide/pakistan/agency/nca.htm.

Ferguson, Charles D., and William C. Potter. 2004. *The Four Faces of Nuclear Terrorism*. Monterey, Calif.: Center for Nonproliferation Studies.

Frost, Robin M. 2005. *Nuclear Terrorism after 9/11*. Adelphi Paper 378. London: International Institute for Strategic Studies.

Gershman, John. 2002. "Is Southeast Asia the Second Front?" *Foreign Affairs* 81 (4): 60–74.

Glaser, Charles L., and Steve Fetter. 2001. "National Missile Defense and the Future of U.S. Nuclear Weapons Policy." *International Security* 26 (1): 40–92.

Hoffman, Bruce. 2006. *Inside Terrorism*. New York: Columbia University Press.

Ispahani, Mahnaz. 1992. "India's Role in Sri Lanka's Ethnic Conflict." In *Foreign Military Intervention: The Dynamics of Protracted Conflict*, ed. Ariel E. Levite, Bruce W. Jentleson, and Larry Berman. New York: Columbia University Press.

International Crisis Group. 2003. "Jemaah Islamiyah in South East Asia: Damaged but Still Dangerous." International Crisis Group Asia Report no. 63 (August 26).

———. 2005. "Philippines Terrorism: The Role of Militant Islamic Converts." International Crisis Group Asia Report no. 110 (December 19).

Jane's World Insurgency and Terrorism. 2005a. "Al Qaeda." August.

———. 2005b. "Jemaah Islamiya." December.

———. 2006a. "Liberation Tigers of Tamil Eelam." January.

———. 2006b. "Abu Sayyaf Group." February.

———. 2006c. "Lashkar-e-Tayyiba." February.

———. 2006d. "New People's Army." May.

———. 2006e. "Jesh-e-Mohammadi." August.

———. 2006f. "Harakat-ul-Mujahideen." August.

———. 2006g. "Lashkar-e-Jhangvi." August.

Jenkins, Brian. 2002. "Countering Al Qaeda: An Appreciation of the Situation and Suggestions for Strategy." Santa Monica, Calif.: RAND.

Jervis, Robert. 1989. *The Illogic of American Nuclear Strategy.* Ithaca, N.Y.: Cornell University Press.

Jones, Owen Bennett. 2002. *Pakistan: Eye of the Storm.* New Haven, Conn.: Yale University Press.

Kuppuswamy, C. S. 2002a. "Abu Sayyaf: The Cause for the Return of U.S. Troops to Philippines?" Noida, India: South Asia Analysis Group, Paper no. 417, February.

———. 2002b. "Philippines: The U.S. Campaign against Abu Sayyaf." Noida, India: South Asia Analysis Group, Paper no. 498, July.

Laqueur, Walter. 1999. *The New Terrorism: Fanaticism and the Arms of Mass Destruction.* New York: Oxford University Press.

May, Michael, Jay Davis, and Raymond Jeanloz. 2006. "Preparing for the Worst." *Nature* 443 (26).

Memorial Institute for the Prevention of Terrorism. 2006. "Group Profile: Aum Shinrikyo/Aleph." Available at http://www.tkb.org/Group.jsp?groupID=3956.

Pape, Robert A. 2003. "The Strategic Logic of Suicide Terrorism." *American Political Science Review* 97 (3): 343–61.

Rogers, Steven. 2004. "Beyond the Abu Sayyaf." *Foreign Affairs* (January/February): 15–21.

Rosenau, William. 2001. "Aum Shinrikyo's Biological Weapons Program: Why Did It Fail?" *Studies in Conflict and Terrorism* 24: 289–301.

Santhanam, K. Sreedhar, Sudhir Saxena, and Manish. 2003. *Jihadis in Jammu and Kashmir: A Portrait Gallery.* New Delhi: Sage.

Schelling, Thomas C. 1982. "Thinking about Nuclear Terrorism." *International Security* 6 (4): 61–77.

———. 1966. *Arms and Influence.* New Haven, Conn.: Yale University Press.

South Asia Terrorism Portal. 2001a. "Harkat ul-Ansar." Available at http://www.satp.org/satporgtp/countries/india/states/jandk/terrorist_outfits/harkat_ul_ansar_or_harkat_ul_jehad_e_islami.htm.

———. 2001b. "Harkat-ul-Mujahideen." Available at http://www.satp.org/satporgtp/countries/india/states/jandk/terrorist_outfits/harkatul_mujahideen.htm.

———. 2001c. "Jaish-e-Mohammed." Available at http://www.satp.org/satporgtp/countries/india/states/jandk/terrorist_outfits/jaish_e_mohammad_mujahideen_e_tanzeem.htm.

———. 2001d. "Lashkar-e-Jhangvi." Available at http://www.satp.org/satporgtp/countries/pakistan/terroristoutfits/Lej.htm.

———. 2001e. "Lashkar-e-Toiba." Available at http://www.satp.org/satporgtp/countries/india/states/jandk/terrorist_outfits/lashkar_e_toiba.htm#.

Stern, Jessica. 2000. "Pakistan's Jihad Culture." *Foreign Affairs* (November/December): 115–26.

———. 2003. *Terror in the Name of God: Why Religious Militants Kill.* New York: HarperCollins.

U.S. Department of State. 2004. "Patterns of Global Terrorism 2003." April. Available at http://www.state.gov/documents/organization/31912.pdf.

U.S. Government. 2002. National Security Strategy of the United States of America. Available at http://www.whitehouse.gov/nsc/nss.pdf.

Wirsing, Robert. 1998. *India, Pakistan, and the Kashmir Dispute: On Regional Conflict and Its Resolution.* New York: St. Martin's.

Zimmerman, Peter D., and Jeffrey G. Lewis. 2006. "The Bomb in the Backyard." *Foreign Policy* (November/December): 33–39.

Zubrzycki, John. 2001. "Musharraf Reshuffles His Trump Cards." *The Australian*, October 10.

12

Japan

New Nuclear Realism

MICHAEL J. GREEN AND KATSUHISA FURUKAWA

The possibility of Japan's nuclear armament has been a subject of widespread international attention for many decades. Structural realists since Herman Kahn and Henry Kissinger have found it difficult to accept that Japan's post-World War II pacifist stance would not yield eventually to full-fledged military power commensurate with its economic strength (Green 2001; Kang 2003; Waltz 2000). North Korea's October 2006 nuclear test and the comments of prominent Japanese politicians such as former Prime Minister Yasuhiro Nakasone and Liberal Democratic Party Policy Research Chair Shoichi Nakagawa that Japan should finally begin debating its nuclear weapon options have renewed such international concern.[1] Even Vice President Dick Cheney warned in 2003 that North Korean nuclear capability could cause Japan to turn to nuclear weapons (Cheney 2003).

Japan's "anti-nuclear" culture, rooted in the experiences of Hiroshima and Nagasaki and the institutionalization of postwar pacifist norms, has been posited as the main obstacle to Japan's development of nuclear weapons. Public opinion polls show that even after North Korea's nuclear test approximately 80 percent of Japanese do not want their country to acquire nuclear weapons (*Daily Yomiuri* 2006). Yet it is striking how the traditional taboo on the public discussion of nuclear options has weakened in recent years. As Japan's threat environment has become more complicated, the focus of official and public discourse has shifted from nuclear disarmament—even though that remains critical to Japanese national identity and interests—to maintaining an effective nuclear deterrent against North Korea and China, including more pronounced interest in Japan's own nuclear option. Nuclear strategy discussions, once the domain of a small handful of alliance managers in the Foreign Ministry, are now the currency of national security discussions in the Defense Ministry, the Diet, academia, and the media.

We argue in this chapter that these developments highlight the growing importance of nuclear weapons in Japanese strategic calculations in the context of the increasing perception of threat from China and North Korea. However, unbundling the current debate in Japan, one finds that the increased relevance of nuclear weapons is not connected to war-fighting scenarios, as one sees with China, or because of a new existential threat, as one sees with Israel vis-à-vis Iran. Rather, it is the specter of political and strategic entropy that would be associated with a collapse of the U.S. extended deterrence commitment that is animating strategic thinking in Japan. Though seldom discussed in such terms, the U.S. extended nuclear deterrence commitment underpins Japan's postwar political order and its international orientation. North Korea's nuclear breakout and changes in Chinese nuclear strategy are raising new questions about the credibility of that extended deterrence commitment.

This preoccupation with sustaining the credibility of extended deterrence is evident in the arguments of the most ardent advocates of independent Japanese nuclear armament. For them indigenous weapons would be a hedge or augmentation to the U.S. nuclear umbrella rather than a substitute. Further, while there is increasing discussion in Japan about nuclear weapons and Japan's options, there is little or no serious consideration of how a fully independent nuclear deterrent would work (in terms of doctrine, operations, or maintenance) or its consequences. In reviewing the evolution of the nuclear weapon debate in Japan, we find a pattern in which Japanese exploration of independent nuclear armament is followed by reaffirmation and strengthening of the U.S.-Japan alliance and the U.S. nuclear umbrella. In other words, the increasing public interest in nuclear weapons in Japan today appears designed to keep the "nuclear card" as a hedge and a signal or warning to the United States to sustain a strong extended deterrence commitment. This is not a new story.

What is new, however, is the interest of Japan's security managers not only in reaffirming extended U.S. nuclear deterrence as in the past, but also in seeking greater participation in and possibly even exercising some control over U.S. nuclear weapon strategy. This will present new challenges for U.S. policy makers, whose previous experience along such lines is limited to the North Atlantic Treaty Organization (NATO). Yet just as the United States had to confront these issues with NATO allies in the 1980s when the Soviet Union deployed SS-20s, it may also become necessary in the new strategic environment unfolding in East Asia.

This chapter begins with a discussion of the evolution of Japan's nuclear policy and past examinations in that country of the nuclear option, reviews the current threat environment and debate about nuclear weapons in Japan, and then explicates the comprehensive strategy evolving in Japan to reinforce the extended nuclear deterrence commitment of the United States. The chapter concludes with an assessment of the possible directions the nuclear debate and nuclear strategy might take under different circumstances.

The Evolution of Japan's Nuclear Policy and Past Examinations of the Nuclear Option

Japan entered the post-World War II nuclear world dependent on the United States for its security but without clarity as to how far nuclear proliferation would proceed or how long the United States would stay. The evolution of Japan's post-war nuclear policy was therefore accompanied by periodic and quiet reassessments of Japan's own nuclear options at times of strategic shifts in U.S. policy or in the international system.[2] The Japanese government then leaked these reviews to remind Washington and potential adversaries of Japan's nuclear options. The U.S. government usually responded by taking steps to reaffirm its extended deterrence commitment.

Evidence of Japanese government exploration of the nuclear weapon options dates back at least to 1957 when the Cabinet Legal Affairs Bureau of Prime Minister Nobosuke Kishi confirmed that nuclear weapons were not unconstitutional (Campbell and Sunohara 2004: 221). Kishi speculated in a meeting with U.S. Secretary of State Dean Rusk that Japan might some day need nuclear weapons (Memcon, Ushiba, and Katzenbach, December 2, 1966, POL JAPAN-US, 1/1/66, Box 2383, CF, RG59, NA, cited in Kurosaki 2006: 80–81). Though Hayato Ikeda, Kishi's successor, was a pacifist, he was interested in nuclear weapons to reduce Japan's defense budget—not an unusual thought in the wake of the Eisenhower administration's "New Look" policy (Kurosaki 2006: 42). Ikeda was also encouraged to think about nuclear weapons by French President Charles de Gaulle, who criticized Japan's dependence on the United States (*Asahi Shimbun* 2007b), and in subsequent discussions with the German chancellor, who was contemplating his nation's options (Ito 1985: 234).[3] Ikeda's successor, Eisaku Sato, broached the idea of Japan developing nuclear weapons with U.S. Ambassador Edwin O. Reischauer in 1964 after China's first nuclear test (Embtel 1964; Kase 1999: 24). He raised the issue again with President Lyndon B. Johnson in a summit the following year (*Asahi Shimbun* 2007b).

Ironically, it was not only the Chinese nuclear test that prompted thinking about nuclear weapons in Japan but also the beginning of negotiations to establish the Non-Proliferation Treaty (NPT), which Japanese officials feared would lock Japan into second tier status in the international system (*Asahi Shimbun* February 18, 1966, cited in Kurosaki 2006: 196). Senior Foreign Ministry officials conveyed their concerns to the U.S. government that Japan might be tempted to pursue nuclear weapons if India or other non-NPT signatories did so or if the Chinese nuclear threat increased (Memcon, Ushiba, and Katzenbach, December 2, 1966,

POL JAPAN-US, 1/1/66, Box 2383, CF, RG59, NA, cited in Kurosaki 2006: 80–81; Ota 2004: 212–13).

It was in the context of the NPT negotiations and the Chinese nuclear test that Prime Minister Sato decided to end the increasingly problematic Japanese debate about nuclear weapons by announcing the so-called Three Non-Nuclear Principles to the Diet in December 1967. The Three Principles, which still govern Japanese nuclear policy, prohibit Japan from manufacturing, possessing, or permitting the entry of nuclear weapons into the country or in its air or sea space.[4] Originally, Sato had planned on only two principles: banning the manufacture of and the possession of nuclear weapons (Kurosaki 2006: 210). However, under pressure from his cabinet colleagues and some members of the ruling Liberal Democratic Party, he added a third prohibition against the entry of nuclear weapons into Japan's territorial waters, air space, or land (Tanaka 1997: 222). Sato soon became concerned that this third principle might weaken the U.S. nuclear umbrella and possibly complicate negotiations with Washington over the return of Okinawa (Budget Committee of the Upper House of the Diet, Record of the 58th session, March 25, 1968: 21, cited in Kurosaki 2006: 210). Thus, in 1968 he prepared a new formulation known as the "Four-Pillars Nuclear Policy," which explicitly declared Japan's reliance upon U.S. extended deterrence for the first time in the alliance's history. Specifically, the Four Pillars are to (1) maintain the original Three Non-Nuclear Principles; (2) pursue global nuclear disarmament; (3) limit the use of nuclear energy to peaceful purposes as regulated by the 1955 Atomic Energy Basic Law; and (4) rely on the U.S. extended nuclear deterrent based on the 1960 U.S.-Japan Security Treaty. Sato contemplated further reinforcing the importance of U.S. extended deterrence by declaring that the Three Non-Nuclear Principles were secondary in importance to reliance on the U.S. nuclear umbrella. However, he had to drop the idea after the pacifists and the antinuclear Japanese press embraced the Three Non-Nuclear Principles and enshrined them as the national norm in Japanese public opinion (Wakaizumi 1994: 140–41).

All of this ferment over changes to the international system and the role of nuclear weapons prompted the Cabinet Office of Research (*Naikaku Chousashitsu*) to commission a secret study on Japan's independent nuclear options in 1967 by a quasi-governmental corporation named, euphemistically, "The Study Group on Democracy" (*Asahi Shimbun* 1994). In a provisional report in September 1969, the group concluded that Japan had the ability to produce a few plutonium-based atomic bombs. However, it argued that International Atomic Energy Agency (IAEA) inspectors would quickly notice such activities given their access to Japanese facilities, and that the cost in yen would exceed ¥2 trillion at a time when Japan's overall annual budget was only ¥2.34 trillion (Ota 2004: 250–51). In a second report focused on geostrategic considerations in 1970, the group recommended against independent nuclear weapons for Japan, noting the lack of strategic depth on the Japanese islands and the likelihood that an independent Japanese nuclear armament would end the U.S. nuclear umbrella, thus weakening deterrence vis-à-vis China and adding the United States as an additional adversary in a new nuclear arms race (Ota 2004: 252). Significantly, the group also focused on the impact on domestic stability and warned that Japanese society would be divided and radicalized by the move, undermining Japan's national security from within (*Asahi Shimbun* 1994). Repeating a pattern of alerting Washington to Japan's concerns and options during times of strategic shift, the Japanese government quietly shared the report with the U.S. government (Kristensen 1999: 17–20).

Other examinations of the nuclear option occurred in key parts of the Japanese government and reached the same conclusion as the Study Group on Democracy. In 1969, the Foreign Ministry produced an internal document, "Waga Kuni no Gaiko Seisaku Taiko" (Guidelines of Japan's Foreign Policy), which recommended continued opposition to nuclear armament but noted the importance of maintaining the economic and technical capabilities necessary to produce nuclear weapons (Kurosaki 2006: 278; Mainichi Shimbun Shakaibu [ed.] 1995). In 1970, Defense Minister Yasuhiro Nakasone ordered a group of experts to examine hypothetical options for nuclear weapons after he failed to secure a reaffirmation from U.S. Secretary of Defense Melvin R. Laird that the United States would send troops to defend Japan under the 1965 U.S.-Japan Joint Declaration (Ota 2004: 256–57). Laird was pushing the new Guam Doctrine that sought to shift the burden of conventional defense to Asian allies while reaffirming that the United States was still prepared under the terms of the Mutual Security Treaty "to use all types of weapons in Japan's defense" (Note by the Secretaries to the Joint Chief of Staff on Talk between the Secretary of Defense and the Director-General, Japan Defense Agency [U], cited in Ota 2004: 257–58). However, Nakasone saw the shift as more fundamental. He was something of a Gaullist at that point in his career and may have chosen to interpret Laird's statements in ways that would allow him to explore options hitherto off the table for the Defense Agency.

The Nakasone group's research on nuclear weapons continued for two years. During that time, Nakasone's most ambitious plans for the Defense Agency were shelved as Japan began negotiating normalization with China in 1972, and the United States demonstrated its readiness to continue using massive force in Asia in its war against North Vietnam. Eventually, the Defense Agency study group concluded that a nuclear weapon program would take five years at maximum and an investment of ¥200 billion yen, which was almost 40 percent of the FY1970 defense budget. According to Nakasone, the lack of a nuclear testing site, effective early warning and basing facilities, and technology for delivery systems (or submarines), all created significant technical hurdles (Nakasone 2004: 224–25; Ota 2004: 259). The group concluded that the U.S. nuclear umbrella was by far the most realistic and effective tool to protect Japan. The Japanese Defense White Paper commissioned by Nakasone in 1972 stated: "as for defensive nuclear weapons, it would be possible in a legal sense to possess small-yield, tactical, purely defensive nuclear weapons without violating the Constitution. In view of the danger of inviting adverse foreign reactions and large-scale war, we will follow the policy of not acquiring nuclear weapons at present" (*Japan Times,* "Gist of White Paper on Defense," October 1970, cited in Campbell and Sunohara 2004: 222). Yet many in the Defense Agency also recognized the utility of a latent potential for nuclear weapons. Defense Policy Bureau chief Takuya Kubo wrote under a pseudonym in the famous 1974 KB Memo, "if Japan prepares a latent nuclear capability which would enable Japan to develop significant nuclear armament at anytime, . . . the United States would then be motivated to sustain the Japan-U.S. security system by providing nuclear guarantee to Japan, because otherwise, the U.S. would be afraid of a rapid deterioration of the stability in the international relations triggered by nuclear proliferation" (Kubo 1971). In the October 1976 National Defense Plan Outline, the Japanese government reaffirmed unequivocally that "Japan relies upon US nuclear deterrence vis-à-vis nuclear threats" (*Asahi Shimbun* October 29, 1976, cited in Kurosaki 2006: 214). However, the thinking expressed in the KB Memo did not disappear.

The pillars put in place by the Three Non-Nuclear Principles, the Four-Pillars Nuclear Policy, and the 1976 National Defense Plan Outline during a period of strategic flux in the 1960s and 1970s clearly led to a stronger U.S. extended nuclear deterrence commitment without eliminating Japanese interest in maintaining a latent capability for purposes of leverage. The credibility of the U.S. extended nuclear deterrence was challenged next by the conclusion of the Intermediate-Range Nuclear Forces (INF) Treaty between the United States and the Soviet Union in the 1980s. It appeared that Soviet tactical nuclear weapons would simply be moved from Europe over the Ural Mountains to face Japan.[5] Sensitive to his friend Prime Minister Nakasone's concerns, President Ronald Reagan negotiated a "zero option" treaty with Moscow that removed all intermediate-range ballistic missiles (IRBMs) from Europe without their redeployment to Asia. Interestingly, the debate over independent nuclear weapons was fairly quiet in Japan at this time, perhaps because the hawkish team of Nakasone and Reagan reassured Japanese strategic thinkers about the credibility of the U.S. extended deterrence commitment. Assurance measures included strengthening defense cooperation and mutual strategic dependence through the Roles and Missions Review, the Strategic Defense Initiative, and a host of other new security arrangements in the wake of the Soviet military buildup in the Far East. Even with a greater threat, the extended U.S. nuclear deterrence commitment seemed more secure because the alliance was based on mutual strategic dependence.

The end of the Cold War prompted new consideration of Japan's nuclear options. It was not by coincidence that the exploration occurred in the context of deteriorating U.S.-Japan relations amid a wave of trade friction and mutual suspicion between Washington and Tokyo after the demise of the common Soviet enemy.[6] In 1995, the Japanese Defense Agency prepared "A Report on the Problems of the Proliferation of Weapons of Mass Destruction," which once again reviewed Japan's nuclear options and again concluded that Japan's strategic interests were better served by avoiding participation in any nuclear arms race (*Asahi Shimbun* 1999). When President William Clinton and Prime Minister Ryutaro Hashimoto issued the April 1996 joint U.S.-Japan Declaration on Security, which reaffirmed the nuclear umbrella and charted a new vision for the alliance in the twenty-first century, the nuclear debate and internal Japanese government reviews again subsided.[7]

It is important to note that none of these internal reviews and examinations occurred in a vacuum or because Japan was developing new technological capabilities or self-confidence. In each case there was an immediate challenge to the strategic assumptions that had underpinned the Japanese confidence in the U.S. extended nuclear deterrent, including China's nuclear test, the Guam Doctrine and withdrawal from Vietnam, and the post-Cold War drift in the U.S.-Japan alliance. The one exception was the stimulus of the NPT negotiation process, in which Japan was concerned about being frozen into an unequal position vis-à-vis nuclear weapon states. In each case, including the NPT negotiations, the U.S. government took steps to reaffirm extended nuclear deterrence and the U.S. defense commitment in ways that caused the debate or examination of nuclear options to recede. Japan consistently concluded that the U.S. nuclear umbrella would be the *best* if not *only* choice for Japan, and successive U.S. administrations—even after momentary drifts and trade battles—eventually took steps to ensure that the extended deterrence remained the best choice. At the same time, Japanese officials rarely rejected the concept of retaining a latent or potential deterrent for leverage and in several cases explicitly endorsed it. It is also noteworthy that each episode concluded with the nuclear question fading from public and political view and reverting to the handful of experts in the Foreign Ministry and the U.S. government who quietly ensured the continuation of the nuclear umbrella.

The New Strategic Environment

Japan today is again entering a period of strategic flux with the rise of China, the North Korean nuclear and missile breakout, the potential threat posed by international terrorism, and proliferation of weapons of mass destruction to rogue states and nonstate actors. Concerns about Russia's future, potential threats to Middle East energy supplies, and ongoing territorial disputes with all of Japan's neighbors further complicate the strategic picture for Tokyo.

The rise of China and uncertainty about long-term Chinese intentions represent the gravest strategic challenge to Japan, in spite of the massive economic interdependence between the two countries (Morimoto 2005: 107). According to Japan's Defense White Paper, China holds a "significant number" of IRBMs and medium-range ballistic missiles (MRBMs), including DF-3 and DF-21, that can target the Asian region, including Japan (Boueichou 2007: 52). Specifically, the DF-21, which has a range of 1,800 kilometers (km) and is capable of carrying a nuclear warhead, is believed to be targeting the U.S. military bases in Japan (Boueichou 2007: 52). Japanese experts estimate that about 50 DF-21s are deployed (Kaneda, Kobayashi, Tajima, and Tosaki 2006: 62). Together with DF-21A, an improved version of the DF-21, China is estimated to have more than 100 MRBMs (Kaneda, Kobayashi, Tajima, and Tosaki 2006: 62). In addition, China has deployed more than 700 short-range ballistic missiles, including DF-15 and DF-11, many of which are deployed on mobile platforms. These missiles, when moved northward, are capable of striking targets in Okinawa (Japan Defense Agency 2006). China also continues to develop cruise missiles, which the Japanese Ministry of Defense believes could target Japan and other Asian countries and complement China's ballistic missile forces (Boueichou 2007: 53). Additionally, a rapid increase in the number of China's fourth-generation fighters, including the J-10, Su-27, and Su-30, is a concern because they can reach the western part of Japan.

China's procurement of Kilo-class submarines and development of new indigenous submarines constitutes another challenge to Japan's security. China's deployment of these latest submarines could in due course overturn Japan's current supremacy in naval forces both quantitatively and qualitatively. Japanese defense officials are concerned that the supremacy Japan has traditionally enjoyed in air and naval power vis-à-vis China is rapidly eroding and could possibly be overturned in the near future. Furthermore, China's continuing efforts to modernize its intercontinental ballistic missiles (ICBMs), including DF-5, DF-31, and DF-31A, together with submarine-launched ballistic missiles (SLBMs), including the JL-2, are also of concern as these could potentially make the U.S. homeland vulnerable to Chinese nuclear attack, opening the old question of whether the United States would protect Japan even at the risk of inviting nuclear strikes against U.S. cities.

National security officials in Tokyo have expressed particular concern that China may decide to step beyond its current nuclear posture of minimum deterrence and decide to develop a robust second-strike capability, perhaps with Japan as a primary target. Simultaneously, some Japanese experts worry that U.S. absolute supremacy in nuclear forces may erode in the future, given the projected decrease in U.S. ICBM (retirement of Minuteman III) and SLBM/SSBN forces (retirement of Ohio-class strategic submarines) (Japanese government 2007). The worst-case scenario for these strategic thinkers is that increase in Chinese capabilities and decrease in U.S. capabilities may lead the United States to conclude a bilateral arms control agreement with Beijing that endorses protection of a Chinese limited nuclear strike capability against the United States, with a decoupling effect that would be devastating for Japan. This concern underlies the growing desire of Japanese strategists to have more say in U.S. nuclear strategy and an opportunity to forestall any strategic arms control agreements that might disadvantage Japan.

Japan's economic interdependence with China complicates strategic thinking. In part this is why some Japanese security experts have argued that the immediate North Korean threat is important to mobilize resources and the will to manage the longer-term challenge posed by the rising Chinese political influence and military modernization (Japan Institute of International Affairs 2007b; Japanese government 2007).

Since the mid-1990s, with the revelations of the abduction of Japanese citizens, deployment of 200 Nodong missiles aimed at Japan, and the development of long-range Taepodong missiles (Bell 2006), North Korea emerged as a serious security concern and a rationale for security normalization in Japan. North Korea is believed to be preparing to field a new IRBM that could easily reach U.S. facilities on Okinawa, Guam, and possibly in Alaska (Bell 2006). Its successful development of the SCUD-ER, with an extended range of 1,000 km, can target the western part of Japan (Kaneda, Kobayashi, Tajima, and Tosaki 2006: 57–58). North Korea's acquisition of Kh-55 cruise missiles adds to the list of potential new delivery systems aimed at Japan (Kohata 2005: 52–53). And North Korea's detonation of its first nuclear device in October 2006 demonstrated its nuclear weapon capability. In light of these developments, North Korea has come to be viewed as a serious security threat.

The Six-Party Talks are viewed in Japan as essential to reduce that threat, but there is also deep anxiety that the United States may agree to arms control measures with Pyongyang that capture only the plutonium-based facilities at Yongbyon without ever dismantling North Korea's existing nuclear weapon inventory, missiles, or highly enriched uranium programs and sufficiently addressing Japan's concern over the abduction issues. There is also concern in Tokyo that broader peace agreements in Northeast Asia may institutionalize peaceful coexistence with a North Korea that promises to abandon nuclear weapons but never actually does. The diplomatic process is thus viewed as indispensable yet fraught with potential complications for Japanese security (*Nikkei Shimbun* 2007).

In the view of Tokyo's strategic planners, another key uncertainty that may significantly affect Japan's strategic environment is the Russia factor. Former Russian President Vladimir Putin suggested that Russia may abrogate the INF Treaty, which would enable Russia to deploy MRBMs, at least theoretically and legally. Japanese realists worry that Russian MRBM deployment could further constrain Japan's resources available for a missile system vis-à-vis China (Japanese government 2007).

The nature of the current Chinese and North Korean threats, and the complications associated with Russia, present new and different challenges to the credibility of extended nuclear deterrence. As Matake Kamiya of Japan's National Defense Academy has pointed out, during the Cold War Japan's defense posture was premised on the assumption that any nuclear attack on Japan would be part of a larger global nuclear war between the superpowers, and there was relatively little concern about decoupling (Kamiya 2007; Nakajima 2006; Wakatsuki 2006). However, it is no longer unthinkable that China would use nuclear weapons against Japan and the United States separately or that Japan might become the sole target of nuclear attack in a Sino-Japanese conflict. North Korea, of course, had no nuclear attack options against Japan during the Cold War, but today it threatens Japan with a well-developed and well-protected arsenal of delivery systems that can carry chemical, biological, and nuclear warheads. Furthermore, if North Korea develops the capability to strike the continental United States, decouplement would become an even greater fear, evoking parallels to De Gaulle's famous question of whether the Americans would be willing to trade New York for Paris (or in this case, Los Angeles for Tokyo). China's increasingly survivable, solid-fuelled intercontinental nuclear missiles, and the danger that Beijing may move from a minimim deterrence strategy to a more flexible war-fighting strategy, compounds this concern, particularly if Sino-Japanese political relations deteriorate. There is therefore greater intensity and immediacy to the present nuclear debate in Japan.

A More Public Debate

The escalation of the North Korea crisis since late 2002 has ignited a new public debate in Japan about whether it should acquire nuclear weapons. Those arguing for an independent Japanese nuclear deterrent are mostly on the right and on the fringes of the public intellectual debate. However, they enjoy extensive media coverage. Typical is the February 2003 issue of *Shokun!,* a conservative opinion journal in Japan in which Kyorin University Professor Tadae Takubo and the former Japanese Ambassador to Poland Nagao Hyodo argue that Japan certainly has a "nuclear card," asserting that a principle of "never say never" dominates international politics. The August 2003 issue of *Shokun!* featured a special section debating whether Japan should have nuclear weapons, introducing the perspectives of forty-five experts and opinion leaders on this subject. Among them, Kyoto University Professor Terumasa Nakanishi argues that Japan should acquire capabilities to go nuclear whenever it deemed appropriate. He predicts that the credibility of the U.S. commitment to Japan would inevitably erode, China would develop a blue water naval presence in Japan's strategic sea-lanes, and the international community would acquiesce to North Korea's nuclear weapons and allow the NPT regime to collapse (Nakanishi 2003, 2006: 14–58). Nakanishi also deploys the Gaullist decoupling argument to argue that nuclear weapons would enhance Japan's diplomatic position vis-à-vis China rather than weaken and isolate it. However, it is important to note that even those such as Nakanishi who advocate pursuit of independent Japanese nuclear weapons, still assume that a nuclear arsenal would be developed within the framework of the U.S.-Japan alliance and with the assistance of the United States (Nakanishi 2003, 2006).

Others in the debate advocate a more explicit exploration of nuclear weapons to increase Japan's strategic leverage and demonstrate the Japanese public's concern about the threat posed by proliferation. Parliamentary Vice Minister of Defense Shingo Nishimura was forced to resign in 1999 when he argued in the Japanese edition of *Playboy* that failure to consider the nuclear weapon option left Japan open to "rape" by the international community. In 2002, Deputy Chief Cabinet Secretary Shinzo Abe came under severe criticism after he told a group of students at Waseda University that they should know of Japan's constitutional right to possess nuclear weapons. Abe's boss, Chief Cabinet Secretary Yasuo Fukuda (not known as a hawk) was then attacked by the press when he tried to explain that Abe was theoretically correct and questioned whether Japan's nonnuclear principles would be immutable over time (*Sunday Mainichi* 2002). Iconoclastic Tokyo Governor Shintaro Ishihara also made news in that same period by arguing that Japan should state its readiness to develop nuclear weapons if China does not cease its rapid military modernization. After the North Korean nuclear test, the chairman of the Policy Research Council of the ruling Liberal Democratic Party, Shoichi Nakagawa, made news by calling for an open debate and examination of Japan's nuclear options. Rather than repudiating him, Foreign Minister Taro Aso explained to the press why Japan's interests would be served by "thinking the unthinkable" before returning once again to the conclusion that Japan's interests are better served by the U.S. nuclear umbrella (Aso 2007: 108).

The current public debate about nuclear weapons reveals several important trends. First, while the debate is less taboo—as measured by pages in print and the willingness of senior politicians to speak out on the subject—there is still a public reaction against those who actually advocate nuclear weapons. Japan's so-called "nuclear allergy" is still quite strong. *Asahi Shimbun's* opinion poll in 2005 found that 86 percent of the public opposed Japan's possession of nuclear weapons (*Asahi Shimbun* 2005), and those numbers have not diminished even in the wake of the North Korean nuclear test (*Daily Yomiuri* 2006).

Second, many of those who advocate greater attention to a nuclear weapon option explicitly do so to increase Japan's leverage with the United States and with potential adversaries such as China and North Korea, without actually exploring the utility of those weapons once deployed (Nakanishi 2006: 56–58).

Third, there is far more public attention given to understanding and shaping the extended U.S. nuclear deterrence commitment than to developing actual plans for an independent nuclear arsenal. As moderate conservative Tokyo University Professor Shinichi Kitaoka explains, it would be irresponsible for modern Japanese scholars, politicians, and officials not to strengthen their understanding of nuclear weapon issues in this way:

> The American people believe that the Japanese would think [about security affairs] in the same manner as they do. The Americans do not have a negative view toward possession of nuclear weapons since they think that these weapons are needed to protect the country and take it for granted to possess nukes. As such, they also believe that the Japanese must be thinking in the same way as they do . . . (Kitaoka 2007: 289 [translated by the authors])

> I am reluctant to support the view that Japan should arm itself with nuclear weapons . . . Nuclear weapons can bring benefit to the security of those countries with large territories, but not to those countries with narrow territories with dense population centers, such as Japan. Japan is in a disadvantageous position in nuclear arms race. However, Japan should at least conduct and continue some type of research on nuclear weapons in peace time. Should nuclear weapons be used against Japan, the Japanese government would be blamed as irresponsible if it would not have any idea as to how to respond to such a crisis. For example, it would have to be ready to provide medical treatment [in such an event]. Some type of relevant research is needed. In addition, I do not go so far as to argue that Japan would never possess nuclear weapons even if a major change might take place [in Japan's security environment]. The context [in which Japan makes strategic decisions] might change, for example, if both North and South Korea should possess nuclear weapons, and if the NPT should collapse, while the credibility of the U.S. [extended deterrence] erodes for some reason. (Kitaoka 2007: 287–89 [translated by the authors])

Indeed, rather than take an anti-American or Gaullist stance, Kitaoka reflects the realists' argument by calling for Japanese experts to understand the role of nuclear weapons just as their American counterparts do. This call for a new realism about nuclear weapons is a striking contrast to previous debates, which were essentially designed to ensure that examination of the role of nuclear weapons quietly went away. As argued in this chapter, unlike earlier examinations of Japan's nuclear options, the present debate considers the conditions under which it might be forced to think about developing such a capability—the paramount variable being the credibility of the U.S. nuclear deterrent.

A Comprehensive Approach to Extended Nuclear Deterrence

How does Japan shore up the credibility of the U.S. extended deterrent? One important consideration is the degree to which the Japanese public continues to have confidence in extended deterrence even after the increased nuclear threats from China and North Korea. As Japan's leading nuclear arms control expert

Shinichi Ogawa noted, the Japanese public's suspicion about the credibility of the U.S. extended deterrent was far higher during the Cold War than it is today, even after North Korea's nuclear test (Ogawa 2003). For example, in May 1969, *Mainichi Shimbun* conducted a public opinion poll which asked, "Do you think that Japan is protected by US nuclear weapons or not?" 35 percent of the respondents said "Yes," 24 percent said "No," and 29 percent replied that U.S. nuclear weapons would endanger Japan's security (*Mainichi Shimbun* May 12, 1969, cited in Kurosaki 2006: 212). In another opinion poll by *Mainichi Shimbun* in June 1968, only 17 percent predicted that Japan would never arm itself with nuclear weapons. In an opinion poll by *Yomiuri Shimbun* in 1969, 32 percent predicted that Japan would possess nuclear weapons within the next decade (both cited in Kurosaki 2006: 279). Opinion polls today indicate a higher level of confidence in the credibility of the U.S. commitment to defend Japan. In the opinion poll by *Yomiuri Shimbun* in December 2006, 71 percent predicted that the United States would help Japan militarily if Japan should come under armed attack by another country (*Yomiuri Shimbun* 2006c).

But nuclear strategy is not determined by public opinion polls. The strategic thinkers in Tokyo are seeking new ways to ensure defense, dissuasion, and deterrence in a context of increased nuclear threat. As Llewelyn Hughes argued in an important 2007 article in *International Security,* the Japanese strategy on nuclear weapons involves investment in a series of "insurance policies" (Hughes 2007: 73). We argue that there are four dimensions to such insurance policies: (1) reinforcing the credibility of U.S. extended nuclear deterrence; (2) building a multilayered defense; (3) arms control, disarmament, and nonproliferation; and (4) hedging.

Reinforcing U.S. Extended Nuclear Deterrence

Above all else, Japanese strategic thinkers are seeking ways to reinforce the credibility of the U.S. extended deterrence commitment in the eyes of the Japanese public and Japan's potential adversaries. Japanese officials are not only interested in statements of reaffirmation, as in the past, but also institutionalized and regular consultations on U.S. nuclear doctrine and strategy. The search for information is aimed primarily at arming the defenders of the credibility of the U.S. nuclear umbrella with a better understanding of its modalities so that they can win internal arguments as the external threat increases. A secondary purpose is to better anticipate the direction of the U.S. extended deterrence policy in order to ensure that alliance managers on the American side keep the declaratory policy harmonious with Japan's increased need for reassurance (the statements by President George W. Bush and Secretary of State Condoleezza Rice reaffirming the nuclear umbrella in the wake of the October 2006 North Korean nuclear test are examples of such attempts on the part of the United States).[8] A third aim may be to ultimately have a say in how the United States dissuades and deters (and if necessary, defeats) North Korea or even China (*Asia Times* 2004; *Yomiuri Shimbun* 2006a). Finally, Japanese strategists are increasingly concerned about arms control negotiations the United States might enter into with China or North Korea that could leave Japan in a vulnerable position (Japanese government 2007; Sakamoto 2003: 82).

Japanese officials and scholars close to the government have floated the idea of announcing an intention to revise the Three Non-Nuclear Principles, specifically as a means to strengthen the credibility of the U.S. extended deterrent. The purpose would be to enable the introduction of U.S. nuclear weapons onto Japan's soil (taking out the third principle that Sato had so disliked), though the overall "revision" would be a reminder to potential foes that Japan has its own options with respect to the first principle (nonpossession). In 2003, as tensions mounted with North Korea over its nuclear weapon program, a Japanese foreign minister's advisory board had already recommended the relaxation of the third principle that bars the entry of foreign nuclear weapons into Japanese territory. The panel argued that if North Korea developed deliverable nuclear weapons, it would be critical for Japan to take the steps necessary to reinforce deterrence. The panel also argued that as the Japanese government had for a long time tacitly permitted the entry of U.S. naval assets with nuclear weapons into Japan, the Three Non-Nuclear Principles had been in fact "the Two-and-a-Half-Non-Nuclear Principles" (*Kyodo News* 2003).

There are obvious constraints on any strategy that would allow U.S. tactical nuclear weapons back on Japanese soil. Even after the October 2006 North Korean nuclear test, 79.9 percent of the Japanese public expressed support for the continuation of all three of the Three Non-Nuclear Principles (*Yomiuri Shimbun* 2006b). Also, there is the question of whether such a revision of The Three Principles would enhance U.S. extended deterrence, given the fact that the United States has abolished MRBMs under the INF Treaty and may no longer have the tactical nuclear weapon assets that would be useful to deter China or North Korea when deployed on Japanese soil or territorial waters (Japanese government 2007). As a matter of military strategy, U.S. nuclear forces could be better protected by being deployed away from Japan, considering Japan's vulnerability due to the lack of strategic depth.

In addition, there is increasing aspiration among Japan's strategic planners to secure some notional influence or ownership in the U.S. nuclear umbrella. What exactly ownership means is not clear even to the advocates of this approach. There is the "German model" of dual-controlled tactical nuclear weapons that Japan would not be able to operate without the United States. But the advocates of more ownership in the strategy of extended deterrence are less interested in operational control than doctrinal input at this point. Specifically, the Ministries of Foreign Affairs and Defense have indicated interest in initiating a regularized consultation mechanism with the U.S. government to discuss nuclear strategy or an Asian version of the NATO Nuclear Planning Group (which was originally an institutional pillar of NATO's nuclear strategy), perhaps including South Korea as well. The appearance of such a mechanism would be as reassuring as the actual content of the discussions, at least initially (Green 2007).

The increasing interest in asserting some ownership over U.S. extended deterrence policy faces complications on the U.S. side of the alliance. First, the Japanese government has a weak record on leaks and would need to establish a stringent mechanism for protection of sensitive information, much of which is not available even to close U.S. allies with strong information protection records like Australia. Second, U.S. discussion of nuclear weapon doctrine with key NATO allies has advanced to a stage that could not be easily replicated with Japan, where the pressure for information is as much political as operational. Third, the growing Japanese appetite for a clear and robust declaratory policy vis-à-vis North Korea will be a challenge for the management of U.S. strategic relations with South Korea, where public sentiment is quite opposed to threatening rhetoric towards the North. Finally, the fact that the United States and Japan do not have a joint and combined command structure and still do not engage in operational planning in the way the U.S. military does with South Korea or NATO would be an impediment to concrete discussions of the linkage between defense strategies and nuclear deterrence. Despite these complications, the United States will likely come under increasing pressure to demonstrate a commitment not only to extending the nuclear umbrella over Japan, but also to explaining how it works.

Building a Multilayered Defense

Since the 1990s Japan has developed a multilayered national security concept that combines various aspects of assurance, dissuasion, deterrence, denial, passive defense, active defense, and damage confinement as well as crisis management, to meet the changing security environment. At the core of this strategy—and critical to ensuring the credibility of U.S. extended deterrence—has been closer defense cooperation with the United States on a regional and global basis. Japan has deployed forces to support U.S. coalition operations in Iraq in the reconstruction phase after Operation Iraqi Freedom and in the Indian Ocean as part of Operation Enduring Freedom. Japan has agreed to pay at least US$6 billion to assist with redeployment of U.S. forces from Okinawa to Guam, in part to ease the burden on the local Okinawans, but in large measure to help the United States develop a more agile air and naval presence in the Western Pacific as part of the U.S. Global Posture Review (United States-Japan Security Consultative Committee Document 2006). Japan has also been a partner of the United States in global counterproliferation and dissuasion efforts, such as the Proliferation Security Initiative (PSI), hosting the *Team Samurai* exercise in 2004 and the *Pacific Shield 07* exercise in 2007.

Missile defense has also been a key pillar of Japan's multilayered response to the new threat environment, beginning with the December 1998 decision to collaborate on joint research on sea-based systems (a decision made easier after North Korea's launch of the Taepodong-1 missile in August 1998). The August 1999 joint Memorandum of Understanding was the basis for shared research on a Block IV missile defense system. In December 2003 it was decided to deploy a two-tiered integrated missile defense system consisting of sea-based systems (deployed on Aegis destroyers) and a land-based Patriot system (Kanbou Choukan 2003).[9] The timeline for deploying the full system was accelerated after Pyongyang's 2006 missile and nuclear tests. Completion of the full system is expected by the end of 2011 (with successful field tests of the Kongo-class Aegis systems in the spring of 2007 keeping things on schedule). The system is designed primarily to defeat North Korea's Nodong missiles. While not stated openly, there is also an expectation that the capability would complicate Chinese strategic planning and reinforce the effect of the U.S. extended nuclear deterrent against a Chinese threat.

One question still unresolved is whether Japan should develop a capacity for anticipatory self-defense or preemption. The government has determined that Japan has the constitutional right to attack an enemy's forces if an attack on Japan is imminent and no other recourse is available. The Mid-Term Defense Capability Development Plan (*chuki boueiryoku seibi keikaku*) for FY2005–10 authorized a budget to study the question that could potentially be applied to developing Japan's preemptive capabilities. The discussion of preemption in Japan is fraught with complications. For one thing, it would complicate the U.S. ability to maintain escalation control in any conflict if Japan developed a unilateral capability. However, if Japan developed the capability in conjunction with the United States, it would most likely be symbolic. Preemptively eliminating hardened underground Nodong missile sites would require massive ground attack sorties, if not highly advanced cruise missiles; both expensive assets are available only to the United States. And a Japanese tactical offensive capability would be far more likely to trigger a security dilemma in Asia. As a result, the majority of Japanese political leaders and defense experts oppose such a capability, though certain prominent political leaders such as former Defense Minister Shigeru Ishiba argue that the capacity is needed. (Ishiba had made such statement prior to his second appointment as defense minister in 2007.)

While Japan's multilayered defense has not led to significant internal balancing against the Chinese and North Korean threats (defense spending is still below 1 percent), there has been a striking interest in acquiring new capabilities such as the F-22 Raptor to maintain capabilities vis-à-vis the People's Liberation Army Air Force and to have platforms with stealth technologies that aid penetration for counterstrikes. This is a contrast to past procurement decisions on military aircraft where industrial base concerns and technology development have often trumped operational considerations. However, in 2007 the Bush administration denied Japan the option of importing the F-22, and the next-generation aircraft decision is still pending.[10]

Meanwhile, external balancing has become an increasingly prominent aspect of Japan's effort to maintain security in the region. While neither Australia nor India is likely to retaliate with nuclear weapons against countries threatening Japan, it is striking that part of Japan's overall strategy in a more fluid and threatening environment is to strengthen strategic ties and defense cooperation with these other maritime democracies. Japan signed its first security agreement ever with a third party when then Australian Prime Minister John Howard visited Tokyo in March 2007, and Japanese naval forces exercised with U.S. and Indian naval forces in April that year.

Arms Control, Disarmament, and Nonproliferation

Arms control, disarmament, and nonproliferation have been central to Japan's "insurance policy" against the nuclear threat. Even after the serious challenges posed by the nuclear programs of North Korea and Iran, the evidence is strong that the Japanese public still has faith in the credibility of the international regimes for nuclear arms control, disarmament, and nonproliferation (*Yomiuri Shimbun* 2006b).[11]

Yet there has always been an uncomfortable tension between Japan's active support for complete nuclear disarmament under Article VI of the NPT and its no less active effort to strengthen the U.S. nuclear umbrella. As Japan's Foreign Ministry has noted: "on the one hand Japan does rely on the United States' nuclear deterrent against nuclear threats, on the other hand Japan, being the sole country to have suffered nuclear devastation, adopts a realistic and incremental approach to realize a peaceful world free of nuclear weapons through practical disarmament measures to improve [the] Japanese security environment" (Japan Institute of International Affairs 2007a: 46).

In pursuit of the longer-term goal of total nuclear disarmament, Japan has proposed resolutions on ultimate elimination of nuclear weapons to the U.N. General Assembly every year since 1994. Japan has also been a strong supporter (and funder) of the IAEA safeguards and the Comprehensive Nuclear-Test-Ban Treaty (CTBT) (Japan Institute of International Affairs 2007a: 47). In addition, Japan concluded the Additional Protocol in December 1999 and urged other parties to do the same through multilateral diplomacy in the United Nations, Asia-Pacific Economic Cooperation forum, and other institutions. Finally, Japan has pushed for a Fissile Material Cutoff Treaty as the next significant issue to the CTBT in the multilateral disarmament and nonproliferation negotiations (Japan Institute of International Affairs 2007a: 48).

In the wake of the 1998 North Korean Taepodong test, Japan has matched its emphasis on the *negotiation* of treaties with a new emphasis on counterproliferation, enforcement, and compliance. Japan began hosting the Asian Senior-Level Talks on Nonproliferation in November 2003 and the Asian Export Control Dialogue in October 2004, respectively, with the purpose of strengthening Asian states' export control systems (Japan Institute of International Affairs 2007a: 186). Japan has also urged other Asian states to join in the PSI.

On the whole, interviews with Foreign Ministry officials involved in arms control suggest a waning confidence in the ability of the annual U.N. Conference on Disarmament in Geneva to have any impact on the growing Chinese and North Korean nuclear challenges. However, there is new interest in using the NPT Review Conference and other multilateral mechanisms to try to establish an international consensus on halting the expansion of existing nuclear arsenals.

Hedging

Not surprisingly, hedging continues to be an implicit element in Japan's strategy for maintaining deterrence. In reviewing the public debate, we noted that senior politicians flagged Japan's nuclear options in the wake of the North Korean nuclear test to signal or increase its leverage with both Washington and Beijing. Perhaps not by coincidence, another review of Japan's nuclear weapon options was leaked to the press in December 2006. That review went into considerable detail on the technical capabilities and limitations Japan would face in developing a nuclear weapon capability (Tamura 2006). The Japanese government disavowed any role in that report. However, few observers accepted that claim, given the clear technical proficiency of the authors. The 2006 report argued that it would take at least three to five years for Japan to produce a prototype small nuclear warhead, with an investment of ¥200 to ¥300 billion (approximately US$1.9 to 2.8 billion, assuming an exchange rate of US$1 = ¥106) and require the mobilization of hundreds of experts and engineers (Tamura 2006). The elements necessary for a nuclear weapon exist in Japan's nuclear fuel-cycle programs that produce plutonium, although it is reactor-grade plutonium in the form of mixed-oxide for civilian purposes.

Presented to a senior journalist by a senior Japanese official (Tamura 2007),[12] the report again reaffirms the technical constraints on Japan's nuclear weapon development, while highlighting the fact that the technical expertise and facilities to develop such weapons can be harnessed should it become necessary. Japan also has the M-V and H2-A rockets, which have potential ICBM capabilities. The M-V rocket operates with solid fuel and is capable of placing a 1.8-ton payload into orbit, while the H2-A rocket operates with liquid fuel and is equipped with advanced aerospace engineering capabilities.

In addition to technical restraints, Japan would face organizational and bureaucratic obstacles as well. For many decades, engineers and especially nuclear physicists have been socialized against nuclear weapons. A lack of secrecy laws and intrusive IAEA inspections would make a clandestine program impossible. An overt program would be prohibitively expensive without the kind of international collaboration Japan receives for peaceful nuclear use.

Conclusion

As Lawrence Freedman, the British strategist, once observed: "acquiring nuclear capability is a statement of a lack of confidence in all alternative security arrangements" (Freedman 1994/1995: 36). Put in the context of Japan's national security, Japan has so far retained faith in "alternative security arrangements" that are anchored in the U.S.-Japan security relationship. The history of the development of the U.S.-Japan alliance demonstrates one consistent pattern: whenever Japan has debated new security arrangements at a time of strategic shift in the environment, it has consistently selected pragmatic arrangements. Through the careful calculation of relative costs and benefits associated with each option, Japan eventually adopted new security measures within the renewed framework of the U.S.-Japan alliance. In the words of Victor Cha, "[a]s long as US commitments remain firm, the likelihood of Japan seeking alternative internal or external balancing options is low. In other words, the causal arrow is more likely to run in the direction from weakened U.S. alliance to alternative balancing options, rather than from alternative balancing options to weakened U.S. alliance" (Cha 2003: 9–10).

How might Japanese thinking about nuclear weapons evolve from here? The pattern is well established and repeated. Japan may likely retain a latent nuclear weapon capability for leverage and hedging purposes, but the primary effort will be to strengthen the U.S. extended nuclear deterrent that underpins Japan's security in terms of regional engagement and domestic political stability. Given the new challenges in the strategic environment, however, Japan will expect more of the United States in terms of information about and management of the extended nuclear deterrent and will be less easily satisfied. When declaratory policy alone fails, Tokyo may focus on changes in the Three Non-Nuclear Principles to allow the reintroduction of U.S. tactical nuclear weapons or seek more explicit counterstrike capabilities, such as procurement or basing of systems like the F-22. Should extended deterrence weaken, the preference could be for something akin to the "German model" of dual-keyed tactical weapons rather than an independent nuclear weapon capability. Finally, judging from the current debate, should deployment of nuclear weapons in Japan become the only credible choice, the clear preference would be for tacit support from the United States to avoid creating a new enemy and to sustain as much extended deterrence as possible. The clandestine path to strategic surprise and the unveiling of a Japanese bomb is highly unlikely, given the intrusive IAEA presence in Japan, the technical obstacles, the lack of support and secrecy within Japan's nuclear community, the likely domestic polarization and instability, and the risk of destroying whatever remains of extended deterrence and turning the United States from ally into enemy.

If the causal arrow will travel through the alliance, what would force Japan to consider the path described above? The debate would be accelerated by U.S. accommodation of North Korea or China in arms control negotiations that appeared to leave Japan more vulnerable or by the development of Nodong, Taepodong, or other capabilities by North Korea that increased the danger of decoupling. More catastrophic scenarios for the credibility of extended deterrence would be a failure to defeat Chinese aggression against Taiwan or Japan or North Korean aggression against Japan or South Korea. The trend in U.S. capabilities and strategy would also have an impact. Japanese strategic planners will carefully watch the direction of the U.S. nuclear arsenal and strategy and the state of forward-deployed U.S. forces in the Pacific, particularly air and naval units. Should South Korea, Taiwan, or another U.S. ally in the region develop nuclear weapons, this would intensify the Japanese debate, leading to a strategic preference for further reinforcement of the extended deterrence, this time possibly complicated by the intangible factors of pride and nationalism.

None of these scenarios leads directly to an independent Japanese nuclear arsenal without efforts to first strengthen, revive, or reaffirm U.S. extended nuclear deterrence. This means that Japan will signal its intentions and concerns in ways that will be hard for Washington to miss. In that sense, the debate about nuclear weapons in Japan is not necessarily negative. Certainly, some extreme opinions that support Japan's possession of indigenous nuclear weapons might seem shocking in the initial phase of such discussions. However, as many political leaders, officials, and experts join such discussions, more pragmatic perspectives will begin to shape them. This will help the Japanese public understand the costs and benefits of the nuclear option and shape their view of what is in the best national interests of Japan. It will also educate the American side about what must be done to keep the U.S. commitment credible.

There is a context within which Japan's neighbors will view this debate. The more that pragmatic discussions about future strategy become confused by outside audiences with internal Japanese political fights about how to treat the past, the greater the danger that Japan's realism will be mistaken for revisionism or militarism in North Korea, South Korea, or China. Japanese leaders will also have to consider carefully how their own discussion plays in the United States. Throughout the postwar period, Japan has signaled that it has the option to develop nuclear weapons to secure reaffirmation of the U.S. defense commitment and nuclear umbrella during times of shifting strategic terrain. With each challenge to previous assumptions about the alliance, the United States and Japan have ended up crafting a tighter and more interdependent security arrangement. That trend is likely to continue with the growing threats posed by North Korea's nuclear program and China's rising power. However, it is possible for Japan to overplay its hand and inadvertently risk undermining U.S. trust in the alliance.

For its part, the United States must recognize that Japan's steady recalibration of its national security framework will make the Self-Defense Forces a more effective and committed partner in international security, but these changes will also open new opportunities for independent action by Japan. Similarly, the growing Japanese interest in ending the taboo on discussing nuclear strategy at home and with the United States will lead to decreased opposition to the alliance and the U.S. nuclear umbrella. However, it will also create more hard questions for U.S. policy and doctrine. The United States cannot make these changes go away. It should see that Japan's choice is clearly for a more effective and integrated alliance rather than the autarkic capabilities that were more popular among Japanese politicians between the 1950s and 1970s. The increasing salience of nuclear weapons in Japanese strategic calculations should lead naturally to a closer alliance, not a pursuit of autonomy in nuclear weapons. Much, however, will depend on the future of U.S. strategy toward Japan and Asia.

Notes

The views expressed here are those of the authors and do not represent those of the Center for Strategic and International Studies, the Research Institute for Science and Technology for Society, or its research sponsors. The authors would like to thank David Fedman of the CSIS Japan Chair for assistance with research for this chapter.

1. On September 5, 2006, Yasuhiro Nakasone stated at a press conference: "There is a need to also study the issue of nuclear weapons . . . There are countries with nuclear weapons in Japan's vicinity . . . we are currently dependent on U.S. nuclear weapons (as a deterrent) but it is not necessarily known whether the U.S. attitude will continue." (As reported in *Japan Policy & Politics* 2006). On October 27, 2006, at a press conference in Washington, D.C., Shoichi Nakagawa stated: "My proposal is to have a nuclear debate. Much debating should be done . . . Debating is one of the options to prevent the situation [of a nuclear attack] . . . We should discuss various options." (As reported in *Japan Economic Newswire* 2006.)

2. See the following reference materials for a comprehensive overview of Japan's examination of the nuclear option: Kurosaki 2006 and Michishita 2006.

3. After talking to Charles de Gaulle, however, Hayato Ikeda discussed the idea with his West German counterpart as well. See Ito 1985: 234.

4. These principles were first enunciated by Prime Minister Eisaku Sato in 1968 and were formalized in a Diet resolution in 1971. However, the third principle of prohibiting the entry of nuclear weapons into Japan has been seen as having little credibility in Japan or other Asian countries. These principles became moot only after the George H. W. Bush

administration publicly announced in 1992 that U.S. ships, aircraft, and submarines would no longer carry tactical nuclear weapons after the end of the Cold War.

5. The official name of the INF Treaty is "Treaty between the United States of America and the Union of Soviet Socialist Republics on the Elimination of Their Intermediate-Range and Shorter-Range Missiles."

6. These studies were initiated at a time when overseas concerns were mounting due to Japan's reluctance to sign the extension of the NPT. According to the Japanese officials who were in charge of the international negotiation for the indefinite extension of the NPT, Japan wanted to get nuclear weapon states' firm and clear commitments to total nuclear disarmament, but could not get such confirmation from them, which led to Japan's reluctance to sign the revised treaty swiftly. However, foreign countries misunderstood Japan's reluctance as a reflection of Japan's intention to keep a future nuclear option. The Japanese Defense Agency studies were intended to expel overseas misunderstanding about Japan's nuclear ambition, according to the agency official who led this study group.

7. This declaration, officially known as the "U.S.-Japan Joint Declaration on Security-Alliance for the 21st Century," was signed in Washington on April 17, 1996. For the full version of the declaration visit http://www.mofa.go.jp/region/n-america/us/security/security.html.

8. On October 9, 2006, immediately following confirmation of North Korea's nuclear test, President Bush stated: "The United States remains committed to diplomacy, and we will continue to protect ourselves and our interests. I reaffirm to our allies in the region, including South Korea and Japan, that the United States will meet the full range of our deterrent and security commitments." On October 18, 2006, during a visit to Tokyo following North Korea's October nuclear test, Secretary of State Condoleezza Rice stated: "The role of the United States is to make certain that everybody, including the North Koreans, know very well that the United States will fully recognize and act upon its obligations under its mutual defense treaty with Japan . . . The United States has the will and the capability to meet the full range, and I underscore the full range, of its deterrence and security commitment to Japan." On October 19, 2006, during a press conference prior to her visit with Prime Minister Shinzo Abe in Tokyo, Secretary of State Condoleezza Rice asserted that "the United States regards Japan's security as US security." She continued, "North Koreans should not believe they can change the security environment . . . the Japan-US alliance has an ability to respond to their challenge." (As reported in *Associated Foreign Press* 2006.)

9. The final architecture of Japan's MD system will consist of four Aegis destroyers equipped with ballistic missile defense function, sixteen FUs of the Patriot PAC-3 system, four FPS-XX radars, and seven improved FPS-3 radars, all of which will be connected by an integrated command and communication system.

10. For a more detailed overview of the debate surrounding Japan's acquisition of F-22 fighters see *The Financial Times* (2007). For information regarding the debate surrounding Japan's acquisition of FX fighters see *Defense Industry Daily* (2006).

11. In a February 2006 survey conducted by the Cabinet Office of Japan, 76 percent of respondents felt that Japan should "continue with the present arrangement of protecting peace with the U.S.-Japan Security Treaty" and 74 percent of respondents thought that Japan "benefits from its current security arrangement." For a full report on the results of this survey visit http://www.mansfieldfdn.org/polls/poll-06-20.htm.

12. While then-Prime Minister Abe flatly denied the existence of such examination by the Japanese government, Hideo Tamura, an editorial staff member of *Sankei Shinbun* and an author of this news article, is confident about the authenticity of this internal government document. According to Tamura, the examination was led by a senior official within the government who was in a position to mobilize necessary resources and whom Tamura knows well personally. Tamura assumes that this examination might have been made without the knowledge of political leaders and that the document might have been produced to enable the bureaucrat to be ready to respond promptly to any question by the political leaders pertaining to Japan's latent nuclear capability, should the politicians truly ask such questions. The senior official prepared this document preemptively, but to the surprise of this senior official, no political leader seems to have ever asked such a question.

References

Asahi Shimbun. 1994. "Kakubuso Kano daga Motenu" (Nuclear Armament Technically Possible, but Not Recommendable). November 13.

———. 1999. "Hikaku Power: Haibokushugi Tsuranuki Ginen Harae" (Non-nuclear Power: Sustain 'Defeatism' and Expel Skepticism of Other Countries). August 4.

———. 2005. "Kaku wo Ou, 60-nen to Korekara: Kakukakusan, Hirogaru Kigu, Nikkan Chu Bei Futsu Doku, 6 kakoku Yoron Chousa" (Tracking the Nukes, 60 years After the End of the Second World War and Hereafter: Nuclear Proliferation, Widespread Concerns, Opinion Poll in 6 Countries; Japan, Korea, China, US, France and Germany). August 6.

———. 2007a. "Beikoku heni Dandou Misairu Geigeki ga Hitsuyou de Icchi, Yuushikishakon" (The Blue Ribbon Panel Unanimously Agreed that Japan Should Intercept Ballistic Missiles Heading toward the US). June 29.

———. 2007b. "Kaku wo Ou, Kenshou Nihon no Seisaku: Jou: Nihon 'Hikaku' ni Jirenma" (Tracking the Nukes: Reviewing Japan's Policy, Part I. Japan's Non-Nuclear Posture Faced with Dilemma). August 1.

Asia Times. 2004. "Seoul, Tokyo and the Forbidden Nuclear Card." October 7.

Aso, Taro. 2007. *Jiyu to Hanei no Ko* (Arc of Freedom and Prosperity: Japan's Expanding Diplomatic Horizons). Tokyo: Gentosha.

Associated Foreign Press. 2006. "Japan, US Step Up Work on Missile Shield." October 19.

Bell, B. B. 2006. Commander, United Nations Command; Commander, Republic of Korea-United States Combined Forces Command; and Commander, United States Forces Korea, "Statement Before the Senate Armed Services Committee," March 7 (official document).

Boueichou (Japanese Ministry of Defense). 2007. *Bouei Hakusho 2007 nendoban* (White Paper of Japanese Defense 2007).

Campbell, Kurt M., and Tsuyoshi Sunohara. 2004. "Japan: Thinking the Unthinkable." In *The Nuclear Tipping Point,* ed. Kurt M. Campbell, Robert J. Einhorn, and Mitchell B. Reiss. Washington, D.C.: Brookings Institution Press.

Cha, Victor D. 2003. "Defensive Realism and Japan's Approach toward Korean Reunification." *NBR Analysis* 14 (1). 5–32.

Cheney, Dick. 2003. "Interview with Vice President Dick Cheney." Meet the Press, NBC, March 16.

Daily Yomiuri. 2006. "Poll: 80% Support Upholding Japan's Nonnuclear Principles." November 21.

Defense Industry Daily. 2006. "F-22 Raptors to Japan?" February 20.

Embtel 2067. 1964. Tokyo to SecState, December 29, NSA, No. 400 (official document).

Financial Times. 2007. "Stealth Debate Precedes Abe US Visit." April 23.

Freedman, Lawrence. 1994/1995. "Great Powers, Vital Interests and Nuclear Weapons." *Survival* 36 (4) (Winter). 35-52.

Green, Michael J. 2001. *Japan's Reluctant Realism: Foreign Policy Challenges in an Era of Uncertain Power.* New York: Palgrave Press.

———. 2007. Background interviews with the Japanese Minister of Foreign Affairs and the Japanese Ministry of Defense officials, July–November.

Hughes, Llewelyn. 2007. "Why Japan Will Not Go Nuclear (Yet): International and Domestic Constraints on the Nuclearization of Japan." *International Security* 11 (4) (Spring): 67–96.

Ito, Masaya. 1985. *Ikeda Hayato to Sono Jidai* (Hayato Ikeda and the Epoch). Tokyo: Asahi Shimbunsha.

Japan Defense Agency. 2006. Remarks of former senior official, at meeting of Graduate Research Institute of Policy Studies, Tokyo, Japan, June 7.

Japan Economic Newswire. 2006. "Japan's LDP Policy Chief Again Calls for Debate on Nuclear Possession." October 28.

Japan Institute of International Affairs. 2007a. *Japan's Disarmament and Nonproliferation Policy*. Tokyo: Japan Institute of International Affairs.

———. 2007b. Remarks of the Japanese experts, at a meeting, Tokyo, Japan, May 11.

Japan Policy & Politics. 2006. "Ex-premier Nakasone Proposes Japan Study Nuclear Option." September 11.

Japanese government. 2007. Remarks and presentation of the Japanese officials and experts, at a study group meeting of the government, Tokyo, Japan, May 11.

Kamiya, Matake. 2007. Professor, National Defense Academy, remarks, at meeting of Japan Institute of International Affairs, Tokyo, Japan, May 11.

Kanbou Choukan (Chief Cabinet Secretary) 2003. *Kanbou Choukan Danwa* (remarks by the Chief Cabinet Secretary), Tokyo, Japan, December 19.

Kaneda, Hideaki, Kazumasa Kobayashi, Hiroshi Tajima, and Hirofumi Tosaki. 2006. *Nihon no Misairu Bouei* (Japan's Missile Defense). Tokyo: Japan Institute of International Affairs.

Kang, David. 2003. "Getting Asia Wrong: The Need for New Analytical Frameworks." *International Security* 27 (4) (Spring): 57–85.

Kase, Miki. 1999. *Daitouryou ate Nihonkoku Shushou no Gokuhi Fairu* (Secret Files for the U.S. Presidents Concerning the Japanese Prime Ministers). Tokyo: Mainichi Shimbunsha.

Kitaoka, Shinichi. 2007. *Kokuren no Seiji Rikigaku* (Political Power Dynamism at the United Nations). Tokyo: Chukou Shinsho.

Kohata, Kensuke. 2005. "Ukuraina kara Ryushutsushita Junkou Misairu no Eikyou" (The Effects of the Proliferation of Cruise Missiles from Ukraine). *Sekai Shuhou,* May 10, 52–53.

Kristensen, Hans M. 1999. *Japan Under the Nuclear Umbrella: U.S. Nuclear Weapons and Nuclear War Planning in Japan During the Cold War.* San Francisco: The Nautilus Institute.

Kubo, Takuya. 1971. *Boueiryoku Seibi no Kangaekata* (A Framework to Consider the Arrangement of Japan's Defense Capabilities), February 20. Available at http://www.ioc.u-tokyo.ac.jp/~worldjpn/documents/texts/JPSC/19710220.O1J.html.

Kurosaki, Akira. 2006. *Kaku Heiki to Nichibei Kankei* (Nuclear Weapons and Japan-U.S. Relations). Tokyo: Yushisha.

Kyodo News. 2003. "Kaku Tousai Kan no Ichiji Kikou Younin wo, Gaishou no Shimon Kikan" (Foreign Minister's Advisory Board Recommended to Permit the Temporary Visits of U.S. Nuclear Ships to Japanese Ports). September 18.

Mainichi Shimbun Shakaibu, ed. 1995. *Usagi no Mimi to Hato no Yume: Nihon no Kaku to Jouhou Senryaku* (Rabbit's Ears and Dove's Dream: Japan's Nuclear and Information Strategy) Tokyo: Liberta Shuppan.

Michishita, Narushige. 2006. *Kaku Mondai ni kansuru Nihon no Ugoki* (Japan's Actions regarding Nuclear Problems), a briefing material produced for the purpose of Professor Michishita's class at the Graduate Research Institute of Policy Studies in Tokyo, Japan, August.

Morimoto, Satoshi. 2005. *Morimoto Satoshi no Me* (Eyes of Satoshi Morimoto). Tokyo: Gurafu-sha.

Nakajima, Shingo. 2006. *Sengo Nihon no Bouei Seisaku* (Japan's Defense Policy After the Second World War). Tokyo: Keio University Press.

Nakanishi, Terumasa. 2003. *Nihonkoku Kakubushou heno Ketsudan* (Japan's Decision to Be Armed with Nuclear Weapons). *Shokun!*, August. 22–37.

———, ed. 2006, *Nihon Kaku Busou' no Ronten* (Issues of Japan's Nuclear Armament). Tokyo: PHP Publishing.

Nakasone, Yasuhiro. 2004. *Jiseiroku* (Record of Reflection). Tokyo: Shinchosha.

Nikkei Shimbun. 2007. "Aribi Gaiko wa Komaru" (We Are Distressed at "Alibi" Diplomacy). March 11.

Ogawa, Shinichi. 2003. "Seinen shiteiru Nihon no Kakubusou wo meguru Giron ni tsuite" (A Perspective on a Revival of US Debate on Japan's Nuclear Armament). Briefing Memo. Tokyo: National Institute of Defense Studies. May 9.

Ota, Masakatsu. 2004. *Meiyaku no Yami* (The Shadowy Pact). Tokyo: Nihonhyouronsha.

Sakamoto, Kazuya. 2003. "Imaha Hitsuyounaikeredo . . ." (Although Nuclear Option is Not Necessary Now . . .). *Shokun!* August. 82.

Sunday Mainichi. 2002. "Seikai Gekishin, Abe Shinzo Kanbou Fukuchoukan ga Katatta Monosugoi Nakami, Kaku Heiki no Shiyou ha Iken deha nai" (Political World Shaken Severely by the Remarks of Deputy Cabinet Secretary Shinzo Abe: The Use of Nuclear Weapon Would Not Violate Japan's Constitution). June 2.

Tamura, Hideo. 2006. "Kaku Danto Shisaku ni 3 nen Ijo" (More than Three Years Are Needed to Produce a Prototype of Nuclear Warhead). *Sankei Shimbun*, December 25.

———. 2007. Editorial staff member, *Sankei Shimbun*, interview, Tokyo, Japan, May 1.

Tanaka, Akihiko. 1997. *Anzen Hoshou* (National Security). Tokyo: Yomiuri Shimbunsha.

U.S.-Japan Security Consultative Committee. 2006. "United States-Japan Roadmap for Realignment Implementation," May 1.

Wakaizumi, Kei. 1994. *Tasaku Nakarishi wo Shinzemu to Hossu* (Believing that There Was No Other Option Available). Tokyo: Bungei Shunju.

Wakatsuki, Hidekazu. 2006. *Zenhoui Gaikou no Jidai* (An Era of Multidirection Diplomacy). Tokyo: Nihon Keizai Hyoronsha.

Waltz, Kenneth. 2000. "Structural Realism After the Cold War." *International Security* 5 (21) (Summer): 5–41.

Yomiuri Shimbun. 2006a. "Japan Reassured of U.S. Nuclear-Umbrella Deterrence." October 19.

———. 2006b. "Hikaku 3 Gensoku, Kongo mo Mamorubeki 80% . . . Yomiuri Yoron Chousa" (Public Opinion Poll by Yomiuri Shinbun: Over 80% Support to Continue the Three-Non-Nuclear Principles). November 20.

———. 2006c. "Nichibei Kyodo Yoron Chousa" (Public Opinion Polls Jointly Conducted in Japan and the United States). December 1.

13

South Korea
Fears of Abandonment and Entrapment

KANG CHOI AND JOON-SUNG PARK

On October 9, 2006, the Democratic People's Republic of Korea (DPRK or North Korea) conducted a nuclear test, informing the world of its arrival on the international scene as a de facto nuclear weapon state. Despite that provocative action, the Republic of Korea (ROK or South Korea) remains committed to a nonnuclear posture. At the same time, the once formidable and seemingly unbreakable military alliance between South Korea and the United States is under stress and undergoing a process of adjustment that is recognized as essential by both countries. That adjustment is occurring in the context of President Roh Moo Hyun's paradoxical national security doctrine of "cooperative self-reliant national defense,"[1] popularly known as the "Koreanization of Korean defense." These developments raise the following questions: why does Seoul still desire a strong U.S. commitment to defend South Korea, and why does it maintain a nonnuclear posture?

Opinion polls taken before and after North Korea's nuclear test indicate that a majority of South Koreans favor the nuclear arming of their country, though they prefer a negotiated solution to the nuclear crisis.[2] Conservatives especially seemed to believe that the nuclear option might be unavoidable should Washington fail to provide a credible "nuclear umbrella." At the same time, there was widespread international concern that North Korea's nuclear test may have a domino effect on Japan and South Korea.[3]

However, this chapter argues that a nuclear-armed South Korea is highly unlikely, and probably impossible, in the foreseeable future. Development of an indigenous nuclear weapon capability would be counterproductive for South Korea's security and work against its long-term goal of unification. Reaffirming and strengthening the U.S. extended nuclear deterrence commitment and maintaining its nonnuclear posture make eminent security sense for South Korea. Our argument is based on an analysis of South Korea's security policy, including nuclear policy since World War II. The chapter posits that South Korea's fear of abandonment (FoA) by the United States (of its defense commitment to South Korea) and its fear of entrapment (FoE) by U.S. strategic concerns have been the key determining factors in the evolution of South Korea's security policy. In turn, these fears have been shaped by changes in four variables: (1) the international security environment, (2) the North Korean threat, (3) the U.S. security commitment and strategy, and (4) South Korea's threat perception.

Historical Overview

Mid-1950s to Early 1960s: Deployment of U.S. Tactical Nuclear Weapons

After the signing of the Korean War Armistice agreement in July 1953, South Korea's highest security priority was to prevent another war on the Korean peninsula. As U.N. forces withdrew, the United States also gradually pulled out its troops. Fearing that hostilities could resume if South Korea were left alone again, President Rhee Syngman strongly desired a long-term U.S. military presence in Korea (Kim, Tae Woo 2005: 211). The ROK-U.S. Mutual Defense Treaty signed in October 1953 was a joint product of South Korea's desperate effort to keep U.S. forces committed to its defense and the U.S. recognition of Korea's strategic value in fighting the spread of communism in Northeast Asia (Kim and Cho 2003: 70–74).[4]

It is noteworthy that South Korea agreed to leave the command authority over its armed forces in the hands of the United Nations Command (hereafter UNC) as a way of ensuring continued U.S. military commitment (Jung 1993: 85–86). Although the command authority of the UNC was later replaced with a somewhat limited form of "operational control" (hereafter OPCON), it helped create the structural link between the ROK and U.S. forces.[5] The integration of command authority strengthened the U.S. security commitment, but the U.S. forces in Korea (USFK) decreased significantly in number.[6] To compensate for the troop withdrawal and make the U.S. commitment more credible, the Eisenhower administration announced the nuclear arming of the USFK in July 1957, based on a new strategy known as the "New Look" (Tow 1991: 182–85).[7] Soon thereafter, the United States deployed tactical nuclear weapons in South Korea and implemented further reduction in the USFK.[8] Since then, the United States has provided military assistance to South Korea worth about US$34 billion, including the Military Assistance Program, International Military Education and Training, Military Assistance Service Fund, and Foreign Military Sales to help build the ROK armed forces (Ham 1998: 156–58).[9]

In January 1958, the United States began deploying tactical nuclear components into South Korea.[10] The 7th Infantry Division (ID) of the 8th U.S. Army was transformed into the "Pentomic Division,"[11] a specially organized new force structure to fight a nuclear war (Jang 2002: 268–72). It was equipped with an unspecified number of 280-millimeter artillery pieces that were capable of firing both conventional and nuclear warheads along with Honest John surface-to-surface missiles. In 1959 the U.S. Air Force dispatched a squad of Matador missiles, which with a maximum range of 1,100 kilometers could target all of North Korea, key areas of China, and the Soviet Far East. The U.S. tactical nuclear force in South Korea was further strengthened by the introduction in 1961 of Mace missiles with a range of 1,800 kilometers (*Donga Daily* 2006).

1960s and 1970s: South Korea Pursues Its Own Nuclear Option

Throughout the 1960s and 1970s, South Korea's security situation was tested repeatedly. The country's sense of insecurity was acute during this period. First and foremost, DPRK military provocations increased in frequency and intensity. In the early 1960s, upon the completion of its postwar recovery, North Korea accelerated its military buildup under the "Four-Line military policy" (Ham 1998: 163).[12] From the late 1960s, a militarily more confident Pyongyang committed a series of armed provocations as well as acts of terrorism: attempting to assassinate President Park Chung Hee (January 1968, June 1970, and August 1974), capturing USS *Pueblo* (January 1968), armed guerrilla infiltrations (July 1965 and October 1968), and shooting down the U.S. EC-121 reconnaissance plane (April 1969), to name a few (Spector 1990: 121–22).

Second, unfavorable international security circumstances exacerbated South Korea's insecurity. The United States was dragged more deeply into the Vietnam quagmire (Krepinevich 1986: 56–99). The Vietnam War was particularly troublesome to South Korea. As Washington could not afford to risk another war, it failed to satisfy Seoul's desire for a tough U.S. military response to North Korea's provocations (Cho 2001: 105). This undermined the credibility of the U.S. security commitment in the perception of South Korea (Jung 1993: 92–93). Moreover, concerned about further drawdown of the USFK, South Korea contributed to the U.S. war effort in Vietnam by dispatching its own contingent—it sent approximately 320,000 soldiers to Vietnam over an eight-year period (1964 to 1973) and suffered more than 16,000 casualties including 5,000 killed in action (Choi 1996: 274). The Vietnam War ended in a communist victory after the U.S. withdrawal under the Nixon Doctrine. The Nixon Doctrine, announced in July 1969, emphasized the lead role of each Asian country in its own defense.[13] In essence, the doctrine was meant to scale down the U.S. presence in Asia to reduce its political, economic, and military burdens (Jung 1993: 92–93). Based on this doctrine, the United States planned major reductions in the USFK. In July 1970, Secretary of State William Rogers notified the South Korean government of the U.S. plan to withdraw some 20,000 U.S. troops from South Korea. And in August that year, Vice President Spiro Agnew indicated that the United States would withdraw the USFK completely over the next five years (Oh 2006: 107–9).[14]

The unilateral nature of those decisions and the manner in which they were delivered deeply disturbed President Park (Lee, Dong Hyun 2002: 148–50; Lee, Heung Hwan 2003: 142–50). In spite of his opposition, the withdrawal of the U.S. 7th ID was completed in March 1971,[15] and the 2nd ID remained as a "strategic reserve." For the first time since the end of the Korean War, this left the ROK forces deployed alone at the Demilitarized Zone (DMZ)—except for the Joint Security Area (JSA). Many South Koreans interpreted this as a loss of U.S. automatic engagement in the event of a North Korean invasion (Cho 2001: 102–3). To address such concerns, the United States agreed to provide South Korea with US$1.5 billion to modernize the ROK armed forces and establish the ROK-U.S. Combined Field Army.

It is in this context that President Park called for a "self-reliant national defense"[16] and began to implement a series of policies to modernize the capabilities of the ROK armed forces (Jung 1993: 96–97). However, he recognized that building a robust defense industry would be a painstakingly slow process and that South Korea's industrial base was in an early development stage (Ham 1998: 179). Further, without its own deterrent option, South Korea would remain vulnerable for the foreseeable future. He considered it implausible to deal with the North Korean threat by relying solely on conventional means and began to think radically about arming South Korea with nuclear weapons. President Park's secret nuclear weapon program still remains a "popular mystery," though recent academic research has begun to shed new light.

Evidence suggests that South Korea's nuclear weapon program dates back to the early 1970s.[17] In 1970, President Park established the Agency for Defense Development and the Weapons Exploitation Committee to produce or acquire weapon systems and military supplies (Cho 2001: 95; U.S. House of Representatives, Committee on International Relations 1978: 33–35, 79–80). By late 1973, President Park's nuclear weapon program had begun to take a concrete form, with the reinforcement of nuclear research teams and the effort to acquire nuclear reprocessing plants as well as associated core designs and technologies from France (Lee, Dong Hyun 2002: 153).

Concurrently, following India's nuclear test in 1974, nuclear nonproliferation became a high priority for the international community. Having observed South Korea's suspicious nuclear activities, the United States pressured President Park to halt the nuclear weapon program (Lee, Dong Hyun 2002: 159–61). It warned that it would pull out the USFK and stop providing military and financial assistance (Lee, Heung Hwan 2003: 75–83). From the U.S. standpoint, South Korea's possession of nuclear weapons was unacceptable, as it would destabilize and endanger East Asian regional security.

President Park had to address the U.S. concern. To assuage U.S. suspicion about its intentions, South Korea showed signs that it was renouncing its nuclear weapon program (Spector 1990: 122). It suspended major nuclear projects, including plans to import a French reprocessing plant and research reactors. In April 1975, South Korea ratified the Non-Proliferation Treaty (NPT), which it had already signed in 1968.[18] Nonetheless, President Park's nuclear ambition did not simply go away: a nuclear "hide-and-seek" game unfolded between Seoul and Washington. In a press interview with the *Washington Post* on June 26, 1975, President Park said, "If South Korea were not provided with a *U.S. nuclear umbrella,* South Korea would *do anything* to protect its security, *including the development of nuclear weapons*" (emphasis added; see Kihl 1977). In January 1976, most South Korean nuclear programs were simply renamed and reorganized. For example, the reprocessing plant project was renamed the "Alternative Project on Chemical Processing"[19] to avoid U.S. monitoring. The research nuclear reactor was to be developed independently (Lee, Dong Hyun 2002: 162–65).

However, the revelation that South Korea planned to construct two Canadian-designed heavy water reactors deepened U.S. suspicion. The South Korean government explained that the plan was intended to reduce its dependence on the United States and diversify the import sources of nuclear technology. The United States viewed it differently (Lee, Heung Hwan 2003: 73–79). From the U.S. standpoint, the heavy water reactors were known to be far less proliferation resistant. South Korea's intention seemed clear; it was seeking another avenue for nuclear weapon development. This intensified bilateral friction between South Korea and the United States.

When the next U.S. administration, under President Jimmy Carter, directly linked the USFK withdrawal plan with human rights conditions in South Korea, the ROK-U.S. relationship deteriorated further (Ham 1998: 179). Tensions spiraled downward as South Korea's nuclear program made noticeable progress, including the completion of nuclear fuel fabrication facilities in October 1978. Even though President Carter's openly harsh rhetoric on the human rights violations of President Park continued, his plan to withdraw U.S. forces did not materialize in the face of strong resistance from South Korea and the U.S. military (Ham 1998: 179–81).[20] The North Korean military threat was judged far too great to justify such withdrawals (Tow 1991: 188). Except for a symbolic withdrawal (3,400 troops), no substantial reduction of the USFK took place. The Carter administration terminated the withdrawal plan in 1979.[21] To shore up the eroding South Korean confidence in the bilateral alliance, both governments agreed to establish the Combined Forces Command (CFC), an integrated command and control system under a single command structure. The formal inauguration of the CFC in November 1978 was an important turning point in the ROK-U.S. military relationship, reducing South Korea's feeling of insecurity (Jung 1993: 97).

With the assassination of President Park in October 1979,[22] two decades of authoritarian leadership came to an end, and so did South Korea's nuclear weapon program (Kim, Jong Ryum 1997: 297–98). Today, many South Korean security experts and nuclear scientists, some of whom actually took part in President Park's nuclear weapon program, do not hesitate to point out that had the program continued, South Korea could have accumulated enough weapon-grade plutonium to manufacture a couple of nuclear bombs by the mid-1980s (Lee, Dong Hyun 2002: 165).

1990s: South Korea Adopts a Nonnuclear Policy

Termination of the Cold War resulted in many pivotal changes: the demise of the Soviet bloc, a new unipolar world order with the United States as the sole superpower, and growing economic prosperity facilitated by globalization and interdependence. The new era was perceived as ushering in a period of peace and prosperity. On the Korean peninsula, however, the 1990s were turbulent.

The First Nuclear Crisis. In 1988, President Roh Tae Woo set forth a bold new foreign policy initiative known as *Nordpolitik* (or Northern Policy). South Korea made a series of diplomatic efforts to normalize its relations with the communist bloc states (Jung 1993: 51). It normalized relations with the Soviet Union (in 1990) and China (in 1992), along with most of the other communist states. South Korea expanded its diplomatic sphere and influence through the Nordpolitik policy while North Korea became increasingly isolated from the international community.

Notwithstanding the success of the Nordpolitik policy, the security situation on the Korean peninsula became tense for two primary reasons: the emergence of the North Korean nuclear problem and the elimination of U.S. "ground-based" nuclear deterrence in South Korea. Although North Korea did have a nuclear weapon program in the 1970s, it had not drawn much attention (Kim, Myoung Ki 1999: 115). When the United States detected suspicious North Korean nuclear activities and demanded an International Atomic Energy Agency (IAEA) inspection, North Korea rejected the demand. Pyongyang reiterated its propaganda of a "nuclear-free Chosun" (Kim, Myoung Ki et al. 1999: 77, 137) and demanded an immediate withdrawal of the USFK along with U.S. tactical nuclear weapons as a condition for accepting the IAEA inspection and safeguards.

The second problem came from the United States. In September 1991, President George H. W. Bush announced his plan to unilaterally withdraw all land- and sea-based tactical nuclear weapons that had been deployed in foreign countries.[23] The plan included all forward-deployed tactical nuclear weapons in South Korea (Lee and Ji 2004: 182). In its execution, however, the U.S. policy of "neither confirm nor deny" (NCND), which underscored strategic ambiguity, was hastily discarded. The withdrawal of tactical nuclear weapons and the termination of the U.S. NCND policy may have been considered necessary to pressure Pyongyang to accept IAEA inspection (Kim, Myoung Ki et al. 1999: 182–84). However, South Korea was forced to review its security and defense policy in the absence of U.S. "ground-based" nuclear deterrence.

President Roh's response was to seek a negotiated solution to the North Korean nuclear problem, though other officials believed strongly that the North's nuclear program must be stopped at once, even by military means (Carter and Perry 1999: 128–31; Ham 1998: 197).[24] In December 1991, South Korea and North Korea adopted the "Agreement on Reconciliation, Non-aggression, and Exchanges and Cooperation," commonly known as the "Basic Agreement." It included many confidence-building measures such as "control of major movements of military units and major military exercises, the peaceful utilization of the DMZ, exchanges of military personnel and information, phased reductions in armaments including the elimination of weapons of mass destruction and attack capabilities and verifications thereof."[25]

A month later, the two Koreas signed another important agreement, the "Joint Declaration of the Denuclearization of the Korean Peninsula."[26] The declaration clearly spelled out that South and North Korea must "eliminate the danger of nuclear war" and "create an environment and conditions favorable for peace and peaceful unification . . . and contribute to peace and security in Asia and the world." It required both Koreas not to "test, manufacture, produce, receive, possess, store, deploy or use nuclear weapons."

Although the two agreements became effective in February 1992, they were never meaningfully implemented. Worse, they did little to stop Pyongyang's nuclear weapon program and eliminated any possibility that Seoul could develop reprocessing or uranium enrichment facilities, even for purely scientific and peaceful purposes (Kim, Myoung Ki et al. 1999: 110–15). It was undoubtedly a gesture of goodwill by South Korea to improve nuclear transparency as well as inter-Korean relations. But with that declaration South Korea lost important leverage that could be used to compel North Korea to give up its nuclear weapon program.

The Second Nuclear Crisis and Growing Strains in the U.S.-ROK Alliance. In October 2002, the second North Korean nuclear crisis began to unfold. The U.S. intelligence community learned that North Korea was secretly pursuing uranium enrichment. It was considered a material breach of the 1994 Agreed Framework, in which North Korea agreed to freeze all nuclear-related activities in exchange for the provision of two light water reactors by the United States.

When the U.S. assistant secretary of state for East Asian and Pacific Affairs, James Kelly, visited North Korea in October 2002, he heard "shocking news." Kang Suk Joo, the first vice foreign minister, was said to have admitted that North Korea had nuclear weapons and argued that it was "entitled" to such arms because of the continuing hostile U.S. policy and threats (*New York Times* 2002).[27]

For President Roh Moo Hyun, who took office in 2003, the most pressing issues were the North Korean nuclear problem and the adjustment of the ROK-U.S. alliance. With his progressive and pacifist political orientation, President Roh initially sought to play the role of mediator between the United States and North Korea in dealing with the nuclear crisis, creating controversies in Seoul and Washington.[28]

The U.S. war in Iraq became another source of friction between Seoul and Washington. President Roh considered it necessary to send troops to Iraq to secure U.S. cooperation in resolving the North Korean nuclear issue. However, because of the South Korean public's opposition and delays in preparation, troop deployment was slow. The George W. Bush administration's unilateral conduct of the global war on terror after the 9/11 terrorist attacks and its unilateral adjustment of the USFK amid the North Korean nuclear problem were also partly responsible for the growing tensions between the two countries.[29]

The response to the North Korean nuclear problem was to be multilateral, with more witnesses, better burden sharing, and stronger punishment if necessary. The result was the Six-Party Talks, a multilateral diplomatic process that included all concerned states in the region: the two Koreas, the United States, Japan, China, and Russia. The underlying objective of this process was to persuade North Korea to end all its nuclear weapon programs in exchange for economic aid packages from the other five countries.

The first round of Six-Party Talks was held in Beijing in late August 2003. However, as North Korea rejected the U.S. proposal for complete, verifiable, and irreversible dismantlement, the talks proved to be difficult from the outset. The intermittent talks finally made a meaningful breakthrough in September 2005, when in the fourth round the participants adopted the "9.19 Joint Statement."[30] However, follow-up meetings produced no meaningful progress. And after the United States imposed new financial sanctions, North Korea refused to participate in the Six-Party Talks.[31]

North Korea exacerbated the situation by launching seven missiles into the East Sea on July 5, 2006. Among them was a three-stage ballistic missile, the Taepodong 2, which was later found to have failed. North Korea's test firing of missiles resulted in an exceptionally harsh response from the international community. Japan played a leading role in formulating a U.N. resolution demanding that U.N. member states be allowed to monitor North Korea's missile development and that they not purchase North Korean missiles, related components, or technologies. North Korea's position remained unchanged. On the same day that the U.N. Security Council Resolution 1695 (UNSC RES 1695) was adopted, North Korea announced its rejection of such an "unreasonable" Resolution and stated its determination to test additional missiles to further develop its self-defense capability.

North Korea's Nuclear Test. On October 9, 2006, North Korea's Central News Agency released the following statement:

> The DPRK successfully conducted an underground nuclear test under secure conditions . . . a great leap forward in the building of a great prosperous powerful socialist nation . . . a historic event as it greatly encouraged and pleased the Korean People's Army (KPA) and people that have wished to have powerful self-reliant defense capability. It will contribute to defending the peace and stability on the Korean Peninsula and in the area around it.[32]

About a week after North Korea's nuclear test, the U.N. Security Council unanimously adopted Resolution 1718 (UNSC RES 1718) imposing weapon and financial sanctions on North Korea. Both Moscow and Beijing joined South Korea and the United States in condemning Pyongyang's nuclear adventurism.

Pyongyang's nuclear test presented perhaps the toughest security challenge to Seoul since the end of the Korean War. In the midst of adjusting the ROK-U.S. security alliance, South Korea was unprepared to tackle the North Korean nuclear threat by itself. Instead of seeking its own countermeasures, South Korea responded in traditional ways to secure a U.S. commitment to defend South Korea. At the same time, it sought to maintain its nonnuclear posture. The importance of the U.S. commitment was emphasized in the thirty-eighth ROK-U.S. annual Security Consultative Meeting (SCM). South Korea argued strongly for the inclusion of the term *extended deterrence* in the joint communiqué in addition to a nuclear umbrella, whereas the United States was reluctant to do so (*Yonhap News* 2006). Reference to the U.S. extended deterrence commitment was eventually included in the Joint Statement, once again restoring the salience of the U.S. nuclear umbrella.

Despite the tense situation, around December 2006 the United States began to show willingness to engage in bilateral talks with the DPRK, which it had earlier rejected. One such bilateral meeting took place in Beijing in November 2006, and another meeting was held in Berlin in January 2007. Only then did the Six-Party Talks begin to make progress. On February 13, 2007, all six parties agreed to take "initial phase" actions to "disable" the North Korean nuclear weapon programs based on what is known as the "2.13 Agreement."

In October 2007, two meaningful events occurred. At an inter-Korean summit meeting in Pyongyang, President Roh and Chairman Kim agreed on the "Declaration on the Advancement of South-North Korean Relations, Peace and Prosperity." And the six parties reached a "second-phase" agreement, which gave some hope for making significant progress to complete North Korea's nuclear disablement by the end of 2007.

Nevertheless, some South Koreans still have concerns over the U.S. approach to the North Korean nuclear problem. They worry that the United States might adopt the "Indian model" and implicitly acknowledge North Korea as a nuclear weapon state as long as it does not proliferate. If so, South Korea would remain subject and vulnerable to a North Korean nuclear threat. Such a U.S. orientation toward North Korea would most likely damage the credibility of the U.S. security commitment and ROK-U.S. relations.

Dynamics and Interactions of Policy Considerations

In each time period discussed above, nuclear weapons were important—first reflected in the deployment of U.S. tactical nuclear weapons in South Korea and thereafter in South Korea's own policy initiatives. In the 1970s, South Korea's security policy emphasized the development of an indigenous nuclear weapon program. Beginning in the 1990s, the importance of nuclear weapons for South Korea's security declined. Since the 1991 Joint Declaration of the Denuclearization of the Korean Peninsula, South Korea has unilaterally adhered to a nonnuclear posture despite North Korea's nuclear challenge. It has abided by the spirit and principles of the Declaration as well as international nuclear nonproliferation norms.

The dramatic shift in South Korea's nuclear policy is a rather unusual case. It is difficult to find a country that once actively pursued a nuclear weapon program, has since renounced its nuclear ambition, and maintains a strict nonnuclear posture. South Africa and Libya are other rare cases. As history shows, once a country decides to go nuclear, international pressures (such as economic sanctions) and other disincentives seldom succeed in reversing that decision. The cases of India and Pakistan, and the more recent instances of North Korea and Iran, exemplify this point.

What explains the change in South Korea's nuclear security orientation? This chapter argues that it was a combination of FoA and FoE.[33] These two factors are broadly affected by changes in four variables: (1) the international security environment, (2) the North Korean threat, (3) the U.S. security commitment and strategy, and (4) South Korea's threat perception. These variables are closely interconnected and determine the type and degree of the FoA and FoE. South Korea's strategic choices and nuclear policy were distinct in each time period.

The International Security Environment

South Korea's security has been influenced by the larger structure of the international security environment during and after the Cold War. Each period has differently affected South Korea's overall security situation and produced fundamentally different outcomes in its security policy.

Initially, the influence of the international environment was benign for Korea. The Allied victory in World War II liberated Korea from Japanese colonial rule. Soon thereafter, however, the international environment became very negative. The Korean War and the subsequent division of Korea was an unfortunate product of the Cold War confrontation. Also, the U.S. failure to save Vietnam from communism revealed the weaknesses in U.S. security and military policies. When South Korea's sense of insecurity increased as a result, it began to pursue its own nuclear weapon program (Cho 2001: 104–5, 112).

The beginning of the 1990s was a significant turning point. The collapse of the Soviet Union and the end of the Cold War led to the downfall of communist states, leaving North Korea more isolated. Accordingly, the threat posed by North Korea was considered to have decreased substantially (Ham 1998: 244). All in all, this produced a strategically, diplomatically, and militarily advantageous circumstance for South Korea and relieved its security concerns.

The North Korean Threat

North Korea's military strategy can be summarized by two core principles: surprise preemptive attack and simultaneous attack from the front and the rear. As North Korea could not engage in a long war of attrition against the combined ROK-U.S. forces, it would need to achieve strategic and tactical surprise, take the initiative in the early stages of war, and occupy core areas of South Korea before U.S. reinforcements could arrive. In short, North Korea's military strategy calls for a "blitzkrieg," or lightning war (Ham 1998: 35–36, 189–90).[34]

To this end, North Korea has amassed its troops along the DMZ, strengthened its multidimensional infiltration capability, maintained a large number of specially trained guerrilla warfare units, and developed strategic weapons, all of which could threaten South Korea's strategic center of gravity. Despite its economic hardship, North Korea stubbornly maintained a million-person army and developed missiles and weapons of mass destruction (WMD), including biochemical agents and nuclear weapons (Jeon 2005: 94–100; Kim, Kyoung Soo 2004: 122–48). This North Korean threat has been a major security challenge not only for South Korea but for Northeast Asia as a whole.

Until the early 1970s, the North Korean military enjoyed numerical superiority over South Korea. Although the North Korean threat has been mostly conventional in nature, its engagement in terrorism and irregular warfare should not be overlooked. From the 1960s to the 1990s, North Korea committed as many as 550 acts of armed provocation against South Korea (Ham 1998: 190–91). In response, South Korea began its own military buildup, mainly focusing on developing a qualitative edge in military capabilities, to augment the USFK presence. South Korea felt it necessary to have its own capability for military deterrence. For that reason, President Park sought to acquire retaliatory capabilities to prevent North Korean acts of terrorism as well as other military provocations. His conclusion was to develop nuclear weapons.

In the mid- and late 1970s, North Korea's economy began to stagnate under the inherent contradictions and inefficiencies of a socialist economy. To make matters worse, the death of Kim Il Sung and massive floods took place in the mid-1990s.[35] Unable to pursue its conventional military buildup and modernization, North Korea began to focus on asymmetric capabilities: biochemical agents and their delivery means, such as mid- and long-range missiles (Ham 1998: 295). This time, however, South Korea chose not to develop nuclear or biochemical weapons.

The U.S. Security Commitment and Strategy Transformations

Changes in U.S. security policy and its security commitments were especially important. The interaction among shifts in U.S. policy, changes in the USFK posture, and South Korea's response to them have been the strongest determinant of South Korea's nuclear policy.

In the 1950s, the ROK-U.S. alliance and the introduction of tactical nuclear weapons provided a credible deterrence for South Korea. In the 1970s, however, the Nixon administration began to withdraw the U.S. 7th ID over President Park's strong objection.[36] Fearing further reductions in the USFK and concerned that Washington would eventually abandon South Korea, President Park undertook a secret nuclear weapon program, proclaiming his strategic objective of "self-reliant national defense" (Lee and Ji 2004: 164–73). Notwithstanding the Carter administration's decision to cancel the troop withdrawals and the creation of the CFC, President Park's nuclear weapon programs continued until the last moment of his presidency.

In the wake of the termination of the Cold War, the United States discarded its long-maintained NCND policy. And the U.S. nuclear deterrence on the Korean peninsula, based on physical presence, was converted to "off-shore deterrence." Further, in line with its mid- and long-term strategic assessment, the George H. W. Bush administration planned to reduce and readjust its level of military presence in East Asia, including the USFK. Despite Washington's abrogation of the NCND policy and its force readjustment plans, no substantial change materialized with respect to U.S. security policy and the USFK. Overall, the strategic environment favored South Korea, and it did not pursue a nuclear option.

The emergence of the first North Korean nuclear crisis in the early 1990s and the U.S. contemplation of a surgical military strike on selected North Korean nuclear facilities created insecurity in South Korea. Though the 1994 U.S.-DPRK Agreed Framework helped prevent the crisis from escalating to a war, South Korea became alienated in the bilateral negotiations. The South Korean government did not openly reconsider its position of denuclearization, but it is noteworthy that a domestic debate over "nuclear sovereignty" surfaced during that time.

Since the turn of the twenty-first century, the ROK and the United States have worked cooperatively to readjust their alliance by focusing on bilateral issues such as the relocation of U.S. bases, the transfer of ten specific missions, OPCON, and strategic flexibility. Both Seoul and Washington agreed on a substantial reduction in the number of USFK. And South Korea's sense of insecurity about further reductions has become less pronounced.

South Korea's Threat Perceptions

In the 1950s, the Korean War's terrible devastation caused enormous psychological stress among South Koreans. Thus, while the 1953 ROK-U.S. Mutual Defense Treaty was an institutional mechanism to assuage South Korea's feeling of insecurity, the later U.S. deployment of tactical nuclear weapons was the tangible manifestation of U.S. security commitment. Still, in South Korea's view, the U.S. responses to North Korea's open hostilities were disappointingly weak and unreliable. And during the late 1960s and the 1970s, South Korea's threat perception rose dramatically in response to the Nixon Doctrine and USFK withdrawals. It can be argued that the weakening of the U.S. security commitment and South Korea's increased threat perception were the two catalysts in Seoul's decision to pursue a secret nuclear weapon program.

After the 1980s, as North Korea became more actively involved in terrorist acts than in direct military provocations, South Korea's threat perception became less strictly military and focused more on the asymmetric and quasi-military aspects. Due to its own rapid economic growth, South Korea could also accelerate the building of its defense industry and acquisition of major weapon systems, thus regaining confidence in its conventional military capability. In short, South Korea's perception of the North Korean threat alternated throughout the 1990s. The early 1990s unfolded with a strategically favorable environment for South Korea. Continued economic growth, hosting of the 1988 Seoul Olympic Games, and Nordpolitik's diplomatic success galvanized South Korea's confidence. With the onset of the North Korean nuclear crisis, this favorable atmosphere quickly reversed. North Korea's nuclear development undermined South Korea's efforts to address the imbalance in conventional military capability and raised the level of perceived threat from North Korea. Furthermore, when the United States contemplated military strikes against North Korea's nuclear facilities, South Koreans

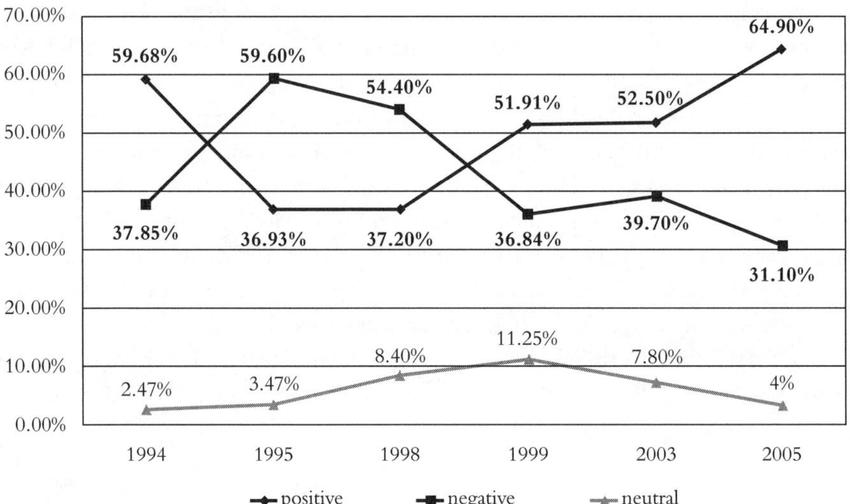

FIG. 13-1. Recent Changes in South Korea's Threat Perception: South Korean Public's General Perception Toward North Korea.
SOURCE: Annual National Survey on Unification Issues (1994–2005), Korea Institute for National Unification (KINU), http://www.kinu.or.kr.

recognized the real possibility of a war on the peninsula. They panicked when a North Korean official threatened that "Seoul would be a sea of flames" in the event of war.[37]

South Korea's threat perception showed this vacillating pattern until the turn of the twenty-first century, whereupon, to everyone's surprise, it diminished rapidly. Survey results showed a significant reduction in threat perception among South Koreans (Korea Institute for National Unification [KINU] 1994–2005; see also Figures 13-1 and 13-2). President Kim Dae Jung's "sunshine policy" greatly contributed to this perceptual change. The perception of a reduced threat from North Korea made for a new way of thinking about North Koreans as "brothers" in need of support and cooperation, rather than as intimidating "enemies" who should be contained.

Fear of Abandonment Versus Fear of Entrapment

The relationship of these four variables to South Korea's FoA and FoE is not directly causal or even temporal or substantive. However, the pattern of their interaction shows that certain variables—the U.S. security commitment and South Korea's threat perception—carry more weight than others (see Table 13-1).

South Korea has always feared abandonment, but its fear of entrapment is a more recent phenomenon. In the past, any sign of weakening U.S. security com-

Do you believe that North Korea possesses nuclear weapons?

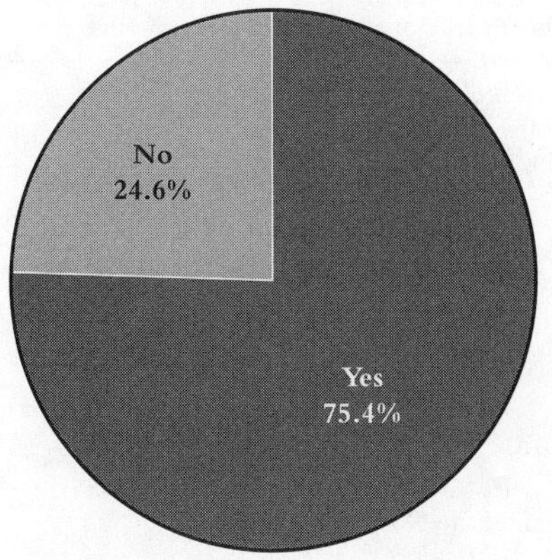

Do you consider North Korea's possession of nuclear weapons a threat?

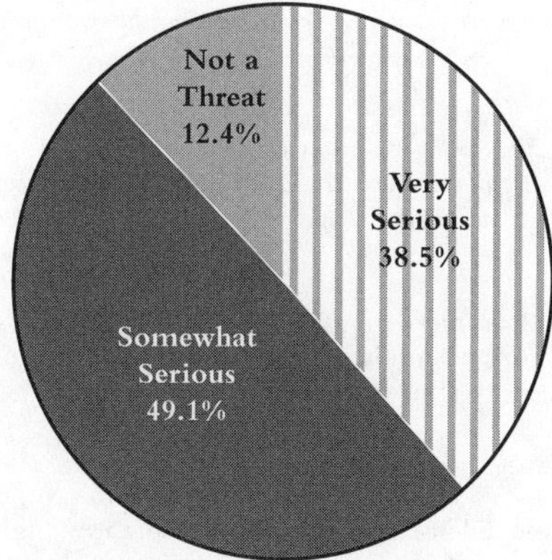

Who is responsible for North Korea's nuclear test??

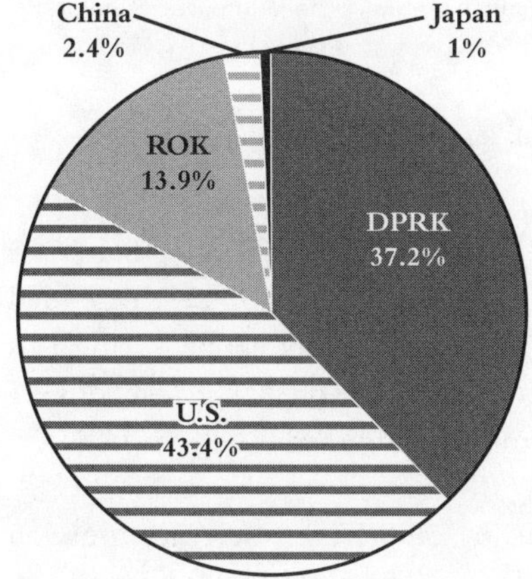

How uneasy are you after the North Korean nuclear test?

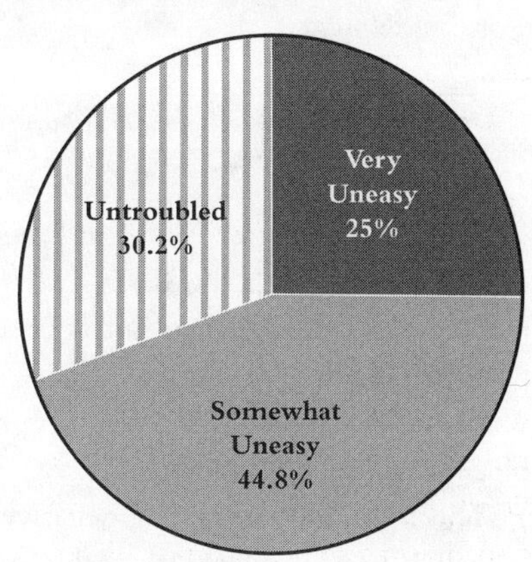

FIG. 13-2. South Korea's Threat Perception After North Korea's Nuclear Test.

mitment strengthened the FoA. But the proactive and aggressive military policy of the United States is worsening South Korea's FoE. In particular, South Koreans worry that the widening scope of U.S. military intervention beyond the Korean peninsula will increase the risk of their country's involvement in regional and international conflicts. From this point of view, it could be argued that FoA and FoE have opposite effects on the security policy of South Korea.

During the earlier periods, FoA was the main reason for the greater salience of nuclear issues in South Korea; the later periods saw the emergence of FoE, which brought with it a new dynamic. The distinctive features of each period influenced South Korea's strategic choices and nuclear salience as follows.

TABLE 13-1

Effect of Four Variables on South Korea's Fear of Abandonment (FoA) and Fear of Entrapment (FoE), 1958–2007

1958–68
Very poor international security environment; heightened threat from North Korea; very high confidence in U.S. security assurances; very high perception of the North Korean threat → low FoA
1970–80
Poor international security environment; extremely high threat from North Korea; medium to low confidence in U.S. security assurances; very high perception of the North Korean threat → extreme FoA
1990–2000
Good international security environment; diminishing threat from North Korea; high confidence in U.S. security assurances; high perception of the North Korean threat → medium FoA, low FoE (newly appeared)
2000–07
Good international security environment; change in the nature of the North Korean threat (asymmetrical threats); medium confidence in U.S. security assurances; medium perception of the North Korean threat → low FoA, medium FoE (FoE ≥ FoA)

NOTE: The four variables are (1) the international security environment, (2) changes in the North Korean threat, (3) the U.S. security commitment and strategy, and (4) South Korea's perception of the threat.

South Korea under President Rhee relied completely on the United States for its security through the ROK-U.S. alliance. The completion of U.S. extended nuclear deterrence by the introduction of tactical nuclear weapons during this period shaped the initial rise of nuclear salience in South Korea. The level of FoA was kept low by a strong U.S. security commitment with the help of U.S. extended nuclear deterrence.

The 1970s saw extremely negative changes in South Korea's security situation as well as in its security ties with the United States. The Cold War environment, North Korea's armed provocations and acts of terrorism, a weaker U.S. security commitment under the Nixon Doctrine, and the subsequent high level of South Korea's threat perception all played a part in heightening the FoA. Hence, in the 1970s, South Korea made considerable effort to lay the groundwork for enhancing its own defense capability. At that time, South Korea's strategic objective became what President Park called a "self-reliant national defense," which was to include the development of nuclear weapons. With these negative variables, the salience of nuclear weapons for South Korea's security was unusually high. This was manifest in the continued presence of U.S. tactical nuclear weapons and South Korea's pursuit of a secret nuclear weapon program.

In the early 1990s, security conditions turned in favor of South Korea. Although the North Korean threat was still formidable, it began to diminish as

South Korea's Nordpolitik policy succeeded in diplomatically encircling and isolating North Korea. And the U.S. security commitment remained firm. Although the withdrawal of U.S. tactical nuclear weapons and the official end of the NCND policy put an end to ground-based nuclear deterrence, the status of the USFK and the U.S. nuclear umbrella did not change. Despite the positive turn, South Korea was still wary of North Korea's nuclear activities. But that perceived threat did not raise South Korea's FoA, thanks to other positive conditions. With a moderate level of FoA, South Korea could confidently maintain a nonnuclear posture.

In the first half of the 1990s the new concern over FoE began to appear in South Korea's security equation. Seoul began to fear becoming involved in a conflict unilaterally initiated by the United States, as would have happened if, for example, Washington had pursued a surgical strike on North Korean nuclear facilities at Yongbyon during the first nuclear crisis. U.S. military action against North Korea would certainly trigger retaliation from Pyongyang and endanger the South Korean people. The lack of prior consultation on the part of the United States fueled this new fear.

Later, through its Nordpolitik policy, South Korea's strategic objective altered further to change the nature of North Korea itself. During the late 1990s and early 2000s, President Kim Dae Jung's "sunshine policy" attempted to transform North Korea from a hated enemy to a trustworthy partner.

Notwithstanding positive developments, South Korea faces another wave of major security challenges in the twenty-first century: nuclear tests by North Korea and the ongoing adjustment of the ROK-U.S. alliance. Although the overall international security environment is favorable to South Korea, the new challenges complicate its strategic position. The South Korean government remains confident that the USFK will remain on the Korean peninsula for the foreseeable future, but it also believes that the USFK's involvement in global conflicts has become more likely. Will South Korea's FoA and FoE continue in the future? If so, how will they evolve and affect South Korea's nuclear strategy?

First, regarding FoA, the current readjustment of the ROK-U.S. alliance includes weakening or dismantling the structural links between the ROK military and the USFK. The OPCON transfer to South Korea will likely lead to an eventual end of the CFC, which has organically united the two armies.[38] After a final resolution of the North Korean nuclear problem and the establishment of a permanent peace regime on the Korean peninsula, a complete withdrawal of the USFK cannot be ruled out. If that happens, South Korea could once again find itself fearing abandonment, since the USFK has been not only a strong deterrent against the North Korean threat but also a stabilizer in the region.

Second, South Korea's FoE will likely remain in place for some time. In the event of further escalation of the North Korean nuclear problem, the international community would certainly impose tougher sanctions on Pyongyang. If international sanctions included military measures, South Korea would be incapable of managing and controlling its own security. Having placed its priority on resolving the nuclear problem through peaceful negotiations, Seoul has expressed reservations about participating in the U.S.-led missile defense program and the Proliferation Security Initiative (PSI) to avoid unnecessarily provoking Pyongyang. Moreover, the expansion of the strategic role of the USFK not only to counter the North Korean threat, but also other regional and international conflicts, could jeopardize South Korea's security.

A decision by South Korea to pursue its own nuclear deterrent could be viewed as a logical conclusion to resolve the tension between FoA and FoE. Nevertheless, South Korea's seemingly illogical strategic choice of a nonnuclear posture makes perfect sense for the following reasons.

First and foremost, the United States is believed to be the key determinant of South Korea's FoA and FoE. The U.S. security commitment influences South Korea's strategic choices and shapes the salience of nuclear issues. A strong U.S. security commitment and the provision of its nuclear umbrella play the role of a "bottle cap" that keeps South Korea from thinking it needs to develop nuclear weapons. Thus the current nonnuclear posture of South Korea is a direct result of the strength and credibility of the U.S. commitment.

Second, South Korea voluntarily renounced the nuclear option. It announced the Joint Declaration of the Denuclearization of the Korean Peninsula in 1991. Since then, the South Korean government has faithfully abided by international nonproliferation norms. Although it pursued a nuclear weapon program during the 1970s, South Korea today is widely recognized as a responsible middle power, based on its success in economic development and political democratization. South Korea has extensive bilateral and multilateral ties with many countries. It has more to gain from increased interdependence on various fronts. If it were to develop nuclear weapons, a short-term security interest might be served, but the cost would surely outweigh the benefit. Simply put, the nuclear option is not an attractive alternative for South Korea.

Third, South Korea's choice of a nonnuclear posture makes even more sense when looking far into the future. Unquestionably, unification of the Korean peninsula is the strongest desire of all Koreans. Yet unification will have to accompany fundamental changes in Northeast Asia. It is essential that South Korea maintain the trust of the major regional players, including the United States, Japan, China, and Russia to eliminate external obstacles to unification. Only then can a unified Korea be born with the blessings of its neighbors and the international community. However, a South Korea with nuclear weapons would seriously set back the goal of unification. It would not only weaken the U.S. security commitment and the ROK-U.S. alliance, but also turn South Korea's neighbors into potential enemies. These are turns of event that South Korea cannot afford, either militarily or politically.

In sum, South Korea's strategic choice regarding the nuclear option must be viewed in a context that is not purely military. The continued U.S. security commitment, the improved international status of South Korea, and the desire for a unified Korean peninsula should all be taken into account when forecasting South Korea's strategic policy. To secure and maintain international support for unification, to attain that goal, and to have a reliable ROK-U.S. security partnership, South Korea will continue to make its best effort to envisage a common future with the United States. As long as it is able to do so, it is very likely that South Korea will maintain its nonnuclear posture.

A Cooperative, Self-Reliant Defense and Extended Deterrence

For the past fifty years, South Korea's strategic thinking has been reactive in nature. Most of its security policy choices were made in response to changes in the security environment, both foreign and domestic. Recently, however, South Korea has become more proactive in pursuing its security policy agenda (Kim, Young Ho 2004: 202–3). Most notable are South Korea's active participation in the Six-Party Talks and its new doctrine, known as "Cooperative Self-Reliant National Defense." Although the public has supported the former, the latter policy initiative has been controversial among the South Korean public as well as Korea watchers elsewhere. In August 2003, President Roh stressed the necessity of achieving self-reliant defense capabilities:

> It is unbecoming for us to allow our defense policy to unravel and national opinion to go into a tailspin every time the strategy of the United States changes. Things will not work out simply by crying out against the withdrawal of the American troops. Now it is time for us to accept the changes in reality. During my remaining term in office, I intend to help lay a firm foundation for our armed forces to be fully equipped with self-reliant national defense capabilities within the next 10 years.[39]

This stance was criticized by conservative circles who feared the new doctrine could seriously damage the very foundation of the ROK-U.S. alliance. On the other hand, progressive groups and leftists have argued that the alliance would increase the chances of South Korea's involvement in regional conflicts. This domestic debate has helped resurrect South Korea's FoA and FoE.

To address this problem, the ROK National Security Council explained that the core concept of cooperative self-reliant defense is the development of self-reliant national defense capabilities while maintaining a mutually beneficial ROK-U.S. alliance to cope with present and future security challenges. Put differently, improving Seoul's own military readiness and adjusting the ROK-U.S. alliance would work "in tandem." The new policy presupposes close consultation and cooperation between South Korea and the United States in their respective security policies.

Since then, Seoul's policy makers have devised an ambitious defense reform program, known as "Defense Reform 2020," to make the ROK defense posture less vulnerable to external changes and expand its areas of responsibility—not confining them to the North Korean threat, but preparing to meet other needs for security cooperation with regional and global scope (Republic of Korea 2005). The primary objectives of the new policy are to address increased defense requirements, particularly with respect to North Korea's asymmetric capabilities; to efficiently allocate a limited defense budget and resources;[40] and to forge a better functioning ROK-U.S. alliance. In short, the new policy of cooperative self-reliant defense and its defense reform program are both a reflection of South Korea's present security reality and a projection of its strong determination to cope with future challenges.

After Seoul's policy makers clarified the policy concept for the South Korean public and its counterpart in the United States, the debate receded somewhat. Still, the most important prerequisite for attaining this policy objective remains unchanged: the peaceful resolution of the North Korean nuclear problem. Today, one of the most serious security concerns for South Korea and Northeast Asia as a whole is the fear of nuclear proliferation.

The possibility of either a decision by South Korea to go nuclear or a regional nuclear arms race still seems remote, but neither can be ruled out completely. Unless timely and appropriate measures are taken, nonnuclear states in the region, including South Korea and Japan, may be compelled to consider their own nuclear options. At this time, the United States is believed to hold the key to preventing this worrisome development. The key is the continued provision of the U.S. nuclear umbrella.[41] The latest reaffirmation of the U.S. extended deterrence commitment to South Korea was made at the thirty-eighth SCM in 2006. What is notable about the SCM was that the term *extended nuclear deterrence* was inserted in the Joint Communiqué upon South Korea's insistence.[42] Due to this, the excessive fear of nuclear threat in South Korea has been largely mitigated. The insertion of the term altered nothing significant in the ROK-U.S. security relationship. Why then did South Korea so persistently request this wording in the Joint Communiqué? To answer this question, it is important to revisit the evolution of the ROK's defense strategy.

As discussed earlier, it is now clear that "ground-based" nuclear deterrence has been replaced by "offshore" deterrence. The former was viewed as particularly strong since it consisted of a "trip-wire" strategy with forward deployment of the USFK and the presence of U.S. tactical nuclear weapons on South Korean soil. Though more flexible, "offshore" deterrence is mainly conventional and is largely symbolic in nature.

The trip-wire strategy, which deliberately made the USFK "hostage" in the event of a North Korean attack, was perceived to ensure an automatic U.S. military involvement. It assuaged the FoA among South Koreans. Despite the recent drawdown of USFK strength, the remaining U.S. 2nd ID still serves this function. Nowadays, though, U.S. officials say that a trip-wire strategy is outdated and no longer valid;[43] yet they argue that the United States is firmly committed to the defense of South Korea.

Having agreed on a wide range of outstanding military-related issues, such as the relocation of the Yongsan garrison and the 2nd ID, the USFK's strategic flexibility, and the transfer of OPCON to the ROK Joint Chiefs of Staff (JCS), all of which would ultimately dissolve the trip-wire strategy, South Korea and the United States have already moved from trip-wire deterrence to real "offshore deterrence."

The present problem is that both Seoul's and Washington's efforts to compensate for the loss of physical links and a weaker security guarantee have fallen short of each other's expectations. Certainly the United States will provide a "bridging capability" for South Korea in the form of time and know-how as the ROK military prepares to assume the current roles and missions of the USFK.[44] These military preparations will inevitably take considerable time and money. In particular, their enormous budgetary implications could impede policy implementation. There is only a slim chance that South Korea would acquire enough strategic assets, such as C^4ISR, counter-ABC (atomic/biological/chemical), air-defense, long-range strike, and lift capabilities, to meet the schedule. Something has to fill the security gap, and this is exactly why the insertion of the term *extended deterrence* matters to South Korea.

Strangely, though, the continued provision of U.S. extended deterrence seems to have opposite effects on FoA and FoE in South Korea: The continued provision of the U.S. nuclear umbrella for South Korea helps reduce FoA, but the new U.S. nuclear doctrine also increases the level of FoE. Basically, the FoA and FoE issues relate to how the United States will handle the North Korean nuclear problem. South Korea's FoA could soar if the United States tacitly accepted North Korea's nuclear weapon status with a condition of nonproliferation. Conversely, the FoE would linger as long as the public believes that a U.S. military strike on North Korea is possible.[45] U.S. missile defense and PSI are concerns as well.

To assuage Seoul's concerns, the United States has shown greater flexibility and enthusiasm for diplomatic negotiations while maintaining a strong combined military deterrence.[46] Strong reaffirmation of the U.S. extended deterrence commitment has raised South Korea's confidence in its security and strengthened the U.S. position when dealing with North Korea.

The question of whether extended deterrence will continue to be credible over the long term is somewhat problematic. From South Korea's perspective, the challenge for U.S. extended deterrence lies in its credibility, not its capability. The main reason that U.S. credibility is at issue is simply that extended deterrence cannot be taken for granted. Because of the manner and atmosphere in which U.S. "extended deterrence" commitment was made, some have questioned the sincerity of that commitment. After the thirty-eighth SCM, Seoul's policy makers explained to the public that the inclusion of the term signaled meaningful progress since they interpreted it as a more specific manifestation of the nuclear umbrella. But to Seoul's disappointment, U.S. officials, among them Burwell B. Bell, the commander of the USFK and the CFC, refused to acknowledge this interpretation and publicly downplayed the significance of the term's inclusion.[47] As the sharp difference of opinion over the interpretation of the term continued, the two countries made little progress on the follow-up questions, such as under what circumstances and how U.S. extended deterrence will be implemented, what kinds of response measures are available, whether this kind of consideration should be reflected in the combined war plan of OPLAN 5027, and so forth.

To enhance the credibility of the U.S. extended nuclear deterrence commitment, the United States must pay more attention to how that commitment is perceived in South Korea. This is not, however, to suggest that Washington alone is responsible for this task. Seoul's policy makers also need to be more forthright about what they can and cannot do to meet the U.S. regional and global strategic priorities. Doing so may include cooperating on the realignment of the forward U.S. military presence, devising a new method of keeping the ROK and U.S. militaries closely linked even after the OPCON transfer, and expanding the scope of the ROK-U.S. alliance to include cooperation on nonproliferation and counterterrorism. Frequent meetings and consultations at various levels will also be essential. Through these measures, both South Korea and the United States will be able to build a shared understanding of extended deterrence. In bilateral consultations, both sides need to be sure that they understand each other's words and intentions. Finally, it should be emphasized that U.S. extended deterrence will be effective only if it is backed up by strong U.S. political determination.

Conclusion: Future Policy Implications

In 1991, South Korea chose a strategy of managing the North Korean threat by denuclearizing the Korean peninsula. Along with the Joint Declaration, South Korea permanently abandoned the nuclear option. Even after North Korea's recent nuclear test, South Korea maintains a nonnuclear posture and seeks peaceful resolution of the North Korean nuclear problem.

South Korea's policy decisions are undoubtedly due to changes in external conditions; the post-Cold War security environment is unfolding favorably for South Korea. This trend is believed to be irreversible. Once South Korea and

North Korea settle the "nuclear problem" peacefully, South Korea believes that it will be in a position to determine North Korea's future.

With respect to the looming concern about "nuclear dominos" in East Asia, there is no ambiguity in South Korea's position. That is, the nuclear domino game is not a "winnable" one from a South Korean viewpoint. Even if South Korea were to become involved in a nuclear arms race by initiating another nuclear weapon program, time is not on its side. And surrounding conditions would prove to be extremely unfavorable for South Korea. Furthermore, choosing the nuclear option would jeopardize the security commitment from the United States, South Korea's long-time security partner. Fortunately, the U.S. nuclear umbrella (or extended nuclear deterrence) was reaffirmed at the thirty-eighth SCM. However, the credibility of that commitment matters the most. High credibility of the U.S. commitment is key to preventing a decision by South Korea to develop nuclear weapons.

Some advocates of "nuclear sovereignty" argue that South Korea must possess reprocessing and enriching capabilities to manufacture nuclear weapons if it becomes necessary (Yang 2006: 163). However, the emergence of the nuclear sovereignty issue is a transient phenomenon and would have little impact on South Korea's policy or strategic choices.

Some policy elites, including political leaders, express the view that South Korea's possession of nuclear weapons would protect it from North Korea and ensure its survival for the time being. But a nuclear weapon program would ultimately become a major obstacle to reunification. Hence, no South Korean political leader is likely to consider the nuclear option seriously. A brief summary of the argument is presented in Table 13-2.

In retrospect, much of the discourse relating to the salience of a nuclear weapon capability for South Korea has centered on two fronts: (1) dealing with the North Korean threat and (2) preserving security ties with the United States. Recent changes in the security environment on the Korean peninsula, in Northeast Asia, and in the rest of the world, however, necessitate a reexamination of South Korea's nonnuclear posture in the context of current inter-Korean relations and adjustments in the ROK-U.S. alliance. In particular, the North Korean nuclear test and, more remotely, the aftermath of the 9/11 terrorist attacks on the United States, have brought many significant changes to strategic considerations in both countries. South Korea must pay close attention to developments that could affect Northeast Asia's security environment and consider how it can quickly readjust the current alliance as well as maintain and strengthen the U.S. extended nuclear deterrence. Thus the discussion of South Korea's future security should not focus on whether it might once again choose to develop nuclear weapons but on how to maintain a strong ROK-U.S. alliance that preserves regional order and stability without the fear of nuclear proliferation. Finally, as South Korea looks beyond

TABLE 13-2

Major Factors in South Korea's Nuclear Orientation

Variable	Historical Period			
	Initial period of U.S. provision of nuclear umbrella, 1958–68	Nuclear option, 1970–80	Denuclearization policy, 1990–2000	Maintaining and strengthening nonnuclear posture, 2000–07
Quality of the international security environment	Very poor	Poor	Good	Good
North Korean threat	Heightening • Postwar recovery and rebuilding military • Quantitative superiority	Extremely high • Armed provocations • Four-Line military policy • Quantitative superiority • Acts of terrorism	Diminishing • 1st nuclear crisis • Quantitative superiority • Increased asymmetric threats (WMD, missile)	Changed • 2nd nuclear crisis • Quantitative superiority • Increased asymmetric threats (WMD, missile, plus nukes)
U.S. security commitment and strategy	Very high • Tactical nukes • Massive retaliation strategy • NCND	Medium → Low • Nixon Doctrine • Carter's USFK withdrawal plan • CFC • NCND	High • Bottom-up review • QDR • EASI • NCND(x)	Medium • NSS • NMS • NPR • GPR • QDR • PSI, etc.
South Korea's perception of threat from North Korea	Very high	Very high	High	Moderate
FoA and FoE	FoA low	FoA extreme	FoA medium, FoE low (newly appeared)	FoE medium, FoA low (FoE ≥ FoA)
South Korea's strategic choice	Recognizing importance of atomic energy	Nuclear arming option	Denuclearization policy	Denuclearization policy

ABBREVIATIONS: CFC, Combined Forces Command; EASI, East Asia Strategic Initiative; FoA, Fear of Abandonment; FoE, Fear of Entrapment; GPR, Global Posture Review; NCND, Neither confirm nor deny; NMS, National Military Strategy; NPR, Nuclear Posture Review; NSS, National Security Strategy of the United States; PSI, Proliferation Security Initiative; QDR, Quadrennial Defense Review; USFK, United States forces in Korea; WMD, Weapons of Mass Destruction.

simple military calculations and toward ultimate national reunification, arming itself with nuclear weapons cannot be an alternative.

Notes

The views and ideas contained in this chapter are those of the authors. They do not represent any official position of the ROK government and its agencies.

1. The name of this policy is somewhat paradoxical since the juxtaposition of "co-operation" and "self-reliance" could be construed as contradictory.

2. An opinion survey conducted by the Social Trend Institute in October 2006 found that 67 percent of the 700 adult respondents were in favor of South Korea possessing nuclear weapons (*Newsis* 2006). A similar poll taken by the *Joongang Ilbo* and the East Asia Institute in 2005 found that 66.5 percent supported South Korea's development of nuclear weapons (*Joongang Ilbo* 2005).

3. According to a Yomiuri-Gallup poll in November 2006, 78 percent of 1,008 surveyed Americans named the Middle East as the biggest threat, and 75 percent named North Korea. And 71 percent were worried that Japan and South Korea might nuclearize because of North Korea's nuclear test (*KBS Global* 2006).

4. On October 1, 1953, ROK Foreign Minister Pyun Young Tae and U.S. Secretary of State John Foster Dulles signed the ROK-U.S. Mutual Defense Treaty in Washington, D.C. But, the ratification of the treaty did not follow immediately. The ROK and the United States differed over Article 6 of the treaty, which read: "This Treaty shall remain in force indefinitely. Either party may terminate it one year after notice has been given to the other Party." South Korea wanted to remove the written terms of validity from the treaty, but the United States did not. Both sides made a compromise by signing the ROK-U.S. Agreed Minutes, which provided the basis for allowing large-scale military-economic assistance to the ROK and for retaining U.S. operational control over ROK forces. Finally, without changing the terms of validity, the treaty came into effect on November 18, 1954, more than a year after it was signed. Though later explained in detail, the process of making the alliance treaty and agreed minutes reflected Seoul's fear of abandonment and Washington's fear of entrapment.

5. On November 17, 1954, South Korea signed an agreement with the United States that reads as follows:

> It is the intention and policy of the Republic of Korea to:
>
> 1. Cooperate with the United States in its efforts to unify Korea, including possible efforts through the United Nations to secure this objective;
> 2. Retain *Republic of Korea forces under the operational control of the United Nations command* [emphasis added] while the Command has responsibilities for the defense of the Republic of Korea, unless after consultation it is agreed that our mutual and individual interest would best be served by a change (from "Agreed Minutes and Agreement Thereto Between the Government of the Republic of Korea and the United States of America Relating to Continued Cooperation in Economic and Military Matters and Amendment to the Agreed Minute of November 17, 1954," signed at Seoul and Entered into force November 17, 1954; amended at Washington and entered into force August 12, 1955).

6. As the Korean War ended, the strength of the USFK, which had reached about 325,000 men during the war, was reduced to approximately 85,000 (a single corps consisting of two divisions: the 2nd and 7th infantry divisions) by 1955. This major withdrawal of Korean War veterans was made possible by the Armistice as well as the signing of the ROK-U.S. Mutual Defense Treaty.

7. Even before that announcement, to justify the ratification of the ROK-U.S. Mutual Defense Treaty, Secretary of State Dulles argued that the American nuclear trip wire was more appropriate in Korea than in Europe. Accordingly, at the 75th plenary session of the Military Armistice Committee on June 21, 1957, the UNC unilaterally declared the

abrogation of Section D, Article 13, of the Armistice Agreement, which prohibits the introduction of weapons from outside onto the Korean peninsula. See Dulles's testimony in the Selected Executive Hearing before the House Foreign Affairs Committee, "U.S. Policy in the Far East: Part I" (1954). Also see Tow 1991.

8. These included Honest John rockets, 280-millimeter and 8-inch artillery tubes, Nuclear Gravity Bombs, Lance missiles, nuclear mines, and others. The exact number of weapon systems is not known. According to some unofficial accounts, the number reached 700 before 1977.

9. In addition, the United States provided about US$6.4 billion in economic assistance between 1954 and 1968.

10. The introduction of U.S. tactical nuclear weapons in South Korea had multiple meanings. First, it bolstered the conventional military capability of the ROK-U.S. forces. Second, it was a clear demonstration of the U.S. security commitment. Third, the tactical nuclear weapons were the last resort for crisis or escalation management and reserved for retaliation, not for preemptive use. Fourth, the United States showed its unilateral decision-making power, as it managed the whole decision-making processes unilaterally, from introducing the Pentomic Division to controlling nuclear weapon stockpiles in Korea.

11. In the mid- and late 1950s after the Korean War, the U.S. Army recognized the need for reorganization. Hard-pressed and alarmed by the looming masses of the Soviet Union's Warsaw Pact military as well as the likelihood of nuclear warfare, the U.S. Army contrived a solution: the Pentomic Division. By encouraging smaller, more independent, yet lethal units, the army was able to build "nuclear war capable" combat divisions and improve the survivability of troops as well: "Adjusting to atomic strategy and tactics, the Army announced a complete reorganization of 18 active divisions . . . Under radically different tables of organization and equipment . . . the regiments of all 18 divisions . . . [will] be transformed into five smaller combat groups (pent) that can group quickly for major-division operations and disperse as quickly to escape atomic retaliation (-omic)" (*Time* 1957).

12. In December 1962, North Korea adopted the Four-Line military policy as a means to realize its *juche* ideology (translated as "independent stand" or "spirit of self-reliance"). The four components of this policy are: (1) arming the entire population, (2) fortifying the entire territory, (3) training all military personnel as leaders, and (4) modernizing military equipment.

13. As announced on July 25, 1969, at a press conference in Guam, the Nixon Doctrine stated:

> But as far as our role is concerned, we must avoid that kind of policy that will make countries in Asia so dependent upon us that we are dragged into conflicts such as the one that we have in Vietnam . . . [A]s far as the problem of military defense, except for the threat of a major power involving nuclear weapons, . . . the United States is going to encourage and has a right to express that this problem will be increasingly handled by, and the responsibility for it taken by, the Asian nations themselves." The doctrine's three main points are that the United States will (1) keep its treaty commitments; (2) provide nuclear deterrence for allies and those threatened by nuclear powers; (3) furnish military and economic assistance, but not manpower. (From President Nixon's informal remarks in Guam with journalists on July 25, 1969. The full text can be found at http://www.presidency.ucsb.edu/ws/index.php?pid=2140.)

14. Oh Won Chul, President Park's science and engineering advisor, provides a detailed account of the ROK-U.S. security relations during Park's presidency based on what he saw and heard (see Oh 2006). Also see http://www.owonchol.pe.kr/10ceoi(text)/10ceoi(text9).htm (November 21, 2007).

15. With the withdrawal of 7th ID, the administration, though not the jurisdictional control authority, of the DMZ was handed over to the ROK JCS, except in the JSA, known as Panmoonjeom.

16. "Our country must be defended by our own people. Our ally, the U.S., will cooperate with and support us only if we resolutely push forward what we need to do for our own defense, and also only if we demonstrate our ability to do just that even when there is no help from the U.S. This is exactly what self-reliant defense means." Commencement speech at the National Defense University, July 20, 1972.

17. For a detailed description of President Park's decision making on a "self-reliant" defense, see Kim, Jong Ryum 1997: 269–98.

18. *Yonhap News* (2005). During the late 1960s, the ROK and the United States differed sharply with respect to joining the NPT. The ROK Ministry of National Defense released secret diplomatic documents about Korea's participation in the Vietnam War in the late 1960s. According to the documents, both Foreign Minister Choi Kyu Ha and U.S. Ambassador Porter held fast to their respective opinions in the negotiations over the ROK's signing of the NPT. The U.S. position was that ROK participation was required for the safe establishment of the NPT regime. The ROK, however, primarily concerned about potential nuclear attacks from China or a possible nuclear arms transfer to North Korea, was not willing to join the NPT, reasoning that doing so would inevitably limit its policy choices. When the United States provided reassurance of its security commitment to Korea, the ROK finally agreed to sign the NPT.

19. The given rationale for this project was to localize the production of nuclear fuel.

20. For example, in 1977, Major General John Singlaub, then USFK chief of staff, publicly criticized President Carter's decision to withdraw U.S. troops from Korea. His open challenge to the civilian leadership led to his early retirement.

21. Initially, the Carter administration had intended to withdraw about 6,000 troops in 1978.

22. President Park was assassinated by Kim Jae Kyu, then head of the Korean Central Intelligence Agency (KCIA), on October 26, 1979.

23. "Foreign countries" referred to key U.S. allies and security partners in Europe and Asia.

24. *Chosun Daily* (1991). In April 1991, the minister of national defense, Lee Jong Gu, spoke of the need to consider "strong measures" such as preemptive strikes against North Korea. He expected the construction of a North Korean nuclear reprocessing facility to be completed by 1993. Based on this expectation, he cautiously warned that North Korea could have a nuclear weapon manufacturing ability as early as the mid-1990s. He therefore thought the ROK would be compelled to take preventive military action before it was too late. His remarks about preventive military action were presented as an option that might be pursued only after diplomatic efforts had been exhausted. But the defense minister's hawkish remarks immediately backfired, stirring up criticism among opposition politicians. They said the remarks were too potentially fatal to inter-Korean relations to be simply

a slip of the tongue. To prevent further political uproar, the defense minister offered an apology and withdrew his remarks.

25. On December 13, 1991, the Basic Agreement was signed at the South-North High-Level Talks between ROK Prime Minister Chung Won Shik and DPRK Premier Yon Hyong Muk.

A full text of this agreement in English can be found at the following website: http://www.nautilus.org/DPRKBriefingBook/agreements/CanKor-VTK-1991-12-13-agreement-on-reconciliation-non-agression-exchanges.pdf (PDF/Adobe Acrobat format).

26. For the full text see http://www.nautilus.org/DPRKBriefingBook/agreements/CanKor-VTK-1992-01-20-joint-declaration-denuclearization-korean-peninsula.pdf.

27. There remains some controversy over what Kang did or did not say. However, it can be assumed that Kang at least hinted at the existence of an alternative nuclear weapon program.

28. After his inauguration, President Roh announced three principles related to the North Korean nuclear issue: (1) no tolerance of North Korean nuclear weapons, (2) the resolution of North Korean nuclear problems peacefully through dialogue, and (3) a lead role for the ROK in the process.

29. After the U.S.-led invasion of Iraq in March 2003, South Korea dispatched two supporting units, "Seohee" and "Jema," which consisted of 575 military engineers and 100 medics respectively. When the Bush administration asked for additional combat troops in September 2003, President Roh agonized over the decision, since so many South Koreans were opposed. About a month later, the Roh administration decided in principle to send troops to Iraq, but no concrete action followed immediately (Kim and Dresser 2003). Following a February 2004 vote by the National Assembly, the ROK military then formed the "Zaytun" Division (meaning *olive* in Arabic) consisted of 2,800 soldiers. After selecting the stationing location, training and equipping the troops, and dealing with other logistical problems the troops arrived in Iraq about a year after the U.S. request. Meanwhile, the United States moved 3,600 USFK troops from the U.S. 2nd ID to Iraq in August 2004, despite the new nuclear crisis on the Korean peninsula.

30. Ministry of Foreign Affairs and Trade (ROK), Press Release, September 20, 2005. South Korea took a cautious position on resuming the Six-Party Talks. South Korea lowered its expectations that North Korea would comply with the joint declaration a year after it was made. Available at http://epic.kdi.re.kr/epic_attach/2006/R0609347-1.pdf.

31. In September 2005, the U.S. Treasury Department froze US$25 million of North Korean funds in a bank account at the Banco Delta Asia. The United States blacklisted this Macau-based bank as a "primary money laundering concern."

32. http://www.kcna.co.jp/index-e.htm (October 11, 2006).

33. For a detailed discussion of the fears of abandonment and entrapment, see Cha (2000).

34. For more information on North Korea's military doctrine, see http://news.bbc.co.uk/2/hi/asia-pacific/3096265.stm; http://www.globalsecurity.org/military/world/dprk/doctrine.htm; and http://www.fas.org/nuke/guide/dprk/doctrine/index.html.

35. Later, North Korea began what it called the "March of Hardship," enduring shortages of food, widespread famine and disease, energy crises, and foreign currency troubles.

36. Here, Washington's unilateral decision making and the lack of prior consultation were particularly problematic.

37. On March 21, 1994, a North Korean official, Park Young Soo, said this to his South Korean counterparts in a working-level meeting about exchanging special envoys. Once his remarks were broadcast, the South Korean public responded in fear by buying up necessities, withdrawing their savings from banks, going overseas, and so forth. A sharp drop in South Korean stock prices also reflected the public's agitation.

38. The other system, the UNC, has only weak political, military, and legal foundations and is not expected to completely replace the current role of the CFC.

39. From President Roh's address at the ceremony of the 58th Anniversary of National Liberation on August 15, 2003. Available at http://english.president.go.kr/cwd/en/archive.

40. Over the past decade, the ROK defense budget has shrunk and is currently fixed at less than 3 percent of South Korea's GDP, which equates to approximately 15–16 percent of government budget expenditures. Although the figure is slightly higher than the world average military expenditure of 2.5 percent, the total amount is much smaller than that of other regional powers such as the United States, Japan, China, and Russia. This budgetary constraint on the ROK military could be a major obstacle to realizing its defense reform programs. For details, see Stockholm International Peace Research Institute (2006), chapter 8.

41. The United States has repeatedly made it clear that the provision of the U.S. nuclear umbrella will remain in effect. The 2002 NPR reads, "U.S. nuclear forces will continue to provide assurance to security partners . . . This assurance can serve to reduce the incentives for friendly countries to acquire nuclear weapons of their own to deter such threats and circumstances."

42. The relevant text of the Joint Communiqué reads as follows: "Secretary Rumsfeld offered assurances of firm U.S. commitment and immediate support to the ROK, including continuation of the *extended deterrence* [emphasis added] offered by the U.S. nuclear umbrella, consistent with the Mutual Defense Treaty." Available at http://www.defenselink.mil/news/Oct2006/d20061020uskorea.pdf (April 30, 2007).

43. The critics include General Leon LaPorte, former commander of UNC/CFC/USFK. Commander LaPorte has argued that U.S. troops should not be regarded, or treated, as hostages. The U.S. position is that the real trip wire is the "letter and spirit" of our mutual defense treaty, backed up by the substance of our alliance and our strong military forces.

44. For the ROK military to independently exercise wartime OPCON, it will need to acquire enhanced C^4ISR capabilities. The ROK military is still behind schedule in achieving the required level of capability and has yet to purchase necessary weapon systems such as AWACs and UAVs. The United States will play a "bridging" role and continue to provide this type of capability until South Korea is ready.

45. Therefore, when the U.S. 2002 NPR was unveiled, South Koreans became alarmed that the new U.S. nuclear strategy introduced the doctrine of a "preemptive nuclear strike." See excerpts from the NPR available at the following links: www.defenselink.mil/news/Jan2002/d20020109npr.pdf and www.globalsecurity.org/wmd/library/policy/dod/npr.htm.

46. On April 23, 2003, the United States, North Korea, and China held three-party talks in Beijing, which was in effect the first direct U.S.-DPRK bilateral negotiation. After that, the United States refused to talk directly with North Korea, leaving the possibility of such direct communication open only within the framework of the Six-Party Talks.

However, concerned about losing the momentum gained through multilateral negotiation, China and South Korea stated that they would welcome any direct contact between Washington and Pyongyang—whether within or outside the Six-Party Talks framework. After the negotiation process had been stalled for more than a year owing to U.S. financial sanctions against North Korea's money-laundering activities, the United States finally agreed to direct bilateral talks and began to show more flexibility in dealing with North Korea. Washington's negotiators met their North Korean counterparts in Berlin, Germany, in January 2007. A month later a similar meeting took place in Beijing before the third phase of the fifth round of Six-Party Talks.

47. *Hankook Ilbo* (2006).

References

Carter, Ashton B., and William J. Perry. 1999. *Preventive Defense: A New Security Strategy for America.* Washington, D.C.: Brookings Institution Press.

Cha, Victor D. 2000. "Abandonment, Entrapment, and Neoclassical Realism in Asia: The United States, Japan, and Korea." *International Studies Quarterly* 44 (2): 261–91.

Cho, Chul-ho. 2001. "Transitions in Park Chung-hee's Nuclear Policy and ROK-U.S. Relations" (in Korean). In Jin-Young Suh and Nae-Young Lee, eds., *World Order and East Asia in Transition* (in Korean). Seoul: Oreum.

Choi, Dong-joo. 1996. "A Reexamination of the Motives for South Korea's Participation in the Vietnam War" (in Korean). *Korean Political Science Association (KPSA) Journal* (Seoul) 30 (2).

Chosun Daily. 1991. "The Opposition Request to Dismiss the Defense Minister Lee for His Improper Remarks" (in Korean). April 14. *Donga Daily.* 2006. "U.S. Kept 700 Tactical Nukes in South Korea . . . All Withdrawn in 1991" (in Korean). October 13.

Ham, Taek-Young. 1998. *Political Economy of National Security: Economy, National Capacity, Military Power* (in Korean). Seoul: Bobmunsa.

Hankook Ilbo. 2006. "Nuclear Umbrella Also in Dispute" (in Korean). October 31.

Jang, Myoung-Soon. 2002. "A Study of the Transformation and Development Directions of U.S. Army Divisions" (in Korean). *National Defense Policy Review* 58 (Winter). Seoul: KIDA Press.

Jeon, Jei-Guk. 2005. *Strategic Environment and Military Expenditure in the Times of Knowledge Information* (in Korean). Seoul: KIDA Press.

Joongang Ilbo, "NK Nuclear Weapons Influence . . . ROK Too Should Have Nuclear Weapons". October 14, 2005.

Jung, II-young, ed. 1993. "Revisiting the Last Half-Century's ROK Diplomacy" (in Korean). Seoul: Nanam.

Kihl, Young Whan. 1977. "Korea's Future: Seoul's Perspective." *Asian Survey* 17 (11): 1064–76.

Kim, Il-young, and Seong-ryoul Cho. 2003. *USFK: Retrospect and Prospect.* Seoul: Hanul Books.

Kim, Jong Ryum. 1997. *Oh, Park Chung Hee* (in Korean). Seoul: Joonang M&B.

Kim, Kyoung-soo, ed. 2004. *North Korea's Weapons of Mass Destruction: Problems and Prospects.* Seoul: Hollym Corporation.

Kim, Myoung-ki, et al. 1999. *A Nuclear-Free Korean Peninsula and International Law* (in Korean). Seoul: Sowha.

Kim, Sung-Han, and Heather Dresser. 2003. "The ROK-U.S. Alliance: How to Envision It?" *IFANS Review* 11 (2): 121–47. Seoul: IFANS.

Kim, Young-ho. 2004. "Cooperative Self-Reliant National Defense and Directions of Reorganizing Force Structure" (in Korean). In Jung-in Moon and Sung-hoon Lee, eds., *Self-Reliant Defense Policy and Making Defense Reform Work* (in Korean). Seoul: Oreum.

Kim, Tae-woo. 2005. *Should We Let Go of the USFK or Keep Them?* (in Korean). Seoul: KIDA Press.

Korea Institute for National Unification (KINU). 1994–2005. "Annual National Survey on Unification Issues." Available at http://www.kinu.or.kr.

Krepinevich, Andrew F., Jr. 1986. *The Army and Vietnam.* Baltimore: The Johns Hopkins University Press.

Lee, Dong-hyun. 2002. *Written History, Unwritten History: Korea's Modern History at Issue* (in Korean). Seoul: Minyeon.

Lee, Heung-hwan. 2002. *The Bush Administration and North Korea* (in Korean). Seoul: Samin Books.

———, ed. 2003. Kison Report 2. *The 35 Scenes of Korea's Modern History in the U.S. Secret Documents* (in Korean). Seoul: Samin Books.

Lee, Sung-hoon, and Hyo-geun Ji. 2004. "Changes in the ROK-U.S. Alliance and ROK Military Buildup" (in Korean). In Jung-in Moon, Ki-Jung Kim, and Sung-hoon Lee, eds. 2004. *Self-Reliant Defense Policy and Making Defense Reform Work* (in Korean). Seoul: Oreum.

Newsis. 2006. "67 Percent of South Koreans Say Their Country Needs Nuclear Bombs" (in Korean). October 10. *New York Times.* 2002. "North Korea Says It Has a Program on Nuclear Arms". October 17. Oh, Won-chul. 2006. How *Did Park Chung-Hee Establish an Economic Power?* (in Korean). Seoul: Dongsuh Books.

Park, Chung-hee. 1970. *Major Speeches by Korea's Park Chung-hee.* Seoul: Hollym Corporation.

Republic of Korea. 2004. National Security Council. 2004. *Peace, Prosperity, and National Security: National Security Strategy of the Republic of Korea.* Seoul.

———. 2005. Ministry of National Defense. *Defense Reform 2020.* Seoul.

Spector, Leonard S. 1990. *Nuclear Ambitions: The Spread of Nuclear Weapons 1989–1990.* Boulder, Colo.: Westview Press.

Stockholm International Peace Research Institute (SIPRI). 2006. *SIPRI Yearbook 2006: Armaments, Disarmament and International Security.* Oxford: Oxford University Press.

Time. 1957. "The Pentomic Division." January 7.

Tow, William T. 1991. "Reassessing Deterrence on the Korean Peninsula." *Korean Journal of Defense Analysis* 3 (1): 179–218. Seoul: KIDA Press.

U.S. House of Representatives, Committee on International Relations. 1978. Subcommittee on International Organization Report, "Investigation of Korean-American Relations." Washington, D.C.: U.S. Government Printing Office, October 31.

Yang, Chang-guk. 2006. "The Joint Declaration of Denuclearization Is Already Abrogated . . . Dare to enrich uranium to secure nuclear fuel!" (in Korean). In *South Korea's Nuclear Sovereignty,* pp. 154–63. Seoul: Shindonga.

Yonhap News. 2005. "Vietnam War: The Background of South Korea's Joining the NPT." December 2. *Yonhap News.* 2006. "ROK-US SCM, Adopting the Joint Statement in Agony." October 21.

14

Taiwan
Conventional Deterrence, Soft Power, and the Nuclear Option

VINCENT WEI-CHENG WANG

Taiwan (officially Republic of China [ROC]) meets most definitions of existential insecurity—through its entire experience as a separate political entity—in a way that few other Asian cases do (Solingen 2007: 115). Not only does it face the People's Republic of China's [PRC's]) unremitting political, economic, and military pressure, but its statehood is unrecognized by most major states and intergovernmental organizations. China's rapid military buildup since 1990 has raised the concern that the cross-Strait military balance has begun to shift in China's favor (Office of the Secretary of Defense 2006: 37; Shambaugh 2000). The military imbalance is seen as further endangering Taiwan's political survival and way of life.

Yet Taiwan has no recourse to global or regional security organizations. No major power except the United States has a commitment to Taiwan's security. And that commitment is not unconditional. Taiwan exemplifies Michael Mandelbaum's definition of "orphan"—a state that was aligned with the United States during the Cold War but "felt more threatened and less protected than the allies" because it faced neighbors that did not accept the legitimacy of its existence as a sovereign state and had "neither formal treaties of alliance nor American troops on [its territory]" (Mandelbaum 1995: 28–29).

Nonetheless, Taiwan figures prominently in the security picture in twenty-first-century Asia for two reasons. First, facing an acute threat, Taiwan has been labeled a "virtual nuclear power" or "virtual proliferant" (Mack 1997)—that could acquire nuclear weapons in a relatively short time due to its well-developed industrial infrastructure, civilian nuclear expertise, and past attempt at developing a nuclear weapon program. The October 2006 North Korean nuclear test rekindled speculation as to whether Taiwan, Japan, and South Korea might become the "next nuclear states" should a nuclear arms race ensue in East Asia (Rosen 2006).

Second, Taiwan is important to Asian regional security because of the possibility of a conflict between two major nuclear powers. China claims the right to use force against Taiwan while the United States, under the Taiwan Relations Act, *might* choose to intervene in a cross-Strait conflict.

This chapter makes four main arguments. First, to cope with its unique security situation and challenge, Taiwan has adopted a broad strategy combining elements of "hard power" and "soft power" (Nye 2004). Since 1949 Taiwan's security strategy has incorporated four elements: (1) self-defense, (2) alliance (explicit or implicit), (3) economic statecraft, and (4) democracy.[1] Second, while Taiwan's economic power and democratic example increase the international community's stake in Taiwan, ultimately its survival depends on its own conventional deterrence capability and the U.S. security commitment. Third, since Taiwan has forsworn its own nuclear weapon program and China's objective concerning Taiwan is mainly political (unification), nuclear weapons play only an indirect role in Taiwan's defense strategy. The important question is whether the U.S. security commitment to Taiwan (including an implicit nuclear umbrella) remains credible. Fourth, while it is plausible to speculate that Taiwan might reconsider its nuclear option under certain conditions, its most realistic security strategy remains a prudent blend of strengthened self-defense, credible U.S. political and military support, increased international community stake in Taiwan, and denying China excuses to launch an unprovoked attack.

These arguments are developed in the rest of the chapter, which has four sections. The first section discusses the nature of the China threat to Taiwan. The subsequent section investigates how Taiwan has dealt with that threat. The third section reviews Taiwan's past attempt at developing nuclear weapons and draws some lessons. The final section explores the conditions under which Taiwan might reconsider nuclear or other offensive options.

The China Threat

Ever since the ROC moved to Taiwan in 1949 as a result of the Chinese civil war between the Kuomintang and the Chinese Communist Party, the PRC has sought to bring Taiwan under its control. While China's strategic objective of unifying Taiwan has remained unaltered, its tactics have evolved over time. In the 1950s–60s, China threatened to "liberate" Taiwan by force. However, as it lacked amphibious warfare capabilities, China's threats were more rhetorical than real. China's bombardment of the ROC-held islands of Kinmen and Matsu constituted arguably the most serious military episode during that period (Tsou 1959).

After the United States and the PRC established diplomatic relations in 1979, China shifted its emphasis to "peaceful reunification" but did not renounce the use of force against Taiwan. Over time, the China threat to Taiwan became multifaceted, including constricting Taiwan's international space, manipulating fissures in Taiwan's young democracy, and absorbing Taiwan's outward investment and trade flows. However, it is China's military buildup in recent years that poses the greatest threat to Taiwan's security.

Until the end of the 1980s, China's military modernization was low priority—ranking last in Deng Xiaoping's "Four Modernizations"—mainly due to budgetary constraints. China's rapid economic growth and the availability of military hardware from Russia spurred China's military modernization. Beginning in 1990, China's defense expenditure has grown at double-digit rates. The Pentagon's annual reports on China's military power point out that while preparing for a "Taiwan contingency" remains the primary focus of China's military modernization, it also aims to project military power in the broader Asia-Pacific region (Office of the Secretary of Defense 2006). In 2005, China passed the Anti-Secession Law, sanctioning the use of "non-peaceful means and other necessary measures to protect China's sovereignty and territorial integrity" under certain conditions yet to be defined.

China's military options against Taiwan include (1) persuasion and coercion; (2) limited force options—such as employing information operations, special operation forces on Taiwan, and missile or air strikes on key military or political sites—to try to break the will of Taiwan's leadership and population; (3) air and missile campaign; (4) blockade; and (5) amphibious invasion. In recent years, China's military modernization has placed greater emphasis on developing the capabilities to achieve air and naval superiority over Taiwan, deny or complicate possible U.S. intervention, and compel Taiwan to accept China's terms for unification.[2] If China decides to use force against Taiwan, its most plausible course of action would be a conventional war aimed at achieving quick victory and keeping Taiwan's economic infrastructure intact.

This raises questions about the nuclear dimension. Unlike most analysts, James Nolt (1999) argues that China has no real military option in dealing with Taiwan and can only defeat Taiwan by using nuclear weapons. But as China's goal is primarily political (unification), do nuclear weapons serve any purpose? China officially espouses a no-first-use (NFU) policy—it will not be the first to use nuclear weapons against other states. But former Chinese chief arms control negotiator, Sha Zukang, claimed that China's NFU commitment does not extend to Taiwan, because "Taiwan is a province of China, not a state, so the policy of no-first-use does not apply" (*Straits Times* 1996: 3). Sha's statement was later corrected by the Chinese government. In 1999 a Foreign Ministry spokesman, Sun Yuxi, when asked if China would use nuclear weapons against Taiwan, extended China's NFU principle to Taiwan: "We will not be the first to use nuclear weapons and will not use nuclear weapons against non-nuclear weapon countries and regions, let alone against our Taiwan compatriots" (*New York Times* 1999).

From time to time certain statements by senior Chinese military officers raised doubt about China's NFU pledge and possible use of nuclear weapons in a Taiwan contingency.[3] In October 1995, Xiong Guangkai, who is now the deputy chief of the general staff of the People's Liberation Army, told Chas Freeman, a former Pentagon official, that China would consider using nuclear weapons in a Taiwan conflict. Freeman quoted Xiong as saying that Americans should worry more about Los Angeles than Taipei (*New York Times* 2005). In July 2005, General Zhu Chenghu, then at National Defense University, said: "If the Americans draw their missiles and precision-guided ammunition on to the target zones on China's territory, I think we will have to respond with nuclear weapons" (*New York Times* 2005). His statement raised the possibility of miscalculation and escalation in a Sino-American war over Taiwan.

Given the opaque nature of the PRC military, it is difficult to know whether these nuclear threats represented the generals' own opinions or a test balloon for official policy. It is reasonable to argue that China's main threat to Taiwan is conventional, such as missile or amphibious attack, and that Beijing is gaining the upper hand in the conventional military balance across the Strait.

Taiwan's Response: Conventional Deterrence and Possible U.S. Intervention

Taiwan's grand strategy in coping with the China threat includes the key "soft power" dimension. In keeping with the purpose of this book and space constraint, here I provide only a brief overview of the soft power dimension. During the first two decades of the Cold War, Taiwan was a key frontline state in the U.S.-led geostrategic containment of the international communist threat (Garver 1997). It was protected by the U.S. defense commitment that included extended deterrence. In the 1960s–70s, its export-led economic development model became successful, but its diplomatic fortunes declined. Taiwan's importance in global trade and production became a key pillar of its security. And, starting in the late 1980s, Taiwan evolved into a vibrant democracy, in contrast to China's 1989 crackdown on democracy protestors and its continued poor human rights record. Taiwan positioned itself as a model in global Third Wave democratization worthy of international support and recognition. In the early 1990s, Taiwan launched a "Go South" policy—buttressed by trade and investment—toward Southeast Asia, an important region to Taiwan. In 1999, the global information industry was disrupted as a result of Taiwan's earthquake. This disruption demonstrated Taiwan's vital role in the global semiconductor industry, leading one analyst to argue that Taiwan had a "silicon shield" against Chinese attack (Addison 2001). "Soft power" instruments such as democracy, trade, and popular culture are key elements of Taiwan's comprehensive security strategy.

Although Taiwan's security is embedded in world trade and global democratization, the realist premise of self-help in an anarchic international system is critical. Given the asymmetry vis-à-vis China, Taiwan's defense preparation against the Chinese military threat rests on two pillars: a formidable conventional military force and a close relationship with the United States (Hickey 1997: 37). Taiwan appears to have a three-layered strategy: (1) deterring China by making the cost of invasion unacceptably high; (2) if that fails, engaging China independently long enough for (3) assistance from a powerful outside actor (the United States).

With the world's sixteenth largest active troop size (290,000) and nineteenth highest military expenditure (US$7.9 billion in 2005), Taiwan has a considerable conventional military force. However, its adversary has the world's largest active troop size (2.25 million) and the second largest military expenditure (US$65 billion in 2004).[4] Purchasing advanced weapons has been important for Taiwan's security. According to Stockholm International Peace Research Institute (SIPRI) data, between 1977 and 2006 Taiwan imported US$28.4 billion worth of arms, making it the seventh largest importer of arms in the world (for the same period, China was the eighth largest arms importer, receiving US$28.2 billion, mostly after 1999).[5]

Maintaining a close relationship with the United States is crucial for Taiwan. Its armed forces are equipped with weapons obtained primarily from the United States. In recent years, it has also procured some weapons from other Western countries (e.g., sixty French Mirage fighter jets in 1992) and has emphasized indigenous military production in certain fields to achieve greater "self-reliance." U.S. arms sales enabled Taiwan to maintain sufficient self-defense capabilities. From FY1950 to FY2006, the United States sold Taiwan US$18.3 billion of military equipment under the foreign military sales program and US$3.2 billion worth of commercial exports licensed under the Arms Export Control Act (Defense Security Cooperation Agency n.d.). In 2007, Taiwan's legislature approved funds for the purchase of certain weapon systems approved by the George W. Bush administration in 2001, including P-3 Orion antisubmarine aircraft, the Patriot Advanced Capability (PAC-2 upgrade) missile defense system, and a feasibility study of a diesel-electric submarine.

In recent years, to cope with the growing China threat, Taiwan has taken measures to counter a possible three-phased Chinese attack: (1) a sudden, overwhelming attack on critical strategic and military targets using air power and special forces designed to force a rapid end to the war; (2) an effective naval blockade of major ports, to be followed by an extended air campaign to cripple Taiwan economically and militarily; and (3) an amphibious landing to facilitate a multi-divisional armored and mechanized attack on the political center (Yang 2007). To survive air strikes, Taiwan has hardened command, control, and communication centers and improved its air defense system. To counter a naval blockade, the ROC Navy has put increasing emphasis on antisubmarine warfare. To thwart an amphibious landing, Taiwan's ground forces have undergone a major streamlining and restructuring into composite brigades capable of conducting two-dimensional operations. Taiwan is also developing offensive countermeasures in an attempt to destroy or degrade PLA war-fighting assets on the mainland.

Although Taiwan's efforts are considerable, its conventional deterrence capability may be in relative decline for three reasons. First, the rapid pace of Chinese military modernization—double-digit growths in annual defense spending since 1990—makes it difficult for Taiwan to keep pace with China. Second, in recent years, as a result of spending more on health care and social welfare, Taiwan's defense expenditure has declined in absolute and relative terms.[6] Third, because the United States is mired in Iraq and is increasingly dependent on Chinese cooperation on various issues (e.g., North Korea), its commitment to Taiwan, whose leadership seems to be pushing for de jure independence, has become more ambiguous and contingent.

The last point illustrates an inherent alliance dilemma. In a seminal work, Glenn Snyder discusses the logics of "abandonment" and "entrapment" and concludes "alliance bargaining considerations . . . tend to favor a strategy of weak or ambiguous commitment" (Snyder 1984: 467). In the U.S.-Taiwan relationship, Taiwan has always feared abandonment by the United States. In contrast, the United States fears entrapment, "being dragged into a conflict over an ally's interests that one does not share, or shares only partially."

Historically, the United States has played a critical role in Taiwan's security. Under its defense treaty with Taiwan (1954–78), the United States dispatched the Seventh Fleet to patrol the Taiwan Strait and extended its nuclear umbrella to Taiwan. Recently declassified material shows that from January 1958 to July 1974, the United States stored nuclear weapons on Taiwan.[7] U.S. protection prevented a Chinese attack on Taiwan.

In December 1978, as one of the conditions for normalizing relations with the PRC, the United States abrogated the 1954 defense treaty with Taiwan. U.S. Congress enacted the Taiwan Relations Act (TRA) to shore up Taiwan's security. However, it is debatable whether the "residual" U.S. commitment to Taiwan's security under the TRA constitutes an *implicit* nuclear umbrella. The TRA declares that it is the policy of the United States to "consider any effort to determine the future of Taiwan by other than peaceful means . . . a threat to the peace and security of the Western Pacific area and of grave concern to the United States," to provide Taiwan with "arms of a defensive character," and to "maintain the capacity of the United States to resist any resort to force or other forms of coercion that would jeopardize the security, or the social or economic system, of the people on Taiwan" (Taiwan Relations Act 1979). But the TRA is silent on whether the United States will defend Taiwan in the event of a Chinese attack. Snyder's insights on entrapment help explain why the United States adopts a policy of "strategic ambiguity" toward the Taiwan Strait. It is intended to keep both China and Taiwan in check. Unlike Japan or South Korea—both treaty allies of the United States—Taiwan cannot for certain rely on America's extended deterrence commitment. It must work hard to cultivate American support.

Given its existential insecurity and the implicit and ambiguous commitment of its only ally, Taiwan has often been identified as a country with good reasons for possessing nuclear weapons as part of its comprehensive strategy of survival. Andrew Mack grouped Taiwan along with Japan, South Korea, and North Korea in a category called "virtual nuclear powers" who could acquire nuclear weapons in a relatively short time but have chosen not to do so (Mack 1997).

Taiwan's Nuclear Programs and U.S. Policies During the Cold War

It is useful to discuss Taiwan's past, present, and future nuclear policy in the context of the larger issue of why states build nuclear weapons. The Taiwan case confirms insights from theories on the role of nuclear weapons in a country's security policy but also adds to its unique complexity. It can be fruitfully compared with other countries like Israel that face existential insecurity.

States seek nuclear weapons for many reasons: coping with an acute threat, prestige, political clout, technology, and economic benefits (Cirincione 2007; Pomper 2005). Scott Sagan (1996–97) advances three "models" of states' nuclear decisions: (1) "the security model": states build weapons to increase national security against foreign threats, especially nuclear threats; (2) the "domestic politics model": nuclear weapons are viewed as political tools to advance parochial domestic and bureaucratic interests; and (3) "the norms model": nuclear weapon decisions are made because weapons acquisition, or restraint in weapons development, provides an important normative symbol of a state's modernity and identity.

Goldstein (2000) argues that despite the end of the Cold War, nuclear deterrence will remain at the core of the security policies of the world's great powers and will continue to be an attractive option for many less powerful states worried about adversaries whose capabilities they cannot match. America's extended deterrence during the Cold War persuaded many, but not all, of its allies to forego nuclear weapons, thus contributing to the success of the U.S.-led nonproliferation regime (Mandelbaum 1995: 25–26).

A patron can bolster the credibility of its extended deterrence commitment by establishing treaty obligations for the defense of the client state or storing nuclear weapons on the soil of the client state. Recently declassified material shows that the United States secretly deployed nuclear bombs in twenty-seven countries and territories during the Cold War (*National Security Archive Electronic Briefing Book* 1999; Norris, Arkin, and Burr 1999).

During the Cold War the United States sought to achieve three goals in the nuclear domain: (1) nonproliferation and arms control (to enhance global security and norm development), (2) extended deterrence (to preserve alliance solidarity and U.S. reputation), and (3) commercial gain (to benefit the American nuclear power industry). This three-pronged strategy was linked by the quid pro quo mandated in the 1968 nuclear Non-Proliferation Treaty (NPT): the five nuclear weapon states (the United States, the USSR, Britain, France, and the PRC) agreed not to transfer nuclear weapons or other nuclear explosive devices to other states, and nonnuclear weapon states agreed not to seek or develop nuclear weapons in return for their "inalienable right" to use nuclear energy for peaceful purposes (Article IV, Sec. 1), subject to International Atomic Energy Agency (IAEA) safeguards. Under the NPT, nuclear powers have a responsibility to assist developing countries with their energy needs (Article IV, Sec. 2).[8] These multiple goals—sometimes complementary and sometimes contradictory—were clearly at work in the various roles the United States played in Taiwan's civilian and military nuclear programs during the Cold War.

Taiwan's Nuclear Program During the Cold War

Taiwan's civilian nuclear power and nuclear weapon programs started at about the same time—in the 1960s. It is useful to consider these two programs together because the United States played key roles in both, and because there is substantial technological overlap between them (the first stage of making nuclear weapons—the production of fissile materials, such as uranium-233, uranium-235, or plutonium-239—is the same as for generating nuclear power) (Chung 2004a: 137). Taiwanese officials are still reticent about Taiwan's abandoned nuclear weapon program, but in recent years more information has emerged. Table 14-1 summarizes the key developments of Taiwan's nuclear program during the Cold War.[9]

The table reveals several important lessons. First, Taiwan's nuclear weapon aspirations were driven by an acute sense of insecurity. The genesis of the Hsin Chu Project was a direct result of China's successful explosion of a nuclear bomb in 1964. The prospect that the PRC could now use nuclear weapons to wipe out Taiwan was deeply unsettling to ROC President Chiang Kai-shek. Chiang tried to persuade U.S. President Lyndon Johnson to take out China's nascent nuclear arsenal but to no avail. So he, and especially his son, Chiang Ching-kuo, decided to develop an indigenous nuclear weapon program.

There was dissent. Professor Ta-you Wu, former president of Academia Sinica in Taipei and then director of the Science Development Advisory Committee of

TABLE 14-1.

Timeline of Taiwan's Nuclear Program During the Cold War

1955	Atomic Energy Council (AEC) founded to promote peaceful use of nuclear energy. Taipower created Atomic Power Research Commission. National Tsinghua University (NTHU) reopened in Hsin Chu, with a Graduate Institute of Atomic Science.
1956	Taiwan opened its first nuclear reactor, provided by the United States, at NTHU.
1964	China successfully tested nuclear weapons, stimulating Taiwan to develop a full-scale nuclear program.
1965	The predecessor of the military-run Chungshan Institute of Science and Technology (CSIST) was established. The proposed First Institute would become the Institute for Nuclear Energy Research (INER).
1967	The US$140 million Hsin Chu Project was launched, consisting primarily of procuring and operating a heavy-water reactor, a heavy-water production plant, a reprocessing research lab, and a plutonium separation plant.
1968	ROC joined the Non-Proliferation Treaty (NPT). Supervision of INER was moved to AEC.
1969	INER purchased a small heavy-water reactor (40 megawatt), dubbed Taiwan Research Reactor (TRR), from Canada, which became operational in 1973. INER served mainly to facilitate Taiwan's procurement of elements to produce plutonium.
1971	IAEA negotiation of safeguard agreement short-circuited by the U.N. transfer of recognition. Eventually, agreement reached so the United States became the ultimate legal guarantor of Taiwan's nonnuclear status.
1974	CIA concluded that Taiwan was working toward a nuclear weapon capability and would be capable of producing a nuclear weapon within five years.
1976	Premier Chiang Ching-kuo promised Taiwan would not acquire its own reprocessing facilities or engage in any activities related to reprocessing.
1977	United States pressured Taiwan to dismantle reprocessing facilities and return U.S.-supplied plutonium. Taiwan's nuclear program was brought under control, but concerns remained.
1978	President Jimmy Carter normalized relations with the PRC. Taipower's first nuclear reactor began producing electricity. Over the years, the amount of electricity generated by Taipower's six reactors, all U.S.-made, increased to 20 percent of Taiwan's electricity needs. The fourth nuclear plant, with two more modern reactors, is scheduled to begin operation in 2006–07 (with the delay in 2000, it was not finished as of March 2008).
1987	INER began building a multiple hot cell facility.
1988	Colonel Chang Hsien-yi, deputy director of INER and a CIA spy, defected and revealed Taiwan's plans. The CIA estimated that Taiwan was within one or two years of developing a nuclear bomb. President Chiang Ching-kuo died. U.S. government agencies and IAEA inspectors shut down TRR and the hot cell. President Lee Teng-hui promised President Ronald Reagan that Taiwan would agree to conclusively and verifiably end its nuclear weapon program.

SOURCES: Author's compilation using information in Mitchell (2004), Albright and Gay (1998), Burr (1999), and Chung (2004a).

National Science Council, wrote to Chiang to oppose the Hsin Chu Project on the grounds that the plan underestimated the true costs, risked confrontation with the United States, and overestimated the chance of success.[10] Yet Taiwan's authoritarian political leaders at the time overruled protests like that of Wu, thwarted an informed public debate, and permitted the clandestine execution of the project. The military fully supported the Hsin Chu Project by providing manpower and resources. The five-year US$140 million (NT$4.8 billion) project amounted to 15 percent of the central government net expenditures of NT$32.2 billion in 1968 (Chung 2004a: 158).

National pride was another impetus. In 1957, Drs. Chen-ning Yang and Tsung-dao Lee of the University of Chicago became the first ethnic Chinese scientists to win the Nobel Prize in physics. This inspired many young, bright, and idealistic students in Taiwan to study nuclear physics, and the military tapped into this talent pool.

"Dr. H's" experience is illustrative. After graduating from one of Taiwan's top high schools, he chose to study physics at the military-run Chung-cheng Institute of Technology (CCIT). CCIT, Chungshan Institute of Science and Technology (CSIST), and the Institute for Nuclear Energy Research (INER) are all located in Lung Tan, about forty minutes by car from Taipei. After college, Dr. H was assigned to INER and after two years was sent to study in the United States, where he received a Ph.D. and had a postdoctoral fellowship before returning to INER. He recalled: "At that time, INER employed over one thousand people. On average, each researcher had two support staffers. The pay was excellent and the morale was high. I felt proud about what I was doing, because I was young and prone to following orders."[11]

The reactor purchased by INER, the Taiwan Research Reactor (TRR), was the same design as Canada's National Research eXperimental reactor; it had a "cousin" in South Asia—the CIRUS reactor India purchased in 1960. (Fourteen years later, in 1974, India made and tested a nuclear device fabricated from the plutonium produced by that reactor.) At full operation, TRR could produce ten kilograms of weapon-grade plutonium each year; in twelve years it could have produced sufficient weapon-grade plutonium for a small number of nuclear weapons.[12] TRR reached critical mass on January 3, 1973.

Taiwan's nuclear weapon program accelerated in the 1970s. The quickening pace correlated directly with the nation's growing diplomatic and security concerns: the ROC was expelled from the United Nations (U.N.) in 1971, and thereafter from all U.N.-affiliated organizations.[13] The Nixon Doctrine signified the U.S. desire to reduce its military burden in Asia, culminating in the fall of Saigon in 1975. In 1972, Nixon visited mainland China and signed the Shanghai Communiqué, committing the United States to normalize relations with China. On

December 15, 1978, President Jimmy Carter announced that the United States would recognize Beijing and sever diplomatic ties with Taipei on January 1, 1979. These diplomatic setbacks heightened Taiwan's insecurity and fear of abandonment by the United States.

The second lesson is that the attitudes and actions of the United States—informed by its national interests—was a key enabling or constraining factor in Taiwan's tortuous nuclear weapon development program. During the Cold War, the United States sought to pursue several goals—including preventing the spread of communism, nuclear nonproliferation, and commercial interests of its nuclear energy industry.

In 1954, Presidents Eisenhower and Chiang signed a mutual defense treaty, incorporating Taiwan in the United States alliance system in East Asia. Taiwan benefited from Eisenhower's Atoms for Peace program. During the Offshore Island Crises of 1955 and 1958, Eisenhower contemplated using nuclear weapons against the PRC but was also concerned about "embroilment" in Chiang's futile campaign to militarily retake the mainland, which could have triggered a wider conflict involving the two superpowers (Tsou 1959). His dilemma illustrated the patron state's fear of entrapment.

Taiwan's civilian and military nuclear programs benefited from direct and indirect U.S. assistance. The United States was both the guarantor of Taiwan's nonnuclear weapon status and the chief supplier of key materials, facilities, and technologies to Taiwan's nuclear power industry. Consequently, both the United States and Taiwan reached a reciprocal "bargain" under the NPT. All of the state-owned Taipower's eight light-water reactors used to generate electricity were provided by leading American companies (General Electric and Westinghouse) that sold package deals, including fuel and repossession of spent fuel.

Other than some hydraulic power, Taiwan lacks any significant raw energy sources. It imports over 97 percent of raw materials for its energy needs. Compared to other sources of energy, nuclear fuel is a better choice from a strategic standpoint (it is less susceptible to wartime energy shortage or blockade) because of its compactness and density. Its importance will increase in the future. So will the nuclear expertise.

The U.S. attitude toward Taiwan's military nuclear program was even more intriguing. The United States assisted Taiwan in acquiring the TRR from Canada, and enriched uranium from South Africa. Most of Taiwan's scientists in nuclear physics and related fields studied in the United States or Canada. Thus it appears that the United States permitted (or wanted) Taiwan to possess certain nuclear capabilities as a potential strategic counterweight to China. Yet as the main architect and chief enforcer of the nonproliferation regime, the United States did not want Taiwan's nuclear program to get out of control.

In January 1988, a U.S.-trained scientist and spy dealt a decisive blow to Taiwan's nuclear weapon program. Colonel Chang Hsien-yi, deputy director of INER, defected to the United States, carrying with him sensitive information about the nuclear weapon program at INER. While studying in the United States, Chang had been recruited by the Central Intelligence Agency (CIA). At the INER, he monitored Taiwan's nuclear program for the U.S. government.[14] Armed with incriminating evidence provided by Chang, President Reagan demanded that the new president of Taiwan, Lee Teng-hui, conclusively and verifiably shut down Taiwan's nuclear weapon program. The Chang Hsien-yi incident marked the end of Taiwan's nuclear weapon program and the associated Tien Ma (Sky House) missile program (Minnick 2002).

Since 1988, Taiwan's official position has been that it will not apply its scientific know-how to build nuclear weapons (*China Post* 1997). Those closely involved in Taiwan's nuclear weapon program (e.g., President Chiang Ching-kuo and General Hau Pei-tsun, chairman of the Joint Chiefs of Staff) viewed Chang as a traitor who caused the fatal setback to Taiwan's nuclear aspirations. Americans generally viewed the end of Taiwan's nuclear weapon program as a success. The *Bulletin of the Atomic Scientists* hailed this as a "nuclear nightmare averted" (Albright and Gay 1998). Ambassador James Lilley said that he believed it was time for the Chang Hsien-yi case to be "publicly acknowledged as a success, a classic in the annals of intelligence" (Weiner 1997).[15]

However, today in Taiwan's open environment, opinions about Chang seem to be changing. Those who believe that reviving the nuclear option is a bad choice for Taiwan generally have a more balanced view on Chang (there were technical and nontechnical limitations to Taiwan's nuclear project, and what Chang did may have averted a disaster for Taiwan). Others argue that in Taiwan's democratic and open society today it is highly unlikely that a serious undertaking such as developing nuclear weapons could proceed secretly without public knowledge or media scrutiny. A former national security aide to President Chen Shui-bian opines that it would be hard to prevent a second "Chang Hsien-yi incident" from happening.[16]

The Chang incident threw INER into disarray. Many INER researchers suddenly lost their raison d'etre. Although the United States took decisive measures to end Taiwan's nuclear weapon program, it did not ask (or allow) the INER to disband. What explains the United States' mixed response? One view is that the United States regarded these researchers with concern, so having them in one place facilitated monitoring and control and prevented "proliferation" of nuclear manpower.[17] Another view is that the United States wanted Taiwan to maintain some kind of "near-nuclear capability" by retaining these researchers' expertise. An author of Taiwan's Defense White Paper, Chien Chung, opined that the United States wanted Taiwan to "keep the engine warm and await further instructions" (*nuanji daiming*). He estimates that there are still over 800 "national treasures" today. He notes: "It would have been quite easy to totally dissolve Taiwan's nuclear manpower; just give all these people U.S. passports! This is one reason why, although it is difficult to obtain the material, Taiwan's capability to research and develop nuclear weapons can never be completely ruled out."[18]

The key is U.S. interests and attitudes. The George W. Bush administration's forceful approach toward the nuclear challenges posed by Iraq, North Korea, and Iran notwithstanding, if changing national interests due to geopolitical shifts (e.g., if the United States sees China as the main threat) require that the United States choose a reliable nuclear partner or proxy with sufficient technological capabilities and compatible national values, Chung thinks Taiwan is a good choice.[19] The concern, however, is that a nuclear-capable Taiwan may become intransigent in disputes with China due to its confidence in America's support, causing the United States to lose escalation control in a conflict with China. Entrapment thus becomes plausible for the United States.

The third lesson is that Taiwan's deep dependence on the U.S. security commitment gave the United States exceptional leverage over Taiwan's nuclear aspirations. Taiwan's dependence on the United States is more acute than that of Japan and South Korea. It is no longer under explicit treaty protection of the United States and U.S. support for Taiwan would have to factor in China's reaction. This gives the United States unusually large leverage over Taiwan's nuclear aspirations. For the foreseeable future, the United States can manage Taiwan's nuclear program using a mixed strategy of preventing proliferation, maintaining near-nuclear capability, and sharing the fruits of peaceful use of nuclear energy.

Needing access to international markets and nuclear technology, dependent on the United States, and concerned about China's possible preemptive strike, Taiwan's best choice was and is nuclear restraint.

Taiwan's Current Nuclear Orientation

Today Taiwan does not have nuclear weapons (Federation of American Scientists, n.d.), but it has a fairly sophisticated civilian nuclear power industry, which produced over 20 percent of Taiwan's total electric power in recent years (Government Information Office 2004: 149). Many sources put Taiwan in the category of "abstaining countries"—industrialized nations with the technical capacity but not the political desire to develop nuclear weapons (Cirincione 2007: 44; Manning 1997–98: 80; Spector, McDonough, and Medeiros 1995: 8).

Officially, Taiwan adheres to the nuclear nonproliferation regime.[20] Its 1988 commitment to the United States went beyond the obligations mandated by the NPT (Mitchell 2004: 301). Although Taiwan is not a member of the IAEA, the

AEC conforms to IAEA code and guidance (Atomic Energy Council 2005). The government position on nuclear weapons is a categorical "four no's" policy—Taiwan will not "develop, produce, store, or use" nuclear weapons (*Agence France Presse* 2004), or a stricter "five no's" policy (the four no's plus no acquisition) (Ministry of National Defense 2004: 221)[21] —intended to dispel any doubt. The ruling party from 2000 to 2008, the Democratic Progressive Party (DPP), went a step further by espousing a "nuclear-free homeland" (*feihe jiayuan*) on Taiwan (Executive Yuan Nuclear-Free Homeland Commission 2003).[22]

Since the termination of Taiwan's nuclear weapon program in 1988 there has been a normative change in Taiwan's nuclear research (Chien 2005: 475; also cited in Chung 2005: 21, 28). Today, all of Taiwan's nuclear programs are ostensibly for peaceful use. The DPP espouses a fundamentally antinuclear policy. To maintain its security, Taiwan counts on America's tacit security commitment and the international norm against the use of nuclear arms against nonnuclear weapon states, and maintains itself as a "virtual proliferant" through the technological infrastructure of a thriving civilian nuclear program. But is a "nuclear option" completely out of the question?

Assessing the Nuclear "Option"

Although it is not a member of the United Nations, as a state dependent on the United States for its security, it is important for Taiwan to adhere to the nonproliferation regime to ensure U.S. support. However, Taiwan has never felt completely comfortable about the U.S. commitment to its security. Every few years certain news reports or official comments would surface that called into question whether Taiwan still has a secret nuclear weapon program.

Rather than judging these inconclusive reports and subsequent official denials and clarifications, I analyze the role of nuclear weapons, if any, in Taiwan's security strategy, by taking into account both capabilities and intentions. These two interrelated aspects roughly correspond to "supply-side" and "demand-side" factors, respectively. The former relates to *feasibility* (whether Taiwan can do it), whereas the latter relates to *desirability* (whether Taiwan ought to do it). In the arms control lexicon, supply-side strategies seek to prevent the transfer of weapons technologies to would-be proliferators, whereas demand-side strategies seek to address the security concerns behind the drive for the bomb (Mack 1997: 51–52).

For Taiwan, both its capabilities and intentions are influenced by broader factors, such as the international nonproliferation regime, technological availability, the regional security environment, and its threat perception, but none is more important than the relationship with the United States and the robustness of the U.S. security commitment. As the history of Taiwan's nuclear program shows, these larger strategic and diplomatic factors on the demand side played a key part

TABLE 14-2
Factors Influencing Taiwan's Nuclear Decision

	Desirability (demand side)	Feasibility (supply side)
Enabling factors	To offset acute power asymmetry between China and Taiwan (quick "equalizer") To ensure survival (existential deterrence) Last-ditch effort after being abandoned by the patron state	Military nuclear technical expertise can be reconstituted? Civilian nuclear technical expertise Progress made in missile technology
Inhibiting factors	Opposition from the patron state (even a pretext for abandonment?) Opposition from within Taiwan's democratic society PRC's possible preemptive strike	Military nuclear technical expertise degraded Difficulty acquiring materials Lack of test sites Secrecy can't be assured

in shaping Taiwan's nuclear choices. They will also be crucial for understanding, or even predicting, Taiwan's nuclear future. Table 14-2 summarizes the enabling and inhibiting factors that would influence Taiwan's decision to develop nuclear weapons in terms of feasibility and desirability.

Overall, although several enabling factors favor Taiwan's development of nuclear weapons from the standpoints of both desirability (the demand side) and feasibility (the supply side), the *cost* outweighs the benefit, suggesting that a "virtual" nuclear capability is the more plausible option.

Under what conditions can and should Taiwan cross the nuclear threshold to formally incorporate a nuclear weapon capability in its national security planning? Both capabilities and intentions are important in this calculus.

There are divergent views on feasibility. Some believe that if Taiwan decided to develop nuclear weapons, it could do so quickly, perhaps within a year or two (Mitchell 2004: 301). With the infrastructure for nuclear research (INER and National Tsinghua University [NTHU]) and experience with nuclear power generation, as the world's sixteenth largest economy, and with the fourth largest foreign exchange reserve,[23] Taiwan appears, prima facie, to possess the human and financial capital needed to resume its nuclear weapon program. Others are skeptical. They point to the high cost to restart the program (US$10 billion), the predictable resistance by opposition parties, the tight monitoring and control by the United States and the IAEA,[24] and the inability to find suitable locations on the island to conduct nuclear tests as reasons why the nuclear option is infeasible.[25]

There are divergent views on the desirability of nuclear weapons as well. For the rare voices that advocate the development of nuclear weapons, it is unclear whether their unorthodox comments reflect simply bravado or hint at the existence of a secret program. Officials who have made these types of remarks have invariably retracted their comments to defuse unwanted attention. Former President Lee Teng-hui, replying to a question in the National Assembly on July 28, 1995 about Taiwan's nuclear intentions, said: "Whether or not we need the protection of nuclear weapons, we should restudy the question from a long-term point of view." Reuters ran a story saying that Taiwan meant to reconsider the use of nuclear weapons. This prompted Taiwan's foreign minister, Fredrick Chien, to issue a categorical denial that Taiwan had any intention of developing nuclear weapons, blaming the reporters for misunderstanding and misinterpreting a Chinese phrase that President Lee had used (Lin 1995: 13).

A vocal minority stresses Taiwan's need to have offensive weapons, including nuclear weapons, to deter China from attacking the island. A researcher affiliated with the Taiwan Research Institute, which is closely tied to former President Lee Teng-hui, argues that Taiwan cannot rely on China's pledge not to use nuclear weapons against Taiwan and should instead develop a counter-value nuclear deterrent against possible Chinese use of nuclear arms against Taiwan (Liao 1999). A *Taipei Times* (2004) editorial argues that "the ability to obliterate China's ten largest cities and the Three Gorges Dam would be a powerful deterrent to China's adventurism." To rally support for arms procurement, on September 25, 2004, former premier Yu Shyi-kun said that Taiwan should rely on a Cold War-style "balance of terror" to safeguard national security in the face of intimidation from Beijing (Hille 2004). It is unclear how much weight to give to these voices, but they are clearly a minority in Taiwan.

A cautious international relations scholar who was close to the DPP government believes that Taiwan should forgo the production and development of nuclear weapons to avoid the predictable intense international scrutiny and pressure, but keep quiet about acquiring nuclear weapons.[26] He hinted that the international black market would be the fastest way for Taiwan to acquire nuclear weapons. However, Chung disagrees: "Without testing, the quality of acquired weapons cannot be assured, and the numbers so acquired would be insufficient to constitute a deterrent, but Taiwan's reputation would surely suffer."[27] Andrew Yang of the Council on Advanced Policy Studies, a top think tank on security issues, thinks that nuclear weapons are actually a liability for Taiwan's security because they further complicate Taiwan's security challenge.[28]

There are good instrumental reasons for Taiwan to choose nuclear restraint owing to what international relations scholars call "security interaction": Taiwan's development of nuclear weapons for self-defense might be seen as offensive by China and a casus belli. In an article criticizing Premier Yu's call for a "balance of terror," Chien Chung concludes that developing WMD for the sake of engaging in a "balance of terror" with the adversary is not indispensable to Taiwan's national strategy nor will it enhance Taiwan's national security (Chung 2004b). Most government officials think that there cannot be any ambiguity in Taiwan's nuclear policy and that 100 percent transparency is the best option.[29]

However, Table 14-2 illustrates the scenarios for contemplating the "nuclear option": Taiwan may cross the nuclear Rubicon if it believes that the cross-Strait military imbalance has become so lopsided and the prospect for Beijing to use force to unify Taiwan has become so imminent that only nuclear weapons can serve as a quick "equalizer" to preserve Taiwan's independence or as a last-ditch effort to draw the United States into the conflict (Rosen 2006: 12).

Table 14-3A shows that China has all classes of WMD and delivery systems, but Taiwan only has short-range ballistic missiles capable of carrying conventional

TABLE 14-3 A AND B

Military Power of China and Taiwan

A. Status of Weapons of Mass Destruction (2004)

Indicator	China	Taiwan
Nuclear weapon status	Confirmed	None
Chemical weapon status	Probable	Suspected
Biological weapon status	Suspected	Suspected
Short-range ballistic missile status	Confirmed[a]	Confirmed[g]
Medium-range ballistic missile status	Confirmed[b]	None
Intermediate-range ballistic missile status	None	None
Submarine-launched ballistic missile status	Confirmed[c]	None
Intercontinental ballistic missile status	Confirmed[d]	None
Strategic bomber status	None	None
Strategic submarine status	Confirmed[e]	None
WMD commitments	BTWC, CWC, NPT[f]	NPT[h]

SOURCES: Author's compilation of National Bureau of Asian Research (NBR) Research Team findings, 2004, obtained through *Strategic Asia* data query service, available at http://strategicasia.nbr.org/Data/DataSheet/Criteria.aspx; and Nuclear Threat Initiative (NTI).

[a]CSS-6 (DF-15/M9), CSS-7 (DF-11/M-11), CSS-8 (DF-7). Over 650 DF-11 (M-11) and DF-15 (M-9) are deployed opposite Taiwan.

[b]CSS-2 (DF-3), CSS-5 (DF-21). Several dozen that can reach Japan, India, and Russia.

[c]CSS-N-3 (J-1)

[d]30+: 24 CSS-4 (DF-5A), 8 CSS-9 (DF-31), CSS-3 (DF-4). Two dozen or so can reach the U.S. and Europe.

[e]1

[f]BTWC: acceded; CTBT: signed but not ratified; CWC: signed and ratified; NPT: acceded.

[g]Ching Feng, Tien Chi.

[h]The ROC ratified the NPT in 1970. After its expulsion from the United Nations in 1971, ROC said it would abide by CWC, BTWC, and NPT.

B. Defense Spending and Economy (1990–2005)

	China			Taiwan		
	GDP ($ billions, PPP)	Defense expenditure ($ billions)	Defense expenditure (% of GDP)	GDP ($ billions, PPP)	Defense expenditure ($ billions)	Defense expenditure (% of GDP)
1990	413	11.3	3.1	151	8.7	5.4
1995	3,500	33.0	5.9	291	13.1	5.0
2000	4,500	42.0	3.9	386	17.6	5.6
2005	8,182	81.5	4.3	612	7.9	2.4

SOURCES: Author's compilation of IISS, Military Balance data obtained from Strategic Asia data query service (http://strategicasia.nbr.org/Data/DataSheet/Criteria.aspx); and CIA, *The World Factbook* (http://www.odci.gov/cia/publications/factbook/index.html).

warheads. Table 14-3B shows the rapid increase in China's defense spending since 1990, powered by the huge expansion of China's economy. As the Pentagon's recent reports on China's military power indicate, China has devoted substantial resources to weapon systems that can be used in asymmetric war to intimidate or actually attack Taiwan and prevent U.S. intervention (Office of the Secretary of Defense 2006).

The only imaginable scenario in which Taiwan could pursue the nuclear option is if three conditions were present concurrently: (1) there is a serious problem in the credibility of America's tacit extended deterrence commitment; (2) the United States is perceived as ready to abandon Taiwan in the face of Chinese assertiveness; and (3) the cross-Strait military balance has become so lopsided in favor of China that only nuclear weapons could restore some (semblance of) balance. These are extraordinary conditions under which the unthinkable could happen. Only a "perfect storm" caused by an increasing Chinese military threat, deteriorating regional security, and abandonment by the United States might force Taiwan to cross the nuclear Rubicon.

The impact of Taiwan becoming a nuclear weapon state on regional security is expected to be largely negative. China has declared that Taiwan's development of nuclear weapons would be a casus belli.[30] The dual shock caused by the "demonstration effect" of America's abandonment of Taiwan and a militarily more belligerent China could cause Japan to renounce its decades-old pacifist policy and reconsider the nuclear option.

However, there is at least one scenario in which nuclear weapons might be used on behalf of Taiwan. The U.S. Nuclear Posture Review (2002) listed "a military confrontation over the status of Taiwan" as one of the "immediate contingencies" that the United States must prepare for and mentions China by name as a nuclear target. That scenario, representing a breakdown of deterrence, risks escalation with incalculable consequences.

Assessing Taiwan's Nonnuclear Options

Taiwan can certainly explore two political strategies of security: (1) negotiating with the PRC—the only state that threatens Taiwan's survival—to establish confidence-building measures; and (2) joining regional or global institutions to socialize the international community and mitigate the risk China poses to Taiwan's security. However, the first strategy is fraught with problems. At the very least, it would require Taiwan to renounce the pursuit of de jure independence in return for Beijing's promise not to use force against Taiwan. The DPP government is unwilling to consider this compromise, although the incoming Ma Ying-jeou administration may be so inclined. Some question Beijing's trustworthiness. It seems confidence-building measures result from, rather than give rise to, a long period of fostering mutual trust. Given the deep mistrust between the two sides, counting on China for Taiwan's security requires a leap of faith unsupported by evidence.

The second political strategy is also impractical. Beijing's isolation strategy—that demands all states and international organizations to respect its "one China" principle—means that few are willing to take on the issue of Taiwan's security for fear of antagonizing China. Beijing's refusal to permit Taiwan more "international space" contributes to Taiwan's alienation from China.

This leaves only the United States as a possible counterweight to China. As long as Taiwan feels reasonably assured by the U.S. security commitment, albeit implicit and not unconditional, it can forgo the costly nuclear option. Pursuing such an option might alienate its chief security backer.

Can Taiwan address its security challenges with conventional military force and other "low politics" measures? As argued earlier, Taiwan relies on economic globalization, democracy, self-defense, and possible U.S. intervention to protect its security. On the self-defense front, apart from nuclear weapons, Taiwan has enjoyed a qualitative edge and is currently improving its conventional capability.

Military conflict in the Taiwan Strait is likely to be conventional in nature, launched by China to either punish Taiwan for taking measures Beijing deems as crossing the "red line" or to compel Taipei to accept unification on Beijing's terms. Because China's *political* objective is to unify and not destroy Taiwan's economy and infrastructure, its nuclear arsenal is basically irrelevant to that objective. If China were to threaten nuclear weapons against Taiwan, it would result in worldwide condemnation and sanctions. Any hope of winning Taiwanese hearts would be dashed.

China's rapid acquisition of ballistic and cruise missiles and power projection capabilities suggests it is pursuing coercive diplomacy. As section two showed, Taiwan has responded by adopting various defensive measures, such as hardening critical facilities, creating redundancy in command and control systems, maintaining air superiority, strengthening antisubmarine capability, and developing ballistic missile defense (BMD) capability.

Taiwan also has achieved some progress on offensive conventional force. In 2006, Chinese-language media reported that Taiwan's Ministry of Defense was building the country's first-ever "strategic force" that would have a small-scale fighting capability in 2007 (*United Daily News* 2006). This capability will rely on Taiwan's improved missiles, which now have a range of 600–1,000 kilometers—enough to reach Chinese cities like Shanghai; the aim is to further improve the range to 2,000 kilometers, the distance to Beijing. In April 2007, upon completing its Han Kuang computer war games, Taiwan's Defense Ministry informed the American observers that Taiwan now has "Tactical Shorebase Missiles for Fire Suppression" (TSMFS) with a range of up to 1,000 kilometers. The Ministry said that TSMFS is a passive system designed to counter an attack by China and will only target the mainland's airports and missile batteries, not civilian installations (*China Post* 2007). Although the United States did not support Taiwan's development of such systems, Taiwanese officials argued that such systems are necessary for self-defense, enabling the island to counter a mainland attack for some time before friendly countries can come to Taiwan's assistance. To assuage the United States, President Chen Shui-bian promised that Washington would have the last say over the island using such weapons against the mainland (*South China Morning Post* 2007; *New York Times* 2007).

Taiwan's progress in missile technology represents a notable technological accomplishment for countering China's rapid missile buildup. It is inconceivable that Taiwan will fire the first shot, because it would be met with massive retaliation by China. Yet from Taipei's standpoint, possessing some longer-range missiles might complicate China's force calculus and raise the cost of coercive diplomacy. Until BMD becomes more reliable, many countries will find that offense is much cheaper than defense. Taiwan will thus simultaneously pursue BMD and quietly develop TSMFS. In light of China's continual missile buildup and improved performance, the United States will soon face two critical choices that could cause diplomatic controversies—whether to sell Taiwan the Aegis-equipped destroyers ("postponed" in 2001) and whether to include Taiwan in the U.S.-led BMD in East Asia.

If the improved missiles carry only conventional warheads, they are unlikely to deter a China that is willing to use nuclear weapons against Taiwan, although China would have to pay a very high political price for such blatant deviation from its NFU policy. The missile accomplishment has rekindled speculation on the status of Taiwan's strategic (including nuclear) capabilities. Might Taiwan's missile program provide China with a pretext for a "preventive war"? While the Bush Doctrine may have lowered the bar for countries to justify this traditionally dubious concept in international law, it is difficult to deny that Taiwan developed these missiles as a reaction to China's missile intimidation.

Given the current security situation in East Asia, Taiwan has to walk a tightrope with its security strategy. It must continue increasing the stake for the international community in its economic and democratic example. It must do everything possible to maintain U.S. political and military support. It must not give China any excuse to make an unprovoked attack. If it should seek to acquire a nuclear weapon capability, Taiwan must do so in the most discreet manner. These are stringent requirements. Nevertheless, the "nuclear option" will always exist for a Taiwan facing existential threat from a powerful adversary. Meanwhile, Taiwan needs a comprehensive strategy that combines hard and soft power to ensure its continued survival as a separate state.

Notes

1. For more discussion, see Tan, Walker, and Yu (2003) and Swaine (1999).

2. Swaine, Yang, Medeiros, with Mastro (2007) examine the various military options.

3. Roberts (2007) explores the "how likely?" and "how stable?" of the nuclear dimension in a Taiwan contingency.

4. Military Balance (2007: 373–75) and www.globalsecurity.org.

5. SIPRI Arms Transfer Database. Available at http://www.sipri.org/contents/armstrad/output_types_TIV.html.

6. Welfare spending absorbed 17.7 percent of government expenditure in 2004, but only 8.9 percent in 1994. The share of defense spending dropped from 23.7 percent in 1994 to 15.4 percent in 2004. Defense expenditure has been in decline in the last decade: 5.7 percent of GDP or US$11.2 billion in 1994; 3.2 percent or US$9.1 billion in 1999; 2.4 percent or US$7.9 billion in 2005 (Ministry of National Defense 2004: 144).

7. Norris, Arkin, and Burr (1999), Appendix B: Deployment by Country.

8. For the text of the NPT, see http://disarmament2.un.org/wmd/npt/npttext.html.

9. For details of Taiwan's nuclear weapon program, see Mitchell (2004), Albright and Gay (1998), and Burr (1999). The best and hitherto most detailed work written in Chinese is Chung (2004a: 133–68).

10. Albright and Gay (1998: 55); Wu (1988), quoted in Albright and Gay (1998).

11. Interview with Dr. H, former INER researcher, Taipei suburb, Taiwan, December 21, 2005.

12. Chung (2004a: 155); interview with Dr. H.

13. The U.N.'s recognition of the PRC as the only legal government of all China—the so-called "one China" policy—raised the interesting possibility that Taiwan could claim nuclear weapon state status, but in the end, Taiwan decided to accede to the requirements of the NPT and the IAEA, and through a trilateral nuclear agreement the United States became the ultimate guarantor of Taiwan's nonnuclear status, facilitated by IAEA inspections (Mitchell 2004: 297–98).

14. Weiner (1997); China Post (2000). Chang had apparently been recruited by the CIA some ten years earlier during his doctoral study at the University of Tennessee. There were more suspected moles planted by the CIA inside INER. Interview with Dr. H.

15. See also Lilley's testimony at the "Hearing of the Commission on the Roles and Capabilities of the United States Intelligence Community," U.S. Senate, January 19, 1996. Available at http://www.fas.org/irp/commission/testlill.htm.

16. Interview with Dr. Cheng-yi Lin, research fellow, Academia Sinica, Taipei, Taiwan, December 16, 2005.

17. Interview with Arthur Ding, December 23, 2005.

18. Interview with Chien Chung, National Tsing-hua University, Hsinchu, Taiwan, December 20, 2005.

19. Interview with Chien Chung.

20. Interview with Michael Tsai, deputy minister of national defense, Taipei, Taiwan, December 23, 2005.

21. See also ibid.; and interview with Chien Chung.

22. Interview with Dr. Min-sheng Ouyang, minister, Atomic Energy Council, Taipei, Taiwan, December 20, 2005.

23. Taiwan's gross domestic product (in purchasing power parity) in 2006 was estimated at US$668.3 billion, and its foreign exchange reserves as of 2006 were US$280.6 billion (CIA, The World Factbook).

24. Interview with Dr. Chong-pin Lin, former deputy defense minister, Taipei, December 16, 2005.

25. Arthur Ding, interview.

26. Interview with an international relations scholar, Taipei, Taiwan, December 16, 2005.

27. Chien Chung, interview.

28. Interview with Andrew Yang, December 21, 2005, Taipei, Taiwan.

29. Interviews with Deputy Minister Michael Tsai and Minister Ouyang.

30. Over the years, depending on the changing situation in the Taiwan Strait, China has altered the conditions under which it might use force against Taiwan, despite its professed policy of "peaceful reunification." The most recent such conditions are included in the 2000 white paper on the Taiwan issue and the 2005 Anti-Secession Law.

References

Addison, Craig. 2001. *Silicon Shield: Taiwan's Protection against Chinese Attack.* Irving, Tex.: Fusion Press.

Agence France Presse. 2004. "Taiwan Will Never Develop Nuclear Weapons: Military Spokesman." October 20.

Albright, David, and Corey Gay. 1998. "Taiwan: Nuclear Nightmare Averted." *Bulletin of the Atomic Scientists* 54 (1): 54–60.

Anti-Secession Law. 2005. Available at http://english.peopledaily.com.cn/200503/14/eng20050314_176746.html.

Atomic Energy Council. 2005. "Overview of Civil Nuclear Situation in Taiwan." PowerPoint presentation, November 1.

Burr, William. 1999. "New Archival Evidence on Taiwanese 'Nuclear Intentions,' 1966–1976." *National Security Archive Electronic Briefing Book* 19. October 13. Available at http://www.gwu.edu/~nsarchiv/NSAEBB/NSAEBB20/.

Campbell, Kurt M., Robert J. Einhorn, and Mitchell B. Reiss, eds. 2004. *The Nuclear Tipping Point: Why States Reconsider Their Nuclear Choices.* Washington, D.C.: Brookings Institution.

Chien, Fredrick. 2005. *Memoir of Minister Chien,* Part I. Taipei: Commonwealth Publishing.

China Post. 1997. "MND Refutes Nuclear Bomb Ploy." December 23.

———. 2000. "Former Top General Reveals Secret Nuclear Weapons Program." January 6.

———. 2007. "MND Unveils New Tactical Missile System for Defense." April 25.

Chung, Chien. 2004a. *Core of the Bomb, Zero Hours: How the Two Sides of the Taiwan Straits Went Nuclear* (in Chinese). Taipei: Maitian Press.

———. 2004b. "Perspectives on Strategy: Omni-directional Thinking: Speaking about Premier Yu's 'Balance of Terror'" (in Chinese). *Cutting-edge Technology* (November): 21–27.

———. 2005. "Proliferation of Weapons of Mass Destruction in the Second Nuclear Age in Asia." *Taiwan Defense Affairs* 5 (3): 21–28.

Cirincione, Joseph. 2007. *Bomb Scare: The History and Future of Nuclear Weapons.* New York: Columbia University Press.

Defense Security Cooperation Agency. n.d. *DSCA Historical Factbook of September 30, 2006.* Available at http://www.dsca.osd.mil/data_stats.htm.

Executive Yuan Nuclear-Free Homeland Commission. 2003. *Taiwan's Choice: A Nuclear-Free Homeland.* Taipei.

Federation of American Scientists. n.d. Report on Taiwan. Available at http://www.fas.org/nuke/guide/taiwan/nuke/index.html.

Garver, John W. 1997. *The Sino-American Alliance: Nationalist China and American Cold War Strategy in Asia.* Armonk, N.Y.: M. E. Sharpe.

Goldstein, Avery. 2000. *Deterrence and Security in the 21st Century.* Stanford, Calif. Stanford University Press.

Government Information Office (Taiwan). 2004. *Taiwan Yearbook 2004.* Taipei.

Hickey, Dennis Van Vranken. 1997. *Taiwan's Security in the Changing International System.* Boulder, Colo.: Lynne Rienner Publishers.

Hille, Kathrin. 2004. "Taiwan Is Seeking Missiles That Could Hit China." *Financial Times,* September 27.

Liao, Hung-hsiang. 1999. "Taiwan Should Develop Strategic Nuclear Weapons" (in Chinese). *Defense International* 175 (March): 18–21. Available at http://www.taiwanesevoice.net/cyber/09/19990300.htm.

Lin, Teo Paul. 1995. "Taipei Says Categorically: No Building of N-arms." *Straits Times,* August 9.

Mack, Andrew. 1997. "Potential, Not Proliferation." *Bulletin of the Atomic Scientists* 53 (4): 48–53.

Mandelbaum, Michael. 1995. "Lessons of the Next Nuclear War." *Foreign Affairs* 74 (2): 22–37.

Manning, Robert A. 1997–98. "The Nuclear Age: The Next Chapter." *Foreign Policy* 109 (Winter): 70–84.

Military Balance. 2007. London: International Institute for Strategic Studies.

Ministry of National Defense (Taiwan). 2004. *2004 National Defense Report.*

Minnick, Wendell. 2002. "Taiwan Has No Tien Ma Ballistic Missiles." *Jane's Missiles and Rockets* (October).

Mitchell, Derek J. 2004. "Taiwan's Hsin Chu Program: Deterrence, Abandonment, and Honor." In *The Nuclear Tipping Point: Why States Reconsider Their Nuclear Choices,* eds., Kurt M. Campbell, Robert J. Einhorn, and Mitchell B. Reiss, pp. 293–313. Washington, D.C.: Brookings Institution.

National Security Archive Electronic Briefing Book. 1999. "Companion Page to the *Bulletin of the Atomic Scientists* 20 (October 20). Available at http://www.gwu.edu/~nsarchi/news/19991020.

New York Times. 1999. "China Says It Will Not Use Nuclear Weapons against Taiwan." September 3.

———. 2005. "Chinese General Threatens Use of A-Bomb if U.S. Intrudes." July 15.

———. 2007. "Taiwan Plans to Produce Missiles Able to Hit China." September 29.

Nolt, James H. 1999. "The China-Taiwan Military Balance." In *Across the Taiwan Strait: Exchanges, Conflicts, and Negotiations,* eds., Winston L. Yang and Deborah A. Brown, pp. 181–220. Jamaica, N.Y.: St. John's University Center of Asian Studies.

Norris, Robert S., William M. Arkin, and William Burr. 1999. "Where They Were." *Bulletin of the Atomic Scientists* 55 (6): 26–35.

Nuclear Posture Review [Excerpts]. 2002. 8 January. Available at http://www.globalsecurity.org/wmd/library/policy/dod/npr.htm.

Nye, Joseph. 2004. *Soft Power: The Means to Success in World Politics.* New York: Public Affairs.

Office of the Secretary of Defense. 2006. Annual report to Congress, *Military Power or the People's Republic of China 2006.* Available at http://www.defenselink.mil/pubs/pdfs/China%20Report%202006.pdf.

Pomper, Miles A. 2005. "Is There a Role for Nuclear Weapons Today?" *Arms Control Today* 35(6): 6–12.

Rosen, Stephen Peter. 2006. "After Proliferation: What to Do if More States Go Nuclear." *Foreign Affairs* 85 (5): 9–14.

Roberts, Brad. 2007. "The Nuclear Dimension: How Likely? How Stable?" In *Assessing the Threat: The Chinese Military and Taiwan's Security,* eds. Michael Swaine et al., pp. 213–40. Washington, D.C.: Carnegie Endowment for International Peace.

Sagan, Scott D. 1996–97. "Why Do States Build Nuclear Weapons? Three Models in Search of a Bomb." *International Security* 21 (3): 54–86.

Shambaugh, David. 2000. "A Matter of Time: Taiwan's Eroding Military Advantage." *Washington Quarterly* 23 (2): 119–33.

Snyder, Glenn H. 1984. "The Security Dilemma in Alliance Politics." *World Politics* 36 (4): 461–95.

Solingen, Etel. 2007. *Nuclear Logics: Contrasting Paths in East Asia and the Middle East.* Princeton, N.J.: Princeton University Press.

South China Morning Post. 2007. "Chen Qualifies Missile Use Against Mainland; US Advice Would be Sought Before Attack." October 30.

Spector, Leonard S., and Mark G. McDonough, with Evan S. Medeiros. 1995. *Tracking Nuclear Proliferation: A Guide in Maps and Charts, 1995.* Washington, D.C.: Carnegie Endowment for International Peace.

Straits Times. 1996. "N-weapons Use Does Not Apply to Taiwan." August 6.

Swaine, Michael D. 1999. *Taiwan's National Security, Defense Policy, and Weapons Procurement Processes.* Santa Monica, Calif.: RAND.

Swaine, Michael D., Andrew N. D. Yang, and Evan S. Medeiros, with Orinana Sklar Mastro, eds. 2007. *Assessing the Threat: The Chinese Military and Taiwan's Security.* Washington, D.C.: Carnegie Endowment for International Peace.

Taipei Times. 2004. "Taiwan Needs Nuclear Deterrent." Editorial (13 August): 8.

Taiwan Relations Act. 1979. Public Law 96-8. Available at http://www.ait.org.tw/en/about_ait/tra/.

Tan, Alexander, Scott Walker, and Tsung-chi Yu. 2003. "Taiwan's Evolving National Security Policy." In *Conflict in Asia: Korea, China-Taiwan, and India-Pakistan,* ed. Uk Heo and Shale A. Horowitz, pp. 41–55. Westport, Conn.: Praeger.

Tsou, Tang. 1959. *The Embroilment over Quemoy: Mao, Chiang and Dulles.* Salt Lake City: Institute of International Studies, University of Utah.

United Daily News. 2006. "Special Missiles Are Deployed on Offshore Islands Near the Mainland" (in Chinese). October 16. Available at http://udn.com/NEWS/NATIONAL/NAT1/3559805.shtml [accessed 16 October 2006].

Weiner, Tim. 1997. "How a Spy Left Taiwan in the Cold." *New York Times.* December 20.

The World Factbook, available at https://www.cia.gov/cia/publications/factbook/index.html.

Wu, Ta-you. 1988. "A Historical Document—A Footnote to the History of Our Country's 'Nuclear Energy' Policies" (in Chinese). *Biographical Literature* 52 (2). [Quoted in Albright and Gay 1998],

Yang, Andrew N. D. 2007. "Taiwan's Defense Preparation Against the Chinese Military Threat." In *Assessing the Threat: The Chinese Military and Taiwan's Security,* eds. Michael Swaine et al., pp. 265–84. Washington, D.C.: Carnegie Endowment for International Peace.

15

Australia
Back to the Future?

ROD LYON

Studies of Australia and nuclear weapons usually assume something of an archaelogical form. They are "digs" to explore lost worlds: either the lost world of Australia's own nascent nuclear weapon program, or the lost world of the Cold War era, when nuclear weapons and nuclear strategy were central features of the international security landscape. But there is another side to the story not usually told—the side where Australia's previous patterns of thinking about nuclear weapons and nuclear strategy provide useful insights into its possible future behavior. Australia's thinking has traditionally reflected a basic level of "fit" between the existing security environment and its own role in the world. The comfort of that fit has shifted with time, so much so that over the past fifty years Australia has been everything from a possible nuclear proliferator, to a supporter of extended nuclear deterrence, to an important advocate of global nuclear arms control. Those previous shifts suggest Australia's twenty-first century nuclear identity might not yet be fixed.

Indeed, a relatively long period of stability in Australian nuclear policy may be coming to an end. The core of Australia's traditional policy—a belief that nuclear weapons have value because of the stability they bring to the global order—has been progressively devalued by the lower profile of nuclear weapons in great-power relationships since the end of the Cold War. Further, the stability belief itself is under challenge from a new, diverse nuclear "club" and from a new species of adversary apparently less susceptible to nuclear threats. The foundations of Australian nuclear doctrine are eroding at precisely the point that Australia's own sense of engagement with nuclear issues is quickening. Public debate has intensified over the possible construction of nuclear power stations in the country.

The previous government openly canvassed the development of an enrichment capability to add value to Australia's uranium exports. That new sense of national engagement with nuclear issues, and the rising level of debate about the same, is given greater strategic relevance by its broader regional context: a backdrop of accelerating change in the Asian security environment, as the region's great powers all stake claims for larger roles. National and regional factors seem likely to become the principal determinants of Australia's future nuclear policy, while the relative influence of global considerations will probably decline.

The core of Australian thinking about nuclear weapons was established during the Cold War period, when Australian perceptions and judgments about nuclear strategy were heavily influenced by the bipolar security environment and the country's alliance with the United States. Many of those perceptions and judgments outlasted the Cold War, but almost twenty years after the end of the Cold War the sense of erosion in what we might call Australia's nuclear "doctrine" is marked. The ending of that period of doctrinal stability should not be taken to suggest any imminent covert or malign agenda on the part of Australian policy makers. Canberra has no plans to develop a nuclear arsenal, and it has no need for such an arsenal. Australia lacks both the infrastructure and the regulatory environment to support the rapid development of civil nuclear power. Still, the next ten to twenty years might see the development of a more substantial civil nuclear industry within Australia and, in parallel with that development, the nurturing of a greater expertise among Australian nuclear scientists across the full range of the nuclear fuel cycle. Australia's capacity to head down the nuclear weapon path will grow in the coming years. Many other countries will be in a similar position.

Contradiction or Coherence?

Some might find Australia's nuclear history bizarrely contradictory. Australia is simultaneously one of Washington's closest allies and also the only major Western country to hold formal membership in a regional nuclear-free zone. British nuclear testing in Australia during the 1950s provides the only case in history where a country without a nuclear arsenal agreed to provide nuclear testing facilities for a nuclear weapon state; yet today Australia is recognized as one the world's strongest opponents of nuclear testing, and one of the strongest proponents of the Comprehensive Test Ban Treaty (CTBT). Australian uranium mining was initially undertaken to supply material to the U.S. and British nuclear weapon programs, but Australia now applies some of the most stringent safeguards in the world to ensure that its uranium exports are used only for civil nuclear purposes.

Notwithstanding first impressions, Australian thinking about nuclear issues has been marked by a surprising degree of coherence. At the heart of that thinking is a judgment that nuclear issues and the global security order are closely intertwined. Policies have wavered over time, but principally because secondary judgments—about the sort of contribution that Australia can make to that security order—have shifted. So Australia has supported the U.S. nuclear deterrent as a major contributor to global stability and earlier supported the more limited British arsenal for exactly the same reason. It has pursued the objective of nuclear arms control and nonproliferation because of the inherently destabilizing consequences of an unregulated nuclear competition for global order. And it has become, in recent years, a uranium-exporter to civil nuclear programs—and anticipates a marked growth in that role in coming years—precisely because it hopes to feed global nuclear civil requirements in a way that minimizes the risk of nuclear materials slipping into covert nuclear weapon programs.

Australia's Threat Perceptions and Nuclear Strategy

Australia's threat perceptions have traditionally lacked both immediacy and proximity. The exceptions to that observation—Japanese attacks on northern Australia in World War II and *Confrontasi* with Indonesia in the 1960s—were both comparatively brief historical episodes. The isolation from immediate, direct threats has allowed Australians to be more extroverted in their thinking about security threats and more interested in a security architecture that inhibits direct threats. Australia's strategic policy has for decades been founded upon a belief that distant events matter. The former prime minister, John Howard, argued this line in September 2006: "The belief that the protection of our continent and citizens starts well beyond our shores has formed an essentially unbroken line in Australian strategic thinking—from the sacrifices on the Western Front 90 years ago to our commitments today in places like Iraq and Afghanistan. Geography alone has never determined our strategic horizons" (Howard 2006a: 1).

Australians derived their core impressions about nuclear weapons from the end of World War II and the onset of the Cold War. Those impressions were shaped by their understandings about three main issues: key security challenges, nuclear actors, and the Asian security order.

Starting with the first of those issues—the key security challenges—the Cold War, like the period that preceded it, was a time when Australians believed their principal strategic threat came from large revisionist powers. As one observer has written: "The half-century from 1935 was probably the most insecure in Australia's history . . . This extreme insecurity stemmed from two related developments. One was the proliferation of strong revisionist powers, at odds with the prevailing regional and international orders. The other was the acquisition by those powers of historically novel weapons of mass destruction" (Reynolds 2005: 352). During colonial days, Australians believed their security was intimately tied to the fortunes of the British empire. The onset of the nuclear age only hardened the national belief that great and powerful friends would be needed to help safeguard national security from revisionist great powers.

But Australian political leaders also saw some positive elements from the nuclear age. One positive element concerned the actors who were developing nuclear arsenals. Great powers tended to be risk averse in their behavior, and nuclear weapons reinforced their natural caution. Great powers could be trusted not to stray idly into nuclear conflict. Prime Minister Robert Menzies argued this position back in 1957:

> There is an advantage for the world in having nuclear and thermo-nuclear weapons in the hands of the United States, the United Kingdom and the Soviet Union, and in no others. These Great Powers . . . are sufficiently informed about the deadly character of these weapons to find themselves reluctant to cause a war in which they are used. The possession of these violent forces is, in the case of these great nations, a deterrent not only to prospective enemies but to themselves. (Menzies 1957: 798)

The "exclusivity" of the nuclear club was therefore a critical strategic factor: the identity of the nuclear actors was central to the judgment that nuclear weapons could play a stabilizing role in international affairs. Menzies spoke in 1957 about a world of three nuclear powers, each of them "sufficiently informed" great powers. The world of three powers did not last. But even when the Non-Proliferation Treaty (NPT) was concluded, it was still a world of only five nuclear powers, each a member of the Permanent Five (P5) on the United Nations Security Council. When the Cold War ended, it was broadly understood that we lived in a world where the P5 had overt nuclear weapon programs and a small handful of countries had covert, bomb-in-the-basement programs. Australia's foreign minister could still talk of nuclear weapons as having helped to instill "a certain discipline" in great-power relationships (Evans and Grant 1995: 79).

The third element of Australia's traditional thinking about nuclear weapons was a judgment that nuclear weapons were relatively less central to the strategic balance in the Asian theater than they were in the European theater. The Soviet Union was not really an Asia-Pacific power, after all, although the country stretched across to Vladivostok. Within the USSR itself, all the "weight" was on the European end. Moscow found it far easier to "overloom" in the narrow geographic confines of the European theater than it did in the broad expanses of Asia. In the bipolar international strategic contest, the Asian theater was not one where Soviet conventional capabilities needed to be offset by Western nuclear policies. Moreover, the Chinese arsenal was small. The U.S. nuclear forces in the theater were primarily sea-based rather than land-based. And no U.S. nuclear weapons were ever deployed on Australian soil.

Alliance

Further, Australian policy makers were perfectly ready to believe that if nuclear weapons were ever needed, some would be close at hand. The alliance signed in

September 1951 between the governments of Australia, New Zealand, and the United States (ANZUS) made Australia the direct beneficiary of U.S. extended deterrence. Even during the Cold War days, the nuclear connection often seemed remote and abstract. Unlike its North Atlantic Treaty Organization counterpart, the ANZUS alliance had no Nuclear Planning Committee. The remoteness of the connection had its benefits: in particular, it helped to make the security relationship between the two countries much less fraught than it might otherwise have been, and by doing so allowed a broad bipartisan consensus to develop across the Australian political spectrum that the ANZUS alliance was an important strategic partnership.

The benefits of alliance membership were of course much wider than the mere provision of extended nuclear deterrence; they carried with them the understanding that allies would have privileged access to U.S. conventional weapon technologies, as well as training and exercising opportunities that would be unavailable to non-allies. A general understanding has emerged that Australia is capable of "punching above its weight" in international security matters, principally because of the particular capabilities of the Australian Defence Force (Thomson 2005). Further, the improvements that came to U.S. allies from conventional weapons transfers have been of particular value in deflecting specific concerns about the strength and effectiveness of nuclear deterrence, since the bar for nuclear intervention was always perceived to be a rising one as a direct result of such improving conventional capacities.

The role that nuclear weapons played in Australian strategic thinking might well have been less remote had Indonesia taken a different historical path. The long period of stability offered to the Southeast Asian region by President Suharto's "New Order" Indonesia was instrumental in allowing Australians to develop a sense that their country faced no serious threat from the north. The emergence of New Order Indonesia, as former Prime Minister Paul Keating once noted, constituted "the event of single greatest strategic benefit to Australia after the Second World War" (Keating 2000: 126). Certainly, Australia's relationship with Indonesia has often been a fragile one, mired in a set of historical anxieties and fears (Philpott 2001). Keating's own speechwriter, Don Watson, once used the image of a screen door to give a sense of Australians' perceptions of their northern neighbor:

> The Indonesian archipelago was in the nature of a screen across Australia's front door and on it over the years the rents in Australia's collective consciousness were imprinted. Indonesia was Asia's numberless hordes. In Sukarno's last years that dread was allied to the equally potent fear of communism. It reminded Australians of their extreme isolation from the world they trusted and knew and of their suffocating proximity to one they didn't. (Watson 2002: 166)

It would be hard to overstate the formative impact of a stable Indonesia on Australian security planning in the decades since the 1960s. But even today, it is Indonesia's "going bad" that might constitute the single factor that could drive a resuscitation of Australia's own long-abandoned nuclear weapon program, in large measure because of those deep national fears of isolation.

The Domestic Face of Stability

The ANZUS alliance and nuclear deterrence in general enjoyed broad mainstream support in Australia; the major political parties were closely identified with a broadly bipartisan approach to security and defense policy. Still, as in all Western democracies, nuclear weapons were undoubtedly the source of some contention among minor political parties and occasionally noisy pressure groups. At times, those influences were also important in attempting to shape Australian strategic policy from the left wing of the Australian Labor Party (ALP), one of the two major parties in the country. But the antinuclear, antialliance movement has been broadly "contained" within the framework set by the major political parties. And where vocal pronuclear or antinuclear movements have burst beyond mainstream boundaries, they have usually enjoyed only a limited political lifespan. The minor Democratic Labor Party's support for an independent Australian nuclear capability during the 1960s passed with the party's fall in 1974. And on the opposite end of the spectrum, the Nuclear Disarmament Party's (NDP) advocacy of nuclear abolition in the mid-1980s essentially expired when the party tore itself apart from within, testifying to the continuing marginalization of single-issue political causes within the Australian political system (Kerr 1985; Prior 1987). The fate of the NDP's principal leaders is itself revealing. Peter Garrett joined the ALP and was elected in the safe House of Representatives seat of Kingsford Smith in 2004. Jo Valentine helped to establish the West Australian Greens Party after leaving the NDP and became their senator in the Australian Senate. In brief, the figureheads of the antinuclear movement were either co-opted by major parties or drifted off to the broader issue profile of other left-wing groups. So too did most of their supporters.

Helping to Deter

As a commitment to the nuclear deterrence policy of its major ally, Australia hosted a small number of key U.S. facilities during the Cold War. The facilities were clearly constructed to enhance the command and control capacities of the U.S. military. At North-West Cape in Western Australia, a VLF radio station supported U.S. submarine deployments in the Pacific and Indian Oceans. At Nurrungar in South Australia, a Defense Support Program satellite-support station provided tracking of ballistic missile launches across a broad range of the Earth's surface. And at Pine Gap in the Northern Territory, a signals intelligence station supported U.S. intelligence collection efforts. The facilities were established during the 1960s, and all were represented by Australian governments as stabilizing in nature, that is as reinforcing deterrence by bolstering U.S. early warning capacities or second-strike capabilities. This sophisticated presentation of the strategic merits of the facilities reached its most disarming articulation under the ALP government of Bob Hawke in the 1980s, when antinuclear groups had their greatest purchase among the Australian public. Pine Gap and Nurrungar were then said to be indispensable for the verification of arms control agreements.

The Australian "Nuclear Option"

Australia was at one time a possible candidate for nuclear proliferation. That face of Australian nuclear thinking has been more fully explicated in recent years as classified material from the 1960s has been declassified. A number of articles and books have examined the Australian "case study" of nonproliferation, including Jim Walsh's (1997) "Surprise Down Under," Jacques Hymans's (2002) "Isotopes and Identity," and Wayne Reynolds's (2000) *Australia's Bid for the Atomic Bomb.* Some of the thinking behind Australia's hedging strategy can be traced from the 1960s. T. B. Millar's book *Australia's Defence,* for example, published in 1969, canvasses some of the reasoning. A 1965 article by University of New South Wales Professor J. H. Green, "The Australian Atom Bomb," assessed Australia's production capacity for a small nuclear arsenal and the cost required to undertake such a program. Such calculations usually sat alongside a profound sense of the probable limitations of proposed nuclear arms control solutions, including the NPT. As Millar himself concluded, "it would seem that little can be gained by denying ourselves the option of ever having nuclear weapons, and little can be lost by moving closer to being able to have them" (Millar 1969: 168).

This thinking must be seen in its historical context, a context heavily shaded by a sense of Britain's impending departure from the region, China's crossing of the nuclear threshold, the Vietnam War, and the enunciation by President Nixon of the Guam (Nixon) Doctrine of 1969. Those events helped to propel a current of vulnerability in Australian strategic thinking, a current driven by a perception that Australia was a large, vulnerable, underpopulated continent that had to take advantage of the opportunities offered by nuclear weaponry to raise the perceived cost of attack to a potential aggressor. Moreover, it was far from clear that the nuclear NPT would be successful in attracting adherents. Australian policy makers of the time worked to keep open a range of options just in case the strategic environment were to sour abruptly.

Jacques Hymans has argued that the key motivation for Australia's shift from a "nuclear nationalism" to a "non-nuclear nationalism" had less to do with strategic reality and more to do with issues of national identity. Australians, claims Hymans, became more confident about their own identity, and expressed that confidence in ways that did not depend on the development of a national nuclear arsenal. During the 1970s, he argues, a particular form of Australian nationalism emerged that "shared a strong sense of Australia's potential strength and independence with the [pronuclear nationalists] but . . . lacked the latter's fear of Chinese and Asian communism" (Hymans 2000: 3). Hymans's theory is intriguing, but it may understate the importance of traditional security-materialist variables in driving the shift that he correctly observes. A confluence of events, which included the emergence of New Order Indonesia, and a normalization of relations with China (symbolized by the visit of President Nixon to China in 1972), was responsible for a series of Australian governments reaching the conclusion that Australian security was better served by policies of alliance and nonproliferation than by an indigenous nuclear program.

By the 1980s, Australian strategists had started to articulate more fully a doctrine of self-reliant defense that drew upon conventional weapons, exploited Australia's growing economic and technological strengths, and made the requirements for an indigenous nuclear arsenal seem much more remote. The possibility of an indigenous arsenal allowed Australia a sense that extreme options were available in extreme need. But in reality the strategy had little comfort to offer. Australia's procurement of nuclear weapons would have excited nuclear proliferation in Southeast Asia and more widely. And the weapons themselves would probably have pulled money away from conventional force improvements and left Australia with a much less usable military force than the one it now possesses.

Extended Nuclear Deterrence

Besides, the extended deterrence available to Australia courtesy of its alliance with the United States meant Australians could have some of the benefits of nuclear weapons without the attendant costs. A former defense minister, Kim Beazley, has argued that the extended nuclear deterrence provided to Australia under the ANZUS treaty had a little-noticed but key benefit for Australia: it allowed the country to avoid a politically volatile discussion of the possible merits of an independent nuclear deterrent:

> We . . . accepted for ourselves that an element of the nuclear umbrella was inevitable in the United States relationship. We did not conduct nuclear exercises with the United States, that is true, but since Gough Whitlam's day one of the arguments in favor of the U.S. alliance was that it avoided a discussion in Australia of an independent nuclear deterrent. You might say to that, "Well, no big deal," but recollect that we were acquiring F-111s with nuclear triggers, we were going to develop a nuclear facility at Jervis Bay, and we were refusing to sign the nuclear non-proliferation treaty. (Beazley 1997: 51)

In one sense it seems odd to claim that extended nuclear deterrence was a central feature of Australian strategic doctrine, because Australians throughout the Cold War remained uncertain about the specific nature of the extended nuclear deterrence guarantee. In large part this was because the guarantee itself lacked specific content. Beazley suggested in 2003 that there had been a protracted effort—"two decades of struggle"—by Australian policy makers to clarify the doctrine during the days of the Cold War (Beazley 2003: 329). Australians themselves have long rated the prospect of an armed attack on their own continent as low, and the further prospect that the attack would be of such a nature that it would require the engagement of the U.S. nuclear arsenal was still more remote. Under the doctrine of self-reliance, Australia had pressed toward a strategic objective that said Australia should not need to rely on the combat forces of another nation to defend the Australian continent, and that objective applied even to conventional combat forces, let alone the U.S. nuclear arsenal.

Most Australians came to believe that there were few, if any, threats in the Asia-Pacific of sufficient gravity to require nuclear deterrence, save other nuclear threats. This condition led many to conclude that nuclear deterrence existed solely to deter the use of other nuclear weapons. One of the side effects of that belief was a ready acceptance of the doctrine of mutual assured destruction (MAD). But the belief also yielded some important ground to antinuclear groups, for it allowed them to argue that if nuclear weapons did not exist then nuclear deterrence would not be necessary to prevent their use.

The majority of the Australian population saw extended nuclear deterrence as serving only one remote but crucial possibility: deterring the possibility of a nuclear attack on Australia. This notion also pervaded the official establishment: see, for example, former Deputy Secretary of Defense Hugh White's explanation of extended deterrence before a parliamentary committee in 2004:

> Today, and for that matter, for many decades in the past, Australia's approach to defending ourselves from missile attack has been the extended deterrence provided by the United States. And that is quite explicit extended deterrence. That principle was reinforced in a 2000 white paper. That statement in a 2000 white paper was based on explicit discussions with U.S. officials. The position of the United States is that they would threaten nuclear retaliation against a country that attacked Australia with nuclear missiles. That will make people think pretty seriously. I think that will work in a high proportion of cases. (White 2004: 59)

Such views helped to sustain within the Australian policy-making community a sense that this was, in fact, the proper role of nuclear weapons. It is not at all hard to find members of that community talking, over the years, in terms that constrain the appropriate application of nuclear deterrence to deterring the possible use of an adversary's nuclear weapons. Robert Ray, Beazley's successor in the defense portfolio, also spoke of nuclear deterrence as though it deterred only "nuclear attacks" on Australia (see Ray 2003). And the small booklet published by the Department of Foreign Affairs in 2005 detailing Australia's role in countering weapons of mass destruction (WMD) paints a similar picture: that MAD was essentially the basis for deterring nuclear attacks (Department of Foreign Affairs and Trade [DFAT] 2005: 53).

This limitation is important because it suggested that extended nuclear deterrence had a rather limited mandate to fulfill. The number of nuclear weapon states in the world was small. As a simple matter of arithmetic, extended nuclear deterrence did not have to be extremely robust in order to play an important part in the possibilities canvassed by reasonable actors. Still, important in that equation was the identity of the nuclear actors: it was critical that the wielders of nuclear power were serious players—cautious and risk averse—however much they might be at ideological loggerheads.

For Australian policy makers, the important questions about extended nuclear deterrence were not ones that necessarily focused solely on Australia's own security imperatives. Many worried about the efficacy of extended nuclear deterrence in relation to more exposed allies in the broader Western strategic community, including Western Europe and Northeast Asia. But it is still true that the relatively low level of security threat that Australia faced directly meant that nuclear weapons were usually seen as offsetting other nuclear weapons, that the credibility of the U.S. extended nuclear deterrent guarantee was never severely tested within Australia, and that the nuclear debate was often dominated by relatively marginal issues.

Doctrinal Erosion

A broad overview of the history of Australian thinking about nuclear weapons would run as follows. During the 1950s, Australia faced a world of two nuclear powers and helped a third country—the United Kingdom—to cross the threshold into that world. During the 1960s, Australia strengthened its tie to the United States, deliberately building the link through the acceptance of U.S. nuclear command and control facilities on Australian soil, while keeping its own nuclear option open. The 1970s brought closure to the indigenous nuclear option, through signature and ratification of the NPT, the prospect of a more stable Indonesia and more engaged China, and the articulation of a nonnuclear Australian identity.

The 1980s brought a political environment more tolerant of nonmainstream views and a growing concern about the way in which nuclear deterrence policies were evolving. Among the Australian public, that concern often found expression in the form of a burgeoning peace movement and a visceral worry about the stridency of the Reagan administration then in power in the United States. At the level of the political elite, some of that concern can be traced in the report published in 1986 by an Australian parliamentary committee, the Joint Committee on Foreign Affairs and Defence (JCFAD), entitled "Disarmament and Arms Control in the Nuclear Age" (JCFAD 1986). The committee spent three years working through issues of disarmament and arms control in the nuclear age. Its final report reflected a set of worries that deterrence was moving away from its "basic" position in favor of a "countervailing" model. The countervailing theory of deterrence was criticized by the committee on the basis that it implied lower levels of international stability, greater complexity in international security, and a potentially open-ended arms competition. While not directly advocating a return to basic deterrence per se, the report argued for a condition of mutual deterrence at much lower levels of armaments, a reversal of the trend toward "conventionalization" of nuclear weapons, and a return to a situation where nuclear weapons were maintained only in order to deter nuclear attack by another nuclear power.

It was this line of thinking that led the then Labor government to conclude that deterrence was not a perfect condition. Gareth Evans, then minister for foreign affairs, told the Australian Senate in 1986 that "nuclear deterrence is justified only as a means of holding the line, as it were, until disarmament is achieved rather than being something good or desirable in itself" (Evans 1986: 2487). It was this judgment that empowered the Keating government in the 1990s to seek a more sweeping solution to the whole issue of nuclear weapons.

The Post-Cold War Visions

The post-Cold War period can be divided into two different "visions" of nuclear weapons and strategy. The visions are essentially chronologically separate, although joined by a short historical "bridge" in the years 1996–97. It might be no accident that the bridge occurs at a time when a long period of rule by the ALP comes to an end in Australia and a more conservative Coalition government is elected (suggesting that a further bridge might yet result from the 2007 federal election). The end of the Cold War began a slow erosion of the idea that nuclear weapons were central to sustaining global order and maintaining great-power peace. The belief in that principle eroded most noticeably within the ALP, which was in government during the First Gulf War and witnessed the new marvels of conventional weapon wizardry, and which had the more compelling antinuclear wing of either of the major parties. The subsequent Coalition government was more reluctant to abandon the idea that nuclear weapons were central to global order but was to find new challenges to the idea on its own watch.

The first of the post-Cold War visions was founded upon a belief that nuclear weapons would remain relatively exclusive in international security and that U.S. conventional weapons were picking up more of the burden of deterrence in the era of unipolarity. This vision was optimistic in regard to controlling horizontal proliferation. That optimism was built upon the counterproliferation success of

Desert Storm in Iraq and the subsequent United Nations Special Commission (UNSCOM) monitoring regime, the conclusion of the 1994 Framework Agreement with North Korea, the reversal of South Africa's nuclear weapon program, and the sound management of nuclear weapons by those members of the Commonwealth of Independent States (CIS; Ukraine, Byelorussia, and Kazakhstan) that had inherited parts of the Soviet arsenal after the breakup of the Soviet Union. The indefinite extension of the NPT at the 1995 Review Conference was seen as solidifying those gains.

Some of this optimism was evident in the Defence White Paper 1994, *Defending Australia,* which argued:

> The Government does not accept nuclear deterrence as a permanent condition. It is an interim measure until a total ban on nuclear weapons, accompanied by substantial verification provisions, can be achieved. In this interim period, although it is hard to envisage the circumstances in which Australia could be threatened by nuclear weapons, we cannot rule out that possibility. We will continue to rely on the extended deterrence of the U.S. nuclear capability to deter any nuclear threat or attack on Australia. (Department of Defence [DOD] 1994: 96)

However, for the Labor government this position lacked stability, precisely because the "circumstances" in which nuclear weapons would be useful were so "hard to envisage." The result was that Australian leaders quickly found themselves on something of a slippery slope. Under Keating, by the mid-1990s, we see a much more determined rejection of the whole nuclear deterrence strategy. In his speeches Keating cited Fred Kaplan, claiming that the strategy of deterrence served essentially to disguise the nature of the weaponry and that the nuclear threat had been "the nightmare of two generations" (Keating 1995: 4).

The Canberra Commission was created to explore paths to nuclear disarmament. Keating insisted: "The world must extricate itself from the circular argument that we need nuclear weapons because we have nuclear weapons . . . As we saw in the Gulf War, new technology has given weaponry an accuracy that substitutes precision for brute explosive force, and with far less risk to civilians than those from nuclear weapons" (Keating 1995: 5). The nuclear disarmament proposal was also designed to free the Labor party from its long campaign against nuclear testing. It allowed the government to argue that nuclear tests were a "symptom" of the nuclear problem and not its cause. They were a symptom of "the deeper and more troubling problem of nuclear weapons in the world" (Keating 1995).

For Keating, the Canberra Commission filled a variety of roles. It was timed to appeal to left-wing antinuclear voters during the 1996 election. But it was also a statement about a specific historical window of opportunity and an attempt to advance a particular model of middle-power activism in international relations (Hanson and Ungerer 1998). In one of history's ironies, the commission's recommendations about nuclear disarmament ended up being presented to the incoming

Conservative government of John Howard. The new government was unenthusiastic about the whole antinuclear mission, but unwilling to fight an esoteric foreign policy battle in the first year of its incumbency. Howard himself was not then especially interested in foreign policy, and other ministers lacked the weight and arguments to be persuasive. But in the longer term, the election of a Conservative Coalition government in 1996 was to prove a decisive turning point.

The second vision of the post-Cold War era began to unfold in the late 1990s, particularly after the Asian financial crisis of 1997–98. This view was centered on the Indian and Pakistani nuclear tests of 1998, U.S. nonratification of the CTBT, Iraq's expulsion of UNSCOM inspectors in 1999, the gradual erosion of the 1994 Framework Agreement with the Democratic People's Republic of Korea (DPRK), the terrorist attacks of 9/11, and the revelations concerning the activities of A. Q. Khan's proliferation ring. This vision was much less optimistic about the prospects for controlling proliferation and so less optimistic about maintaining the exclusivity of the nuclear club. This vision focused on the limitations of nuclear deterrence in asymmetrical contests, the rise toward nuclear status of a group of actors less tied to international norms, and the dangers of terrorist acquisition of nuclear weapons. Various "props" to traditional deterrence came to be seen as more compelling: including both ballistic missile defense and the Proliferation Security Initiative (Lyon and Dellit 2001). Deterrence itself was seen as less of a central motif in the post-Cold War environment, with the emergence of nuclear weapon states outside the major blocs. Proliferators were of a different ilk. Motivations for nuclear weapon development were thought to include coercion, blackmail, and intimidation rather than deterrence (DFAT 2005: 53). In this vision, the goal of nuclear disarmament was distant, and the barriers to proliferation were eroding.

The 9/11 Attacks and After

The terrorist attacks of September 11, 2001, brought matters to a head. They pulled directly counter to Australians' traditional understanding that security threats usually emanated from the strong rather than the weak. And they suggested the emergence of a new species of global adversary that might not be so readily addressed by existing security arrangements. In a major address on Australian strategic policy in June 2004, Prime Minister John Howard cited the thinking of Philip Bobbitt and Joseph Nye to argue that 9/11 had "recast" Australia's thinking about security threats in the twenty-first century. Major power relations appeared "more benign." But we were, he argued, at a "pivotal time in world affairs"; a time when "the privatization of war . . . could drastically alter civilization itself" (Howard 2004).

In the post-9/11 environment, a debate quickened within Australian politics about the durability and efficacy of deterrence in relation to those new security challenges. On one side of that debate we find a marked uneasiness about the utility of deterrence in an era of risk-tolerant adversaries. Speeches by government ministers and publications by government departments suggest that this uneasiness was felt in official circles. Robert Hill, the defense minister, suggested that deterrence worked best against predictable, traditional adversaries (Australian Broadcasting Corporation [ABC] 2003). Alexander Downer, the minister for foreign affairs, observed that "the strategic doctrine of deterrence or the game theory calculus of mutually assured destruction don't apply when the strategic environment is one of asymmetric threats" (Downer 2004: 5). In 2005, the DFAT rehearsed and defended the contributions that Australia could best make to fighting proliferation. It described a government much less certain about the place of deterrence as a stabilizing factor in global security: "Deterrence remains a part of defence postures but is no longer sufficient or as central as it was in the Cold War, especially in dealing with WMD threats from states of concern armed with ballistic missiles and, potentially, from non-state actors" (DFAT 2005: 3).

On the other side of that debate was a set of strange bedfellows. Some were realists, or at least pragmatists, like noted commentator Owen Harries and former senior official Richard Woolcott. They argued that deterrence remained an operative mechanism in the world (Harries 2005; Woolcott 2003). Others were patently apprehensive about the possible replacement of defense and deterrence concepts that previously lay at the core of Australian defense strategy with something more proactive, preemptive, and offensive. In brief, post-9/11, thinking about nuclear deterrence in Australia underwent a partial inversion. Those closest to new paradigms of thinking within Australian defense circles were more inclined to talk about the limitations of deterrence and the need for proactivism in security policy. Those least attracted to that new paradigm were more inclined to talk about the continued utility of deterrence and the fact that proactive security policies are dangerous and destabilizing.

The government was hesitant about formally committing Australia to new concepts in defense, and that hesitancy showed most tellingly in the constricted nature of the DOD update papers published in 2003, 2005, and 2007. However, recent research supports the notion that among officials and advisers the 9/11 attacks produced a more uncertain picture of the world and its hazards. That picture was frequently dominated by a new sense of the importance of nonstate actors and asymmetrical threats (Hirst 2005–06: 84).

What does all that mean for Australian thinking about nuclear weapons? The implications are unclear. But throughout the two post-Cold War visions, and especially in the wake of 9/11, Australian policy makers increasingly came to question their three premises of the Cold War era: the premises about key challenges, actors, and the Asian security environment. The idea that revisionist great powers constituted the single greatest threat to Australian security gradually faded. The notion that the nuclear club was composed of actors "sufficiently informed" of the deadly dangers of nuclear weapons became less compelling. And the structure of the Asian security order came under greater question as the hegemonic order established by the San Francisco arrangements—the set of alliance agreements devised in the early phase of the Cold War—began to yield ground to the dynamic rise of the regional powers. This third factor added a particular layer of complexity to the consideration of nuclear issues.

The Asian Security Order and the Future of Nuclear Weapons

Notwithstanding its prominence in global missions involving coalitions of the willing, Australia usually sees the Asia-Pacific region as its top strategic priority. Within that region, it is conscious of the role that nuclear weapons play. Indeed, within the region it sees six nuclear-armed states: the United States, Russia, China, India, Pakistan, and North Korea. Only three nuclear-armed states live outside the region: Britain, France, and Israel. The number of regional nuclear players is itself a source of concern: more players make the nuclear competition more complicated.

At the time of the 1998 nuclear tests by India and Pakistan, Australia's initial reaction emphasized the similarities between Indian and Pakistani proliferation. But within a year or two, a normalization of the Canberra-New Delhi relationship provided much clearer evidence that Australia would treat the Indian case differently from the Pakistani case, again suggesting that Australia was more prepared to cede the right of responsible great powers to have nuclear weapons than it was to cede the same status to others. The differing treatment of the two proliferation cases from the subcontinent also implied that Australian policy makers saw the nuclear "club" breaking down into two distinct groups, "responsible states" and "states of concern." India, like China, was included in the first group; Pakistan, like North Korea, in the second. Pakistan's case for inclusion in the first group was never especially compelling, but it has been eroded by worries about Pakistan's fragility and genuine concern about the transfer and spread of nuclear capabilities facilitated by the A. Q. Khan network. North Korea clearly fell into the second group. Although its nuclear program had been edging forward in slow motion for the better part of two decades, the regime could never show that it had sufficient wisdom to be self-deterred. And North Korea's own poor record on technology transfers of WMD-related materials gave good cause for concern about the possibility that the regime in Pyongyang might make similar transfers to extremist Islamic groups if the price were right.

Australia's comfort with the notion that the great powers are legitimate nuclear club members is also clear in the decision to sell Australian uranium to China, and the "in-principle" decision by the Howard government to supply uranium to India, for their respective civil nuclear power programs. The foreign minister defended this approach by observing that China already possessed a sizable nuclear arsenal and so already had access to fissile materials for that program. Again, the idea of nuclear weapons being held by the responsible members of the international order permeates this view of the issue. And after his 2006 trip to New Delhi, where the issue of Australian willingness to supply uranium for India's civil nuclear program arose, Howard defended the Indian government's "responsibility" on nuclear matters. At a joint press conference with U.S. Secretary of State Condoleezza Rice on March 17, 2006, Howard told journalists they should "bear in mind that India has a good record in the 30 years or more since she exploded a nuclear device in . . . 1974, has had a very good record in relation to nonproliferation" (Howard 2006b: 4).

Australia derived enormous advantages from an Asian security order centered on its principal ally's hegemonic role (Tellis 2000). That order worked to privilege some regional countries over others, slowly reconfiguring intraregional force balances over the long run, and thereby shaping the political equation within which nuclear deterrence policies played their part. But that type of order is beginning to weaken. Australia would see its own national security interests best served by some type of arrangement that drew China and India, the two nuclear great powers of Asia currently outside the existing security order, more closely into patterns of partnership and cooperation with that order. The Howard government had already signaled that it saw China and India as two countries that satisfy the classic Menzies definition of fit and proper wielders of nuclear arsenals: they are both great powers smart enough to be deterred from ready use of the weapons. The issue of supplying uranium to India certainly proved something of an early hurdle for the new Rudd government, though the new foreign minister, Stephen Smith, signaled in January 2008 both a commitment to the existing policy on uranium supply—under which Australia does not sell uranium to nonmembers of the NPT—and a willingness to "give consideration" to the India-United States Civil Nuclear Cooperation Agreement if it progressed to the International Atomic Energy Agency and the Nuclear Suppliers Group (Smith 2008: 5). That attempt to square a difficult circle revealed an ALP government that, like its predecessor, was acutely conscious of the imperatives of great-power politics on this issue.

The rise of the Asian great powers has not pulled Australia away from its traditional belief that great powers are responsible actors in nuclear matters. Rather, it has reinforced that view. Implicit in this position is the idea that Australian policy makers could probably accept Japan's crossing the nuclear threshold, although they would think such an act destructive of nuclear arms control and potentially worrisome in relation to possible great-power contests in the region. But within the Asian nuclear order it would be fair to conclude that great-power proliferation has not been the greatest concern to Australian policy makers. Instead, it is Asian weak-power proliferation that has been of particular concern—North

Korean proliferation especially, but Pakistani proliferation as well. Down the track it is possible that other non-great-power proliferators, such as South Korea and Taiwan, might begin developing indigenous nuclear arsenals. If status quo-supporting U.S. allies in Northeast Asia began such programs, Australian policy makers would likely revisit the central strategic question of whether Australia needed a nuclear arsenal of its own.

A New Domestic Context

The gradual erosion of Australia's traditional nuclear doctrine has not occurred in a domestic vacuum. But the domestic context of the shift has been given greater importance by a recent burst of interest in Australia's own engagement as a nuclear actor. Australia is home to a substantial share of the world's proven uranium resources. And a debate is under way about the extent to which the country might benefit commercially from greater processing of its uranium exports.

This new prominence of nuclear issues on the domestic political agenda was especially evident in 2006, when the former Howard government opened a discussion about whether a domestic civil nuclear power industry made sense for Australia given the pressing requirements to lower greenhouse emissions, and whether it might make economic sense for the country to develop a uranium enrichment capability. Presently, Australia processes its uranium only to the uranium oxide concentrate stage. The Howard government argued that further development would keep in Australia the monies spent for enrichment of Australian uranium to the relatively low levels required for nuclear power generation.

A decision to embark on the enrichment path was never taken, and with the defeat of the Howard government in the 2007 election, such a decision may be indefinitely postponed. The Rudd Labor government now in power is likely to be more cautious about moving down that path. For Australia it raises a host of issues, including whether the construction of an enrichment industry would be—or could be—a proliferation hazard. Such a program could only be undertaken with a reasonable degree of international support, as well as a set of reassurances by Canberra that its program was fully safeguarded and intended wholly for civil and commercial purposes. The need for such reassurances was spelled out by a former Indonesian government official, Dewi Anwar, in early September 2006 (ABC 2006). The Australian defense minister's subsequent public endorsement of the doctrine of extended nuclear deterrence (Nelson 2006: 3) was probably intended to constitute just such a reassurance, cast as it was in the context that Australia did not need to pursue a doctrine of self-reliance in this one very important area of security.

Even the extent to which Australia heads down the path of a civil nuclear program remains uncertain. The report from a review committee set up by the former government to consider Australia's options for uranium and nuclear power was equivocal in its treatment of the nuclear option (Department of Prime Minister and Cabinet [DPMC] 2006). Shrewd political observers interpreted the Howard government's move not as a subtle plan to position Australia for possible nuclear weapon breakout but, as a commitment to the health of Australian industry and the economy, and a challenge for the then main opposition party, the ALP, within which divisions typically run deep on nuclear matters (Grattan 2006). The return of the Labor party to the government benches has made the prospect of a civil nuclear power industry less likely.

Pathways to Indigenous Nuclear Weapons

At this point, it is worth considering the hard question, what might drive Australia to develop its own nuclear arsenal? Within Australia there is no important constituency that favors heading down that path. No political party or individual political leader campaigns on the notion that Australia needs its own nuclear arsenal. No recognized Australian strategic analyst publicly argues such a case. In short, there are no domestic drivers within the current Australian body politic for an indigenous nuclear arsenal. For that situation to change, Australians would have to perceive that an indigenous nuclear arsenal would have a direct relevance to their own security needs.

There are three possible "pathways" that might entice Australia toward the production of an indigenous nuclear arsenal, and they echo earlier historical concerns: the return of revisionist great powers to the regional system, an energized local security dynamic, or a collapse of the international nonproliferation framework. The first pathway would have great historical resonance with the Australian people. Were a revisionist China to reemerge on the Asian landscape, for example, it would awaken a range of fears that would play upon Australians' concerns about their relative lack of power assets. This world would resemble the one before Nixon's visit to China, but in conditions where the rapid growth of Chinese power would threaten a fundamental reorientation of regional security architecture. In this world, an Australian government would be keen to see a much more specific extended nuclear deterrence assurance, and there would be some who would argue that the policy of self-reliance should apply in the nuclear area as well as in the conventional.

The second pathway, the energized local security dynamic, would play upon a different historical resonance. This pathway would remind Australians of their concerns about the Indonesia of the pre-New Order days, and it would play upon a set of historical anxieties related to potent fears of being cut off from the world most familiar to them. Such a local security dynamic would be set in motion if Indonesia were to proliferate: that would, in turn, drive Australia to focus much more closely upon a strategic contest with its close neighbor. Unlike the first pathway, the second pathway would have the worry of geographical proximity; the proximity factor would place considerable stress upon the credibility of the

U.S. extended nuclear deterrent. An indigenous nuclear arsenal would look much more attractive.

The third pathway—the return of the multipolar nuclear world—would remind Australians of their concerns in the late 1960s about the potential limitations of an NPT regime that failed to command widespread support. This pathway would emerge not from the actions of a particular country but from a much broader issue: the collapse of the current nonproliferation regime. A world in which status quo powers started to abandon that regime, and where the number of nuclear weapon states in the world increased rapidly, would be a world in which Australia would certainly revisit the issue of its own nuclear identity. A substantial increase in the number of Asian nuclear weapon states would seem especially menacing. In that world, one of Australia's guiding foreign policy principles—that it should endeavor to find itself "in good company"—would start to work in favor of proliferating and not merely against it. And in this world, Australia is much more likely to judge that the mathematics of potential nuclear contests would not favor the continued credibility of the U.S. extended nuclear deterrence assurance.

The three pathways are all more closely related to external factors (beyond Australia's control) than to internal ones. Australia already sees a security environment in flux. Both the pace and the direction of change in that security environment could be altered in important ways in the years ahead. In some circumstances Australia might well judge that its own continued reliance on the U.S. extended guarantee was strategically unwise. If nuclear weapons were in the hands of many more countries that Australian policy makers believed might be potential strategic adversaries, and especially if it were to become something of an international "norm" for well-heeled middle powers to possess small nuclear arsenals, it is not unreasonable to imagine that Australia—alongside many other countries—would contemplate the proliferation option. And in such circumstances the conceptual core of extended deterrence—that Washington was willing to risk its own security to protect its ally from every nuclear threat—would be inherently less credible. Still, that sort of world is relatively distant from the one we inhabit today.

Thoughts about an independent Australian nuclear arsenal remain distant. Given the dominant model of security thinking that informs the Australian government's policy on such issues—and stresses the intimacy of Australia's connection to the United States and good relationships with the neighbors—it might plausibly be argued that the circumstances in which Australia might contemplate the development of an independent nuclear arsenal are exceedingly remote. Those circumstances would seem to require both a loss of faith in U.S. engagement in ultimate Australian security concerns and a savage deterioration of good regional and neighborly relations, most particularly with China and Indonesia. Neither event is seen as likely.

Outlook

The erosion of the traditional core of Australian nuclear policy adds a degree of fluidity to future Australian thinking about its nuclear options. Australia sees no circumstances in which it might wish to abrogate the ANZUS Treaty. It values its security connection to the United States and the broad "deterrent" effects that the Treaty itself might generate in the mind of any potential aggressor. Further, the Treaty assists with the development of Australia's conventional defense forces. And the framework of defense cooperation can be expected to have ongoing benefits; the continuing proliferation of ballistic missile technologies, for example, suggests that the early warning and intelligence functions of the Pine Gap facility will not soon become strategically redundant.

But we might well see a greater debate in coming years about the meaning and credibility of the extended nuclear deterrence component of the ANZUS alliance relationship. That debate would be excited in particular by an accelerating rate of nuclear proliferation among what Australians would think of as non-great-power states or by shifts in the Asian security order that brought the issue of great-power rivalries to the fore. Even in those circumstances, it is not self-evident that Australia would see its security best served by a crossing of the nuclear Rubicon. On the whole, Australians have moved away from a belief that nuclear deterrence is a central pillar of the global order, and they are more likely to question the utility of the doctrine of deterrence across a larger fraction of the spectrum of possible threats. If the strategic future of twenty-first-century Asia is toward greater reliance on nuclear deterrence relationships to manage a shifting and dynamic great-power balance, or to offset high-level security threats, then Australia will feel uneasy. In consequence, it will be more drawn to exploring ways of "contextualizing" the environment within which deterrence operates, much as it did in the 1980s. That response would work—to some extent, perhaps—for the first group of nuclear actors, those whom Australia regarded as genuine members of the nuclear club. But it would not work well for a second group: those who in Menzies' definition would seem unlikely to have the good sense to be self-deterred by nuclear weapons. Addressing the challenges posed by that second group might be much harder.

References

Australian Broadcasting Corporation (ABC Online). 2003. "Australia Signs Up to U.S. Missile Defence Plans," December 4. Available at www.abc.net.au/pm/content/2003/s1003689.htm.

———. 2006. "Indonesia Concerned about Uranium Enrichment Talk in Australia." September 3. Available at www.abc.net.au/news/newsitems/200609/s1731694.htm.

Beazley, Kim. 1997. "ANZUS after 45 Years." Symposium organized by the Joint Standing Committee on Foreign Affairs, Defence and Trade. Parliamentary Paper 186.

———. 2003. "Whither the San Francisco Alliance System." *Australian Journal of International Affairs* 57 (2): 325–38.

Department of Defence (DOD). 1994. *Defending Australia.* Defence White Paper. Canberra: Australian Government Publishing Service.

———. 2003. *Australia's National Security: A Defence Update 2003.* Canberra: Commonwealth of Australia.

———. 2005. *Australia's National Security: A Defence Update 2005.* Canberra: Commonwealth of Australia.

———. 2007. *Australia's National Security: A Defence Update 2007.* Canberra: Commonwealth of Australia.

Department of Foreign Affairs and Trade (DFAT). 2005. *Weapons of Mass Destruction: Australia's Role in Fighting Proliferation.* Canberra: Commonwealth of Australia.

Department of Prime Minister and Cabinet (DPMC). 2006. *Uranium Mining, Processing and Nuclear Energy—Opportunities for Australia.* Canberra: Commonwealth of Australia.

Downer, Alexander. 2004. "The Threat of Proliferation: Global Resolve and Australian Action." Speech to the Lowy Institute, February 23. Available at http://www.foreignminister.gov.au/speeches/2004/040223_lowy.html.

Evans, Gareth. 1986. Question without Notice: Liberal Party Video on Nuclear Issues. *Senate Hansard,* November 19, p. 2487.

Evans, Gareth, and Bruce Grant. 1995. *Australia's Foreign Relations In the World of the 1990s.* Melbourne: Melbourne University Press.

Grattan, Michelle. 2006. "Put Up Your Nukes." *The Age,* June 4.

Green, J. H. 1965. "The Australian Atom Bomb." *Australian Quarterly* 37 (4): 36–44.

Hanson, Marianne, and Carl Ungerer. 1998. "Promoting an Agenda of Nuclear Weapons Elimination: The Canberra Commission and Dilemmas of Disarmament." *Australian Journal of Politics and History* 44 (4): 533–51.

Harries, Owen. 2005. "Costs of a Needless War." *The Australian,* July 18.

Hirst, Christian. 2005–06. "Reformers and Defenders: Perceptions of Change in Australian Defence Strategy since 11 September 2001." *Australian Army Journal* 3 (1): 77–93.

Howard, John. 2004. Transcript of the Prime Minister's address to the Australian Strategic Policy Institute, Westin Hotel, Sydney, June 18. Available at http://pandora.nla.gov.au/pan/10052/20061221-0000/www.pm.gov.au/news/speeches/speech921.html.

———. 2006a. Transcript of the Prime Minister's address to the ASPI Global Forces 2006 conference, Canberra, September 26. Available at http://pandora.nla.gov.au/pan/10052/20061221-0000/www.pm.gov.au/news/speeches/speech2150.html

———. 2006b. Transcript of the Prime Minister's joint press conference with the U.S. Secretary of State, Sydney, March 17. Available at http://pandora.nla.gov.au/pan/10052/20061221-0000/www.pm.gov.au/news/interviews/Interview1824.html

Hymans, Jacques E. C. 2000. "Isotopes and Identity: Australia and the Nuclear Weapons Option, 1949–99." *Nonproliferation Review* (Spring): 1–23.

Joint Committee on Foreign Affairs and Defence (JCFAD). 1986. "Disarmament and Arms Control in the Nuclear Age." Parliamentary Paper 337/1986. Canberra: Australian Government Publishing Service.

Keating, Paul. 1995. "The 50th Anniversary of the United Nations, Australia, and a World without Nuclear Weapons." Speech at Parliament House, Canberra, October 24.

Available at http://parlinfoweb.aph.gov.au/piweb/view_document.aspx?id=3800&table=PRESSREL

———. 2000. *Engagement: Australia Faces the Asia-Pacific.* Sydney: Macmillan.

Kerr, Bill. 1985. "The Politics of the NDP Split." *Arena* 72: 51–56.

Lyon, Rod, and David Dellit. 2001. "Ballistic Missile Defence: An Australian Perspective." *Australian Journal of International Affairs* 55 (3): 445–51.

Menzies, Robert. 1957. Ministerial Statement on Defence, Australian House of Representatives, Canberra, September 19.

Millar, T. B. 1969. *Australia's Defence.* Melbourne: Melbourne University Press.

Nelson, Brendan. 2006. "The ANZUS Alliance." Address to the Bradfield Forum, September 8.

Philpott, Simon. 2001. "Fear of the Dark: Indonesia and the Australian National Imagination." *Australian Journal of International Affairs* 55 (3): 371–88.

Prior, Sian. 1987. "The Rise and Fall of the Nuclear Disarmament Party." *Social Alternatives* 6 (4): 5–11.

Ray, Robert. 2003. Senate Parliamentary Record, March 26, p. 10193.

Reynolds, David. 2005. "Empire, Region, World: The International Context of Australian Foreign Policy since 1939." *Australian Journal of Politics and History* 51 (3): 346–58.

Reynolds, Wayne. 2000. *Australia's Bid for the Atomic Bomb.* Melbourne: Melbourne University Press.

Smith, Stephen. 2008. Doorstop interview, Perth, January 17. Available at http://www.foreignminister.gov.au/transcripts/2008/080117_doorstop.html.

Tellis, Ashley. 2000. "Smoke, Fire and What to Do in Asia." *Policy Review* 100 (April–May).

Thomson, Mark. 2005. "Punching above Our Weight? Australia as a Middle Power." Australian Strategic Policy Institute. *Strategic Insight* 18 (August 31).

Walsh, Jim. 1997. "Surprise Down Under: The Secret History of Australia's Nuclear Ambitions." *Nonproliferation Review* (Fall): 1–20.

Watson, Don. 2002. *Recollections of a Bleeding Heart: A Portrait of Paul Keating PM.* Sydney: Random House.

White, Hugh. 2004. Testimony before the Australian Parliamentary Joint Standing Committee of Foreign Affairs, Defence and Trade on the issue of U.S.-Australia defence relations, March 26.

Woolcott, Richard. 2003. "Threadbare Basis to the Homespun Yarn That Led Us into Iraq." *Sydney Morning Herald,* November 26.

16

ASEAN
The Road Not Taken

TAN SEE SENG

The challenges of nuclear proliferation in Asia have been described as the most pressing in the world, owing to an overabundance of conditions that favor proliferation and a mixed regional record of compliance with international conventions on nonproliferation (Cha 2003). Be that as it may, nuclear weapons do not figure prominently in the security calculations and policies of Southeast Asian countries. Unlike China and North Korea in Northeast Asia, and India and Pakistan in South Asia, Southeast Asian states do not see nuclear weapons as critical for their national and regional security. Rather, regional preferences have emphasized the development of conventional military capabilities, the promotion of regional security cooperation, the pursuit of economic development, and reliance on alliance arrangements with major powers. In fact, Southeast Asian countries have made a deliberate decision to make their region a nuclear weapon-free zone. Furthermore, major human resource, technological, and infrastructural hurdles stand in the way of any plan to develop and acquire nuclear weapons by regional states. Both demand conditions (desire for and policy of nuclear weapon procurement) and supply conditions (access to necessary technologies, infrastructures, and finances for nuclear weapon development and acquisition) that could motivate countries to acquire nuclear weapons are absent in Southeast Asia. Lack of security need, abundance of supply-side constraints, and normative commitments that deemphasize nuclear weapons appear likely to continue the nonnuclear orientation of the Southeast Asian countries in the foreseeable future.

Nevertheless, there are two concerns that could complicate the extant regional consensus against nuclear weapons and, given the right conditions, even undermine it. The first concern arises from the growing interest in certain Southeast

Asian countries in the development of nuclear power. The likelihood that growing energy needs may induce some countries to consider civilian uses of nuclear power—a use authorized by the global nuclear Non-Proliferation Treaty (NPT)—raises the possibility that nuclear safety, nuclear theft and the black market, and nuclear terrorism could become more prominent in regional security considerations. Less immediate but no less important is the consideration that the centralization and control typical of national nuclear programs may affect the social and political transitions taking place in Southeast Asian societies in harmful ways. The second concern is the spillover effect from nuclear proliferation and the nuclear policies of countries in the adjoining Northeast and South Asian regions. These could negatively affect the Southeast Asian security environment and compel certain countries in the region to rethink the nuclear option.

In responding to these concerns, the Southeast Asian region has principally resorted to regional mechanisms and supported global nonproliferation and disarmament norms, rules, and institutions. Foremost among these is the regional members' commitment to the Southeast Asian Nuclear Weapons Free Zone (SEANWFZ) Treaty, which entered into force in 1995 (though not yet ratified by all signatory countries); the NPT; and other U.N.-based frameworks. Second, Southeast Asian countries have relied on regional institutions such as the ASEAN Regional Forum (ARF) and the Asia-Pacific Economic Cooperation (APEC) forum to advance their security interests. While these institutions have been slow to formulate or enforce nonproliferation obligations, they have issued declaratory statements that serve as platforms for developing regional awareness of the proliferation threat and the apposite norms for discussing and dealing with it. Finally, Southeast Asian countries seem to be turning to ad hoc and functional regional arrangements to focus attention on particular security issues in culturally sensitive ways that eschew the ideological and political clashes that have occasionally hampered both ARF and APEC.

However, competing interests and strategic perceptions among Southeast Asian states have weakened the regional riposte reducing it to issue-specific and limited cooperation, and, for the most part, lacking coherence. Short of a greater shared perception of nuclear threat, regional security cooperation is unlikely to graduate beyond its largely declaratory character. Nevertheless, the regional response has not been unimportant. Given the largely instrumental character of the extant security order in Southeast Asia (Alagappa 2003), regional management of nuclear security, at least in the foreseeable future, would most likely be accomplished through ad hoc modalities. In the long term, formal regionalisms that would have evolved into normative-contractual arrangements—as in the case of the Association of Southeast Asian Nations (ASEAN)—could serve as the vehicle to systematically pursue and enhance regional nuclear security. But until an effective rule-based regionalism emerges in Southeast Asia, the likelihood is that a functional, issue-based approach conducted bilaterally and, to the extent possible, multilaterally, will work; indeed it has worked to focus high-level attention on the growing nuclear challenges confronting the region.

The Security Environment of Southeast Asia

For strategic and economic purposes, many Southeast Asian countries have actively sought to cultivate ties with major powers, particularly the United States. The involvement of major Asian powers—Japan since the 1960s, China since the 1990s, and most recently India—has also been accepted and promoted in the region. The perceived success of Beijing's "charm diplomacy" toward Southeast Asia has sparked a debate over whether the strategies of Southeast Asian states toward China are best explained in terms of balancing, bandwagoning, hedging, or enmeshing (Acharya 2003–04; Kang 2003). Such debates aside, regional states have assiduously avoided the China threat discourse, preferring to see the rise of China as a challenge and an opportunity (Goh 2005). The singular achievement of the ASEAN states has been to engage all external powers—China, Japan, Russia, the United States, and India—in an institutionalized multilateral security dialogue through ARF (Khong 1997).

Against the backdrop of growing regionalism and multilateral diplomacy, Asia's alliances forged during the Cold War era have endured, though not without difficulties (Tow 2001). Some see these alliances in Northeast and Southeast Asia as providing predictability and deterrence; others are less convinced of their relevance to the contemporary milieu (Fukuyama 2005). Most analysts view Asia as existing between a balance of power and a community-based security order—with alliances as part of that complex architecture (Alagappa 2003; Ikenberry and Tsuchiyama 2002). Although constructivist international relations scholars quibble with their realist counterparts over the significance of the contributions by ARF and ASEAN to regional security, it is instructive that few among them would deny the relevance of U.S.-led alliances to the security of Southeast Asia (Acharya and Tan 2006). However, even if alliances lose their salience in the security strategies of Southeast Asian countries, it is unlikely that they will opt out of the SEANWFZ regime and choose nuclear militarization. In contrast to the Northeast and South Asian states, which either have become nuclear weapon states, harbor such aspirations, or ally with a nuclear weapon power, Southeast Asian countries have emphasized nonnuclearization.

National Security Conceptions and Strategies

The following strategies have figured in almost every regional state's security approach at one time or another: self-help, usually articulated in terms of a comprehensive conception of security (or, in ASEAN parlance, *national resilience*);

regional cooperation on a bilateral and multilateral basis; and community building through ASEAN (Alagappa 1998). The five cases discussed below highlight the fact that nuclear weapons have not figured in the security calculus of these Southeast Asian countries.

Indonesia

The primacy of domestic considerations in Indonesia's foreign and security policy has essentially meant that nuclear weapons have largely been irrelevant to Indonesia's defense or at least to its conception of national resilience. Despite Sukarno's supposed dalliance with the notion of an Indonesian bomb, beginning with Suharto's New Order, Indonesia has pursued security strategies aimed at preserving its archipelagic integrity by modernizing its conventional military capability, fostering regional cooperation with its Southeast Asian neighbors, and promoting confidence-building measures (Anwar 1998; Cornejo 2000). In a region characterized by bilateral alliances and alignments with extraregional powers, Indonesia's foreign policy is distinctive for its grounding in nonalignment and a "free and active" (*bebas-aktif*) orientation (Leifer 1974; Sebastian 2006).[1] Indonesia's regional orientation is evident in its pursuit of strong bilateral relations and its emphasis on ASEAN as a key vehicle for realizing its vision of regional order. And despite its initial concern that ARF would be dominated by extraregional powers, Indonesia has since embraced the forum, as long as ASEAN remains its primary driving force.

However, Jakarta's current aspiration to develop nuclear power for civilian use has raised concerns. Indonesia has been identified on international watch lists—including those maintained by the Stockholm International Peace Research Institute (SIPRI) and First Watch International—as well as by the United States, as a state of "strategic nuclear concern" (Taylor et al. 2004).[2] Indonesia has recently announced the selection of possible sites at Ujung Lemahabang and Madura (both in Java), as well as an agreement with Russia for assistance in the construction of power reactors (Moore 2003). The paucity of indigenous technology and specialized manpower in Indonesia—a predicament that applies to other Southeast Asian aspirants of civil nuclear power programs—implies that International Atomic Energy Agency (IAEA)-approved international assistance remains crucial to Jakarta's nuclear power development. Thus, even if Indonesia harbors nuclear weapon ambitions—an unlikely prospect at best—major supply-side hurdles would render its realization highly problematic. For a country for which the transition from a counterinsurgency to a conventional military force proved difficult, the quantum leap to nuclear militarization would likely be even more difficult. Further, Indonesia has been the principal sponsor of the SEANWFZ Treaty and is unlikely to pursue policies that undermine it.

Malaysia

Nuclear weapons have also not figured in Malaysia's security calculus. Although it supports nonalignment, Malaysia has bilateral defense and security arrangements with several countries, including Australia and the United States (Mak 2004). Kuala Lumpur does not view its involvement in the Five Power Defense Arrangements (FPDA) as a contradiction of its nonaligned stance. Echoing the Indonesian perspective and approach, Malaysia has focused on developing its national resilience—its "first line of defense"—as elaborated in the Malaysian doctrine of comprehensive security (Alagappa 1988). This holistic understanding of security was evident in Kuala Lumpur's Defense White Paper, released in 1998 amid the financial crisis that was then wrecking various Asian economies. The white paper's principal focus was on economic policy autonomy as a critical component of Malaysian security and defense (Mak 2004: 131). Finally, Malaysia also views its own security as inextricably tied to a strong and effective ASEAN community (Nathan 1998). As articulated by its former premier Mahathir Mohamad: "ASEAN remains in the forefront of [Malaysia's] foreign policy priorities" (Pathmanathan and Lazarus 1984: 103–4).

Malaysia does not harbor a nuclear weapon aspiration. Such an aspiration would run counter to Malaysia's significant contributions to the idea of a Zone of Peace, Freedom, and Neutrality (ZOPFAN) in Southeast Asia. One consideration that could conceivably propel Malaysia to acquire nuclear weapons is its perennially difficult relationship with Singapore, described in one instance as a "national security concern" in the Malaysian perspective (Nathan 1998: 525). Should the Malaysia-Singapore bilateral relationship deteriorate to a military confrontation, Malaysia could consider a nuclear option as a way to equalize Singapore's real or perceived conventional military power advantage (Cha 2003: 471). To date, however, Malaysia has shown no indication that nuclear weapon acquisition is on its agenda. And its civilian nuclear power exploration is still in a preliminary stage.

Singapore

Similarly, Singapore has no need of nuclear weapons. Of all the Southeast Asian countries, Singapore stands out as the one state that has not only made a virtue of self-help and power balancing but has also stridently proclaimed their importance (Dunne 1997; Ganesan 1998). As in the case of Indonesia and Malaysia, Singapore's articulation of self-help has taken the form of a comprehensive security doctrine known as Total Defense (Alagappa 1988; Leifer 2000). Like Malaysia, Singapore is an FPDA member. However, unlike Indonesia and Malaysia, where counterinsurgency has long been the primary focus of their respective militaries, Singapore has built a sophisticated, conventional armed force that no other Southeast Asian country's military can rival (Huxley 2000). More than America's Southeast Asian allies (Thailand and the Philippines) Singapore is the most enthusiastic supporter of American strategic dominance in Asia (Kwa and Tan 2001). In the view of Singapore's leaders, the United States is peerless in its role as a security guarantor and key balancer in Asia; in the absence of preponderant U.S. power, Singapore would be at risk (Chin 2004; Kwa and Tan 2001). Should the U.S. security guarantee prove unreliable, particularly in response to a militarily aggressive China, Singapore may be tempted to acquire a nuclear weapon capability. Its long-standing, deep engagement of China, however, makes this an unlikely prospect. Apart from the accent on defense and deterrence, regional cooperation through ASEAN also figures prominently in Singapore's security strategy. The Association provides an institutional framework within which Singapore can manage its complex relations with Indonesia and Malaysia (Ganesan 1998).

Singapore has yet to join its regional neighbors in the quest for nuclear energy. Its efforts to further transform its already formidable military assets have raised concerns in some quarters about a possible nuclear option given its conspicuous lack of natural resources (Freeman 2006). In July 2006, Singapore's defense minister hinted that Singapore may invest in ballistic missile defense (*Straits Times* 2006). But it is highly unlikely that a Singaporean missile defense, if or when operational, would include a nuclear weapon component. More likely, Singapore will continue to rely on the sea-based missile defense shield provided by U.S. warships deployed to the region. A decision to acquire nuclear weapons would violate Singapore's commitment to SEANWFZ and the NPT.

Vietnam

Possession of a nuclear deterrent has also not been crucial to Vietnam's security. Hanoi's "renovation" (*doi moi*) strategy adopted in 1986 marked a crucial turning point that gave rise to a series of significant foreign policy developments, including its withdrawal from Cambodia, rapprochement with both China and the United States, and membership in ASEAN (Ninh 1998). These developments enhanced Vietnam's security (Le 2005). Renovation also strengthened the political legitimacy of the Vietnamese Communist Party.

Still, whether Vietnam, which is currently exploring the feasibility of nuclear power for civilian use, may become a nuclear weapon state merits consideration. Three decades ago, Vietnam engaged in a brief, bloody—and for Beijing, ego-bruising—border war with China. It is not inconceivable that Hanoi may build a nuclear deterrent if bilateral ties with Beijing deteriorate dramatically to a military confrontation. There was also speculation in Hanoi that Vietnam could become a target of regime change in the context of Washington's preemptive policy articulated in its 2002 National Security Strategy (Vuving 2007). Like North Korea, Vietnam could see nuclear weapons as crucial for regime survival. Nevertheless, there is no evidence to suggest that Vietnam harbors nuclear weapon ambition. Nor is there evidence to suggest that Vietnam's proposal to develop nuclear energy has a defense motivation. In 2004, Vietnam's president, Tran Duc Luong, strongly supported the call for a complete abolition of weapons of mass destruction (WMD), including nuclear weapons—possibly an oblique message to both China and the United States (*Viet Nam News* 2004). Diplomacy remains Vietnam's best hope for restraining Chinese adventurism and improving its own position vis-à-vis its northern neighbor (Ninh 1998).

Myanmar

Historically, it is safe to assert that Myanmar has not needed or sought nuclear weapons, although its ties with North Korea have led some to speculate that the Burmese leadership may be interested in such an option. Myanmar's security policy has emphasized self-help (including isolation and neutrality), strategic ties with regional powers (China and India), and, to a lesser extent, regionalism in Southeast Asia (Han 1988; Johnstone 1963; Liang 1990). Isolationism and neutrality did not preclude Myanmar's long-standing strategic ties with China, with whom it has enjoyed a "brotherly" (*paukphaw*) relationship from the 1950s to the present (Steinberg 2006).

Following the military coup of 1988, Myanmar's security perspective and approach, while still essentially internal in orientation, developed an international dimension as well. Its security concerns remain overwhelmingly domestic, focused on regime survival, national unity, and law and order (Than 1998).

At the same time, Myanmar's geopolitical horizon widened to include an international dimension via a regional strategy that emphasized strategic ties with China and later India and membership in ASEAN. Myanmar's entry into the Association in 1997 provided an opportunity for the assimilation of that country into the international community and to gain the support of fellow members in countering Western criticism and boycotts (Seekings 2005). However, ASEAN's pressure for change, its criticism of the failure of the junta to enter into a dialogue with Aung San Suu Kyi, and its condemnation of the junta's crackdown on the September 2007 antigovernment demonstrations may be diminishing Myanmar's interest in ASEAN. Myanmar's ties with China, and increasingly India, take on added significance in this context (Lall 2006).

An answer to the question of whether Myanmar aspires to become a nuclear weapon state depends on whether its growing isolation compels it toward that end. Myanmar has been reported to be exploring nuclear power for civilian use (Boyd 2006; Lintner 2002). This has led some in the United States to identify it as a potential nuclear rogue, due in part to (unconfirmed) reports of alleged deals struck between Myanmar and North Korea for the supply of nuclear equipment (Ogilvie-White 2005). Much may depend on the outcome of the ongoing effort by the United States and its regional partners to denuclearize the Korean peninsula. An amicable settlement that leads to the peaceful dismantling of North Korea's nuclear program and the successful integration of that country into the international community could prove to be a crucial lesson for the Burmese leadership.

The above case studies suggest that Southeast Asian countries do not have the security need or capability to become nuclear weapon states. Although future aspirations cannot be ruled out, it is highly improbable that regional states, in light of their commitments to SEANWFZ and the NPT, their highly limited technological and infrastructural capabilities and consequent reliance on external assistance, and their readiness to subject their civilian nuclear explorations to IAEA standards and controls, would cross the nuclear Rubicon in the foreseeable future.

The Extant Regional Commitment to Nonproliferation

Speculations aside, there exists in Southeast Asia a relatively durable, normative commitment to nonproliferation. The region has long been susceptible to great-power influence and intrusion. As small and medium-size states with limited defense capabilities and with economies that are highly dependent on international trade, ASEAN countries have had to rely on a regional strategy of diplomatic suasion against domination of their region by external powers. This led to the adoption in 1971 of a declaration that committed the Southeast Asian region—then divided along Cold War ideological lines—to a Zone of Peace, Freedom, and Neutrality (ZOPFAN).

Neutrality with Southeast Asian Characteristics

ZOPFAN was deemed to have the potential to relieve tensions, achieve a "lasting peace" in Southeast Asia, and ensure that regional states can avoid external interference in their internal affairs (Hanggi 1991). However, this strategy did not preclude security ties between Southeast Asian states and external powers. Malaysia and Singapore were members of the consultative FPDA that included the United Kingdom, Australia, and New Zealand. Thailand and the Philippines had bilateral defense treaties with the United States. The dual approach of neutrality and alliance served the region well during the Cold War. The emphasis on neutrality meant that responsibility for the region's security lay with Southeast Asians themselves. At the same time, their continued membership in alliance and other defense arrangements was viewed as providing indemnity against the pernicious designs of aggrandizers and the communist powers.

The concept and practicality of neutrality were contested from the outset. There were also competing visions of neutrality. The Indonesian vision of neutrality, which placed sole responsibility for the region's security with Southeast Asians, ultimately triumphed. The earlier Malaysian vision of regional neutrality would have relied on strategic guarantees by external powers (the United States, the Soviet Union, and China). The vagueness of the Indonesian ZOPFAN formula enabled Jakarta to tacitly accept continued American military presence in the region—a situation favored by Singapore, Thailand, and the Philippines (Khong 2006). However, by the end of the Cold War, the meaning of ZOPFAN had taken on a new hue, even for Indonesia: the maintenance of strategic great-power balance in the region, particularly that involving China and the United States. This was clear from Jakarta's discourse of a "balance of interests" in response to Singapore's offer of naval facilities to the U.S. Pacific Fleet following the closure of U.S. bases in the Philippines in the early 1990s (Sebastian 2006).

Crucially, insofar as ASEAN members are concerned, this revised understanding of ZOPFAN—that Southeast Asian states remain the drivers of the region's security even if that means having to "invite" external powers to contribute to the regional power balance—forms the basis of ASEAN's security approach for the Asia-Pacific region (Leifer 1996). In this respect, ARF, which institutionalized the participation of external powers in Southeast Asia's security, and the accession by some external powers (though not the United States) to ASEAN's Treaty of Amity and Cooperation (TAC) suggest that Southeast Asia's rendition of regional security management has largely been accepted (Khong 1997). Yet this strategy of appealing to external powers has also complicated the regional desire to keep Southeast Asia free of nuclear weapons.

A Southeast Asia Free of Nuclear Weapons

The idea of Southeast Asia as a zone free of nuclear weapons germinated in 1977 when ASEAN leaders attempted to define and elaborate what would constitute a violation of ZOPFAN (Abad 2005). However, because of the competing security perspectives of member states, the idea lay dormant. Following the official acceptance of ASEAN as a forum for regional security in 1992, the foreign ministers of Indonesia and Malaysia called on ASEAN to take advantage of the renewed interest in nuclear nonproliferation to revitalize the SEANWFZ Treaty. Reintroduced in December 1995 and entering into force in March 1997, the Treaty reflected the region's desire to avoid a spillover of nuclear proliferation from Northeast and South Asia into Southeast Asia (Simon, n.d.). The Treaty passed primarily because it imposed no significant cost on its signatories, unlike in the 1980s when it was initially broached (Alagappa 1987).

Although the region's antinuclear weapon treaty is a notable achievement by regional states in renouncing the development and possession of nuclear weapons, it has not halted the transit of nuclear weapons through Southeast Asian waters. Nevertheless, the treaty, at least in a limited fashion, underscores the low or nonsalience of nuclear weapons in the security calculations of Southeast Asian states.

Nuclear Challenges Facing Southeast Asia

The NPT recognizes the "inalienable right" of all countries to develop and employ nuclear energy as long as they do not make nuclear weapons and allow international inspection of their nuclear assets. Some states claim that this "inalienable right" extends to the acquisition of enrichment and separation technologies, which could conceivably be used for making weapons as well as for fueling peaceful nuclear reactors (Bunn 2004). The tension between entitlement and the concern over proliferation appears unavoidable (Williams and Wolfsthal 2005).

While the preceding concern could well describe a future dilemma, it is not significant at this point. Regional states that have indicated interest in nuclear energy include Indonesia, Malaysia, Myanmar, Thailand, and Vietnam. These countries view nuclear power as a necessary and viable way to meet the burgeoning energy demands of their developing economies (Imai 2001; Symon 2006). The Cebu Declaration on East Asian Security of January 2007 commits East Asia Summit participants to work together to "reduce dependence on conventional fuels" and to facilitate the pursuit of alternative energy sources, including civilian nuclear energy (East Asia Summit 2007). The lure of the promise of nuclear energy is understandable, particularly for highly populated countries in Southeast Asia that suffer energy shortages. The region has at least eight known operating nuclear research reactors, and the number is expected to rise in the future (see "Asia's Nuclear Energy Growth" 2002; Lintner 2002; Ogilvie-White 2005, 2006; Roston 2002; *Viet Nam News* 2006).

The region's growing interest in nuclear energy for civilian use raises questions about nuclear safety, theft and illegal sale of nuclear materials, and the danger of nuclear terrorism by extremist millenarian and other militant groups. Further, the development of national nuclear programs could lead to excessive technocratic centralization and control, which may bring with it important ramifications for society and politics. Another grave challenge facing Southeast Asia is the prospect that proliferation trends in adjacent regions, Northeast and South Asia, may spill over into Southeast Asia.

Nuclear Safety, Theft, and Terrorism

Although regional aspirations to acquire nuclear weapons do not appear salient at this juncture, the prospects of nuclear safety, theft, and terrorism are likely to bedevil the security of Southeast Asia and, as some analysts argue, require urgent comprehensive responses from the ASEAN states (Taniguchi and Nilsson 2004). Regarding the risk of nuclear terrorism, while most discussions of nuclear proliferation in Asia focus on Northeast and South Asia, of late the Southeast Asian region has come under closer international scrutiny. Counterterrorism specialists often point out that international terrorist networks, notably Al-Qaeda and its regional affiliates, have sought to acquire nuclear and radiological materials purportedly to secure a nuclear strike capability, no matter how rudimentary (Abuza 2003; Carter 2001–02; Ferguson 2006). The Australian government, for example, warned in late 2004 that in Southeast Asia the Jemaah Islamiyah "may step up its terror campaign with nuclear weapons" (*New Zealand Herald* 2004). The acknowledgment that such scenarios are possible has been sufficient to encourage both American and Asian military establishments to engage in joint security exercises such as coordinated naval and air patrols in the Malacca Straits involving the littoral states (e.g., MALSINDO, Eye-in-the-Sky) (Ho and Raymond 2005; Prabhakar, Ho, and Bateman 2006). But such responses are at best "second and third line responses." If unsubstantiated by "first line responses" that emphasize interdiction at the source, they would merely palliate but not solve the problem (Roston 2002).

With regard to nuclear safety and security, concerns include the potential theft of and trade in nuclear materials. The disclosures of a secret nuclear black market network involving the Pakistani scientist A. Q. Khan, ostensibly with Malaysian commercial links, and the arrest of an individual in Thailand who attempted to sell cesium-137, underscore the risks associated with poorly secured nuclear and radiological materials in Southeast Asia (Andreoni and Ferguson 2003; Simon 2004). There is also concern over potential theft of highly enriched uranium (HEU) for the purpose of fabricating and detonating crude or improvised nuclear devices; of radioactive isotopes for radiological dispersion devices (RDD), otherwise known as "dirty bombs" (Ferguson 2003: 12) or radiation emission devices; and of spent fuel, of both the HEU and low enriched uranium (LEU) varieties. Indeed, where RDD are concerned, despite major successes in nonproliferation, the spread and potential use of "dirty bombs," according to a recent IAEA report, remain real (Timerbaev 2004).

At present, programs initiated by the United States, such as the Reduced Enrichment for Research and Test Reactors (RERTR) program and the Foreign Research Reactor Spent Nuclear Fuel (FRRSNF) acceptance program, serve as preventive mechanisms (Ogilvie-White 2005: 13–22). Under the guidance of the RERTR program, research reactors in the Philippines, Malaysia, Thailand, and Indonesia would either convert to or opt to use only LEU, whereas the FRRSNF program has facilitated the removal of irradiated fuel from regional reactors and its repatriation to the appropriate reprocessing and waste management facilities (Barrow 2004). Although these U.S.-initiated programs are important, the IAEA has pointed out that research reactor operators in Southeast Asia cannot rely on such programs indefinitely. They must eventually find their own solutions for the permanent disposal of spent fuel (Ritchie 2006). This obligation is particularly worrisome given the apparent inability of consecutive Indonesian administrations to manage intermittent environmental problems, including severe flooding in

Jakarta caused by torrential monsoons and pollution caused by forest fires in Sumatra. The dangers of nuclear contamination could prove far more serious to the region than floods and haze.

The ultimate nightmare scenario involving nuclear failure, nuclear theft, and nuclear insecurity provoked by decentralization gone wrong must surely belong to the former satellites states of the now defunct Soviet Union (Imai 2001: 59–60). While the Central Asian situation may not apply to Southeast Asia—there are no "loose nukes" in Southeast Asia—it nevertheless provides a sense of just how bad things could get should regional nuclear aspirants unexpectedly experience severe domestic turmoil. Such turmoil and disruptions could spawn virulent nationalisms and/or secessionisms that put at risk the safety and security of nuclear assets, including civilian ones (Mansfield and Snyder 2002).

Excessive Centralization and Control

Barring developments of the type discussed above, the more plausible challenge for Southeast Asia could well be just the opposite—excessive centralization and control without proper democratic accountability for nuclear assets. The historical experiences of the Northeast Asian states (Japan, South Korea, Taiwan, and China) with nuclear energy have for the most part involved the long-term evolution of highly centralized arrangements and technicalized power complexes comprising power reactors, research reactors, and nuclear fuel-cycle facilities (Byrne and Hoffman 1988; Kim and Byrne 1996). According to Lovins (1997), this type of "hard path" strategy encourages strong interventionist central control, increases bureaucratization and alienation, enhances vulnerability and the "paramilitarization" of civil life, and nurtures elitist technocracy at the expense of democratic governance. Exaggerated versions of hard-path strategies could constitute a type of organizational pathology. Bluntly put, where national nuclear management is concerned, Northeast Asia's past could well be Southeast Asia's future, not least because of the shared reliance throughout Asia on elitist technocracies and performance-based legitimacies that emphasize results and outcomes without care for the social and political costs borne by Asian societies (MacIntyre 1996). Whether such excessive centralization and control would be detrimental to democratic political change in Southeast Asia remains to be seen. It could mean a prolongation of soft authoritarian rule—or worse, authoritarian reversal in democratic regimes—in the region if only because that system best accommodates the type of technocratic governance that hard-path strategies require.[3]

Spillover Effects of Proliferation

A crucial concern in Southeast Asia is the possible spillover effect of nuclear proliferation in adjacent regions. So critical has this consideration been to the security calculations of Southeast Asian states that it helped give new life to the SEANWFZ

Treaty in 1995. In Northeast Asia, the emergence of North Korea as a nuclear weapon state could arguably encourage horizontal proliferation by Japan and South Korea, and vertical proliferation by China. In South Asia, both India and Pakistan could end up accelerating their respective nuclear weapon development should efforts to establish a viable peace process fail. Both eventualities would undoubtedly prove highly destabilizing for the entire Asia-Pacific region, including Southeast Asia. But as discussed earlier, more disconcerting for the Southeast Asian region would be the potential for trade in nuclear weapon components from these adjacent regions to terrorist organizations in Southeast Asia. Again, the case of the black market nuclear proliferation network involving a Malaysian business company is instructive. If the Southeast Asian region can manufacture and ship high-quality centrifuge components destined for Libya, then it also has the ability to produce and sell them within the region (Simon 2004).

There is little question that Southeast Asian nuclear concerns are at least partly affected by the policies and actions of external powers. The regional decision to formulate SEANWFZ, though fraught with disagreement among ASEAN members, clearly responded to the shared concern over the potentially adverse effects of Cold War-related great-power engagement and rivalry in the Southeast Asian region (Abad 2005). At least three aspects of external power engagement in Southeast Asia, direct or otherwise, are noteworthy.

First, the foreign and defense policies of external powers, whether directed toward the region or one another, clearly matter to Southeast Asians. The security guarantee provided by the United States for its Asian allies, including Thailand and the Philippines, has been important. Likewise, as members of the FPDA, Malaysia and Singapore conceivably benefit from the extended British nuclear deterrent (Jones 2003). Nevertheless, a state may forgo its nuclear ambition even if the security guarantee of the great power to which it is allied has weakened or is weakening. For instance, it has been argued that South Korea did not develop a nuclear weapon capability despite compelling reasons to do so—a rising North Korean nuclear threat, a waning U.S. security guarantee, a vibrant domestic economy—largely owing to a mix of a carrot-and-stick approach and moral suasion that successive U.S. administrations employed on Seoul (Siler 1998).

The contrasting approach of the United States toward North Korea's nuclear test, on the one hand, and the U.S.-India nuclear cooperation agreement, on the other, could have far-reaching implications. Washington's discriminatory policy could compel nuclear aspirants to follow the example of India, particularly if they are integral to a U.S. countervailing coalition against China. Related to this is the ongoing U.S.-led effort to construct a ballistic missile defense system in partnership with strategic allies and partners, such as Australia, Japan, Taiwan, and possibly Singapore (U.S. Department of State 2006). How this would affect security calculations in Southeast Asia remains unclear. However, given the North

Korean nuclear challenge and other factors such as Asian partners' repeated requests for greater access to U.S. defense technology (Simon 2003), the possibility exists that more technologically advanced Southeast Asian states (like Singapore) might seize the opportunity afforded to acquire nuclear weapons. Furthermore, China's supply of missile technology and armaments to Pakistan is well established—a development that could provide more delivery platform options for Pakistan's nuclear assets (Paul 2003). This too could conceivably encourage some Southeast Asian states—Myanmar, for example—to seek Chinese assistance in their nuclear weapon development. Providing such assistance, however, would clearly contravene China's commitment to the NPT, which in recent times has been exemplary despite its past contributions to proliferation.

Second, and related to the preceding point, is the war on terror. For Southeast Asians, while the war may have refocused America's attention on Southeast Asia, it initially did so in a way that rendered the region a problem to be solved—namely, Southeast Asia as the "second front" in the Global War on Terrorism, rather than a region that deserved to be deeply engaged for all the right reasons (Gershman 2002). That said, in contrast to the unilateralism in Washington's policies in the Middle East, U.S. engagement in Southeast Asia has demonstrated sensitivity to regional concerns and support for multilateral security cooperation (Liow and Tan 2006). A cozy relationship with Washington has its drawbacks given the tide of anti-Americanism in some regional quarters (Walt 2005). And references to preemption and regime change in U.S. official security discourse elicit angry rejoinders from Malaysia and Indonesia. Yet the readiness with which the United States provided military and economic assistance to Southeast Asian partners, along with significant counterterrorism cooperation and intelligence sharing, clearly facilitated and enhanced long-standing bilateral ties. But whether these ties have moderated regional circumspection concerning the United States is an open question.

Third, the "hypocrisy" of first-generation nuclear powers in preaching the virtues of nonproliferation and preventing aspirants from acquiring nuclear weapons—while maintaining strategic doctrines and policies that insist on keeping their own nuclear deterrents—is the single most powerful argument for horizontal proliferation (Tyson 2004). But while this refrain is not uncommon in regional policy circles and public opinion—along with a host of other contentions of Western hypocrisy—there is no evidence to suggest that Southeast Asian states are seeking to proliferate on this basis.

Regional Mechanisms

How have Southeast Asian countries responded to challenges arising from emerging regional aspirations for civilian nuclear power and possible spillover effects of proliferation in adjacent regions? Besides the self-help strategies discussed earlier, Southeast Asian states have principally resorted to regional mechanisms and support for global norms, rules, and institutions oriented toward nonproliferation and disarmament. In this regard at least three areas deserve attention: (1) the normative commitment of Southeast Asian states to keep themselves and their region free of nuclear weapons through the SEANWFZ Treaty; (2) the use of formal regionalisms such as ARF and APEC to develop a common understanding of the challenges nuclear proliferation poses to Southeast Asia; and (3) the instrumental significance of ad hoc regional arrangements that facilitate focused attention and functional cooperation among regional states on specific regional security concerns, including proliferation.

The SEANWFZ Treaty

There is little doubt that the purpose and expectations of the SEANWFZ Treaty among its signatories are limited. Extraregional powers have been even less enthusiastic about the treaty. Although SEANWFZ is an extension of TAC, it is unlikely that signatories to TAC who possess nuclear weapons would accede to the SEANWFZ Treaty in the foreseeable future. China, however, has apparently indicated such willingness. China may support it because the Treaty prohibits the passage and placement of nuclear weapons by another nuclear weapon state in a region Beijing regards as being in its natural sphere of influence. The accession by France, a first-generation nuclear weapon state, to TAC could signal a shift among some nuclear weapon states toward SEANWFZ in the future (Vatikiotis 2006).

In regard to visits and deployments of foreign air and maritime assets bearing nuclear weapons to Southeast Asia, the Treaty places the decision squarely in the hands of the Southeast Asian country involved (Abad 2005). Complicating the issue further is the apparently paradoxical position adopted by some Southeast Asian states. Just as Japan's stand on nuclear disarmament contradicts Tokyo's reliance on the U.S. nuclear umbrella (Limaye 2000), Thailand and the Philippines simultaneously support SEANWFZ and rely on the U.S. security guarantee.[4] Finally, as noted previously, should Singapore participate in the U.S. missile defense program in Asia, it would find itself in the company of Bangkok and Manila.

Despite the obvious strategic and political complexities that confront and confound the realization of the Treaty's stated aims, the self-renunciation of nuclear weapons remains strategically significant, and an important confidence-building measure among Southeast Asian states in the collective management of their region's security (Simon n.d.). For a region whose members have never been bashful about their security preferences and predominantly realist thinking, the collective self-renunciation is not a gimmick but a robust statement of their normative commitment to nonproliferation.[5]

Formal Regionalisms (ARF and APEC)

Without exception, Asian regional security institutions such as ARF have been slow to assume nonproliferation obligations. Concrete actions to prevent WMD-related terrorism took a long time to emerge; declaratory statements tend to be vague and not particularly innovative, often rehashing extant affirmations on nuclear testing moratoriums and the importance of disarmament. ARF is useful as a forum for developing shared understandings; as a norm brewery, the forum has largely been "confined to debate and discussion of the appropriate norms" to facilitate trust and reassurance among member nations, including shared regional dispositions regarding the importance of nuclear security (Alagappa 2003: 586; Katsumata 2006). While recent ARF meetings have highlighted greater awareness of the need for regional and international cooperation against nuclear terrorism, outcomes still lack the discussion of practical steps to prevent and detect theft and misuse of sensitive nuclear materials (Ogilvie-White 2006: 15–17).

ARF's 2004 Statement on Nonproliferation is a step in the right direction. It calls for reinforcing obligations outlined in UNSCR 1540, strengthening national legislation regarding WMD, enhancing intra-ARF regional cooperation among countries and also with the IAEA and the Organization for the Prohibition of Chemical Weapons, and securing political commitment by ARF participants to follow the IAEA Code of Conduct on the Safety and Security of Radioactive Sources. Adherence to IAEA protocols could conceivably include commitment to the Model Additional Protocol, which calls on signatories to provide far greater transparency for their nuclear activities. Specifically, extant safeguards would be reinforced with requirements that states provide broader declarations to the IAEA about their nuclear programs and nuclear-related activities and by expanding the agency's access rights (International Atomic Energy Agency [IAEA] 1997).

In the case of APEC, the push by Washington, shortly after the 9/11 terrorist attacks, to expand the forum's purview to include security and counterterrorism concerns, were greeted positively by Singapore and Thailand but opposed by Indonesia and Malaysia (Bennett 2003). What is interesting for our purposes is the failure of Malaysia, in its counterterrorism action plan report submitted to the APEC Counterterrorism Task Force (CTTF), to describe steps it has taken to eradicate the dangers posed by WMD proliferation and their delivery means by strengthening nonproliferation regimes and adopting and enforcing effective export controls (Ogilvie-White 2006: 13). Nevertheless, by 2006 Malaysia had achieved a turnaround committing, among other things, to the 2005 International Convention on the Suppression of Acts of Nuclear Terrorism (Asia-Pacific Economic Cooperation [APEC] 2006).

The point here is not to belabor the marginal relevance of formal regionalisms to nuclear security in Southeast Asia. But the larger the geographic footprint of a regional institution, the more diverse would be its membership, interests, and issues, and the greater is the likelihood that agreement would be difficult to broker (Oga 2004; Rapkin 2001). ARF and APEC experiences underscore how the complexities of comprehensive, formal regional processes can hinder the search for regional cooperation on nuclear issues. In an important sense, less could be more to gain traction on nuclear security collaboration in Southeast Asia. At the same time, experience also highlights the normative utility of ARF and APEC in raising regional awareness about proliferation and developing the appropriate management norms.

Functional Regionalism

While North Korea's intransigent behavior has raised doubts about the value and success of the Six-Party Talks, it should be recalled that some countries have proposed institutionalizing the Talks as a security forum for Northeast Asia (Cerami 2005). Grand designs aside, an instrumental, ad hoc multilateral initiative like the Six-Party Talks that addresses the singular issue of nuclear security on the Korean peninsula could conceivably be successful, and in some respects it has been. Likewise, the Asian Senior-Level Talks on Nonproliferation (ASTOP), held in Tokyo in 2003, 2005, and 2006, have been relatively productive, bringing together high-level officials from across the Asia-Pacific region to discuss and evaluate regional commitments and efforts to prevent the proliferation of WMD (Bolton 2004). The third ASTOP meeting, in February 2006 aimed to establish a common understanding of pressing international concerns, such as North Korean and Iranian nuclear proliferation; strengthen the existing nonproliferation regime and its ancillary mechanisms, export controls, and the Proliferation Security Initiative (PSI); and deepen understanding among the participating countries of the difficulties and obstacles confronting Asian countries in their disarmament and nonproliferation efforts (Ministry of Foreign Affairs of Japan 2006). The ASTOP process has helped to raise awareness and has enhanced nonproliferation through "soft" strategies (capacity building) and "hard" strategies (improved equipment and facilities).

In contrast to the acrimony and distrust that have pervaded ARF and APEC security discussions, ASTOP sessions, by emphasizing "Asian" diplomatic conventions, seem to foster a greater level of trust, consensus, and agreement among the participants (Center for Nonproliferation Studies [CNS] 2005: 7–8). For example, interactions among officials from the United States, China, and Southeast Asian states is conducted in the consultative, nonconfrontational "ASEAN way" that allows for politically sensitive and potentially controversial issues to be discussed (Ogilvie-White 2006: 18). While some criticize ASTOP for its slow progress, it has nevertheless diminished regional resistance to the U.S.-led PSI and increased regional concurrence on the benefits of interdicting WMD and missile-related shipments on an informal, cooperative basis (Ogilvie-White 2006: 19).

Launched by the United States in 2003, PSI is a multilateral security initiative aimed at preventing the spread of WMD and WMD-related materials by empowering participating countries to conduct air and maritime interdiction (Joseph 2004; Shulman 2006). Critics have assailed the initiative for its tacit rejection of U.N. and other global frameworks; except in Singapore, support for the initiative in the Asian region has been tepid (Valencia 2006). Concerns have also been raised over instances when American security interests collide—preventing WMD proliferation versus preserving the counterterrorism coalition, for example—and their ramifications for international security, as highlighted by Washington's apparent concession to Pakistan's inability or unwillingness to halt the export of WMD (Shulman 2006). Despite the significance the United States has assigned to PSI, it is safe to assume that America's counterterrorism partners who are also suspected proliferators—particularly Pakistan but possibly even China—would likely not be targeted. This lesson would not be lost on Southeast Asian nuclear aspirants, especially the key U.S. allies in the war on terror.

Notwithstanding its shortcomings and the politics underlying its implementation, PSI, remains useful for the detection and prevention of proliferation. The ASTOP process has been instrumental in helping to alleviate regional circumspection about PSI, paving the way for Cambodia, the Philippines, Thailand, and Malaysia to either join PSI or at least provide verbal backing for it. Indonesia has yet to join PSI. However, in June 2006 the Indonesian defense minister hinted that Indonesia might seek an informal arrangement and participate in the initiative "in a limited and ad-hoc manner rather than permanently" (Defense Threat Reduction Agency [DTRA] 2006: 20). As a form of informal regionalism for enhancing awareness of the need for, and, to the extent possible, mustering nuclear security cooperation, ASTOP is an example of a functional, issue-based approach that has worked to focus sustained, high-level attention on and commitment to the region's nuclear challenges.

Conclusion

This chapter has argued that despite the proliferation trends characterizing Northeast and South Asia, the countries of Southeast Asia have made clear that acquiring nuclear weapons is not important to their security interests at this juncture. Its deficiencies notwithstanding, the SEANWFZ Treaty stands as a firm expression of self-renunciation of such weapons by all Southeast Asian states. A clear line has been drawn between the pursuit of nuclear energy for civilian use and the quest to obtain nuclear weapons. This is not to suggest that security considerations regarding nuclear weapons would remain unchanged indefinitely. Apart from deterrence and defense considerations, future quests for nuclear weapons could be driven by considerations of prestige, status, and national pride. However, absent pressing security concerns, these are likely to be insufficient motives (Bracken 1999).

Should certain Southeast Asian countries decide in favor of a nuclear option, it would likely be because they perceive SEANWFZ and NPT as irrelevant to their security needs (Müller 2004). Even then it is not certain that these countries would necessarily pursue a nuclear option. In this regard, Japan's response to the North Korean nuclear test in 2006 is instructive. Japan decided to refrain from becoming a nuclear weapon state despite its status as a civilian nuclear power. According to Foreign Minister Taro Aso, Japan "is absolutely not considering" developing nuclear weapons and will continue to place itself under the U.S. nuclear umbrella (Kessler 2006). Japan's decision demonstrates a readiness to exercise strategic restraint in its policy choices—an example that Southeast Asian countries will do well to emulate. But whether Japan would countenance a reduction in U.S. commitment with the same measure of restraint is much less certain. Should the future military balance be tipped heavily in favor of a stronger and politically aggressive China, the possibility exists for a major shift in the security posture of Indonesia, Singapore, or Vietnam, particularly if the U.S. strategic guarantee can no longer be relied upon.

In the foreseeable future, the more likely challenges for Southeast Asia would consist in managing the effects of nuclear proliferation, triggered through theft or trade, on terrorist groups operating in the region. The regional response has comprised normative mechanisms and regional confidence building oriented toward nonproliferation and disarmament. The largely declaratory nature of these responses has raised important concerns about their efficacy in stemming and eradicating proliferation. Short of a more robust collective perception of the nuclear threat, and greater convergence in the security interests of Southeast Asian states, the likelihood of regional enforcement mechanisms emerging anytime soon remains slim. The ASEAN Charter will clearly be an important step toward rule-based regionalism, although its current emphasis is on regional economic integration, not security cooperation, much less cooperation on nonproliferation. Yet regional responses have also revealed the value of ad hoc modalities, such as ASTOP. Through such methods, the resistance of some regional states to PSI has considerably lessened.

For reasons discussed, the countries of Southeast Asia have elected to avoid the road of nuclear proliferation. Robert Frost's celebrated poem, from which this chapter's title borrows, memorably concludes with the intimation that unpopular but ultimately appropriate decisions make all the difference. It remains to be seen whether the road not taken by Southeast Asian countries will prove to be a wise one for the security of their region.

Notes

1. Interestingly, it has been argued that most Indonesians did not regard the "security agreement" signed with Australia in 1995 as a contravention of Jakarta's foreign policy principles (Sukma 1997).

2. SIPRI, for example, defines such states as having components of a nuclear fuel cycle. Such states therefore play an important role in the context of nuclear nonproliferation while having the technological potential for developing nuclear weapons.

3. To be sure, the mere existence of strict, centralized controls over nuclear assets does not fundamentally compromise democratic governance and legitimacy. But it could complicate extant as well as embryonic political transitions.

4. The U.S. exception to its "no-first-use" promise allows for the use of nuclear weapons against a nonnuclear-weapon NPT member if the latter attacks another nonweapon NPT member while the attacker is in alliance with a state that has nuclear weapons (Bunn 2004).

5. In this respect, Southeast Asian security thinking is more defensive-realist than offensive-realist in approach (Taliaferro 2000). As such, their commitment to SEANWFZ could arguably be understood as a collective exercise in strategic restraint.

References

Abad, M. C., Jr. 2005. "A Nuclear Weapons-Free Southeast Asia and Its Continuing Strategic Significance." *Contemporary Southeast Asia* 27 (2): 165–87.

Abuza, Zachary. 2003. *Militant Islam in Southeast Asia: Crucible of Terror.* Boulder, Colo.: Lynne Rienner.

Acharya, Amitav. 2003–04. "Will Asia's Past Be Its Future?" *International Security* 28 (3): 149–64.

Acharya, Amitav, and See Seng Tan. 2006. "Betwixt Balance and Community: America, ASEAN, and the Security of Southeast Asia." *International Relations of the Asia-Pacific* 6 (1): 37–59.

Alagappa, Muthiah. 1987. "Towards a Nuclear Weapon-Free Zone in Southeast Asia." ISIS Research Note. Malaysia: Institute for Strategic and International Studies.

———. 1988. "Comprehensive Security: Interpretations in ASEAN Countries." In *Asian Security Issues: Regional and Global,* ed. Robert A. Scalapino, Seizaburo Sato, Jusuf Wanandi, and Sung-Joo Han. Berkeley: University of California Press.

———. 1998. "Preface." In *Asian Security Practice: Material and Ideational Influences,* ed. Muthiah Alagappa. Stanford, Calif.: Stanford University Press.

———. 2003. "Managing Asian Security: Competition, Cooperation, and Evolutionary Change." In *Asian Security Order: Instrumental and Normative Features,* ed. Muthiah Alagappa. Stanford, Calif.: Stanford University Press.

Andreoni, Alessandro, and Charles D. Ferguson. 2003. "Radioactive Cesium Seizure in Thailand: Riddled with Uncertainties." *Research Story of the Week,* July 17. Monterey, Calif.: Center for Nonproliferation Studies, Monterey Institute of International Studies. Available at http://cns.miis.edu/pubs/week/030717.htm.

Anwar, Dewi Fortuna. 1998. "Indonesia: Domestic Priorities Define National Security." In *Asian Security Practice: Material and Ideational Influences,* ed. Muthiah Alagappa. Stanford, Calif.: Stanford University Press.

Asia-Pacific Economic Cooperation (APEC). 2006. "Counter Terrorism Action Plans: Malaysia" (February). Available at http://www.apec.org/apec/apec_groups/som_special_task_groups/counter_terrorism/counter_terrorism_action_plans.html.

"Asia's Nuclear Energy Growth." 2002. Uranium Information Centre Nuclear Issues Briefing Paper 2, November. Available at http://www.uic.com.au/nip02.htm.

Barrow, Kristie. 2004. "Dirty Deeds Done Dirt Cheap: Dealing with RDDs." *Trust and Verify* 155 (July–August).

Bennett, Bruce. 2003. "APEC's Response to Terrorism." UNISCI Discussion Papers (Oct.): 1–5. Available at http://www.ucm.es/info/unisci/Bennett3.pdf.

Bolton, John R. 2004. "Stopping the Spread of Weapons of Mass Destruction in the Asian-Pacific Region: The Role of the Proliferation Security Initiative." U.S. State Department, October 27. Available at http://www.nti.org/e_research/official_docs/dos/dos112704.pdf.

Boyd, Alan. 2006. "Myanmar Aims for Missiles and Misses." *Asia Times Online,* April 19. Available at http://www.atimes.com/atimes/Southeast_Asia/FE13Ae03.html.

Bracken, Paul. 1999. "Asia's Militaries and the New Nuclear Age." *Current History* (Dec.): 415–21.

Bunn, George. 2004. "The World's Non-Proliferation Regime in Time." *IAEA Bulletin* 46 (2). Available at http://www.iaea.org/Publications/Magazines/Bulletin/Bull462/nonproliferation_regime.html.

Byrne, John, and Steven M. Hoffman. 1988. "Nuclear Power and Technological Authoritarianism." *Bulletin of Science, Technology and Society* 7: 658–71.

Carter, Ashton B. 2001–02. "The Architecture of Government in the Face of Terrorism." *International Security* 26 (3): 5–23.

Cerami, Joseph R. 2005. "From the Six-Party Talks to a Northeast Asian Security Regime? Cooperative Threat Reduction Strategies and Institutional Development." Bush School Working Paper 525. College Station, Tex.: Bush School of Government and Public Service, Texas A&M University. Available at http://bush.tamu.edu/research/working_papers/jcerami/CeramiISA2005.pdf.

Cha, Victor D. 2003. "Nuclear Weapons, Missile Defense, and Stability: A Case for 'Sober Optimism.'" In *Asian Security Order: Instrumental and Normative Features,* ed. Muthiah Alagappa. Stanford, Calif.: Stanford University Press.

Center for Nonproliferation Studies (CNS). 2005. "Regional Cooperation: Senior Asia-Pacific Officials Meet to Discuss Nonproliferation." *Asian Export Control Observer* 6 (February/March), Center for Nonproliferation Studies, Monterey Institute of International Studies. Available at http://cns.miis.edu/pubs/observer/asian/pdfs/aeco_0502.pdf.

Chin, Kin Wah. 2004. "Singapore's Perspective on the Asia-Pacific Security Architecture." In *Asia-Pacific Security Cooperation: National Interests and Regional Order,* ed. See Seng Tan and Amitav Acharya. Armonk, N.Y.: M. E. Sharpe.

Cohen, Stephen. 1989. "Leadership and the Management of National Security." In *Leadership Perceptions and National Security: The Southeast Asian Experience,* ed. Mohammed Ayoob and Chai-Anan Samudavanija. Singapore: Institute of Southeast Asian Studies.

Cornejo, Robert M. 2000. "When Sukarno Sought the Bomb: Indonesian Nuclear Aspirations in the Mid-1960s." *Nonproliferation Review* 7 (2): 31–43.

Defense Threat Reduction Agency (DTRA). 2006. "Indonesia May Join PSI in Informal Arrangement." OSCINFO document SEP 20060614053003, June 14. *Weekly Treaty*

Review, Defense Treaty Inspection Readiness (DTIRP) Program, June 9–15. Available at http://dtirp.dtra.mil/tic/WTR/wtr_15jun06.pdf.

Dunne, Timothy. 1997. "Realism." In *The Globalization of World Politics: An Introduction to International Relations,* ed. John Baylis and Steve Smith. Oxford: Oxford University Press.

East Asia Summit. 2007. "Cebu Declaration on East Asian Energy Security." Available at http://www.sunstar.com.ph/blogs/asean/?p=241.

Ferguson, Charles D. 2003. "Reducing the Threat of RDDs." *IAEA Bulletin* 45 (1). Available at http://www.iaea.org/Publications/Magazines/Bulletin/Bull451/.

———. 2006. *Preventing Catastrophic Nuclear Terrorism.* CSR 11. New York: Council on Foreign Relations.

Freeman, Marsha. 2006. "A Renaissance in Nuclear Power Is under Way around the World." *Executive Intelligence Review,* February 24. Available at http://www.larouchepub.com/other/2006/3308nuclear_revival.html.

Fukuyama, Francis. 2005. "Re-Envisioning Asia." *Foreign Affairs* 84 (1): 75–88.

Ganesan, Narayanan. 1998. "Singapore: Realist cum Trading State." In *Asian Security Practice: Material and Ideational Influences,* ed. Muthiah Alagappa. Stanford, Calif.: Stanford University Press.

Gershman, John. 2002. "Is Southeast Asia the Second Front?" *Foreign Affairs* 8 (4): 60–74.

Goh, Evelyn. 2005. "Introduction." In *Betwixt and Between: Southeast Asian Strategic Relations with the U.S. and China.* IDSS Monograph 7. Singapore: Institute of Defense and Strategic Studies.

Han, Daw Than. 1988. *Common Vision: Burma's Regional Outlook.* Occasional Paper. Washington, D.C.: Institute for the Study of Diplomacy, School of Foreign Service, Georgetown University.

Hanggi, Heiner. 1991. *ASEAN and the ZOPFAN Concept.* Singapore: ISEAS.

Ho, Joshua H., and Catherine Zara Raymond, eds. 2005. *The Best of Times, the Worst of Times: Maritime Security in the Asia-Pacific.* Singapore: World Scientific.

Huxley, Tim. 2000. *Defending the Lion City: The Armed Forces of Singapore.* St. Leonards, NSW, Australia: Allen and Unwin.

Ikenberry, G. John, and J. Tsuchiyama. 2002. "Between Balance of Power and Community: The Future of Multilateral Security Co-Operation in the Asia-Pacific." *International Relations of the Asia-Pacific* 2 (1): 69–94.

Imai, Ryukichi. 2001. "2000 Nuclear Non-Proliferation Treaty (NPT) Review Conference." *Asia-Pacific Review* 8 (1): 51–62.

International Atomic Energy Agency (IAEA). 1997. *Model Protocol Additional to the Agreement(s) between States and the International Atomic Energy Agency for the Application of Safeguards.* Vienna: IAEA. Available at http://www.iaea.org/Publications/Documents/Infcircs/1998/infcirc540corrected.pdf.

Johnstone, William C. 1963. *Burma's Foreign Policy: A Study in Neutralism.* Cambridge, Mass.: Harvard University Press.

Jones, Matthew. 2003. "Up the Garden Path? Britain's Nuclear History in the Far East, 1954–1962." *International History Review* 25 (2): 306–33.

Joseph, Jofi. 2004. "The Proliferation Security Initiative: Can Interdiction Stop Proliferation?" *Arms Control Today,* June 1. Available at: http://www.armscontrol.org/act/2004_06/Joseph.asp.

Kang, David C. 2003. "Getting Asia Wrong: The Need for New Analytical Frameworks." *International Security* 27 (4): 57–85.

Katsumata, Hiro. 2006. "Establishment of the ASEAN Regional Forum: Constructing a Talking Shop or a Norm Brewery?" *Pacific Review* 19 (2): 181–98.

Kessler, Glenn. 2006. "Japan, Acting to Calm U.S. Worries, Rules Out Building Nuclear Arms: Rice Affirms American Protection in Wake of N. Korean Test." *Washington Post,* October 19, p. A24.

Kim, Jong-Dall, and John Byrne. 1996. "The Asian Atom: Hard-Pathed Nuclearization in East Asia." In *Governing the Atom: The Politics of Risk,* ed. John Byrne and Steven M. Hoffman. New Brunswick, N.J.: Transaction.

Khong, Yuen Foong. 1997. "Review Article: Making Bricks without Straw in the Asia-Pacific?" *Pacific Review* 10 (2): 289–300.

———. 2006. "Michael Leifer and the Pre-requisites of Regional Order in Southeast Asia." In *Order and Security in Southeast Asia: Essays in Memory of Michael Leifer,* ed. Joseph Chinyong Liow and Ralf Emmers. London: Routledge.

Kwa, Chong Guan, and See Seng Tan. 2001. "The Keystone of World Order." *Washington Quarterly* 24 (3): 95–103.

Lall, Marie. 2006. "Indo-Myanmar Relations in the Era of Pipeline Diplomacy." *Contemporary Southeast Asia* 28 (3): 424–46.

Le, Linh Lan. 2005. "Vietnam." In *Betwixt and Between: Southeast Asian Strategic Relations with the U.S. and China.* IDSS Monograph 7. Singapore: Institute of Defense and Strategic Studies.

Leifer, Michael. 1974. "Indonesia's Regional Vision." *World Today* 30 (10).

———. 1996. *The ASEAN Regional Forum.* Adelphi Paper 302. London: Oxford University Press for IISS.

———. 2000. *Singapore's Foreign Policy: Coping With Vulnerability.* London: Routledge.

Liang, Chi Shad. 1990. *Burma's Foreign Relations: Neutralism in Theory and Practice.* New York: Praeger.

Limaye, Satu P. 2000. "Tokyo's Dynamic Diplomacy: Japan and the Subcontinent's Nuclear Tests." *Contemporary Southeast Asia* 22 (2): 322–39.

Lintner, Bertil. 2002. "Myanmar Gets a Russian Nuclear Reactor: Deal Vexes China's Efforts to Expand Its Influence by Courting Yangon." *Wall Street Journal,* January 3. Available at http://www.asiapacificms.com/articles/myanmar_nuclear/.

Liow, Joseph Chinyong, and See Seng Tan. 2006. "A New Era in U.S.-ASEAN Relations?" *IDSS Commentaries* 119/2006.

Lovins, Amory B. 1977. *Soft Energy Paths: Towards a Durable Peace.* Cambridge, Mass.: Ballinger.

MacIntyre, Andrew J. 1996. "Grappling with Legitimacy." *Journal of Democracy* 7 (3): 170–73.

Mak, J. N. 2004. "Malaysian Defense and Security Cooperation: Coming Out of the Closet." In *Asia-Pacific Security Cooperation: National Interests and Regional Order,* ed. See Seng Tan and Amitav Acharya. Armonk, N.Y.: M. E. Sharpe.

Mansfield, Edward, and Jack Snyder. 2002. "Democratic Transitions, Institutional Capacity, and the Onset of War." *International Organization* 56 (2): 297–337.

Ministry of Foreign Affairs of Japan. 2006. "The Third Asian Senior-Level Talks on Non-Proliferation (ASTOP)," February 3. Available at http://www.mofa.go.jp/announce/event/2006/2/0203-3.html.

Moore, Matthew. 2003. "Jakarta's Nuclear Dream." *The Age Online* (Australia), August 22.

Müller, Harald. 2004. "Farewell to Arms: What's Blocking Nuclear Disarmament?" *IAEA Bulletin* 46 (2). Available at http://www.iaea.org/Publications/Magazines/Bulletin/Bull462/farewell.html.

Nathan, K. S. 1998. "Malaysia: Reinventing the Nation." In *Asian Security Practice: Material and Ideational Influences,* ed. Muthiah Alagappa. Stanford, Calif.: Stanford University Press.

Ninh, Kim. 1998. "Vietnam: Struggle and Cooperation." In *Asian Security Practice: Material and Ideational Influences,* ed. Muthiah Alagappa. Stanford, Calif.: Stanford University Press.

New Zealand Herald. 2004. "Jemaah Islamiyah Nuclear Warning from Downer." November 8. Available at http://www.nzherald.co.nz/section/story.cfm?c_id=2&objectid=360798.

Oga, Toru. 2004. "Rediscovering Asianness: The Role of Institutional Discourses in APEC, 1989–1997." *International Relations of the Asia-Pacific* 4: 287–317.

Ogilvie-White, Tanya. 2005. "Preventing Nuclear and Radiological Terrorism: Nuclear Security in Southeast Asia." Occasional Paper. Brisbane: Australian Centre for Peace and Conflict Studies, University of Queensland.

———. 2006. "Non-proliferation and Counterterrorism Cooperation in Southeast Asia: Meeting Global Obligations through Regional Security Architectures?" *Contemporary Southeast Asia* 28 (1): 1–26.

Pathmanathan, Murugestu, and David Lazarus, eds. 1984. *Winds of Change: The Mahathir Impact on Malaysia's Foreign Policy.* Kuala Lumpur: Eastview.

Paul, T. V. 2003. "Chinese-Pakistani Nuclear/Missile Ties and Balance of Power Politics." *Nonproliferation Review* 10 (2): 21–29.

Prabhakar, Lawrence W., Joshua H. Ho, and Sam Bateman. 2006. *The Evolving Maritime Balance of Power in the Asia-Pacific: Maritime Doctrines and Nuclear Weapons at Sea.* Singapore: World Scientific.

Rapkin, David P. 2001. "The United States, Japan, and the Power to Block: The APEC and AMF Cases." *Pacific Review* 14 (3): 373–410.

Ritchie, Iain G. 2006. "Growing Dimensions: Spent Fuel Management at Research Reactors." *IAEA Bulletin.* Available at http://www.iaea.org/Publications/Magazines/Bulletin/Bull401/article7.html.

Roston, Michael. 2002. "Nuclear Archipelagos? Secure Nuclear Materials in Southeast Asia." *PacNet Newsletter* 25 (June 21). Available at http://www.csis.org/pacfor/pac0225.

Sebastian, Leonard C. 2006. "Domestic Security Priorities, 'Balance of Interests,' and Indonesia's Management of Regional Order." In *Order and Security in Southeast Asia: Essays in Memory of Michael Leifer,* ed. Joseph Chinyong Liow and Ralf Emmers. London: Routledge.

Seekings, Donald M. 2005. "Burma and U.S. Sanctions: Punishing an Authoritarian Regime." *Asian Survey* 45 (3): 437–52.

Shulman, Mark R. 2006. "The Proliferation Security Initiative as a New Paradigm for Peace and Security." Strategic Studies Institute (SSI) monograph. Carlisle, PA: Strategic Studies Institute of the U.S. Army War College.

Siler, Michael J. 1998. "U.S. Nuclear Nonproliferation Policy in the Northeast Asian Region during the Cold War: The South Korean Case." *East Asia: An International Quarterly* 16: 41–86.

Simon, Sheldon W. 2003. "Theater Security Cooperation in the U.S. Pacific Command: An Assessment and Projection." *NBR Analysis* 14 (2). Available at http://nbar.org/publications/analysis/pdf/vol14no2.pdf.

———. 2004. "A WMD Discovery in Malaysia and Counter-Terrorism Concerns in the Rest of Southeast Asia." *Comparative Connections: A Quarterly E-Journal on East Asian Bilateral Relations* 6 (1). Available at http://www.csis.org/media/csis/pubs/0401q.pdf.

———. n.d. "Nuclear Weapons and Southeast Asia: The Path Not Taken." Paper prepared for the U.S. Department of Energy and the National Bureau of Asian Research.

Steinberg, David I. 2006. "China's Burma Connection." *Brown Journal of World Affairs* 7 (2).

Straits Times (Singapore). 2006. "Third-Generation RSAF May Go for Anti-Missile Shield." July 2.

Sukma, Rizal. 1997. "Indonesia's Bebas-Aktif Foreign Policy and the 'Security Agreement' with Australia." *Australian Journal of International Affairs* 51 (2): 231–41.

Symon, Andrew. 2006. "Nuclear Power: A Case for International Control." *Straits Times* (Singapore), October 21, p. S16.

Taliaferro, Jerry W. 2000. "Security Seeking under Anarchy: Defensive Realism Revisited." *International Security* 25 (3): 128–61.

Taniguchi, Tomihiro, and Anita Nilsson. 2004. "Hot Spots, Weak Links: Strengthening Nuclear Security in a Changing World." *IAEA Bulletin* 46 (1). Available at http://www.iaea.org/Publications/Magazines/Bulletin/Bull461/.

Taylor, Carolyn, Yana Feldman, Charles Mahaffey, Brett Marvin, and Jack Boureston. 2004. "Countries of Nuclear Strategic Concern: Indonesia." *SIPRI Nuclear Arms Control* (July). Available at http://www.sipri.org/contents/expcon/cnsc1ins.html.

Than, Tin Maung Maung. 1998. "Myanmar: Preoccupation with Regime Survival, National Unity, and Stability." In *Asian Security Practice: Material and Ideational Influences*, ed. Muthiah Alagappa. Stanford, Calif.: Stanford University Press.

Timerbaev, Roland. 2004. "What Next for the NPT? Facing the Moment of Truth." *IAEA Bulletin* 46 (2). Available at http://www.iaea.org/Publications/Magazines/Bulletin/Bull462/what_next.html.

Tow, William T. 2001. *Asia-Pacific Strategic Relations: Seeking Convergent Security*. Cambridge: Cambridge University Press.

Tyson, Rhianna. 2004. "Reframing the Debate against Nuclear Weapons." *IAEA Bulletin* 46 (2). Available at http://www.iaea.org/Publications/Magazines/Bulletin/Bull462/reframing_debate.html.

U.S. Department of State. 2006. "Japan Emerges as America's Largest Missile Defense Partner." International Security, USInfo.State.Gov., March 9. Available at http://usinfo.state.gov/is/Archive/2006/Mar/13-473943.html.

Valencia, Mark J. 2006. "The Proliferation Security Initiative in Perspective." Policy Forum Online 06-41A, May 25. Available at http://www.nautilus.org/fora/security/0641Valencia.html.

Vatikiotis, Michael. 2006. "Vivre la France in ASEAN." *OpinionAsia: Global Views on Asia*. http://www.opinionasia.org/VivrelaFrance.

Viet Nam News. 2004. "Viet Nam Opposes Use of Nuclear Weapons: President." August 4. Available at http://vietnamnews.vnanet.vn/2004-08/03/Stories/02.htm.

———. 2006. "Calculating the Costs of Nuclear Energy," April 9. Available at http://vietnamnews.vnanet.vn/showarticle.php?num=01SUN090406.

Vuving, Alexander L. 2007. "Power Shift and Grand Strategic Fit: Explaining Turning Points in China-Vietnam Relations." Paper presented at "Living with China" Conference, S. Rajaratnam School of International Studies, March 8–9, Singapore.

Walt, Stephen M. 2005. *Taming American Power: The Global Response to U.S. Primacy.* New York: W. W. Norton.

Williams, Joshua, and Jon Wolfsthal. 2005. "The NPT at 35: A Crisis of Compliance or a Crisis of Confidence?" Policy Brief. Washington, D.C.: Carnegie Endowment for International Peace. Available at http://www.carnegieendowment.org/publications/index.cfm?fa=view&id=16850.

PART III

Conclusion

17

Nuclear Weapons and National Security

Far-Reaching Influence and Deterrence Dominance

MUTHIAH ALAGAPPA

A chief conclusion of this study is that nuclear weapons exert an indirect but far-reaching influence on the security thinking, practice, and interaction of nuclear weapon states, their allies, and nuclear weapon aspirant states in the Asian security region. On the surface nuclear weapons appear to play a modest role. Except for a brief period (1998–2002) in India-Pakistan relations, they have been less visible in comparison to the Cold War era, and they appear less salient than conventional military force in dealing with the immediate security challenges confronting states in the region. Even in the small number of situations where they are relevant, nuclear weapons remain in the background and appear to augment conventional forces. The emphasis in the region on modernizing and building conventional military capabilities would seem to further support the contention that nuclear weapons play a modest role in national security. A closer look, however, suggests that they are much more consequential.

Nuclear weapons cast a long shadow that informs in fundamental ways the strategic policies and behavior of major powers (all but one of which possess nuclear weapons), their allies, and those states facing existential threats. They induce caution and set boundaries to the strategic interaction of nuclear weapon states and condition the role and use of force in their interactions. The danger of escalation limits military options in a crisis between nuclear weapon states and shapes the purpose and manner in which military force is used. Although relevant only in a small number of situations, these include the most serious regional conflicts that could escalate to large-scale war. Nuclear weapons help prevent the outbreak of hostilities, keep hostilities limited when they do break out, and prevent their escalation to major wars. Nuclear weapons enable weaker powers to deter stronger adversaries and help ameliorate the effects of imbalance in conventional military capability. By providing insurance to cope with unanticipated contingencies, they reduce immediate anxieties over military imbalances and vulnerabilities. Nuclear weapons enable major powers to take a long view of the strategic environment, set a moderate pace for their force development, and focus on other national priorities, including mutually beneficial interaction with other nuclear weapon states. Although nuclear weapons by themselves do not confer major power status, they are an important ingredient of power for countries that conduct themselves in a responsible manner and are experiencing rapid growth in other dimensions of power.

For allied states, the extended deterrence protection provided by a nuclear weapon major power assuages security concerns, reduces or eliminates the incentive to develop their own nuclear weapon capability, influences their force mix and posture, and enables them to gradually develop bridging capabilities to assume greater security responsibilities including strengthening their own conventional deterrence. It also restricts their military options, induces caution in their behavior, and enables them to pursue other national priorities without intensifying existing security dilemmas. For states and regimes confronting existential threats, nuclear weapons (their own or those of an ally) are perceived as the ultimate security guarantee. Although they do not rely solely or even primarily on nuclear weapons, possession or availability of such capability is perceived as essential to deter much stronger adversaries. The risk of uncertainty and potential for escalation induces caution and limits the military options available to adversaries. Under certain conditions nuclear weapons may enhance the diplomatic leverage of nuclear weapon states. The long shadow cast by nuclear weapons is also evident in the widespread international concern over the spread of nuclear weapons to additional states and especially nonstate actors, the danger of nuclear theft, smuggling, formal and black market trade in dual use technology and material, and in the national and international safeguard measures instituted to prevent such occurrences and practices.

The influence of nuclear weapons is manifest in the national security policies of states, their nuclear doctrines, in the modernization and development of nuclear arsenals, and in the development of ballistic missile defense (BMD) and counterforce capabilities. It is also evident in changes in regional security dynamics (strengthening alliances, mitigating or intensifying security dilemmas, stimulating regional initiatives), and in the international measures instituted to address concerns relating to the spread of nuclear weapons, technology, and material to additional states and nonstate actors. The influence of nuclear weapons in the contemporary era, however, is more subtle and implied than the explicit threats and deployments that characterized the Cold War period.

The study advances four propositions on the role of nuclear weapons in national security in the twenty-first century strategic environment. First, the primary role of nuclear weapons now and in the foreseeable future is basic or central deterrence. Nuclear weapons also prevent blackmail, preserve strategic autonomy (freedom to act), and provide insurance to cope with unanticipated developments in a changing strategic environment. The offensive and defensive roles of nuclear weapons are relatively marginal in utility and appear unlikely to surpass the deterrence role or even increase much in importance in the foreseeable future. Only the United States is developing significant offensive and defensive capabilities. Technological limitations, funding constraints, the relatively low cost of maintaining a strike force that can penetrate ballistic missile defense systems, the preferences and capabilities (conventional and nuclear) of other states, and the generally stable political and strategic environment in the Asian security region are likely to limit the employment of nuclear weapons in these roles.

Second, although deterrence continues to be the dominant role and strategy for the employment of nuclear weapons, the conception and practice of deterrence is different from the mutual assured destruction condition that characterized the Soviet-American nuclear confrontation during the Cold War and varies across countries. Deterrence in the contemporary era is largely asymmetric in nature with weaker powers relying on nuclear weapons to deter stronger adversaries. Variations in goals and a broad range of capabilities have resulted in a spectrum of overlapping deterrence strategies ranging from existential deterrence through minimum deterrence to assured retaliation. At base all deterrence strategies rely on the threat of punishment. They differ in the force level required to deter, certainty of retaliation, and in the threats to be deterred. Existential and minimum deterrence rely more on uncertainty, the risks of escalation and early launch, and the absolute destruction that would result from a nuclear attack. As the name implies, there is a much higher degree of certainty in the capability to retaliate and inflict catastrophic damage in a strategy of assured retaliation. Existential deterrence is concerned primarily with state or regime survival; minimum deterrence is a default option for a state with a small nuclear arsenal concerned with deterring a stronger adversary. Assured retaliation seeks to deter a nuclear attack, including a first strike by a substantial nuclear weapon state. Both established and new nuclear powers are still defining and developing nuclear strategies to cope with a new strategic environment that is likely to further evolve. In addition, "new" nuclear weapon states often do not have the requisite capability to effectively implement their professed strategies. Consequently, there are inconsistencies between declaratory and operational doctrines, as well as behavior in a crisis situation.

Third, the absence of severe confrontations and the limited capabilities of the relatively small Asian nuclear arsenals have resulted in general deterrence postures. The United States seeks capabilities to deal with a wide array of threats, but it does not confront an immediate conflict or crisis situation that warrants actor-specific threats that could result in nuclear retaliation. Its threats to rogue states, for example, tend to be general; and those in relation to contingencies involving China are usually vague and implied. Other countries have chosen to focus on their principal concerns. With the exception of India and Pakistan, they too do not confront situations that warrant nuclear threats. There are very few instances in which intense and immediate hostilities have resulted in the issuance of specific nuclear threats or the development of capabilities to carry them out. In all other cases, nuclear deterrence in Asia is implied and indirect. States maintain a broad range of capabilities, including nuclear weapons, and issue general threats to dissuade other states from thinking seriously about aggression.

Finally, extended nuclear deterrence continues to be important to the national security of U.S. allied states in East Asia. China and certainly India and Pakistan do not have the capability or the strategic imperative to provide strategic protection to an ally against a threat from another nuclear power. Russia has the capability and plans to extend the deterrence function of its nuclear arsenal to protect Byelorussia and Armenia. The circumstances in which such strategic protection would become necessary, however, are fuzzy. Only the United States has the capability and strategic imperative to extend the deterrence function of its nuclear arsenal to Japan, South Korea, Australia, and implicitly Taiwan. All these countries desire the strategic protection of the United States. Japan does not confront an imminent nuclear or large-scale conventional threat, but it is concerned about a rising China that is modernizing its nuclear force and a nuclear-armed North Korea. Viewing the U.S. extended deterrence commitment as essential for Japan's security, Tokyo not only seeks reaffirmation of that commitment but also to increase its credibility in the eyes of potential adversaries and its domestic public. Since the early 1990s the salience of extended nuclear deterrence for South Korea's security has declined. Nevertheless, Seoul sees the U.S. commitment as critical to maintain its nonnuclear posture in the context of a nuclear-armed North Korea and as a fallback while building a "national self-reliant defense" capability. For Australia, the U.S. extended deterrence commitment serves a rather remote but crucial function: to deter a nuclear attack on that country. The probability of an attack that would warrant U.S. nuclear retaliation is very low. Nevertheless, Canberra values the U.S. commitment because it is believed to contribute to global and regional security order and to provide other benefits to Australia. The American security guarantee continues to be critical for Taiwan, but nuclear weapons feature only indirectly in that guarantee.

The above discussion highlights the importance of the U.S. extended deterrence commitment to the security of America's allies in East Asia, especially Japan and South Korea. The U.S. commitment serves crucial symbolic and psychological functions; it reassures allies against long-range threats and prevents them from pursuing independent nuclear options. At the same time, it is relevant only in a narrow set of rather unlikely circumstances. And the competing interests and demands of allies make it difficult for the United States to move beyond declaratory statements. The pressure from Japan to consult and operationalize the U.S. extended deterrence commitment could create complications for the United States and possibly intensify security dilemmas in Northeast Asia.

Indirect but Far-Reaching Influence

Evidence can be adduced to support two competing claims on the salience of nuclear weapons for national and international security in Asia. One reading is that nuclear weapons are only marginally relevant to the many security challenges confronting the United States, Russia, and the Asian nuclear weapon states. They are irrelevant in dealing with internal ethnic and religious conflicts, political legitimacy challenges, international terrorism, and most international territorial disputes. And they appear only indirectly relevant in the management of the conflicts across the Taiwan Strait and on the Korean peninsula. China has articulated force as a key element of its Taiwan policy but its emphasis has been on building short- and medium-range conventional warhead missiles and an amphibious capability. Nuclear threat and nuclear attack will work against its political goal of unifying Taiwan with the mainland. However, nuclear weapons may be implicitly relevant in deterring U.S. intervention in the event of cross-Strait hostilities. Conventional deterrence seems strong on the Korean peninsula. South Korea and the United States have sufficient conventional military capability to defeat North Korean aggression. Although North Korea has tested a nuclear device, it does not have an operational nuclear arsenal. Pyongyang's primary instrument for defense and deterrence is still its large and lethal conventional military capability. Conventional military capability is also the mainstay of the force postures of Israel and Iran, both of which perceive existential threats. Nuclear weapons are in the forefront only in the India-Pakistan dyad. Even here, the two countries rely on their substantial conventional military capabilities as the first line of defense and deterrence.

All countries in the Asian security region are modernizing and building up their conventional military capabilities. And, except for the United States and Russia, the nuclear arsenals of the Asian countries are rather small. Nuclear modernization and development of additional capabilities are under way, but the pace is relatively moderate. There is no rush to build large nuclear arsenals, and there is no nuclear arms race in the region. All these elements would suggest that states rely primarily on their conventional military capabilities and other policy instruments (political compromise, diplomatic negotiations, economic incentives, international law) to deal with most of the immediate security challenges. In this line of argument the overall salience of nuclear weapons is low.

The second reading would be that, from about the late 1990s, nuclear weapons have become more significant in the national security policies and strategies of states in the Asian security region. The 1998 nuclear tests by India and Pakistan, the ensuing crisis between those two countries, and their ongoing development of operational nuclear forces; the 2002 Nuclear Posture Review (NPR) of the

United States (U.S. Department of Defense 2002), which identified several nuclear contingencies in Asia, including China, North Korea, Iraq, and Iran; the ongoing U.S. effort to develop a multilayered missile defense system; Moscow's emphasis on nuclear weapons as the ultimate guarantee of Russia's sovereignty and its vocal opposition to the United States' missile defense plans; North Korea's nuclear test and Iran's quest for nuclear weapons; the demand by Japan and South Korea for explicit reaffirmation of the U.S. extended deterrence commitment; continued Chinese nuclear modernization; the U.S. concern that Chinese nuclear modernization has proceeded faster than anticipated and that China is developing antisatellite weapons (U.S. Department of Defense 2007); and the ratification of the Southeast Asian Nuclear Weapons Free Zone (SEANWFZ) Treaty in 1997: All these developments attest to the growing significance attached to nuclear weapons.

This study supports the second reading and argues that nuclear weapons are becoming a crucial component of national security policies and postures of states in the Asian security region. Though less visible, their influence is far reaching in the strategic interaction of major powers, in the management of critical conflicts, including limiting military options in crisis situations, in addressing the national security threats confronting weak and isolated states, and in the international concern and response to the possible spread of nuclear weapons to additional states and nonstate actors.

Bound Major Power Strategic Interaction

The fear of escalation to nuclear war conditions the role of force in major power relations and circumscribes strategic interaction among them. By restraining measures and actions that could lead to conflict escalation, nuclear weapons limit the competitive strategic interaction of major powers to internal and external balancing for deterrence purposes; constrain their resort to coercive diplomacy and compellence; and shift the burden of international competition and adjustment in status and influence to the economic, political, and diplomatic arenas. They also render remote the possibility of a hegemonic war should a power transition occur in the region. More immediately, nuclear weapons enable Russia and China to deter the much stronger United States and mitigate the negative consequences of the imbalance in conventional military capability. Nuclear weapons reinforce India's confidence in dealing with China. By reducing military vulnerabilities and providing insurance against unexpected contingencies, nuclear weapons enable major powers to take a long view and engage in competition as well as cooperation with potential adversaries. Differences and disputes among them are frozen or settled through negotiations. Though they are not the only or even primary factor driving strategic visions and policies, nuclear weapons are an important consideration, especially in the role of force in major power strategic interaction. They prevent the outbreak of large-scale war. Military clashes when they occur tend to be limited.

Condition Regional Conflict Management

Nuclear weapons have a low profile in the conflicts across the Taiwan Strait and on the Korean peninsula. Conventional military capability dominates deployment, perception of immediate threat, and response to them. However, the danger of escalation to nuclear war determines the role and deployment of conventional military force. That danger also shapes the range and choice of military options in a crisis and the risks that states are willing to take in pursuit of their objectives. The risk of nuclear war not only tempers the means but also influences short- and medium-range goals. Although the nuclear threat is implicit in the Taiwan conflict, the danger of nuclear escalation and retaliation induces caution, deters large-scale conventional attack by China, restrains American military intervention, and limits the military options available to both countries. The nuclear consideration, along with others, also tempers the urgency of Beijing's unification goal and induces Washington to restrain Taiwanese leaders advocating the independence option. Similarly on the Korean Peninsula, nuclear weapons provide an important backdrop. North Korea views nuclear weapons as the ultimate guarantee of its security; this in turn has increased the relevance of the American nuclear umbrella for South Korea. Nuclear weapons figure more prominently in the India-Pakistan conflict. Pakistan attempted to exploit the danger of escalation to nuclear war to alter the status quo. However, that risk also conditioned how it used force and the Indian response to the Pakistani military action. In all three conflicts, the shadow of nuclear escalation circumscribes military action. Though small in number and appearing relatively stable, these conflicts are the most likely sources of major war in the region. Nuclear weapons condition their management in significant ways and in essence take large-scale war off the table.

Ultimate Security Guarantee

Among the states that perceive existential threats, Pakistan relies more immediately and substantially on its nuclear weapon capability to mitigate the negative effects of the imbalance in conventional military capability and deter large-scale conventional and nuclear attack by India. It also seeks to exploit the danger of escalation to nuclear war to support its Kashmir policy. Israel relies primarily on its strong conventional forces to deter and defeat Arab aggression. Its substantial nuclear arsenal remains opaque, and Israel has avoided explicit nuclear threats or reference to nuclear weapons in its security strategy. Despite this, nuclear weapons are perceived as providing the ultimate security guarantee, and Israel has steadily built up its nuclear arsenal. For North Korea, although it still has a large and lethal conventional military capability, its advantage in the conventional military balance has steadily declined. Diplomatically isolated and economically weak, North Korea sees nuclear weapons as an essential reinforcement of its conventional military capability to deter American aggression. Likewise, Iran, witnessing the reluctance of the United States to attack a nuclear capable North Korea and the lack of regional support for such an attack, may perceive nuclear weapons as essential to deter a U.S. attack. Taiwan does not have nuclear weapons, but the implicit American security guarantee including its nuclear umbrella deters large-scale Chinese military attack.

Concern Over New Proliferation

The influence of nuclear weapons is also evident in the international concern over and response to the possible spread of nuclear weapons to additional states and nonstate actors. That the acquisition of a nuclear weapon capability by North Korea and Iran may undermine the nuclear nonproliferation regime, threaten neighboring states, and alter regional security dynamics in Northeast Asia and the Middle East underscores the international effort through the United Nations, the Six-Party Talks, and the European Union to address the nuclear challenges posed by these two countries. In addition to multilateral efforts, the United States initiated the Proliferation Security Initiative (PSI) to interdict transportation of nuclear material and technology from North Korea, retains the force option in dealing with the Iranian challenge, has reaffirmed its extended deterrence commitment to Japan and South Korea, and has taken measures to strengthen its security ties with allies and friends in the Middle East. The North Korean test has generated substantive discussion in Japan on its own nuclear option and on the effort to make the U.S. commitment more credible. At the regional level, Asian states have initiated the Asian Senior-Level Talks on Nonproliferation to discuss and evaluate regional commitments and efforts to prevent proliferation of weapons of mass destruction (WMD); some have joined the PSI; and the Southeast Asian countries have revived the idea of a nuclear weapon-free Southeast Asia to prevent spillover effects from the nuclearization of the Northeast and South Asian subregions (see Tan, Chapter 16 of this volume).

Also of grave concern is the challenge posed by the possible acquisition of nuclear and other WMD by nonstate extremist groups. Though the possibility of such groups acquiring nuclear weapons is low, even a small possibility is considered highly dangerous because of the enormous damage that can be inflicted by such weapons (see Kapur, Chapter 11 of this volume). "Rogue" states like North Korea and Iran may be difficult to deter, but it is believed that traditional deterrence cannot work against nonstate groups that have no return address. This fear and the associated concerns relating to theft and illegal trade in nuclear weapon-related material and technology have resulted in a wide range of countermeasures with consequences for security interaction at the global and regional levels. In sum, though less visible, nuclear weapons have far-reaching influence on national security strategies, on the strategic interaction of nuclear weapon states and their allies, and in the international response to the possible further spread of nuclear weapons. They have and could further alter security dynamics in Northeast Asia, South Asia, the Middle East, and the Asian security region as a whole. For nuclear weapon states and their allies, nuclear weapons serve important deterrence functions, help them cope with unexpected contingencies (insurance), and preserve their freedom to act (strategic autonomy). The nuclear arsenals of Asian states are likely to grow in quantity and quality, although such growth will be gradual. As capabilities increase, the salience of nuclear weapons in national security strategies would further increase. However, nuclear weapons appear unlikely to occupy center stage as they did during the Cold War. Barring unforeseen circumstances, the present development-focused national priorities and the generally stable Asian security environment are likely to prevent severe confrontations and intense strategic competition among major powers (see Alagappa, Chapter 1 of this volume).

The Primary Role of Basic Deterrence

The primary function of nuclear weapons in the Asian security region is basic deterrence—that is, preventing large-scale conventional attack and deterring any form of nuclear attack against the homeland of a nuclear weapon state. China, Russia, India, and Pakistan all see nuclear weapons as essential to balance and deter stronger powers that threaten or might threaten their interests and to preserve policy autonomy in a context of American dominance and a rising China and India. The United States views nuclear weapons as necessary for contingencies involving China and to deter Russia if relations with that country deteriorate. It is unclear if the U.S. nuclear arsenal has a counterforce role against Russia and China and if it is developing BMD against both these countries. Even if the United States were successful in developing these capabilities, the political purposes for which it would use them is unclear. Some states see a role for nuclear weapons to deter chemical and biological attacks on their homelands as well. And some countries have attempted to deploy nuclear weapons in coercive diplomacy, war fighting, and strategic defense roles. In 1999, Pakistan engaged in coercive diplomacy by exploiting the risk of escalation to nuclear war. In response, India too engaged in coercive diplomacy and explored limited war under nuclear conditions. In its 2002 NPR (U.S. Department of Defense 2002), the United States indicated a shift in emphasis from deterrence to offensive and defensive strategies. The ensuing discussion of nuclear policies and strategies of relevant states and their behavior in conflict situations reveals the limitations of the offensive and defensive roles of nuclear weapons and highlights basic deterrence as the most important role for nuclear weapons.

China-United States Dyad

The United States is the principal international security concern for China (see Chu and Rong, Chapter 5 of this volume). Although there are bilateral concerns and disputes, China views Russia as too weak and India as too distant to constitute significant security threats. Further, relations with Russia are good and those with India are on the mend. In China's view, after the United States, Japan is the country most likely to present a future security threat. However, Japan is not a nuclear weapon state, and China has deliberately deemphasized its nuclear forces in relation to that country for fear of provoking it into acquiring nuclear weapons. For the foreseeable future, the principal Chinese nuclear concern centers on the United States.

For the United States, China is the principal concern in Asia. The 2006 Quadrennial Defense Review Report states "of the major and emerging powers, China has the greatest potential to compete militarily with the United States" (U.S. Department of Defense 2006: 29). Earlier, the 2002 U.S. NPR (U.S. Department of Defense 2002) identified China as a potential nuclear contingency because of the uncertainty over that country's strategic objectives and because it is rapidly modernizing its nuclear forces. That NPR also identifies Taiwan as an immediate nuclear contingency, although the public version does not state why it is a nuclear contingency and how nuclear weapons may be relevant to that conflict. The U.S. Defense Department's 2007 report on China's military power asserts that China's expanding military capability is a major factor in changing the East Asian military balance, that improvement in Chinese strategic capabilities may provide that country with new options, and that China's antisatellite programs have significant implications for antiaccess/area denial in Taiwan Strait contingencies and beyond.

War or intense rivalry between the United States and China could arise from one or more of three developments: escalation of a military conflict across the Taiwan Strait, an explicit U.S. strategy to prevent or contain the rise of China, or a Chinese decision to challenge the primacy of the United States. As highlighted in Chapter 1 of this volume, although Beijing is increasing its international power and influence, it does not have the capability or the imperative to challenge American primacy in the foreseeable future. For its part, Washington seeks to engage and constrain China, not contain it. The U.S. purpose is to integrate China as a responsible power into an international system dominated by American values. Neither country views confrontation as inevitable or useful. Except possibly on the Taiwan issue, it is in China's interest to avoid confrontation with the United States.

In regard to the Taiwan conflict, the primary function of nuclear weapons is to deter intervention and aggression. China does not threaten nuclear attack to prevent Taiwan's independence or to forcefully unify that island state with the People's Republic of China (PRC). It would be self-defeating for the PRC to threaten use of nuclear weapons against a territory and people it claims as its own. Further, because Taiwan is geographically close to China, the fallout from a nuclear attack on Taiwan would affect parts of China as well. Threatening to use nuclear weapons against Taiwan would also tarnish Beijing's international image. For all these reasons, any use of force by China against Taiwan is highly likely to be conventional. For its part, Taiwan seeks to deter the PRC through its own conventional military capability and the American security commitment.

For the present, nuclear weapons are relevant only in the U.S.-PRC dimension of the Taiwan conflict. Beijing hopes that the implicit risk of escalation to nuclear war and the prospect of a nuclear retaliatory strike on the United States will induce caution in Washington, deter American military intervention, and compel Washington to rein in Taiwanese leaders who espouse independence. In some ways, the Chinese approach is akin to Thomas Schelling's "threats that leave something to chance," in which deterrence flows from a situation rather than from an explicit threat to escalate or retaliate (Schelling 1966: 121n). The American military objective is to deter Chinese military action against Taiwan and prevent unification by force. American deterrence is primarily conventional. However, by virtue of its nuclear arsenal, American deterrence of China inevitably includes a nuclear dimension. The 2002 NPR identifies Taiwan as a nuclear contingency. Although neither the United States nor China has articulated a policy or a strategy that would involve the use of nuclear weapons, this does not imply that nuclear weapons are irrelevant. The risk of conflict escalation is an ever-present possibility. That risk, however, helps deter the outbreak of hostilities and makes large-scale conventional war unlikely.

A few analysts in both countries have suggested that nuclear weapons could have an intrawar role in the conflict. Keir Lieber and Daryl Press (2006, 2007), for example, suggest that, in the event of military conflict across the Taiwan Strait, the United States might deploy its nuclear primacy to threaten China with a disarming first strike to prevent China from alerting its strategic forces and to keep nuclear weapons out of the conflict. This presumes China would introduce nuclear weapons in the event of overt hostilities. Despite remarks by some Chinese analysts that China should reconsider its no-first-use (NFU) policy and that the United States should expect nuclear retaliation if it intervenes in the Taiwan conflict, it is not in China's interest or its policy to pursue such a course of action (see Chu and Rong, Chapter 5 of this volume). And the United States would likely respond to Chinese military action in the Taiwan Strait with conventional military force unless Beijing attacks U.S. territory.

Beijing's objective in the nuclear arena is to build a robust strategic force to deter an American attack (conventional and nuclear) on its homeland. If deterrence fails, it wants to have a survivable and capable force to retaliate and inflict catastrophic damage on the U.S. mainland. As observed earlier, in the case of the Taiwan conflict, Chinese nuclear weapons have an implicit deterrence role. It is not in China's interest to introduce nuclear weapons into that conflict in support of coercive diplomacy or for war-fighting purposes.

Though not publicly articulated, it seems reasonable to assume that a primary function of the U.S. nuclear arsenal is to deter large-scale Chinese conventional and nuclear attack on American territory. Implicitly, the U.S. nuclear capability also deters a Chinese attack to alter the status quo across the Taiwan Strait. It is unclear how and when the United States will respond to a Chinese attack on Taiwan and whether nuclear retaliation will be contemplated. Much will depend on the situation and whether China introduces nuclear weapons. The United States appears increasingly concerned that Chinese space programs may undermine traditional American military advantages in relation to the Taiwan conflict. The deterrence function of the U.S. nuclear arsenal is not controversial, but some have argued that the United States is intentionally building nuclear primacy and that it is on the cusp of achieving the capability to disarm the long-range nuclear arsenals of Russia and China (Lieber and Press 2007).

Whether the U.S. has a disarming capability against Russia is open to debate. Against China, which has a much smaller nuclear force, it is likely that the United States has substantial counterforce capability. Nevertheless, from an operational perspective, unless the United States can be absolutely certain it can destroy all Chinese strategic assets, having a substantial capability may not provide a military advantage. Even if the United States has a disarming capability against China, the key question is what political purpose would it serve. As noted earlier, an intense confrontation with the United States is not in China's interest, and Beijing has deliberately avoided such confrontation. In the absence of serious provocation, a disarming U.S. strike against China seems hardly credible. If the rise of China is posited as a credible reason, why has the United States refrained from striking China while its nuclear capability is still relatively weak? That Washington contemplated such a strike in 1964 is irrelevant. China was not a rising power then, and it was also not a nuclear power. Even under those conditions the United States chose not to carry out a preventive strike. It seems incredible that Washington might now or in the future carry out a disarming strike against a powerful and nuclear-armed China. The uncertainty of success and the catastrophic cost to both countries would outweigh any rational gain.

Lieber and Press posit that the United States may gain coercive leverage from its nuclear primacy in a future crisis over Taiwan. Washington could warn Beijing that China would face a disarming first strike if it alerted its strategic forces. As noted earlier, it is in China's interest to keep nuclear weapons out of the conflict. It does not have to be threatened with a disarming first strike to do so. The same coercive leverage can be had from a secure second-strike capability that can inflict unacceptable damage. The Lieber and Press argument is similar to the second-wave theorizing of deterrence that accorded priority to technology, military capability, and the logic of the destructive power of nuclear weapons rather than to politics and policy. Although scenarios for the offensive use of nuclear weapons could be imagined, the indisputable primary role of U.S. nuclear weapons in relation to China is deterrence.

China relates its strategic deterrent force to American capability. If the United States develops effective counterforce and BMD capabilities that can threaten the credibility of its strategic deterrent, China will likely respond by increasing the number and effectiveness of its long-range missiles, MIRVing them, and developing counter-BMD capability, including antisatellite weapons. The purpose would be to sustain a strong deterrent force that can survive a first strike and retaliate. Such a nuclear force would also be able to deal with threats from other nuclear weapon states in its neighborhood. China may develop additional capabilities to further strengthen its deterrent posture, which appears to be transitioning from minimum deterrence to assured retaliation, and to increase its policy options.

Russia-United States-China

Russia's international security concerns derive not from any specific threat but from the perceived negative consequences of developments that have weakened its position and influence in the post-Cold War world (see Fedorov, Chapter 4 of this volume). The Russian elite has come to view the United States and its unilateral approach to international governance as marginalizing Russia and threatening its interests in Europe, the Middle East, Transcaucasia, Central Asia, and the Pacific region. Although Russia cooperates with China on several international issues and supplies advanced weapons and military technology to that country, the rapid rise of China is a source of apprehension in some Russian quarters.

Seen as compensating for its weakness in conventional military capability, nuclear weapons are depicted as the ultimate guarantee of Russia's "real sovereignty." Their principal function is deterrence of the United States and China, but it is unclear what specific threats that nuclear weapons are supposed to deter. America's development of BMD and its counterforce capability are perceived to weaken Russia's strategic deterrent. In response, Russia appears to be accelerating the production of a new missile system and has called for new arms control measures. Moscow has renounced its NFU policy and now appears to be considering demonstration (conflict deescalation) and war-fighting roles for its nuclear weapons. As with deterrence, the circumstances in which Russia's nuclear weapons might be used in war fighting and their specific intrawar roles remain unclear.

Although Russia-United States relations have soured during the last several years over the eastward expansion of the North Atlantic Treaty Organization, the planned U.S. deployment of missile defense in Eastern European countries, and over other issues, the United States does not view Russia as an adversary. Nevertheless, as indicated in the 2002 NPR, Russia still has a large nuclear arsenal, and deterrence of that country continues to be a function of the U.S. nuclear arsenal. China too does not view Russia as an adversary. Its primary focus is the United

States. Nevertheless, there is a latent apprehension in China of a resurgent Russia, as there is of a fast-rising China in Russia. If necessary, China's strategic deterrent against the United States can also deter Russia.

The Russian emphasis on nuclear deterrence appears to be grounded in symbolic and psychological considerations. Beginning in Vladimir Putin's second term, nuclear weapons, along with the command of vast energy resources in an energy-hungry world, are viewed as key ingredients of national power and proof of Russia's reemergence as a great power.

Pakistan-India-China

In the Pakistan-India dyad the primary role of nuclear weapons is deterrence. Islamabad views nuclear weapons as essential to offset Indian superiority in conventional arms and deter a large-scale conventional military attack on its homeland (see Khan and Lavoy, Chapter 7 of this volume). New Delhi too sees nuclear weapons primarily in a deterrent role, not only against Pakistan but also against China (see Rajagopalan, Chapter 6 of this volume). Despite scholarly and international predictions to the contrary, nuclear deterrence has worked in the Pakistan-India dyad during both the covert and the overt periods (Hagerty 1998). There has not been a large-scale war between the two countries since they acquired nuclear weapon capability. The nuclear shadow limited the objectives, means, and geography of the 1999 Kargil conflict.

In the early years of the overt nuclear period, Pakistan, and in response India, attempted coercive diplomacy and explored limited war under nuclear conditions. Deploying the risk of escalation to nuclear war as a shield, Pakistan sought to alter the actual Line of Control (LoC) and to force India to the negotiating table to discuss the Kashmir issue. Islamabad was partially successful in its effort. However, the defeat of Pakistani forces, their withdrawal from Kargil, and India's insistence that the LoC could not be altered demonstrate the limitation of nuclear weapons in a coercive diplomacy role. International support for India's position and the perception of Pakistan as a dangerous and irresponsible nuclear weapon state also highlight the political liability of using nuclear weapons in a revisionist role. In the wake of the 2001 terrorist attack on the Indian parliament, New Delhi seriously explored ambitious notions of limited war, including strikes on insurgent groups based in Pakistan; but these were considered too dangerous and dropped. India's attempt at coercive diplomacy and limited war failed (Basrur 2005). New Delhi recognized that nuclear deterrence is effective only against a narrow range of threats—essentially against large-scale conventional attack and nuclear attack. Nuclear weapons cannot deter lower-level conventional military incursions, militant insurgencies, or crossborder terrorism. Pakistan's and India's failed attempts revealed the limitations of nuclear weapons in the coercive diplomacy and limited war roles in this dyad. A long view of the recent history suggests that basic deterrence is the primary function of nuclear weapons. Although India has expressed interest in missile defense and supports the American effort in this area, it is unlikely to develop substantial strategic defense capability in the near future. Any Indian advance in strategic defense would likely be neutralized by Pakistan.

Among the major powers, China is the primary concern for India. However, India does not fear an existential threat or a large-scale conventional or nuclear attack from that country. Unlike Pakistan, China is viewed as a responsible nuclear weapon state that is unlikely to engage in adventurism. Further, India is confident that it has sufficient conventional military capability to deal with limited and large-scale conventional attacks by China. India's strategic concern with China is twofold: one is Chinese strategic support for Pakistan; the second is the strategic (nuclear) imbalance with China, which it is believed could compromise India's strategic autonomy and disadvantage its quest for power and influence in the region (see Rajagopalan, Chapter 6 of this volume). Although India is not worried about a Chinese nuclear attack, New Delhi is vigilant and is developing long-range missiles that can reach most major Chinese cities. It aims over time to develop a robust nuclear deterrent against China to add to its already strong conventional deterrence.

North Korea-United States-South Korea

On the Korean peninsula, nuclear weapons are relevant primarily in basic and extended deterrence functions. As indicated earlier, nuclear deterrence has assumed greater salience for Pyongyang (see Park and Lee, Chapter 9 of this volume). In contrast, the salience of nuclear weapons in the security strategies of the United States and South Korea declined in the 1990s (see Choi and Park, Chapter 13 of this volume). The North Korean nuclear test, however, has resurrected South Korea's interest in extended nuclear deterrence.

The primary function of North Korea's small and unproven nuclear weapon capability is basic deterrence: to neutralize the U.S. and South Korean balance of power advantage and deter a preventive attack by the United States (see Park and Lee, Chapter 9 of this volume). North Korea can threaten U.S. forces and allies in East Asia, but it does not have missiles that can reach the United States. Its present very limited capability cannot support offensive strategies. Any attack on U.S. forces deployed in East Asia or on American allies would be suicidal. North Korea's nuclear weapon program provides bargaining leverage in its negotiations with the other five countries in the Six-Party Talks. Pyongyang has skillfully used that leverage to secure economic benefits, political and diplomatic recognition, and security assurances that would help prolong the Kim Jong Il regime. Like Pakistan, North Korea may in due course seek to deploy the risk of escalation to nuclear war by engaging in lower-level violence to extract concessions from its neighbors.

But such action would be risky. Basic deterrence will remain the primary security value of nuclear weapons for North Korea in the next decade or two.

North Korea's nuclear test has resurrected interest in South Korea to reaffirm the U.S. extended deterrence commitment. Seoul views that commitment as crucial to maintaining its nonnuclear posture and as a fallback while building its own "national self-reliant defense" capability and resolving the conflict with North Korea through bilateral and multilateral negotiations. In the highly unlikely event that North Korea uses nuclear weapons against South Korea, other U.S. allies, or American forces in the region, the United States would certainly retaliate, although whether it would use nuclear weapons remains uncertain. In addition to deterring a North Korean attack, the United States may be developing the capability for offensive and defensive counterforce roles to destroy the limited strategic assets of North Korea. Whether the United States has the confidence to embark on an offensive course of action and whether any political and military purpose will be served by it remain unclear.

Israel and Iran

Dissuading preemptive or preventive military attack and deterring large-scale conventional aggression are the primary roles of nuclear weapons for countries that face existential threats. For Israel, nuclear weapons are an insurance against large-scale conventional attack by a coalition of Arab states that could threaten its viability as a sovereign state (see Cohen, Chapter 8 of this volume). Although what constitutes an existential threat has been debated, it appears that the crossing of certain red lines could trigger the retaliatory use of nuclear weapons. Possible scenarios include Arab penetration of Israel's post-1949 borders, destruction of Israel's air force, massive attacks on Israeli cities, and the use of nuclear weapons on Israeli territory. If Israel has developed the technology to produce battlefield tactical nuclear weapons (this is not certain), it would signal a shift in policy to include a war-fighting role for nuclear weapons. Israel's existential deterrence nuclear policy is linked to maintaining nuclear monopoly in the Middle East. To preserve that monopoly, Israel undertook a preventive military attack on the Iraqi Osirak reactor in 1981. In 2007, Israel undertook preventive military action against an alleged nuclear facility in Syria. Some observers believe that it might take similar action against Iranian nuclear facilities (Raas and Long 2007).

Deterrence of a U.S. attack is the primary driving force behind Iran's quest for nuclear weapons. Enhancing the theocratic regime's legitimacy at home and supporting its great power ambitions in the region are important considerations as well (see Hagerty, Chapter 10 of this volume). Should Iran acquire nuclear weapons, like Pakistan it may venture to use them in a coercive diplomacy role, but this is not a near-term prospect. Deterrence will be the key function. A nuclear Iran is likely to make the deterrence function of Israel's nuclear arsenal more explicit and Iran focused. It may also further strengthen the Arab states' security ties with the United States. The U.S. commitment to them may include an implicit extended nuclear deterrence dimension as in the case of the U.S. commitment to Taiwan, although the security commitment itself would be explicit.

From the foregoing discussion, it is evident that basic deterrence is the primary function of the nuclear arsenals of the major powers in the Asian security region. China, Russia, and India all seek to balance and deter a stronger power that is or could become an adversary. The United States seeks to deter a rising China and a Russia that still has a large nuclear arsenal.[1] Deterrence is also the key role for the nuclear arsenals (or nuclear quests) of states with acute or existential security concerns like Pakistan, Israel, North Korea, and Iran. Some states may seek to exploit the coercive potential of nuclear weapons to alter the status quo or blackmail non-nuclear neighbors. Such roles carry a high-risk premium and heavy political and economic costs with a low probability of success. Consequently these will not be central functions of nuclear weapons in the foreseeable future. The United States is developing offensive and defensive capabilities, but it appears unlikely that these will be sufficiently effective to blunt with confidence the strategic deterrent forces of China or Russia. They may be more potent against lesser nuclear powers but residual doubt would still induce caution in employing nuclear weapons against them in these roles.

Asymmetric, Diverse, and Dynamic Deterrence Strategies

The dominant conception of deterrence during the Cold War was grounded in the strategic interaction between the United States and the Soviet Union, two superpowers with vast nuclear and conventional arsenals who were locked in an intense ideological and strategic struggle. Deterrence between them that was focused on the Central European front was specific, immediate, and rested on mutual vulnerability to each other's secure second-strike capability. As elaborated in Chapter 2, other forms of deterrence, including existential, minimum, opaque, and recessed deterrence, also existed during the Cold War. These, however, remained on the periphery because the Soviet-American confrontation dominated international security.

There is no comparable overarching global security dynamic in the present period, and national power including nuclear capabilities span a wide spectrum. Except possibly between the United States and Russia, nuclear deterrence today operates largely in a condition of asymmetric power relationships. Using its still relatively large nuclear arsenal, Russia too seeks to deter a far more powerful United States from a position of weakness. China seeks to deter the dominant United States. India seeks to deter a fast-growing China that has a more advanced nuclear arsenal, as well as a weaker Pakistan, which has comparable nuclear capabilities.

Pakistan seeks to deter a far larger and conventionally stronger India. From its position of undeclared nuclear monopoly in the Middle East, Israel seeks to deter conventional military attack by a coalition of Arab states. And isolated North Korea and Iran seek to deter the world's only superpower, the United States. In all the above cases, weaker powers view nuclear weapons as an important means to deter states with greater nuclear and conventional military capabilities. The United States, on the other hand, seeks to deter multiple threats or contingencies from a position of unmatched military capability. In nearly every case, deterrence is a strategy between unequal powers. Asymmetry is now the dominant condition for deterrence. Combined with the small size of Asian nuclear forces and their limited capabilities, asymmetry has resulted in three basic types of deterrence strategies—existential deterrence, minimum deterrence, and assured retaliation.

No one conception of deterrence dominates thinking about nuclear strategy in the Asian security region. Each state's choice of strategy hinges on its strategic purpose, capabilities, and circumstances. Existential deterrence captures the nuclear postures of Israel and North Korea; it is also likely to be the posture of a nuclear Iran; minimum deterrence is the formal label attached to the nuclear strategies of Pakistan, India, and China; and the United States and Russia retain the capability for assured retaliation. Existential deterrence, minimum deterrence, and assured retaliation strategies are conceptually interconnected and overlapping. All three strategies rely on the threat of punishment but differ in the degree of certainty of retaliation and the force level required to deter. They can be viewed as part of a continuum. Existential and minimum deterrence are not necessarily preferred endpoints but convenient or necessary way stations on the path to assured retaliation.

Existential Deterrence

Existential deterrence is rooted in the belief that the very existence of a stockpile of nuclear weapons would induce caution if the political goal and military engagement were clear. It was advocated during the Cold War (as an alternative to the assured retaliation strategy) to argue against relative destruction capabilities and competitive armaments, and for the credibility of the American extended deterrence commitment in Europe. The idea of existential deterrence has been adapted in the contemporary period as a strategy for states that have only nascent or undeclared nuclear forces and whose primary security concern is survival. In this adaptation, as the stake and resolve are clear, a simple capability to carry out an undifferentiated countervalue strike is adequate to deter the adversary. Such a strategy was deemed to characterize Indian and Pakistani nuclear behavior in the 1980s and 1990s before they became overt nuclear weapon states (Hagerty 1998).

The Cold War-type existential deterrence is discernible now in the nuclear policy of Israel and the adapted version in that of North Korea. For Israel, a strong conventional military capability remains the bedrock of defense. At the same time, it has developed a substantial nuclear arsenal, which is viewed as insurance of last resort. The sole purpose of Israel's undeclared but substantial nuclear arsenal is to deter existential threats and, if absolutely necessary, to retaliate against that adversary. However, it has not issued any explicit nuclear threat. The Israeli political leadership believes that mere knowledge by friend and foe that Israel possesses a substantial and operational nuclear arsenal is sufficient to deter adversaries (see Cohen, Chapter 8 of this volume). Should Israel's nuclear monopoly in the Middle East be threatened, say by a nuclear Iran, its deterrence strategy would become more explicit and possibly move in the direction of assured retaliation or even war fighting.

The adapted version of existential deterrence characterizes the strategy of North Korea. The purpose of its nascent nuclear weapon capability is to offset the growing imbalance in conventional military capability and deter the United States. Although estimates vary, Pyongyang is believed to have enough weapon-grade plutonium for about six to ten bombs (Cirincione, Wolfsthal, and Rajkumar 2005). It has also developed short- and medium-range missiles that can potentially carry warheads to regional targets. North Korea does not have missiles that can reach the United States. A long-range missile was tested in 1998 with mixed success. North Korea still has several problems to overcome before it can be deemed to possess an operational nuclear arsenal. Nevertheless, Pyongyang believes that the possession of even a fledgling ability provides North Korea with a deterrence capability that can augment its conventional deterrence against the United States (see Park and Lee, Chapter 9 of this volume). The potential to inflict quick and substantial damage on targets in South Korea and Japan would deter the United States from undertaking preventive military action against North Korea like the action it took against Saddam Hussein's Iraq.

Existential deterrence of the second kind is also likely to be Iran's strategy if it succeeds in its quest for nuclear weapons (Hagerty, Chapter 10 of this volume). As in North Korea, the foremost concern of Iran's political elite is the survival of the revolutionary Iranian state and the incumbent leadership. Nuclear weapon capability is believed to be essential to regime security. It would offset Iran's weakness in conventional military capability, substantially increase the cost of confrontation with Iran, and deter the United States from invading Iran to topple the theocratic regime and reverse the revolution. Nuclear-capable North Korea has been relatively successful in fending off U.S. aggression, and gaining acceptance of the Kim Jong Il regime that was previously condemned as morally despicable. The other nonnuclear member of the axis (Saddam Hussein's Iraq), however, was invaded twice by the United States, and ultimately the regime in that country was toppled. The lessons from North Korea and Iraq may drive Iran to continue its covert quest for nuclear weapon capability. The danger for Iran, however, is that it is still several years away from acquiring even a fledgling capability. Meanwhile it is subject to preventive attack by the United States or Israel.

Minimum Deterrence

The strategy of minimum deterrence is rooted in the premise that a small, easily concealable nuclear force has an inherent retaliation capability and that the level of damage caused by a small number of nuclear weapons in a countervalue strike is sufficient to deter countries with much stronger nuclear arsenals. Minimum deterrence is the formal label used by governments in Pakistan, India, and China to describe their national nuclear postures. All three countries have made only a few brief official statements on their nuclear strategies. These have at times been contradictory, reflecting the secrecy and ambiguity that surround their nuclear weapon capabilities but also suggesting that their nuclear strategies are still evolving. Official statements and interpretations by analysts suggest that Pakistan, India, and China seek to deter large-scale conventional and any form of nuclear attack on their homeland by threatening nuclear retaliation.

The minimum deterrence strategy of Pakistan appears to place a higher premium on risk and uncertainty than that of India, which emphasizes certainty of retaliation and massive damage, and of China, which appears to have characteristics of an assured retaliation strategy. Pakistan has rejected India's proposal that the two countries adopt an NFU policy. It sees the possibility of first use as strengthening its deterrence strategy. Making public its nuclear threshold would provide space for India to use its huge conventional military capability and reduce the deterrent value of Pakistan's nuclear force (see Khan and Lavoy, Chapter 7 of this volume). Islamabad seeks to constrain and deter India by exploiting the risk of escalation to nuclear war as well as by threat of nuclear retaliation.

India and China have committed themselves to an NFU policy because it serves their strategic interests, but also in the belief that the value of nuclear weapons is primarily political and that they are weapons of last resort. Both countries have since qualified their commitments, and the security value of the NFU policy is now being debated in China. In the wake of the 1998 tests, India quickly committed itself not to use nuclear weapons first and to use such weapons only in retaliation against a nuclear attack. However, subsequent statements that India might retaliate with nuclear weapons against chemical and biological attacks, and against attacks on Indian forces anywhere, have loosened its earlier commitment to limit retaliation to nuclear attack on its territory, opening up the possibility that India might use nuclear weapons first in other situations (see Rajagopalan, Chapter 6 of this volume). China has qualified its earlier absolute commitment that it would "never at anytime or under any circumstances be the first to use nuclear weapons." The emphasis in its NFU commitment has shifted to nonnuclear weapon states. Although NFU is still the official policy, some Chinese analysts believe it should be reconsidered in relation to the Taiwan conflict. They have argued that a first-use policy would strengthen deterrence against American intervention. Others argue that, given the American threat of prevention, a first-use policy would create uncertainty and invite a preemptive strike. In Chapter 5 of this volume, Chu and Rong argue that the NFU policy safeguards China's interests by contributing to greater certainty and preventing escalation to nuclear war. From an operational perspective, the NFU pledge may not be meaningful, as states cannot be certain that the pledge will hold in crisis situations.

The minimum deterrence strategies of India and China have also been trending in the direction of assured retaliation. In India, this shift is more evident as an idea than in terms of capability (see Rajagopalan, Chapter 6 of this volume). Emphasizing credibility, the Indian strategy of minimum deterrence seeks to move beyond the risk and uncertainty that are characteristic of the minimum deterrence strategy. By stressing certainty of retaliation, it opens up the possibility of moving to a full assured retaliation strategy in due course. For now, however, the emphasis remains on a small nuclear force that can survive a first strike and inflict a high level of retaliatory damage on the adversary. The interpretation of minimum deterrence in China has shifted from existential deterrence in the early years to minimum deterrence as understood in the literature; it is now trending toward assured retaliation. Iain Johnston (1995–96) labels China's present strategy as "limited deterrence" while Chu and Rong (Chapter 5 of this volume) call it "large-scale minimum deterrence." Although the labels may be different, there is agreement that the Chinese understanding and practice of minimum deterrence is dynamic. The contemporary Chinese understanding of minimum deterrence reduces the emphasis on risk and places much greater emphasis on survival and certainty of retaliation. Unlike in India, this shift is reflected in the development of capabilities as well. The Chinese conception of minimum deterrence has also become more relational; that is, it has become more sensitive to change in adversaries' force structure. Over the longer term, the minimum deterrence strategies of China, and possibly India and Pakistan, will likely acquire assured retaliation characteristics.

Assured Retaliation

The United States and Russia still have large nuclear arsenals and secure second-strike capabilities that can inflict unacceptable damage on each other and on China. China and Russia believe that the strategic defense capabilities under development by the United States would erode the effectiveness of their strategic deterrent forces. If the United States is successful in building effective strategic defenses against Russia and China, and these two countries are unable to neutralize them, one key basis (lack of defense against nuclear weapons) for deterrence dominance would be undermined. The development of effective defense capabilities by China and Russia would also have a similar effect. However, even if deterrence is no longer technologically dominant, this does not automatically imply that the strategy of deterrence would cease to be the preferred strategy for employment of nuclear weapons. The choice of strategy is a function of both political objectives and capabilities.

In addition to diversity, deterrence strategies in the Asian security region are in the midst of change and likely to evolve further. The late entrants are still coming to terms with their status as nuclear weapon states and are developing strategies appropriate to their security situations and capabilities. The older nuclear weapon states are adapting to new strategic circumstances, threats, and capabilities. The United States made a bold attempt in the 2002 NPR to map its nuclear strategies and capabilities for a new era. Though it is still official policy, the NPR has failed to crystallize support, and with the termination of the Bush administration in January 2009, its future remains uncertain. Although Russia has expressed its view that nuclear weapons remain important, it also has not developed a coherent strategy for the new era. Chinese nuclear strategy has evolved and will likely continue to do so with a focus on the United States.

General Deterrence Postures

Contemporary deterrence postures are more in line with the idea of general deterrence than immediate deterrence; the latter applies in very few cases with limited systemic consequence.[2] The dominance of general deterrence postures is due to the absence of severe confrontations. Although the United States, Russia, China, and India all face several threats, immediate situations that may involve nuclear weapons are small; most other threats are long range and still hypothetical. Of the immediate situations, only in the India-Pakistan conflict are the two protagonists locked in a military confrontation. The Taiwan conflict has witnessed periodic tensions and relatively minor military clashes, but the United States and China are not locked in a military confrontation. A military standoff persists on the Korean peninsula, but the intensity of conflict has declined over time. Although general deterrence postures also existed during the Cold War, in large measure they were extensions of the severe confrontation and the immediate deterrence situation between the United States and the Soviet Union in Europe.

Reflecting the multiple threats confronting the United States, the 2002 NPR categorizes contingencies as immediate (well-recognized current dangers), potential (plausible, but not immediate), and unexpected (sudden and unpredicted). North Korea, Iraq, Iran, Syria, and Libya are identified as countries that could be involved in immediate, potential, and unexpected contingencies. China is an immediate contingency (Taiwan) and a potential contingency (modernization of its military capability combined with conflicting strategic objectives could result in a hostile situation). Russia is identified as a possible concern in the event that Russo-American relations deteriorate. Moscow is dissatisfied with American dominance, and some Russian quarters worry about a rising China; but neither country poses an immediate threat to Russia. For China, the most urgent concern is American military intervention in the event of a conflict across the Taiwan Strait, and a medium-term worry is American containment of China; the formidable nuclear arsenal of Russia and a nuclear India are also of concern. For India, Pakistan is the more immediate challenge; the threat from China is long term but considered more important. For Pakistan, India is an immediate threat; for North Korea the United States poses an immediate threat. The existential threat posed by Arab states is the primary challenge for Israel, but the immediacy of this threat has declined. Iran's nuclear quest is emerging as a key security concern in Israel (see Cohen, Chapter 8 of this volume; Inbar 2008).

Except possibly in the India-Pakistan dyad, the states concerned have attempted to deal with their security concerns by adopting general deterrence postures. The United States, for example, has opted for a nuclear doctrine that Wirtz (Chapter 3 of this volume) terms a "strange mix of deterrent, war-in-sight, and disarmament policies." Although the 2002 NPR (U.S. Department of Defense 2002) identifies several contingencies and seeks to develop an array of capabilities, it does not specify precise actions that would result in nuclear retaliation. Even in relation to North Korea and Iran, despite the rhetoric, Washington has not specified red lines that, if crossed, would cause it to retaliate. In the case of Taiwan too, the American deterrence posture is general. Washington has stated its general goal (no unification by force) and responded to crisis situations like that in 1995–96. It has not specified particular developments that could result in nuclear retaliation. It hopes that U.S. military might, combined with Washington's response to earlier crisis situations, will be sufficient to deter China from taking military action and that uncertainty about the U.S. response would dissuade Taiwan from seeking to alter the status quo.

Likewise, China has opted for a general deterrence posture, toward both the United States and other nuclear weapon states. In the case of Taiwan, the Chinese military buildup emphasizes missile and conventional military capabilities. The deterrent role of nuclear weapons is implied in the situation; there have been no explicit Chinese threats to use nuclear weapons in a war-fighting or deterrent role. Beijing also hopes that its military modernization, its growing power and influence, and political and economic interaction and cooperation will dissuade other nuclear weapon states from contemplating the use of force to resolve disputes with China.

Similarly, India seems to be opting for a general deterrence posture toward China. India's lack of urgency in developing a deterrent force against China should be seen in this light. Despite its bluster, Russia has not identified specific developments that would require nuclear retaliation. Moscow hopes that its formidable nuclear arsenal will induce respect and caution in other states. Finally, although Israel's nuclear force has a very specific mission (the survival of Israel), Tel Aviv has not publicly specified acts that would prompt its nuclear retaliation. Shimon Peres has indicated that it is sufficient for Israel's friends and foes to know that it has this capability (Hoffman 2006).

The effectiveness and shortcomings of general deterrence are discussed in Chapter 18. For now I want to emphasize that an immediate deterrence-like situation exists only in the India-Pakistan dyad and that the consequences of this situation are geographically and strategically limited. In all other instances, general deterrence dominates thinking about nuclear deterrence, including extended nuclear deterrence.

The Continuing Relevance of Extended Deterrence

Among the nuclear weapon states, only the United States possesses the motive and means to extend the deterrence function of its nuclear arsenal. Japan, South Korea, Taiwan, and Australia view the American extended nuclear deterrence commitment as contributing to their national security. Russia has the capability to provide extended deterrence commitment and plans on it for Byelorussia and Armenia, although the threats against which these two countries would require such strategic protection remain unclear. China, India, and Pakistan do not have the strategic imperative or the capability to provide strategic protection to an allied country against a threat from another nuclear power.

U.S. extended deterrence commitments help deter possible attacks against allies. Such attacks, however, are not imminent. Most threats are long range and hypothetical. Thus, for the most part, extended deterrence is general and psychological, designed to reassure allies against long-range threats and to prevent them from pursuing independent nuclear options. Extended deterrence also helps allies preserve their strategic autonomy. However, it also constrains their strategic choices, limits the flexibility in employment of their conventional military force, and creates fears of abandonment and entrapment. Maintaining a fine balance between relying on the U.S. commitment and developing their own defense and deterrence capability is a key challenge for South Korea and in some ways for Taiwan, which has only an implicit U.S. commitment. It is less of a challenge for Japan and Australia. Both these countries seek strong alliance relationships with the United States.

The formidable U.S. nuclear arsenal makes its extended deterrence commitment effective and credible; at the same time national sensitivities, differing threat perceptions, competing demands among its allies, the lack of an integrated command structure, and U.S. worry about entrapment make crafting and implementing a viable strategy of extended deterrence more difficult.

Among America's allies in Asia, nuclear weapons have become a key concern primarily in Japan. It does not face an existential threat and does not have serious international disputes that could involve the use of nuclear weapons. Tokyo's concerns center on the strategic vulnerability of a Japan surrounded by nuclear weapon states, the negative strategic consequences of nuclear weapons in the hands of competitors for the nature and content of order in East Asia, and the constraints they may impose on Japan's policy options (see Green and Furukawa, Chapter 12 of this volume). Although Japan has periodically explored the nuclear option since the Chinese nuclear test in 1964, for a number of reasons (strategic considerations, domestic politics, financial cost, and international repercussions), reliance on the American nuclear umbrella was seen as a better alternative. North Korea's nuclear test in October 2006 stimulated such an exploration, and the conclusion again was to seek reaffirmation of the U.S. extended deterrence commitment.

Tokyo sees the U.S. extended deterrence commitment as the central pillar of its nuclear policy. The other pillars are nuclear disarmament of North Korea, development of BMD, maintenance of a latent nuclear weapon capability, and strong support for the international nonproliferation regime. The key question for Japan is how to ensure the effectiveness and credibility of the U.S. extended nuclear deterrence commitment in a new security environment. Although declaratory statements by high-ranking U.S. leaders were deemed sufficient in the past, Japan now seeks more concrete assurance. Tokyo's credibility concern centers on three issues: (1) a strategic perception gap, (2) a possible decoupling of extended nuclear deterrence for Japan from basic deterrence in defense of the U.S. homeland, and (3) the inequality in the United States-Japan Mutual Security Treaty. That the U.S. approach to China, North Korea, and Russia may differ from that of Japan's underlies the strategic perception gap. Washington may take unilateral policy actions that leave Japan in a vulnerable position. The decoupling concern is informed by a modernizing Chinese nuclear arsenal that can increasingly hit a wide set of targets on the U.S. mainland, and the development of long-range nuclear missiles by North Korea. Would the United States be willing to engage in nuclear retaliation in the defense of Japan if such action could result in substantial damage to its homeland? Finally, prohibitions or restrictions issuing from constitutional, legal, and normative considerations prevent Japan from fully sharing in the collective defense of Japan and the United States. This may weaken American commitment to the security of Japan.

To shore up the credibility of extended deterrence, certain quarters in Japan advocate relaxing its commitment to the Three Non-Nuclear Principles and amending legislation that prevents Japan from intercepting missiles targeted at the United States, building a layered BMD system against North Korea and China, and maintaining a latent capability to develop nuclear weapons. Japan is also seeking greater dialogue with the United States; input into and a measure of control over U.S. nuclear policy in Asia; and institutional mechanisms to implement dialogue, input, and control. These measures would move the U.S. commitment beyond the declaratory position with which the United States has been comfortable. For a number of reasons—including secrecy and lack of trust in Japan's ability to handle highly classified information, inadequate capacity on the Japanese side, perceived constraints on U.S. flexibility, and the complexities of crafting an extended deterrence strategy that would adequately meet not only Japan's requirements but also that of its other allies—Washington has been unwilling to move in the direction urged by Japan. Nevertheless, Washington may have to take some measures to reassure its key ally. Because Japan does not confront an immediate security threat, those measures could still be largely process oriented within the framework of general deterrence, with the United States retaining full control over decision making.

In South Korea, the American extended deterrence commitment can be traced to the 1953 Mutual Defense Treaty and more specifically to the 1957 New Look policy of the Eisenhower administration. The extended deterrence commitment was crucial for the security of South Korea in the first three decades of the Cold War. In the 1990s South Korea's perception of the North Korean threat declined markedly and extended nuclear deterrence became almost a non-issue except during the first nuclear crisis.

The 2006 North Korean nuclear test, however, resurrected South Korean interest in extended nuclear deterrence. Upon Seoul's insistence the term *extended nuclear deterrence* was included in the joint communiqué of the thirty-eighth Security Consultative Meeting that occurred soon after the North Korean nuclear test. The South Korean rationale for insisting on the inclusion of extended nuclear deterrence is that the American commitment provides a bridging capability while South Korea builds its defense capabilities to take the lead responsibility for its own defense. The American nuclear umbrella will remain relevant until North Korea gives up its nuclear weapon capability (see Choi and Park, Chapter 13 of this volume). It also prevents South Korea from exploring a nuclear option. At the same time, the South Korean public and political leaders are deeply conflicted and divided on the security alliance with the United States. They fear becoming entrapped in U.S. preemptive military action against North Korea and elsewhere. Reliance on the American nuclear umbrella is also inconsistent with its nonnuclear posture, its policy to improve relations with North Korea, and its goal to be free of the vagaries of American policy.

For its part, the United States no longer subscribes to a traditional trip-wire strategy. It is reluctant to spell out details of its commitments, including which threats could result in nuclear retaliation or how nuclear deterrence is linked to U.S. and South Korean conventional forces. The United States seeks to deter North Korea by issuing general threats and demonstrating its vastly superior military capability in different parts of the world. Since the United States and the Republic of Korea have sufficient conventional forces to deter and defeat a North Korean military action against South Korea, extended nuclear deterrence is largely symbolic and psychological; the general deterrence posture of the United States can serve this function. However, the commitment will become complicated if North Korea develops long-range nuclear missiles that can hit targets in the United States.

Taipei is less conflicted; in fact, the outgoing Democratic Progressive Party government desires and would be happy to secure a more firm American commitment to the defense of Taiwan against a Chinese attack (see Wang, Chapter 14 of this volume). However, since the Sino-American normalization of relations in 1978, the American security commitment to Taiwan has been implicit under a policy of strategic ambiguity. U.S. nuclear weapons may have an implied role in deterring a large-scale Chinese attack on Taiwan and on any Chinese propensity to escalate hostilities to the nuclear level. However, this is not an explicit commitment. The United States will decide unilaterally whether, when, and how to intervene in a conflict across the Taiwan Strait. As China modernizes its nuclear arsenal and further develops its capability to hit military and civilian targets in the United States, the likelihood that Washington would consider using nuclear weapons in hostilities across the Taiwan Strait will become more remote. Should Washington decide to intervene, it would rely on conventional military capability. The limited American intervention in the 1995–96 crisis served not only to show U.S. resolve against Chinese intimidation of Taiwan, but also to demonstrate American military prowess to restrain China and others from seriously contemplating, threatening, or using force against America's interests in Asia.

Unlike Taiwan, Australia is a formal and close ally of the United States, and Washington is firmly committed to the security of that country. Despite this, the nature of the American extended nuclear deterrence commitment to Australia both during the Cold War and now lacks specific operational content (see Lyon, Chapter 15 of this volume). The only purpose of extended deterrence was and is to deter a nuclear attack against Australia. This is a remote possibility and a limited mandate that could be fulfilled through general assurances without issuing specific threats and developing specific capabilities. Nevertheless, Australia views the extended nuclear deterrence commitment as important in security and symbolic terms and also for other benefits (access to American military technology for conventional force modernization, and the elevation of Australia's international status and role, for example).

Further, Canberra has all along viewed the possession of nuclear weapons by risk-averse, responsible major powers and nuclear deterrence among them as contributing to global and regional stability. The contributions that nuclear deterrence can make to Australia's security and to global and regional stability are the basis on which Canberra rationalizes its conflicting nuclear policies—support for nuclear nonproliferation, opposition to nuclear testing, support for the Comprehensive Test Ban Treaty, and membership in the South Pacific Nuclear Weapon

Free Zone while relying on the American nuclear umbrella and hosting certain U.S. nuclear facilities. In the wake of 9/11 and the entry of new risk-tolerant nuclear weapon states such as Pakistan and North Korea, Australia is reevaluating the salience of nuclear deterrence for its security and for stability in the Asia-Pacific region. Rather than dilute security relations, the changed security environment has deepened Australia's security alliance with the United States and it still values the U.S. extended deterrence commitment.

Conclusion

This chapter has argued that although they appear relevant to a small number of situations, nuclear weapons have a far-reaching influence on the national security strategies and interaction among nuclear weapon states and their allies. They circumscribe the strategic interaction of major powers, play an important role in the management of key regional conflicts that could escalate to major war, and condition the role of force in the international politics in the Asian security region. They also make a significant contribution to regional peace and stability, which is the subject of the final chapter. Before I turn to that, I would like to make brief observations on two issues that were raised in the Introduction. Time and space considerations prevent a more detailed discussion of these issues. One, the roles and strategies of nuclear weapons discussed in this chapter are not unique to Asia. They are a function of specific histories, strategic circumstances, security challenges, and national nuclear capabilities. As these circumstances change, so will the roles and strategies, which are also a function of the nuclear revolution. The dominance of deterrence, for example, is a consequence of the nuclear revolution. Asian countries are not immune to the logic of that revolution. The tendency toward ambiguity and secrecy is not a cultural trait but a function of the belief that such ambiguity and secrecy enhances the deterrent value of small nuclear forces. Ambiguity also characterized nuclear policies and strategies during the Cold War (Kissinger 1957); now it characterizes American policy on the Taiwan issue and Israel's nuclear policy and strategy.

On common discourse, although certain countries use similar terms like *minimum deterrence, limited war, no-first-use,* and so forth, the understanding and operationalization of these ideas vary substantially across countries. The development of a common discourse is hindered by several factors, including the tendency to downplay the significance of nuclear weapons for reasons of political correctness and in the interest of secrecy and ambiguity. As nuclear weapons will continue to exist and national arsenals will grow in size and complexity, it is imperative and useful to begin bilateral and multilateral dialogues to foster common understanding of the roles and strategies of nuclear weapons and their implications for national and regional security. Such dialogues will help build a common vocabulary and contribute to the development of expertise on the subject in Asia.

Notes

1. That deterrence continues to be a key function of the U.S. nuclear arsenal is indicated in a joint statement issued by the U.S. Secretaries for Energy, Defense, and State (National Security and Nuclear Weapons 2007)

2. On the meaning of and distinction between immediate and general deterrence, see Morgan 2003.

References

Basrur, Rajesh M. 2005. "Coercive Diplomacy in A Nuclear Environment." In *Prospects for Peace in South Asia,* Raffiq Dossani and Henry S. Rowen, eds. Stanford, Calif.: Stanford University Press.

Cirincione, Joseph, Jon B. Wolfsthal, and Miriam Rajkumar. 2005. *Deadly Arsenals: Nuclear, Biological, and Chemical Threats.* Washington, D.C.: Carnegie Endowment for International Peace.

Hagerty, Devin T. 1998. *The Consequences of Nuclear Proliferation: Lessons from South Asia.* Cambridge, Mass.: MIT Press.

Hoffman, Gil. 2006. "Peres: Ambiguity has achieved its goal." *Jerusalem Post,* December 12. Online edition.

Inbar, Efraim. 2008. "An Israeli View of the Iranian Nuclear Challenge." Philadelphia, PA: Foreign Policy Research Institute. Available at http://www.fpri.org/

Johnston, Alastair Iain. 1995–96. "China's New 'Old Thinking': The Concept of Limited Deterrence." *International Security* 20 (3): 5–42.

Kissinger, Henry A. 1957. *Nuclear Weapons and Foreign Policy.* New York: Harper Brothers.

Lieber, Keir A., and Daryl G. Press. 2006. "The End of MAD? The Nuclear Dimension of U.S. Primacy." *International Security* 30 (4): 7–44.

———. 2007. Correspondence in "The Short Shadow of U.S. Primacy?" *International Security* 31 (3): 174–93.

Morgan, Patrick M. 2003. *Deterrence Now.* Cambridge, U.K.: Cambridge University Press.

National Security and Nuclear Weapons: A Statement by the Secretary of Energy, Secretary of Defense, and Secretary of State, 2007. Washington, D.C. Available at http://www.nnsa.doe.gov/docs/factsheets/2007/NA-07-FS-04.pdf.

Raas, Whitney, and Austin Long. 2007. "Osirak Redux? Assessing Israeli Capabilities to Destroy Iranian Nuclear Facilities." *International Security* 31 (4): 7–33.

Schelling, Thomas C. 1966. *Arms and Influence.* New Haven, Conn.: Yale University Press.

U.S. Department of Defense. 2002. *Nuclear Posture Review in the DoD Annual Report to the President and the Congress.* Washington, D.C.: Department of Defense. Available at www.defenselink.mil/execsec/adr2002/toc2002.htm.

U.S. Department of Defense. 2006. *Quadrennial Defense Review Report.* Available at http://www.defenselink.mil/qdr/report/Report20060203.pdf.

———. 2007. *Military Power of the People's Republic of China.* 2007. Washington, D.C.: Office of the Secretary of Defense.

18

Reinforcing National Security and Regional Stability

The Implications of Nuclear Weapons and Strategies

MUTHIAH ALAGAPPA

Another major conclusion of this study is that although nuclear weapons could have destabilizing consequences in certain situations, on net they have reinforced national security and regional stability in Asia. It is possible to argue that fledgling and small nuclear arsenals would be more vulnerable to preventive attacks; that the related strategic compulsion for early use may lead to early launch postures and crisis situations; that limited war under nuclear conditions to alter or restore the political status quo can intensify tensions and carry the risk of escalation to major war; that inadequate command, control, and safety measures could result in accidents; and that nuclear facilities and material may be vulnerable to terrorist attacks. These are legitimate concerns, but thus far nuclear weapons have not undermined national security and regional stability in Asia. Instead, they have ameliorated national security concerns, strengthened the status quo, increased deterrence dominance, prevented the outbreak of major wars, and reinforced the regional trend to reduce the salience of force in international politics. Nor have nuclear weapons had the predicted domino effect. These consequences have strengthened regional security and stability that rest on multiple pillars.

The grim scenarios associated with nuclear weapons in Asia frequently rely on worst-case political and military situations; often they are seen in isolation from the national priorities of regional states that emphasize economic development and modernization through participation in regional and global economies and the high priority accorded to stability in domestic and international affairs. The primary goal of regional states is not aggrandizement through military aggression but preservation of national integrity, state or regime survival, economic growth and prosperity, increase in national power and international influence, preservation or incremental change in the status quo, and the construction of regional and global orders in which they are subjects rather than objects. Seen in this broader perspective, nuclear weapons and more generally military force are of greater relevance in the defense, deterrence, and assurance roles than offensive ones. This does not imply that offensive use of force or military clashes will not occur; only that force is not the first option, that military clashes will be infrequent, and that when they do occur they will be limited in scope and intensity. Security interaction in Asia increasingly approximates behavior associated with defensive realism.

The study advances four other propositions on the implications of nuclear weapons and strategies for security and stability in the Asian security region and for the global nuclear order. First, it argues that nuclear weapons have a modifying effect, but they do not fundamentally alter system structure (distribution of power) or the patterns of amity and enmity. By strengthening weaker powers, nuclear weapons have helped offset imbalances in conventional and nuclear capabilities and mitigated the negative consequences of those imbalances. This has affected the distribution and effects of military power in certain bilateral relationships. However, nuclear weapons in and of themselves have not substantially altered the overall regional distribution of power. Likewise, nuclear weapons have not fundamentally altered patterns of amity and enmity in the Asian security region. The one exception may be in the Middle East where a nuclear Iran could bring into sharper relief the Israel-Iran line of enmity and temper that between Israel and certain Arab states (though not the Palestinians). This is still a hypothetical situation, and Israel-Iran enmity is not only a function of nuclear weapons. A nuclear Iran could substantially alter the Middle East security dynamics, broaden and increase the connection of that region to South Asia, and increase the subregion's relevance for regional and global security. In all other Asian subregions, nuclear weapons have not altered security patterns but have affected the intensity of existing security dilemmas. Offensive strategies including first use have intensified certain security dilemmas; deterrence strategies by and large have had ameliorating effects.

Second, the impact of nuclear weapons on alliance formation and sustenance is mixed. In the abstract, nuclear weapons should enhance internal balancing and reduce the need for external balancing; this should reduce the significance of alliances. In certain ways this has been the case with Pakistan, Israel, and North Korea. All these countries see nuclear weapons as enhancing their self-reliant deterrence capability and as their ultimate security guarantee. However, nuclear weapons have not reduced the salience of alliance and alignment relationships for these countries. Nuclear weapon states may still choose to ally or align with each other for different benefits. For nonnuclear weapon states that perceive nuclear or large-scale conventional threats, alliance with a state that can effectively extend the deterrence function of its nuclear arsenal remains attractive. Concern with nuclear threats, along with other considerations, has strengthened the U.S. alliance relationships with Japan, South Korea, and Australia. In certain situations, concern with nuclear threat could also challenge and weaken these alliances.

Third, on conflict resolution, the study posits that the enormous destructive power of nuclear weapons argues against dispute resolution through the physical use of violence. At the same time, nuclear weapons are not a barrier to peaceful conflict resolution. In fact, the grave risks associated with escalation to nuclear war have occasionally induced parties to explore a diplomatic settlement. The settlement of disputes, however, requires conflicting parties to negotiate compromises on political differences. In the absence of such compromise, nuclear weapons can freeze and intensify conflicts.

Finally, the study posits that if it is to continue to be relevant, the nuclear order that emerged during the Cold War must substantially alter to accommodate contemporary strategic realities, including a focus on Asia, which has become a core world region and in which strategic competition is likely to intensify. A "new" nuclear order that is likely to emerge gradually would have to address at least four challenges: (1) sustaining deterrence in a condition of asymmetry and small nuclear forces, (2) accommodating "new" nuclear weapon states, (3) preventing the spread of nuclear weapons to additional states and to nonstate actors, and (4) facilitating the safe and secure development of nuclear energy to meet the growing demand for this clean fuel. Freezing the twentieth-century order would be counterproductive. The gap between the formal order and reality would widen and undermine its viability and effectiveness.

The findings on the roles and implications of nuclear weapons in this study may appear too "benign" and unacceptable to those who view nuclear weapons as the primary drivers of insecurity and arms control, especially nonproliferation scholars and advocates who see preventing the spread of nuclear weapons and their eventual elimination as urgent ends in themselves. Regardless of intellectual and moral persuasions, nuclear weapons will be a feature of the Asian security landscape in the foreseeable future. The ethics of responsibility requires us to investigate and address all their security implications, not just the negative consequences of proliferation. In this connection, security studies and arms control scholarship in the twenty-first century should illuminate, develop, and subject the "new" roles and strategies for the employment of nuclear weapons to more rigorous analysis and contribute to deterrence stability in a condition of asymmetric power relationships. Strategic dialogue among nuclear weapon states that fosters common understandings can also contribute to stability.

Nuclear Weapons Reinforce Security and Stability

Three contending views have been advanced on the consequence of nuclear weapons for peace and security in Europe during the Cold War. One view is that nuclear weapons contributed to the long peace and stability in Europe (Gaddis 1992; Jervis 1988; Waltz 2004).[1] The second view does not contest the idea of a long peace but disputes that nuclear weapons contributed to it (Mueller 1988, 1998). The third view contests the claim that the Cold War was a period of stable peace. In this view, the nuclear standoff during the Cold War was highly dangerous and should be avoided. In terms of relevance for the contemporary era, some Western analysts (mostly nonproliferation scholars and advocates) argue that the contribution of nuclear weapons to the long peace in Europe would not apply to Asia. Asian countries are culturally different; their militaries view preventive war in a favorable light and are not interested in developing invulnerable strategic forces; and insecure command and control arrangements make them more prone to accidents and unauthorized use (Feaver 1992–93, 1993; Sagan 1994, 1995). Adherents of this perspective argue that the Indian, Pakistani, and most recently North Korean nuclear tests would set off a domino effect, with negative consequences for security and stability in Asia and the world. Their arguments connect with the third perspective, which argues that the Cold War nuclear confrontation was highly dangerous, the peace that existed was highly tenuous, Europe was lucky to escape the nightmare scenario, and Asia should at all cost avoid repeating that scenario.[2] The view that nuclear weapons would contribute to insecurity and instability in Asia seems to have become dominant in the West, especially in the wake of the 1999 and 2002 crisis situations between India and Pakistan and the 2006 North Korean nuclear test. It resonates with and reinforces earlier views in Europe and the United States that Asia was ripe for rivalry and that its future would resemble the war-torn Europe of the nineteenth century (Buzan and Segal 1994; Friedberg 1993–94).

In 2003 I argued against the "ripe for rivalry" line of thought, pointing out that Asia had enjoyed relative peace and security for over two decades (now three decades) and that a relatively stable security order based on several pillars had developed in the region (Alagappa 2003a, 2003b). There has not been a major war since the Vietnamese invasion of Cambodia in 1978 and the Chinese punitive attack on Vietnam in 1979. Despite periodic tensions, war has not broken out across the Taiwan Strait or on the Korean peninsula. There has been more military conflict between India and Pakistan, and the probability of an overt military clash between those two countries is higher than in the other two conflicts. Even there, though, and in some ways because of the acquisition of nuclear weapon capabilities, the use of force has been limited and largely confined to the areas adjacent to the line of control (LoC) in Kashmir. The 1999 Kargil conflict did not escalate to a full-scale war. The many territorial disputes in Asia have resulted in only occasional and limited military clashes. Historical memories and contemporary concerns linked to a dominant United States and a rapidly rising China have created mistrust, apprehensions, and long-range threat perceptions among major powers.

Such apprehensions and threat perceptions may intensify competition for power and influence, but they have not resulted in vigorous strategic rivalry and arms competition. Nor has Asia become a hotbed of wars where the survival of states is at issue and countries are constantly jockeying for power.

International political interaction among Asian states is for the most part rule governed, predictable, and stable. The security order that has developed in Asia is largely of the instrumental type, with certain normative contractual features (Alagappa 2003b). It rests on several pillars. These include the consolidation of Asian countries as modern nation-states with rule-governed interactions, widespread acceptance of the territorial and political status quo (with the exception of certain boundary disputes and a few survival concerns that still linger), a regional normative structure that ensures survival of even weak states and supports international coordination and cooperation, the high priority in Asian countries given to economic growth and development, the pursuit of that goal through participation in regional and global capitalist economies, the declining salience of force in Asian international politics, the largely status quo orientation of Asia's major powers, and the key role of the United States and of regional institutions in preserving and enhancing security and stability in Asia.

I extend that argument in this study to include the effects of nuclear weapons and the strategies for their employment. I argue that although there could be destabilizing consequences, on net, nuclear weapons reinforce deterrence dominance and enhance national security and regional stability in the Asian security region. My claim is supported on the following grounds. First, nuclear weapons assuage the security concerns of vulnerable states. Second, nuclear weapons prevent the escalation of regional conflicts to full-scale war. Third, general deterrence postures assure major powers and help stabilize relations among them. Fourth, nuclear weapons strengthen the political and military status quo by making violent change highly dangerous and unlikely. Finally, nuclear weapons further circumscribe and transform the role of force in Asian international politics. Taken together, these political and military effects of nuclear weapons, along with the absence of intense strategic rivalry and competition among the major powers, reinforce the security and stability that have come to characterize the Asian security region over the last three decades. My argument shares certain features of those advanced by Waltz (1995), Hagerty (1998), and Goldstein (2000), but it is also distinct and grounded in two decades of post-Cold War regionwide experience and linked to other political, strategic, and economic factors that also underpin security and stability in the region. It is important to view the roles and effects of nuclear weapons in this larger context.

Critics would contest my claim by pointing to the crisis situations in India-Pakistan relations during the 1999–2002 period, the abstract shortcomings of general deterrence, and the potential domino effect of the Indian, Pakistani, and

North Korean nuclear test. They would also draw attention to two other sets of issues. One set relates to strategic considerations, including the danger of preemptive and preventive action, and the strategic incentive to use a small nuclear arsenal early for fear of losing it in a preemptive strike. The second set relates to dangers that are deemed peculiar to new nuclear weapon states: command-and-control problems, safety issues, the risk of nuclear weapons falling into the wrong hands (extremist groups and rogue regimes, which cannot be deterred because of their irrational behavior), and the dangers associated with nuclear weapons in a failed or failing state. I discuss the strategic arguments in the context of developing and supporting my argument. Here I briefly address the second set of issues.

The risks associated with new nuclear weapon states are indeed plausible and should be of concern. It would take me too far afield to contest the biased assumptions that inform some of these claims in relation to non-Western nuclear weapon states. I would like to make three general points. First, the logic of risk and that of strategic need are different and should be addressed separately. Conflating them makes for a crosspurpose debate that is unproductive. The risk argument is advanced by those who oppose the acquisition and development of nuclear weapon capability by developing countries. Intellectual (and possibly racial) biases and national strategic interests are often cloaked in this argument, which is usually advanced on behalf of the international community. Proponents of this persuasion deny the security need or the relevance of nuclear weapons for that need, and they advance political, status, and bureaucratic arguments as the "real" reasons underlying the quest for a nuclear weapon capability. The country that is seeking the capability advances the strategic logic. That country's political leadership believes that the acquisition of nuclear weapon capability is vital to secure its national interest even if it entails high cost. It is not unaware of the risks, but these are trumped by the security imperative. The logic of risk cannot be the basis for self-denial of a capability deemed vital in a self-help world. An enterprise cannot be forbidden, especially on discriminatory grounds, simply because it entails risks for the so-called international community.

The new nuclear weapon states recognize the command, control, and safety problems and have taken measures to prevent accidents and theft. Outsiders should consider assisting those states by providing suitable technologies and best practices instead of simply isolating and castigating them. Safety of the nuclear arsenal in an unstable state, such as Pakistan, is indeed a serious concern. That concern must be addressed on a case-by-case basis with specific policies but not by a blanket policy that applies to all developing countries. Pakistan has instituted certain measures to safeguard its arsenal and prevent unauthorized use (see Khan and Lavoy, Chapter 7 of this volume). Out of fear that these weapons may fall into the hands of Islamic extremist groups, the United States has assisted in these efforts as well (Sanger and Broad 2007). The strategic logic has to be addressed on its own terms by those acting on behalf of the international community. The United States, for example, is now willing to provide security assurances to the Kim Jong Il regime in the context of the Six-Party Talks to negotiate a settlement of the North Korean nuclear problem. In certain cases, the security need cannot be addressed satisfactorily. And those acting on behalf of the international community (authorized and unauthorized) may have to forcibly eliminate the target state's nuclear capability or will have to live with a new nuclear weapon state. It has been done before.

Second, the new states recognize the revolutionary nature of nuclear weapons; they are not immune to the strategic logic of these weapons. They have not behaved differently from the "rational" Western states. Just like the United States, Russia, Britain, and France, "new" countries see nuclear weapons as being useful in a deterrence role. They are in the process of developing more survivable forces but doing it responsibly in the context of other national priorities, avoiding intense arms competition that characterized the interaction of the advanced countries during the Cold War. Some new nuclear weapon states have attempted offensive strategies in the employment of nuclear weapons, but this attempt is not peculiar to them. The United States is in the forefront in developing offensive and strategic defense capabilities that some Asian states consider destabilizing.

Third, the claim that so-called rogue states cannot be deterred does not withstand scrutiny. The Soviet Union was a revolutionary state seeking to fundamentally transform the international order. Yet deterrence was the primary nuclear strategy in dealing with that country. Deterrence was also the strategy against a China that under Mao was deemed a rogue and irrational state, especially during the Cultural Revolution. Characterization of China as a revolutionary state also did not stop the United States from negotiating with Mao and forming a strategic alignment with that country against the Soviet Union. Despite the claim that rogue states cannot be deterred, deterrence (conventional and nuclear) has been and continues to be the primary U.S. strategy against North Korea. The United States is now negotiating with a regime that it labels as irrational and tyrannical in an effort to freeze and eliminate North Korea's nuclear weapon capability. Certain frustrated arms controllers in the United States now attempt to depict India, the world's largest democracy and the fourth or fifth largest economy in terms of purchasing power parity, as a rogue state, although the Bush administration through its bilateral deal with India is seeking to bring that country into the formal nuclear order. The ongoing debate in Asia over the pros and cons of a first-use policy is not much different from that in the Atlantic alliance during the Cold War or that in post-Cold War Russia. The point here is that the nuclear behavior of non-Western states is not substantively different from that of Western ones. Further, a country like the United States, which has a formidable nuclear arsenal, can deter them. I now turn to supporting my claim that nuclear weapons have contributed to security and stability in Asia.

Assuage Security Concerns

Nuclear weapons contribute to stability by assuaging the security concerns of vulnerable states. This is most evident in the case of Pakistan. Islamabad sees nuclear weapons as having enhanced its security in relation to the existential threat it perceives from India (see Khan and Lavoy, Chapter 7 of this volume). Nuclear weapons neutralize the effects of the large imbalance in conventional military capability, constrain India's military options, and increase Pakistan's deterrence self-reliance. The security effect of an opaque nuclear force like that of Israel is more difficult to demonstrate, especially as that country also has superior conventional military capability. Avner Cohen suggests that Israel has been able to "extract the benefits of an existential nuclear deterrence posture" (see Cohen, Chapter 8 of this volume). Arab countries' tacit acceptance of Israel's nuclear deterrence posture, he argues, has contributed to Israel's security and to regional stability by lowering the intensity of the Arab-Israeli conflict, and in some instances even contributed to peace settlements, like that between Israel and Egypt. Cohen posits that Israel's nuclear capability possibly compelled Saddam Hussein to limit his missile attacks on Israel during the First Gulf War to conventional weapons. Although Israel has superior conventional military capability, nuclear weapons enhance Israel's self-confidence and demonstrate its resolve to survive.

For North Korea, nuclear weapons serve a more immediate deterrence function against the United States. Though still numerically large, North Korea's conventional military capability has steadily eroded and is losing the balance-of-power advantage it had enjoyed for decades. North Korea has also lost the military support of Russia and China. In this context, North Korea's nuclear weapon capability assumes greater importance. Pyongyang believes that nuclear weapons enhance its security and provide it with diplomatic leverage in the Six-Party Talks for securing tangible security, diplomatic, and economic benefits (see Park and Lee, Chapter 9 of this volume). It is a fact that U.S. policy has shifted from a rigid stance that stressed the preventive force option and demanded complete and verifiable disarmament of the North Korean nuclear weapon program to serious engagement in multilateral discussions to arrive at a diplomatic settlement with due regard to Pyongyang's concerns. Several considerations underlie the shift in U.S. policy. North Korea's determination to stay the course, culminating in the 2006 nuclear test, appears to be one of them. Of particular relevance is the impact of Pyongyang's missile and nuclear tests on America's East Asian allies and the ensuing imperative to limit the fallout from those tests.

The U.S. extended deterrence commitments have been a significant factor in assuaging the security vulnerabilities and concerns of Japan and South Korea in the wake of the North Korean nuclear test. As discussed in Chapter 17, both countries insisted on reaffirmation of the U.S. commitment, and Japan is exploring measures to increase the credibility of that commitment. In reassuring Japan, the U.S. commitment is a significant factor along with others in forestalling exploration of an independent nuclear option by that country. For South Korea, the U.S. commitment enables it to maintain a nonnuclear posture, provides time to build a self-reliant defense capability, and is a fallback in dealing with a nuclear-armed North Korea.

Help Stabilize Regional Conflicts

Nuclear weapons contribute to regional stability by preventing the outbreak of major hostilities and their escalation to full-scale war in key regional conflicts across the Taiwan Strait, on the Korean peninsula, and over Kashmir. The restraining effect of nuclear weapons in the Taiwan and Korean conflicts has been discussed in Chapter 17. The fear of escalation to the nuclear level limits China's force options and implicitly deters a major Chinese attack on Taiwan. The United States' response to Chinese threats and intimidations has been calibrated to show firmness and caution. Washington has also reined in provocative behavior by independence-oriented Taiwanese leaders. Similarly nuclear weapons help stabilize the conflict on the Korean peninsula. North Korea feels more assured of its deterrence capability while South Korea is assured by the U.S. extended deterrence commitment. It is possible to argue that there has not been a deep crisis in the conflict across the Taiwan Strait to demonstrate the restraining and stabilizing effect of nuclear weapons and, further, that stability in the Taiwan and North Korea conflicts is due to a number of factors including conventional deterrence. It is difficult to refute these claims, as the deterrence effect of nuclear weapons cannot be isolated and quantified in the absence of severe crisis when the role and effect of such weapons come into sharper relief. However, this does not imply irrelevance or that nuclear weapons do not contribute to stability.

The stabilizing effect of nuclear weapons may be better illustrated in India-Pakistan relations, as the crises between these two countries during the 1999–2002 period are often cited as demonstrating nuclear weapon-induced instability. Rather than simply attribute these crises to the possession of nuclear weapons, a more accurate and useful reading would ground them in Pakistan's deliberate policy to alter the status quo through military means on the premise that the risk of escalation to nuclear war would deter India from responding with full-scale conventional retaliation; and in India's response, employing compellence and coercive diplomacy strategies. In other words, particular goals and strategies rather than nuclear weapons per se precipitated the crises. Further, the outcomes of these two crises revealed the limited utility of nuclear weapons in bringing about even a minor change in the territorial status quo and highlighted the grave risks associated with offensive strategies. Recognition of these limits and the grave consequences in part contributed to the two countries' subsequent efforts to engage in a comprehensive dialogue to settle the many disputes between them. The crises also led to bilateral understandings and measures to avoid unintended hostilities.

Though it is too soon to take a long view, it is possible to argue that, like the Cuban missile crisis in 1962, the 1999 and 2001–02 crises between India and Pakistan mark a watershed in their strategic relations: the danger of nuclear war shifted their focus to avoiding a major war and to finding a negotiated settlement to bilateral problems. Large military deployments along the common border and Pakistan-supported insurgent activities in India continue; and the two countries regularly conduct large-scale military exercises and test nuclear-capable missiles that have each other's entire territory within range. Despite these activities, the situation has become less tense; stability with the ability to absorb shocks has begun to characterize the bilateral relationship over the past five years. Some have termed this "ugly stability" (Tellis 1997: 5), but it is stability nevertheless.

Assurance and Stability in Major Power Relations

The caution induced by nuclear weapons, their leveling effect, the strategic insurance they provide to cope with unanticipated contingencies, and general deterrence postures inform and circumscribe interaction among the major powers, reduce their anxieties, and constrain the role of force in their interaction. This enables major powers to take a long view and focus on other national priorities. Nuclear weapons feature primarily in deterrence and insurance roles. These roles are not necessarily threatening to other parties. Modernization of nuclear arsenals and the development of additional capabilities have proceeded at a moderate pace; they have produced responses but not intense strategic competition. The net effect has been stabilizing.

The stabilizing effect of nuclear weapons in the Sino-American, Russo-American, and Sino-Indian dyads were discussed in Chapter 17. Here I will limit myself to making some additional points. Continuing deterrence dominance underlies China's measured response to the U.S. emphasis on offensive strategies and its development of strategic missile defense. Perceiving these as undermining the robustness of its strategic deterrent force, China seeks to strengthen the survivability of its retaliatory force and is attempting to develop capabilities that would threaten American space-based surveillance and communications facilities in the event of hostilities. However, these efforts are not presented as a direct challenge to or competition with the United States. Beijing has deliberately sought to downplay the modernization of its nuclear force. This is not simply deception, but a serious effort to develop a strong deterrent force without entering into a strategic competition with the United States, which it cannot win due to the huge imbalance in military capabilities and technological limitations. Strategic competition will also divert attention and resources away from the more urgent modernization goals. A strong Chinese strategic deterrent force blunts the military advantage of the United States, induces caution in that country, and constrains its military option in the event of hostilities. Although Russia's response to the U.S. development of offensive and strategic defense capabilities has been more vocal, it lacks specifics. Moscow also does not appear to have allocated significantly more resources to its nuclear force.

India's strategic deterrence force does not compare with China's, but its nuclear, missile, and conventional military capability give New Delhi a relatively high degree of self-confidence in managing relations with Beijing. The insurance provided by its small nuclear force and strong conventional capability, combined with technological and resource limitations, and improving bilateral relations, explain India's gradual development of a nuclear deterrent capability against China. India's minimum deterrence nuclear posture and its gradual nuclear buildup also reassure China, which sees the United States as its principal security concern. In recent times, Japan has been more sensitive than India to China's nuclear force modernization and the development of North Korea's missile and nuclear capabilities. In part, this is due to the lack of its own nuclear weapon capability. However, Japan has not sought its own nuclear weapon capability to compete with China or North Korea, a move that could be destabilizing. Instead it has sought reaffirmation of the U.S. extended deterrence commitment, denuclearization of the Korean peninsula, increase in its own conventional military capability, and development of strategic defense, all of which can be stabilizing.

Because they are not immediately threatening, the general deterrence postures adopted by all the major powers have contributed to regional stability as well. Patrick Morgan (2003: 80–115) has written that government leaders are "often barely moved by general deterrence threats that they ought to take into account." Because the response to it is uncertain, he argues that general deterrence suffers an inherent credibility problem and is vulnerable to military probes that could lead to deterrence failure. It is possible to depict the Chinese missile firings in 1995–96 and the 1999 Pakistani military infiltration into Kargil as probing the general deterrence postures of the United States and India, respectively. The firm and quick response in both cases established the credibility of American commitment to the status quo across the Taiwan Strait and the Indian determination to preserve the status quo in Kashmir. When established, immediate deterrence (as opposed to general deterrence, although the difference between the two is not clear-cut) may be more credible, but this is not certain. But immediate deterrence may not be relevant or practical in all situations. In the absence of intense hostilities or a lack of capabilities, a nuclear weapon state is more likely to adopt a policy of general deterrence. The risk of escalation to nuclear war and the devastation that can be inflicted by nuclear weapons make general deterrence more effective than conventional deterrence. Periodic demonstration of resolve may be necessary to shore up the credibility of general deterrence. From the perspective of stability, which is the primary issue addressed here, general deterrence is less directly threatening than immediate deterrence and more effective than conventional deterrence. It does not aggravate security relations or feed competitive strategic armament; and it is more defensive in character than immediate deterrence, which can have a strong aggressive component. All these features of general deterrence contribute to stability.

Reinforce the Political and Military Status Quo

Reviewing the Cold War experience, Robert Jervis has argued that nuclear weapons strengthen the status quo. However, he qualified that assertion by excluding situations where the status quo is ambiguous or when a revisionist power has the power to implement threats, has high resolve, and sees the domestic and international situations as precarious enough to merit great risk and cost (Jervis 1989: 32–34). Along these lines but in a more detailed fashion, Paul Kapur (2006) argues that nuclear weapons may provide incentives for a weaker, revisionist state to engage in limited conventional military action to alter the status quo. Such a state would not engage in aggressive behavior in a conventional world because it would most likely result in failure. In a nuclear world, the stronger state is inhibited from employing its full military might for fear that hostilities would escalate to nuclear war. This risk of escalation emboldens a highly motivated state to behave aggressively.

In this study, I argue that the risk of escalation cuts both ways and that the net effect of nuclear weapons has been to reinforce the status quo and enhance stability in the Asian security region in two ways: they make change through violence more difficult and highly costly; and they dramatically increase the political cost of "adventurist" behavior by nuclear weapon states. The limit to forcefully alter the status quo and the associated political risks disadvantage the challenger and help entrench the status quo. These points are best illustrated by the India-Pakistan case. They are also evident in a limited manner in the conflict across the Taiwan Strait.

I begin with the basic observation that the attempts by Pakistan to alter the territorial status quo in Kashmir and by China to force a particular political outcome in Taiwan through the threat and use of force failed. Jervis's qualification of his argument and Kapur's extension of that argument may explain why Pakistan resorted to military action in 1999, but cannot account for the failure and implications of that action. To begin with, the relatively small-scale Pakistani military infiltration, even if successful, could not have substantially altered the territorial status quo in Kashmir, although it could have set a precedent for further "salami tactics." In the end, it did not bring about even a minor change in the territorial status quo. On the contrary, the outcome of the military action helped entrench the territorial status quo. India responded firmly to the military intrusion. It defeated and compelled the withdrawal of the Pakistani infiltration force. After initial denials, Pakistan acknowledged that regular troops undertook the military intrusion and eventually had to withdraw that force. The risk of escalation cut both ways. It constrained India's military options, but it also circumscribed Pakistan's response to the Indian military reaction. Pakistan could not openly support its forces in Indian-held Kashmir or escalate the war. By strictly limiting its military response to territory under its control, India gave credence to and legitimated the LoC. And since the conflict, New Delhi has insisted that although it is open to new thinking on the Kashmir issue, it would not condone altering the LoC. International support for this position has since increased.

India emerged from the conflict as a responsible status quo power, whereas Pakistan's "adventurist" behavior further tarnished its shaky international image. The rise of Islamic extremism in Pakistan, Islamabad's support for the Taliban regime when that regime was in power in Afghanistan, the wide and substantial damage done by the A. Q. Khan network, military authoritarianism, and political instability, among others, had raised concerns about Pakistan as a viable state and a responsible nuclear weapon state. The 1999 adventure added to these concerns. The inability to bring about even a minor change in the territorial status quo and the grave risks associated with a limited conflict under nuclear conditions appear to have led to a sober assessment of the role of nuclear weapons in this dyad. The net effect of nuclear weapons has been to enhance deterrence dominance and entrench the political and territorial status quo.

The Taiwan case is less instructive as the role of nuclear weapons is implicit, and there has not been a severe crisis. Further, China was not trying to alter the territorial status quo through force but to influence the political situation on the island in a desired direction. Seeking to affect the outcome of the Taiwan presidential elections in 1995, China fired missiles in the vicinity of the island. That effort failed. Not only did the result of the election go against the outcome desired by Beijing, the United States responded in a firm manner by deploying two aircraft carriers and warning China that it would not tolerate intimidation and forceful change in Taiwan's status. China refrained from escalating the military conflict out of concern that it could not achieve conflict escalation dominance and that escalation would risk bringing nuclear weapons more directly into the conflict. Although China has not renounced the use of force and continues to build up its missile and amphibious capabilities, that crisis highlighted the dangers and drawbacks of relying on the force option (including the negative consequences for its image as a responsible rising power), leading Beijing to deemphasize forceful unification. That incident as well as the public discussion in China of the merits of its no-first-use (NFU) policy and the advocacy in certain Chinese quarters for using nuclear weapons in a war-fighting role in the event of a military conflict across the Taiwan Strait has also chastened the United States. Since the 1995–96 crisis, the emphasis in both China and the United States has been on preserving the status quo. Reversing its earlier strong support, the Bush administration leaned heavily on the Chen administration in Taiwan not to take any unilateral action that would alter the status quo. In the India-Pakistan case and in the conflict across the Taiwan Strait, nuclear weapons have further reduced the prospects for military victory and strengthened the status quo and stability.

The Domino Effect Has Not Materialized

It will be useful at this juncture to address more directly the set of instability arguments advanced by certain policy makers and scholars: the domino effect of new nuclear weapon states, the probability of preventive action against new nuclear weapon states, and the compulsion of these states to use their small arsenals early for fear of losing them in a preventive or preemptive strike by a stronger nuclear adversary.

On the domino effect, India's and Pakistan's nuclear weapon programs have not fueled new programs in South Asia or beyond. Iran's quest for nuclear weapons is not a reaction to the Indian or Pakistani programs. It is grounded in that country's security concerns about the United States and Tehran's regional aspirations. The North Korean test has evoked mixed reactions in Northeast Asia. Tokyo is certainly concerned; its reaction, though, has not been to initiate its own nuclear weapon program but to reaffirm and strengthen the American extended deterrence commitment to Japan. Even if the U.S.-Japan security treaty were to weaken, it is not certain that Japan would embark on a nuclear weapon program. Likewise, South Korea has sought reaffirmation of the American extended deterrence commitment, but has firmly held to its nonnuclear posture. Without dramatic change in its political, economic, and security circumstances, South Korea is highly unlikely to embark on a covert (or overt) nuclear weapon program as it did in the 1970s. South Korea could still become a nuclear weapon state by inheriting the nuclear weapons of North Korea should the Kim Jong Il regime collapse. Whether it retains or gives up that capability will hinge on the security circumstances of a unified Korea. The North Korean nuclear test has not spurred Taiwan or Mongolia to develop nuclear weapon capability.

The point is that each country's decision to embark on and sustain nuclear weapon programs is contingent on its particular security and other circumstances. Though appealing, the domino theory is not predictive; often it is employed to justify policy on the basis of alarmist predictions. The loss of South Vietnam, for example, did not lead to the predicted domino effect in Southeast Asia. In fact the so-called dominos became drivers of a vibrant Southeast Asia and brought about a fundamental transformation in that subregion (Lord 1993, 1996). In the nuclear arena, the nuclear programs of China, India, and Pakistan were part of a security chain reaction, not mechanically falling dominos. However, as observed earlier the Indian, Pakistani, and North Korean nuclear tests have thus far not had the domino effect predicted by alarmist analysts and policy makers. Great caution should be exercised in accepting at face value the sensational predictions of individuals who have a vested interest in accentuating the dangers of nuclear proliferation. Such analysts are now focused on the dangers of a nuclear Iran. A nuclear Iran may or may not have destabilizing effects. Such claims must be assessed on the basis of an objective reading of the drivers of national and regional security in Iran and the Middle East.

Declining Probability of Preventive Military Action in East and South Asia

The prospect of military action to destroy nuclear weapons and facilities in East and South Asia has declined markedly. The Soviet Union contemplated preventive military action against China's nuclear facilities in 1969, but the United States refused to support such action. Several years ago there was concern that India might attack Pakistan's nuclear installations. Even if this was a serious possibility, its probability has declined sharply. The two countries entered into an agreement not to attack each other's nuclear facilities. This agreement held even during the crisis situations in the 1999–2002 period. Since then, India and Pakistan have taken additional measures to prevent an accidental outbreak or escalation of conflict.

More germane to the contemporary context is the emphasis in the U.S. 2002 Nuclear Posture Review on offensive military action against rogue states. The United States seriously contemplated a preventive strike against North Korea's nuclear weapon facilities during the first nuclear crisis on the Korean peninsula in 1993–94 (Perry 2006). And the George W. Bush administration threatened preventive action against North Korea during its first term.[3] However, that policy has lost traction and has no support among states in Northeast Asia, including U.S. allies. Neighboring countries oppose any preventive strike, fearing that it could result in a general war that would have negative consequences for their own national security and regional stability. Although the United States has the military capability to undertake such an action it is unlikely to act without the support of its regional allies. The force option is still on the table, but the approach to resolve the North Korean nuclear problem has decidedly shifted to the diplomatic arena.

In contrast, preventive military action against presumed nuclear facilities has been more common in the Middle East. Israel undertook a preventive strike on Iraq's Osirak reactor in 1981. The United States invaded Iraq in 2003 on the grounds that Saddam Hussein was developing weapons of mass destruction. It is now confirmed that on September 6, 2007, Israel attacked an alleged nuclear facility in Syria supposedly supplied by North Korea. In addition to warning Syria, there is speculation that this strike was intended as a message for North Korea and Iran. For some time now, there has been speculation that the United States or Israel might carry out preventive military action against Iran. In recent times the fear of a nuclear Iran has been compounded by presumed Iranian interference in Iraq, the implosion of that country, and the perceived development of an Iran-centered alignment in the Middle East that would be detrimental to the interests of the United States, its Arab allies, and Israel. Speculation that the United States is contemplating a military strike on Iran waxes and wanes, with Tehran warning of severe consequences for the United States and Israel.

Certainly the United States and Israel have the military capability to carry out a preventive strike on Iran's nuclear facilities (Logan 2006; Raas and Long 2007). However, such action would have to cross several hurdles and success is uncertain. Iran's nuclear complex is large, carefully concealed, and spread throughout the country. The availability of accurate intelligence and the political repercussions of such an attack are primary limiting factors. The ongoing wars in Afghanistan and Iraq are limiting factors as well. A directed military strike against critical nuclear facilities might not strain American military capability, but a full-scale invasion of Iran to bring about regime change would. The political, diplomatic, economic, and military costs of such a war would be high for the United States. Although support for preventive action appears to have increased among certain Western allies, and the Arab allies of the United States might not object, there would be little international support in other regions or domestic support in the United States. Even if it does not carry out a military strike, Washington might not object to an Israeli preventive action. It has been reported that Tel Aviv and Washington shared intelligence before the Israeli strike against the Syrian facility. From the preceding discussion it appears that preventive military strikes are still a possibility in the Middle East. Compared to the rest of Asia, there are far fewer checks and balances in the Middle East. Offensive use of force continues to be important in that subregion.

Incentive for Early Use and Instability: Not an Empirical Reality

It has been argued that states with small or nascent nuclear arsenals might have strategic incentive to use them early in a conflict to secure a military advantage in an impending full-scale war or to prevent the crippling of their nuclear arsenals in the event of a preventive strike. Without survivable nuclear forces, these considerations would encourage launch-on-warning postures that could produce crisis situations and undermine stability. Park and Lee (Chapter 9 of this volume) discuss this theme in relation to North Korea. Although uncertain how this theoretical possibility might materialize, they posit that North Korea's nuclear armaments will generate continuous crises and threats to peace on the Korean peninsula. That North Korea's quest for nuclear weapons and the American responses have generated crisis situations and may do so in the future is not the issue. The question is whether nascent and small nuclear weapon states will adopt early-launch postures that produce crisis and undermine stability. There is little empirical evidence to support such a claim.

In the abstract, it would be illogical for a nascent or small nuclear power to adopt such a posture against a much superior adversary, as for example in the standoff between North Korea and the United States. Even if North Korea were to inflict substantial damage on the United States or its allies, it is unclear what coercive value would accrue to it. It is almost certain, though, that it would not survive a massive retaliatory strike by the United States. An early use posture can only be rationalized on the basis of an irrational regime, as has been the case with North Korea. However, if North Korea develops a partially survivable nuclear force, early use could have some value; but still such use is likely to be deterred by the possibility of massive retaliation and destruction by the more powerful adversary. Early use postures may make more sense between powers of roughly equal capability with partially survivable nuclear forces. However, evidence from the India-Pakistan dyad, which has a relatively longer nuclear history, does not support this abstract possibility. Despite Pakistan's refusal to embrace an NFU policy and its attempt to exploit the risk of escalation to nuclear war, Islamabad has not opted for an early use posture (see Khan and Lavoy, Chapter 7 of this volume). India, which *is* committed to an NFU policy, has also not adopted an early use posture. As Devin Hagerty (1998) points out, despite the tensions between them, both countries have taken unilateral and bilateral measures to avoid early use. Deterrence, not early use, characterizes their nuclear postures.

Evidence from Asia offers little support for the instability arguments. On the contrary, the claim that nuclear weapons have thus far contributed to security and stability rests on a relatively stronger empirical foundation. Stability has also been enhanced by the further circumscription due to nuclear weapons of the role of force in Asian international politics.

Reinforcing the Circumscription of Force

In 2003, I argued that the role of force in Asian international politics was becoming circumscribed (Alagappa 2003b). I attributed the declining salience of force to several developments: the general acceptance in Asia of the prevailing political and territorial status quo, which makes conquest and domination unacceptable and reduces the need for a forceful defense of a state's core interests; an increase in the political, diplomatic, and economic cost of using force in a situation of complex interdependence; and the impracticality of resolving conflicts through force. These considerations reduce the need for the offensive role of force, leaving defense, deterrence, and assurance as the primary missions of armed forces in the region. Over the past three decades, the use of force has been limited to border clashes, militant insurgencies, and occasional clashes at sea, where the danger of escalation is low. A major war could still occur, but the probability has declined dramatically since the early phase of the Cold War, when Asia was the site of several large-scale wars.

Nuclear weapons reinforce the declining salience of the offensive role of force in the Asian security region and increase the importance of deterrence, defense, and assurance. The logic of the enormous destructive power of nuclear weapons and the lack of defense against them also applies to Asia. None of the key regional conflicts can be resolved through the use of force, including conventional military force. The danger of escalation limits the offensive role of conventional military force among nuclear weapon states. The salience of deterrence and defense, already on the rise in the context of wide acceptance of the status quo, is now becoming entrenched. Asian states are becoming defensive realists. Nuclear weapons make nuclear deterrence and conventional defense the dominant strategies. Despite the U.S. effort to build a strategic defense system, deterrence dominance, for reasons advanced in earlier discussion, is likely to continue for the foreseeable future. Target nuclear weapon states can and will take measures to increase the robustness of their strategic deterrent forces. In situations of stark asymmetry, limited strategic defense may make a difference and make offensive use of force under nuclear conditions more attractive. However, it is unlikely to eliminate all uncertainty; continued caution is likely counsel against offensive military action.

Fear of escalation to the nuclear level and the desire to be viewed as a responsible player by the international community appear to have constrained India's military options in 1999. A similar fear constrains Chinese and American options across the Taiwan Strait, and American options on the Korean peninsula. The military, political, diplomatic, and economic costs of using force, especially nuclear force, is very high among nuclear weapon states. Nuclear weapons strengthen the growing trend in the region that emphasizes conventional defense, nuclear deterrence, and political assurance.

Modifying Effect on System Structure and Dynamics

Nuclear weapons have not fundamentally altered system structure, which is defined by the overall distribution of power (that depends on several attributes, including but not only military power) in the system. Nor have they altered the patterns of amity and enmity in the Asian security region, which are a function of threat perceptions rooted in political disputes, competition for international position and influence, historical animosities, and other factors. However, nuclear weapons have strengthened weaker powers and in certain situations have intensified or ameliorated the intensity of threat perception. These consequences have had a leveling effect and affected security dynamics in certain relationships.

Strengthening Weaker Powers

Nuclear weapons strengthen weaker powers by canceling or mitigating the effects of imbalance in conventional and nuclear weapon capability and thereby reducing their strategic vulnerability. By threatening nuclear retaliation and catastrophic damage in the event of large-scale conventional or nuclear attack, and exploiting the risk of escalation to nuclear war, weaker powers with nuclear weapons constrain the military options of a stronger adversary. This is most evident in the India-Pakistan dyad but also in the China-U.S. and North Korea-U.S. dyads.

Pakistan is much weaker than India in several dimensions of national power, including conventional military capability. It suffered defeats in two of the three conventional wars it fought with India in the prenuclear era, with the 1971 war resulting in humiliating defeat and dismemberment. In the nuclear era, which dates from the late 1980s, Islamabad has been able to deter India from crossing into Pakistan proper and Pakistan-controlled Kashmir even in the context of Pakistani military infiltration into Indian-controlled Kashmir in 1999. India did not follow through with the limited-war option in 2001–02 because of the grave risk it entailed. India was also forced in part by the risk of nuclear war to engage in a comprehensive dialogue to settle disputes between the two countries, including the Kashmir conflict. Pakistan's nuclear arsenal has blunted the potency of India's large conventional military force. Although it has not canceled out all the consequences of the large power differential between the two countries, it has had significant constraining impact with carry-on effects for subregional security structure and dynamics.

China viewed nuclear weapons as a cheap and effective way of counterbalancing the United States and the Soviet Union during different phases of the Cold War (Goldstein 2000). Despite its rapid rise, Beijing still views its relatively small nuclear arsenal as a key means of redressing the huge imbalance in military capability with the United States. A small but modernizing nuclear arsenal has enabled it to limit the coercive consequences of the strategic imbalance and restrain American military intervention in the conflict across the Taiwan Strait. Further, by mitigating the effects of military imbalance, a growing China has been able to exploit its other stronger attributes to enhance its power and influence in Asia. Like China vis-à-vis the United States, India sees it nuclear arsenal as necessary to reduce its strategic vulnerability in relation to China. A much weaker Russia now seeks to compensate for its weakness in conventional military power with its still formidable nuclear arsenal.

The leveling and cautionary effects of nuclear weapons are also evident in the relationship of the weak and isolated North Korea with the vastly superior United States. Although North Korea does not have an operational nuclear arsenal and the United States can destroy that country many times over, the risk of quick and substantial damage to its forces and allies in the region induces caution and constrains U.S. military options. If in the future North Korea develops nuclear weapons and marries them to its missile capability, the risks associated with preventive military action against that country would multiply. Instead of simply suffering the will of the mighty United States, North Korea's nascent capability has provided it with security and bargaining leverage in its negotiations with major powers in the region.

Modifying Effect on System Structure

The greater potential for internal balancing and the leveling effect of nuclear weapons modify system structure and its effects. In South Asia, for example, having nuclear weapons has enabled Pakistan to militarily counterbalance India and make Indian dominance of that subregion more difficult. Although Pakistan has all along balanced India, conventional balancing became more difficult after the dismemberment of Pakistan in 1971 and the highly contingent nature of external support. Nuclear weapons enable Pakistan to counterbalance and constrain India's military options in a more sustained manner, relying on its own capability. Likewise, the Chinese nuclear capability has a modifying effect on American dominance. The hegemonic position and influence of the United States in Asia is increasingly constrained by China; nuclear weapons indirectly contribute to this.

At the same time, nuclear weapons in themselves have not fundamentally altered system structure in the Asian security region. The unipolar structure of the present system and the anticipated changes in the distribution of power among states in the Asian security region are consequences of change in the overall national power of states that has several dimensions. Military power is an important component of national power; and, as indicated earlier, having nuclear weapons makes a significant difference in national military capability. However, military power by itself is not a sufficient basis for major power status. Further, without strong political, economic, technological, and demographic foundations, it is difficult to sustain a strong military capability, as demonstrated by the experience of the former Soviet Union. The enormous destructive power of nuclear weapons is important for its modifying effect, but it is less fungible and less relevant in the pursuit of nonsecurity goals. Nuclear weapons add to but are not a sufficient basis of national power.

The present dominance of the United States, the decline in the position of Russia, and the rise of China and India are not due to their nuclear weapon capabilities. U.S. dominance is grounded in its vast lead in several dimensions of power. Although Russia still has a formidable nuclear arsenal, it is not a superpower or even a top-tier regional power in Asia. In fact, the rapid decline of the Soviet Union/Russia from superpower status was due to the fact that it was a one-dimensional (military) power. That lesson has not been lost on China, which seeks to develop comprehensive national power (Wu 1998). China has long had nuclear weapons and is slowly modernizing its nuclear arsenal. The rapid and substantial increase in its national power and the apprehension it creates are primarily due to China's sustained high rate of economic growth, which in turn produces the resources for accumulating and exercising international power and influence. Likewise, the rise in the power and status of India is due in large measure to its economic growth and change in foreign policy. Nuclear weapons contribute to but do not account for India's rise. Political stability, economic growth, technological advancement, and human resource potential and development, along with military capability, contribute to international perception and ranking of states.

I disagree with those who discount or sideline the salience of nuclear weapons in the power and prestige of countries in the contemporary era (Paul 1998), but at the same time it is necessary to locate the importance of nuclear weapons in proper perspective. Military power remains an important component of national power. To be taken seriously as a major power with a voice in international security matters, a country must possess substantial military capability. This is reflected in the defense expenditures and policies of all major states and in the quest of Japan to become a "normal" power. Although it has been an economic superpower for more than two decades and has made substantial financial contributions to the peace and security efforts of the United Nations and those of its alliance partner, the United States, Japan has been unable to gain the international status and recognition it desires. It now seeks to develop its conventional military capability so that it can contribute "blood" and not just "treasure" in meeting its international obligations and security treaty commitments and to play a more assertive role in shaping the emerging international security order in Asia and more broadly the world. Although Japan does not seek to acquire nuclear weapons, it would like to institute measures to increase the effectiveness and credibility of the American extended deterrence commitment to Japan. If the U.S. commitment erodes, it is not improbable though not certain that Japan may develop its own nuclear weapon capability.

Exacerbating Some Security Concerns but Not Others

Nuclear weapons have not fundamentally altered lines of amity and enmity in the Asian security region. The principal effect of nuclear weapons has been their consequence for the intensity of existing animosities, not the creation of new ones except possibly in the Middle East, where a nuclear Iran could substantially alter the subregional lines of enmity. Offensive strategies for the employment of nuclear weapons have intensified existing security dilemmas; but deterrence strategies have not.

Enmity in the India-Pakistan dyad dates to the partition of British India and their conflict over Kashmir and Pakistan's quest for equality with India. Nuclear weapons have both ameliorated and intensified threat perceptions in this dyad. They have mitigated Pakistan's sense of insecurity by constraining India's military options. The large asymmetry in conventional military capability has become less consequential. Nuclear weapons, including Pakistan's first-use strategy, have strengthened deterrence in this relationship. However, Pakistan's policy to exploit the risk of escalation to nuclear war to alter the political and territorial status quo in Kashmir, and India's coercive response to restore the status quo and to demand cessation of Pakistani support for crossborder insurgent movements, intensified both countries' vulnerabilities and threat perceptions, and resulted in crisis situations early in the overt nuclear era. Since then, however, the situation has stabilized. A mixed strategic picture (conflict, dialogue, and negotiations between the two countries, along with other priorities and international pressure) has helped to reduce the threat intensity between them. Recognition of the grave risks associated with offensive strategies under nuclear conditions is a factor as well. Although both countries continue to develop their nuclear and missile capabilities with reference to each other, the anxiety surrounding missile tests and military exercises has declined. Further, the crises precipitated by offensive strategies deepened the security interdependence between the two countries, providing a basis for limited confidence building and arms control measures to prevent unintended escalation of hostilities.

North Korea's quest for nuclear weapons heightened existing security concerns in the United States, Japan, and South Korea, all of which were already in adversarial relationships with that country. U.S. threats of preventive action intensified North Korea's threat perception, providing additional rationale and momentum to its nuclear quest. The net effect has been to intensify threat perceptions in the U.S.-North Korea and North Korea-Japan dyads and to a lesser degree in the North Korea-South Korea dyad. This has contributed to strengthening the security ties between the United States and its allies in Northeast Asia. For different reasons, China too became concerned about North Korea's nuclear program. That program, and particularly the 2006 North Korean nuclear test, heightened Chinese sensitivity to the negative consequences for security and stability in Northeast Asia and for China. These included the increased possibility of American preventive military action to destroy North Korea's nuclear facilities, regime collapse and turmoil in a neighboring country, massive refugee outflows, Japanese involvement on the Korean peninsula, and the further strengthening of U.S.-Japan-South Korea security relations. A nuclear North Korea could also complicate the U.S. focus of China's nuclear strategy. Beijing began to view the North Korean nuclear program as a serious security problem and became active in trying to defuse it by hosting the Six-Party Talks. Such involvement would also have diplomatic gains for China on several fronts and make it a key player in managing security in Asia.

Iran's nuclear quest has created apprehensions in Israel and certain Arab countries in the Middle East. A nuclear Iran is likely to intensify the Israel-Iran line of enmity and bring about change in Israel's nuclear posture, making nuclear weapons more prominent in Middle East security. The animosity between Iran and the Arab states may also intensify, while that between Israel and the Arab states could become tempered.

Among the major powers, nuclear weapons have created apprehensions but not fundamentally altered the basis and nature of their security interaction, which is characterized by cooperation and conflict. The vastly superior American nuclear arsenal, and especially Washington's emphasis on offensive and defensive strategies, have raised concerns in Beijing and Moscow. Talk of U.S. nuclear primacy with a disarming capability created disquiet in these countries. The United States clarified that its offensive and defensive strategies are specifically directed at rogue states, and there is increasing doubt that the United States could develop effective strategic defense capabilities against China and Russia. Nevertheless, these countries can be expected to strengthen their strategic deterrent forces and increase their policy options in relation to the United States. At the same time, China has not abandoned its minimum deterrence strategy to engage in direct nuclear competition with the United States. The Chinese response has been deliberately indirect and muted. By retaining a posture of dynamic minimum deterrence and an NFU policy while continuing to modernize its nuclear force, China seeks to prevent deterioration of its security relations with the United States. In the case of Russia, its strong opposition to the U.S. ballistic missile defense deployment in Eastern Europe and its suspension of the Conventional Forces in Europe Treaty further strained U.S.-Russia relations. However, Russia has not articulated a nuclear strategy to directly challenge or compete with the United States. The United States also does not appear to have altered its view of not treating Russia as an enemy state.

Nuclear weapons have not substantially altered Sino-Indian security interaction, which appears to be proceeding on dual tracks: engagement and cooperation along with mutual suspicion and quiet competition. Although China condemned the Indian nuclear tests, and India is concerned about the strategic imbalance, neither country has emphasized nuclear weapons in their relationship. India seeks to build a robust deterrent against China, but it has not pursued this goal with urgency. China too has deemphasized its nuclear force in relation to India. The low-key general deterrence postures of both countries reflect their common desire to improve bilateral relations.

Evidence from Asia supports the general proposition that arms per se do not create insecurity, but strategies for their employment may intensify or ameliorate insecurity. And nuclear weapons may modify but do not fundamentally alter the pattern of security interaction. The modifying effect of nuclear weapons on system structure is evident in alliances and alignments in the Asian security region.

Mixed and Complicating Effect on Alliances and Alignments

Alliance formation and sustenance is a function of threat perception and balance of military capabilities (Walt 1987). The greater potential of nuclear weapons for internal balancing may reduce the need for a small nuclear weapon state to engage in external balancing by allying with a larger nuclear weapon state, but alliances among them can still be forged or sustained on other strategic considerations. A small nuclear weapon state lacking a secure second-strike capability and, fearing nuclear attack by a stronger adversary, for example, may choose to align or ally with a larger nuclear weapon state. Alignment or alliance among nuclear weapon states may also rest on other benefits (such as status, diplomatic and economic gains, and technological transfer). Perceiving a nuclear threat and lacking its own capability, a nonnuclear weapon state may choose to ally with a nuclear weapon state that can extend the deterrence function of its nuclear arsenal. The alliance relationship of a nonnuclear or small nuclear weapon state with a larger one confronts two problems. One is fear of entrapment; the danger of becoming involved in the patron's broader security commitments that may have negative consequences for it. The larger nuclear weapon state also fears entrapment, as its junior partner could draw it into an undesired confrontation with another nuclear weapon state. The second problem—fear of abandonment—is more applicable to a client or junior partner state in an alliance relationship. The fear is that its security interests may be sacrificed in the national interest of the larger state, especially if that state is vulnerable to retaliatory nuclear attack. In sum, nuclear weapons can strengthen and weaken alliances and make their management more complicated. All these effects of nuclear weapons on alliances are visible in Asia.

As observed in Chapter 17, states perceiving existential threats view nuclear weapons as the ultimate security guarantee. In a worst-case scenario, they can rely on their own nuclear deterrent without the fear of abandonment. Nuclear weapons have reduced the salience of external balancing for Israel, Pakistan, and North Korea. Nevertheless, Israel still values close strategic ties with the United States, and Pakistan with China. Israel derives considerable political, diplomatic, strategic, economic, and technological benefits (and incurs some costs) from its close ties with the United States. Its opaque nuclear status is in part due to an understanding reached between Washington and Tel Aviv (Cohen, Chapter 8 of this volume). Pakistan's nuclear weapon capability has not significantly affected its strategic alignment with China, which is grounded in their common concern over India. Islamabad still relies on China for political and diplomatic support, assistance with nuclear and missile technology, and economic assistance (Khan and Lavoy, Chapter 7 of this volume). For China, Pakistan is still valuable in constraining rising India's power and influence in and beyond South Asia. Pakistan's strategic independence also permits China to adopt a more neutral position on issues such as the Kashmir conflict and improve relations with India without undermining those with Pakistan.

North Korea has no military ally. Beijing's commitment to the security of North Korea has been reduced significantly in the context of China's modernization drive, dramatic improvement in the PRC and the Republic of Korea's (ROK) relations, and the political transition in North Korea. The growing conception in China of North Korea as a security problem has weakened Beijing's support for the Kim Jong Il regime. However, China does not wish collapse of the North Korean regime and opposes preventive military action against North Korea. Pyongyang's security ties with the Soviet Union terminated with the collapse and fragmentation of that country. Russia provides only conditional diplomatic support. Termination of the alliances with China and Russia, its weakening economic and military position, and diplomatic isolation spurred the imperative for North Korea's self-reliant deterrent capability.

Other nonnuclear weapon states like Japan, South Korea, Australia, and Taiwan that perceive military threats from nuclear armed adversaries have taken a different route: sustaining and strengthening their alliance relationships with the United States. As discussed in Chapter 17, North Korea's nuclear weapon and missile programs and China's modernization of its nuclear arsenal are perceived in Japan as increasing its strategic vulnerability. Rather than seek an independent nuclear weapon capability or reduce the salience of the U.S.-Japan security alliance, the nuclear concern provides an additional incentive for deeper security ties between Japan and the United States (see Green and Furukawa, Chapter 12 of this volume). Tokyo is seeking mechanisms for nuclear dialogue with Washington and for input into U.S. nuclear policy toward Asia to increase the credibility of the American extended deterrence commitment. There is concern that the U.S. may enter into understandings or agreements with China and North Korea that do not take full account of Japan's interests. A fear of abandonment lurks in the background and could become stronger, especially if the United States becomes vulnerable to a nuclear strike by North Korea. For now the emphasis is on strengthening the U.S.-Japan alliance. Tokyo also seeks to enhance strategic relations with other like-minded countries, such as Australia and India.

The North Korean nuclear test also resurrected interest in South Korea to reaffirm the American extended deterrence commitment under the U.S.-ROK security treaty. Through much of its post-World War II history, Seoul was worried about abandonment and the need to firmly bind the United States to South

Korea's security (Choi and Park, Chapter 13 of this volume). Since the early 1990s, however, South Korea has been deeply conflicted over its security alliance with the United States. This was reflected in the security policies of the progressive administrations of Kim Dae Jung and Roh Moo Hyun. Seoul was worried about becoming entrapped in an American preventive military action against North Korea and becoming involved in U.S. global security commitments like that in Iraq. The North Korean nuclear test helped heighten the importance of the U.S. security commitment. And the incoming conservative Lee Myung Bak administration is committed to improving South Korea's ties with the United States and transforming the U.S.-South Korea military alliance into a "Korea-U.S. Strategic Alliance" based on three core principles of "common values, trust, and peace" (Lee 2008). Differences in threat perception, competing goals and interests, and future burden and responsibility sharing, along with change in the nature of threats, are likely to complicate future management of U.S. alliances with Japan and South Korea. However, the alliances themselves are likely to continue.

The entry of new, "irresponsible" nuclear powers (Pakistan and North Korea) and the changed security environment have raised questions about the earlier Australian rationale for supporting the U.S. nuclear umbrella and Australia's security alliance with the United States (Lyon, Chapter 15 of this volume). However, this largely intellectual doubt does not appear to have affected the U.S.-Australia alliance, which deepened in the wake of 9/11 and under the John Howard administration. The new Kevin Rudd government seeks closer ties with China and may be less enthusiastic about contributing to U.S. global military ventures, but it is unlikely to substantively alter the close security relationship with the United States.

The fear of abandonment and entrapment are most visible in the Taiwan-U.S. security relationship. The United States is the only and vital security guarantor for Taiwan. However, the U.S. commitment is deliberately ambiguous, implicit, and designed to deter China as well as Taiwan. Taiwan cannot take the U.S. commitment for granted (Wang, Chapter 14 of this volume). Fearing abandonment, it has to continuously work to retain U.S. support. For its part, the United States fears entrapment—being drawn into a war situation not of its choosing. Although the United States seeks to deter China, it does not want a major war with that country, especially one that could escalate to the nuclear level. Management of the U.S. commitment to the security of Taiwan has become more complicated with the rise of China; the modernization of its nuclear, missile, and naval forces; and the need for the United States to cooperate with that country on a wide range of issues.

Not a Barrier to Peaceful Conflict Resolution

The three key conflicts in Asia (on the Korean peninsula, across the Taiwan Strait, and over Kashmir) cannot be settled by force without huge costs. By dramatically increasing the speed and scale of destruction that can occur from their use, nuclear weapons have made the barrier to settlement by force prohibitive. In this sense, it is possible to argue that they have helped freeze conflicts. However, nuclear weapons are not a barrier to peaceful settlement. In fact, the impossibility of military victory and the grave risks associated with nuclear war may have led states to alter their immediate goals and explore a diplomatic settlement.

Nuclear weapons constrain Chinese use of force to alter the status quo and achieve its unification goal. Recognizing the risks associated with military action (including possible escalation to nuclear war), the unlikely prospect that the Taiwan conflict will be resolved peacefully to its satisfaction in the foreseeable future, and a belief that the present trend in cross-Strait relations is in its favor, China has in recent years begun to shift its emphasis from unification to preventing Taiwan independence and preserving the status quo. On the Korean peninsula, recognizing the limits and risks of attempting an offensive strategy, the United States altered course to seek a diplomatic settlement of the nuclear problem and other disputes there. In India-Pakistan relations as well, the grave risks associated with the military standoff between the two countries have forced them to explore negotiated settlement of the multiple disputes, including the status and control of Kashmir.

It should be observed here that multiple factors account for the shift in objective (in the Taiwan conflict) and the decisions to enter into dialogue and negotiate diplomatic settlements (of the North Korea and Kashmir conflicts). Limits and risks associated with nuclear weapons are one inducement. Ultimately, the peaceful settlement of these conflicts will hinge on working out compromise agreements. Such compromises become more (or less) possible with domestic political change. Recent government change in Taiwan and Pakistan has created a positive atmosphere for reducing tension and negotiating bilateral agreements to establish stable and peaceful relations in hitherto tension-ridden dyads. The incoming Ma Ying-jeou administration in Taiwan does not push the independence agenda, desires better relations with China, and is viewed favorably by Beijing. Although the unification issue is unlikely to be resolved soon, the favorable developments are likely to enhance cross-Strait relations and increase Taiwan's security and international space. Likewise, the swing to democratic government in Pakistan may augur well for continuation of the India-Pakistan comprehensive dialogue and movement toward a negotiated settlement. But the presence of spoilers may make even an interim arrangement difficult. In South Korea, change in government may set back North-South relations. Although he favors continued engagement of North Korea, Lee Myung Bak would like to see greater progress on the nuclear issue and greater reciprocity in North-South relations.

It is pertinent to observe here that nuclear weapons may have helped freeze the Cold War confrontation, but they did not prevent its termination. That confrontation came to an end with change in government in the former USSR. Gorbachev's accession to the top position in the Soviet Communist Party and his reform policies were crucial in ending the Cold War and in the eventual dissolution of the USSR. Although China was not locked into a nuclear confrontation, the transition from Mao Tse Tung to Deng Xiao Ping and the latter's open-door policy and modernization program were crucial in changing China's international orientation. The general point is that resolution of disputes hinges on willingness to make deep political compromise; this can only come about through fundamental change in policy, which in turn becomes possible with idea-driven change in government. Nuclear weapons are instruments of policy and need not be a barrier to settlement of political disputes.

Forging a New Nuclear Order

The Cold War nuclear order emerged in the context of the largely Eurocentric Soviet-American confrontation. Although Israel had a serious covert nuclear weapon program and India had conducted a peaceful nuclear explosion in 1974, China was the only non-Western country acknowledged as a nuclear weapon state. The nuclear arsenals of the United States, the Soviet Union, Britain, France, and China were considered legitimate.[4] That nuclear order was founded on the twin concerns of sustaining deterrence between the two superpowers and preventing additional proliferation (Walker 2007). The primary concern was the deterrence strategies of the United States and the Soviet Union and their implications for international security and stability. Arms control measures were designed to prevent the unintended outbreak and escalation of hostilities between them, to manage crisis, and to advance stability in their strategic interaction. There was less worry over the security strategies of the second-tier nuclear weapon states and their implications. The primary effect of the Non-Proliferation Treaty (NPT) that formed the second pillar of the Cold War nuclear order was to legitimize the discrimination embodied in that Treaty and to prevent additional proliferation by denying material and technology to new aspirants, imposing sanctions on them, and delegitimating new nuclear weapon states. It served the strategic interests of the five nuclear weapon states and ranked below the demands of their national security.

Asia was a sideshow in that order. Policies, strategies, and agreements reached in a Eurocentric context were imposed on Asia. The implications for Asia were often an afterthought. The Cold War order is out of sync with present realties; some assert that it is broken and that a "new" nuclear order has to be constructed (Roberts 2007). A new nuclear order must center on the Asian security region, which has six nuclear weapon states (six including Israel; seven if North Korea is included) and which has become a core world region with potential to emerge as the central region of the world in the twenty-first century. As the findings of this study highlight, the nuclear situation in Asia today is dramatically different from that in the Cold War era. Deterrence is still the dominant strategy for employing nuclear weapons, but it operates in a condition of asymmetry and mostly with small nuclear forces. Nuclear weapons have far-reaching implications, but they are not in the forefront as they were in the Cold War confrontation.

Elements of a New Nuclear Order

A new order should take account of the changed strategic realities; the centrality of Asia; and the "new" roles, strategies, and outcomes of nuclear weapons, and not simply seek to continue to impose treaties and regimes that were negotiated in a different context. Further, it must be flexible enough to accommodate new nuclear powers. In an earlier period, the nuclear order did accommodate the new nuclear weapon states of the Soviet Union, China, Britain, and France. The attempt to freeze that order resulted in several undeclared nuclear weapon states outside the system. The effort in 1995 to close loopholes and permanently freeze the discriminatory nonproliferation regime compelled India, followed by Pakistan, to openly declare their nuclear weapon status. In addition, fear of U.S. military action accelerated the nuclear program of North Korea and that of Iran. The new nuclear order must address five issues: It must (1) sustain deterrence in new conditions and discourage offensive roles and strategies, (2) be capable of accommodating new nuclear weapon states, (3) address the security concerns of potential candidates to prevent further spread of nuclear weapons, (4) prevent proliferation to nonstate actors, and (5) support the peaceful use of nuclear energy with adequate safeguards.

Sustain Deterrence in New Conditions and Discourage Offensive Strategies. As discussion in Chapter 17 highlighted, deterrence continues to be the dominant strategy for employment of nuclear weapons, but it now operates primarily in a condition of asymmetry with mostly small nuclear forces. The nuclear order must support measures to strengthen deterrence stability in the new condition and discourage capabilities and strategies that can undermine security and stability.

Accommodate New Nuclear Weapon States. The nuclear order in the 1950s and 1960s did accommodate change by bringing on board new nuclear weapon states. The U.S.-India nuclear deal must be seen in this light. It is an attempt to bring a rising India into the nuclear order with due consideration of its strategic interests and of nonproliferation concerns. This effort cannot be viewed solely or even primarily through the nonproliferation lens. A rigid nonproliferation stance would gradually widen the gap between the formal nuclear order and reality and over time make the formal order largely irrelevant. In due course, country-specific arrangements would have to be worked out for Pakistan and Israel as well. An incremental approach that accommodates change with emphasis on responsible behavior would create a more stable and inclusive nuclear order that can strengthen security and stability.

Slow the Spread by Addressing Demand and Supply. A continuing thrust of the new nuclear order must be to slow the further spread of nuclear weapons by addressing the security concerns of potential nuclear weapon states. One may question why this is an important concern in light of the conclusion of this study that nuclear weapons have thus far contributed to security and stability. My response is as follows. I am not arguing that more is better and that any state that wants nuclear weapons should be able to get them. My argument is that nuclear weapons have contributed to security and stability in the Asian security region. The "new" nuclear weapon states (India, Israel, and Pakistan) acquired the capability over a prolonged period. All three countries believed that nuclear weapons were essential for their security. India and Pakistan were denied technologies, faced sanctions during the covert and overt periods, and incurred high costs in persevering with their quests. Similarly, North Korea and Iran are now confronting sanctions and technology denials. Their nuclear weapon programs may or may not move forward. My point is that if a country strongly believes it needs nuclear weapons for its security, it will persist in that quest and ultimately succeed. At that point the international community has little choice but to accept that country as a nuclear weapon state. The prolonged acquisition period permits adjustments among relevant states. Thus it is still necessary to be concerned with the spread of nuclear weapons to limit it to those countries that consider them vital, are willing to incur high costs, overcome international opposition, and are capable of producing their own weapons and missiles. In the process, the international community should make a serious effort to address the security concerns of such countries (the demand side of the proliferation equation) to obviate the need for these "ultimate" weapons.

In this regard, the U.S. security alliances with Japan, South Korea, and Australia, and its extended deterrence commitments to them, are important in assuaging their security concerns and preventing their pursuit of independent nuclear options. To make its security guarantee even more credible, the United States may have to explore country-specific arrangements. China's continued deemphasis on nuclear weapons in its relations with Japan would also help prevent Japanese pursuit of the nuclear option. In relation to North Korea and Iran, the United States is a prime driver of their quest for nuclear weapons. Washington considers them "bad guys." This they may be, but not addressing their security concerns drives them into a corner from which they see nuclear weapons as their savior. With the failure of its earlier policy, the Bush administration switched to a diplomatic approach that addresses the political, security, and economic concerns of North Korea in an arrangement that would progressively dismantle that country's nuclear weapon capability.

It is premature to draw any firm conclusions from the North Korean case. Progress has been limited and episodic and could take several years, and success is not guaranteed. But a diplomatic approach that addresses the security concerns of the state pursuing a nuclear weapon capability is likely to be more productive than an approach that stresses isolation, denial, and sanctions. Carrot and stick must go together. Despite the ongoing effort, the international community may have to accept and come to terms with a nuclear North Korea. A determined state cannot be prevented from acquiring nuclear weapon capability. However, the process can be made onerous and costly. Military action that brings about regime change may "permanently" stop the program, but regime change may lead to even worse problems. Iraq is a classic recent example. Nonproliferation is not the only objective. National and regional security and stability are as important if not more important. These objectives and national self-interest appear to drive the Chinese approach to the North Korean nuclear problem. The nuclear nonproliferation regime, if it is to remain relevant, must address both demand and supply. It must also accommodate gray zones rather than insist on black-and-white outcomes.

Prevent the Spread to Nonstate Actors. Another thrust of a new nuclear order must be to prevent the spread of nuclear material, technology, and weapons to nonstate groups and organizations. Nuclear weapons in the hands of nonstate actors threaten both specific states and the entire international system. Countries that provide sanctuary to terrorist groups should be legitimate targets for military action by aggrieved states and the international community. The international community has taken several measures to prevent the spread of nuclear material, technology, and weapons to nonstate actors. Based on a 2002 report by the International Atomic Energy Agency (IAEA 2002), several international instruments have been adopted. These include the Code for Conduct for the Safety and Security of Radioactive Sources and the U.N. General Assembly's International Convention for the Suppression of Acts of Nuclear Terrorism adopted in 2005 (IAEA 2005). The U.N. Security Council Resolution 1540 adopted in 2004 calls on states to strengthen their nuclear safeguards and prohibits them from transferring nuclear capabilities to potentially dangerous nonstate actors. In addition, U.N. Security Council Resolution 1373 adopted in 2001 called on states to become parties to international conventions relating to terrorism. The United States has also initiated several measures, including the Proliferation Security Initiative. The challenge now is to bring more states on board and to implement the various conventions and initiatives. Preventing nuclear terrorism requires sustained vigilance, the development of additional countermeasures, and effective implementation.

Facilitate Development of Nuclear Energy with Adequate Safeguards. The final thrust of the "new" nuclear order should facilitate peaceful use of nuclear power to meet rising energy demand, with adequate safeguards to prevent noneconomic use.

The high price and polluting effects of fossil fuels, as well as the concern that known reserves may be inadequate to meet the growing energy demand, have generated much interest in nuclear energy. To meet the growing demand, international governance will be required to support investment and trade in nuclear energy and to institute sufficient controls to prevent the spread of nuclear weapon capability (Sokolski 2007).

The five issues discussed above that have to be addressed by a new nuclear order are not necessarily complementary. Competing demands are likely to make the forging of a new nuclear order more difficult. Grand schemes will be difficult to design, gain acceptance, and implement. Piecemeal and ad hoc measures are more likely. Although some aspects may still be relevant, any effort to freeze or restore the Cold War nuclear order wholesale is likely to fail.

Concluding Thoughts

Asia and the world are entering new strategic and nuclear environments that are dramatically different from those of the Cold War. Though not in the forefront as in the Cold War confrontation, this study has argued that nuclear weapons continue to be important. They cast a long shadow that informs in fundamental ways the strategic thinking, policies, strategies, and interaction of major powers and their key allies. Modernizing their arsenals and building new capabilities, old and new nuclear weapon states envisage new roles and strategies for nuclear weapons in the context of the security challenges they confront. Some states view nuclear weapons as crucial for survival; others see them as a relatively inexpensive way of competing with and deterring stronger adversaries; some see them as insurance to avoid blackmail and cope with strategic uncertainty; and as the world's sole superpower, the United States seeks to employ nuclear weapons and construct a nuclear regime to sustain a U.S.-led global order.

A major conclusion of this study is that deterrence dominance is likely to continue, and deterrence is likely to be the primary role and strategy for the employment of nuclear weapons in the foreseeable future. However, deterrence today functions in a condition of asymmetry and mostly with small nuclear forces. It is further complicated by the development of offensive capabilities and strategic defense. Another important conclusion is that thus far nuclear weapons have contributed to peace and stability in the Asian security region by assuaging national security concerns and reinforcing the circumscription trend in the region on the role of force. Although destabilizing consequences can be imagined, these have been rare and confined to early stages in the acquisition and operationalization of capabilities and strategies. By highlighting the risks and dangers associated with certain roles and strategies, crisis situations have contributed to a more sober assessment of the roles and limitations of nuclear weapons.

These and other observations advanced in this study run counter to some conclusions reached during the Cold War and differ from prevailing conventional wisdoms. It is crucial to reexamine and refine "old" ideas, concepts, and strategies as well as develop "new" ones relevant to the contemporary nuclear era. This study has identified some baseline national nuclear roles and strategies and explored their regional security implications. The propositions advanced here, however, require further development, refinement, and even reformulation. The meaning, content, and operationalization of the various strategies of deterrence, including the required force levels, for example, require detailed inquiry. How to advance deterrence stability in a condition of asymmetry and small nuclear forces is another important issue to explore. Ensuring the effectiveness and credibility of extended deterrence is another. Having developed a comparative understanding of the roles of nuclear weapons in national security strategies of relevant states and their regional security implications, it is now opportune and necessary to embark on more in-depth work on these issues. Such work must be grounded in the changing political and strategic conditions in Asia and accord due consideration to developments in defense science and technology. It is also important to develop a knowledge community on the subject, especially in Asia, and to foster cross-country and regional dialogues to develop a common discourse and understanding. My hope is that this study provides a foundation for these and other undertakings on the subject of nuclear weapons and security in twenty-first-century Asia.

Notes

1. For contending explanations of the long peace, see Kegley (1991).

2. Many Western leaders made statements to this effect after the Indian and Pakistani nuclear tests in 1998. See, for example, Clinton (1998).

3. William Perry, a former defense secretary who handled the 1993–94 nuclear crisis on the Korean peninsula, recommended a military strike to stop the North Korean test of a long-range missile. See Carter and Perry (2006).

4. Mohamed ElBaradei (2006: A23) states that "under the NPT there is no such thing as a 'legitimate' or 'illegitimate' nuclear weapon state." The recognition of five states as holders of nuclear weapons was regarded as a matter of transition. The NPT does not confer permanent nuclear weapon status on the five countries.

References

Alagappa, Muthiah.2003a. "Introduction: Predictability and Stability Despite Challenges. In *Asian Security Order: Instrumental and Normative Features,* ed. Muthiah Alagappa, pp. 1–32. Stanford, Calif.: Stanford University Press.

———. 2003b. "Managing Asian Security: Competition, Cooperation and Evolutionary Change." In *Asian Security Order: Instrumental and Normative Features,* ed. Muthiah Alagappa, pp. 571–608. Stanford, Calif.: Stanford University Press.

Buzan, Barry, and Gerald Segal. 1994. "Rethinking East Asian Security." *Survival* 36 (2): 3–21.

Carter, Ashton B., and William J. Perry. 2006. "If Necessary, Strike and Destroy: North Korea Cannot be Allowed to Test This Missile." *Washington Post,* June 22: A29.

ElBaradei, Mohamed. 2006. "Rethinking Nuclear safeguards." *The Washington Post,* June 14: A23.

Clinton, William. 1998. Remarks on the Patients Bill of Rights. May 28, 1998. Available at http://www.presidency.ucsb.edu/ws/index.php?pid=56039&st=&st1=.

Feaver, Peter. 1992–93. "Command and Control in Emerging Nuclear Nations." *International Security* 17 (3): 160–87.

———. 1993. "Proliferation Optimism and Theories of Nuclear Operations." *Security Studies* 2 (3/4): 159–91.

Friedberg, Aaron L. 1993–94. "Ripe for Rivalry: Prospects for Peace in a Multipolar Asia." *International Security* 18 (3): 5–33.

Gaddis, John Lewis. 1992. *The United States and the Cold War: Implications, Reconsiderations, Provocations.* New York: Oxford University Press.

Goldstein, Avery. 2000. *Deterrence and Security in the Twenty-first Century: China, Britain, France, and the Enduring Legacy of the Nuclear Revolution.* Stanford, Calif.: Stanford University Press.

Hagerty, Devin T. 1998. *The Consequences of Nuclear Proliferation: Lessons from South Asia.* Cambridge, Mass.: The MIT Press.

International Atomic Energy Agency (IAEA). 2002. *Protection Against Nuclear Terrorism: Specific Proposals.* Available at http://www.iaea.org/About/Policy/GC/GC49/Documents/gc49-17.pdf.

———. 2005. *Nuclear Security: Measures to Protect Against Nuclear Terrorism: Progress Report and Nuclear Security Plan for 2006–9.* Available at http://www.iaea.org/About/Policy/GC/GC49/Documents/gc49-17.pdf.

Jervis, Robert. 1988. "The Political Effects of Nuclear Weapons." *International Security,* 13, Fall: 28–38.

———. 1989. *The Meaning of the Nuclear Revolution: Statecraft and the Prospect of Armageddon.* Ithaca, N.Y.: Cornell University Press.

Kapur, S. Paul. 2006. *Dangerous Deterrent: Nuclear Weapons Proliferation and Conflict in South Asia.* Stanford, Calif.: Stanford University Press.

Kegley, Charles W. 1991. *The Long Postwar Peace: Contending Explanations and Projections.* New York: Harper Collins.

Lee, Myung Bak. 2008. "Address by H.E. Lee Myung Bak, 17th President of the Republic of Korea." New York: Korea Society. Available online at http://www.koreasociety.org/dmdocuments/20080415-LeeMyungBak-English.pdf.

Logan, Justin. 2006. *The Bottom Line on Iran: The Costs and Benefits of Preventive War versus Deterrence.* Washington, D.C.: CATO Institute, Policy Analysis No. 583.

Lord, Winston. 1993. " A New Pacific Community: Ten Goals of American Policy." Opening Statement of Confirmation Hearings: East Asian and Pacific Affairs. Washington, D.C.: Subcommittee of the Senate Foreign Relations Committee. Available at http://findarticles.com/p/articles/mi_m1584/is_n14_v4/ai_13784438/pg_8.

———. 1996. "U.S. Relations with Indonesia." Washington, D.C.: Statement before the Subcommittee on East Asian and Pacific Affairs of the Senate Foreign Relations Committee, September 18. Available at http://dosfan.lin.uic.edu/ERC/briefing/dispatch/1996/html/Dispatchv7no38.html.

Morgan, Patrick M. 2003. *Deterrence Now.* Cambridge, UK: Cambridge University Press.

Mueller, John. 1988. The Essential Irrelevance of Nuclear Weapons: Stability in the Postwar World." *International Security,* 13, Fall: 55–79.

———. 1998. "The Escalating Irrelevance of Nuclear Weapons." In *The Absolute Weapon Revisited: Nuclear Arms and the Emerging International Order,* eds. T. V. Paul, Richard J. Harknett, and James J. Wirtz. Ann Arbor: The University of Michigan Press.

Paul, T. V. 1998. "Power, Influence, and Nuclear Weapons: A Reassessment." In *The Absolute Weapon Revisited: Nuclear Arms and the Emerging International Order,* eds. T. V. Paul, Richard J. Harknett, and James J. Wirtz. Ann Arbor: The University of Michigan Press.

Perry, William. 2006. "Proliferation on the Peninsula: Five North Korean Nuclear Crises." *Annals of the American Academy of Political Science,* 607, 1: 78–86.

Raas, Whitney, and Austin Long. 2007. "Osirak Redux? Assessing Israeli Capabilities to Destroy Iranian Nuclear Facilities." *International Security* 31 (4): 7–33.

Roberts, Brad. 2007. "All the Kings Men? Refashioning Global Order." *International Affairs* 83 (3): 523–30.

Sagan, Scott D. 1994. "The Perils of Proliferation: Organization Theory, Deterrence Theory, and the Spread of Nuclear Weapons." *International Security* 18 (4): 66–107.

———. 1995. "More Will Be Worse." In *The Spread of Nuclear Weapons: A Debate,* ed. Scott D. Sagan and Kenneth Waltz. New York: W. W. Norton.

Sanger, David E., and William J. Broad. 2007. "U.S. Secretly Aids Pakistan in Guarding Nuclear Arms." *New York Times.* November 18. Available at http://www.nytimes.com/2007/11/18/washington/18nuke.html?8br=&pagewanted=all.

Sokolski, Henry. 2007. "Towards an NPT-Restrained World That Makes Economic Sense." *International Affairs* 83 (3): 531–48.

Tellis, Ashley. 1997. *Stability in South Asia.* RAND: Documented Briefing.

Walker, William. 2007. "Nuclear Enlightenment and Counter-Enlightenment." *International Affairs* 83 (3): 431–54.

Walt, Stephen M. 1987. *The Origins of Alliances.* Ithaca, N.Y.: Cornell University Press.

Waltz, Kenneth. 1995. "More May Be Better." In *The Spread of Nuclear Weapons: A Debate,* ed. Scott D. Sagan and Kenneth Waltz. New York: W. W. Norton.

———. 2004. "Nuclear Myths and political Realities." In *The Use of Force: Military Power and International Politics,* ed. Robert J. Art and Kenneth N. Waltz. Boulder, Colo.: Rowman and Littlefield.

Wu, Xinbo. 1998. "China: Security Practice of a Modernizing and Ascending Power." In *Asian Security Practice: Material and Ideational Influences,* ed. Muthiah Alagappa. Stanford, Calif.: Stanford University Press.

Index

Index

Also from Muthiah Alagappa

Civil Society and Political Change in Asia: Expanding and Contracting Democratic Space (2004)

Asian Security Order: Instrumental and Normative Features (2003)

Coercion and Governance: The Declining Political Role of the Military in Asia (2001)

Asian Security Practice: Material and Ideational Influences (1998)

Political Legitimacy in Southeast Asia: The Quest for Moral Authority (1995)